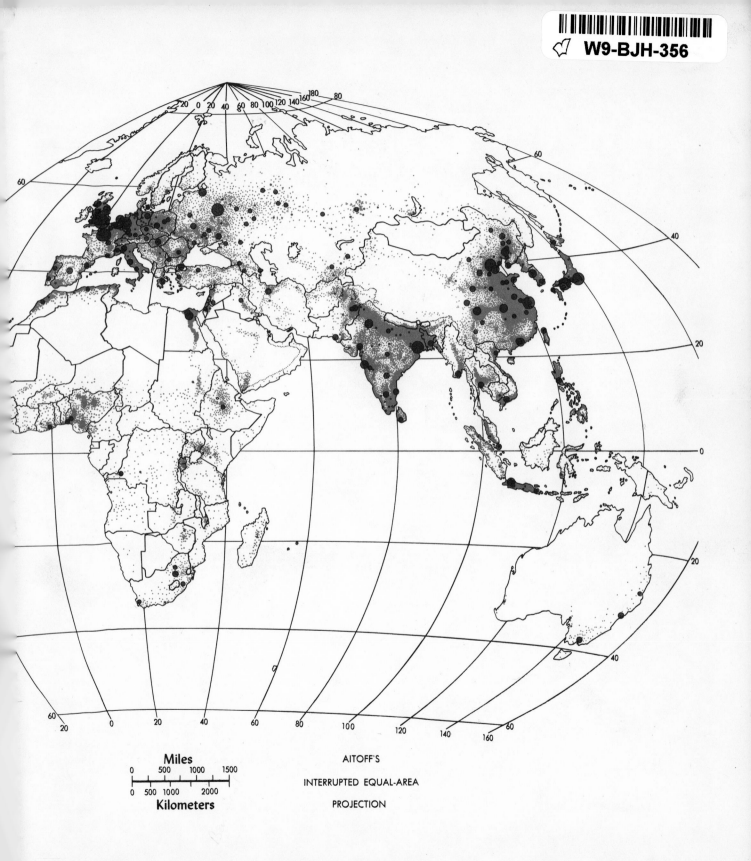

Miles

0    500   1000   1500

0   500  1000    2000

Kilometers

AITOFF'S

INTERRUPTED EQUAL-AREA

PROJECTION

# A GEOGRAPHY OF MANKIND

# McGRAW-HILL SERIES IN GEOGRAPHY

EDWARD J. TAAFFE AND JOHN W. WEBB, *Consulting Editors*

*Broek and Webb*   A Geography of Mankind
*Carlson*   Africa's Lands and Nations
*Conkling and Yeates*   Man's Economic Environment
*Cressey*   Asia's Lands and Peoples
*Demko, Rose, and Schnell*   Population Geography: A Reader
*Detwyler*   Man's Impact on Environment
*Eliot Hurst*   Transportation Geography: Comments and Readings
*Kolars and Nystuen*   Geography: The Study of Location, Culture, and Environment
*Kolars and Nystuen*   Human Geography: Spatial Design in World Society
*Kolars and Nystuen*   Physical Geography: Environment and Man
*Lanegran and Palm*   An Invitation to Geography
*Mather*   Climatology: Fundamentals and Applications
*Murphy*   The American City: An Urban Geography
*Pounds*   Political Geography
*Raisz*   General Cartography
*Raisz*   Principles of Cartography
*Starkey, Robinson, and Miller*   The Anglo-American Realm
*Thoman and Corbin*   The Geography of Economic Activity
*Trewartha*   An Introduction to Climate
*Trewartha, Robinson, and Hammond*   Elements of Geography: Physical and Cultural
*Trewartha, Robinson, and Hammond*   Physical Elements of Geography
   (A republication of Part I of the above)
*Trewartha, Robinson, Hammond, and Horn*   Fundamentals of Physical Geography
*Watts*   Principles of Biogeography: An Introduction to the Functional Mechanisms of Ecosystems
*Yeates*   An Introduction to Quantitative Analysis in Economic Geography
*Yeates*   Quantitative Analysis in Human Geography

THIRD EDITION

# A GEOGRAPHY OF MANKIND

**JAN O. M. BROEK**
Professor Emeritus of Geography
University of Minnesota

**JOHN W. WEBB**
Professor of Geography
University of Minnesota

McGRAW-HILL BOOK COMPANY

New York    St. Louis    San Francisco    Auckland    Bogotá
Düsseldorf    Johannesburg    London    Madrid
Mexico    Montreal    New Delhi    Panama    Paris
São Paulo    Singapore    Sydney    Tokyo    Toronto

# A GEOGRAPHY OF MANKIND

34567890VHVH7832109

This book was set in Optima by York Graphic Services, Inc.
The editors were Donald W. Burden, Janis M. Yates, and David Dunham;
the designer was Nicholas Krenitsky;
the production supervisor was Dennis J. Conroy.
New drawings were done by the Cartographic Laboratory,
Department of Geography, University of Minnesota.
Von Hoffman Press, Inc., was printer and binder.

**Library of Congress Cataloging in Publication Data**

Broek, Jan Otto Marius, date
    A geography of mankind.

    Bibliography:  p.
    1.   Geography—Text-books—1945–     I.  Webb, John
Winter, joint author.  II.  Title.
G126.B79   1978      910′.7     77-12586
ISBN 0-07-008012-7

# CONTENTS

List of Maps and Graphs        ix
List of Tables        xiii
Preface        xv
The Metric System        xvii


PROLOGUE


## PART I   INTRODUCTION

CHAPTER 1   THE GEOGRAPHIC VIEWPOINT        7

The Value of Geography | The Purpose of Geography | Subdivisions of Geography |
The Main Concepts of Geography | Citations and Further Readings

CHAPTER 2   NATURE AND CULTURE        27

Mankind and the Biophysical Environment | Society and Culture | Environmentalism |
The Concept of Culture in Geography | Perception of the Environment | The Cultural Landscape |
The Distribution of Mankind | Citations and Further Readings

CHAPTER 3   TECHNOLOGY: ORIGINS AND DIFFUSION        47

The Old Stone Age (Paleolithic) | The New Stone Age (Neolithic) | The Middle East |
Ancient Civilizations in the Americas | China and the West |
The Modern Technological Revolution | Citations and Further Readings


## PART II   CULTURAL DIVERSITY

CHAPTER 4   RACE: BIOLOGICAL FACTS AND SOCIAL ATTITUDES        73

Geography and Genetics | Problems of Classification |
Present Distribution of the Main Races | Race versus Culture | Racial Tensions |
Blacks in the United States | Great Britain | South Africa | Conclusion | Citations and Further Readings

CHAPTER 5   THE MOSAIC OF LANGUAGES        95

Introduction | World Distribution of Languages | The Indo-European Linguistic Family |
Language and Race | Language and Culture | Language and Society | Bilingualism |
Growth of the French Language | Language and Landforms | Citations and Further Readings

CHAPTER 6  RELIGIONS: ORIGINS AND DISPERSALS    121

Introduction | Influence of Religion on Way of Life | The Variety of Religions |
The Main Religions | Cradlelands of the Main Religions | Judaism |
Christianity | Islam | Hinduism | Buddhism | East Asian Religions | Other Ideologies |
Citations and Further Readings

CHAPTER 7  IDEOLOGIES AND THE POLITICAL ORDER    149

The State: Territory and People | Nationalities and Nations in the European World |
Diversity in Postcolonial Asian and African States | Citations and Further Readings

CHAPTER 8  CULTURE REALMS    179

Problems of Classification and Mapping | Various Proposals for Culture Realms |
Culture Realms in the Fifteenth Century | The Occidental Culture Realm |
The Main Islamic Realm | The Indic Realm | The East Asian Culture Realm |
The Southeast Asian Culture Realm | The Meso-African Culture Realm |
Citations and Further Readings


PART III  PATTERNS OF LIVELIHOOD

CHAPTER 9  FORMS OF ECONOMY:
            GATHERING AND AGRICULTURE IN TRIBAL SOCIETIES    203

A Threefold Division of Societies | Forms of Economy |
Collecting, Hunting, and Fishing in Tribal Societies | Agriculture in Tribal Societies |
Citations and Further Readings

CHAPTER 10  TRADITIONAL LAND·USE: THE PLANTATION: MODERN AGRICULTURE    225

Land Use in Traditional Societies | Pastoral Nomadism | The Plantation |
Land Use in Modern Societies | Citations and Further Readings

CHAPTER 11  INDUSTRIAL COUNTRIES AND REGIONS    261

Factors of Industrial Location | The United States Iron and Steel Industry |
Main Industrial Regions | An Industrial Region: South Wales | Citations and Further Readings

CHAPTER 12  THE RICH AND THE POOR    287

Developed and Underdeveloped Countries | Paths toward Economic Progress |
Citations and Further Readings


PART IV  SETTLEMENTS

CHAPTER 13  FARM AND VILLAGE    309

Geographic Approaches to Rural Settlements | Western Europe | Anglo-America |
Village and House Types in East Asia | The Stilt House in Southeast Asia |
Citations and Further Readings

CHAPTER 14 TOWNS AND CITIES 333

Site and Situation | The Origin and Spread of Cities | Cities in the Modern Era |
Four Facets of Contemporary Cities | Citations and Further Readings

CHAPTER 15 EMERGING URBAN PATTERNS 359

The Distribution of Large Metropolises | The Qualities and Problems of Metropolitan Life |
Citations and Further Readings

PART V POPULATION CHANGE

CHAPTER 16 THE DIFFERENTIAL GROWTH OF POPULATION 391

Population Growth in the Past | Birth and Death Rates | Case Studies in Population Geography |
Future Growth of United States Population | Citations and Further Readings

CHAPTER 17 POPULATION MIGRATIONS 425

Introduction | International Migrations | Internal Migrations | Conclusion |
Citations and Further Readings

CHAPTER 18 PROBLEMS OF POPULATION GROWTH 447

Controversial Views | Nutrition | Infectious Diseases | Future Food Supply | Beyond Food |
Citations and Further Readings

CHAPTER 19 WHAT MAN HAS WROUGHT 463

Is Doomsday Near? | Historical Perspective | Attitudes toward the Environment |
Conservation in the United States | Current Issues | The Way Ahead |
Citations and Further Readings

EPILOGUE 483

INDEX 487

# LIST OF
# MAPS AND GRAPHS

1-1   Scale and Population Density      12
1-2   The Great Plains Region
      Defined      14
1-3   The Twin Cities (Minneapolis-St. Paul)
      Trade Region      15
1-4   Distribution of River Towns in
      Mid-America      17
1-5   Kenya and Texas: Distribution of
      Population      18
1-6   Von Thünen's Circles      21

2-1   Diffusion and Independent
      Invention      28
2-2   The Spread of Hybrid Corn      29
2-3   Canada: Cartogram of Population
      Distribution      35
2-4   World: Important Physical
      Features      38
2-5   World: Climates      40

3-1   Old World: Areas of Origin of Selected
      Plant and Animal Domesticates      48
3-2   New World: Areas of Origin of Selected
      Plant and Animal Domesticates      49
3-3   Early Middle Eastern Agriculture      51
3-4   The Diffusion of the Alphabet      52
3-5   Chinese Culture Hearth      53
3-6   Meso-American Culture Hearth      54
3-7   Central Andean Culture Hearth      55
3-8   The Diffusion of Papermaking from
      China to the West      59
3-9   Europe: Canals Built by 1840      61
3-10  World: Persons per Motor Vehicle and
      Motor Vehicle Production, Mid-
      1970s      62
3-11  Europe: Superhighways,
      Mid-1970s      63
3-12  North America: Superhighways,
      1976      64

3-13  North America: Air Passenger Traffic,
      1969–1970      65

4-1   Distribution of the ABO Blood Group
      Genes in the Aboriginal Populations
      of the World      75
4-2   Isolated Peoples      79
4-3   Early Human Migrations      80
4-4   Negroid Genetic Variations      82
4-5   United States: Black Population      88
4-6   United States: Nonwhite Migrants
      to Selected Metropolitan
      Centers      89
4-7   South Africa: Ethnic Groups      91

5-1   World: Principal Linguistic Families
      and Subfamilies      100
5-2   Europe: Languages      103
5-3   The Ural-Altaic Languages (West
      Eurasian groups)      105
5-4   Dialects of the Eastern United
      States      107
5-5   South Asia: Languages      109
5-6   World: International Languages      112
5-7   France: Languages      114
5-8   Polynesian Linguistic
      Relationships      116

6-1   Cradlelands of the Main
      Religions      125
6-2   Jewish Populations in Europe and the
      Mediterranean, 1933 and 1956      127
6-3   Eastern Christianity      130
6-4   Christianity and Islam in
      Europe      133
6-5   United States: Religious Affiliations,
      1950      135
6-6   Islam      138
6-7   Hindu Pilgrimage Places      143

6-8   Buddhism   145

7-1   East Central Europe: Boundaries and States in the Twentieth Century   153
7-2   Yugoslavia   154
7-3   Areas of German Speech in 1939, and Political Boundaries of Germany before 1918 and after 1945   157
7-4   Switzerland   159
7-5   Belgium   160
7-6   Integration in Europe   162
7-7   Les Franco-Canadiens   164
7-8   South Asia: Political Divisions   169
7-9   Nigeria   171
7-10  Malaysia, Singapore, and Brunei   174

8-1   A. J. Toynbee: Civilizations Current in A.D. 1952   181
8-2   J. O. M. Broek: Culture Realms   182
8-3   Culture Realms about A.D. 1450   184
8-4   The Expansion of Russia   189
8-5   Southeast Asia: Languages   194
8-6   Southeast Asia: Religions   195

9-1   World: Tribal, Traditional, and Modern Societies   205
9-2   World: Forms of Economy (After E. Hahn, 1892)   207
9-3   World: Gatherers, Hunters, and Fishers, about A.D. 1500   209
9-4   Northern Eurasia: Reindeer Herding   213
9-5   World: Forms of Land Use in Tribal Societies   216
9-6   Shifting Agriculture at Fokole, Liberia   218
9-7   Africa: Regions Infested by the Tsetse Fly   220

10-1  Africa and Asia: Forms of Land Use in Traditional Societies   226
10-2  A Village in Himachal Pradesh, India   229
10-3  India: Irrigation Projects   231
10-4  Nile Valley: Irrigation   233
10-5  Afghanistan: Pastoral Nomadism   234
10-6  Malaya: Rubber- and Rice-Producing Areas   240

10-7  World: Tractors per 1,000 Hectares of Arable Land (about 1975)   241
10-8  Percentage of Labor Force in Agriculture in Selected Countries   242
10-9  World: Forms of Land Use in Modern Societies   246
10-10 United States: Major Milksheds in the Northeast   248
10-11 New Zealand: Agricultural Exports   250
10-12 Soviet Union: Land-Use Regions   252
10-13 World: International Trade in Wheat   253

11-1  Michigan: Employment in the Printing and Automotive Industries, 1960, by Counties   263
11-2  Northeastern United States: Family Income below $3,000, 1959   264
11-3  Western Europe: Income per Capita   265
11-4  Distance and Costs for Different Transportation   268
11-5  Transportation Costs to and from a Transshipment Point   268
11-6  Eastern United States and Canada: Steel Production Capacity, 1970   270
11-7  Anglo-America: Labor Force in Manufacturing, by Counties, 1968   272
11-8  Southern New England: Industrial Establishments, 1968   274
11-9  Europe: Industrial Regions   276
11-10 Great Britain: Industrial Districts   277
11-11 Continental Western Europe: Industrial Districts   278
11-12 Soviet Union: Industrial Districts   279
11-13 Japan: Industrial Districts   280
11-14 South Wales   283

12-1  The Americas: Income Per Capita, about 1975   289
12-2  World: Gross National Product per Capita   291
12-3  Percentages of Working Population in Agriculture, Manufacturing, and Services in Selected Countries   292

12-4 World: Energy Consumption per Capita 293

12-5 World: Economic Development and Underdevelopment 294

12-6 World: Percentage of Population under Fifteen Years of Age 299

12-7 World: Illiteracy 300

12-8 World: Daily Newspapers, Number of Copies per 1,000 Inhabitants 301

12-9 World Bank Loans and Credits, 1945-1976 303

13-1 India: A Village in Punjab 311

13-2 Lower Saxony: Open Field (Esch) Village 312

13-3 Europe: Rural Settlement Types 315

13-4 Quebec: Long Lots in the Seigneury of Boucherville 317

13-5 American Settlement Forms 319

13-6 The Southern Plantation 322

13-7 China: Two Agricultural Communes 327

13-8 Southeast Asia: House Types 329

14-1 World Urbanization of National Populations 334

14-2 Pittsburgh, Pennsylvania 335

14-3 Mesopotamia: Ancient Cities 337

14-4 Peking and Changan, China 342

14-5 Ibadan, Nigeria 344

14-6 United States and India: Ranks and Sizes of Cities 348

14-7 Theories of Urban Structure and Growth 349

14-8 Paris: Central Area 351

14-9 Central Place System 353

14-10 Southwestern Saskatchewan: Central Place System 354

15-1 World Metropolitan Populations 360

15-2 Eastern North America: Large and Medium-Sized Cities 364

15-3 Santa Clara Valley, California: Settlement Changes 365

15-4 Western and Central Europe: Large Cities 367

15-5 Metropolitan Subway Systems 373

15-6 Dagenham, England: Population Composition 374

15-7 New York: Racial Segregation, 1970 378

15-8 Growth Axes for the Paris Region 381

15-9 Southeast England: Planned Population Redistribution 382

15-10 Minneapolis-Saint Paul Metropolitan Area: Expected Growth Patterns 384

16-1 World: Population Growth from 8,000 B.C. 392

16-2 The Population of Europe and the European Culture Area since Ancient Times 396

16-3 The Demographic Transformation in England and Wales 399

16-4 World: Mortality, Mid-1970s 400

16-5 Mortality Rates for Selected Countries 401

16-6 World: Fertility, Mid-1970s 402

16-7 Fertility Rates for Selected Countries 403

16-8 World: Demographic Situation in the Mid-1970s 405

16-9 The Fifteen Larger National Populations: 1976 and 2000 409

16-10 Mauritius: Population in the Twentieth Century 410

16-11 India: Population in the Twentieth Century 411

16-12 Mexico: Population in the Twentieth Century 413

16-13 China: Population and Food, Estimates for 1950-1970 416

16-14 Japan: Population in the Twentieth Century 417

16-15 Sweden: Population Since 1750 419

16-16 United States: Population in the Twentieth Century 420

16-17 United States and Zero Population Growth 421

17-1 Spatial Relocation: The Decision to Migrate 427

17-2 United States: Immigrants, 1831-1910 428

17-3 Europe: Migrations, 1944-1951 433

17-4 Europe: Major Sources of Foreign Labor 436

17-5  United States: Interregional Migration, 1960–1965  442

17-6  United States: Net Migration by States, 1960–1970  443

17-7  United States: Components of Population Change, by States, 1960–1970  444

18-1  World: Infant Mortality, about 1975  449

18-2  World: Caloric and Protein Intake per Capita  453

18-3  World: Diseases  455

18-4  World: Arable Land per Capita and Net Cereal Importers, Early 1970s  459

18-5  World: Fishing Grounds and Catches  460

19-1  Prehistoric Man and Mammal Extinction  466

19-2  Reduction in Woodland in Cadiz Township, Green County, Wisconsin  467

19-3  United States: Land Surface Distributed by Strip and Surface Mining  474

19-4  Pollution of the Rhine Drainage Basin  476

# LIST OF TABLES

2-1 Areas of Population Concentration, 1976    36

4-1 Mixed population in Selected Political Units    86
4-2 United States: Percentage of Total Negro Population in Selected Regions, 1790–1970    87

5-1 The Principal Linguistic Families and Languages of the World    96
5-2 The Languages of Europe    102
5-3 Bilingualism or Multilingualism in Selected Countries    111

6-1 Main Religions and Estimated Number of Adherents, 1976    124
6-2 Distribution of Jews    128
6-3 United States Church Membership, 1976    136

7-1 The Population of Yugoslavia, 1971    155

8-1 Subdivisions of the Occidental Culture Realm    183

9-1 Forms of Land Use    208

15-1 City Regions with 2.5 Million Inhabitants or More, and Their Neighbors with Over Half a Million Inhabitants, 1975    362
15-2 Blacks in Central Cities and Metropolitan Areas of the United States    377

16-1 World Population from 8000 B.C. to the Present    393
16-2 The Population of Europe: Ancient to Modern Times    394
16-3 The Populations of the Continents, 1650–1970    395
16-4 Countries with Over 10 Million Inhabitants: Selected Data, Mid-1970s    406
16-5 Forecast of Population Increase, 1975–2000    408
16-6 India, Bangladesh, and Pakistan: Population Growth, 1921–1971    412
16-7 United States: Projections of Population, 1980–2020    421

17-1 Origins of United States Immigrants from Europe by Top-ranking Countries, 1821–1970    429
17-2 Components of United States Population Growth, 1870–1970    430
17-3 Third World Populations and Urban Development, 1976    438
17-4 Estimates of Migrants as a Percentage of Recent Population Increases    439
17-5 Formal and Informal Urban Economic Sectors    439

18-1 Man-Land Ratios for Selected Countries    450

19-1 Misuse of Resources    464

# PREFACE

In preparing this new edition of *A Geography of Mankind,* I was conscious of a personal and professional loss: Jan Broek died in 1974, a year after the publication of the second edition. He lived in Berkeley, California, where he had retired after more than two decades as professor of geography at the University of Minnesota.

The idea for this book originated in a course Broek introduced at the University of Minnesota. It explored the main themes of geography as they related to the diversity of human societies. Later, others of the department joined in teaching it, and now it is given with variations in numerous colleges and universities in America and abroad. Broek and I wrote the text together in the 1960s, each responsible for certain chapters. I also prepared drafts for the maps and diagrams. Ruth Broek smoothed out the differences and infelicities of our writing.

The continued favorable reception of *A Geography of Mankind* persuaded me that the basic character of the two previous editions should be retained for this new one. Many instructors and students offered general comments as well as specific proposals on how to improve the text and maps. Before and during the revision, several critics gave expert and extensive counsel. Many thanks to them and to all others who offered advice. Substantial efforts have been made to enhance the quality and usefulness of the book, taking into account as many of their suggestions as possible.

The entire book has been reviewed and rewritten where necessary so as to present ideas and information clearly. A Prologue describes the purpose and organization of this edition. An important change is the reorganization of the economic section and its reduction from six chapters to four. New material has been added on the developing countries, especially on the growth of cities in the third world. In many countries recent political, economic, and other events altered situations which demanded reassessment. Statistical information had to be updated. Distances and other measures are now in their metric values, though some customary values are retained. Nearly half the maps and graphs for this third edition are new or substantially revised. To improve relevance and quality, new photographs replace many of the old. The endpapers of this book are now an updated map of world population distribution and the well-known "cartogram of national populations"—also brought up to date.

Evidently instructors preparing their lectures, and students pursuing topics of their own, have appreciated the lists of books and articles at the close of each chapter. These bibliographies include some new titles, and a number of the old ones are omitted. Particular attention has been paid to articles in American geographical periodicals, not only because they are widely available in libraries but also because they serve to indicate current interests.

*A Geography of Mankind* incorporates data from various sources, but a survey of this kind does not lend itself to detailed documentation. Some of the ideas and facts came from the Further Readings listed at the end of each chapter. We deeply appreciate the courtesy of those who permitted reproduction of pictures and use of maps; recognition is given in appropriate places. Special thanks are due Thomas Prendergast and Renaldo Reyes, photo librarians of the United Nations, for their help in finding many new photographs.

The Cartographic Laboratory of the Department of Geography at the University of Minnesota prepared the graphic materials. Mei-ling Hsu and Patricia Burwell designed and supervised the drafting of maps and graphs for the previous editions. Much evidence of the high quality of their work remains in this new book. Sandra Haas, now the chief cartographer of the laboratory, worked on the new and revised maps this time; her skill and efficiency are much appreciated. My thanks also go to Su-chang Wang, Si-young Park, Robert Chambers, and Nancy Lestina.

I owe Ruth Broek a debt I cannot repay for her careful revision of the text for stylistic clarity and simplicity. Lapses of fact and opinion must remain my responsibility.

John W. Webb

## THE METRIC SYSTEM

This book uses the international system of units, *Système international d'unités* (SI), otherwise known as the metric system. France, where it originated, adopted it "for all peoples for all time" at the beginning of the nineteenth century. By mid-century the metric system had come into general use in France. Soon it spread to other European countries, and by 1950 its use was worldwide. In the 1970s the United States, the last large country to retain its customary measurements, slowly converts to the metric system. The table below contains the more commonly used SI units and their traditional counterparts.

| SI units (with abbreviations) | Customary U.S. units (approximate) |
| --- | --- |
| **Distance (length)** | |
| 100 millimeters (mm) | 4 inches |
| 1 meter (m) | 3 feet 3 inches |
| 1 kilometer (km) | 1,100 yards |
| 100 km | 60 miles |
| **Area** | |
| 1 hectare* (ha) = 10,000 square meters | 2 acres 80 square rods |
| 10 ha | 25 acres |
| 1 square kilometer (km²) | 310 acres |
| 100 km² | 40 square miles |
| **Liquid (volume)** | |
| 1 liter* (l) = 1,000 cubic centimeters | 1 quart |
| 10 l | 2¾ gallons |
| 100 l | 26 gallons |
| **Temperature** | |
| 100 degrees Celsius (°C) | 212 degrees Fahrenheit (water boils) |
| 25 °C | 77 °F (warm day) |
| 0 °C | 32 °F (water freezes) |
| −20 °C | −4 °F (very cold day) |
| **Weight (mass)** | |
| 1 kilogram (kg) | 2 pounds 3 ounces |
| 1,000 kg = 1 tonne (t) | 2,240 pounds = 1 long ton |
| **Pressure** | |
| 1,000 millibars* (mb) = 100 kilopascals (kPa) | 29.5 inches of mercury |
| **Energy** | |
| 10,000 kilojoules (kJ) | 10,000 British thermal units (Btu) |
| **Frequency** | |
| 60 hertz (Hz) | 60 cycles per second |
| 1.5 megahertz (mHz) | 1,500 kilocycles per second |
| **Power** | |
| 746 watts (W) | 550 foot-pounds per second (1 horsepower) |
| **Multiples** | |
| kilo- (k) | 1 thousand |
| mega- (M) | 1 million |

*Hectare, liter, and millibar are commonly used terms but are not SI units.

# PROLOGUE

In *A Geography of Mankind* we examine, in essence, the social and cultural factors that condition the way the different peoples of the world perceive, organize, and use their habitats and how these factors affect the relations of each group with others.

Most geography textbooks emphasize either man–land relationships or theoretical constructs of spatial organization. While recognizing the merits of both approaches, we find their outlook too restrictive. The first, although of great value in comprehending ecological complexes, neglects the relations between human groups—an omission which makes it impossible to deal adequately with many phenomena of significance, such as cities, plural societies, and migrations. The second approach inevitably concentrates on building models so idealized as to lose touch with the human realities of occupied space in their intriguing variety.

The purpose of this book is to acquaint the student with the main themes of human geography, whether for use as background for a career in this field or as a basis for general education. We can view these geographic themes, of course, from different angles. Our presentation has an accent of its own: It rests on the proposition that each society interprets earth and mankind through the prism of its particular culture. Thus, knowledge of social and cultural diversity is essential to geographic understanding.

Some scholars believe that a uniform cosmopolitan way of life, fashioned in the image of Western civilization, is in the process of replacing the mosaic of cultures. True, Western technology and economy are spreading throughout the world. There is little evidence, however, to prove they erase differences in beliefs, attitudes, or values—in short, ideologies. Even within the United States—paramount example of a vast, integrated economic system—ethnic and regional contrasts have not melted away. Quite to the contrary. Today each group, more conscious of its identity than ever before, insists on the right to follow its own life-style.

Obviously to speculate on trends is less important than to recognize the intrinsic worth of cultural differentiation. This differentiation, comparable to the parallel principle in biology, contains a vital condition for human evolution. Sameness spells sterility. As stated in the Epilogue of this book: "Different cultures, even the most humble ones, may harbor idea strains that could prove highly valuable in breeding new institutions to cope with as yet unforeseen situations."

In the organization of *A Geography of Mankind* we use the thematic or topical approach. This means that we do not begin by dividing the earth into segments or regions such as continents, climatic provinces, economic or political units. Instead, seeking to understand the character of places, we proceed analytically by inquiring into the nature and distribution of various features that shape the earth's variety and interdependence.

This topical approach permits deeper probing into general concepts and principles than allowed by the regional procedure: for example, to explore population, cultural attributes, types of economy. Instead of handing us a preconceived regional system in which to pigeonhole geographic data, the thematic treatment makes us partners in the quest for an intelligible spatial order.

Topical and regional concepts necessarily complement each other. Our chapters on culture realms and economic development explicitly construct a meaningful division of the earth into major cultural and economic regions. Equally important, virtually all chapters contain case studies of specific countries or other places which, together with accompanying maps, offer examples of regional analysis.

By tradition space and time have been sundered and awarded respectively to geography and history. But all events occur in specific places, and all places derive their character from changes through time. Concern with process—that is, with the interaction of forces through time—has particular relevance to social and cultural geography. Observing where people and things are leads us to questions about their place of origin, their routes of dispersal, their transformation within the present location. Accordingly, in this book we reach freely into the past to trace sequences through time and space.

Geography can be more than an academic discipline. A geographic point of view can help us beyond measure to understand the actual world. The present generation faces such problems as rapid population growth, metropolitan disorganization, race relations, degradation of the environment, and the widening gap between rich and poor peoples. Moreover, as students of geography we can learn to appreciate that these and other questions assume different forms in different regions and countries, partly because of the environmental diversity but, even more, because each problem is singularly enveloped within its own cultural matrix.

Reflecting our objectives, we summarize the order of presentation as follows:

Part I introduces fundamental geographic concepts, draws attention to the present population distribution, and surveys the origin and diffusion of skills and tools by which societies in various parts of the world have transformed their habitats.

Part II goes to the heart of the argument by examining race, language, religion, and nation as categories of thought patterns and institutions that unite or separate human groups. After this analysis there follows a provisional synthesis that arranges the earth into broad culture realms.

Part III presents the diverse forms of economy prevailing in tribal, traditional, and modern societies and evaluates their levels of development. These economic patterns, it will be noted, correlate fairly well with the culture realms of the second part.

Part IV compares the forms of settlement in different culture realms, from farmstead and village to town and city, and explores the emerging structure of the metropolitan region with its perplexing problems.

Part V returns to the topic of population but now considers its dynamic aspects of natural growth and movement as seen against the background of spatial variety in cultural tradition, type of economy, and degree of urbanization. The last chapter relates population to habitat by examining the ecological consequences of man's dominance of the earth.

The Epilogue reviews the great forces of change in our era and how they affect the various culture realms. The earth becomes ever more "One World," but not necessarily a uniform world modeled after the Occidental civilization.

This introductory section provides some foundations for the more specialized parts that follow. The Prologue has described the purpose of the book and its organization. Chapters 1 and 2 attempt to explain what geography, especially in its sociocultural aspects, is all about. If some of the concepts appear vague, we hope they will become more meaningful when put to work in the body of the text.

This book has its focus on our present world, but current conditions can be understood only if we recognize them as a phase in a perpetual transformation. Chapter 3 provides a useful historical perspective by tracing origins and dispersals of technology as the means of mankind's increasing control over energy and as a driving force—though certainly not the only one—in the rise and spread of civilizations.

# PART I
# INTRODUCTION

A hillside 400 kilometers north of Santiago, Chile. (Photograph —United Nations)

# 1 THE GEOGRAPHIC VIEWPOINT

## THE VALUE OF GEOGRAPHY

In London one can visit the quarters where Winston Churchill guided the war effort in Britain's darkest hours. The walls of his own room in this underground shelter are covered with maps. They show the lay of the land in the actual and potential battle zones, the locations of cities and manufacturing districts, and reveal at a glance the position of strategic key points in the network of the world's shipping, air, and land routes. This room demonstrates the crucial value of geography in a nation's effort to survive: knowledge of lands and peoples, and of their interrelations.

The average citizen is not likely to find himself in a position where he must make decisions that directly affect the national welfare. But as a member of a democracy he should be well informed so that he can judge current issues, whether of worldwide or local significance, and cast his vote in a responsible manner. Yet, how many Americans understood the vital importance of Greece and Turkey when, after World War II, Russian pressure was mounting toward the Mediterranean? How many in the 1960s when the distant Indochina war burst upon us realized the futility of trying to impose Western objectives upon the peoples of Vietnam, Cambodia, and Laos, whose traditions and ways of thinking are entirely unlike ours?

Quite often we ignore reports about the multinational effort to develop the resources of the Mekong River basin and about petroleum and gas discoveries in northern Alaska or western Europe because we lack the background to grasp the significance of the story. Or we are surprised by news of turmoil in Lebanon or Northern Ireland because we are unaware of age-old differences among ethnic groups. We are puzzled and dismayed when billions of dollars apparently fail to stimulate economic development in poor countries. Safe with the freedom to do what we want with our lives, and lacking knowledge of the variety of human cultures, we cannot comprehend that other peoples cling to their own values.

Geographic ignorance is also common in our own national affairs. As citizens we are concerned with such matters as floods and water shortages, air and stream pollution, chaotic growth of metropolitan areas, lack of adequate health care, and pockets of poverty; but all too seldom do we clearly understand these problems in their regional context.

Geography is not merely useful. It is exciting for its own sake. If we take the trouble to study maps and read books about the places we will visit, our travels become much more meaningful. We become alert to the variety of field patterns, farming types, and cityscapes, to the extent of man-caused erosion, the effect of a new dam or highway, or whatever else may intrigue us about a people and their land.

If we cannot go to see China for ourselves, we can travel in thought with Keith Buchanan while he explains that country's problems and prospects. If we are interested in Mexico, we can learn much about its personality from Carl Sauer, whose writings are based on many years of close observation. The era of discovering new continents is past, but the discovery of new truths about old countries goes on forever.

## THE PURPOSE OF GEOGRAPHY

Geography is organized knowledge of the earth as the world of man. It deals with organic and inorganic phenomena, not for their own sake, but as they help us to understand the earth as the place where people live, work, meet, and mingle, transforming its surface into their habitat.

To speak of "the earth" as a unit fails to bring out its variety of features. Next to terrestrial integration—an ever more meaningful concept in this era of shrinking distances—we should give equal attention to earth differentiation. Geographers want to understand the character of countries, regions, areas—let us say "places" for short—but they realize that no place can be understood by itself. The wealth and welfare of the Dakota grain farmer are linked not only to the precarious rainfall of the northern plains and to methods of farming but, equally or more, to government decisions in Washington or to the movement of grain prices on the world's exchanges. The character of a place is, therefore, always determined by the interplay of its own internal features and its spatial (locational) relations with other places. Taking account of these notions of internal variety and external relationships, we can now restate the aim of geography. It is: *to understand the earth as the world of man, with particular reference to the differentiation and integration of places.*

This statement may surprise some readers. They may hold the notion that geography is vaguely akin to geology and should study plains and mountains, seas and rivers. Or they may think that it is geography's task to demonstrate how nature influences man in different environments. Still others, understanding that geography deals with location, believe that its goal is to map the distribution of any and all phenomena over the earth's surface. Quite true, geographers are interested in land forms, in the effect of environment on man, and in the location of peoples and things. But these tasks are *means,* not the *end.* They all must serve the purpose of geography as described above.

## SUBDIVISIONS OF GEOGRAPHY

Geography comprises a bewildering number of facets. Since there is no generally accepted classification of the subdivisions, the following outline offers no more than a rough guide.

A main partition is that between *regional* and *topical* (also called "systematic") geography, distinguishing the study of areas in the fullness of their interrelated characteristics from the study of single features (topics). This distinction is a matter of emphasis: regional synthesis draws on knowledge of particular features present in the area while, in turn, the analysis of one topic, say manufacturing industries, will necessarily include delineation of the area (region) where it occurs.

Topical geography too has a broad twofold division. The *biophysical* part examines what popularly is called "nature": properties of land, water, and air, also of plants and animals in their distribution and interrelations. *Human* geography, or, more stately, *anthropogeography* deals with man in his geographic aspects. Again the distinction is artificial. Man evermore tames—and taints—nature. At the same time the biophysical environment conditions humanity in both its biological and social aspects.

Like biophysical geography, human geography comprises many specialties. *Economic* geography considers how mankind makes a living. The topic can be further subdivided according to branches of activity, such as agriculture, manufacturing, trade, transportation, and other services. *Cultural* geography is another wide subfield of human geography. The term when introduced from Germany into the United States some fifty years ago referred to the study of how culturally diverse societies have used and changed the earth's surface into "cultural landscapes," which contrast with pristine "natural landscapes." Gradually the subject has come to include all applications of the idea of culture to geographic problems. It analyzes the spatial variations of material traits, such as house types, as well as cultural ones, such as religions.

Each human group—community, society, nation—has its distinctive culture. The investigation of such collective groups in their areal differentiation and interrelations is called *social* geography. This term, used for a long time in Europe, is now catching on in the United States. Inevitably it overlaps cultural geography. One can hardly think of a culture trait without the peoples who invented, spread, or received it. And one cannot imagine a society without its cultural attributes.

*Political* geography examines political phe-

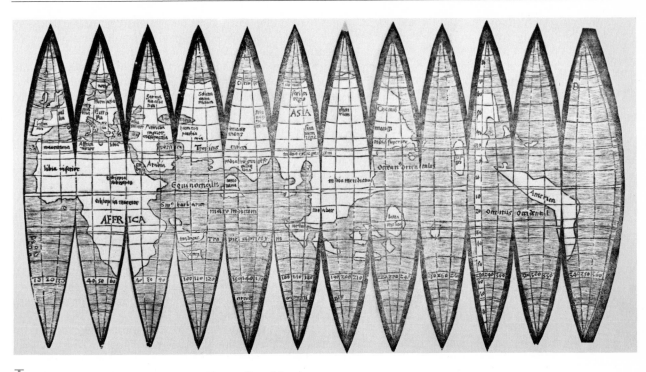

This world map engraved by Martin Waldseemuller of Strasbourg was printed in 1507. It shows, for the first time, the name America for the newly discovered continent. Waldseemuller intended the map to be cut out and pasted on a small globe. (Photograph—James Ford Bell Collection, University of Minnesota, Minneapolis)

nomena in their areal context. In dealing with the territorial manifestations of economic, social, and cultural forces and patterns, political geography relies heavily on the other subfields of human geography.

Understanding of the present usually requires knowledge of how it came into being, in other words, the genetic approach. Thus, geography has a historical component. However, when we speak of *historical* geography, we mean geography of the past for its own sake. Apart from its focus on some former era, historical geography uses the same concepts and asks the same questions as other branches of the discipline.

Another way of cutting the geographic layer cake is to carve out one slice for special examination. *Urban* geography is a good example. Cities and towns were, of course, always considered in geography, but the modern trend toward urbanization and its accompanying problems push this topic into the foreground of current concern. Although the work of some geographers suggests that urban geography is merely an aspect of economic geography, actually the city has social, cultural, and political components that demand equal attention.

Another category concerns not the content but the tools of geographic investigation and presentation. In the forefront stands *cartography.* In recent decades the rapid development of mathematics, statistics, and computerized information has challenged its paramount position. Finally, there are the techniques of *fieldwork,* and their extensions into *remote sensing,* first through the aid of aerial photography, now through powerful new types of infrared sensors, radar, and other scanning devices installed in earth-orbiting satellites.

If we apply this rough sketch of nomenclature to this book, where does it belong? First and foremost, it is in the field of human geography. Second, the approach is topical rather than regional. Third, it views geographic problems mainly from the cultural and social angles, extending to economic and political factors and patterns where relevant. Finally, it pays attention to special phenomena of current concern such as urban and population problems and the transformation of the environment. Maps, graphs, statistical tables, and photographs support and illustrate the text.

## THE MAIN CONCEPTS OF GEOGRAPHY

Geography is a meaningful way of looking at the earth, not a mere inventory of its contents. This geographic viewpoint rests upon a number of fundamental, intertwined concepts. These basic ideas and propositions guide the geographer in his research as well as in teaching. A brief preview will help the reader to spot these concepts as they appear in the following chapters.

### LOCATION

"Where," as the point of reference in earth space, is the first thing the geographer wants to know. To find where something is requires defining its spatial relationship to other points. To locate is to relate. The mathematical position of a specific place can be found on globe or map by means of the grid of meridians and parallels which serve as coordinates. Knowing the mathematical position of a place is like having the address of a person. It tells you only where to find him, but nothing about his home and surroundings. Geographical insight comes with knowledge of the place itself, that is, its *site,* and also with knowing why it is there—that is, its relations with other areas, its *situation.*

*Site* stands for that aspect of place that has to do with the local forces and processes and their interrelations. For instance, one might describe how man has organized his life in an oasis in Central Asia by noting the interrelations of climate, soil, water supply, agriculture, and town life.

*Situation,* also called relative location or geographic position, shows how a place is related to other places. It recognizes that a locality is not an island unto itself but has contacts with other places, which may in part explain the character of the place. For instance, in the case of the oasis,

the town may be the market for exchange of products between farmer and nomad from the surrounding steppe.

Evaluation of an area must always take into account both site and situation, though one may prove to be more important than the other. Extensive ruins in central Asian oases suggest that several hundred years ago there was a much larger and wealthier urban population. Some geographers seek the main cause for the decay in increased aridity which made irrigation more and more difficult; in other words, they hold a local *site* factor responsible. But others deny the evidence of long-range climatic deterioration. They point out that the former wealth of oasis cities rested on their function as trade centers along the caravan routes of inner Asia. When trade was interrupted or shifted to sea routes, the cities lost their source of prosperity. The latter view stresses the change in *situation* as the fundamental cause for the decline.

Site and situation present two aspects of place: site the internal, situation the external. What is "internal" and what "external" depends on how the area is defined. In buying a home, the qualities of the house and lot represent the site, the character and facilities of the neighborhood the situation. In evaluating the strategic position of the United States in the world, the country is the site, the surrounding lands and seas the situation. In each case we are thinking of places and their surroundings, but in the framework of different scales.

### THE MEANING OF SCALE

*Scale,* a familiar term in cartographic presentation, expresses the proportional relationship between map and earth reality. It has important bearing on geographic thought, because the size of the area we observe affects not only the intensity of perception but also the kind of generalizations that can be made about the area (Figure 1–1).

In fieldwork, to record what is observed in a small area, we make use of a large-scale map on which, for instance, 1 centimeter represents $\frac{1}{4}$ kilometer in reality, expressed numerically as a scale of 1:25,000. At this scale we can mark each field, footpath, and house, though we must generalize a bit on shapes. If we want to cover an area four times as wide and long but on paper of the

**ON READING THE MAPS IN THIS BOOK**

Maps, diagrams, and photographs illustrate and supplement the written text. Though most diagrams and photographs explain themselves, maps can be complicated: they symbolize representations or abstractions of the real world. Some represent or picture the earth surface realistically (Figures 10–4 and 13–4). Others are more abstract (Figures 10–7 or 14–7). Each map, regardless of level of abstraction, uses logical principles and concepts through which to code information and ideas. The reader who carefully studies the maps in this book will find that the principles and concepts behind them become clear and more meaningful.

**Symbols**  On most maps, spatial phenomena are depicted by point and areal symbols. For example, dots and circles indicate the distribution of population (Figure 1–5), and different point symbols show several kinds of dispersion (Figure 11-14b). Sequential color combinations in an interval scale may present quantitative distributions (Figures 1–1 and 14–1). Contrasting symbols mark qualitative information (Figures 7–4 and 9–1). Distributions of similar or related phenomena can be represented by means that express their relationships. For example, Figure 6–4 shows events connected with Islam in gray and those associated with Christianity in green.

| PLACE OR SUBJECT | LETTERING EXAMPLE | LETTERING TYPE FACES |
|---|---|---|
| Names of political units: names of countries, provinces, and cities. | **INDONESIA, Borneo,** Dacca | Lydian |
| Names of water bodies: names of oceans, rivers, and lakes. | *INDIAN OCEAN, Yenesey River, Lake Balkhash, Aral Sea* | Futura Book Italic |
| Other areal and regional names. | **TURKESTAN, RUHR, Common Meadows** | Alternate Gothic |
| Explanatory remarks and notes. | 1st to 4th Century | Futura Book |
| Map legend. | **Boundary between East and West** | Optima Semibold |

**Lettering**  Letter sizes vary with the importance of different places and subjects. Various categories of phenomena need contrasting typefaces. Research shows that if the reader knows about the typefaces and the sizes of lettering for different categories of places, he needs less time to understand a map (see diagram).

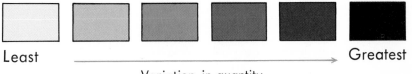

Least ⟶ Greatest

Variation in quantity

**World Maps**  This book uses a standard world base map both for double-page spread (e.g., Figure 15–1) and for single-page (e.g., Figure 12–2). Australia and nearby islands appear twice on these maps, once in the southeast corner in their proper location relative to Asia, and again in the lower left-hand corner with much less distortion of shape.

Mei-Ling Hsu

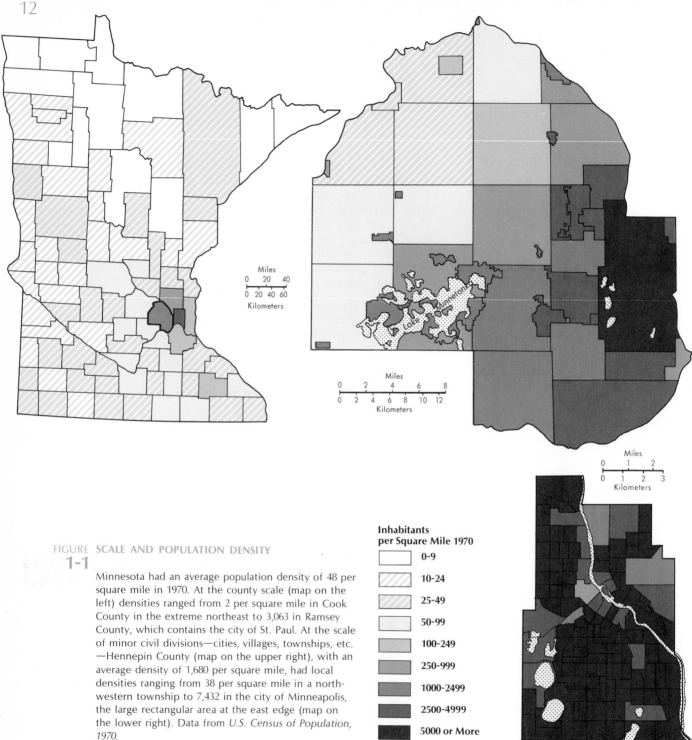

## FIGURE 1-1 SCALE AND POPULATION DENSITY

Minnesota had an average population density of 48 per square mile in 1970. At the county scale (map on the left) densities ranged from 2 per square mile in Cook County in the extreme northeast to 3,063 in Ramsey County, which contains the city of St. Paul. At the scale of minor civil divisions—cities, villages, townships, etc. —Hennepin County (map on the upper right), with an average density of 1,680 per square mile, had local densities ranging from 38 per square mile in a north-western township to 7,432 in the city of Minneapolis, the large rectangular area at the east edge (map on the lower right). Data from *U.S. Census of Population, 1970.*

**Inhabitants
per Square Mile 1970**

| | |
|---|---|
| | 0-9 |
| | 10-24 |
| | 25-49 |
| | 50-99 |
| | 100-249 |
| | 250-999 |
| | 1000-2499 |
| | 2500-4999 |
| | 5000 or More |

same size, we use the smaller scale of 1 centimeter to 1 kilometer (1:100,000).* At this scale we must omit many details; that is, we reduce the individual features into more general patterns of cropland, pasture, house blocks, and roads. By decreasing the scale still further—and keeping the map size constant—we finally arrive at a map of the earth which can show only the gross surface configurations, the larger rivers, and the principal cities.

Another type of map represents only one category of facts as distributed over part or all of the earth. If such a "thematic" or "topical" map, say of population, is on a very large scale, it can show one dot for each enumerated person at the exact location of his residence, but as the scale decreases, one dot must stand for a hundred or a thousand or even more persons.

We cannot say that one scale is better than another, because its value depends on the purpose of the map. But it is important to realize that the level of general conclusions will differ with the scale of the map. There would not be so many disputes about the validity of generalizations if people took careful note of the scale of investigation on which the findings were based (Webb, 1976). For example, while we might conclude from the study of a small area that the location of manufacturing plants is strongly conditioned by taxes, zoning, and terrain, these factors would carry little weight in generalizations about the location of industries in the United States or the world as a whole.

## THE REGIONAL CONCEPT

The places geographers study are of two kinds. First of all, *place* means a specific individual locality identified by its assigned name, be it San Francisco or Paris, Arizona or Albania. These places are given. They are *instituted* by official action and have well-defined boundaries. Also recognizable as place-individuals, though less well defined, are such concrete natural features as Mount Whitney, the Baltic Sea, or Cuba—less well

*In using traditional English and Anglo-American measurements, a parallel example would be the comparison of a map at the scale of 1:15,840—1 inch on the map representing ¼ mile or 15,840 inches in reality—with a map at the scale of 1:63,360 (1 inch representing 1 mile or 63,360 inches in reality).

defined because where exactly does a mountain begin, and where is the boundary between land and sea?

Examples of the second kind of place are the Cotton Belt, the tundra, the American manufacturing belt, the Great Plains. Such places are not "given." Each name denotes an area which is alleged to have a distinct character. Many people deny that there is a Cotton Belt, and while most would concede that the Great Plains exist, no two fully agree as to their exact extent (Figure 1–2). We are dealing here with mental constructs formulated to arrange earth features in some abstract order. The lay person who looks at, say, a map showing climatic regions is apt to take it as a discovery of science, like the table of atomic weights. Instead we should think of it as a useful tool, designed to bring order into the infinite variety of climatic conditions.

A region, then, is a part of the earth that is alike in terms of the specific criteria chosen to delimit it from other regions. An "instituted" place-individual can be in different regions according to the generic order employed—generic in the sense of order by genus or class. Illinois belongs climatically to the humid continental region of North America, agriculturally to the mixed-farming belt, and industrially to the main manufacturing zone.

**Formal and Functional Regions** The examples just mentioned have in common that they are regions defined by the likeness or even homogeneity of specified features or forms. This so-called *formal* or *uniform* region differs from the *nodal* or *functional* region. The latter type is conceived as a spatial entity in terms of organization or linkages, commonly functioning around a central city through a network of circulation. Denver, for example, is the node of an "inland empire" which comprises segments of two very different physical regions, Rocky Mountains and Great Plains, and of diverse economic activities such as crop farming, ranching, forestry, and mining. The limits of Denver's supporting and tributary area, or hinterland, can be determined by the extent and intensity of spatial interaction, such as the in-and-out flow of goods, travelers, long-distance telephone calls, newspaper circulation, wholesale deliveries, and so on. Figure 1–3 shows the tributary region of

FIGURE
**1-2**

## THE GREAT PLAINS REGION DEFINED

Maps in the early 1800s depicted a vast "desert" between the 98th meridian and the Rocky Mountains. By the middle of that century this concept was replaced by that of the "Great Plains," a term apparently first used by Charles Preuss on his map of 1848 and further defined and described in the writings of William Gilpin, who emphasized the short-grass vegetation as the essential feature of the region. According to Lewis, Gilpin's delineation coincides with the "Dry Prairie" shown on a map of 1857 "by D. J. B." and here reproduced as Map A. More recent ways of defining the region (within the political limits of the United States) are: (B) as a "physiographic province" according to Fenneman; (C) as an "agricultural region" according to Baker; (D) as a "semi-arid, treeless, and level environment" by Webb.

SOURCES: Lewis, G. M. "William Gilpin and the Concept of the Great Plains Region," *Annals of the Association of American Geographers,* 56 (1966): 33–51.

Fenneman, N. M. "Physiographic Divisions of the United States," *Annals of the Association of American Geographers,* 6 (1916): 19–98.

Baker, O. E. "The Agriculture of the Great Plains Region," *Annals of the Association of American Geographers,* 13 (1913): 109–168.

Webb, W. P. *The Great Plains,* New York, 1931.

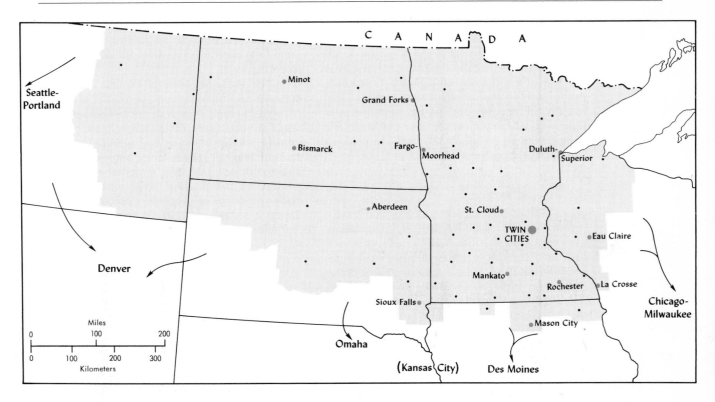

FIGURE **THE TWIN CITIES (MINNEAPOLIS–ST. PAUL)**
**1-3** TRADE REGION

This functional region extends from western Wisconsin to Montana. Beyond the boundaries of the region, unshaded areas gravitate to other named metropolises. Medium-sized and small trade centers within the Twin Cities region are shown. After a map in Borchert, J. R., and Adams, R. B., "Trade Centers and Trade Areas of the Upper Midwest," *Upper Midwest Economic Study Urban Report No. 3*, Minneapolis, 1963, page 25.

● **Metropolitan Center**

▪ **Wholesale-Retail Center**

• **Complete Shopping Center**

Minneapolis–St. Paul (the Twin Cities) as another example. In a worldwide view, sovereign states may assume the character of functional regions. France exemplifies how highly diverse formal regions function as an integrated whole around Paris, the national hub.

**Internally Perceived Regions**   The foregoing discussion asserts that regions do not exist in reality. They are intellectual creations enabling us to order the earth's particular places within meaningful general frames. However, one can argue for the recognition of a type of "real" region: one whose inhabitants share a deep awareness of the historically grown amalgam of life and land. This consciousness of a common bond sets off their territory from its surroundings. Usually this kind of region combines to a high degree both functional coherence and formal homogeneity. Such an area with a distinct personality may be called an "internally perceived" region, or as some would say, a "turf." It exists not only in the sense of the inhabitants' solidarity but also in the experience of outsiders looking in. Compartments like the old French *pays* and the German *Landschaften,* also perhaps in the United States areas like that of the "Pennsylvania Dutch," exemplify this brand of self-differentiating regions. Frequently the regional novelist has found inspiration here where "humanity over centuries entwined with the fabric of the land" to create a particular and unique locality.

## INTERNAL COHERENCE

There are many heterogeneous things that make a region: people, terrain, climate, soil, vegetation, minerals, crops, factories, trade and other services, town and country. If these elements were independent odds and ends, an observer could do no more than make an inventory, like listing the contents of a department store. Actually, each region has an interplay of forces, an interdependence and arrangement of elements, and a common imprint which permits rational inspection and comprehension. This internal consistency unites the particles into a whole, what the French call an *ensemble* and the Germans a *Gestalt.* To be sure, we must verify the assumption that such internal integration exists. The anthropologist who thinks that there is more to culture than a hodgepodge of unrelated traits uses a similar approach to the subject. The historian too, when facing the multitude of events in some bygone period, takes it for granted that there are relationships.

Biologists use the term *ecology* for the study of the mutual relations among all organisms living together in a particular habitat.* The organisms depend on their environment, both physical and biological and, in turn, affect and modify that environment. The mutual interaction between organisms and environment can be conceived as a functioning spatial organization and is called an "ecosystem." The concept of the ecosystem serves as a useful analogy to illustrate the geographic notion of internal coherence. "Analogy" is the word rather than "identity," because we cannot safely transfer these biological con-

cepts to the world of mankind. True, we depend on nature, transform it, are part of it, but at the same time apart from it—because of our culture (see Chapter 2).

The study of elements in their interaction does not presuppose that all are part of one great chain of causality. Obviously the major landforms result from entirely other forces than climate. Climate, though affecting the distribution of organisms and soil types, does not explain their origin and evolution. Nor is humanity merely a product of the physical environment. Clearly, many and disparate processes combine to create the earth and its parts. How then can we hope to find internal coherence in an area where diverse forces happen to meet? The answer lies in viewing human society as the organizer of its habitat. Each society molds the forces and features of its biophysical environment to its singular purpose. In this way it organizes space into a coherent entity such as a country, a region—in short, a place.

This seems a good opportunity to point out the difference in viewpoint between the so-called "systematic" sciences (economics, sociology, biology, geology, and such) and geography. The students of each of those disciplines extract from reality one particular set of phenomena to study. Some of them criticize geographers because they are interested in all things at once and thus constantly trespass into fields already neatly divided among the systematic sciences. They should understand that the geographer studies peoples, industries, cities, climates, not for their own sake but because they are parts of a whole that give character to a place. Geography practiced the integrative, functional approach long before "ecology" became the popular term to express this all-inclusive outlook on reality.

In this holistic position geography resembles history. The historian, too, uses any and all facts—a constitution, a muddy battlefield, a statesman's ulcer—to explain a historic event. Both history and geography should take a comprehensive view of mankind and earth, one stressing time bonds, the other place bonds. This approach counterbalances artificial partitions. Geographers feel that the greater the fragmentation of knowledge, the more the need for putting the bits together again in an orderly way, to understand the reality of places.

*The term *ecology,* coined in 1869 by the German biologist Ernst H. Haeckel, derives from *oikos,* meaning "house" or "household," and *logos,* meaning "word" or, in this context, "knowledge" or "science."

FIGURE 1-4 **DISTRIBUTION OF RIVER TOWNS IN MID-AMERICA**

"Places" have many and diverse characteristics. The towns shown on this map all have one property in common: they belong to the generic class of "river towns."

## SPATIAL DISTRIBUTION

Each individual place has its specific location on the earth's surface. If we select one element or property of that place to compare it with the location of like elements or properties in other places, we record a *distribution*. For instance, there is only one Keokuk, Iowa. But if we think of it as a river town, and now record the location of all river towns in the central United States, we have a map of a distribution (Figure 1-4). The same can be done with all other elements or properties that give character to a place, be they distribution of precipitation in Kansas, of Puerto Ricans in New York, of Chinese in Malaya, or of houses on stilts in Southeast Asia.

Analysis of distributions is a highly important part of geographic study. Some geographers declare it to be the hallmark of geography, but this seems an error. The purpose of geography is to understand the character of places; the study of distributions is one of the means to pursue that end. Many other disciplines also use distributions. The plant pathologist who studies wheat diseases

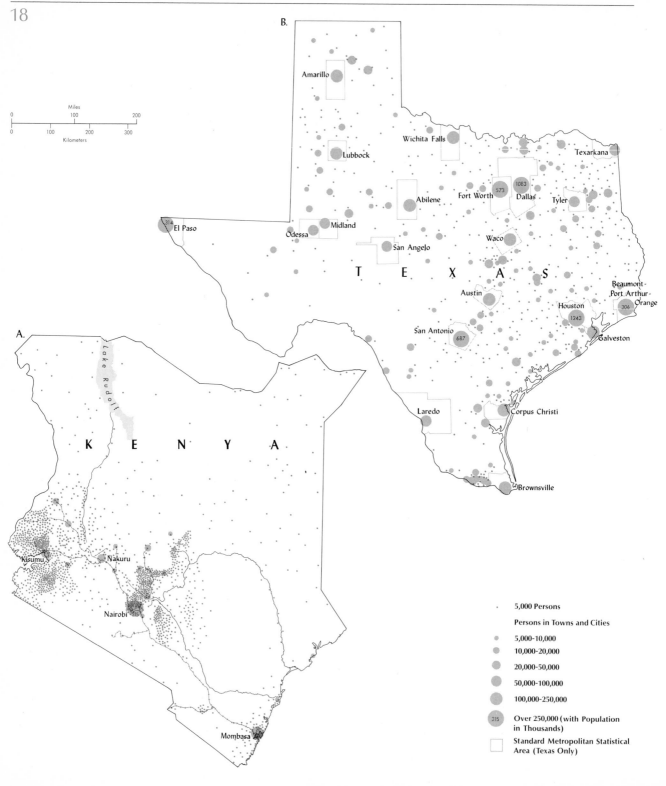

B.

Amarillo

Wichita Falls

Texarkana

Lubbock

Abilene    Fort Worth    Dallas    Tyler
                    573      1083

El Paso

Odessa    Midland

San Angelo

Waco

T    E    X    A    S

Beaumont-
Port Arthur-
Orange

Austin                    Houston    306
                          1243

San Antonio                    Galveston
        687

A.

Lake Rudolf

K    E    N    Y    A

Laredo    Corpus Christi

Kisumu    Nakuru

Nairobi    315

Brownsville

Mombasa

· 5,000 Persons

Persons in Towns and Cities

5,000–10,000

10,000–20,000

20,000–50,000

50,000–100,000

100,000–250,000

315    Over 250,000 (with Population
       in Thousands)

       Standard Metropolitan Statistical
       Area (Texas Only)

Miles
0        100        200

0    100    200    300
       Kilometers

FIGURE
1-5

**KENYA AND TEXAS: DISTRIBUTION OF POPULATION**

These maps are at the same scale. Texas has almost 20 percent more area than Kenya, but their populations are about the same. The uneven distributions of rural population reflect not only the influences of soil, climate, terrain, and vegetation but also the culture of different human groups. The history of land allocation has also been important in both places. In Kenya, note the large size of Nairobi (the capital city) and Mombasa (the main port) compared with other towns; also note the high numbers and density of rural populations in a number of regions. In Texas, note the huge metropolises of Dallas-Fort Worth and Houston; the many other large, medium, and small-sized towns; and the low number and densities of rural populations. The map of Kenya is modified from survey of Kenya, *Atlas of Kenya,* Nairobi, 1962, Map 25A, and that of Texas is based on the *U.S. Census of Population, 1970.*

relative to the size of the study area. *Pattern* means the geometric arrangement without regard to the size of the study area. These distinctions are vital to the correct understanding of distribution. To illustrate, compare the country of Kenya in East Africa and the state of Texas in the United States (Figure 1-5). Kenya is slightly smaller in area, but has a larger population than Texas, leading to a density of population for Kenya of 22 per square kilometer (56 per square mile) compared with 17 per square kilometer (44 per square mile) for Texas.* Although the average densities are fairly close, the dispersion of population is quite different: most Kenyans live in the country, most Texans in the city. Their settlement patterns contrast from village clusters in Kenya to isolated farms in Texas, from urban life in Kenya, dominated by Nairobi and Mombasa, to that of Texan metropolises and cities of all sizes.

## SPATIAL INTERACTION

Interaction between places implies mobility of things, ideas, or people over the earth's surface. Movements of air masses make the local weather, ocean currents condition the temperature and salinity of the sea, and runoff from the highlands affects the lowlands. In human affairs migration brings strangers into new lands, and diffusion of an invention carries a novel idea beyond its area of origin. Division of labor makes people dependent on each other. Territorial specialization demands the exchange of goods and services with other areas. Thus, spatial differentiation goes together with spatial interaction. This interaction requires overcoming distance through communication and transportation or—to adopt a French term covering all forms of movement—through "circulation." Accessibility measures the degree to which a place is approachable from other places by means of circulation.

*Central location* is usually an advantage because it signifies that a place is accessible from all directions, the focus for the surrounding area, its market, its forum, from where in turn goods and ideas radiate. Being in the center of things is not always a blessing, as in a war or tornado. Apart from such destructive forces, however, great ad-

certainly will make a map of their occurrence. While doing that, the pathologist is not suddenly transformed into a geographer. The geographer, however, who is investigating the wheat regions in the United States will welcome the map.

By presenting distributions on a map, we can detect areal associations. For instance, we may note the presence of fruit orchards near the shores of Lake Ontario in those areas where late spring and early autumn frosts are rare. In some cases visual comparison of different distributional patterns may suffice, but in others much more sophisticated statistical methods are needed to establish as exactly as possible the extent of areal correlation between different phenomena. High correlation between two variables is no proof of causal relationship; it is possible that the correspondence in areal extent of the two variables is the unrelated result of a third, unknown, factor. Or the association may be coincidental and of little significance, as in the case where a geographer observed a close correspondence between the American manufacturing belt and the area where Ben Davis apples are grown.

Spatial distribution presents three aspects: density, dispersion, and pattern. *Density* is defined as the overall or average frequency of occurrence of a phenomenon within the area under study, relative to the size of this area. *Dispersion* refers to the extent of the spread of the feature

*See page xvii.

vantages accrue to being in the middle of events. We see this easily when we contrast central and marginal locations in a city, a country, or a wider realm. *Marginal* in the sense here used means being offside, removed from the flow of circulation. Backwaters tend to be stagnant. It is no accident that—before the Europeans came—the southern tips of South America and Africa, as well as Australia and Tasmania, were the homes of very primitive peoples. Knowledge of new ideas and tools hardly reached these remote dead ends.

Distance from the centers of innovation is not the only factor. Any barrier to circulation lessens accessibility and thus acts to preserve traditional ways. The rain forests of the Congo Basin, the jungle-covered uplands of central India, and the "green desert" of the Amazon lowland hide tribes of a culture considerably less developed than that of the people in surrounding regions. Even the inhabitants of the Appalachians, the Scottish Highlands, and the marshes of western Soviet Russia have old-fashioned economies, compared to their compatriots in more accessible areas. All suffer more or less from isolation.

**Von Thünen's Model**   Distance from the market is an important factor in determining where economic activities locate. Johann Heinrich von Thünen (1783–1850), a German estate owner with a thorough knowledge of local agrarian conditions and with a great interest in economic theory, examined the spatial interaction between market and types of farming (*Der Isolierte Staat*, Part I, 1826).* He assumed a circular state consisting of a plain with the same climate and fertility throughout and surrounded by a wilderness that isolated it completely from other countries. He envisioned the population as a homogeneous group practicing a commercial economy, each entrepreneur striving for the highest possible return. In the center of this state the one and only city served as the marketplace, thus setting the price for all commodities. With all these factors held constant, von Thünen introduced the only

*The German geographer Leo Waibel wrote in 1933 a lengthy essay on von Thünen's theory and its significance for geography. Apparently it remained unknown to later American authors. See end of this chapter for citations. The effects of distance on land use are discussed further in Chapter 10.

variable: transportation to the market, its cost increasing at the same rate as distance. His design, conceived in prerailroad days, supposed all goods were moved by horse-drawn wagons (Figure 1–6).

Von Thünen showed how under these conditions different types of land use would develop in concentric rings. The ring adjacent to the city would produce perishables (vegetables, milk) and commodities heavy in proportion to their value (fuel wood, lumber). On the periphery, where transport costs were highest, there would be only animal husbandry requiring minimal investment (livestock ranching on natural pasture). Between these extremes other forms of agriculture prevailed, from intensive farming near the city to single-crop growing in the outer area.

To understand this, one should keep in mind that all farmers were paid the same market price for, say, rye. Those near the market, with small transportation costs, enjoyed a big return, enabling them to grow rye as part of a rotation scheme, with high input of capital and labor. In contrast, those living far from the city received a low return for grain and thus could not afford big expenses. They grew rye only, leaving the fields fallow before sowing again. The point is that the same crop or animal could be produced in several concentric zones but as part of quite different types of farming.

Von Thünen's rational construction—what now is usually called a model—has inspired others to develop location theories for manufacturing industries (Chapter 11) and for towns as central places (Chapter 14). In recent years this theoretical approach to spatial interaction has won many converts among geographers, especially those engaged in economic and urban aspects of the discipline. However, one should remember that a scientific model does not represent a miniature of reality. Rather, it is a highly abstract design set up to examine the effect of one or, at most, a few variables.

Von Thünen's rigorous deductive logic clarifies our thought on spatial interaction. It demonstrates that, under the given assumptions, identical physical environments (sites) will be put to very different uses, depending on the location relative to the market (situation). But by the very nature of its abstraction, this theory ignores many other factors—physical, technical, cultural, his-

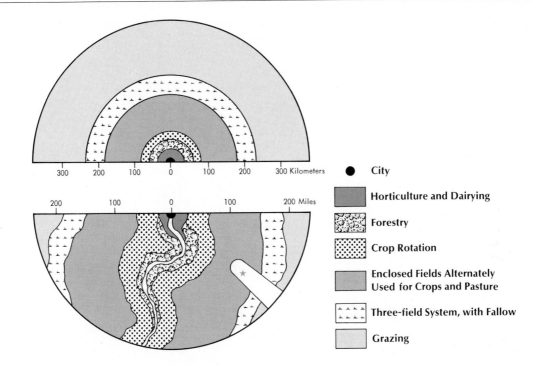

- ● **City**
- **Horticulture and Dairying**
- **Forestry**
- **Crop Rotation**
- **Enclosed Fields Alternately Used for Crops and Pasture**
- **Three-field System, with Fallow**
- **Grazing**

FIGURE **VON THÜNEN'S CIRCLES**
**1-6**

The upper half (A) illustrates the differentiation of land use under von Thünen's basic assumptions. The lower half (B) shows what happens, according to von Thünen, if one relaxes the original assumption by introducing a river (lowering transport cost) and a small market town with its own sphere of influence. The kilometer scale is adopted from Waibel, L., "Das Thünensche gesetz und seine Bedeutung für die Landwirtschaftsgeographie," in Waibel, L., *Probleme der Landwirtschaftsgeographie,* Breslau, 1933.

torical—which the geographer must consider to understand the endless diversity and intricacy of places. Also, changes in transportation technology have greatly altered the nature of the one variable on which von Thünen based his theory.

### THE THEME OF CHANGE

To say that geography deals with place, and history with time, is only part of the truth. The historian always treats events in specific places, be it colonial rule in India or feudalism in western Europe. And the geographer perceives each place as the product of change through time.

"The abiding earth" is a comforting phrase, but reality is different. Everything is in process of change. Even an equilibrium is maintained only by dynamic forces, like that of a rider on a bicycle. The word *process* refers to an interaction of forces that causes a series of changes through time. The process of erosion creates a valley. The process of urbanization swallows up the countryside. To understand the nature, direction, and rate of change requires knowledge of the processes that cause the change. We must view events in time scales appropriate to the process. For instance, weather is subject to daily and seasonal cycles; climate has fluctuated around a relatively constant mean over the last several thousand years, but has actually changed over much longer time spans. Confusion of time scales leads to errors (much like confusion of area scales), such as interpreting the succession of a few cold years as the advent of a new ice age.

In human affairs there are similar short- and long-term changes, though even the longest are brief compared to the geologic time scale. Some are part of daily, seasonal, and annual cycles or fluctuations (e.g., commuter traffic, livestock

The Netherlands: A village perched along a dike, 40 kilometers north of Amsterdam. Vegetables are grown on almost all farm plots. Because for centuries farmers have dredged the drainage ditches to spread the fertile mud over the fields, one-fourth of the surface is water. (Photograph—KLM Aerocarto, Airport Amsterdam)

drives, manufacturing output); others are long-term processes modifying the way of life and the landscape (such as the European migrations or the Industrial Revolution).

Old cities like Rome and Istanbul are living exhibits of what different societies have contributed to city building and architecture. Elsewhere, and particularly in the countryside, the impact of the past may be less striking; nevertheless, the past is there and affects the present. Property lines, for instance, are very stubborn space dividers. In coastal California, alignment of farms and house lots quite commonly conforms to the pattern of Spanish land grants. In each case, an action in the remote past is to be reckoned with today.

The legacy of the past plagues many cities. The problem often is one of site. The first European settlers found the small island of Manhattan and the narrow hilly peninsula at the Golden Gate suited to their needs. They could hardly foresee the modern metropolitan centers that would evolve on these sites.

Changing geographic situations also affect, often severely, the fortunes of cities, countries, and even larger parts of the earth. The New York and San Francisco metropolitan regions, in spite of cramped sites for their central cities, have prospered because they commanded, and still command, the funnels of trade between ocean and continent. But Samarkand and Venice are only shadows of their glorious past when they were on the world's main trade routes. In the rise of the ancient civilizations the favorable situation of the Middle East was an important factor. Here, at the junction of land and sea routes, peoples, ideas, and goods mingled. Later the centers of progress moved to the shores of the Mediterranean Sea. When the positional advantage shifted to the ocean coasts, western Europe developed into the center of innovation. The Mediterranean became a backwater after the Great Discoveries but regained some of its former value when the Suez Canal was opened.

In the historical perspective, regions may be conceived as expanding and contracting entities, perhaps even migrating ones. Somewhere a certain type of economy or a culture trait starts (nomadic herding, irrigation, the cotton plantation), puts its mark on society and landscape, then spreads from there as far as conditions favor its expansion. But a new resource may be discovered, or a different economy may invade and transform the area. The new forces may then even overgrow and smother the old regional pattern until at last only some relict forms of the old order remain.

Even if geographers concentrate on current conditions, they must always remember that the present is but an interim phase in an ever-changing existence. Behind the dominant features they will note the inheritance of the past, but they also may detect mutations or innovations that point toward new directions in the way of life and the use of habitat.

The seven concepts discussed in this introduction express the geographic turn of mind. Another theme has been repeatedly mentioned but not explicitly examined: the relationship between mankind and nature. We will look more closely at this in the following chapter.

## CITATIONS AND FURTHER READINGS

Ad Hoc Committee on Geography, Earth Sciences Division, National Academy of Sciences—National Research Council, *The Science of Geography,* Washington, D.C., 1965. This report contains suggestions for new avenues of research, particularly in theoretical and deductive studies.

Broek, J. O. M. *Compass of Geography,* Columbus, Ohio, 1966. A brief, nontechnical introduction. Also published as *Geography, Its Scope and Spirit,* Columbus, Ohio, 1965, with an additional chapter suggesting methods for elementary and secondary teachers by R. H. Muessig and V. R. Rogers.

Buttimer, A. *Values in Geography,* Commission on College Geography, Resource Paper no. 24, Association of American Geographers, Washington, D.C., 1974.

Chorley, R. J., and Haggett, P. (eds.). *Models in Geography,* London, 1967.

Grotewold, A. "Von Thünen in Retrospect," *Economic Geography,* 35 (1959): 346–355.

Haggett, P. *Locational Analysis in Human Geography,* London, 1966.

Hartshorne, R. *The Nature of Geography,* Lancaster, Pennsylvania, 1939 (and several later editions). A survey of geographic thought in the light of the past. Based in part on the work of the German geographer Alfred Hettner.

Harvey, D. *Explanation in Geography,* London, 1969.

James, P. E. *All Possible Worlds: A History of Geographical Ideas,* Indianapolis and New York, 1972.

Johnson, H. B. "A Note on Thünen's Circles," *Annals of the Association of American Geographers,* 52 (1962): 213–220.

Kostrowicki, J. "A Key Concept: Spatial Organization," *International Social Sciences Quarterly,* 27 (1975): 328–345.

Peet, J. R. "The Spatial Expansion of Commercial Agriculture in the Nineteenth Century: A von Thünen Interpretation," *Economic Geography,* 45 (1969): 283–301.

Sautter, G. "The Discipline and Its Setting: Some Thoughts on Geography in 1975," *International Social Sciences Quarterly,* 27 (1975): 231–249.

Waibel, L. "Das Thünensche Gesetz und seine Bedeutung für die Landwirtschaftsgeographie," in Waibel, L., *Probleme der Landwirtschaftsgeographie,* Breslau, 1933.

Webb, J. W. "Geographers and Scales," in Kosinski, L. A., and Webb, J. W. (eds.), *Population at Microscale, Special Publication No. 8,* New Zealand Geographical Society, Hamilton, N.Z., 1976.

Wright, J. K. *Human Nature in Geography,* Cambridge, Mass., 1966.

## IMPORTANT INTERNATIONAL BIBLIOGRAPHIES

*Bibliographie géographique internationale* (annual), Centre National de la Récherche Scientifique, Paris, 1891–. Annotated bibliography covering a vast amount of geographical literature.

*Current Geographical Publications,* Additions to the Research Catalogue of the American Geographical Society (monthly, except July and August), American Geographical Society, Broadway and 156th St., New York, N.Y. 10032, 1938–.

*Documentatio Geographica: Geographische Zeitschriften- und Serien-Literatur,* Bundesforschungsanstalt für Landeskunde und Raumordnung, 532 Bad Godesberg, German Federal Republic, 1966–. Detailed bibliography of articles and notes in geographical serials and periodicals of the world.

*Geographical Abstracts,* University of East Anglia, Norwich, NR4 7TJ, England, 1966–. Each of the following seven parts appears six times a year. Landforms and the Quaternary, Climatology and Hydrology, Economic Geography, Social and Historical Geography, Sedimentology, Regional and Community Planning, Remote Sensing and Cartography. Brief informative abstracts in English of papers, reports, and books originally published in many languages.

## IMPORTANT GEOGRAPHICAL PERIODICALS

*Annals of the Association of American Geographers* (quarterly), Association of American Geographers, 1710 16th St. N.W., Washington, D.C. 20009, 1911–. High-quality journal with many articles of a philosophical and methodological nature.

*Canadian Geographer—Géographe canadien* (quarterly), Canadian Association of Geographers, Morrice Hall, McGill University, Montreal 2, P.Q. Canada, 1951–. Professional journal of Canadian geographers.

Commission on College Geography, Association of American Geographers, 1710 16th St. N.W., Washington, D.C. 20009. Beginning in 1965 the Commission published three series of interest to college teachers and students: General Series; for example, Church, M., et al.

*A Geographical Bibliography for American College Libraries* (1970): Resource Papers; for example, Tuan, Y.-F. *Man and Nature* (1971): Technical Papers; for example, Fielding, G. J., and Rumage, K. W. (eds.). *Computerized Instruction in Undergraduate Geography* (1972).

*Economic Geography* (quarterly), Clark University, Worcester, Mass., 1925–. The scope of articles is broader than the title would suggest.

*Geographical Journal* (quarterly), Royal Geographical Society, London, 1893–. Published under other titles since 1830.

*Geographical Review* (quarterly), American Geographical Society of New York, New York, 1911–. Contains articles and reviews of high quality.

*Professional Geographer* (bimonthly), Association of American Geographers. For address, see *Annals of the Association of American Geographers*, 1949–. Contains articles, news of members and centers of geographic work, official notices and reviews.

*Progress in Geography*, Arnold, London, 1969–. Each issue (approximately annual) contains review articles by eminent geographers on topics of importance.

*Soviet Geography: Review and Translation* (monthly, except July and August), American Geographical Society, New York, N.Y., 10032, 1960–. Contains full translations into English from Russian of major articles in the principal Soviet geographical periodicals.

*Transactions of the Institute of British Geographers* (quarterly), Institute of British Geographers, 1 Kensington Gore, London, SW7 2AR, England.

## OTHER NOTEWORTHY PERIODICALS

*Antipode, Area, Australian Geographer, Australian Geographical Studies, Focus, Geoforum, Geographia Polonica, Geographical Analysis, Geographical Bulletin, Geographical Magazine, Geographical Review of India, Geography, Journal of Geography, Journal of Historical Geography, Landscape, New Zealand Geographer, Pacific Viewpoint, Scottish Geographical Magazine.*

## IMPORTANT FOREIGN-LANGUAGE PERIODICALS (often containing articles in English)

*Annales de Géographie, Cahiers d'Outre-mer, Die Erde, Erdkunde, Geografiska Annaler* (Series B, Human Geography), *Méditerranée, Oesterreichische Geographische Gesellschaft, Petermanns Geographische Mitteilungen, Revista Geográfica, Revue de Géographie Alpine, Tijdschrift voor Economische en Sociale Geografie.*

# 2 NATURE AND CULTURE

## MANKIND AND THE BIOPHYSICAL ENVIRONMENT

Ever since our prehistoric ancestors became thinking human beings—Homo sapiens—people must have reflected on how the world around them affected their daily lives. They tried to placate the spirits, ghosts, or gods that controlled the forces of the environment. Although we today seem far removed from those crude fears and practices, we also must reckon with nature. One might think that science has already provided a clear view of the relationships between mankind and nature, but this is not so. Some scientists say that new techniques when widely put to use will give almost complete control over the environment, promising a bright future. Solar or nuclear energy, mining of the oceans, air conditioning the tropics, rainmaking over deserts, or irrigating with desalinated seawater—these and many more inventions will free us from nature's tyranny. Others argue that our massive interference with nature has brought erosion of soils, depletion of groundwater, exhaustion of minerals, pollution of air and water, and destruction of wildlife, all pointing up the lack of control over environment which, if continued, may lead to catastrophe (see Chapter 19).

In trying to understand the character of places, the geographer must face the issue of environmental relations. In essence, current geographic thought rejects the notion that the biophysical environment controls the course of human action. To the contrary, it considers mankind as the active and dominant agent who manipulates and modifies the habitat. Nevertheless, we are not independent of the environment; nor are we immune from the consequences of our own follies. The greater mankind's seeming conquest over nature, the more catastrophic may be the fall if modern systems of human existence stumble.

As a biological phenomenon, mankind is relatively constant in both time and space; almost all human beings have the same inborn capabilities and needs. The biophysical earth, changing slowly but comparatively constant in time, varies greatly in space. Yet the differences we see among human groups are not a direct response to their diverse biophysical environments. Rather, each society perceives and interprets the place where it lives through the selective prism of its own way of life, its culture. As time passes, a people may influence their habitat so much that it becomes a part of them and no longer apart from them. Thus, nature and culture intertwine as complementary elements of a whole rather than as opposing forces.

We will elaborate these points later in a discussion of the so-called environmentalist point of view. First, however, we must get to the heart of the matter—*society* and *culture*.

## SOCIETY AND CULTURE

The terms *society* and *culture* defy exact definition and lead to circular arguments. A society is an organized group of human individuals possessing a distinct culture. This shifts the burden to the definition of culture. Perhaps it is simplest to say that a specific culture is the total way of life of a people. Or, if one wants to stress the idealized standards rather than the practice, one might say that a culture is a people's design for living. The content of each culture includes systems of belief (ideology), social institutions (organization), in-

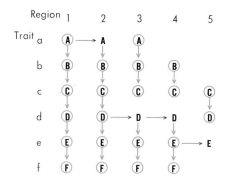

**DIFFUSION AND INDEPENDENT INVENTION**

These diagrams show two hypothetical cases of invention and diffusion. In "A" the different regions acquire most culture traits by diffusion (horizontal arrows). In "B" most traits are acquired by independent invention within the region itself (vertical arrows).

dustrial skills and tools (technology), and material possessions (resources). A composite and more explicit characterization of a culture is: a historically derived system of standardized forms of behavior, which the individual acquires as a member of a society. This statement stresses that culture consists of learned behavior, in contrast to the direct response to inherited biologic drives which are common to all animals including man.

All cultures differ, but their differences stem from variations on universal themes, such as language, religion, economy, law, technology. Since these are universals, there is much potential for interaction between peoples. Another language may be adopted, one religion discarded for another, new ways of making a living borrowed, and so on. As cultures influence each other, they are in constant change. Whether an invention or an idea comes from within or from without, a society must accept it before it can become part of the culture.

**Invention** The question whether local intervention or borrowing from other cultures more effectively shapes the ways of life should be resolved by facts. Our preconceived notions doubtless influence how we interpret these facts. Do we think people are inherently creative or—just the opposite—limited in their inventive ability? One who believes that the natural environment conditions, if not determines, the way of life will probably emphasize local invention as a response to the challenges of nature.

Our modern Western society, with its purposeful drive for technical innovations, makes invention seem to be the obvious and major starter of change, everywhere and at all times. Numerous anthropological studies, however, demonstrate that the truth is very different. Indeed, one must conclude that introductions of ideas and know-how from without, not local inventions, bring about most cultural changes (Figure 2-1).

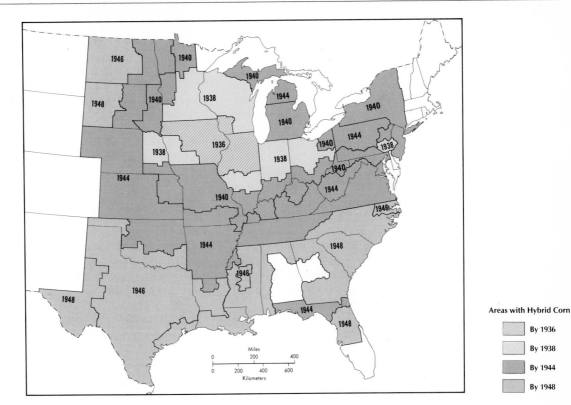

Areas with Hybrid Corn

By 1936

By 1938

By 1944

By 1948

FIGURE
2-2

THE SPREAD OF HYBRID CORN

Innovations may spread rapidly, especially if they improve the economic position of individuals and are promoted by government information agencies.

**Diffusion**  The spread of culture elements or complexes within a society or from one society to another is called *diffusion.* The manner of its transfer between peoples may be by direct contact or by indirect transmission through a chain of intermediaries. As an example of the latter form, it is well known that the Indian tribes of the northern Great Plains adopted the horse, as well as the art of riding and much that went with it, without ever having met a Spaniard. Innumerable ideas and things which we now consider as our European heritage actually came into Europe from cradlelands in the Middle East or even China or India. In turn, many culture traits of the modern Occidental world—be they soft drinks, atomic energy, or even the idea of progress itself—spread to other peoples. The same thing happens with new inventions within our own society. A good example, well documented by various studies, is the diffusion of hybrid corn from its area of origin in Iowa to other states during the 1930s and 1940s (Figure 2-2). Many other examples throughout this book, from religious systems to the steam engine, show the importance of such diffusion studies for human geography.

**Acculturation**  The study of diffusion is concerned with the spread of a culture trait or complex. However, one can also focus attention on a specific culture and see how it is affected by the adoption of foreign traits. The result of the transmission may range from a relatively minor change to virtual assimilation. Somewhere in between these two extremes lies *acculturation,* a useful concept if one can accept its somewhat indeterminate position. The term is most commonly used for "the process of interaction between two societies by which the culture of the society in the subordinate position is drastically modified to conform to the culture of the dominant society" (Hoebel, 1966, 559).

The dominant society—for instance, the Spanish or Portuguese in colonial Latin America—is usually called the donor; the dominated one the recipient, for example, the Indian. However, these positions are not absolute, because the donor group is also a recipient to the extent that it accepts elements (a tool, a food plant, a word) from the other party. Nevertheless, it is in the nature of the definition that the donor society makes the real impact on the other. Even so, the entire culture of the donor may not be available to the recipient, or the latter may not accept all that is offered. A people do not take a foreign element like a patient swallowing a pill from his doctor. Rather, they chew on it, adding their own juices to make it digestible—or they chew it around and reject it.

The present century witnesses great modifications in non-Occidental cultures under the impact of Western civilization. In Japan acculturation has gone quite far. If the term *acculturation* implies interaction *in process,* most would agree that non-Occidental peoples are largely in the position of recipients, thus becoming more similar to Occidental peoples. However, if we want to judge acculturation by the *result* achieved, we must reserve judgment. The process has not yet run its course; there may be recoils and reversals; and conditions vary greatly from society to society. With the degree of acculturation-in-the-end so uncertain, complete cultural assimilation (resulting in conformity) seems most unlikely. We live in One World, but it is not likely to become a uniform world. This may be all to the good. Mankind has, on the whole, profited from diversity of ideas and customs. It will continue to do so in the future.

## ENVIRONMENTALISM

In geography a different approach, called "environmentalism," downplays the importance of diffusion and acculturation; it puts in the forefront the view that human activities are strongly conditioned or even determined by the biophysi-

cal environment. A clear doctrine of this kind appears to have been formulated first in the book *Airs, Waters, Places,* ascribed to Hippocrates. This work was written by a physician, who lived in the fifth century B.C., for colleagues going abroad; it gives therefore a medical rather than a geographical theory. The author described the effect of each natural habitat on the people. For example, because the climate of Europe is more variable than that of Asia (as known to Hippocrates) "the physique of Europeans varies more than that of Asians." The same reasoning applies also to character. "In such a [European] climate arise wildness, unsociability and spirit. For the frequent shocks to the mind impart wildness, destroying tameness and gentleness." In contrast, the uniformity of the seasons in "Asia" explains why its inhabitants are less warlike.

Aristotle repeated the generalization about national character and added the political element: "The nations inhabiting the cold places and those of Europe are full of spirit but somewhat deficient in intelligence and skill, so that they continue comparatively free, but lacking in political organization and capacity to rule their neighbors. The peoples of Asia on the other hand are intelligent and skillful in temperament, but lack spirit, so that they are in continuous subjection and slavery. But the Greek race participates in both characters, just as it occupies the middle position geographically" (van Paassen, 1957, 324–328).

The theme reappeared in the Renaissance and found strong support by the French political philosopher Jean Bodin (1530–1596). He, too, attributed the main differences between peoples to three climatic belts. The northern cold zone produced a physically vigorous but mentally slow type, tending toward democratic government; the hot south had lazy people, intelligent but politically passive, and thus satisfied to live under despotism; in between, in the temperate zone, natural conditions brought about the right mixture of intelligence and industry, and favored the existence of the true monarchy. The influence of Aristotle is obvious, except that Bodin claimed France to be representative of the ideal climatic conditions, thereby underscoring neatly the subjectivity of the generalization.

The works of eighteenth-century writers

A census taker (back to camera) records a family in a highland village in Peru. Some 7 million Indians live in Peru, Ecuador, and Bolivia in isolated parts of the Andes mountain ranges at altitudes between 3,000 and 5,000 meters. (Photograph—United Nations)

such as Montesquieu (*The Spirit of Laws,* 1748), Buffon (*Natural History of Man,* 1749), and Voltaire (*Essay on the Customs and the Spirit of Nations,* 1756) reveal similar environmental notions. A century later Henry Buckle applied the methods of the natural sciences to history. In his view, the mild and moist climate of England had distinct advantages for steady work and perseverance. In contrast, the cold dark winters of Scandinavia or the dry, hot summers of Spain interrupted year-round work, leading to irregular habits and vacillation.

In the late nineteenth century, the theory of evolution through adaptation to the environment appeared to explain why human societies developed individually. Geographers always had found

it difficult to determine what caused the coherence between a people and its habitat. Now "adaptation to the physical environment" gave—or rather seemed to give—the scientific answer. It was in this period that the emphasis in geography shifted from the study of places to the study of environmental influences. In the United States the preoccupation with environmentalism lasted until the 1920s, when professional geographers turned away from it. The old notions, however, survived much longer in primary and secondary school education (Rostlund, 1956).

The fault of the environmentalists lay not in the issue they raised—How do the physical surroundings affect human action?—but in the sweeping generalizations they drew from scattered data, for they often ignored contrary evidence. Having defined geography in a narrow way as the study of environmental influences on mankind, they concentrated on proving the doctrine rather than objectively examining the facts. A favorite theme was the effect of climate. The Industrial Revolution began in northwestern Europe because of its variable weather, which stimulated mental activity and thus caused progress there. The birth of Judaic-Christian monotheism was linked to the desert environment, and the beginnings of free democracy to the influences of the landforms and climate of Greece.

Geographers today have become wary of such grand but simple explanations. Instead of reasoning from physical environment to human worth, they now ask how a particular society at a given time perceives its physical milieu and exploits the resources. This more sophisticated view has led in recent years to a renewed interest in the investigation of environmental factors. With full consideration of human elements, biogeography, sometimes called plant and animal geography, has rapidly moved toward the forefront in geographic research and teaching. The term human ecology now describes the study of relationships between a people and their habitat. Thus, the traditional geographic concern with the interaction between society and habitat enjoys a welcome revival.

## THE CONCEPT OF CULTURE IN GEOGRAPHY

Though a former generation of geographers emphasized environmental controls on human action, they did not ignore cultural factors. One of the founders of modern geography, Alexander von Humboldt (1769–1859), though mainly known for his studies of landforms, climate, and vegetation in Latin America, also examined cultural differences. For instance, he noted that no pastoral nomads inhabited pre-Columbian America, and therefore questioned the popular view that this form of existence is a universal stage in social evolution.

Another outstanding German geographer, Carl Ritter (1779–1859), was primarily interested in the historical growth of cultures in different parts of the world. He thought that divine will had created the earth as a school for man, in which he would advance from crude barbarism to spiritual greatness. Different "natural regions" (mainly defined by landforms) each served a specific purpose in this march of progress. Although this teleological approach (that is, the concern with ultimate ends) is foreign to modern scientific attitudes, Ritter did assemble a huge amount of factual information about different regions of the earth.

Even when Darwinistic notions of adaptation to the environment were at their height, not all geographers subscribed to this view. Friedrich Ratzel (1844–1904), a geographer and ethnologist, was at first beguiled by environmentalism, but afterwards saw the flaws in the argument. In one of his essays he underscored the paramount significance of the cultural factor by declaring: "I could perhaps understand early New England without knowing the land, but never without knowing the Puritan immigrants" (Ratzel, 1904, 407).

The founder of modern French geography, Paul Vidal de la Blache (1845–1918), consistently expressed outright opposition to environmental determinism. According to him the earth does not dictate man's behavior; it only offers opportunities. Human society makes the choice. To use his own words:

One must start from the notion that a land is a reservoir containing dormant energies of which nature has planted the seed, but whose use depends on man. It is he who by molding them to his purpose demonstrates his individuality. Man establishes the connection between disparate elements by substituting a purposeful organization of forces for the random effects of local circumstance. In this manner a region acquires identity differentiating it from others, till at length it becomes, as it were, a medal struck in the likeness of a people. (Vidal, 1903, 8)

The "choice" we make is not free and arbitrary. It is guided and restrained by the mental and social patterns of the group and its level of technology, in short, its culture. We see the habitat through the filter of our habits. Vidal's ideas have been refined and new ones added, but he deserves our appreciation for placing the human group and its way of life, or its life-style (genre de vie), in the center of geographic study.

The fundamental truth of his observations becomes clear to anyone who reflects on the vastly different ways in which succeeding societies have used the same area. For instance, the physical features of the Upper Great Lakes area are now virtually the same as they were 400 years ago. Yet, it saw in succession Indian hunting tribes, French fur traders, American lumbermen, miners, and dairy farmers. Today, the opportunity for recreation is one of its main assets.

## PERCEPTION OF THE ENVIRONMENT

Culture shapes what we see in our surroundings. Studies of environmental perception, quite fashionable now, have their roots in ideas expressed some fifty years ago by Vidal de la Blache and others of his generation. The British geographer Halford J. Mackinder, for instance, wrote in 1918:

The influence of geographical conditions upon human activities has depended . . . not merely on the realities as we now know them to be and to have been, but even in greater degree on what men imagined in regard to them. . . . Each century has its own geographic perspective. (Mackinder, 1942, 28–30)

When the Portuguese on their initial voyages along the west coast of Africa approached the equator, they worried about the hazard of the boiling seas, much the same as airplane builders and pilots discussed the sound barrier not many years ago. Columbus planned his voyage to Asia believing the earth to be much smaller than it is. Americans early in the nineteenth century thought the western interior of their country to be a great desert. The familiar Mercator world map, showing the Americas separated from the Old World by broad ocean moats, bolstered American isolationism.

### OPERATIONAL AND PERCEPTUAL ENVIRONMENT

The environment we live in, affecting us in some way or other, whether or not we are conscious of it, is called the *operational environment.* The portion of the operational environment of which we are aware is usually called the *perceptual environment.* The awareness may result directly from physical sensitivity to environmental stimuli or indirectly from learning and experience.

Although one can maintain that all individuals have their own perceptual environment, it is more important to note that persons belonging to the same culture or subculture most likely share basic ideas about and attitudes toward the environment; in other words, the perceptual environment is the external world as culturally conceived.

The difference between perceptual and operational environment becomes clear when one compares the perception Columbus had of the Atlantic with the operational reality. The former explains why Columbus decided to sail and why he thought he had reached the Indies; the latter accounts for what he actually accomplished.

Perception of Resources   The perceptual approach clarifies the meaning of a "natural resource." It is a useful element or property of the earth. Human needs and skills determine what is useful; in other words, cultural appraisal decides what constitutes a natural resource. Obsidian was just a glassy volcanic rock, no resource, until prehistoric man discovered its value as a cutting tool. Acorns were a major resource to the Californian Indians, but have very little value now. Rare metals and other substances unknown or ignored fifty years ago, such as uranium and thorium for nuclear fuel, are eagerly sought for today. Districts and whole regions rise or decline when natural resources are discovered, exhausted, or replaced by cheaper substitutes. But even things long known can take on new meaning as a resource. For instance, skiing and water sports have brought prosperity to many mountain and lake districts. A natural resource, then, is a relative concept, relative to culture. It is a cultural achievement.

Divergent cultural views often cause misunderstanding when technicians from Western countries, coming into another culture area, introduce new tools or practices. Occidental culture looks upon nature as physical matter to be manipulated for material comfort or power. Many other cultures regard people as part of nature; they do not dominate it, but must conform to the rules. An innovation that may threaten the cosmic harmony is apt to be viewed with suspicion. For instance, in various parts of Indonesia rice is harvested with a little knife no larger than a safety-razor blade. According to local beliefs this preserves the soul of the rice or appeases the rice goddess. Any other way of harvesting is bound to bring disaster.

We know it is easier to see the mote in another person's eye than the beam in one's own. Western societies have their own restrictive attitudes which thwart better use or conservation of resources. In the United States the tradition of local self-government impedes the better organization of metropolitan areas. More importantly, the high respect for technology and science, coupled with veneration of "progress" and ever-expanding demand for industrial products, increasingly threatens the quality of life.

**Behavioral Environment**  Within the perceptual environment one can focus more narrowly on the portion that draws out a behavioral response or toward which behavior is directed. This *behavioral environment* receives much attention in current research from social scientists, including geographers (Saarinen, 1969). For instance, among questions they ask is: What image do people have of a wilderness? An investigation in northern Minnesota showed that motorboaters were less bothered by the presence of roads, crowding, or noise than were canoeists. Therefore, the areal concept the latter had of a wilderness was more demanding, and thus more restrictive, than that of the former (Lucas, 1963). How do people living in areas of natural hazard (e.g., volcanic eruptions, earthquakes, floods, droughts, tornadoes) perceive and estimate the risk, and how do they adjust to the danger (Burton and others, 1969)? What parts of the United States rate high or low as good places to live, in the opinion of respondents residing in different parts of the country? As a final example: Are there national and regional differences in landscape tastes, and thus in the manner in which different societies strive to mold their habitat? These and similar inquiries revolve around the notion that "it is in this behavioral environment that physical features acquire values and potentialities which attract or repel human action" (Kirk, 1951).

## THE CULTURAL LANDSCAPE

Instead of asking how the earth influences man, one can reverse the question: How has man changed the earth? The surface of the earth, as modified by human influence, is called the cultural landscape.

Creation myths of many peoples express the thought that the earth was designed for man. The Old Testament contains the same idea: the Creator commands man to take possession of the earth. Opinions differ on how well man has managed his domain. For many centuries the dominant thought was that man and nature lived in harmony, although more critical views were not lacking. Already Plato observed that Attica had become "a skeleton of a body wasted by disease" owing to man-caused soil erosion. In modern times the theme of man as a destructive agent was eloquently expressed by the American statesman and scholar George Perkins Marsh (1801–1881) in his book *Man and Nature, or Physical Geography as Modified by Human Action* (1864). In his view, it was not the earth that made man, but man who made the earth, and worse, who despoiled it by ruthless exploitation. He warned Americans to exercise restraint in taming their vast new domain, lest it be turned into a wasteland like parts of the Old World. For this reason Marsh has been called "the fountainhead of the conservation movement in the United States" (Mumford, 1931, 78).

Whether we act in a destructive or in a constructive manner, there is no doubt that our actions transform the earth's surface. Mankind must be ranked with the forces of the physical and biotic world as a landscape-forming agent. The American geographer mainly responsible for the modern interest in the study of the cultural landscape was Carl O. Sauer (1889–1975), for many years professor of geography at the University of California, Berkeley. He stressed the need to understand the present landscape as the result of long-time processes involving the changing relations between man and land. Sequent occupance by different cultures has left its marks. Each new generation of inhabitants must take into account what its predecessors have wrought. What we call so glibly "natural prairie," "primeval forest," and "wildlife" actually are ecosystems induced or at least modified by mankind during the course of thousands if not hundreds of thousands of years. And such "natural disasters" as floods and dust storms are often in part due to human intervention with nature. We also interfere with natural

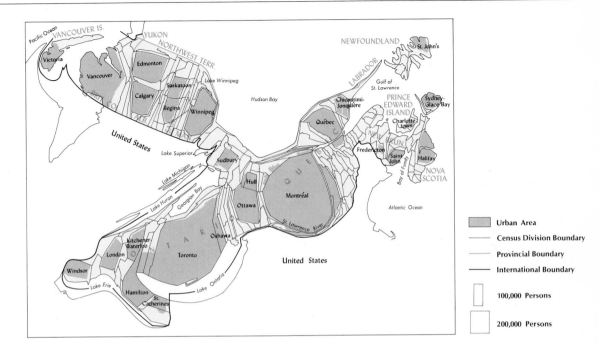

FIGURE CANADA: CARTOGRAM OF POPULATION
2-3 DISTRIBUTION

This "isodemographic map accurately represents the distribution of the Canadian people over their vast territory [and] recreates the image held by many travellers. Air transport accounts for more passenger miles than train and bus combined. Montreal and Toronto are less than four-and-a-half hours by air from Vancouver, but three days and nights by train. The conventional map of Canada [see front end-paper map] is the experience of the landborne traveller." Jackson, C. I., "Wide Open Spaces on the Map of Canada," *Geographical Magazine,* 44, no. 5 (February 1972): 342–351. The map is based on Skoda, L., and Robertson, J. C., "Isodemographic Map of Canada," *Geographical Paper No. 50,* Lands Directorate, Department of the Environment, Ottawa, 1972, with permission, Crown copyright reserved.

processes by restricting disasters such as floods, fires, and avalanches.

In addition to the intellectual satisfaction of comprehending the earth as our home, there is great practical worth in the study of the cultural landscape. Environmental planning aims to bring harmony and efficiency, with "a place for everything and everything in its place." A prerequisite for any plan is knowledge, understanding, and appreciation of the existing landscape so that we may preserve what is of psychological, social, or economic value and, if necessary, change what no longer has these merits. No wonder geographers are called upon to analyze and explain the growing environmental problems of our times. Many find careers in regional and city planning.

## THE DISTRIBUTION OF MANKIND

Even a cursory inspection of the world's population distribution makes readily apparent the complexity of interrelations between culture and nature (see the world map inside the front cover of the book).* Most of the more than 4 billion

*This map of the world distribution of population is most important and will repay careful study. It is a dot and circle distribution map and has an advantage over density maps because it shows the actual locations and concentrations of people. Careful observation can reveal the relative densities of population in different parts of the earth.

human beings crowd together in only a few parts of the earth, while wide areas remain virtually empty. The three major areas of concentration are East Asia, South Asia, and Europe; two minor ones are Southeast Asia and the central-east part of North America (Figure 2-3). These lands together contain almost 3 billion people, or well over two-thirds of the world's population. Adding a few scattered small clusters in Africa, Southwest Asia, Latin America, and on the West Coast of the United States brings the proportion of those living in areas of relatively high density to more than four-fifths of the total population. (See Table 2-1

and the cartogram of national populations inside the back cover of the book.*)

It is tempting to link this gross distribution to the physical alignments of the earth. Indeed, there are broad correlations between the arrangement of the population and the features of the earth (Figures 2-4 and 2-5). Lands deficient in moisture (deserts) and those deficient in heat (polar ice caps, tundras, and subpolar forests) are very sparsely occupied, if at all. In equatorial lowlands, the opposite condition—abundant mois-

*On this cartogram, the area occupied by each country is proportional to its population as estimated for 1976.

**AREAS OF POPULATION CONCENTRATION, 1976 (MILLIONS)***

TABLE 2-1

| East Asia | | South Asia | | Europe† | |
|---|---|---|---|---|---|
| China, mainland | 964 | India | 653 | Southern Europe | 134 |
| Taiwan | 16 | Bangladesh | 83 | Central Europe | 107 |
| North Korea | 17 | Pakistan | 74 | Northwest Europe | 235 |
| South Korea | 37 | Sri Lanka | 14 | U.S.S.R. in Europe | 185 |
| Japan | 112 | Nepal | 13 | | |
| Hong Kong | 4 | Other states | 1 | | |
| Total | 1,150 | | 838 | | 661 |
| Percent of world population | 27.1 | | 19.8 | | 15.6 |
| Southeast Asia | | East Central North America | | Other Clusters | |
| Indonesia | 143 | Northeast U.S.A. | 104 | Pacific Coast, U.S.A. | 25 |
| Philippines | 46 | Southeast Canada | 18 | Central Mexico | 40 |
| Other islands | 3 | | | Southeast South America | 70 |
| | | | | Northwest Africa | 41 |
| Burma | 32 | | | East Africa | 45 |
| Thailand | 43 | | | West Africa | 100 |
| Vietnam | 47 | | | Levant | 54 |
| Malaya | 11 | | | | |
| Other mainland | 10 | | | | |
| Total | 335 | | 122 | | 375 |
| Percent of world population | 7.9 | | 2.9 | | 8.7 |

*Figures for China, India, Nigeria are considerably greater than official estimates. The world total for this enumeration amounts to 4,136,000,000.

†Southern Europe: Portugal, Spain, Italy, Albania, Yugoslavia, and Greece. Central Europe: Bulgaria, Romania, Hungary, Czechoslovakia, Poland, East Germany. Northwest Europe: All other countries in Europe including Finland and Austria.

SOURCES OF DATA: Population Reference Bureau, *World Population Data Sheet 1976*, Environmental Fund, *World Population Estimates 1976*, Washington, D.C. N.B. People living outside these concentrations and clusters number about 860 million, or 20.3 percent of the total population.

The electric pylon symbolizes the spread of Occidental technology in West Bengal, India. With international assistance the Damodar River and its tributaries, which often caused disastrous floods, have been regulated through dams and reservoirs. Controlled irrigation aids the farmer, who tends his rice field with bullocks and simple plow; hydro-electricity powers the steel, aluminum, and chemical plants in what is called "the Ruhr of India." (Courtesy of United Nations)

ture and heat throughout the year—also appears to deter settlement. Mountain lands, whether because of inaccessibility, low oxygen content of the air, low temperatures, or stony soils, also tend to be areas of light settlement. Most people in the more attractive highlands occupy tablelands and relatively flat basins. In contrast, the lowlands of the humid mid-latitudes and subtropics are, on the whole, where most of the world's population live.

WORLD: IMPORTANT PHYSICAL FEATURES

**FIGURE 2-4** A comparison of this map with the one inside the front cover shows that most of the world's population lives at low elevations, whether plains or hill lands. However, note significant exceptions, especially in the tropical highlands of Africa and Central and South America.

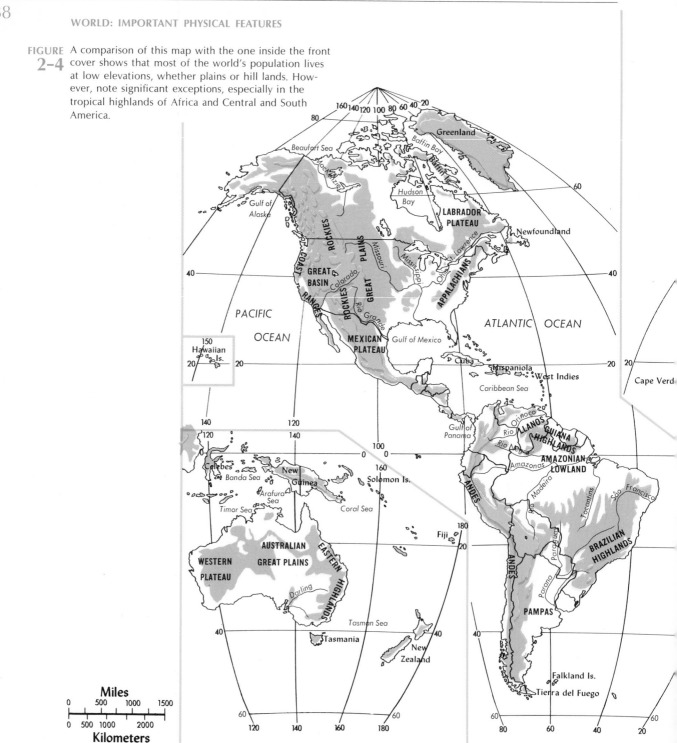

AITOFF'S

INTERRUPTED EQUAL-AREA

PROJECTION

Land Over 5,000 Feet (Over 1,525 Meters)

Land 1,000 to 5,000 Feet (305 to 1,525 Meters)

Land Under 1,000 Feet (Under 305 Meters)

Iceland

Barents Sea

Novaya Zemlya

SCANDINAVIAN HIGHLANDS

Gt. Britain

Ireland

North Sea

RUSSIAN PLAIN

SIBERIAN

PLAIN

Yenesey

Bering Sea

Sea of Okhotsk

60

40

Bay of Biscay

EUROPEAN PLAIN

Volga

Dnepr

Don

CASPIAN DEPRESSION

Ob'

Irtysh

Lena

Amur

Sakhalin

Hokkaido

ALPS

Caspian Sea

Syr Darya

ALTAI

MONGOLIAN PLATEAU

Japan Sea

Honshu

IBERIAN PLATEAU

Black Sea

TURKISH PLATEAU

Amu Darya

TIENSHAN

TARIM BASIN

NORTH CHINA PLAIN

Huang Ho

East China Sea

Kyushu

ATLAS

Mediterranean Sea

IRANIAN PLATEAU

HINDUKUSH

TIBETAN PLATEAU

HIMALAYAS

Chiang

Taiwan

20

nary Is.

Red Sea

ARABIAN PLATEAU

Persian Gulf

Indus

Ganges

DECCAN PLATEAU

Bay of Bengal

South China Sea

Luzon

PACIFIC OCEAN

SAHARAN PLATEAU

Nile

Arabian Sea

Mekong

Sulu Sea

Mindanao

Gulf of Aden

Gulf of Guinea

CENTRAL

ETHIOPIAN PLATEAU

Ceylon

Celebes Sea

Sumatra

Borneo

Celebes

0

CONGO BASIN

Congo

AFRICAN

EAST AFRICAN HIGHLANDS

Java Sea

Banda Sea

New Guinea

Java

Timor Sea

Arafura Sea

Coral Sea

INDIAN OCEAN

Zambezi

Mozambique Channel

Madagascar

20

20

PLATEAU

Limpopo

AUSTRALIAN

GREAT

PLAINS

EASTERN HIGHLANDS

20

Orange

WESTERN PLATEAU

ATLANTIC OCEAN

DRAKENSBERG

Darling

40

40

60

20

0

20

40

60

80

100

120

140

160

60

Tasmania

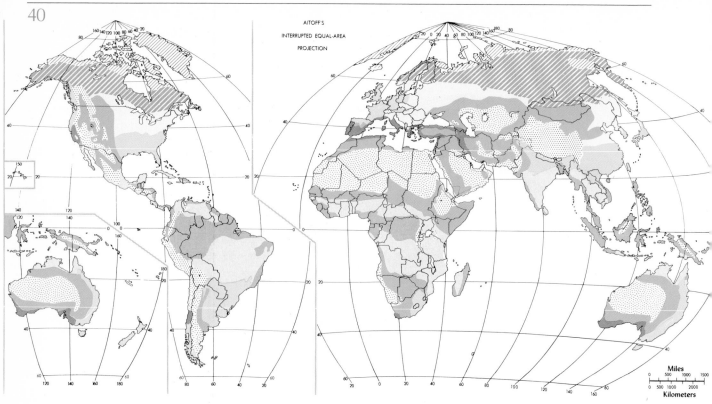

AITOFF'S
INTERRUPTED EQUAL-AREA
PROJECTION

Miles
0    500    1000    1500
0   500 1000        2000
Kilometers

FIGURE **WORLD: CLIMATES**
**2-5**

A comparison of this map with the one inside the front cover shows a fair visual correlation between population concentrations and the humid mid-latitude climates. However, there are numerous and significant exceptions, demonstrating that climate is not the determinant of population distribution.

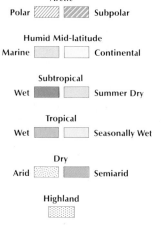

**Arctic**
Polar ▨  ▨ Subpolar

**Humid Mid-latitude**
Marine ▨  ☐ Continental

**Subtropical**
Wet ▨  ☐ Summer Dry

**Tropical**
Wet ▨  ☐ Seasonally Wet

**Dry**
Arid ⬚  ▨ Semiarid

**Highland**
⬚

But closer scrutiny of the map points up many situations which cannot be squared with environmental factors. For example, in the wet tropical lowlands the population densities are in general highest in Asia, lower in Africa, and quite low in South America. Many of India's "teeming millions" live in a hot climate with a short and uncertain rainy season, not much different from the almost empty wet-and-dry savanna lands of Brazil. Or, within Asia, there is a striking contrast between the crowded conditions in India, China, North Vietnam, and Java and the moderate-to-low density that prevails in most of Southeast Asia. The ice-scoured subpolar forest lands of northern Europe support a population which, though sparse, greatly exceeds that of the similar environment in North America, which is still virtually outside the *ecumene* (the inhabited world). In many parts of Central and South America, and of Africa, more people live in highlands than in lowlands.

These anomalies—and many more could be cited—support the contention that we must consider the quality of the habitat in the context of a society's capacities and needs. Among these cultural factors the level of technology and form of economy are the immediate and concrete forces through which societies manipulate their environments. Less tangible but nonetheless important are the spiritual forces that shape cultural values and attitudes. These affect economic behavior and, in turn, are conditioned by the economy. Furthermore, historical circumstance always must be taken into account. Many contrasts between Europe and the Americas in density, dispersion, and pattern of population are due to the fact that Europeans colonized the New World only recently.

With these thoughts in mind, the inspection of a population map becomes more than learning mere data on the whereabouts of people. It should raise a multitude of exciting questions about the ways different societies have met the challenge of their particular physical environments. The next chapter suggests answers to some of these questions by examining the role of technology in the rise of civilizations.

## CITATIONS AND FURTHER READINGS

FOR A DISCUSSION, OR A SAMPLING, OF THE (TRANSLATED)
THOUGHTS OF THE FOUNDING FATHERS OF MODERN GEOGRAPHY:

Brunhes, J. *Human Geography*, New York and Chicago, 1952. (A translation of an abridged French edition of 1947; this classic was first published in 1910.) While Vidal stressed the *genre de vie*, Brunhes emphasized the impress of the way of life on the landscape.

Buttimer, A. *Society and Milieu in the French Geographic Tradition*, Chicago, 1971. A fresh view on the French school.

Dickinson, R. E. *Makers of Modern Geography*, London, 1969.

Freeman, T. W. *The Geographer's Craft*, Manchester and New York, 1967.

Humboldt, A. von. *Views of Nature* or *Aspects of Nature*. (Translated from *Ansichten der Natur*, Stuttgart, 1808, 1849.)

Ratzel, F. "Einige Aufgaben einer politischen Ethnographie," *Zeitschrift für Sozialwissenschaft*, 3 (1900): 1–19. Reprinted in Helmolt, H., *Kleine Schriften von Friedrich Ratzel* 2, München-Berlin, 1904.

Sorre, M. *Les Fondements de la géographie humaine*, Paris, 1943–1952, (Vol. 1, *Fondements biologiques*; vol. 2, *Les Techniques*; vol. 3, *L'habitat*).

———— "The Concept of Genre de Vie," in Wagner, P. L., and Mikesell, M. W. (eds.), *Readings in Cultural Geography*, Chicago, 1962, 399–415. Originally printed in *Annales de géographie*, 57 (1948): 97–108, 193–204.

Stoddart, D. S. "Darwin's Impact on Geography," *Annals of the Association of American Geographers*, 56 (1966): 683–698.

Van Paassen, C. *The Classical Tradition in Geography*, Groningen, Netherlands, 1957.

Vidal de la Blache, P. *Tableau de la géographie de la France*, Paris, 1903.

———— *Principles of Human Geography*, New York, 1926; London, 1959. This translation of an incomplete and posthumously published manuscript gives a fairly good idea of Vidal's views.

Wanklyn, H. *Friedrich Ratzel, A Biographical Memoir and Bibliography*, Cambridge and New York, 1961. In the absence of translations of Ratzel's writings, this is a valuable introduction to the father of "anthropogeography."

Wrigley, E. A. "Changes in the Philosophy of Geography," in Chorley, R. J., and Haggett, P. (eds.), *Frontiers of Geographical Teaching*, London, 1965, 3–20. Useful overview of important shifts in geographical thinking since the eighteenth century.

## REPRESENTATIVE OF "ENVIRONMENTALISM"

Brigham, A. P. *Geographic Influences in American History*, New York, 1903.

Bryan, P. W. *Man's Adaptation to Nature*, London, 1933.

Huntington, E. *Civilization and Climate*, New York, 1920.

———— *Mainsprings of Civilization*, New York, 1945. Reprinted in paperback edition.

Semple, E. C. *American History and Its Geographic Conditions*, Boston and New York, 1903.

———— *Influences of Geographic Environment*, New York, 1911.

Taylor, G. T. *Environment and Nation: Geographical Factors in the Cultural and Political History of Europe*, Toronto and Chicago, 1936.

## COMMENTS ON "ENVIRONMENTALISM"

Chappell, J. E., Jr. "Climatic Change Reconsidered: Another Look at 'The Pulse of Asia,'" *Geographical Review*, 60 (1970): 347–373.

Febvre, L. *A Geographical Introduction to History*, London, 1950. (Translation of *La terre et l'évolution humaine*, Paris, 1923.)

Isachenko, A. G. "Determinism and Indeterminism in Foreign Geography," *Soviet Geography: Review and Translation*, 13 (1972): 421–432, 544–557.

Lewthwaite, G. R. "Environmentalism and Determinism: A Search for Clarification," *Annals of the Association of American Geographers, 56* (1966): 1–23.

Matley, I. M. "The Marxist Approach to the Geographic Environment," *Annals of the Association of American Geographers, 56* (1966): 97–111.

Rostlund, E. "Twentieth Century Magic," *Landscape, 5* (1956): 23–26. Reprinted in Wagner, P. L., and Mikesell, M. W. (eds.), *Readings in Cultural Geography*, Chicago, 1962, 48–53.

Spate, O. H. K. "Toynbee and Huntington: A Study in Determinism," *Geographical Journal,* 118 (1952): 406–428.

Tatham, G. "Environmentalism and Possibilism," in Taylor, G. T. (ed.), *Geography in the Twentieth Century*, London and New York, 1957.

## ATTITUDES TOWARD AND PERCEPTION OF THE ENVIRONMENT

Brookfield, H. C. "On the Environment as Perceived," *Progress in Geography, International Reviews of Current Research,* 1 (1969): 51–80.

Brown, R. H. *Mirror for Americans: Likeness of the Eastern Seaboard, 1810,* New York, 1943. A fascinating portrait of the Atlantic Coast, seen through the eyes of a fictitious geographer of the period.

Burton, I., and others. *The Human Ecology of Coastal Flood Hazard in Megalopolis,* University of Chicago, Department of Geography Research Paper no. 115, Chicago, 1969.

Gould, P., and White, R. *Mental Maps,* Harmondsworth, England, 1974.

Lowenthal, D. (ed.). *Environmental Perception and Behavior,* University of Chicago, Department of Geography Research Paper no. 106, Chicago, 1966.

———— and Prince, H. C. "The English Landscape," *Geographical Review,* 54 (1964): 309–346.

———— and ———— "English Landscape Tastes," *Geographical Review,* 55 (1965): 186–222.

Lucas, R. C. "Wilderness Perception and Use: The Example of the Boundary Waters Canoe Area," *Natural Resources Journal,* 3 (1963–64): 394–411.

Mackinder, H. J. *Democratic Ideals and Reality,* London, 1942 (first issued in 1918).

Marsh, G. P. *Man and Nature, or Physical Geography as Modified by Human Action,* New York, 1864; 2d ed. *The Earth as Modified by Human Action,* New York, 1874.

Merrens, H. R. "The Physical Environment of Early America: Images and Image Makers in Colonial South Carolina," *Geographical Review,* 59 (1969): 530–556.

Mumford, L. *The Brown Decades,* New York, 1931.

Saarinen, T. F. *Perception of Environment,* Association of American Geographers, Commission on College Geography Resource Paper No. 5, Washington, D.C., 1969.

Thompson, K. "Insalubrious California: Perception and Reality," *Annals of the Association of American Geographers,* 59 (1969): 50–64.

Tuan, Y.-F. "Ambiguity in Attitudes toward Environment," *Annals of the Association of American Geographers,* 63 (1973): 411–423.

——— *Topophilia. A Study of Environmental Perception, Attitudes, and Values,* Englewood Cliffs, N.J., 1974.

——— "Images and Mental Maps," *Annals of the Association of American Geographers,* 65 (1975): 205–213.

OTHER STUDIES ON THE RELATION OF
MAN AND ENVIRONMENT, INCLUDING SOME
RECENT WORK ON THE ECOLOGICAL APPROACH IN GEOGRAPHY:

Bates, M. *Where Winter Never Comes,* New York, 1952. An optimistic view of the tropical lands.

Chappell, J. E., Jr. "The Ecological Dimension: Russian and American Views," *Annals of the Association of American Geographers,* 65 (1975): 144–162.

Detwyler, T. R., and Marcus, M. G. (eds.). *Urbanization and Environment. The Physical Geography of the City,* Belmont, Cal., 1972.

Eyre, S. R. "Determinism and the Ecological Approach to Geography," *Geography,* 49 (1964): 369–376.

Gourou, P. *The Tropical World,* London, 1953. A pessimistic view of the tropical lands.

Herbertson, A. J. "The Major Natural Regions: An Essay in Systematic Geography," *Geographical Journal,* 25 (1902): 300ff.

Manners, I. R., and Mikesell, M. W. (eds.). *Perspectives on Environment,* Association of American Geographers, Washington, D.C., 1974.

Stoddart, D. R. "Geography and the Ecological Approach: The Ecosystem as a Geographic Principle and Method," *Geography,* 50 (1965): 242–251.

Tuan, Yi-Fu. *Man and Nature,* Commission on College Geography, Resource Paper no. 10. Association of American Geographers, Washington, D.C., 1971.

——— "Geopiety: a Theme in Man's Attachment to Nature and to Place," in Lowenthal, D., and Bowden, M. J. (eds.), *Geographies of the Mind,* New York, 1976, 11–39.

THE CONCEPT OF CULTURE HAS BEEN
DISCUSSED BY NUMEROUS ANTHROPOLOGISTS.
ESPECIALLY HELPFUL IN RELATION TO GEOGRAPHY ARE:

Forde, C. D. *Habitat, Economy, and Society,* London, 1934.

Foster, G. M. *Culture and Conquest: America's Spanish Heritage,* New York, 1960. A discussion of "conquest culture," culture transfer, and acculturation.

Goldschmidt, W. *Man's Way,* Cleveland and New York, 1959.

Hall, E. T. *The Silent Language,* New York, 1959.

Hoebel, E. A. *Anthropology,* 3rd ed., 1966. 4th ed., 1972. New York.

Kluckhohn, C. *Mirror for Man,* New York, 1949. Also in paperback reprint.

Kroeber, A. L. *Anthropology,* New York, 1948.

White, L. A. *The Science of Culture,* New York, 1949. Also in paperback reprint.

FROM THE LARGE AND GROWING LITERATURE ON CULTURAL,
SOCIAL, AND HISTORICAL GEOGRAPHY A FEW TITLES HAVE BEEN
SELECTED ON THEIR OWN MERIT AS WELL AS A GUIDE TO FURTHER READING:

Bobek, H. "The Main Stages in Socioeconomic Evolution from a Geographical Point of View," reprinted in Wagner, P. L., and Mikesell, M. W. (eds.), *Readings in Cultural Geography,* Chicago, 1962, 218–247.

Brown, R. H. *Historical Geography of the United States,* New York, 1948.

Darby, H. C., and others. *The Domesday Geography of England,* 5 vols., London, 1952–1967.

Glacken, C. J. *Traces on the Rhodian Shore: Nature and Culture in Western Thought from Ancient Times to the End of the Eighteenth Century,* Berkeley, Calif., 1967.

Harris, C. "Theory and Synthesis in Historical Geography," *Canadian Geographer,* 15 (1971): 157–192.

Kirk, W. "Historical Geography and the Concept of the Behavioral Environment," *Indian Geographical Society Jubilee Souvenir,* monograph no. 3 (1951): 152–160.

Lowenthal, D. "Past Time, Present Place: Landscape and Memory," *Geographical Review,* 65 (1975): 1–36.

Lukermann, F. "The Concept of Location in Classical Geography," *Annals of the Association of American Geographers,* 51 (1961): 194–210.

Prince, H. C. "Real, Imagined, and Abstract Worlds of the Past," *Progress in Geography, International Reviews of Current Research,* 3 (1971): 51–80.

Sauer, C. O. *Land and Life: A Selection from the Writings of Carl Ortwin Sauer* (edited, with introduction, by John Leighly), Berkeley and Los Angeles, 1963. An excellent collection of stimulating essays on historical and cultural geography by one of America's leading scholars.

Thomas, W. L. (ed.). *Man's Role in Changing the Face of the Earth,* Chicago, 1956. An international symposium in the footsteps of G. P. Marsh.

Wagner, P. L., and Mikesell, M. W. (eds.). *Readings in Cultural Geography,* Chicago, 1962. A valuable collection of papers on social and cultural geography.

Wheatley, P. *The Pivot of the Four Quarters, A Preliminary Enquiry into the Origins and Character of the Ancient Chinese City,* Edinburgh, 1971.

Zelinsky, W. *The Cultural Geography of the United States,* Englewood Cliffs, N.J., 1973.

Zube, E. H. (ed.), *Landscapes. Selected Writings of J. B. Jackson,* Boston, 1970.


WORKS ON POPULATION DISTRIBUTION,
INCLUDING MAPS: (SEE ALSO THE ENDPAPERS OF THIS BOOK)

Beaujeu-Garnier, J. *Géographie de la population,* 2 vols., Paris, 1956 and 1958.

Burgdorfer, F. (ed.). *World Atlas of Population,* Hamburg, 1954–. A loose-leaf atlas of small-scale dot population maps for major regions of the world.

Hooson, D. J. M. "The Distribution of Population as the Essential Geographical Expression," *Canadian Geographer,* 17 (1960): 10–20.

Hsu, Mei-Ling. "Taiwan Population Distribution, 1965," *Annals of the Association of American Geographers,* 59 (1969): 611–612, Map Supplement no. 11.

Kormoss, I. B. F., and Kosinski, L. A. *Population Mapping 1973,* Commission on Population Geography, International Geographical Union, Bruges, 1973.

Monkhouse, F. J., and Wilkinson, H. R. *Maps and Diagrams: Their Compilation and Construction,* New York, 1963. Contains much information on the mapping of distributions and densities.

Peucker, T. K. *Computer Cartography,* Commission on College Geography, Resource Paper no. 17, Association of American Geographers, Washington, D.C., 1972.

Porter, P. W. "East Africa: Population Distribution," *Annals of the Association of American Geographers,* 56 (1966): 180 and Map Supplement no. 6.

Prothero, R. M. *Reports of Commission on the Geography and Cartography of World Population, 1964–68 and Commission on Population Geography, 1968–72,* University of Alberta, Edmonton, Canada, 1972.

Wild, M. T. "Recent Trends in the Distribution of Population in the Federal Republic of West Germany," *Tijdschrift voor Economische en Sociale Geografie,* 66 (1975): 349–357.

Wright, J. K. "Some Measures of Distribution," *Annals of the Association of American Geographers,* 27 (1937): 177–211.

Zelinsky, W. *Prologue to Population Geography,* Englewood Cliffs, N.J., 1966.

# 3 TECHNOLOGY: Origins and Diffusion

Tools and skills are part of culture. They provide the means to control and transform nature and to increase productivity. Progress in making tools set our ancestors apart from other primates. Tremendous technical achievements distinguish the modern Western world from other cultures. Singling out technology for special attention at this point does not say that it is the mainspring in the progress and differentiation of human groups. Certainly, technology affects other facets of culture, but the reverse is equally true. Tools, after all, are not just things. They express the inner world of ideas, which comprises the total experience of a culture.

The purpose of this chapter is (1) to review how early societies manipulated the natural environment, especially in the Middle East, but also in America and China; (2) to describe briefly the emergence of the West to a position of technological dominance in the modern era. Essentially, the technical assemblage achieved by ancient civilizations governed the ceiling of productivity for many centuries—until the advent of modern science and industry. In sequence, different places at different times led in technical progress. Ideas spread from the centers of invention to other parts of the world, but not all. The contrast between "developed" and "underdeveloped" countries, of which we are now so keenly aware, has persisted throughout human history.

## THE OLD STONE AGE (PALEOLITHIC)

So far, the earliest evidence of manlike beings (hominids) dates back over 2 million years. During the Pleistocene epoch, periods of widespread glaciation alternated with milder conditions.

Throughout these long ages plants, animals, and early man adjusted to slow but drastic alterations of their habitat. It is far from clear how mankind became a species so different from other primates, but it was toward the end of the ice age that humans like us evolved and mastered speech, tools, and fire—"the tripod of culture."

Articulate speech, a function of the brain, means using sound clusters to express symbols, a very different matter from the sounds apes make to transmit direct experience. Language enabled our ancestors to communicate thoughts to companions, to exchange and accumulate experience, and to unite a group in a common world of meanings and values. Not only did they learn from others, but with reflective generalizing thought they improved on what they learned—to innovate, reorganize, and create.

Apes use tools—a stick to reach a fruit, a stone to kill a scorpion—and may even occasionally fashion a piece of wood into a device for an immediate purpose. But human beings became habitual toolmakers, deliberately preparing implements for future use. They supplemented tools for hands and teeth, thus greatly increasing their ability to use the environment and, in time, to become hunters of larger animals. They fashioned wooden clubs, pointed shafts for spears, and shaped stones with sharp cutting edges for tools. Though no evidence survives, they may have found sinews, cordage, or plant fibers valuable for snaring prey.

Undoubtedly, human beings first captured fire from natural conflagrations caused by volcanic activity, lightning, burning coal or gas seepages, or from spontaneous combustion. When it came to *making* fire, they had to depend on tools. From the widely differing devices that tribes with simple technologies still use, we as-

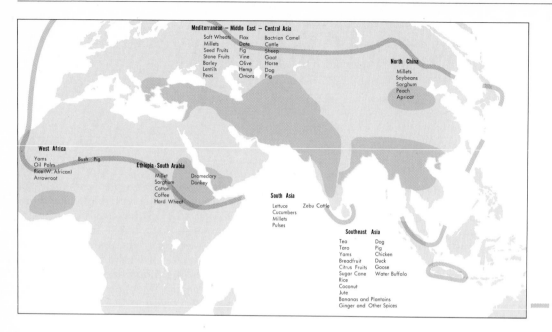

Mediterranean — Middle East — Central Asia

| | | |
|---|---|---|
| Soft Wheats | Flax | Bactrian Camel |
| Millets | Date | Cattle |
| Seed Fruits | Fig | Sheep |
| Stone Fruits | Vine | Goat |
| Barley | Olive | Horse |
| Lentils | Hemp | Dog |
| Peas | Onions | Pig |

North China

Millets
Soybeans
Sorghum
Peach
Apricot

West Africa

Yams            Bush Pig
Oil Palm
Rice (W. African)
Arrowroot

Ethiopia-South Arabia

Millet        Dromedary
Sorghum       Donkey
Cotton
Coffee
Hard Wheat

South Asia

Lettuce       Zebu Cattle
Cucumbers
Millets
Pulses

Southeast Asia

| | |
|---|---|
| Tea | Dog |
| Taro | Pig |
| Yams | Chicken |
| Breadfruit | Duck |
| Citrus Fruits | Goose |
| Sugar Cane | Water Buffalo |
| Rice | |
| Coconut | |
| Jute | |
| Bananas and Plantains | |
| Ginger and Other Spices | |

████ The Limits of Plow
Cultivation in A.D. 1492

FIGURE **OLD WORLD: AREAS OF ORIGIN OF SELECTED**
**3–1** **PLANT AND ANIMAL DOMESTICATES**

The line shows the limits of plow cultivation in A.D. 1492: In the pre-Columbian world the use of the plow coincided fairly well with the spheres of influence of the major civilizations of the Old World.

sume that this invention occurred independently in various places. Using fire to prepare food widened the range of edibles and caused changes in nutrition by chemically transforming the organic matter. Fire also provided light, thus lengthening the workday and extending the living space into deep caves.

What was life like in those times? It was logical that the task of keeping the hearth fire going became that of the women, who had to stay close to the home base because of the children. The helpless young during their protracted state of immaturity needed care, nurture, and protection. The division of labor between the sexes and the sharing of food became a feature of human existence. The women, however, foraged around their campsites for roots, seeds, berries, and edible leaves as well as for grubs and easily caught creatures. The men were the hunters, roaming over much wider areas, banding together to over-

power the prey, and sharing the kill among themselves and their families.

Were early human beings essentially hunters and thus carnivorous? Or were they chiefly vegetarians like their simian relatives? Most likely they were both, depending on where they lived and what foods were available. Tropical forests contained few game animals on the ground level but had plenty of tubers and other edible plant parts. In contrast, subpolar steppes (tundra) and woodlands were rather poor in plants fit for man's consumption, but rich in game animals. Tidal beaches and the shores of rivers and lakes also must have provided a large and secure diet of animal protein.

Mankind's progress during the early and middle Old Stone Age (Paleolithic) was very slow. People like us—*Homo sapiens*—appeared perhaps a quarter of a million years ago. Beginning about 100,000 years ago, great advances spread to form the late Paleolithic cultures, which made specialized tools in wide variety for hunting, fishing, collecting, and domestic tasks. They had used flint for a long time, but now they also adapted bone and ivory. Tools found hundreds of miles from their source of raw material prove that there

Beans
Squashes
Maize
Tomato
Cacao
Peppers
Avocado

Turkey
Dog

Manioc     Dog
Pineapple   Guinea Pig
Potato     Llama
Sweet Potato  Alpaca
Tobacco
Cacao
Squashes
Beans

FIGURE **NEW WORLD: AREAS OF ORIGIN OF SELECTED**
**3-2** **PLANT AND ANIMAL DOMESTICATES**

*The place of origin of many agricultural plants and animals is not known for certain. On these maps some domesticates are shown as originating in more than one region. Based on Sauer, C. O., Agricultural Origins and Disposals, Bowman Memorial Lecture Series, American Geographical Society, New York, 1952, and later research by others.*

was long-distance trade in certain stones for these early crafts.

Archaeological discoveries indicate that the hunting peoples of 25,000 to 15,000 years ago in western Europe and in northern Africa enjoyed comparative comfort and had a fairly complex social life. With bow and arrow and probably spear-thrower, they killed what they needed of the large mammals that roamed the tundralike steppes and open woodlands south of the re-treating ice cap. The cave paintings in the Sahara, Spain, and southern France, probably intended as hunting magic, are not only impressive as art but also give an idea how these hunters lived (Collins, 1976).

# THE NEW STONE AGE (NEOLITHIC)

The Paleolithic was the era of hunting and gathering with chipped stone tools. The term *Neolithic* formerly referred to the cultural stage when man learned to grind and polish stone, but present-day usage emphasizes the achievement of agriculture and often also of pottery.

Domestication of plants and animals apparently began independently and at different times in several parts of the tropics and subtropics. How it started is not known. Perhaps the initial and unintentional steps came about by protecting useful wild plants and by adopting young animals as pets. Gradually the manipulation of the biotic environment became more purposeful and intensive. The transition from a collecting to a producing economy must have taken a long time. Since evidence of domesticated crops and animals dates from about ten thousand years ago, it seems likely that the first gropings toward agriculture reach back much, much further (Figures 3-1 and 3-2).

Archaeological research has revealed three sites of early agriculture: the Middle East, Meso- and Andean-America, and Southeast Asia. This does not exclude the possibility of early and independent origins elsewhere, such as China, India, and parts of Africa (Harris, 1967). Because the record of the transition from incipient agriculture to civilization is best known for the Middle East, we will consider this area first.

## THE MIDDLE EAST

The Middle East stretches from the eastern Mediterranean lands to Iran and from the Black Sea to the Indian Ocean. It shows how situation and site complement each other in explaining the historical significance of an area. Geographical position on the crossroads of Asia, Europe, and Africa made it highly accessible. Here peoples and ideas met, and out of the encounter by concord and conflict arose innovation and change which were carried outward again.

Within the confines of the Middle East, site differences in climate and landform induced a variety of biotic environments. Surrounding the Syrian Desert lies a sickle-shaped zone traditionally called the "Fertile Crescent" (Figure 3-3). It curves from the coastal areas of Palestine and Syria eastward to the alluvial plain of the Euphrates and Tigris and is backed by the heights of the Lebanon-Taurus-Zagros mountains. Recent archaeologic finds indicate that the origin of agriculture lay not in the bottomlands of the great rivers but at some 800 to 1,500 meters (about 2,500 to 5,000 feet) altitude in the intermontane basins and valleys. These uplands receive some 250 to 650 millimeters (10 to 25 inches) of rain, mainly in winter; it appears that the precipitation some ten thousand years ago was approximately the same. In the open woodlands roamed the wild ancestors of goats, sheep, and cattle, and among the grasses were the forebears of wheat and barley.

This hilly zone offered a great variety of natural niches, each with its own complex of plant and animal communities. It was almost like a field experiment station as peoples of the region approached the threshold of agriculture. Evidence of farming villages, beginning as much as 10,000 years ago, have been found on the inward slopes of the Zagros Mountains at Jarmo, at Haçilar and Çatal Hüyük in southwestern Turkey, and near Jericho, Jordan. Archaeologists also discovered remains of six-row barley, domesticated wheat, peas, lentils, and bones of domesticated goats, sheep, and possibly cattle and pigs (Braidwood, 1960, 134; Harris, 1967, 93). Tools made of obsidian point to external trade, since this material must have been brought from Anatolia, well to the north.

## THE BEGINNINGS OF CIVILIZATION

Early grain and animal agriculture in the uplands depended on rainfall. The small gardening plots, worked by hand tools, were probably abandoned after a few years for new clearings of fresh fertility. Before 5000 B.C. cultivators began to move down the mountain flanks into the lowland of the Tigris and Euphrates. Here they had to adjust to a very different set of environmental conditions. As the meltwater from the mountains runs off, the rivers flood the lower plain in April or May and deposit their silt. The fertility of the soil, however, is countered by the arid climate and the fierce summer heat. Crops planted in the fall need irrigation from the rivers, which by that time have retreated to their channels.

It is not known exactly how and when the lowland farmers devised the system of canals and ditches to divert river water to their fields. Most likely, water management allowed the use of permanent fields instead of the shifting cultivation as practiced in the hills. Another important advance came with the invention of the plow and the use of oxen to pull it. The triad of grain, plow, and draft animal established field agriculture in its essentials.

The arts of pottery and probably weaving were already known in the early farming communities. Metallurgy came later. It started with the use of native copper, followed by silver and gold. More important for practical purposes was the discovery, around 3500 B.C., that a mixture of copper and tin produced the hard alloy, bronze. But tin was scarce. Probably bronze weapons and tools were for the rich only, while the common people continued to use stone, wood, and bone, or baked brick. In time most of the tin had to be brought from large deposits in the Danube Basin and along the coasts of western Europe. This attests to the existence of long-distance commerce. Doubtless goods other than tin—as well as ideas—spread along these trade routes.

Transportation had relied on man and beast as pack carriers and on rowing vessels until be-

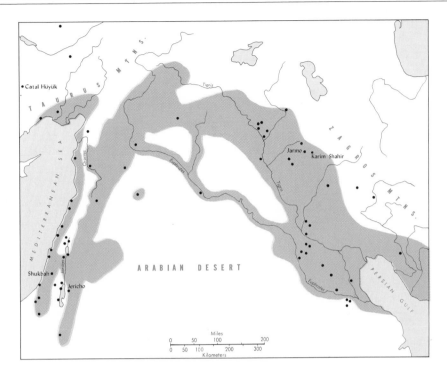

FIGURE **EARLY MIDDLE EASTERN AGRICULTURE**
3-3

The dark area is the Fertile Crescent. The Persian Gulf penetrated further inland in ancient times than it does now. The dots indicate locations of very early agriculture and also the sites of the earliest cities.

tween 3500 and 3000 B.C. Then the wheel came into use for vehicles and the sail for ships, both permitting greater loads. The Minoans of Crete and the Phoenicians rose to importance chiefly because they served as middlemen between the civilizations of the south and east and the less developed peoples who lived to the north and west and produced raw materials.

The horse was a relative latecomer in the field of transportation. It may have been domesticated in the grasslands of Hungary or the steppes bordering the Black and Caspian seas, and was introduced into the ancient civilizations early in the second millennium B.C. when Indo-European peoples invaded the Middle East from the north. After that until recent times, the man on the chariot, and later on horseback, dominated the battlefield as well as the ceremonial procession.

With improvements in agricultural tech-

niques and in transportation, populations increased and occupations became more specialized and stratified. Fewer workers were needed in agriculture. The surplus concentrated in towns, even large cities. By 4000 B.C. the trend toward urban living was well under way, chiefly in lower Mesopotamia, that is, south of the present Baghdad. In these urban centers resided the priest-rulers, who used large labor battalions to construct extensive canal networks and to build monumental temples and palaces. Writing, mathematics, astronomy, and a calendar attest further to the intellectual level of this culture, which truly can be called a civilization.

Thus the civilizing process was one of mutually interacting elements. Economic change had social and political consequences, but also was conditioned, as it is now, by spiritual, social, and political forces. For instance, canal irrigation was a highly important advance, but it would not have been possible without some tradition of cooperative enterprise. In the same way, before cities could grow there had to be a food surplus. In turn, the sociopolitical power of the urban ruling

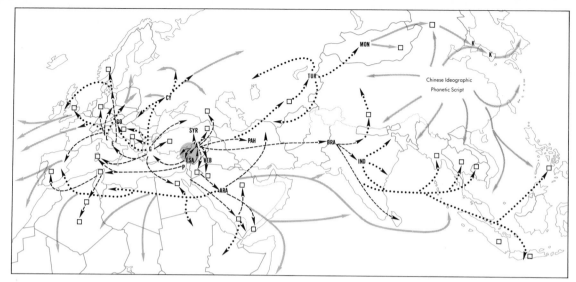

FIGURE
3-4

**THE DIFFUSION OF THE ALPHABET**

The invention of the alphabet in the Middle East in the second millennium B.C. can be considered comparable to the discovery of agriculture and the development of modern science in its effect on the life of mankind. Of forms of ancient writing other than the alphabet, only the Chinese ideographic script remains in use today. This map shows the routes of diffusion of the alphabet, which was accomplished largely through the spread of religion and trade. In the course of time, the alphabet has been adapted to scores of different languages and has proved itself to be one of the most versatile of human inventions. This map is based on information in Diringer, D., *Writing* (Ancient Peoples and Places Series), London, 1962.

|  |  |
|---|---|
| ⟶ | Second Millennium B.C. |
| - - -⟶ | First Millennium B.C. |
| ·····⟶ | First Millennium A.D. |
| ⟶ | Second Millennium A.D. |
| G | Important Alphabets |
| ☐ | Other Alphabets |

| | |
|---|---|
| ESA | Early Semitic Alphabets |
| A | Aramaic |
| P | Phoenician |
| SYR | Syriac |
| HEB | Hebrew |
| ARA | Arabic |
| E | Ethiopic, etc. |
| L | Latin |
| G | Greek |
| GO | Gothic |
| CY | Cyrillic |
| PAH | Pahlavi |
| BRA | Brahmi |
| IND | Indian Alphabets |
| TUR | Turkic, etc. |
| MON | Mongol Alphabets |

group may well have initiated new ways toward greater production and more efficient collection and storage. Societies are interacting organizations. No exclusive ultimate cause—environmental, religious, economic, or political—can fully explain them.

Two later achievements of importance deserve mention. One was the development of a successful method for extracting iron in quantity and its conversion, as wrought iron, into a multitude of things, from pots to swords and plowshares. Now for the first time a metal came within reach of the working folk. The place of origin was

in eastern Anatolia or Armenia, the date about 1500 B.C.

A further great achievement, also in ancient times, was the alphabet, devised by Semitic peoples living in the Sinai peninsula. It was much superior to the older Sumerian cuneiform and Egyptian hieroglyphic systems. Easily learned and adaptable to other languages, this alphabet with minor modifications displaced all other kinds of writing in the Old World except the Sinitic (Figure 3-4). Thus, as it spread, it became a unifying means of communication.

Ideas and things radiated from the Middle

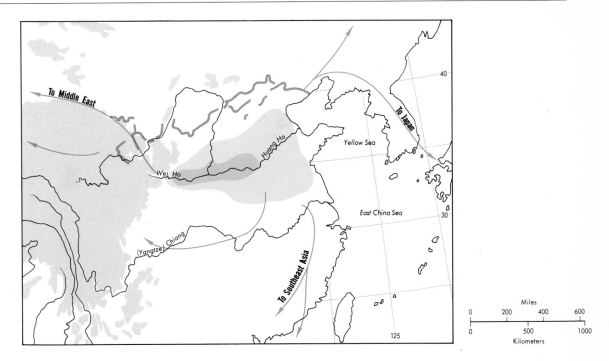

FIGURE **CHINESE CULTURE HEARTH**
3-5

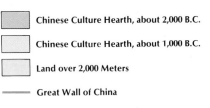  Chinese Culture Hearth, about 2,000 B.C.

Chinese Culture Hearth, about 1,000 B.C.

Land over 2,000 Meters

———— Great Wall of China

◄——— Directions of Spread of Chinese Culture

East, but not all of them, nor at the same speed. Agricultural village life reached Egypt by 5000 B.C. or somewhat later and developed from then onward into a civilization with a style of its own. Middle Eastern accomplishments spread north and then east through Turkestan and the oases of Central Asia to northern China. Here, in the loess-covered uplands near the confluence of the Huang (Yellow) and Wei rivers, evidence has been found that grain cultivation, cattle and sheep raising, and pottery making were well established by 3000 B.C.

Not all traits or techniques filtered through the Asian heartland and some that did may have been rejected. For instance, milking did not be-

come part of the agricultural complex of China or, for that matter, of East and Southeast Asia as a whole. Early presence in China of indigenous cultivated plants, such as kaoliang (a kind of sorghum) and millets, suggests local development, but the question remains open whether this preceded the borrowing from the Middle East. Whatever the answer, it is certain that by the time the Chinese had spread over the great alluvial Huang Ho plain, they had achieved a civilization distinctly their own (Figure 3-5).

The dry regions of inner Asia and North Africa discouraged crop production beyond the stream-fed areas. Here the ancient association of livestock and grain farming broke down and was replaced by nomadic herding. In its earliest phase the pastoral nomads depended on sheep and goats, with the ass as beast of burden. All are well adapted to spare brush and scrub vegetation. Bovine cattle were important only in the less dry areas where grass was available for pasture. The Old Testament gives us glimpses of this precarious life on the steppe and desert, and of the yearning for a more settled existence in the land of milk and honey.

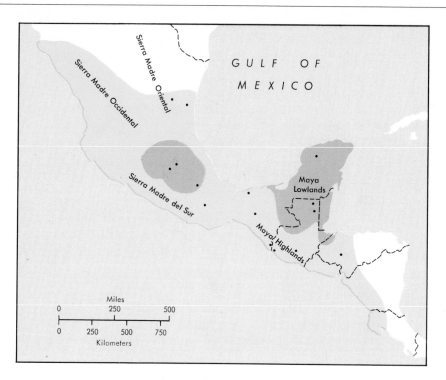

FIGURE **MESO-AMERICAN CULTURE HEARTH**
3-6

The lightly shaded areas represent regions of advanced culture, darker areas represent the cores of Mexican and Mayan societies. Dots show the locations of important archaeological sites where evidence of early or incipient agriculture has been found. From a map in Braidwood, R. J., and Willey, G. R. (eds.), *Courses Toward Urban Life: Archaeological Considerations of Some Cultural Alternatives,* Viking Fund Publications in Anthropology, No. 32, New York, 1962. By permission of Aldine Publishing Company.

Domestication of the horse and later the camel gave nomadic herding a boost. Both provided a powerful means of transportation. The camel was particularly well adapted to the desert, the horse to the steppe. Moreover, the horse and the dromedary—the one-humped camel—proved valuable in forming fast-moving armies. The mounted nomads gained military superiority over settled farming communities and became capable of controlling large empires (see Chapter 11). Although livestock herding spread southward into Africa over the eastern highlands, neither the horse nor camel followed it. The Meso-African always remained a herdsman-on-foot.*

Archaeologic evidence from India suggests that many Middle Eastern innovations, including agriculture, had reached the Indus Valley by 3000 B.C., if not earlier. Europe also turned to agriculture, but beyond the Alpine ranges cooler and wetter conditions changed its character. Moreover, it appears that European forest dwellers, who had developed a relatively efficient form of intensive food collecting, resisted and slowed down the progress of farming. Even so, some crops were grown in the lands near the North Sea as early as 4000 B.C. But stock raising predominated, with crop cultivation a poor second, both supplemented by the old and well-established skills of fishing and hunting.

In Africa the Sahara formed a severe barrier to the dispersal of new ideas. The Nile Valley, however, offered a route southward to central

*"Meso-Africa" is used in this book in preference to Negro Africa. See Chapter 8.

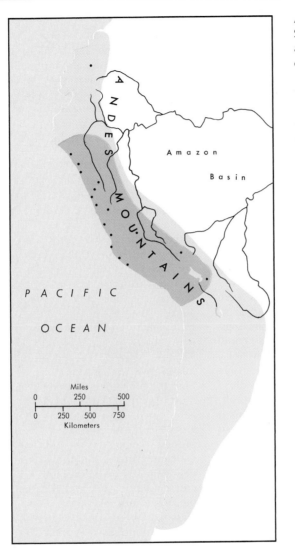

FIGURE **CENTRAL ANDEAN CULTURE HEARTH**
3-7

The lightly shaded area represents the region of
advanced culture, and the darker area the core of
Andean society. Dots show important sites where evi-
dence of incipient or early agriculture has been found.
From a map in Braidwood, R. J., and Willey, G. R. (eds.),
*Courses Toward Urban Life: Archaeological Consid-
erations of Some Cultural Alternatives,* Viking Fund
Publications in Anthropology, No. 32, New York, 1962.
By permission of Aldine Publishing Company.

Africa. Several crops spread that way into the
Sudan. Others may have come overseas from India
and even the Malay Archipelago. Some had their
origins in Africa itself, such as the guinea yam,
palm, and, in Ethiopia, sorghum, coffee, and cotton. The practice of migratory agriculture and the
prevalence of the tsetse fly (Chapter 9) discouraged the use of draft animals and the plow (Figure
3-1). To this day the main field tool of the Meso-
African farmer is the hoe.

In perspective, it is truly remarkable what
the peoples of the Middle East wrought in the
time span from 8000 to 1500 B.C. The following
centuries saw few if any additional basic inventions and discoveries. Even the Greek and Roman
civilizations, whatever their achievements in
other spheres, were technologically only extensions and proliferations of the Middle Eastern
accomplishment.

## ANCIENT CIVILIZATIONS IN THE AMERICAS

The first human immigrants entered the Americas
some 30,000, perhaps even 50,000, years ago by
way of the land corridor now occupied by the
Bering Strait. They had the use of fire, made stone
tools, kept dogs, and possessed other techniques
and equipment typical for north Asian hunters
and collectors of that time. They adjusted to different environments as they spread southwards,
hunting big game in the forests and grasslands of
humid North America, but collecting seeds and
plants in the arid and semiarid southwest. Eventually they spread all the way through South
America, reaching the southern parts over 10,000
years ago.

Advances toward civilization occurred in
two areas: one generally called Meso-America,
the other in the central Andean region—each
with its peripheral zones (Figures 3-6 and 3-7).
Also it is possible that a region between these
two, say about the present Colombia, had the
earliest agriculture, from where it spread north
and south (Sauer, 1952). However that may be, the
two nuclei had interconnections, although they
matured somewhat independently into centers of
civilization.

## MESO-AMERICA

Even more so than in the Middle East, the diverse physical environment of Meso-America offered a wide choice of places to live and plants to cultivate. It varied from moist tropical lowlands to semiarid temperate tablelands and high volcanoes.

It appears that by 7000 B.C. inhabitants of Mexico supplemented their gathering and hunting activities by growing a few crops: pumpkin or squash, and chili pepper. Later they domesticated maize, the bottle gourd, cotton, and several species of beans. Village life, polished-stone tools, and pottery were slow to develop as compared to their early association with agriculture in the Middle East. Not before 1500 B.C. did most of Meso-America have well-established agricultural communities, depending mainly on the cultivation of squash, beans, and—especially—improved varieties of maize. Apparently the fields were cleared by the slash-and-burn method, and abandoned after a few years to make new clearings.

One would not think such land use could support a dense population, and certainly not a large nonfarming one. Yet, after 1000 B.C. massive public structures were erected. These grandiose temples, instead of giving evidence of a well-developed urban life, may have been inhabited only by a small elite. The largely agrarian Mayan population lived in dispersed hamlets amid their fields, but they came in great crowds to these ceremonial centers on market days and for religious festivals.

From 300 B.C. onward, cities developed. The largest one, Teotihuacan in the Valley of Mexico, at one time may have had at least 100,000 inhabitants. It seems reasonable to assume that irrigation was used then, though direct proof of this is lacking. We know for certain that when the Spaniards arrived in 1519, irrigation was being practiced in the Valley of Mexico and other highland basins. In Yucatan and adjacent areas, the lowland Maya may have retained migratory-field (milpa) agriculture; however, much land was given over to intensively worked and permanent garden plots.

On this economic base rested an impressive social superstructure, which included a priestly hierarchy and other forms of social stratification. Astronomy, mathematics, and a calendar system were well developed, especially by the Maya. There was a system of writing, but its application to daily economic and administrative tasks came quite late. Sculpture and pottery show great creativity. Metallurgy was slow to develop and remained restricted to gold, silver, and copper, with little use in fashioning tools. Among the few domesticated animals were the dog and the turkey. The wheel was known, but used only in toys.

## THE CENTRAL ANDES REGION

Excavations by archaeologists on the northern desert coast of Peru have disclosed the existence of sedentary village communities at 2500 B.C., and perhaps as early as 4000 B.C. The settlements, located at the river mouths, depended more on fishing and hunting than on farming. But they cultivated squash, chili pepper, lima beans, and cotton, the latter perhaps used with gourds to provide materials for net fishing. Tuberous crops such as manioc, potato, and sweet potato may have been introduced around 2500 B.C. Maize (from the north?) and peanuts were added about 1400 B.C. After 750 B.C. agricultural villages spread inland over the coastal lowlands. In leaving behind the moist river bottoms near the coast, they must have relied more and more on irrigation. The early presence of monumental architecture suggests that these interior settlements had a surplus of food available for the full-time employment of craftsmen, artists, and priests. From then on, gradually, agriculture intensified, the population increased in density, and the social organization became more elaborate. State formation and class-structured society came into being nearly two thousand years ago.

Cities developed late—after A.D. 800—and never reached the size or complexity of those in Mexico. The famed road system with its efficient courier service dates back no further than A.D. 900. By that time a numerical notation system had been devised by means of knotted strings which served to keep the statistical and fiscal records for the elaborate organization of the Inca Empire. The complete absence of a writing system—in contrast to Meso-America—helps to explain the weak development in mathematics, astronomy, and calendrics.

We know little about events in the intermontane valleys and on the plateaus, but we have

The ruins of the fifteenth-century Andean fortress town of Machu Picchu (the words mean "high mountain") near Cuzco, Peru, a silent reminder of the Inca civilization which united much of present Chile, Peru, Bolivia, and Ecuador in a common social, political, and religious community. (Photograph—United Nations)

proof that fields were terraced, fertilized with guano, and intensively irrigated. The potato was domesticated in the highlands. Animal husbandry became important, the llama serving mainly as pack animal and the alpaca prized for wool. Weaving and metal casting spread after the first century of the present era, especially in the central Andes, which had wider use for copper tools and weapons than Meso-America. When the technique of making bronze became known, this alloy found practical use during the last centuries of pre-Columbian times.

## AMERICAN CIVILIZATIONS AND THE OLD WORLD

The rise of American civilizations shows many parallels with the Old World, though progress from incipient agriculture to real civilization seems to have been slower. This poses the question whether the stimulus toward higher levels of culture came from the Old World to the Americas. The discussion around this problem is too complex for full exposition, but we must set forth a few pro and con arguments.

Those who favor the notion that many New World culture traits were introduced from the Old World minimize the ocean barrier by pointing to the Malayo-Polynesian voyages far eastward into the Pacific, the successful *Kon-Tiki* expedition by raft westward across that ocean, and the not infrequent drifting of fishing vessels from Japan to the west coast of North America. More recently, Thor Heyerdahl sailed the *Ra,* a boat of ancient Egyptian design, from northwest Africa to the Caribbean, and he argues effectively that there was wholesale cultural transmission from east to west in ancient times. Other advocates of contact before Columbus point to numerous similarities between the Old World and the New, from alcoholic beverages to the zodiac. But there is no consistent process of diffusion to explain the various isolated items. Why couldn't people in different parts of the world hit on the same individual ideas?

But there is one sector of civilization where man's creative thought is not enough. He cannot invent plants, and this is the trump card of the diffusionists. Plant domesticates present in both parts of the world in pre-Columbian times are the sweet potato, bottle gourd, coconut, and cotton. There have been various arguments raised against accepting these crops as evidence of pre-Columbian trans-Pacific cultural contacts, but least effectively against the sweet potato. This plant (not to be confused with the Old World yam) is apparently of American origin. When the first Europeans visited New Zealand, the Maoris were using the sweet potato as a common food crop. If this is valid evidence, one can hardly rule out the possibility of movements in the other, eastward, direction. Were these movements infrequent and accidental, or part of a constant trickle, if not free flow, of men and ideas? The latter must be postu-lated if it is to support the hypothesis that much of the American civilizations originated in the Old World. But if many advanced culture traits were imported, why were other, equally valuable, ideas not transferred, or not accepted? If America got the notion of the zero and zodiac from the Old World, why did not such eminently useful inventions as the wheel for pottery and transportation, the plow, manufacture of iron, and more advanced forms of writing cross the ocean?

Present knowledge favors the concept of a largely independent cultural evolution in the Americas. Nevertheless, since research occasionally discovers unsuspected links, it may be wise to agree that "a verdict of 'not proven' must . . . be accepted by all but convinced diffusionists—and their equally convinced opponents" (Singer, 1954, vol. 1, 84).

## CHINA AND THE WEST

We must now return to the Old World, first to consider briefly the influence of China on western Eurasia, second to outline the emergence and spread of modern technology. We have seen that several innovations moved from west to east into China, thereby contributing much to its early agricultural assemblage. Chinese culture developed a character of its own and independently made important advances in technology. These inventions filtered slowly south and westward by land and sea routes. There can be little doubt that much of the spurt in technical progress during the European Renaissance was due to the introduction of ideas or skills that originated in China. These included papermaking, printing with blocks and movable type, gunpowder, the crossbow, suspension bridge, canal lock, watertight compartments for ships, and the use of the magnetized needle in navigation.

In this transmission, the Islamic world of the Middle East and Central Asia played the key role. This may be illustrated by the diffusion of papermaking (Figure 3–8). About A.D. 100 the Chinese invented paper, using a process similar to that of today. In 751 the Chinese attacked Samarkand, a trade center astride the route between China and the West. The Arab garrison successfully defended it and even took Chinese prisoners. Among them were some papermakers who taught the Arabs

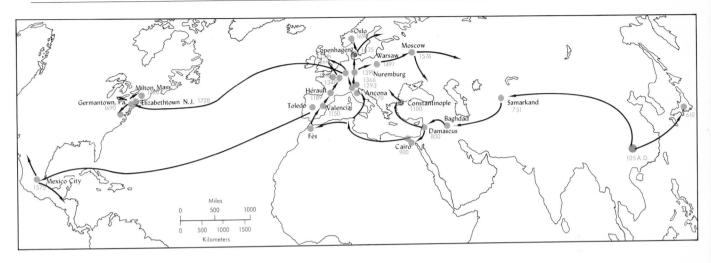

FIGURE **THE DIFFUSION OF PAPERMAKING FROM CHINA**
**3-8** **TO THE WEST**

● **Papermaking with Approximate**
**Date of First Mill**

Papermaking spread through the Moslem world from Samarkand and reached Christian Europe in 1189. It crossed the Atlantic to Mexico City in 1575 and to Pennsylvania (Germantown) in 1690. Based in part on information in Blum, A., *La Route du Papier*, Grenoble, 1946.

their trade. Within two centuries paper mills had been established at Baghdad and Cairo. Diffusion to Europe came by way of Sicily and Moorish-dominated Iberia. Paper mills were set up in Toledo and Valencia by 1150. Moorish papermakers helped to found a mill in Hérault in southern France. By the fourteenth century papermaking had spread to northern Italy, from where Italian artisans carried their craft over the Alps into Germany. England had its first mill probably in the fifteenth century. Across the Atlantic papermaking began in Mexico City in 1575, and in 1690 a German migrant to Philadelphia began business in nearby Germantown. After that, papermaking spread throughout the colonies.

## THE MODERN TECHNOLOGICAL REVOLUTION

In the last two centuries a new way of life has arisen. The Industrial Revolution increased productivity of labor, transformed patterns of organization, sparked new theories of economic management, and stimulated political thought regarding distribution of wealth. Communication, transportation, and sources of energy in manifold forms gave people a freedom never before imagined. A. R. Hall wrote of the change in attitudes that accompanied the Industrial Revolution:

Men looked to the future now, not to the past, and perhaps for the first time in history had some inkling of the road to be traversed in time to come. They saw science as the inspiration of technology, and technology as the key to a life of richness and prosperity. (Singer, 1954, vol. 3, 721)

## THE NEW TRANSPORTATION TECHNOLOGY

The most spectacular results of the new ways of thought in science and technology have been those involving transport of goods, men, and ideas: the ocean-going sailing ship; the steam engine as used in vessel and locomotive; the internal-combustion engine of car, truck, and plane; knowledge of electromagnetic impulses, as employed in telephone, radio, television; perhaps soon, atomic power applied to space flight. These carriers by their very nature spread their use, together with other technical paraphernalia, far from their points of origin. They enabled Europeans, and later Americans, to invade all parts of the globe, and with armaments, trading companies, and colonial administrations, to control regional and world politics and to shape economies to their own ends. The West rose to dominance through its command of new means of circulation.

**Ocean Sailing** The fifteenth century saw European sailing ships venture from coasts and enclosed seas out into the open oceans. The Portuguese, putting together many technical improvements in ship construction, built the three-masted caravel, the type of ship used by Columbus, da Gama, Magellan, and other seamen of the great age of discovery. Concurrently they improved navigation methods originally learned from the Arabs, developed the arts of chart and map making from earlier Mediterranean examples, and mastered the use of the ship-mounted cannon. During the period from 1400 to 1800 when Europeans explored the land and sea configuration of the earth and brought its peoples into new contact with one another, the sailing ship was the most complex and ingenious invention mankind had achieved.*

Portugal founded a sea empire around the southern Atlantic and Indian oceans as far as the Moluccas and Japan. Seamanship, zeal for exploration, a knack for commerce, and religious fervor changed her from a small peripheral European state into the mistress of a great empire. Spain appropriated most of the New World and reached across the Pacific to claim the Philippines. This Iberian world hegemony waned by the end of the sixteenth century as the English, Dutch, and French challenged the joint Spanish-Portuguese monopoly of overseas dominion. The Dutch, having wrenched independence from their Spanish masters, took to the oceans and carved an empire of their own from Portuguese possessions, mostly in Southeast Asia. The Dutch held the world's stage during the mid-seventeenth century, for a time keeping other empire seekers in check.

The English under their vigorous Tudor sovereigns made conquest of the sea and colonization a national concern. They settled along the Atlantic coast of North America and undertook commercial and imperial ventures that led to the

creation of an Indian empire. France also entered the competition, sent settlers to North America, and acquired a trading empire in the Orient. While the Dutch managed to hold onto most of their Southeast Asian possessions, the French lost their claims in India and in America to the British, who emerged in the nineteenth century as masters of the seas and arbiters of world affairs.

All these enterprises combined to expand trade in spices and condiments, sugar, tobacco, the more valuable metals, and slaves. Western Europe became the geographical focus for the new ocean trade that increasingly concentrated in the "narrow seas," the waters bounded by England, France, and the Netherlands. This commerce, together with the burgeoning farm production at home, brought wealth to the rising populations of western Europe, though the distribution of these new riches varied considerably.

To found commercial empires with sea connections was one thing; to settle permanently overseas was another. First Spain, then Portugal, England, France, and the Netherlands, and to a lesser extent Denmark, Sweden, Germany, and other European nations sent out a growing number of colonists, who created overseas societies from New Spain, New France, New England, and New Netherlands to New Zealand and New South Wales.

The age of discovery had barely closed when iron ships propelled by steam engines revolutionized ocean transportation in the first half of the nineteenth century. Before long, goods in enormous quantities were being carried between the Americas and Europe, and between southern Asia and Europe. The opening of the Suez Canal in 1869 and of the Panama Canal in 1914 greatly reduced the length of ocean voyages.

The Europeans became expert in channeling their own work and abilities into profitable ways and in harnessing the energy of other peoples to their advantage. They formed a market, not only for the old luxuries, but also for vast quantities of meat, wheat, and other foods, for cotton and wool, metal ores, and industrial raw materials. In return, Europe sent out manufactured goods, capital for investment in plantations, mines, and railways, and armies of administrators, engineers, and soldiers to manage and protect the colonial enterprises.

*The same could be said of the subsequent steam-driven ocean-going warship and liner. In our day the spaceship continues the theme that the most advanced forms of technology develop in transportation systems.

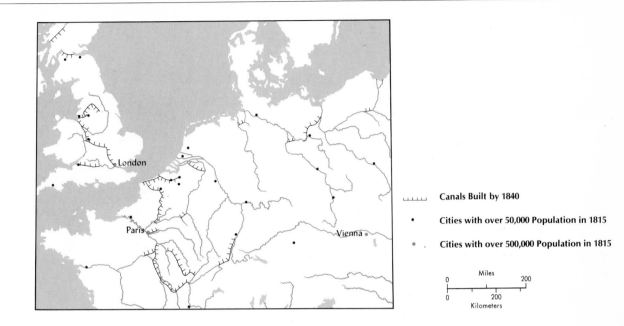

FIGURE **EUROPE: CANALS BUILT BY 1840**
**3-9**

Map legend:

‖‖‖‖‖   Canals Built by 1840

•   Cities with over 50,000 Population in 1815

•   Cities with over 500,000 Population in 1815

Miles 0 — 200
Kilometers 0 — 200

**Land and Air Transportation** Land transportation until the nineteenth century remained primitive as compared to that of ocean ship and river boat. Indeed, most of the roads were mere tracks; even the heavily traveled ones were less well constructed than those left by the Romans. Rivers still served as the chief inland highways, though coastal routes also were used. The Rhine, Elbe, Danube, and rivers further east carried heavy traffic. This was also true in North America, where most of the settlements depended on river or coastal traffic.

The need to improve land transportation brought about the grading and surfacing of roads with binding materials to subdue dust and enhance drainage. The well-constructed toll road (turnpike) became a common feature in the late eighteenth and early nineteenth centuries in western Europe and along the Atlantic Seaboard of North America. Some countries developed a system of fast horse-drawn coaches to carry mail and passengers overland.

Another way of breaking the bottleneck of land transportation was by digging canals. China, Italy, and the Netherlands had long supplemented their rivers in this manner. The need for trans-porting bulky goods inland brought about a canal-building era that reached its high point late in the eighteenth century and lasted until about 1840 (Figure 3-9). England connected the industrial towns of the Midlands with the seaports of London and Liverpool; France joined her principal rivers; the United States attempted, with only partial success, to unite the eastern seaboard with rivers and lakes of the interior. These prodigious feats in canal building alleviated, for a time, the paucity of inland transportation.

The railroad dramatically improved the accessibility of landlocked places. Soon after the reciprocating steam engine became the prime mover for industrial machines, the steam locomotive was developed by adapting it to wheels. England built the first steam railway in the 1820s; soon rails began to extend over western Europe and eastern North America. Not since the time of the mounted-nomad society in Central Asia had it been possible to link together and develop large inland areas as economic units. Now railways connected seaboard with interior in Europe, North America, southern South America, Australia, and, to a lesser extent, India and Russia.

Cities no longer needed to locate on impor-

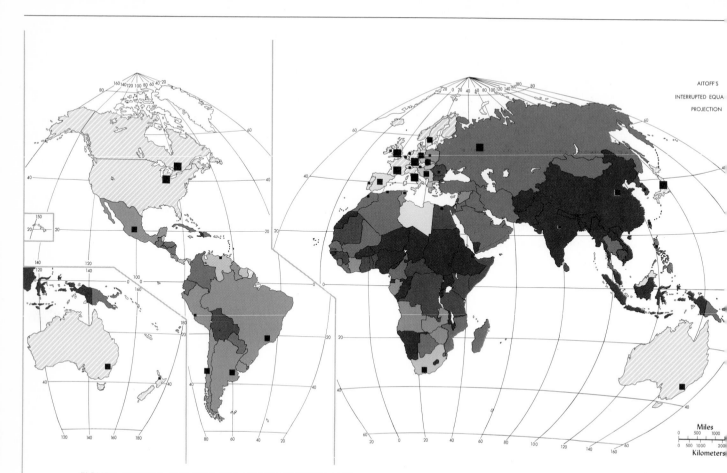

FIGURE **WORLD: PERSONS PER MOTOR VEHICLE AND**
**3-10** **MOTOR VEHICLE PRODUCTION, MID-1970S**

By 1980, vehicle registrations will be much larger in many countries, moving them into the next higher category. Based on data from United Nations, *Statistical Yearbook,* 1975, New York, 1976.

**Persons per Motor Vehicle**
- 250 and over
- 100-249
- 50-99
- 25-49
- 10-24
- 5-9
- Under 5

**Motor Vehicle Production, 1975**
- ■ Over 1 Million
- ■ 100,000 - 1,000,000
- ▪ Under 100,000

tant waterways. Americans could settle in their Midwest and Great Plains, yet feel that their lives and economy were tied by railroad to the Atlantic Coast, and ultimately with overseas markets and suppliers. In Russia, industry and cities developed more slowly than in western Europe. The coming of the railroad emancipated what industry there was and stimulated expansion as far east as the Ural Mountains. The building of the Trans-Siberian Railroad (1891–1901) connected Europe with the Pacific and made Russian settlement of Siberia much easier. Earlier (1880–1885) the Canadian Pacific transcontinental railroad had joined eastern Canada with the West, helping bring British Columbia into the confederation.

The advent of the motor vehicle around 1900 brought a whole new type of transportation into being. Since then the car and truck have furnished a personal and convenient way of getting from one place to another. After the automo-

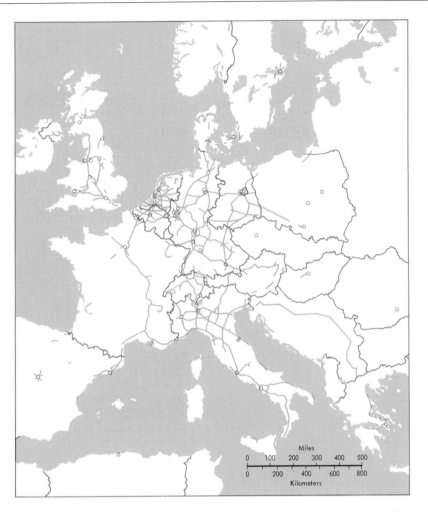

FIGURE **EUROPE: SUPERHIGHWAYS, MID-1970S**
3–11

National differences are evident from this map. Much of the German system dates from the 1930s and 1940s and has been upgraded in more recent years. The Dutch and Italian roads are relatively new. France, long known for its fine highway system, has not yet felt the need to build many long superhighways.

bile diffused throughout Anglo-America and western Europe, it spread to other countries. Figure 3–10 shows that regions of early invention and development still have most of the motor vehicles, but now other areas are beginning to manufacture or import cars in considerable quantities. The densest road networks, too, still lie in western Europe and North America, which also have many excellent superhighways (Figures 3–11 and 3–12).

In all industrialized countries the use of the car for personal transportation and the truck for freight increases rapidly. Indeed, in some countries freight transportation by road expands faster than private-car use, notably in planned economies like the Soviet Union and the Central European states. Trucks offer more flexibility than freight cars for terminals and routes, which often enables them to capture new markets and offer special services. In the United States, Europe, and the Soviet Union, the railroads are readjusting to functions they are best able to perform in the new competitive situation.

FIGURE
3-12

**NORTH AMERICA: SUPERHIGHWAYS, 1977**

Construction of the United States "interstate and defense highway system" began in 1956. By the mid-1970s most of the system was completed. The map includes these highways as well as some built by state authorities. Canada has some superhighways, especially in Ontario. Short sections in and near some Canadian towns are not shown.

Logically, the same regions that developed the railroad and automobile produced the airplane. Airlines transport passengers and more and more goods—the latter especially to areas lacking roads such as northern Canada and interior Australia—but it may be decades before they rival the truck, railroad car, or ship as freight carriers (Figure 3-13).

Cultures vary in how they utilize technological advances. Japan has built a dense railway web, and its road traffic is increasing rapidly.

Countries where economic development began to accelerate only two or three decades ago may never acquire a complete railway system. More probably, roads complemented by air routes will serve most of their needs. Airplane and helicopter afford immediate access to spots in trackless deserts, rain forests, and mountains. They demonstrate once more the vital significance of transportation in mankind's conquest of the earth.

## POWER AND THE MANUFACTURING REVOLUTION

The Industrial Revolution saw great changes in sources of energy. Late in the eighteenth century the steam engine, after much experimentation, began to replace waterwheel and muscle as a prime mover of machines. Before long, James Watt's designs were copied and installed in many places in Britain. Early in the nineteenth century British engineers helped to set up the first steam

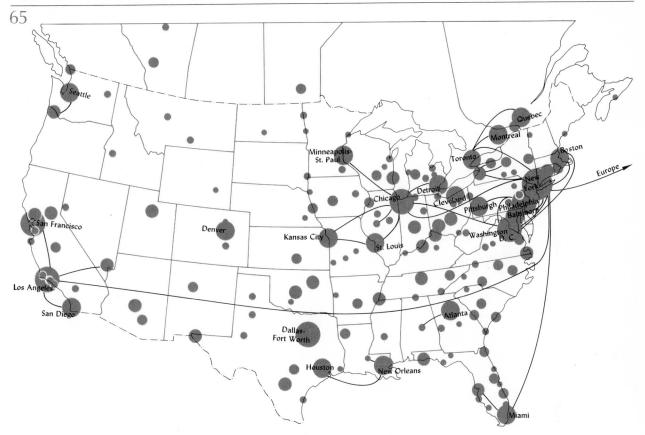

FIGURE **NORTH AMERICA: AIR PASSENGER TRAFFIC,**
**3-13** 1969-1970

The data refer to the number of scheduled incoming flights per week. When several airports serve one city their combined traffic is shown by one symbol. For example, the New York symbol represents arrivals at John F. Kennedy, La Guardia, and Newark Airports. Data from *Oxford Economic Atlas of the World,* London, 1972, page 87.

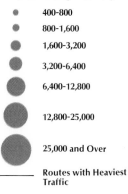

**Incoming Flights per Week**
**(Scheduled Passenger Service)**

| | |
|---|---|
| • | 400-800 |
| • | 800-1,600 |
| ● | 1,600-3,200 |
| ● | 3,200-6,400 |
| ● | 6,400-12,800 |
| ● | 12,800-25,000 |
| ● | 25,000 and Over |
| ——— | Routes with Heaviest Traffic |

engines on the European continent near Liège in the Meuse Valley. Soon thereafter France and Germany followed, then the United States and other countries.

Prior to the steam engine, spinning and weaving were carried on in small rooms, often in farm homes. In contrast, a steam engine of sufficiently advanced design could turn the spindles and looms of a whole factory. Soon other

Like all native Americans the Indians of Ecuador, South America, are of Mongoloid genetic stock. The llamas, long ago domesticated in the Andes, serve as beasts of burden in this high mountain environment. (Photograph—United Nations)

power-driven tools were invented to melt, bore, shape, and test. Manufacturing became a series of processes concentrated at point locations: groups of "mills" located near one another, surrounded by dwellings for the workers. Thus began a new kind of settlement aggregation: the industrial town (Chapter 14). First in Britain, then Belgium, later northern France, eastern United States, and western Germany, these industrial towns usually developed at or near coalfields, where they had cheap fuel to supply the boilers of the steam engines. Often factories were grafted onto the outskirts of already existing towns. As manufac-

turing and service industries attracted more labor, the proportion of people living in urban areas surpassed, for the first time in history, that in the countryside.

## DEVELOPMENT OF MODERN AGRICULTURE
Science and technology also helped to create a modern "agricultural revolution." Many advances came to the landed estates of the northwestern European countries during the seventeenth and eighteenth centuries when capital earned overseas was invested in land reclamation and in new methods of production (see Chapter 10). Improvements in farming included, briefly: crop rotation to replace medieval fallowing of fields, introduction of disease-resistant plant varieties, and better qualities of seed and breeding stock. Productivity increased with the use of

chemical fertilizers. As machinery took over many farm jobs, agricultural transformation greatly increased the productivity per worker. Scientific forestry ensured and conserved timber supplies and reduced soil erosion. Marketing arrangements and transportation facilities efficiently moved products to the consumer. Regional and worldwide networks of production, trade, and consumption replaced the localized patterns of earlier times.

Beginning in the eighteenth century, massive increases in population and revolutions in political and social affairs accompanied these developments in industry and agriculture. The profits from farm, factory, and commerce became the right of many to enjoy and no longer the prerogative of only a wealthy few. As the modern economy diffused from its hearth, population numbers and attitudes also changed. Ideas of social justice, which first flowered in Europe and America, spread to other parts of the world where they took on various forms and degrees of emphasis.

Today the most complex forms of technology appear in the application of atomic science to armaments, space exploration, power production, and medicine; in the use of high-speed computers and other "thinking machines"; and in the introduction of automation in the process of manufacturing. The North Atlantic countries that spearheaded the drive toward full industrialism lead the others, though the Soviet Union and Japan are catching up and surpassing them in some sectors. Newly developing nations just entering the industrial age are finding it more and more difficult to lessen the gap between their simpler economies and those of countries where scientific and technologic complexities speed ahead at an unprecedented rate.

The spread of industrialism has fateful consequences for the life of different societies and for the earth's ability to provide general life support systems for mankind.

## FURTHER READINGS

### DOMESTICATION AND DIFFUSION OF PLANTS AND ANIMALS

Ames, O. *Economic Annuals and Human Cultures,* Botanical Museum, Harvard University, Cambridge, Mass., 1939.

Anderson, E. *Plants, Man, and Life,* Boston, 1952.

Braidwood, R. J. "The Agricultural Revolution," *Scientific American,* (September, 1960): 130–148.

Candolle, A. de. *Origin of Cultivated Plants* (translated from the French edition of 1855), New York, 1885.

Cutler, H. "Food Sources in the New World," *Agricultural History,* 28 (1954): 43–49. Reprinted in Wagner, P. L., and Mikesell, M. W. (eds.), *Readings in Cultural Geography,* Chicago, 1962, 282–289.

Epstein, H. "Domestication Features in Animals as Functions of Human Society," *Agricultural History,* 29 (1955): 137–146. Reprinted in Wagner, P. L., and Mikesell, M. W. (eds.), *Readings in Cultural Geography,* Chicago, 1962, 290–301.

Hahn, E. *Die Haustiere und ihre Beziehungen zur Wirtschaft des Menschen,* Leipzig, 1896.

Harris, D. R. "New Light on Plant Domestication and the Origins of Agriculture: A Review," *Geographical Review,* 57 (1967): 90–107.

Isaac, E. *Geography of Domestication,* Englewood Cliffs, N.J., 1970.

Johannesen, C. L., and others. "The Domestication of Maize: Process or Event?" *Geographical Review,* 60 (1970): 393–413.

Kramer, F. L. "Eduard Hahn and the End of the 'Three Stages of Man,'" *Geographical Review,* 57 (1967): 73–89.

Reed, C. A. "Animal Domestication in the Prehistoric Near East," *Science,* 130 (1959): 1629–1639.

Sauer, C. O. *Agricultural Origins and Dispersals,* Bowman Memorial lectures, Series 2, American Geographical Society, New York, 1952.

———— *Seeds, Spades, Hearths, and Herds,* Cambridge, Mass., and London, 1969.

Simoons, F. J. "The Antiquity of Dairying in Asia and Africa," *Geographical Review,* 61 (1971): 431–439.

———— "Contemporary Research Themes in the Cultural Geography of Domesticated Animals," *Geographical Review,* 64 (1974): 557–576.

Solheim, W. G., II. "Southeast Asia and the West," *Science,* 157 (1967): 896–902.

———— "New Light on a Forgotten Past," *National Geographic Magazine,* 139 (1971): 330–339.

Ucko, P. J., and Dimbleby, G. W. (eds.). *The Domestication and Exploitation of Plants and Animals,* Chicago and London, 1969.

Vavilov, N. I. "The Origin, Variation, Immunity and Breeding of Cultivated Plants" (translated from the Russian), *Chronica Botanica,* 13 (1951): 1–366.

## ORIGINS AND SPREAD OF TECHNOLOGY

Ashton, T. S. *The Industrial Revolution,* London, 1950.

Boxer, C. R. *The Dutch Seaborne Empire,* London, 1965.

Butzer, K. W. *Environment and Archeology: An Introduction to Pleistocene Geography,* Chicago, 1965.

Cameron, R. "The Diffusion of Technology as a Problem in Economic History," *Economic Geography,* 51 (1975): 217–230.

Carter, G. F. "Plant Evidence for Early Contacts with America," *Southwestern Journal of Anthropology,* 6 (1950): 161–182.

———— "Movement of People and Ideas across the Pacific," in Barrau, J. (ed.), *Plants and the Migrations of Pacific Peoples,* Honolulu, 1963.

Chambers, J. D., and Mingay, G. E. *The Agricultural Revolution 1750–1880,* London, 1966.

Childe, V. G., *Man Makes Himself,* London, 1936, 1941, 1951. Also in paperback edition.

Clark, G. *World Prehistory: An Outline,* Cambridge, 1961.

———— and Piggott, S. *Prehistoric Societies,* London, 1965. A fine introduction to the subject.

Crosby, A. W., Jr. *The Columbian Exchange: Biological and Cultural Consequences of 1492,* Westport, Conn., 1972. Also in paperback edition.

Daniel, A. G. *Ancient Peoples and Places,* London and New York, various dates. A multivolume series, each book of which deals with a particular society or topic in ancient and prehistoric times. Among the most interesting are Powell, T. G. E. *The Celts;* Harden, D. *The Phoenicians;* Talbot-Rice, T. *The Scythians;* Bloch, R. *The Etruscans;* Wheeler, M. *Early India and Pakistan;* and Bushnell, G. H. S. *Peru.*

Hawkes, J. *Prehistory,* in *History of Mankind, Cultural and Scientific Development,* vol. 1, part 1, New York, 1963. The first volume of a multivolume series on the history of mankind; sponsored and published by UNESCO.

Kirk, W. "The Role of India in the Diffusion of Early Cultures," *Geographical Journal,* 141 (1975): 19–34.

Levison, M., Ward, R. G., and Webb, J. W. *The Settlement of Polynesia: A Computer Simulation,* Minneapolis and Sydney, 1973.

Lüthy, H. "Colonization and the Making of Mankind," *Economic History,* 21 (1961): 483–495.

McNeill, W. H. *The Rise of the West: A History of the Human Community,* Chicago, 1963. Also in paperback edition.

Marsak, L. M. (ed.). *The Rise of Science in Relation to Society,* New York, 1964.

Mellaart, J. *Earliest Civilizations of the Near East,* London, 1965.

Needham, J. *Science and Civilization in China,* 4 vols., London, 1954–1962.

Nef, J. U. *Cultural Foundations of Industrial Civilizations,* New York, 1960.

Parry, J. H. *The Establishment of the European Hegemony,* New York, 1961. Also in paperback.

———— *The Spanish Seaborne Empire,* London, 1966.

Price, A. G. *The Western Invasions of the Pacific and Its Continents: A Study of Moving Frontiers and Changing Landscapes, 1513–1958,* London, 1963.

Sauer, C. O. "The End of the Ice Age and Its Witnesses," *Geographical Review,* 47 (1957): 29–43. Reprinted in Leighly, J. (ed.), *Land and Life,* Berkeley and Los Angeles, 1963, 271–287.

Singer, C., Holmyard, E. J., Hall, A. R., and Williams, T. N. (eds.). *A History of Technology,* 5 vols., London, 1954–1958.

Skelton, R. A. *Explorers' Maps: Chapters in the Cartographic Record of Geographical Discovery,* New York, 1958.

Stanislawski, D. "Dark Age Contributions to the Mediterranean Way of Life," *Annals of the Association of American Geographers,* 63 (1973): 397–410.

———— "Dionysus Westward: Early Religion and the Economic Geography of Wine," *Geographical Review,* 65 (1975): 427-444.

Steward, H. H., and others. *Irrigation Civilizations: A Comparative Study,* Pan-American Union Social Science Monographs no. 1, Washington, D.C., 1955.

Sykes, P. *A History of Exploration,* New York, 1961. Also in paperback edition.

Thompson, J. E. *The Rise and Fall of Maya Civilization,* Norman, Okla., 1956.

Washburn, S. L. (ed.). *Social Life of Early Man,* Viking Fund Publications in Anthropology no. 31, New York, 1961.

Willey, G. R. (ed.). *Prehistoric Settlement Patterns in the New World,* Viking Fund Publications in Anthropology no. 23, New York, 1956.

The word *culture* commonly embraces the entire way of life of a people. It can also be used, however, in a more limited sense to express manifestations of the inner world of spirit. Culture in the latter meaning forms the subject of this part. Its main themes are race, language, religion, and polity.

Race as such is both a biological and a sociocultural concept. Language provides the main instrument for transmitting culture within a group and, at the same time, is one of its important characteristics. Religious and political ideologies condition, if not determine, consciously held beliefs and unconscious assumptions; in turn, they reflect cultural traditions. These traits provide the psychic energy of people and bind them together in a society set apart, though not isolated, from other societies.

The last chapter of this part proposes a division of the earth into broad culture realms and briefly describes each one. This gives us the context for understanding economy, settlement, and population—the subjects to be examined in subsequent sections.

# PART II
# CULTURAL
# DIVERSITY

Stephanos, a Greek Ortho-dox monk who lives on the island of Cyprus. (Photograph —United Nations)

# 4 RACE: Biological Facts and Social Attitudes

Geographers consider the term *race* from two angles, the scientific and the cultural. *Race* applies to the biologically distinct types of mankind that have developed in various parts of the earth, inheriting their physical traits through the generations. In a more popular meaning, *race* also refers to the way each human group perceives its own physical character and that of others through the lens of its culture. Because these sentiments—however ill-conceived—are realities which may deeply affect the fabric of a country as well as its external associations, they fall within the purview of human geography.

## GEOGRAPHY AND GENETICS

Mankind is a single subspecies (*Homo sapiens sapiens*), an interbreeding population descended from the same source. But within the subspecies are groups with distinctive features living in different locations around the earth. Genetics, the biological science dealing with heredity, can help answer the question how these human races came about.

Children inherit from their parents nose shape, skin color, blood type, and so on. The inheritance units are called genes. Each nucleus of a human cell contains a complete double set of genes. However, each male and female reproductive cell carries only one of each pair of genes. At fertilization these single genes join to form a new complete set of pairs in the cells of the offspring. For example, a child receives two genes for hair color, one from each parent.* If both signal "brown hair," the child will have brown hair. If one calls for brown and the other for red hair, the

dominant gene (in this case for brown hair) will prevail over its alternate, the recessive one. Genetic signals do not merge but remain segregated in their effect. Dominant genes can come from either parent, thus giving each generation an *independent assortment* of inherited characteristics. Although differences in nurture and environment may help produce variations, most come from the mixing and reshuffling of the genes at each generation.

New variety is added by *mutation,* a permanent structural change in a gene—as in the rearrangement of atoms in a complex molecule—resulting in the alteration of some feature. Accumulation of mutations within a group can bring about striking changes. Whether or not a mutation will survive depends on *selection* and *isolation.*

The principle of *selection* is that some individuals are more capable of survival than others because they cooperate better with the conditions of life. Physical and social environments may select (but do not cause) some mutations and genetic combinations. They tend to preserve those individuals that are preadapted to them and to eliminate the others. Differing physical environments undoubtedly have led to the selection of distinctive features of specific groups in the distant past before culture, from homemade fires to clothing, began to insulate man from the direct effects of cold, heat, dampness, dryness, brightness, and darkness.

Social and cultural conditions may create artificial barriers that regulate unions and do away with random breeding. Until recently parts of the United States forbade by law (and still restrict by social pressure) marriage between blacks and whites. Some religious groups discourage outside marriages. In India, marriages between persons of different castes are normally taboo. Fashions of

*Actually most features, including hair color, result from not one but several genes.

 mother and her child in a village of Guinea-Bissau in west Africa.
(Photograph—United Nations)

time and place affect the norm of sexual attrac-
tiveness of males and females, leading to the
preservation, increase, or decrease of certain
characteristics.

Genetic *isolation* is the separation of one
breeding group from others in the same species.*
Because mutation is random, all isolated communities, if not too large, will after a time diverge
physically from other groups, whether or not their
environments are similar. Mutations of no particular advantage diffuse throughout a small isolated
population. This is called *genetic drift.* If such

*The opposite of isolation is *propinquity* (nearness).

communities occupy unlike environments, the
combination of natural selection and genetic drift
increases the chance that they will evolve into
physically quite distinct groups, each with its own
genetic inheritance common to all persons within
the group. When two or more such communities
meet and blend, the genetic mixing results in a
physically diverse population.

Physical and cultural conditions, together
with relative location, have strongly affected the
processes of selection and the formation of *homogeneous* (literally, "born from the same") and
*heterogeneous* ("born from the different") human
groups. Distinct features, evolved during the ages

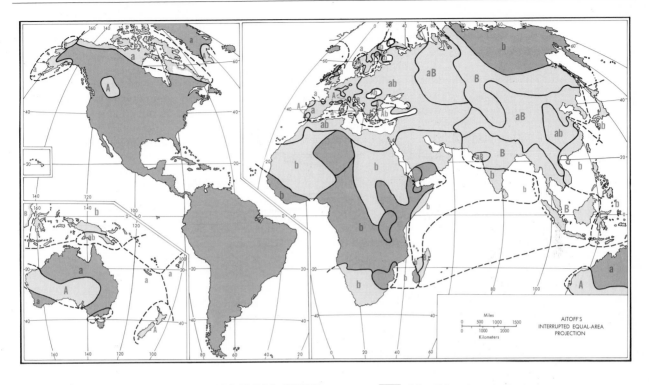

FIGURE **DISTRIBUTION OF THE ABO BLOOD GROUP**
**4–1** **GENES IN THE ABORIGINAL POPULATIONS OF THE WORLD**

The frequency categories used in this map reflect the much higher proportion of blood type O and the lower proportions of blood types A and B in the human population. Based on maps and data in Mourant, A. E., et al. *The ABO Blood Groups,* Oxford, 1958.

when isolated groups lived under widely different biophysical conditions, have become, through subsequent dispersion and mixing, characteristic of large populations that now include almost all of the human species.

## BLOOD TYPES

Despite the differences in skin color and other features commonly used to identify human races, little is understood about the individual genes through which we inherit them. Well known, however, after many years of research and data gathering, are the specific genetic systems responsible for blood types.

Among the genetically independent blood systems is that known as ABO, which gives blood types A, AB, B, and O. The last one indicates an absence of A and B, two substances which cause clotting of the red blood cells when mixed with blood that does not contain them. In the genetic system A and B are dominant over O, but neither A nor B dominates over the other. A person with A and B genes has blood type AB. The ABO genes follow the laws of segregation. That means the types do not merge: an individual with type AB has both substances and not a blend of them.

Figure 4–1 shows that the ABO blood type genes have strong regional concentrations. High proportions of the A gene are found among some outlying European populations, North American Indians, Balkan and Middle Eastern peoples, and some groups of Australian aborigines. Type A is almost absent in Middle and South America, with low frequencies in Africa, South Asia, and northeastern Asia. The B gene, while not as numerous in total as A, occurs in relatively high proportions in Central and Southeast Asia and with moderate frequency in parts of Africa. The O gene is the most widespread and numerous. It has high frequencies among some western European populations, Australian aborigines, American Indians, and some African peoples; somewhat lower frequencies occur in East and Central Asia.

These distributions pose problems as yet unsolved. Some scholars think that all mankind in its early history was of type 0. Then, when mutation A occurred, it replaced 0 in some regions. Type B, a later mutation, followed the same course. The higher incidence of B in eastern Europe as against A in western Europe, and a similar division between northern and southern India, can be explained in terms of nomadic armies from Central Asia with high B frequencies invading the agricultural peripheries of Eurasia and breeding with the O and A peasant peoples. Type B, which is associated with "Mongoloid"* groups in their later stage of evolution, is uncommon among American Indians.

Such sweeping explanations fail to account for the existence of B genes in central Africa, the Pacific islands, and among some groups in the Americas. It seems unlikely that independent but parallel mutations occurred among peoples so remote from each other. Perhaps early migrations were more extensive than so far realized, including, for instance, widespread diffusion of Mongolian features among African populations.

In short, the meaning of these distributions is not yet clear. It is hoped that further patient sifting of serological clues will make more evident their value in tracing the migrations of mankind.

## PROBLEMS OF CLASSIFICATION

Ideally speaking, a race is a population which is homogeneous. Most peoples, however, consist of individuals with different genetic patterns and varied inheritance. Thus, classification of human

*The suffix -oid, from the Greek, means "having the form of," "like."

races is difficult if not impossible. Another trouble is that although much is known about the distribution and diversity of body features (*phenotypes*), little has been established about underlying genetic structures (*genotypes*).

Relying on phenotypes creates further issues. Phenotypes do not change in a set combination from group to group. For example, mankind can be broadly divided according to skin color, but such division fails to match the one based on head shape. Only by excluding some peoples and by selecting a few traits can we find yardsticks that vary together. Moreover, because most phenotypes derive from many genes, with independent assortment, they fall into subclasses that merge gradually into each other. This makes it virtually impossible to delimit races by hard-and-fast lines. Some traits—for example, the ABO blood types—are inherited through the presence or absence of a single gene. In these cases there is no merging of phenotypes; unfortunately these traits do not covary with others from group to group.

To most people *skin color* is the hallmark of race. Pigments such as melanin, when increased in amount, darken the skin and appear to protect blood and tissue from excessive exposure to solar radiation. Some scholars claim that the early humans, who lived in tropical regions with strong sunlight, were dark of skin. Lighter pigmentation developed, it is thought, when they migrated to regions where the sun was less intense. Many genes control skin color phenotypes, and shades range from very fair to black; attempts to divide this continuum into sections remain quite arbitrary.

Color subdivisions among mankind persist where breeding groups are relatively isolated and where groups of different color living close together are regulated by patterns of social segregation. When isolation decreases and social norms change, color distinctions blur as in South America, especially Brazil, where there is much intermarriage between persons of African, American, and European ancestry.

*Head shape* also has been used extensively to classify races. What we know of prehistoric man necessarily depends on skeletal remains, and the skull is easy to measure. There are indeed marked differences in the head shape of peoples,

This Indonesian man is fairly representative of the Southeast Asian type of Mongoloid. (A Shell photograph)

but these differences do not covary with other traits. Among light-skinned peoples, most Russians have broad heads but most Norwegians long heads. Mongols also have broad heads but most Japanese long heads; both black Africans and West Europeans have long heads.

*Hair form and texture* show significant racial differences. Between the straight hair of the Mongol and the woolly hair of the West African there are intermediate forms of wavy and curly hair, as found among Europeans and North Africans. Though environment and manipulation may temporarily change hair form, heredity is the basic control; the types do not seem to merge. Whether different kinds of hair have selective value is not known, although there is much speculation about this.

The shape of jaw and nose, the presence or absence of the Mongolian eye fold, stature, the amount of body hair—these and other features vary from one group to another. However, as with features for which the genetic mechanism is well known, they do not vary together, which makes any attempt at dividing mankind into races artificial and arbitrary. Nature gives us no classification. What we call "human races" are only statistical averages. As Blumenbach, founder of modern physical anthropology, wrote in 1775:

Although there seems to be [such a] difference between widely separated nations, that you might easily take the inhabitants of the Cape of Good Hope, the Greenlanders, and the Circassians for so many species of men, yet when the matter is thoroughly considered, you see that all do so run into one another, and that one variety of mankind does so sensibly pass into another, that you cannot mark out the limits between them. (Blumenbach, 1865, 99)

It is no wonder then that many different classifications have been proposed. Blumenbach himself identified five races by using skin color as the criterion. A century later Deniker listed twenty-nine races based on hair form, skin color, and nose shape. Most modern classifications recognize three main stocks; some give consideration to mixtures and others sharply distinguish each group.

A good geographical classification will take into account the distribution of important physical traits as well as the genetic nature and origins of distinctive human groups. The following discussion, based on the locational concepts of isolation and propinquity, moves from small homogeneous groups to the main divisions of mankind, which are heterogeneous in character.

### ISOLATED PEOPLES

Easiest to classify are several small isolated groups. Their isolation means that their genes play only a minor role in determining the physique of the mass of mankind. Figure 4–2 summarizes the nature and location of these peoples. It has been suggested that such peoples represent the prototypes of modern man, resembling the human beings from whom have developed the present main racial stocks outlined below. The widespread distribution of the Australoids (and also the Negritoids) lends credence to this idea. On the other hand, slight differences within each of these isolated groups suggest either a series of roughly parallel developments in different places or migration to their present locations during a relatively recent stage of human evolution. Perhaps the Negritoids originated in southern Asia, spread widely, then were pushed back to their present refuge areas by invaders.

The Bushmen pose a riddle with their eye folds and slanting eyes which resemble those of Asians. Perhaps these features are due to independent natural selection in environments where sunlight is very intense. Formerly Bushmen ranged over wide areas of southern Africa; only a few

thousands survive. The more numerous Hottentots appear to derive some traits from Negroid peoples of southeastern Africa.

### THE MAIN RACIAL STOCKS

The great mass of people belong to large heterogeneous groups with variable genetic structures. Identifying three sets of distinct genetic features allows a broad division into Negroid, Mongoloid, and Caucasoid racial stocks.

The Negroid set includes genes for black skin and black woolly hair, dark eyes, broad and flat nose, thick and everted lips, long head, prognathous jaw, and stocky body build. The regions of selection appear to have been the hot, bright savanna lands of West Africa.

Among the Mongoloid genes are those for light yellow to brown skin, brown eyes, straight and coarse black hair, flat face and nose, broad head, epicanthic eye fold, high cheekbones, and short and stocky build. The regions of selection were probably the dry and bright mid-latitude steppes with pronounced summer and winter seasons of Central Asia.

The Caucasoid genetic set includes fair skin and eyes, light and wavy hair, prominent and narrow nose, thin lips, and abundance of body hair. The regions of selection most likely were the damp, cool, cloudy tundras and forests of western Eurasia.

The climatic-vegetational environments here noted are the ecological conditions in the Old World during the last glaciation. In that period the mountain belts of Eurasia from the Atlantic to the north Pacific became impassable or at least hazardous to cross. However, to the south lay a zone of more genial climate. We can postulate that *Homo sapiens* (probably only a few scattered thousands) lived in this tropical and subtropical region, but that some groups moved into outlying regions and were overtaken by climatic change. Where isolated for long periods in extreme environments, the people were modified by natural selection and genetic drift. Distinctive adaptations became common to each of the isolated groups: for example, black skin, hair, and eyes, the eye fold and flat face, the fair hair and skin.

In the central belt, it can be further conjec-

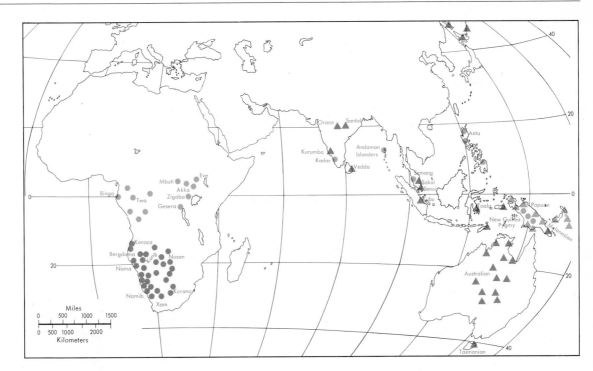

FIGURE **ISOLATED PEOPLES**
4-2

The symbols indicate locations of groups genetically
isolated from the main mass of mankind until modern
times.

| Group | Features | Examples | |
|---|---|---|---|
| ● Negritoid | Yellow to Brown Skin | Congo River and Upper Nile Pygmy | Negrillo |
| | Black Spiral (Peppercorn) Hair | | |
| | Short Stature | Andaman Islanders | |
| | Negrito and Negrillo Have Different Blood Types | Semang of Malaya New Guinea Pygmy Aeta of Luzon | Negrito |
| ● Bushmanoid | Hair and Skin like Negritoid | Bushmen and Hottentots of Southern Africa | |
| | Flat Face | | |
| | Epicanthic Eyefold | | |
| | Steatopygy in Female | | |
| ▲ Australoid | Dark Skin and Eyes | Australian Aborigines Ainu of Hokkaido and Sakhalin Vedda of Ceylon Sakai of Malaya Kurumba of Deccan Plateau Bhil, Gond of Deccan Plateau Oraon, Santal of Chota Nagpur | |
| | Dark, Wavy Hair | | |
| | Broad Nose | | |
| | Full Lips | | |
| | Long Head | | |
| | Hirsute | | |
| | A and O Blood Types (No B) | | |
| ▲ Papuan- Melanesian | Much like the Australoid, but More Frizzly Hair | Papuans of New Guinea Melanesians of Solomons | |

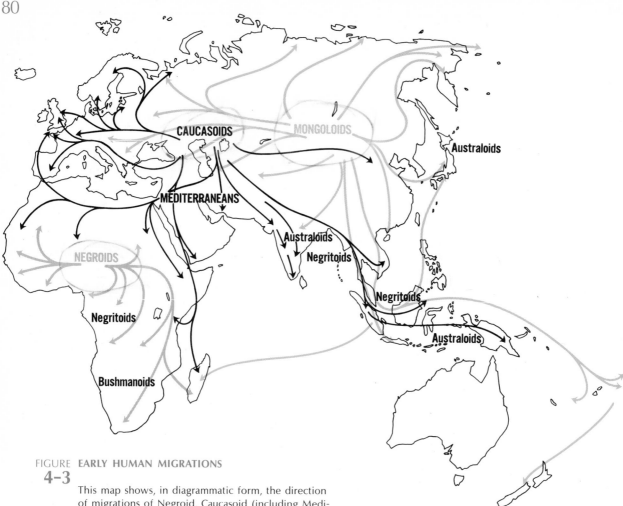

FIGURE **EARLY HUMAN MIGRATIONS**
**4-3**

This map shows, in diagrammatic form, the direction
of migrations of Negroid, Caucasoid (including Mediterranean), and Mongoloid genetic elements into regions occupied by Negritoid, Bushmanoid, and Australoid peoples.

tured, the peoples continued to maintain a pool
of diverse hereditary factors. Toward the end of
the glaciation when climatic conditions amelio-
rated, contacts were reestablished between the
formerly extreme areas and the central belt. Much
migration and intermixing took place, especially
along the margins of the regions where specialized types had evolved. This explains why peoples
of the central belt are hardest to classify. Here
groups, probably quite diverse to begin with, have
absorbed over a long time features from the Caucasoids, Mongoloids, and Negroids. Though these

are usually grouped together as "Mediterraneans"
under the broad heading of Caucasoid, many
other peoples identified as Negroid or Mongoloid
show similarly varied genetic provenance (see
Figures 4-3 and 4-4).

For example, we will trace how Mongoloid
features spread after the climate of the northern
zone of the Old World warmed up. The survivors
of the cold in isolated inner Asian intermontane
basins increased in numbers and spilled out to
east, north, and south, settling in central and
north China, in Mongolia, and in parts of Siberia,
mingling with other peoples with different physical traits. Some of the Mongoloids crossed by the
Bering Strait and the Aleutian chain to North

America, where earlier migrations of similar basic stock had preceded them (Coon et al., 1950, 83–84).

Sometime after 4000 B.C. farming peoples of Mediterranean physique moved eastward through central Asia from oasis to oasis. When they reached the Yellow River plain of northern China, they mixed heavily with the aborigines and in time acquired some Mongoloid features. As Chinese they later pushed southward, driving ahead of them most of the unassimilated indigenous Mongoloid tribes who, in turn, invaded Southeast Asia's mainland and the Malay Archipelago. These Mongoloids, in migrations beginning perhaps earlier than 2000 B.C., absorbed some of the earlier inhabitants, producing a local Mongoloid variety, the ancestors of the Polynesians.

Caucasoid peoples, in a series of migrations from the north into the Mediterranean region and into southwestern Asia, infused lighter color into the populations of these areas. Migrations in Africa spread Negroid traits from the western part of the continent through the southern and northern sections and reached even portions of southern Europe and southwestern Asia. Figure 4–3 summarizes the main directions of these Old World migrations up to historic times.

## PRESENT DISTRIBUTION OF THE MAIN RACES

The natural selection of distinctive *Negroid* features probably occurred in the hot and bright savanna lands of West and Central Africa. Moving away from this region, we meet many types with some Negroid features but also with traits common to peoples of the Mediterranean and Middle East. Figure 4–4 shows the presumed genetic relations of different groups within the Negroid division. Black skin gives way to brown and lighter shades, broad flat nose to narrow nose, stocky build to slender, tightly curled hair to wavy or even straight, thick lips to thin.

Other differences are obvious in the descendants of the Africans who were brought as slaves to the New World from West Africa. We know for a fact that many Europeans in the Americas interbred with their slaves. From this developed an Afro-American population possessing on the average numerous Caucasoid features. Also in Africa, we can assume, populations show such mixtures of traits resulting from similar unions.

The "classic" *Mongoloid* individual of Mongolia is round-faced, relatively hairless, and stocky. In this region, isolated by mountain ranges and ice sheets, distinctive features evolved through "climatic engineering." As one moves away from this area, there are strong indications that Mongoloid genes decrease in frequency. In north China the people are often slim in build, and the facial features of a significant proportion—perhaps one in twenty—remind us of Mediterranean-Southwest Asian types. In southern China the epicanthic eye fold is less evident. The Japanese are often narrow-faced, hirsute, and slightly built. The Eskimo have many Mongoloid features but a prominent narrow nose. American Indians, often lumped together as a variety of Mongoloid, actually are diverse in physique, some with almost pure Mongoloid characteristics, others resembling Southeast Asians.

It is not so easy to divide the *Caucasoid* peoples into distinct subgroups living in separate regions. This is particularly true of Europe, where many migrations have resulted in much mixing and remixing. Three principal types can be recognized, however: (1) Nordic people have fair skin, wavy blond or red hair, blue eyes, narrow noses, and long heads; they form only a bare majority of the Scandinavians, a large minority in the British Isles, North Germany, and the Low Countries, and occur in still lower proportions farther afield. (2) The Alpines have broad heads, thick-set bodies, light skin, and straight to wavy brown hair; they too are found in varying proportions throughout Europe, with a wedgelike zone of concentration from Central Asia penetrating into western France. One view claims that Alpine traits represent a blend of Nordic and Mediterranean features with those of prehistoric European populations. Another view contends that they evolved from an intermixing of Nordic with Mongoloid after invasions from Central Asia. (3) The Mediterranean types occupy lands from Portugal and Morocco to the Indian subcontinent. The nose is generally large, the head long, eyes dark, and facial features smooth. But other traits show considerable range: the skin from light olive to dark, and the hair from brown to very dark brown

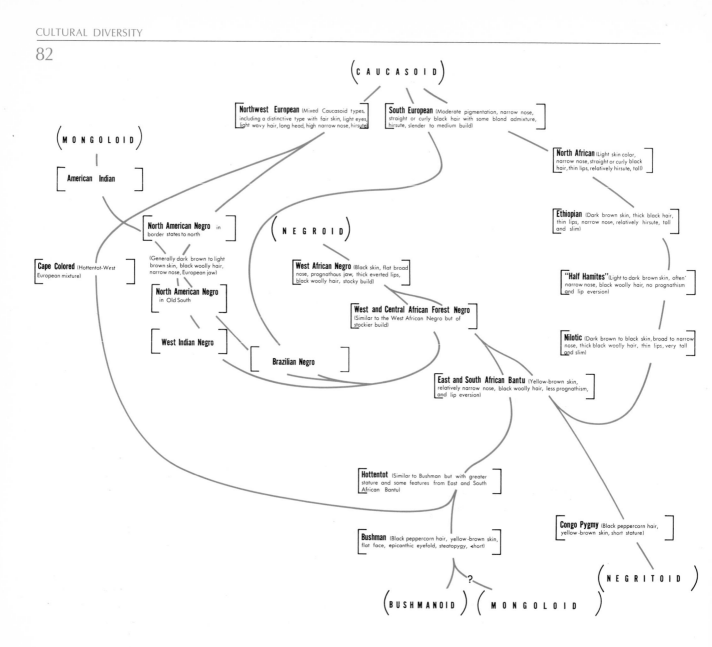

FIGURE **NEGROID GENETIC VARIATIONS**
4-4

The lines on this diagram do not represent lines of descent, but rather are unmarked scales of increasing and decreasing Negroid gene frequencies.

and from straight to wavy. In North and East Africa, Mediterranean features shade into Negroid. Complexions become darker in India, almost black in south India, although many other fea-

tures are similar to those of the lighter folk farther north. Mediterranean traits gradually fade away in Southeast Asia and the islands of the Pacific Ocean; they are replaced by those of Mongoloid peoples and by characteristics associated with Australoid and perhaps Negritoid peoples.

The white populations of South Africa, Australia, and New Zealand are similar to their counterparts in northwestern Europe, while those of North America reflect the more diverse racial origins of its immigrants. In South America the peoples of European background are principally Mediterranean in physique. In Siberia the white settlers, having come from eastern Europe, show high proportions of Alpine features.

In each of these cases the Caucasoid Europeans have mixed to a greater or lesser extent with peoples of other genetic backgrounds. In Anglo-America the offspring of blacks and whites are referred to as blacks and are generally classed with those of solely Negro ancestry. The term *mulatto*, meaning "black and white mixture," is not now used in North America, although it is elsewhere. South African whites mating with Hottentots created the Cape Coloreds, most of whom live in Cape Province. Latin Americans of European origin combined with indigenous American stock to produce the Mestizos, who are very numerous and form the bulk of the population in several Latin American countries.

## RACE VERSUS CULTURE

Often one can observe some correspondence between physical and cultural characteristics: the English are Caucasoid, the Chinese Mongoloid, the Ghanaians Negroid. A common saying is, "He looks like a Frenchman (Mexican, Filipino)." This is understandable, because both biological inheritance and learned behavior stem mostly from parents. Some people, though, are not aware of the essential difference between race and culture. They carelessly use such terms as "German race," "Jewish race," and "Arab race," instead of "nation," "religious community," and "cultural group." Others go much further; they assert that race determines culture. To them the achievements of Western civilization are uniquely great, owing to the innate superiority of the white race, while what they perceive to be lower levels of material and spiritual life in Africa and Asia, or among blacks in the United States, results from the inferiority of the "colored races." Such attitudes are ingrained in the historical experience of white Anglo-American culture.

It is nonsense to say that skin color is a key to mental worth. So far as we know, physical differences among human populations cannot express or affect mental qualities one way or the other. But it is possible that the inheritance of mental qualities varies from one physically distinct group to another. Are general intelligence, artistic sense, or an energetic disposition inherited in different degrees or forms by different racial groups? A satisfactory answer is impossible. To experiment is extremely difficult, because the influences of nurture cannot be stripped away to discover what is nature. Tests that try to distinguish inborn mental traits or capabilities of racial groups only succeed in being gauges of economic or social opportunity.

The history of civilized man shows no evidence that race determines the level of technical achievement. For instance, the many inventions in agriculture originated among various races. As Boris Pasternak wrote: "Mankind does not live in a state of nature, but in history." People's attainments appear to be governed by the culture in which they are embedded rather than by the racial group to which they belong. Confucius put it more simply: "Men's natures are alike; it is their habits that carry them far apart."

## RACIAL TENSIONS

Geographers' concern with racial relations follows from their interest in the comparative study of places: Why do racial tensions occur where they do and how do they affect the character of a country? Racial relations derive from attitudes that are part of culture. Knowledge of the biological character of ethnic groups in a region of racial tension provides no answer to these questions. It only serves to set the stage for investigating the locational, historical, and social conditions that may account for the conflict.

In modern history, colonization by Europeans has often created situations conducive to race prejudice. But colonization itself is not the cause of racial tension, for there have been cases where racial discord has not followed it. In Brazil, for example, the Portuguese imposed a colonial system on the American Indians and later imported large numbers of African slaves; despite these events, that country seems to have a low level of race prejudice, although it doubtless exists.

A man of Caucasoid stock from Cyprus, in the eastern Mediterranean, where genetic mixing has been going on for thousands of years. (Photograph—United Nations)

The emergence of racial bias, then, depends on the specific nature and circumstances of the encounter between ethnic groups. Confrontations have occurred in different ways: in colonial settlement, like that of Europeans in the Americas, Africa, Australia, and Siberia; through economic enterprise as represented by European and American trading companies and plantations in less developed tropical regions; or in colonial imperialism as, for instance, the division of Africa between European powers in the nineteenth century.

On the whole, contacts in the economic sphere have been, and are, most common. Among various racial groups, the different levels of technological attainment turn into a division of work along ethnic lines. The use of cheap labor came to be justified on the assumption that the workers were of an inferior race and thus worthy only of menial tasks. The dominant group employed the same rationalization to support their political control—the inferior should be governed by the superior. Such views, of course, are not confined to peoples of European culture.

Much racial prejudice has the same kind of economic and political motivation as class prejudice, and the two may be related in origin. In former times, and in some places today, intolerance was directed toward class. The ruling class considered the lower classes as "born to their station in life." As long as an economy required a force of "hewers of wood and drawers of water," the menial workers could be perpetuated by treating them as a race apart. It is still common in many societies, regardless of racial character, to have rigid class if not caste systems with strictly confined marriage circles. In Europe, when the eighteenth-century Enlightenment promoted the idea of human equality, class barriers began to crumble, leading to more or less "open societies." In this respect the United States, less burdened by tradition than Europe, took the lead.

Unfortunately race prejudice appears to have taken the place of class prejudice. Thus, although slavery was abolished in Western countries in the nineteenth century, attitudes held toward the lower classes were transferred to the descendants of slaves, especially those of African ancestry. The motivation was still one of economic and political power, but skin color became the test of who belonged to the low-caste laboring group. This explanation of racial relations is not all-inclusive; nevertheless it may help to understand the situation in countries like the United States, Rhodesia, and South Africa.

## INTERBREEDING

In almost all cases of race prejudice the final argument of those who favor segregation is that the children of mixed marriages are inferior.* They may well be inferior in their upbringing or accomplishments if they are discriminated against. There is no evidence that they are biologically inferior. Some authorities go further and express the view that crossbreeding results in

*"Race mixture" and "miscegenation" are misleading terms since true races in the sense of homogeneous populations rarely are involved in interbreeding, at least in modern times. The terms "mixed-blood," "half-blooded," and "full-blooded" are liable to misinterpretation (although perhaps justified by continuous usage) because each individual's blood is his own. As pointed out before, blood types cut across the normally used racial divisions of mankind.

biologically superior specimens. As L. C. Dunn wrote:

The limited amount of in-breeding which occurs within a marriage circle tends to produce gene differences between different circles. When members of different circles marry, the children are liable to contain more gene pairs with unlike partners than the parents. In some animals and plant populations this condition appears to be conducive to greater biological vigor—the "mixed bloods" or hybrids are superior in some respects to either parent stock. In fact it may be that variety is good because it makes unlike combinations commoner. We know very little about this sort of thing in man, but the very mixed biological make-up of all present day human individuals and groups suggests that there may be something in it.

Biologically then, men belong to one mating circle, and share in a common pool of genes. Thus there is no biological justification for race hatred or prejudice. One should be careful to recognize this prejudice for what it is, and not try to conceal it behind a "scientific" rationalization.

The conditions of the modern world, deplorable as they are for many peoples over whom hangs the threat of insecurity and war, are nevertheless just those which tend to remove and reduce the factors which created biological race differences. If given a chance to continue in operation, they have the power to restore the unity which the human race lost by geographical dispersion. (UNESCO, 1952, 283–284)

It has been suggested that the status of "half-breeds" indicates the degree of assimilation between the two parent groups. The offspring of European-Asian mixing (often called "Eurasians") usually have not been fully accepted either by Asians or by Europeans, thus pointing up the marked cleavage between the colonized and the colonizers. On the other hand, people of mixed parentage in Hawaii and Brazil meet with little overt racial discrimination.

Table 4–1 shows the ethnic composition in a number of countries where the inhabitants are of different racial origin. The table is of less value for its figures, which should be used with caution, than for the variety of ethnic or racial concepts it reveals. The explanatory footnotes demonstrate again how significant cultural perception is in the classification of racial groups.

## BLACKS IN THE UNITED STATES

The United States Census divides the population into "Whites" and "Nonwhites," and the latter into "Nonwhite Races," among which are "Negro, American Indian, Japanese, Chinese, Filipino, Korean, Asian Indian, and Malayan." For the Bureau of the Census, "the concept of race is derived from that which is commonly accepted by the general public. . . . [It] does not reflect clear-cut definitions of biological stock, and several categories obviously refer to national origin." In responding to census questions, individuals assign

**MIXED POPULATIONS IN SELECTED POLITICAL UNITS\***

TABLE
4-1

| Political unit | Date | Description | Population | |
|---|---|---|---|---|
| | | | Thousands | Percent |
| Guatemala | 1964 | Indigenous | 1,809 | 42.2 |
| | | Nonindigenous | 2,479 | 57.8 |
| Malawi | 1966 | African | 4,021 | 99.5 |
| | | Asiatic | 11 | 0.3 |
| | | European | 7 | 0.2 |
| South Africa | 1970 | Asiatic | 620 | 2.9 |
| | | Bantu | 15,057 | 70.2 |
| | | Colored | 2,018 | 9.5 |
| | | White | 3,751 | 17.5 |
| Sri Lanka | 1963 | Burgher and Eurasian | 46 | 0.4 |
| | | Malay | 33 | 0.3 |
| | | Moor | 682 | 6.4 |
| | | Sinhalese | 7,513 | 71.0 |
| | | Tamil | 2,288 | 21.6 |
| | | Vedda | Unknown | Unknown |
| | | Other | 20 | 0.2 |
| United States | 1970 | Chinese | 435 | 0.2 |
| | | Filipino | 343 | 0.2 |
| | | Indian (indigenous) | 793 | 0.4 |
| | | Japanese | 591 | 0.3 |
| | | Negro | 22,580 | 12.0 |
| | | White | 177,749 | 86.5 |
| | | Others† | 721 | 0.4 |

\*From Table 15, United Nations *Demographic Yearbook 1971*, New York, 1972, and Table 29, United Nations *Demographic Yearbook 1973*, New York, 1974. These books contain a discussion of these and other compilations. "The heterogeneity of the concepts used in collecting these data is their basic defect. This lack of uniformity is evidenced by the variety of terms used: ('nationality,' 'race,' 'color,' 'race and color,' 'color and geography,' 'stock,' 'origin,' 'socio-economic characteristics,' etc.). Furthermore, different shades of meaning have been attached to these words, so that the connotations range from a rough biological concept . . . to a question of cultural affiliation. . . . In addition, more than one concept has sometimes been employed in a single distribution, so that, for instance, 'French' and 'Negro' may appear as two of the items in a classification. . . . It goes without saying that the terms and figures of the table should be treated with circumspection."

†Comprises Aleut, Eskimo, Hawaiian, Korean, Malayan, Thai, and others not covered by specific categories. See also the text at the top of this page for further information on the U.S. Census use of the concept of race.

themselves to the "racial" category with which they identify. Presumably, many individuals of mixed ancestry make the decision on sociocultural grounds.

The majority of American blacks exhibit physical characteristics derived from both African and European ancestry. Most of the interbreeding took place before the emancipation of the slaves. The institution of slavery was succeeded by the color bar. Many states, especially in the South, had laws forbidding the marriage of Negroes and whites. In many cities and states the racial bar still exists in custom. Nevertheless, numerous light-colored persons of mixed ancestry have been, and are being, absorbed into the white population. At present there is little intermarriage between blacks and whites. The marriage circles of the two groups are almost mutually exclusive. If the social barriers to marriage remain, the Afro-American population may stabilize in physical appearance somewhere near the midpoint between the Northwest European and West African.

According to the 1970 census, Negroes number 22.6 million, or almost 11 percent of the national population. Table 4-2 shows how their distribution has changed since 1790. The table is largely self-explanatory and only needs a few comments. The northern border states of the South were the first to experience a relative decline in their black population. In the twentieth

century, losses spread to rural districts of other Southern states. The cities of the South maintained and, in the case of the large cities, even increased their proportion of blacks. Since the Civil War the shares of the Northeast and Middle West and, in more recent times, of the Pacific Coast states have steadily grown (see also Figure 4-5).

The dominant feature of change at mid-twentieth century was the migration of the Afro-American to the cities. Figure 4-6 shows two things: the large numbers moving from the South to northern cities, and the relationship between southern areas of origin and northern cities of destination. The proportion of the national black population in each of three pairs of regions—South Atlantic–Northeast, Central South–Midwest, Southwest–Pacific—has remained almost constant since 1890 (Hart, 1960).

At the height of the black migration from the rural South in the 1960s, the average rural black family had an income less than half that of the urban blacks who, in turn, had little more than half that of the urban whites. Furthermore, the income of a black family in northern cities was substantially higher than in southern cities, double in some instances. Also, northern cities and states had rapidly developed welfare income systems for the poor and the jobless, whereas most of the South had not. These circumstances made

**UNITED STATES: PERCENTAGE OF TOTAL NEGRO POPULATION IN SELECTED REGIONS, 1790-1970**

TABLE 4-2

| Region | 1790 | 1860 | 1910 | 1960 | 1970 |
|---|---|---|---|---|---|
| Northeast | 24.3 | 8.2 | 9.1 | 21.8 | 25.3 |
| East North Central | 1.0 | 1.4 | 3.1 | 15.3 | 17.1 |
| Pacific | | 0.1 | 0.3 | 5.1 | 6.7 |
| Southwest | | 24.3 | 30.6 | 19.5 | 16.9 |
| Border | 42.4 | 26.7 | 15.9 | 10.6 | 9.7 |
| Southeast | 32.3 | 39.2 | 40.1 | 26.1 | 18.3 |
| Other | | 0.1 | 0.9 | 1.6 | 6.0 |
| United States total, thousands | 757 | 4,442 | 9,828 | 18,872 | 22,580 |

Definitions of regions:
Northeast: New England, New York, New Jersey, Pennsylvania, Delaware, Maryland, West Virginia, District of Columbia.
East North Central: Ohio, Indiana, Illinois, Michigan, Wisconsin.
Pacific: Washington, Oregon, California, Alaska, Hawaii.
Southwest: Mississippi, Arkansas, Louisiana, Oklahoma, Texas.
Border: Virginia, Kentucky, Tennessee, Missouri.
Southeast: North Carolina, South Carolina, Georgia, Alabama, Florida.
SOURCE: Hart, 1960, and *U.S. Census of Population, 1960, 1970.*

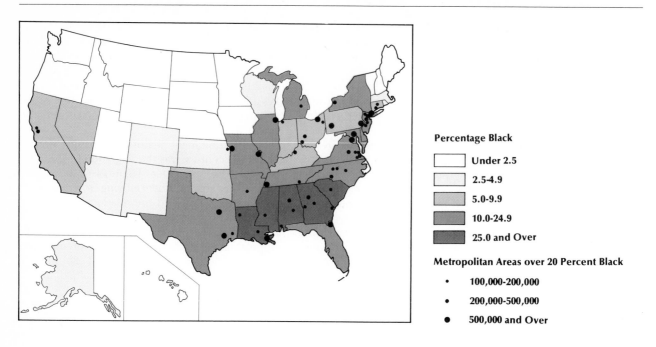

**Percentage Black**

| | |
|---|---|
| ☐ | Under 2.5 |
| ☐ | 2.5-4.9 |
| ☐ | 5.0-9.9 |
| ☐ | 10.0-24.9 |
| ☐ | 25.0 and Over |

**Metropolitan Areas over 20 Percent Black**

- • 100,000-200,000
- • 200,000-500,000
- ● 500,000 and Over

FIGURE UNITED STATES: BLACK POPULATION
4-5

The colors show the black population as a percentage of the total population of each state. The dots show central cities in which blacks make up more than 20 percent of the total population. Source of data: *U.S. Census of Population, 1970.*

it hardly surprising that the South-to-North migration continued throughout the 1960s. However, it slackened gradually in the early 1970s as the pool of potential rural migrants dwindled. Burgeoning large southern cities with improved race relations began to attract many more migrants than those of the North, where living conditions appeared to deteriorate.

On a different scale we can examine the changing distribution of white and black populations within large metropolitan areas. When blacks were held in slavery, indenture, or other servile status, most lived among the whites to whom they were bound. The legal, social, and economic institutions of segregation made blacks outcasts, unable either to develop their culture or to be assimilated into white society. Because the black did not threaten white supremacy, residential intermixture posed no problems to the whites. Putting it in another way, social distance was so immense that segregation was unnecessary. Such cities as Charleston and New Orleans had a low degree of segregation; others, including those of the Northeast, had few blacks, though here they sometimes lived in clusters.

Major changes occurred in American life during the twentieth century, particularly from 1920 onward. White immigration from Europe slowed to a trickle. The massive movement from the rural South to the urban North got under way, reaching its peak in the 1960s. Many of the legal props of social segregation were pronounced unconstitutional; blacks became aware of their own worth. As social distance lessened, most whites, unable to accept integration, favored residential segregation—intensifying an old and characteristic feature of American cities to have the poor (formerly penniless immigrants) live around the urban centers near the menial and low-paying jobs.

The formation of black ghettos proceeded rapidly during the 1950s and 1960s. As whites moved to the suburbs, blacks crowded into the vacated centers. For example, between 1960 and

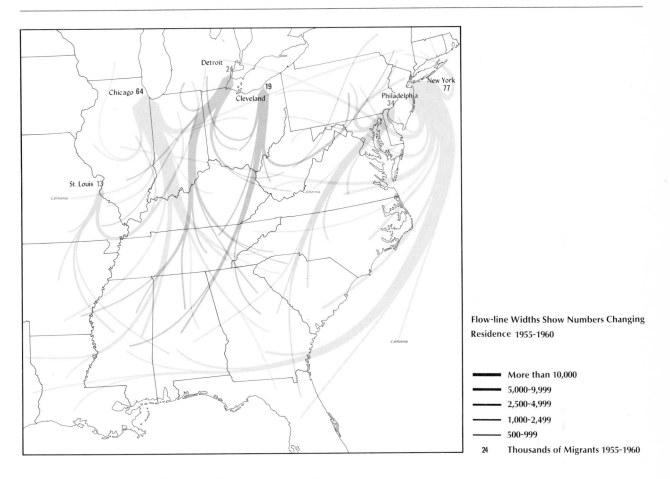

**Flow-line Widths Show Numbers Changing
Residence 1955-1960**

━━━ **More than 10,000**
━━ **5,000-9,999**
─── **2,500-4,999**
── **1,000-2,499**
── **500-999**
**24 Thousands of Migrants 1955-1960**

FIGURE UNITED STATES: NONWHITE MIGRANTS TO
**4-6** SELECTED METROPOLITAN CENTERS

Black migrations from the rural South to the urban
North were at their height in the late 1950s. The flow
lines join states of residence in 1955 to places of residence in 1960. Compiled from data in U.S. Bureau of
the Census, *Census of Population, 1960,* Subject Reports, *Mobility for Metropolitan Areas,* Washington,
D.C., 1963.

1970 in the New York metropolitan area the five
counties which make up New York City gained by
migration 435,000 blacks and other minority races
and lost 955,000 whites (see Figure 15–8). Four
nearby counties in New Jersey added 97,000
blacks by migration and lost 203,000 whites. In
nine surrounding suburban counties, on the other

hand, an estimated 680,000 whites moved in but
only 94,000 blacks and other minority races.*

By the early 1970s black ghettos and white
suburbs of small and middle-sized cities experienced some social integration by dismantling
neighborhood school districts and substituting
citywide school systems, with much busing of
students across the old boundaries. Most of these
arrangements were devised by or followed court
actions supporting the legal policy of integration.
In the large metropolitan areas, however, similar
procedures proved difficult if not impossible to
implement.

*These figures from the U.S. Census may be inaccurate
because blacks in New York City were undercounted.
The correct figures would reinforce the point made here.

Because of these developments and their differing impact from city to city and from region to region, the old idea of the national "melting pot" (actually for whites only) has given way to a confusion of voices on the current situation and the trends in social relations among ethnic groups.

Many hold the notion that America is becoming a plural society in which blacks, Indians, Mexican-Americans, Puerto Ricans, and so on should be considered as having distinct cultures with the right to remain distinct, especially since they have been effectively barred from participating in the "American dream." Undoubtedly the perpetuation of metropolitan residential segregation and its accompanying social and cultural separatism will deepen the consciousness of pluralism among the population at large (see also Chapter 7). Nevertheless, to the extent that the national policy of integration succeeds, it can halt the formation of more or larger ghettos and thus reduce tension and promote the cooperation and harmony so necessary among the various communities within American society.

## GREAT BRITAIN

In Europe racial tensions are rare because its population has a relatively homogeneous composition. However, recent immigration of West Indians and Pakistanis into Britain provides an interesting case of racial confrontation on the home ground of a European nation.

The West Indies, especially densely populated Jamaica, Barbados, and the Leeward Islands, have large numbers of blacks, once imported as slaves. Because the small white minorities for a long time marked their upper-class status by a strong color bar, the West Indian black is genetically closer to the West African than is the North American Negro. An East Indian element also has been added to the black, white, and mixed groups in the Windward Islands, Trinidad, Tobago, and Guyana.

Many West Indians, especially Jamaicans, migrated in the 1950s and early 1960s to Britain, where they now form a small but conspicuous minority. Severe restrictions have been imposed against further immigration from the West Indies,

Africa, and South Asia; however, those who already had come suffer no legal discrimination. Just the same, they have been relegated to the lower levels of what remains of the old British social-class structure. Most have "working-class" jobs in London and other large cities. Racial tension exists and there have been confrontations from time to time.

An instructive sidelight on the nature of race relations and prejudice is that the Britons tend to show more bias against Pakistanis, who are physically Caucasoid like themselves but are Moslems and do not speak English, than against the West Indians, who fit more easily into the English milieu because they are culturally Christians and speak English.

## SOUTH AFRICA

Severe racial discrimination and oppression prevail in the Republic of South Africa. Of the 26 million inhabitants over two-thirds are black Africans belonging to various Bantu-speaking tribes. Less than one-fifth of the population is of European descent; of these well over half use Afrikaans (a version of Dutch) as their mother tongue and adhere to the stern religious traditions of the Reformed Church Calvinism. The remainder of the whites are mostly of British origin, speak English, and generally are of much weaker religious persuasion. The Cape Coloreds—10 percent of the population—stem from the time when white settlers and sailors frequently mixed with the Hottentots, the indigenous people of the south tip of Africa. Other groups recognized as culturally and physically distinct include the Cape Malays and the Indians. The latter, originally imported to work on the plantations and railroads of Natal, now are mostly engaged in crafts and retail trade in that part of the country (Figure 4–7).

In this plural society (see also Chapter 7) each ethnic component performs a well-defined role in the economy. The whites everywhere occupy the top positions, but also are the skilled workers. The Coloreds and the Indians, where present, form the lower middle class, active in semiskilled jobs and services. The Bantu as a whole are at the bottom as unskilled laborers on farms, in mines, and in factories. This stratification

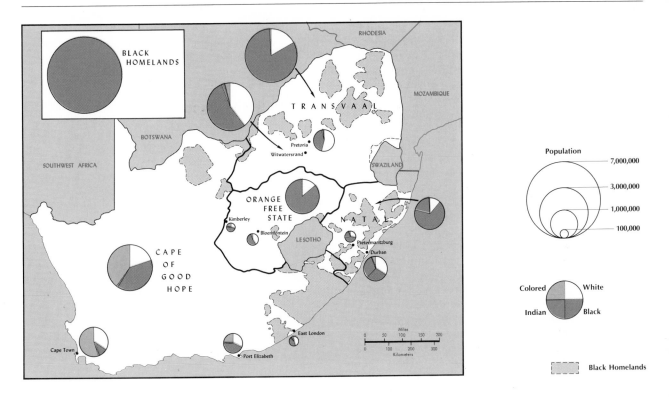

FIGURE  **SOUTH AFRICA: ETHNIC GROUPS**
4-7

This map shows the ethnic groups present in each of the large cities of South Africa and for the rest of the population of each province. The population of the "black homelands" is almost entirely Bantu.

of ethnic groups within the economic order is accompanied by strict segregation in the social-cultural sphere. The whole structure is governed by decisions of the whites, though other ethnic groups press for political power.

Since the 1940s the white minority—with the Afrikaners in the vanguard—has become more and more concerned about maintaining its identity and power amidst the rising consciousness of the other groups in the Republic and against the independent Meso-African states to the north. From various possible means to protect their way of life, they have chosen the hard-line policy of "separate development" (apartheid)—social, economic, and political—for whites and nonwhites. To bring this about, the government has estab-

lished within its territory eight "Bantustans" (Bantu homelands) to which all blacks must move. Each Bantustan has a measure of autonomy and has been promised independence before 1980.

This radical policy of territorial partition and racial segregation suffers, however, from so many contradictions and injustices that it is impossible to realize it on an equitable basis. At present about half of the 18 million blacks live in white areas, the other half on tribal reserves, the new homelands, which cover some 186,000 square kilometers (71,000 square miles)—about 15 percent—of South Africa. If the Bantustans were to absorb the full complement of their official citizens, their average population density would be no less than 80 per square kilometer (200 per square mile) (ignoring the rapid growth of the Bantu peoples), and this in rural areas largely of low agricultural potential. In contrast, the 85 percent of the country occupied by nonblacks would have only 7 persons per square kilometer.

Obviously the blacks would not be able to support themselves in these homelands. Nominal independence would not bring freedom. Reliance on temporary jobs in the white state, combined with the need to accept financial assistance from the South African government, would create dependent ghetto-states, in spite of all promises of independent Bantustans.

Meanwhile, South Africa needs labor to maintain its high level of economic activity. Many blacks come to the cities to find work, and then remain. Their urbanized way of life is much lower than the standard of the whites, but higher than the circumstances they left behind. Huge black residential zones, populated by unskilled workers living in servile conditions, are like so many powder kegs around the white-dominated core of Johannesburg.

The Cape Coloreds, unlike the Bantu people, have no tribal territories to which they can return. The policy of apartheid moved them from where they lived among the whites and placed them in segregated settlements, sometimes far from their places of employment. Foreign countries, including the United States, pressure South Africa to solve the problems concerning the Coloreds and Bantus as well as those of Indians, Malays, and other groups.

While all this goes on, the job reservation walls are crumbling. As the severe labor shortages spread, South Africa continues with the development of its modern economy. Coloreds, and to some extent also Bantu, are now admitted to higher rungs of the job ladder formerly assigned to whites only. Here lies the fateful paradox: The government ruthlessly pursues its policy of segregation, while the economy moves toward more integration.

## CONCLUSION

Research in the biological nature of mankind belongs to the fields of genetics, anatomy, and physical anthropology. The geographer uses the findings because they throw light on the relations between race and place.

There is no biological justification for race prejudice. Nevertheless, race prejudice exists among many peoples, in some to such a degree that tension and fear are critical features of their society. To understand these situations, one must switch from the biological to the sociocultural approach. The geographer can contribute to this line of investigation by focusing on place: Why does confrontation of "races" lead to discord in one area and not in others? And how do these conditions affect the character of countries?

Far too little is known as yet to give satisfactory answers to these questions. However, it is clear that racial intolerance is not inborn, but acquired. If bias is learned, it also can be unlearned. Nevertheless, such changes can hardly be expected to occur overnight. It has been said that to split the atom has proved easier than to eradicate race prejudice. Unless and until rational thought and desire for justice catch up with the findings of the biological sciences, racial discrimination will remain as proof of man's inhumanity to man.

## CITATIONS AND FURTHER READINGS

Blum, H. F. "Is Sunlight a Factor in the Geographical Distribution of Human Skin Color?" *Geographical Review*, 61 (1971): 557–581.

Blumenbach, J. F. *The Anthropological Treatises of Johann Friedrich Blumenbach* (translator and ed. T. Bendyshe), London, 1865.

Boyd, W. C. *Genetics and the Races of Man*, Boston, 1950.

——— and Asimov, I. *Races and Peoples*, New York, 1955.

Collins, D. *The Human Revolution: From Ape to Artist*, Oxford, 1976.

Coon, C. S., Garn, S. M., and Birdsell, J. B. *Races: A Study in the Problems of Race Formation in Man*, New York, 1950.

Davis, C. A., and Donaldson, O. F. *Blacks in the United States: A Geographic Perspective,* Boston, 1975.

De Laubenfels, D. J. "Australoids, Negroids, and Negroes: a Suggested Explanation for Their Disjunct Distributions," *Annals of the Association of American Geographers,* 58 (1968): 42–50.

Dobzhansky, T. *Evolution, Genetics, and Man,* New York, 1955.

Dunn, L. C., and Dobzhansky, T. *Heredity, Race, and Society,* New York, 1952.

Fabre, M., and Oren, P. *Harlem, Ville Noire,* Paris, 1971.

Fellows, D. K. *A Mosaic of America's Ethnic Minorities,* New York, 1972.

Haley, A. *Roots: Saga of an American Family,* New York, 1976.

Hart, J. F. "The Changing Distribution of the American Negro," *Annals of the Association of American Geographers,* 50 (1960): 242–266.

Hoebel, E. A. *Anthropology: The Study of Man,* 4th ed., New York, 1972.

Hooton, E. A. *Up from the Ape,* New York, 1958.

"The Human Species," *Scientific American,* 203 (1960).

Jordan, W. D. *White over Black: American Attitudes toward the Negro, 1550–1812,* Chapel Hill, N.C., 1968.

Livingstone, F. B. "Anthropological Implications of Sickle Cell Gene Distribution in West Africa," in Montagu (1970): 271–299.

Lowry, M. "Race and Socioeconomic Well-being: A Geographical Analysis of the Mississippi Case," *Geographical Review,* 60 (1970): 511–528.

———— "Population and Race in Mississippi, 1940–1960," *Annals of the Association of American Geographers,* 61 (1971): 576–588.

McEntire, D. *Race and Residence,* Berkeley, Calif., 1960.

Montagu, M. F. A. *Man's Most Dangerous Myth: The Fallacy of Race,* New York, 1942 (4th ed. Cleveland, 1964).

———— *An Introduction to Physical Anthropology,* Springfield, Ill., 1951.

———— (ed.). *Culture and the Evolution of Man,* New York, 1970.

Rose, H. M. *Social Processes in the City: Race and Urban Residential Choice,* Association of American Geographers Commission on College Geography, Resource Paper no. 6, Washington, D.C., 1969.

———— *The Black Ghetto: A Spatial Behavioral Perspective,* New York, 1971.

———— (ed.). "Contributions to an Understanding of Black America," *Economic Geography,* 48 (1972), no. 1. A symposium.

Sabbagh, M. E. "Some Geographical Characteristics of a Plural Society: Apartheid in South Africa," *Geographical Review,* 58 (1969): 1–28.

Simpson, G. E., and Yinger, J. M. *Racial and Cultural Minorities,* New York, 1953.

Taeuber, K., and Taeuber, A. *Negroes in Cities,* Chicago, 1965.

Tax, S. (ed.). *The Evolution of Man,* Chicago, 1960.

———— (ed.). *Horizons of Anthropology,* Chicago, 1964.

UNESCO. *The Race Question in Modern Science,* Paris, 1952.

Wiesenfeld, S. L. "The Sickle Cell Trait in Human Biological and Cultural Evolution," *Science,* 157 (1967): 1134–1140.

# 5 THE MOSAIC OF LANGUAGES

## INTRODUCTION

Language is a part of culture, a part of society's equipment for living. In this respect it is like social organization, government, and law. But language is more than just another segment of culture, because it also serves as the vehicle of communication among all components of society and as the main means of culture transmission from one generation to another. Furthermore, writing and reading also involve language, for systems of writing are symbolized language.

The thousands of different languages spoken by human beings suggest a mosaic on a world map. Their character, relationship, and significance are of great value to geographical study. To help us understand something of their complexities, here are a few definitions.

*Speech* is a system of meaningful sounds produced by the human voice tract. Each individual has his or her own speech, an *ideolect* unlike that of anyone else, acquired mostly during childhood as *mother tongue* but modified continuously throughout life. A *dialect* is the speech of a community, that is, an interactive group who understand one another and who share similar ideolects in pronunciation, vocabulary, and grammar. A *language* is speech whose core is intelligible to all its users, including subgroups that have quite different dialects. The concept of a community is less important for the idea of language than for the idea of dialect. Indeed, peoples of various societies may use the same language, not because of any close contacts at present but because of some connection in the distant past.

In cases where it is difficult to decide whether or not a particular speech is a dialect or separate language, national or sectional feelings may brush aside academic distinctions and de-mand recognition as a language. Extreme dialects may be almost mutually unintelligible to other speakers of the language. They may be related to the speech in an adjacent country, or a vestige of speech no longer in common use. Also one may ask: At what point can a regional variation in accent and vocabulary justify the label of dialect?

A *living language* is any mother tongue spoken today; a *dead language* is not used so but was, at some time in the past. Some dead languages such as Latin or Sanskrit are learned for religious or scholarly reasons. The term *vernacular* usually denotes the tongue used by ordinary folk of a region when another language, imposed from outside, has become the medium of government and education.

A *linguistic family* (or *linguistic stock*) is a group of languages which show evidence of having diverged through time from one original tongue. Languages of one family resemble each other in systematic ways, usually through similar sounds or clusters of sounds, frequently with the same meaning and also sometimes through likeness in grammatical and vocabulary structure.

A *standard language* (sometimes called "official language") is a version that is recognized for education, government, and other public affairs. In a *script,* written symbols are used to express a language on paper or other substance. Often a standard written form of language emerges. With the development of *literacy* (the ability to read and write), the written standard spreads widely and may lead to submersion of local or provincial variations.

Almost all *communication* comes through language or symbolized language, such as writing, smoke signals, drumbeats, and codes. The use of standard spoken and written versions of a language facilitates communication within a country.

# THE PRINCIPAL LINGUISTIC FAMILIES AND LANGUAGES OF THE WORLD

| TABLE 5-1 | Linguistic family and language | Speakers, millions | Regions where standard language | Other regions | Remarks |
|---|---|---|---|---|---|
| | Indo-European | | | | |
| | English | 340 | U.K., U.S., South Africa, also Canada, Jamaica, and other (British) Commonwealth countries | Republic of Ireland, other old colonial territories | Worldwide lingua franca of commerce, science, and diplomacy |
| | Hindi | 280 | India and Pakistan, the Urdu dialect in the latter | | Lingua franca of north India; Urdu dialect used by Moslems in much of south Asia |
| | Spanish | 320 | Spain, all Latin American republics except Brazil, Haiti | Parts of northwest Africa | |
| | Russian | 150 | Russian Soviet Federated Socialist Republic | Other parts of U.S.S.R. | Official language of U.S.S.R. |
| | Portuguese | 125 | Portugal, Brazil | Parts of Africa, etc. | A dialect in northwest Spain is Galician |
| | Bengali | 130 | Bangladesh, West Bengal (India) | Assam and other parts of northeast India | About 80 million speakers in Bangladesh, 50 million in West Bengal |
| | German | 93 | Germany, Austria, Luxembourg, Switzerland | Alsace and Lorraine | Area of German speech much contracted since 1944 |
| | French | 80 | France, Belgium, Haiti, Canada, Switzerland | Parts of the French Union | Widely used as a lingua franca |
| | Italian | 62 | Italy, Switzerland | Corsica | |
| | Ukrainian | 47 | Ukrainian S.S.R. | Other U.S.S.R., Canada | Closely related to Russian |
| | Marathi | 45 | Maharashtra (India) | Nearby India | |
| | Punjabi | 50 | Punjab (Pakistan and India) | Adjacent regions of South Asia | |
| | Polish | 36 | Poland | Nearby U.S.S.R. | Area much changed since 1944 |
| | Gujarati | 22 | Gujarat (India) | | |
| | Persian | 35 | Iran | To northeast, esp. Afghanistan and Tajik S.S.R. | Lingua franca in Central Asia |
| | Sino-Tibetan | | | | |
| | Chinese | 700 | China, Taiwan | | Standard dialect is Mandarin. |
| | Cantonese | 60 | | South China, Southeast Asia | The southern Chinese speak many languages; these four are the most important. Others are Shant'ou and Tai-Shan. Most "overseas" Chinese speak Cantonese, Wu, or Min |
| | Wu | 50 | | Chechiang, Chiangsu | |
| | Min | 45 | | Fuchien, Taiwan | |
| | Hakka | 25 | | South China | |
| | Vietnamese | 40 | North and South Vietnam | Southeast Cambodia | |
| | Thai | 40 | Thailand | Nearby Southeast Asia | Has many related dialects |

**Table 5-1  continued**

| Linguistic family and language | Speakers, millions | Regions where standard language | Other regions | Remarks |
|---|---|---|---|---|
| Dravidian | | | | |
| Telegu | 55 | Andhra Pradesh (India) | Nearby South India | |
| Tamil | 45 | Tamil Nadu (Madras) (India) | Nearby South India, Ceylon | Spoken by most Indians in Burma and Malaya |
| Kannada | 30 | Mysore (India) | Nearby South India | Also called Canarese |
| Malayalam | 25 | Kerala (India) | | |
| Japanese-Korean | | | | |
| Japanese | 110 | Japan | Pacific Islands, Korea | |
| Korean | 54 | North and South Korea | | |
| Semitic-Hamitic | | | | |
| Arabic | 145 | Morocco, Algeria, Tunisia, Mauritania, Libya, Egypt, Sudan, Iraq, Saudi Arabia, Kuwait, South Yemen, Yemen, Oman, Syria, Trucial States | Western Sudan, east coast of Africa, Lebanon | The lingua franca of Islam in the west |
| Austroasiatic | | | | |
| Indonesian | 100(?) | Indonesia | | A new standard language, based on a Sumatran tongue |
| Javanese | 60 | | Java | The main vernacular on the island of Java |
| Ural-Altaic | | | | |
| Turkish | 36 | Turkey | | Formerly more widespread |
| Niger-Congo- | | | | |
| Bantu | | | West, central, and southeast Africa | A large grouping with scores of languages and dialects |
| Swahili | | Tanzania, Kenya | Other parts of East Africa | |

SOURCES: United Nations *Demographic Yearbook* and *Statistical Yearbook,* various years; official yearbooks of different countries.

Communication is also possible among peoples with different versions of the same language or its dialects or with similar closely related languages, though classified as distinct. Persons who are *bilingual* or *multilingual* speak, write, or read two or more languages. Without them there could be little communication among peoples with different languages. Ability to use a language other than one's mother tongue varies from a "smattering" to a fairly complete knowledge of the standard version.

To sum up, we can use the following example: English is a language spoken by some 320 million people in many parts of the world. Its standard versions differ in the United Kingdom, the United States, Canada, and Australia. Its dialects include Cockney, Brooklynese, American Southern speech, and Scottish. English, and such languages as German, Swedish, Dutch, and Danish, belong to the Germanic group, a subfamily of the Indo-European linguistic family.

# WORLD DISTRIBUTION OF LANGUAGES

The most useful way of making a world survey is to identify families of languages; that is, to make a *genetic* classification, showing relationships by origin and development. Of course one can classify languages in many other ways, for instance, by using the frequency of certain kinds of sounds. This aspect might interest the linguist, but it would be of little value from the historical and cultural point of view.

In countries with a long literary tradition, such as parts of Asia and Europe, the genetic associations of related languages are easier to observe than where the literary record goes back only a few decades. For example, Anglo-Saxon, Old High German, and Old Norse preceded the modern tongues of English, German, and Danish. From writings in these ancient languages we know that they had similar grammatical forms, sounds, and vocabularies. We can study the development of each into its modern equivalent in the voluminous literature written over the last thousand years.

Figure 5–1 (pp. 100–101) shows the location of the principal linguistic families and subfamilies. Table 5–1 (pp. 96–97) summarizes the distribution and importance of all individual languages spoken by more than 20 million persons. The world map of linguistic families and subfamilies has some shortcomings. Many different families and subfamilies of languages spoken by relatively small groups have been combined, for example, those of the American Indians and those in New Guinea. Moreover, the structure and relationships of numerous tongues in Africa and eastern Asia are far less known than those of the Indo-European languages. Further research by linguists is now clarifying the familial relationships of these languages. Thus, the map reflects the inadequacy of our present state of knowledge. In spite of these limitations, world distribution maps and detailed tables like Figure 5–1 and Table 5–1 contain enormous amounts of information which in textual form would cover scores or even hundreds of pages.

## THE INDO-EUROPEAN LINGUISTIC FAMILY

The study of linguistic affiliations can shed light on migrations and contacts among different human groups in prehistoric as well as historic times. The following discussion will help to illustrate the way linguistic materials can supplement other information in re-creating past human geography.

The Indo-European linguistic stock includes the principal languages of Europe and of areas colonized by Europeans, together with many tongues of southern and southwestern Asia (for Europe see Table 5–2 and Figure 5–2). Member languages are spoken by about one-third of mankind. This family can be divided into two broad branches. The western one comprises the Greek, Romance (also called Italic), Celtic, Germanic (or Teutonic), Tokharian, and Anatolian languages; these last two, now extinct, were used in western Asia and Asia Minor, respectively. To the eastern branch belong the many Indo-Aryan languages, Iranian, Armenian, Illyrian (including Albanian), and the Balto-Slavic tongues.

In the nineteenth century, comparative and historical study of these languages and their predecessors established that all were descended from a cluster of related dialects spoken in prehistoric times. The speakers of these dialects left no documents to read or inscriptions to decipher; however, their language has been partly retrieved by linguistic methods. The reconstructed language, called Proto-Indo-European, should not be confused with the family after which it is named. From the study of words in Proto-Indo-European it is possible to infer the way of life of the peoples who spoke it and the approximate location of their homeland.

Since these ancient folk had words for oxen, sheep, pigs, the plow, and cereals used for bread making, we may assume they were farmers and had connections with the Middle East, where this kind of agriculture originated. However, they had no words for tropical or Mediterranean animals such as the elephant, donkey, or camel, or for cultivated plants such as the vine and fig. They knew how to refine metal ores and make alloys, and how to fashion axes and other implements. They hunted the goose and duck but did not know the lion and tiger. The conclusion that they resided in a temperate, not a tropical, climate is reinforced by the fact that they had words for winter and snow. From their knowledge of the beech, birch, pine, apple, and oak we can narrow down the location of their habitat to the western

Literacy—the ability to read and write—helps individuals to a fuller life as human beings within their society. Here two schoolgirls use a narrow pavement to do their homework on their way home from school in Kisangan, Zaire. (Photograph—United Nations)

part of the Eurasian landmass. Almost all scholars agree that they lived in Europe north of the Alps–Black Sea line. From this area of general agreement opinions diverge: some advocate a Scandinavian homeland, others the extensive plains of north Germany and the Baltic lands, still others the Danubian basin. It seems best to think of the original distribution as covering a broad continuous area in east-central Europe. From here the speakers of the Proto-Indo-European language, or rather its various dialects, dispersed in several directions, broke up into divergent groups, and intermingled with others, leading in the course of thousands of years to the present linguistic mosaic.

Knowledge of the Indo-Europeans is not

FIGURE **WORLD: PRINCIPAL LINGUISTIC FAMILIES AND**
**5-1** **SUBFAMILIES**

Based in part on the maps in Meillet, A., and
Cohen, M., *Les Langues du monde,* Paris, 1952.

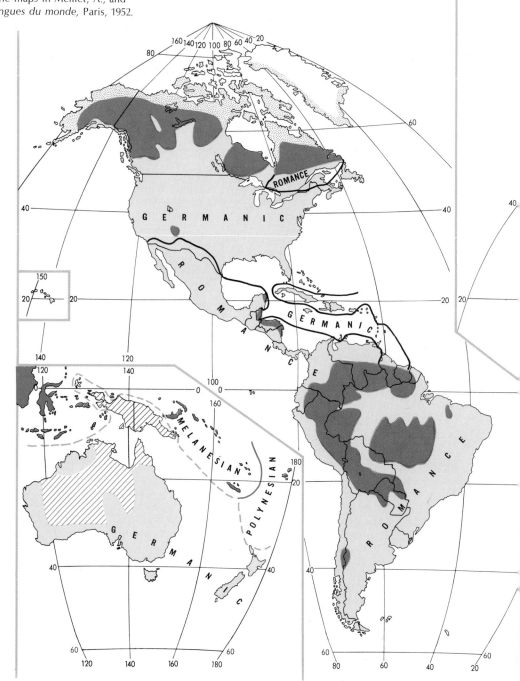

Indo-European
Ural-Altaic
Sino-Tibetan
Japanese-Korean
Austroasiatic
Australian
Papuan
Caucasian
Hamitic-Semitic
Macro-Sudanic
Hottentot-Bushman
Niger-Congo-Bantu
American Indian
Eskimo
Dravidian

**Miles**

0    500    1000    1500

0   500  1000    2000

**Kilometers**

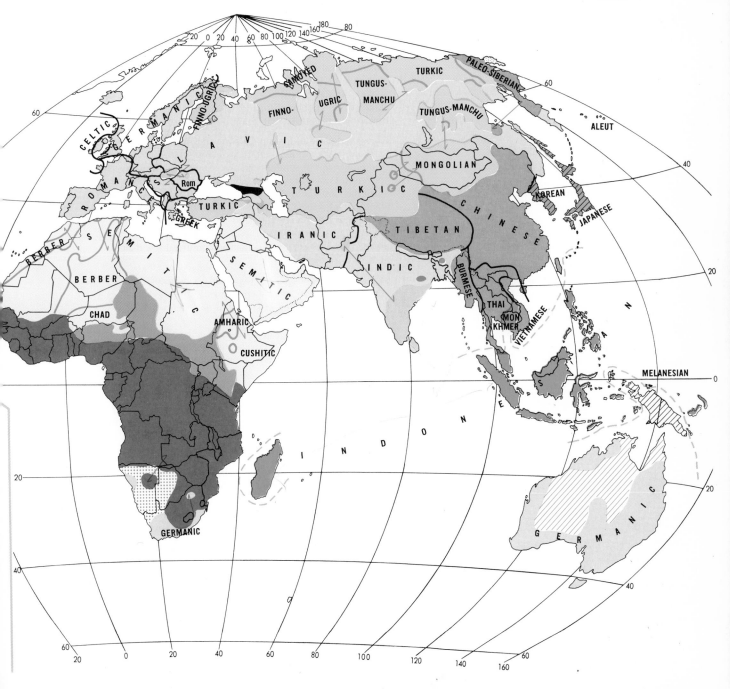

AITOFF'S

INTERRUPTED EQUAL-AREA

PROJECTION

# THE LANGUAGES OF EUROPE (EXCEPT U.S.S.R.)

TABLE
5-2

| Linguistic family Subfamily and language* | | Speakers, millions | Remarks |
|---|---|---|---|
| Indo-European | | | |
| Celtic | *Cornish* | None | Spoken in Cornwall until 1800s |
| | Welsh | 0.6 | Recent revival in Wales as a means of national artistic expression |
| | Breton | 0.7 | Spoken in Brittany, but giving way to French |
| | *Manx* | None | Spoken on Man until 1900s |
| | Irish Gaelic | 0.03 | Standard in Republic of Ireland, where it is learned in school |
| | Scottish Gaelic | 0.08 | In northwest Scotland, but dying out |
| Italic (Romance) | *Latin* | None | Official language of Roman Catholic Church |
| | French | 66 | Standard in France, Belgium, Switzerland; many historic dialects |
| | *Provençal* | None | Written version of southern French dialects; died out long ago |
| | Catalan | 6 | Spoken in Catalonia, Valencia, the Balearics, and Roussillon (France) |
| | Spanish | 27 | Spain has Castilian dialect as the standard. Many other dialects |
| | Portuguese | 10 | Standard in Portugal; Galician is a dialect in northwest Spain |
| | Italian | 62 | Standard in Italy and Switzerland; many dialects; spoken in Corsica |
| | Rhaeto-Romansh | 0.6 | Standard in Grisons (Switzerland); also spoken in Italy |
| | Romanian | 18.0 | Standard in Romania. Zinzar (Balkan countries) is a dialect. |
| | Sardinian | 1 | Spoken in Sardinia |
| Balto-Slavic | Czech and Slovak | 15 | Standard in Czechoslovakia; two similar languages |
| | Polish | 36 | Standard in Poland; area much changed since 1944 |
| | Wendish | 0.01 | Close to Czech; spoken in Lusatia in east Germany |
| | Slovenian | 1.6 | Standard in Slovenia (Yugoslavia) |
| | Serbo-Croat | 14 | Standard in Serbia and Montenegro (Cyrillic alphabet), Croatia (Roman alphabet), and Bosnia-Hercegovina (both alphabets) |
| | Macedonian | 1 | This dialect of Bulgarian is standard in Macedonia (Yugoslavia). |
| | Bulgarian | 6 | Standard in Bulgaria |
| Germanic | Icelandic | 0.2 | Standard in Iceland |
| | Danish | 5 | Standard in Denmark. A dialect is used in the Faeroe Islands |
| | Norwegian | 3.9 | Standard in Norway. Riksmål (southeast); Landsmal (southwest) |
| | Swedish | 8.5 | Standard in Sweden; also spoken in southwest Finland |
| | German | 93 | High German is standard (Germany, Austria, Luxembourg, Switzerland); Yiddish is one of many dialects |
| | Plattdeutsch | (?) | The vernacular of the north German plain |
| | Dutch and Flemish | 18 | Standard in Netherlands and Belgium. Two similar languages |
| | Frisian | 0.4 | Vernacular in Friesland, Netherlands. The closest relative of English |
| | English | 57 | Standard in U.K.; also spoken in Ireland |
| Illyrian | Albanian | 3.2 | Standard in Albania; also spoken in Kosmet district (Yugoslavia) |
| Hellenic | Greek (modern) | 9.5 | Standard in Greece; different from *Homeric* and *Classical Greek* |
| Indic | Romany | 1 (?) | The gypsy language of the Balkans, Czechoslovakia, England, etc. |
| Ural-Altaic | | | |
| Pre-Indo-European | | | |
| | Basque | 0.6 | No known relatives; spoken in northern Spain and southwest France |
| Finno-Ugric | Lappish | 0.01 | Spoken in northern Scandinavia |
| | Finnish | 4.5 | The standard in Finland is Suomi |
| | Magyar | 14 | Standard in Hungary; also spoken in central Romania and in Slovakia |
| Turkic | Turkish | 36 | Standard in Turkey; also spoken in parts of the Balkans |

*Dead languages are in italics.

FIGURE **EUROPE: LANGUAGES**
5-2

The principal linguistic families are shown in color;
linguistic subfamilies and individual languages are
shown by name on the map. For the full distribution
of the Uralic languages see Figure 5–4.

–––– · · Boundaries between Linguistic Subfamilies

–– –– –– Boundaries between Languages

Indo-European

Ural-Altaic

Hamito-Semitic

Basque

deduced solely from the study of languages. Archaeological finds and historical records of the societies which they penetrated or contacted provide us with clues about their migrations and the effects they had on other peoples. It is clear that from about 2000 B.C. the Indo-European speakers began to spread out in all directions. The Aryans supplanted the urban civilization of the Indus Valley. During the first half of the second millennium B.C., Babylonia was under alien, possibly Aryan, rule. In the same period the Hittites were pressing from the northwest. Toward the end of the second millennium the Mycenaeans built a trading empire on the traditions of Minoan Crete. The Persians under Cyrus and Darius stretched their domain from the Aegean Sea to northern India and as far south as the Sahara Desert. In turn, the Phrygians destroyed the Hittites; Dorians and other Greeks superseded the Mycenaean civilization centered on the Aegean and Crete. Peoples speaking Italic tongues subjugated the prehistoric inhabitants of the Italian peninsula. The Celts burst into Europe south of the Danube and west as far as Britain and Gaul. The Germanic peoples pressed behind the Celts and eventually overthrew them and their Roman overlords; they also pushed eastward toward the Vistula River. The Slavic and Baltic folk, at first penned within the backwoods of east central Europe, later supplanted Celts, Germans, and Scythians in more open lands.

What forces caused these migrations is a matter of conjecture. Some scholars think that an unfavorable change in climate brought about the movements. Another view is that technological development, including the use of the horse and the making of superior weapons, led to population pressure and the urge to conquer new lands, especially the richer ones to the south.

## LANGUAGE AND RACE

Migrations such as these affect the spatial association of language groups and human races. At the broad world scale, the distribution of languages corresponds to that of races. Most Negroids speak Niger-Congo-Bantu languages, most Mongoloids Sinitic languages, most Caucasoids Indo-European languages. The correspondence is not surprising,

for all children both inherit physical features and learn their language from their parents.

In the course of time as peoples migrated and mingled, the once coincident boundaries of race and language became blurred. Many Negroid peoples now speak Semitic and Hamitic tongues, formerly the sole possession of Caucasoids. Some groups transported into other cultural areas have taken over the local speech; examples are the blacks who speak English in the United States, a version of French in Haiti, and Portuguese in Brazil. The official language of Liberia is English, which the returned slaves brought along to the state they founded in the early nineteenth century. Peoples speaking the individual tongues of the Uralic and Altaic family include Mongoloids in Asia and Caucasoids such as the Magyars in Central Europe (Figure 5-3). Evidently, race and speech are innate, but the ability to speak a specific language is acquired.

## LANGUAGE AND CULTURE

Each language differs from others not only in vocabulary and structure but also in the effect it has on those who use it. Exact translation from one language to another is virtually impossible because each has its own way of dealing with ideas, facts, and concepts. It is commonplace to say that the culture of a people expresses itself in its language; equally true, the habits of speech affect thought and action. Because logic and perception are functions of language structure, a people's language conditions their view of reality.

European languages, for instance, contain a built-in strong sense of defining actions according to their occurrence in time. In contrast, several east Asian languages appear less adapted to talking about the passage of time. Or, as another example, while Europeans have many terms to express opposites and extremes, such as good—bad, strong—weak, rich—poor, the Chinese have few such pairs. Instead, their speech offers many words that allow for subtle shadings of intent. It is possible, therefore, that the way a given people grasps reality in some measure reflects linguistically structured concepts of time, space, validity, and objectivity.

Many peoples in different parts of the

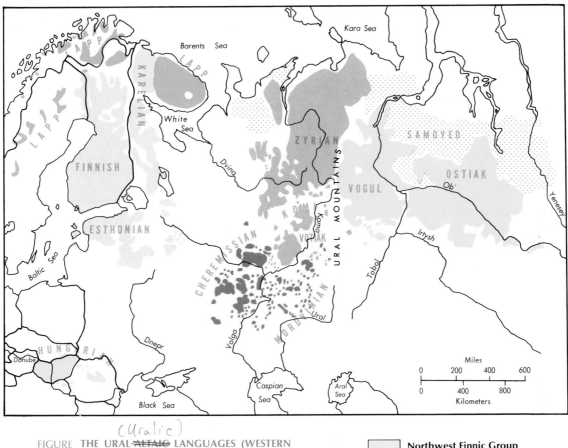

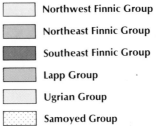

FIGURE
5-3

*(Uralic)*

THE URAL-~~ALTAIC~~ LANGUAGES (WESTERN EURASIAN GROUPS)

| | |
|---|---|
| ▢ | **Northwest Finnic Group** |
| ▢ | **Northeast Finnic Group** |
| ▢ | **Southeast Finnic Group** |
| ▢ | **Lapp Group** |
| ▢ | **Ugrian Group** |
| ▢ | **Samoyed Group** |

These linguistic groups are now dispersed over western Asia and eastern Europe. Present speakers have highly varied cultures from Finns and Magyars in central Europe to the reindeer-herding Lapps and Samoyeds. See also Figure 5–2. Based in part on a map in Meillet, A., and Cohen, M., *Les Langues du Monde,* Paris, 1952.

world, who possess little of the material culture so cherished by modern Western man, express themselves with eloquence in ordinary conversation about life in the immediate present and neighborhood, a richness unmatched by the increasingly basic and colorless idiom of modern societies. For this reason it is unwise—and even unjust—to call some languages "primitive" in comparison to one's own. The truth may be the other way around.

As language is the principal means of communicating culture, it can be useful to identify culture groups. Linguistic families are too broad to be employed for this purpose; for example, the Indo-European family does not form one cultural unit, as it comprises Indians, Pakistanis, Persians, Greeks, and Norwegians. Even linguistic subfamilies are not reliable guides to cultural entities. It is true that the entire Romance subfamily of the Indo-European stock has a common culture.

However, Romanians are culturally more Slavic than Mediterranean, and the cultural likeness of the Italians, French, and Spanish arose not because they spoke related tongues but because their culture traits stemmed from Roman (Latin) heritage of classical times or because they were subject to similar influences of the Mediterranean environment. In examining the relationships between language and culture, it is best, therefore, to consider each language separately. After all, mutual intelligibility is what counts in language as a means of communication. As Philip L. Wagner says:

**Linguistic heterogeneity is one of the most obvious, most absolute, and most fixed of the categories of diversity that apply to human populations. The sharp discontinuities and relatively uniform blocs that characterize modern linguistic communities strongly influence human behavior, and particularly the association of people and their interaction. Political, social, and economic structures are often closely related with linguistic usage, and distributional patterns of these phenomena tend to coincide strikingly with linguistic areal patterns. (Wagner, 1958, 86)**

It should be noted, however, that the identification of language with culture is far from complete: some Frenchmen speak German and most Irishmen speak English. Furthermore, the generalization often fails to apply to colonial areas where language transference has occurred. The peoples of France and Haiti both speak French, but the ties between them are less than the cultural ones between France and western Europe and between Haiti and other Caribbean islands.

Usually differences in dialects are guideposts to determine subdivisions within cultures. In the United States most Southerners are easily recognized by their distinctive manner of speech. In Britain, the Scots use a dialect of English, unless they have consciously learned standard English; like the Southerners, the Scots are recognized as a cultural subgroup.

*Linguistic geography,* a specialized study carried on in many countries, describes the character and extent of languages and dialects. From data gathered in numerous personal interviews, the occurrence of individual words can be ascertained; by combining these findings, one can map dialect regions and ultimately language regions.

Linguistic geographers (linguists by training rather than geographers) for many decades have engaged in unraveling the complexities of local and regional dialects in the United States. Their work shows that thousands of words and phrases have regional usage; these when plotted on maps reveal dialect regions. Nineteenth-century Americans thought there were two basic dialects, Northern and Southern, an assumption reflecting contemporary sectional views. The linguistic geographers made it clear that between the Northern and Southern dialects lay an area of Midland speech that occupied a small stretch of the Middle Atlantic Seaboard but widened westward to include much of Mid-America (Figure 5–4).

The origins of these dialects (and their subforms) go back to the colonial past. By 1790 Anglo-American settlement was continuous from Maine to Georgia. The culture varied, however, with the ways of life that each settlement region (New England, Pennsylvania, Virginia, and so on) had developed when comparatively isolated. Each had its own dialect, some form of mother-country English blended with other elements, perhaps Indian, Dutch, or German. When the settlements coalesced, the dialects and the boundaries between them remained. Only in the twentieth century have they lost ground to a still developing standard American version of English, promoted by universal methods of education and by nationwide radio and television.

The boundary between Northern and Midland speech runs westward through northern Pennsylvania and south of Lake Erie, while that between Midland and Southern goes southwestward through Virginia and the Carolinas and then west. Within the three main regions are dialect subareas like southeastern New England, metropolitan New York, the upper Ohio valley, and eastern North Carolina.

A decade ago one might well have predicted that dialects in the United States would soon be a thing of the past. Now this is less certain. Movements toward diversity have always been potent forces in the lives of human societies; there is little reason to believe that all we can look forward to is a homogenized blend. Linguis-

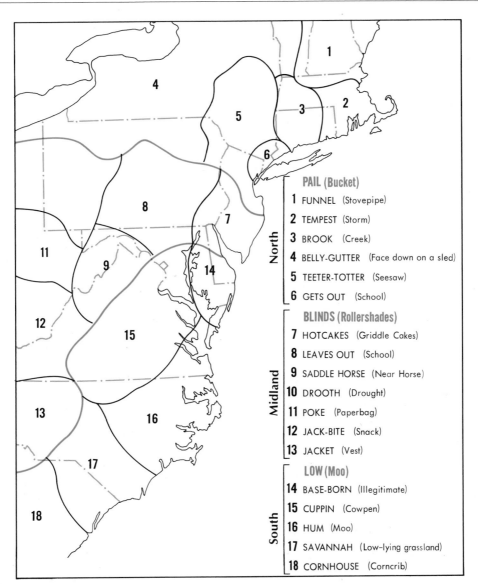

PAIL (Bucket)
1 FUNNEL (Stovepipe)
2 TEMPEST (Storm)
3 BROOK (Creek)
4 BELLY-GUTTER (Face down on a sled)
5 TEETER-TOTTER (Seesaw)
6 GETS OUT (School)

BLINDS (Rollershades)
7 HOTCAKES (Griddle Cakes)
8 LEAVES OUT (School)
9 SADDLE HORSE (Near Horse)
10 DROOTH (Drought)
11 POKE (Paperbag)
12 JACK-BITE (Snack)
13 JACKET (Vest)

LOW (Moo)
14 BASE-BORN (Illegitimate)
15 CUPPIN (Cowpen)
16 HUM (Moo)
17 SAVANNAH (Low-lying grassland)
18 CORNHOUSE (Corncrib)

North

Midland

South

FIGURE **DIALECTS OF THE EASTERN UNITED STATES**
5-4
The three major dialect regions can be divided into a number of subareas. Words shown are examples of the many used to define these subareas. After maps and data in Kurath, H., *A Word Geography of the Eastern United States*, Ann Arbor, 1949.

tic similarity does not necessarily imply friendly relations and vice versa. Widespread disenchantment with the sameness of an institutionalized national American culture leads many citizens to turn away from the traditional "melting-pot" model and to identify instead with smaller groups that give more meaning to everyday individual life. Possibly even new dialect areas may develop in the central cities occupied by blacks and other ethnic minorities with distinctive life patterns. Ease of transportation and communication also stimulates a movement toward specialized speech, such as that among the youth or professions or others, irrespective of location. If America is (or is to be) a pluralistic society in which some groups live in a degree of cultural isolation, then the internal variety that has marked American speech in the past very likely will continue into the future. Many other countries, too, experience a revival of interest in subcultures that are in danger of being erased by trends toward national uniformity.

Language finds another spatial expression in the "names on the land" (Stewart, 1958). Place-names (*toponyms*) and the study of place-names (*toponymy*) reveal the land as perceived or idealized by its inhabitants and can be an important key to understanding the historical geography of a region.

Succeeding generations usually retain old place-names but add others for new towns, villages, farms, and whatever features not previously named. Thus the toponyms of a particular district, if studied in sufficient detail, indicate the contributions from successive groups of settlers. An alternative in toponymy is to examine the origin and spread of a specific kind of place-name. Zelinsky (1967) illustrates this in his study of the diffusion of classical town names in the United States from their first appearance in upper New York State during the late eighteenth century.

## LANGUAGE AND SOCIETY

Individuals learn, usually from their parents, the ability to speak a specific language as part of their cultural equipment. Since languages can also be learned later in life, persons can change their language. Most descendants of immigrant families to the United States lose their mother tongue after two generations. But for a whole society the process of changeover is slow, often taking centuries to complete. And while many people have in the course of time accepted a foreign language, others cling to their native tongue in spite of severe pressures.

If two peoples intermingle, it appears that the language of the more developed culture eventually will be accepted by the other group. When the Romans pushed north of the Apennines into the plain of the Po River (Cisalpine Gaul) and northwestward into Gaul proper, their Latin, with local variants, replaced the Celtic dialects. Centuries later, Germanic-speaking tribes which swept into the western portions of the collapsing Roman Empire often took over the versions the romanized Celts were using. During the Middle Ages, universal submission to the Catholic Church, which used Latin for all secular and religious purposes, helped to spread the Romance languages.

Arabic has been accepted throughout much of North Africa, in southwest Asia as far as the Tigris-Euphrates Valley and in scattered pockets as far east as Afghanistan. In ancient times the peoples of this huge region spoke a variety of Semitic, Indo-European, and Hamitic languages; Arabic was then confined to the Arabian peninsula. Today Hamitic tongues remain only in small areas of northwest Africa and in southern sections of the Nile watershed. The change to Arabic came about during the Middle Ages, not only because it was the language of the conquerors and the ruling class, and thus of all governmental business, but also because it was the language of the Koran, the holy book of Islam. This trend toward acceptance was later reinforced when Arabic also became the vehicle of commerce over a wide region of the Old World.

A similar process is responsible for the present distribution of Indo-European and Dravidian languages in the Indian peninsula. In early times Dravidian languages were spoken over much of the subcontinent; they gave way, from the second millennium B.C. onward, to the languages of the Aryan invaders from the northwest (Figure 5–5).

In our times we see the gradual decline of minor languages in lands where one language dominates. Welsh, Irish Gaelic, and Scottish Gaelic have retreated before the advance of English, and Manx and Cornish have died out completely. Such developments are hastened today because government, business, school, radio, and television use the standard language of the majority.

For a group to accept a new language, there must be a willingness to change, prompted by religious, economic, or other social reasons. For

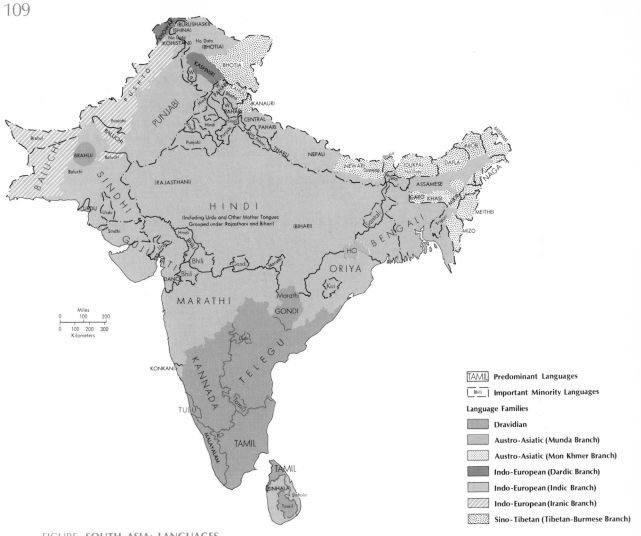

FIGURE **SOUTH ASIA: LANGUAGES**
5-5

This map is a generalization of the complex linguistic mosaic of the subcontinent. In many regions distinct languages, spoken by small groups or minorities, are not shown on the map. Proportions of total populations speaking the different languages within administrative districts are used to define language areas. From an original map designed by J. E. Schwartzberg, South Asia Historical Atlas Project, University of Minnesota.

example, in the sixteenth century the Welsh of the upper and middle classes realized that the recent political union of their country with England could profit them only if they learned to speak English; otherwise social positions would be closed to them because of language. Conversely, a ruling group often promotes its language by conducting all secular and religious business in its own language, to the exclusion of others.

In certain circumstances, groups have retained their language in the face of competition from a dominant and linguistically alien society.

What matters in such cases is the strength of the retentionist movement rather than the pressure exerted by the dominant culture.

Feelings of "loyalty to the group" seem to be the prime motive in resisting the imposition of another language. A community with strong attachment to its way of life will feel a threat to its language as a menace to its entire culture. Since most persons identify themselves with a group foremost through the common language, they feel any outside interference with it as a direct grievance. Thus, language becomes the central symbol around which opposition to foreign domination crystallizes.

Of the Celtic subfamily, Welsh and Irish Gaelic are likely to survive even though they have been declining for centuries. In the case of Welsh, there is an underswell of "cultural nationalism," which aims to preserve the language for cultural purposes, such as in literature, music, and drama. Modern Irish Gaelic, the official language of the Republic of Ireland, is taught in the schools and serves as the medium for conducting much government business. This is, in part, a protest against the use of English, the tongue of the conquerors who exploited Ireland and gave up political control only after a long period of agitation and bloodshed.

In North America the French-speaking inhabitants of Québec and nearby areas of Canada number 7 million, almost one-third of the total Canadian population. They have remained an anomaly in an otherwise English-speaking Canada and United States despite the fact that the French area has received no substantial influx of French immigrants since the eighteenth century. The Roman Catholic traditions and the French language are twin bonds that unite *les Franco-Canadiens*. Politics also worked in favor of retention. After the conquest of Québec in the eighteenth century the French region was administered as Lower Canada. Discussions about the union of British possessions in North America were long and bitter. By the time of confederation and self-government (1867), the inhabitants of Lower Canada had become fully conscious of their linguistic distinctiveness and knew it brought them unity and power. Preservation of their language became a political issue which was resolved by giving French official status in Canada (see also Chapter 7).

A further example of language retention comes from Poland. The old kingdom of Poland, long an outpost of Western Christianity, disappeared at the end of the eighteenth century when Prussia, Austria-Hungary, and Russia divided it among themselves. During the nineteenth century the Polish language was outlawed and officially replaced by German and Russian. But many Poles, resenting foreign rule, kept their mother tongue. They succeeded in reasserting Polish nationality after World War I and again following World War II, during which there had been another German-Russian partition.

Political problems, associated with linguistic divisions, exist in other countries. In Ceylon, the Sinhalese claim supremacy, while the Tamil minority demands equality. In Italian Tyrol a German-speaking minority presses for recognition of its language and for local political autonomy. In northern Spain the Basques and in northeastern Spain the Catalans assert their individuality by covert and occasionally overt action against the decrees of Castilian-speaking Madrid.

Both past and present support the notion that the languages of more developed culture groups remain stable in the face of competition, frequently from much larger groups. For example, the numerous Chinese who settled among the Malay-speaking peoples of Southeast Asia have usually retained their language and customs because of their higher social and economic status. Similarly, Arabs who penetrated south of the dry belt of North Africa kept their language though living among larger groups with other speech. Germans who up to the end of World War II lived in scattered communities all over central and eastern Europe stuck to their language for many centuries, partly because they considered themselves on a cultural level above that of the peoples among whom they lived, and partly because they felt affinity with the increasingly coherent German nation. Chapter 7 views these concepts through a study of ideologies and political order.

## BILINGUALISM

Usually we think of individuals as speaking one language, their mother tongue. Maps of language distributions, such as Figures 5-1 and 5-2,

## BILINGUALISM OR MULTILINGUALISM IN SELECTED COUNTRIES (DATA IN THOUSANDS)

| TABLE 5-3 | Ability to speak | Mother tongue |
|---|---|---|
| **Canada (1971)** | | |
| English only | 14,470 | 12,197 |
| English and French | 2,900 | |
| French only | 3,879 | 5,794 |
| Neither French nor English | 319 | |
| **Cyprus (1960)** | | |
| Greek only | 387 | 442 |
| Turkish only | 60 | 104 |
| Other language only | 19 | 27 |
| Greek and Turkish | 34 | |
| Greek and English | 45 | |
| Turkish and English | 4.5 | |
| Greek, Turkish, and English | 11 | |
| Others | 13 | |
| **Belgium** | (1930) | (1947) |
| French only | 3,039 | 2,911 |
| Flemish only | 3,493 | 3,554 |
| German only | 69 | 59 |
| French and Flemish | 1,046 | 1,326 |
| French and German | 67 | 83 |
| Flemish and German | 8 | 23 |
| French, Flemish, and German | 54 | 216 |
| **Swaziland (1956)** | | |
| Afrikaans | 1.7 | |
| English | 2.4 | |
| English and Afrikaans | 3.8 | |
| Swazi | 218.5 | |
| Swazi and English | 11.2 | |
| Others | 0.2 | |
| **Sri-Lanka (Ceylon) (1963)** | | |
| Sinhala | 5,414 | |
| Tamil | 1,763 | |
| Sinhala and Tamil | 838 | |
| English | 6.6 | |
| English and Sinhala | 494 | |
| English and Tamil | 102 | |
| English, Sinhala, and Tamil | 324 | |
| Unknown | 13 | |
| Others | 14 | |
| **Paraguay (1962)** | | |
| Guaraní | 737 | |
| Spanish | 72 | |
| Spanish and Guaraní | 791 | |
| Others | 35 | |

Sources of data: United Nations *Demographic Yearbook, 1970* and *1973,* New York, 1971 and 1974. For Belgian data: *Annuaire statistique de la Belgique, 1961,* Bruxelles, 1961.

strengthen the notion that people living in each area use only the language shown. Actually, many millions also are fluent in a language additional to the one learned at home because they need it to engage in commerce, a profession, or politics. Bilingualism is particularly necessary in countries where some other force than language has fused a nation, such as religion in India, insular habitat in Sri Lanka (Ceylon), or historical circumstance in Belgium.

Worldwide statistics on bilingualism are at present not available. Only in some countries where more than one language is important have such data been collected. Table 5-3 is taken from these sources. We briefly discuss here some examples of bilingualism.

**India** The Census of India collected information on "mother tongue" and "subsidiary language." Although the published data are suspect owing to political influences at census time, they suggest a substantial amount of bilingualism, despite the fact that only a few of the people can read and write. Bilingualism is most common in regions where there is much fragmentation in the distribution of mother tongues or where those speaking minor languages are isolated among a population that uses one of the major languages. In 1951 the state of Hyderabad (which has since been replaced by other states with different boundaries) had four principal languages: Telegu, Marathi, Urdu, and Kannada, also called Canarese. Of those who spoke one of the four principal languages as their mother tongue, only 14 percent had a subsidiary language. But of those who spoke a minor language as their mother tongue, more than half had a subsidiary language.

**Belgium** Although an important fact of life for the Belgian people is the existence of different language communities, the government of that country no longer publishes up-to-date statistics on languages. This reflects the difficulty of collecting accurate information on a politically explosive subject. Presently available information dates from before and after World War II. In 1947 the Flemish-speaking population was 44 percent, a slight decline since 1930; 36 percent spoke French only as against 38 percent in 1930. Those with both French and Flemish increased from 12

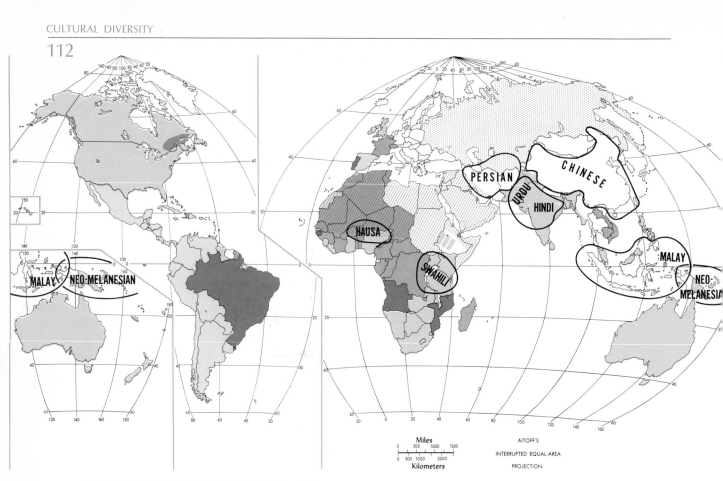

FIGURE
5-6

**WORLD: INTERNATIONAL LANGUAGES**

A few languages have achieved importance as media of communication among groups with diverse languages of their own. Those identified in the key are used in many parts of the world, often far from their original homeland. The languages named on the map have not spread as widely, but have an important function as regional lingua francas.

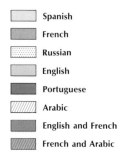

| | |
|---|---|
| | Spanish |
| | French |
| | Russian |
| | English |
| | Portuguese |
| | Arabic |
| | English and French |
| | French and Arabic |

percent in 1930 to 16 percent in 1947. German, although prevalent only in a small eastern border section, is also recognized as a national language. Although in 1930 only 1 percent of the population could speak all three languages, the percentage had risen to 3 in 1947. These small advances in tri- or bilingualism had no effect on the perennial strife between Belgium's language groups (see Chapter 7).

**Cyprus** Two main cultural—and antagonistic—groups occupy Cyprus: Greek Cypriot and Turkish Cypriot. The numbers speaking each language and combination of languages are shown in Table 5-3. The island's independence from the British, who had ruled it for a number of decades, came in 1960 after years of struggle. There followed an uneasy truce, marred by terrorist acts; eventually the United Nations took over supervision of relations between the two main factions. Recently an attempted coup d'etat by a group of dissident Greek Cypriots led to a massive invasion and occupation by Turkish armed forces and the forced relocation of many Greek as well as Turkish Cypriot families. The data show that before the invasion, the Turks as one might expect from their minority position were more bilingual than the Greeks; many more Turks spoke Greek than vice versa. And many more Greeks spoke English than Turkish.

**Lingua Franca** A special kind of bilingualism involves a *lingua franca,* that is, a language used over a wide area as a means of communication among peoples of different speech. For instance, English is the most widely known lingua franca in India and in other parts of the (British) Commonwealth; besides, it has international importance in commerce, science, and diplomacy. Hindi, the lingua franca of northern and central India, is spoken by many millions who have not learned one of its dialects as their mother tongue. Although designated as the official language of all India, it meets strong resistance in the south, where Dravidian languages prevail. Urdu, similar to Hindi, but with many words borrowed from Persian and Arabic—and with a different script—is a lingua franca in Pakistan and is its official language. Most Moslems in India also use Urdu as their lingua franca. In West Africa, Hausa is used for business purposes by perhaps as many as 40 million people who have varied mother tongues. In East Africa, Swahili provides the common means of communication for many groups in Kenya, Tanzania, and Uganda, and for some it serves as the official language (Figure 5-6).

If a lingua franca is greatly changed and simplified, a *pidgin* comes into existence, "pidgin" being a Chinese version of the English word "business." In the southwestern Pacific in the nineteenth century a pidgin developed called "Bêche-de-Mer" (Beach-la-mar) which later broke up into several variants. Related to this development is Neo-Melanesian, a language of Melanesian structure and vocabulary with some English elements. It is spoken as a common tongue around the coasts of New Guinea and in the Solomon Islands. Bazaar Malay, derived mainly from the vernacular of the coastal Malays of Sumatra, is the

lingua franca of the island world of southeast Asia. In the United States the Indians in the Pacific northwest have Chinook jargon, a mixture of Chinook, French, and English. Many Indian tribes in Paraguay and Brazil speak Guaraní as their *lingua geral* (general language); its accents vary under Portuguese and Spanish speech rules.

Sometimes a pidgin becomes the chief language of a group or a set of groups, each abandoning its own in favor of the one they all understand. An example is French Creole, which exists in many varieties, notably in Louisiana and Haiti, where slaves who had no common tongue converted the language of their masters to their own use. Taki-taki in Surinam, a mixture of African and European languages, serves a great number of ethnic groups. The versions of English in Jamaica, the Bahama Islands, and parts of Surinam have a similar function.

## GROWTH OF THE FRENCH LANGUAGE

The development of the French language to its present condition and location (Figure 5-7) illustrates many ideas outlined in this chapter. At the time of Julius Caesar's conquest Celtic languages were spoken in most of Gaul (the ancient name for continental western Europe). By the fourth century A.D. Latin had replaced the old tongues; this was not the classical Latin some of us learn in school, but a vernacular called Romance. After Roman authority collapsed, Romance in Gaul developed local peculiarities, removing it further from classical Latin, and also distinguishing it from other changing local versions of Romance in Iberia and Italy. Within Gaul differences emerged between the north and the south, largely due to dialect alterations made by the Salian Franks who, though they entered Gaul speaking a Germanic dialect, accepted Romance later after conquering the country.

In the ninth century the Frankish Emperor Charlemagne attempted to reintroduce classical Latin as the official language. The attempt was short-lived, for by this time the dialects were far removed from classical Latin; moreover, after his death the empire collapsed. By the twelfth cen-

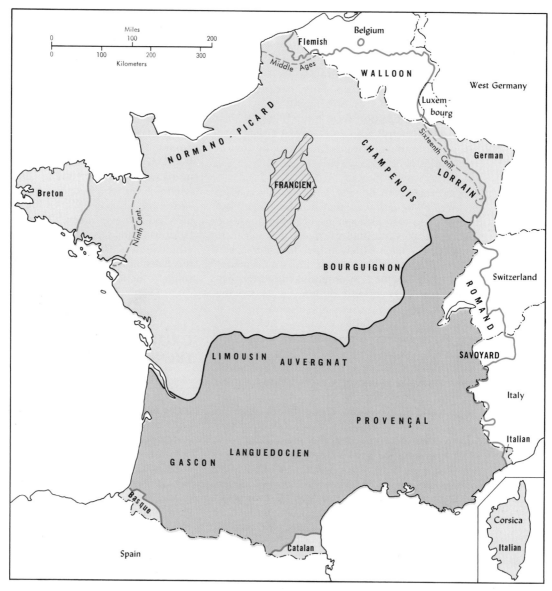

Miles
0    100    200
0  100  200  300
Kilometers

Belgium
Flemish
WALLOON
West Germany
Middle Ages
Luxem-bourg
German
NORMANO - PICARD
CHAMPENOIS
LORRAIN
Sixteenth Cent.
Breton
FRANCIEN
Ninth Cent.
BOURGUIGNON
ROMAND
Switzerland
LIMOUSIN    AUVERGNAT
SAVOYARD
Italy
PROVENÇAL
Italian
GASCON    LANGUEDOCIEN
Basque
Spain    Catalan
Corsica
Italian

FIGURE **FRANCE: LANGUAGES**
5-7

Based on Sheet 70 of the *Atlas de France*, Paris, 1959.

—— **Present-day Border of French Language**

**Langue d'Oïl (in Former Times)**

**Langue d'Oc (in Former Times)**

Breton **Other Languages Spoken in France**

– – – **Borders of these Languages in Earlier Times**

////// **Original National Territory with Parisian French Dialect**

GASCON **Important Historic Dialects of French**

tury the feudal rulers of the region around Paris were gaining political control of the emerging national state of France. The dialect of the capital region, Parisian French, became the court language and later the official written version. The Parisian dialect also had the advantage of standing midway between the dialects of the north and those of the south.

In southern France a literary language, Provençal—developed by strolling lyric poets (troubadours)—was briefly used, but receded before the growing influence of Paris. Today there is a transitional zone where their features intermingle.

The standard written version of Paris was accepted by the seventeenth century, but it took much longer to develop a standard spoken version. In the nineteenth century, military service, universal schooling, and the newspaper helped to establish Parisian French over other dialects. Now it is used almost exclusively except for those regions where another language is the mother tongue. The local *patois*, distinct dialects deeply rooted in the Romance period, have virtually disappeared. These patois should not be confused with provincial ways of pronouncing Parisian French.

Standard French has also made inroads into areas of non-French languages, all on the periphery of France. Basque, spoken in the southwestern corner of the country, seems to have maintained its position in recent decades after having been much reduced in importance during the previous century. Catalan is the language of Roussillon, a province on the Mediterranean which France acquired from Spain in 1659. Italian has declined as the language of the Nice area (Nizza in Italian) taken from Savoy in 1860. Breton, once spoken over the entire Brittany Peninsula, has withdrawn to the interior and the western half. This Celtic language was brought into the region during the fifth and sixth centuries by settlers from southwestern Britain. Flemish in the north has also decreased and undergoes continual erosion. In Alsace and Lorraine, annexed in the seventeenth and eighteenth centuries, German vernaculars still are spoken, though reduced in area. German and French reacquisitions of these provinces resulted in alternating emphasis on the national language of whichever country held control. Figure 5-7 shows the retreat of the non-French languages.

As a result of French colonial rule, French is spoken by many educated people in northwestern Africa, in areas of western and central Africa, in Vietnam, and in some Pacific islands. In addition, because French culture held the dominant position during the eighteenth and nineteenth centuries, its language was adopted as a medium of international diplomacy and commerce. Although French still has significance in this regard, English now overshadows it.

## LANGUAGE AND LANDFORMS

The surface of the earth with all its variety of landforms and climates is like a tremendous stage for the drama of language change, migration, acceptance, and retention. How have these physical features affected the mosaic of language? It might be thought that since language is a part of culture, and thus derives from human beings, there can be no relationship between language and physical environment. This may sound logical, but the truth is more complex. Friedrich Ratzel, pioneer in the study of migration and diffusion, pointed out that when any movement occurs, the routes taken and the places avoided reflect the conditioning influences of the earth.

Easily accessible areas certainly favor rapid and wide dispersal of a language or group of related languages. Germanic languages prevail on the north European plain from Flanders to the Polish border and formerly had many sizable outliers to the east. The subfamily of Indic tongues occupies the plains of the Indus and Ganges, but peters out at the Himalayas and the mountains of Burma, behind which different language families are ensconced. The mounted nomads ranged over the huge arc of flat land from Mongolia to central Europe and brought their languages to present-day Hungary and to many regions further east. Similarly, islands close to others or to the mainland are readily accessible. This explains the spread of Malayo-Polynesian tongues far into the Pacific and Indian oceans.

On the other hand, rough topography tends to turn aside the main streams of movement.

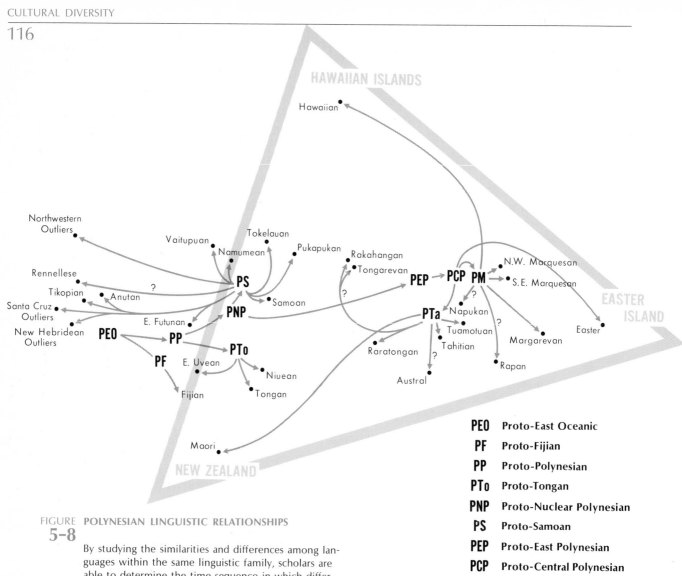

FIGURE **POLYNESIAN LINGUISTIC RELATIONSHIPS**
**5-8**

By studying the similarities and differences among languages within the same linguistic family, scholars are able to determine the time sequence in which different tongues have become separated from their ancestor languages. This diagram shows that the oldest independent Polynesian languages are those at the western edge of the "triangle"; these include Tongan and Samoan. Much later, Hawaiian, Tahitian, and Maori became independent languages associated with the descendants of settlers of particular island groups. These conclusions support the overwhelming mass of evidence that points towards the western margins of the tropical Pacific Ocean as the point of entry of the forebears of the Polynesians into the "triangle." See Levison, M., Ward, R. G., and Webb, J. W., *The Settlement of Polynesia: A Computer Simulation,* Minneapolis, 1973, page 49.

| | |
|---|---|
| **PEO** | **Proto-East Oceanic** |
| **PF** | **Proto-Fijian** |
| **PP** | **Proto-Polynesian** |
| **PTo** | **Proto-Tongan** |
| **PNP** | **Proto-Nuclear Polynesian** |
| **PS** | **Proto-Samoan** |
| **PEP** | **Proto-East Polynesian** |
| **PCP** | **Proto-Central Polynesian** |
| **PM** | **Proto-Marquesan** |
| **PTa** | **Proto-Tahitian** |

| | |
|---|---|
| • | **Existing Languages** |
| ? | **Relationship Uncertain** |

In Dacca, the capital city of Bangladesh, a teacher conducts an outdoor reading class for children of an overcrowded primary school. (Photograph—United Nations)

Where migrants settled in coves and valleys, as did the Scotch-Irish in the southern Appalachians, they remained cut off from the crosscurrents of life within the United States and kept their distinctive speech. The Slavic dialect area in Lusatia (Lausitz), south of Berlin, has survived since medieval times because marshy conditions isolated the folk and prevented their assimilation into the German people.

The mainland part of Southeast Asia in its language distribution shows a marked contrast between lowlands and uplands. Each major lowland is the core of a state—Burma, Thailand, Cambodia, Laos, Vietnam—and is relatively homogeneous in speech, though quite distinct from the next lowland. The highlands between them, however, are occupied by numerous tribal groups whose tongues, although usually related to one or the other of the lowland languages, are a veritable linguistic hodgepodge. In the same way, isolation has produced the hundred or more distinct languages of the Caucasus Mountains in thè southern part of the Soviet Union, and the many linguistic families of New Guinea. The mountains separated groups not only from the main streams of language migrations but also from each other.

Language boundaries tend to correspond with physical features. The Pyrenees divide French from Spanish; the Alpine zone is the complex meeting place of French, German, and Italian; the Pripet Marshes cut Byelorussian from Ukrainian; the swampy belt along the lower Danube lies between Bulgarian and Romanian.

With these and other examples, can we speak of cause and effect? Close inspection of the Pyrenees barrier and of the local distribution of languages reveals that the linguistic boundaries do not follow the mountain crests; in particular, Catalan and Basque occur on either side. The present line between the Czech and German languages runs along the highland rim of Bohemia,

but in this case, the political border is responsible for the linguistic divide. Prior to 1945, German extended well within the highland rim; after 1945, forced migration pushed it back to coincide with the political boundary, located along the crest. In North America the course of the Rio Grande marks the boundary between the standard languages of the United States and Mexico. Nevertheless, many people whose families for generations have lived north of the river retain Mexican Spanish as their vernacular.

At first sight, then, the association of the earth's physical features with linguistic distributions might seem to be a matter of cause and effect. On further thought, we realize that language areas, in common with other products of cultural diffusion, cannot be explained by reference to any one set of factors. They must be understood as the result of a complex interplay of historical forces and environmental conditions that affect individual lives and the groups of individuals that make up societies.

## CITATIONS AND FURTHER READINGS

*Atlas Linguistique de la France,* Paris, 1902–1910.

Belen'kaya, V. D. "Current Tendencies in the Naming of Places," *Soviet Geography: Review and Translation,* 16 (1975): 315–320.

Bowen, E. G., and Carter, H. "The Distribution of the Welsh Language in 1971: An Analysis," *Geography,* 60 (1975): 1–15.

Bruk, S. I., and Aperchenko, V. S. (eds.), *Atlas Narodov Mira* (Atlas of the People of the World), Moscow, 1964.

Brunn, S. D., and Wheeler, J. O. "Notes on the Geography of Religious Town Names in the U.S.," *Names,* 14 (1966): 197–202.

de Carvalho, C. M. D. "The Geography of Languages," in Wagner, P. L., and Mikesell, M. W. (eds.), *Readings in Cultural Geography,* Chicago, 1962, 75–93. Translated from *Boletim Geográfico,* 1 (1943): 45–62.

Hall, R. A. "Pidgin Languages," *Scientific American,* 200 (1959): 124–132.

Haugen, E., and Bloomfield, L. (eds.), *Language as a Human Problem,* New York and London, 1974, especially pp. 23–72.

Hymes, D. *Language in Culture and Society,* New York, 1964.

Jones, E., and Griffiths, I. L. "A Linguistic Map of Wales, 1961," *Geographical Journal,* 129 (1963): 192–196.

Kaups, M. "Finnish Place Names in Minnesota: A Study in Cultural Transfer," *Geographical Review,* 56 (1966): 377–397.

Kiddle, L. B. "The Spanish Language as a Medium of Cultural Diffusion in the Age of Discovery," *American Speech,* 27 (1952): 241–256.

Kurath, H., and Bloch, B. *The Linguistic Atlas of New England,* Providence, R.I., 1939–1943.

Loukotka, C. "Ethno-Linguistic Distribution of South American Indians," *Annals of the Association of American Geographers, Map Supplement* no. 8, 57 (1967): 437–438.

Seibutis, A. A. "Paleogeography, Toponymy and Ethnogenesis," *Soviet Geography: Review and Translation,* 16 (1975): 594–608.

Smith, A. H. *English Place-Name Elements,* English Place-Name Society, vols. 25–26, Cambridge, 1956.

Stewart, G. R. *Names on the Land: a Historical Account of Place-Naming in the United States,* rev. and enl. ed., Boston, 1958.

Trudgill, P. "Linguistic Geography and Geographical Linguistics," *Progress in Geography, International Reviews of Current Research,* 7 (1975): 227–52.

Wagner, P. L. "Remarks on the Geography of Language," *Geographical Review,* 48 (1958): 86–97.

Wolff, P. *Western Languages A.D. 100–1500,* New York, 1971.

Zelinsky, W. "Classical Town Names in the United States: The Historical Geography of an American Idea," *Geographical Review,* 57 (1967): 463–495.

# 6  RELIGIONS: ORIGINS AND DISPERSALS

## INTRODUCTION

A society depends on a common ideology for its existence. The word ideology as used here does not connote a specific—and usually dogmatic—interpretation of all social phenomena as, for instance, when we speak of "the Marxist ideology." Rather, we define it in a wider and more neutral sense: the set of beliefs, sentiments, and values that bind together the members of a group and thereby set them apart from other societies. It includes religious as well as secular thought patterns. Authors have spoken of it variously as the value system, the ethos, the great traditions, or the major themes of a society.

It is easy to assert that each people has its ideology but very difficult to pin down the specific character of any group. It is hard enough to describe and understand the personality of one individual. How can we analyze and comprehend the character of a nation or, still broader, the ways of thought of an entire civilization? This question can be countered by another: Can we afford to ignore the topic because full understanding is beyond our reach? We need to know what peoples are like, including our own. The foreign affairs officer contemplating a potential international conflict, the politician seeking election, the businessman exploring a foreign market, all must formulate some image of the people with whom they deal. A number of social sciences study village communities, tribes, regional societies, and nations to discover the ideals and attitudes that condition the behavior of each group. The results so far are often more impressionistic and speculative than verifiable. Nevertheless, research holds promise for more exact achievement in the future.

Foremost among ideologies is religion. This cultural universal stands open to worldwide inspection and comparison. Each religion has a center of origin, routes of diffusion, and pattern of present distribution. Even the most secularized societies retain many traits rooted in religious tradition.

Like all other cultural universals, religion is not easy to define because it has so many facets in different cultures. In essence, it refers to belief in the supernatural, in what arouses in a human being a feeling of awe or piety, in what he considers sacred. Religion, therefore, includes any form of such beliefs, from monotheism to ancestor worship and even magic.

In concrete situations it is hard to decide where the religious part of an ideology ends and the profane, the secular, begins. Confucianism is usually considered among the religions, though its founder actually taught the ethics of daily life. Among simple tribal folk, and even in some traditional societies such as India, religion is an all-pervading force. On the other hand, modern commercial-industrial societies give religion a more modest position. In the communist countries the official ideology is atheistic, but religion persists not only in the ancient forms but also in the cult of revolutionary heroes.

## INFLUENCE OF RELIGION ON WAY OF LIFE

According to the German sociologist Max Weber, a religion produces a distinct attitude toward life, and this orientation affects the further development of the society in question. In a stimulating work Weber proposed that the Protestant ethic had a strong effect on the development of capitalism in northwestern Europe (Weber, 1904). He did not agree with the Marxist contention that methods of material production determine the social superstructure, including religion. Neither position represents a generalization that is universally valid. In most cultural situations religion and social, political, and economic factors interact mutually.

Numerous examples in history and current international relations illustrate how religion has put a mark on human societies. Take, for instance, the division of India and of Ireland and the establishment of Israel. Political differences, party politics, and minority problems often have religious undertones—or overtones—as in West Germany, the Netherlands, or French Canada (for case studies see Chapter 7).

Religion strongly influences social institutions, and thus law. Marriage contracts in many countries require religious sanction. Islam permits polygyny (polygamy for men); Christianity insists on monogamy. Most high Hindu castes forbid a widow to remarry. Whatever its origin, the caste system in India is closely associated with religion. Religious doctrine regarding marriage may influence the size of the family and, therefore, the growth of population. Major religions spreading to new areas have carried with them the use of language, script, and the calendar of the homeland or, at least, of the adopted homeland.

Our modern economy strives to be so rational that we tend to overlook the religious factor in the daily round of making a living. Traditional peasant societies closely tie religious practices to the production of food, on which their lives literally depend. Rituals accompany the selection of propitious days for planting and sowing and for the beginning of the fishing season. Most diet restrictions have religious significance and affect agriculture. Jews and Moslems exclude the pig from their livestock; they consider it an unclean animal. Hindus in India, because they venerate the cow, refuse to kill it or to eat beef. The huge cattle population may even hinder better land use.

Vast numbers of religious pilgrims visit holy shrines. They inject large sums of money into means of transportation and into the local economy of such places as Jerusalem, Rome, Banaras in India, Mecca in Arabia, Lourdes in southern France, or Ste. Anne de Beaupré in Canada. Often the areal organization of religion led to the growth of settlements whose main function is religious administration or practice, such as the cathedral and abbey towns in Europe.

Ceremonial seasons (holidays, fast periods) also affect the economy because they reduce or ban work while creating a need for goods, from clothing to fish. The search for aromatic gums and woods for incense stimulated commerce—for example, the ancient Egyptian trade with Somaliland for myrrh, and the Chinese quest for sandalwood in Southeast Asia.

Elements of physical environment have played a significant role in most religions: holy mountains and rivers (Mount Sinai, Mount Fuji, Mount Tabor, the rivers Ganges and Jordan), sacred caves, groves, and lakes. Some sanctuaries may be visited only on special occasions and under strict ritual observances. Taboos on the use of plants and animals are common in primitive religions, and a number have survived in more advanced faiths. Specific religions use plants as cult symbols, such as the lotus and pipal or bo tree in Buddhism, the oak and spruce in ancient Germanic ritual (whence the Christmas tree), and the conifer in Shinto.

## THE VARIETY OF RELIGIONS

Religion among primitive peoples consists in the belief in some power or powers beyond man which can be appealed to for aid in times of need. These powers may be souls of the departed, spirits living on mountains, in stones, trees, or animals, or as ghosts and disembodied beings. Such belief and worship is called *animism*. Somewhat different is the faith in *mana*, the supernatural power which manifests itself in persons who have unusual and mysterious skill or in things that possess extraordinary, miraculous properties. Such beliefs and related practices persist among many nonliterate peoples of today.

There is, of course, a continuum from "primitive" to "high" religions as well as from tribal to universal ones. Interesting as these beliefs are, those of tribal level are of minor significance to our study. We must limit our overview to those religions that have many followers or bear an important relationship to ideas that are widespread among mankind.

Lahore, Pakistan: Moslems praying inside the great mosque, built by Moghul Emperor Aurangzeb in the seventeenth century. In this ritual position the faithful, turned toward Mecca (here westward), touch the floor with their foreheads, symbolizing complete submission to Allah. (Courtesy of United Nations)

## THE MAIN RELIGIONS

A useful and important distinction among religions is that between *ethnic* and *universal* (Sopher, 1967). Ethnic religions include tribal ones as well as those of wider scope. They consist of a set of beliefs and practices that individuals share as members of a particular nation or even of an entire civilization. Examples include Judaism, Shintoism (the indigenous cult of the Japanese), Hinduism (the ethos and related caste system of Indic civilization), and the Chinese moral-religious system.

The universal, or universalizing religions—Buddhism, Christianity, and Islam—contrast with the ethnic because they aim at worldwide, supranational acceptance. At first they were reform movements within an ethnic religion. As the new ideas gained universal appeal, they expanded into a spiritual message directed to all mankind. These three religions proselytize actively, admitting new members through individual symbolic acts of commitment.

Ethnic religions do not have such a simple mechanism to gain followers. Individuals must be fully assimilated into the community, nation, or civilization before being accepted as coreligionists. Such religions, therefore, spread slowly. India and China achieved this mainly by gradually absorbing foreign tribes into their dominant and expanding culture. In principle Judaism is reserved for the ingroup, though in ancient times it occasionally engaged in missionary activity.

We observed that universal creeds arose from ethnic religions. Does the reverse also happen? Yes, in the sense that a universal religion adapts to the local culture and thereby to a greater or lesser degree becomes modified. By and large, the geographic pattern of Christendom's chief subdivisions—Eastern Orthodox, Roman Catholic, and Protestant—reflects the interplay of universal and ethnic forces in shaping religious ideologies and institutions. Other and more local examples are the Cao-Dai sect in South Vietnam and the Chondo-Kyo in Korea, both combining Roman Catholic and indigenous features.

On the whole, the faiths in South and East Asia seem to have more interpenetration than those in the Middle East and in Europe. Even Buddhism, though generally characterized as exclusive, shows more adaptability to other religious environments than do the three monotheistic religions. The Chinese tradition of religious thought and ritual appears to be most inclusive because of its ancestor reverence; it mixes Taoism and Confucian ethics in various blends with Buddhism and even Christianity.

How many people belong to each major faith is hard to say, and therefore Table 6–1 gives only a rough approximation. Many countries lack exact data in the form of civil or religious census enumerations; the census does not usually ask questions about religion. Church organizations define their membership in various ways. Individuals who answer the question of religious faith in a civil census make their own decisions. In North America, and especially in Europe where by tradition the population is preponderantly Christian, large numbers do not actively participate in any church affairs and many declare they have no religion. Numerous Latin Americans profess to be Catholics but never attend mass. In China the blend of religions makes it almost impossible to arrive at meaningful separate figures for the followers of each of the various creeds. Most people in communist countries at least outwardly conform to the atheist position of their governments.

Altogether, there are many reasons to use quantitative data with considerable caution. Available facts indicate that Christianity has the largest number of adherents, with Islam, Hinduism, Buddhism, and Confucianism following in that order. If one recalls the intermingling of beliefs in China, however, it is probably more correct to give the Chinese amalgam second place, with Islam, Hinduism, and Buddhism following. The effect of Marxist doctrine in China—not to be ignored—is hard to evaluate among the traditional beliefs of 900 million people.

## CRADLELANDS OF THE MAIN RELIGIONS

Leaving aside the native ancestor cults and moral codes of East Asia, we note how strikingly small is the section of earth where the present main religions originated. Hinduism appeared in northwestern India, its offshoot Buddhism began in the north central part, Judaism and Christianity originated in Palestine, and Islam—partly based on the latter two—had birth in western Arabia (Figure 6–1).

**MAIN RELIGIONS AND ESTIMATED NUMBER OF ADHERENTS, 1976 (IN MILLIONS)**

| TABLE 6-1 | Religion | | Adherents |
|---|---|---|---|
| | Christianity | 955 | |
| | Roman Catholic | | 541 |
| | Eastern Orthodox | | 87 |
| | Protestant* | | 328 |
| | Islam | 538 | |
| | Hinduism | 524 | |
| | Buddhism | 250 | |
| | Confucianism† | 186 | |
| | Shinto | 60 | |
| | Taoism† | 30 | |
| | Judaism | 14 | |

SOURCE OF DATA: Encyclopedia Brittanica, *Book of the Year, 1976.*

*Protestant figures include full members rather than all baptized persons. Not comparable to ethnic religions or those counting all adherents.

†Figures for Confucianism and Taoism are not determinable for China.

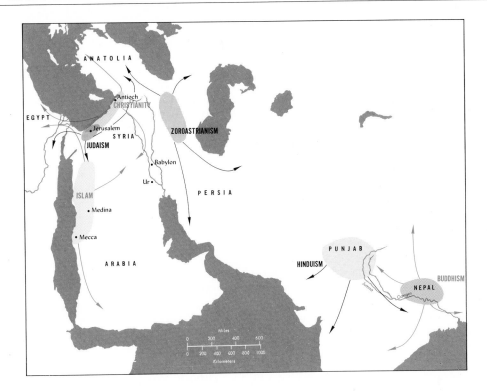

FIGURE **CRADLELANDS OF THE MAIN RELIGIONS**
6-1

This area of origins coincides fairly well with that of ancient civilizations. Spatial correspondence by itself does not prove cause and effect; nevertheless, we know enough of cultural evolution to accept some form of causal relationship, even if its exact nature escapes us. The nomadic herding tribes had to cooperate before they could control water for irrigation in the alluvial valleys of the Fertile Crescent and of the Indus. Group effort increased food production, made the division of labor possible, and gave rise to cities. Tribal rites changed to an elaborate system for the preservation of the state. Backed by religious sanction, laws replaced tribal customs to regulate the activities of the enlarged compound societies.

These are some factors that underlie the development of supratribal religions and of elaborate ethical and social rules. Keep in mind that southwestern Asia was the hub of migrations and trade routes which led to exchange of ideas over wide areas. All this—and much more information could be added—indicates at best that the ground was prepared for the growth of the great religions.

The intriguing point remains that they did not originate in the old hearths of the main civilizations (Mesopotamia, Nile, Huang Ho, and Indus valleys) but on their margins. Many cases in history show that an innovation found more fertile soil for development on the periphery of a culture than in its center. Perhaps well-entrenched institutions in the core area effectively resisted drastic change.

## JUDAISM

Among the Semitic tribes that wandered through the deserts of the Middle East some 3,800 years ago were the ancestors of the Jews. From their contacts with peoples of the irrigated valleys they acquired ideas of more advanced agriculture and also of religion. Abraham and his successors set out from Ur, in southern Mesopotamia, reached

Canaan, in Palestine, went to Egypt, and returned again to Canaan. In Mesopotamia they may well have heard about the great king Hammurabi of Babylon (2067–2025 B.C.), who received from the sun god the tablets with the laws of the kingdom. The idea of one god as sovereign over all other gods appears to have been widespread among ancient Semitic-speaking peoples. What came to distinguish the Hebrew religion was the commitment to the one and only God, who had chosen them in a solemn covenant to bear witness to this belief.

Moreover, Yahweh (Jehovah) demanded ethical virtue of his people. This exclusive monotheism, strengthened by many rituals, together with ethical and civil laws, welded the Jews into a distinct, closely knit religious community quite different from that of other Semitic peoples. Victories over their enemies and political unification of the tribes under a monarchy added to their feeling of national consciousness. But the pressures from the surrounding empires became too much for this small nation. The end of the ancient Jews as an independent people came in 586 B.C., when Babylonian conquerors destroyed Jerusalem and sent them into exile. Later the Jews were allowed to return but remained under control of different foreign masters. A revolt against the Romans led to their full dispersal in A.D. 70.

The civil and economic status of the scattered Jewish communities was fairly high in the Roman Empire before Christianity became the official religion. From then through the Middle Ages the Jews in Europe suffered discrimination, expulsion, or massacre, depending on place and time. For instance, they were expelled from England in the thirteenth century and not admitted again until after the middle of the seventeenth century. Even where they were tolerated, exclusiveness on both sides kept Christians and Jews apart, particularly where the latter were gathered in ghettos. When persecution in Germany became severe during the fourteenth century, the king of Poland offered refuge; thus Judaism concentrated in that country, which then included much of the present Ukraine. The Rhine-Frankish dialect of the refugees, mixed with Hebrew and Slavic words, became known as Yiddish (from the German *jüdisch,* meaning "Jewish").

Under the feudal system the Jews, as strangers, could not own land and were excluded from many occupations. The majority became traders and artisans, the rich ones bankers. In the prevailing agrarian society the Jews assumed the role of middlemen between the ruling landed nobility and the peasants. When and where native groups wanted to take over the position of middle class but felt not strong enough to compete with the Jews, they tried to drive out the "foreign" rivals.*

In contrast, Jews found considerable liberty in the Middle Eastern and North African countries that the Moslems had conquered, and especially in Moslem Spain, which became a center of revival for Jewish culture. After the Iberian Peninsula was cleared of Arab rule (1492), the Jews were expelled unless they accepted Christianity. Many of them—the so-called *Sephardim* of the Spanish-Jewish rite—fled to North Africa and to the Turkish Empire around the eastern Mediterranean. A number moved to Holland, later to England, and thence to the colonies.

Emancipation began toward the end of the eighteenth century when Rationalism demanded religious tolerance. Moreover, the bourgeois Christians of postfeudal Europe matched the Jews in economic prowess. France was the first to give the Jews explicitly equal rights, and in the nineteenth century most countries of western and central Europe followed. The mass of European Jewry, living in agrarian east central Europe, had to wait for emancipation. Meanwhile suppression continued, punctuated by pogroms (organized massacres). The treaties after World War I gave, on paper at least, equal rights and protection to all minorities in the postwar states of East and Central Europe. Actually much discrimination remained. Though the communist revolution in Russia outlawed anti-Semitism, it ruined most Jews economically because it eliminated their role of entrepreneur.

Germany in 1930 had some 600,000 Jews, about 1 percent of its total population. Under Hitler's leadership they were persecuted in medieval fashion. During World War II the Nazis gathered Jews from Germany, the occupied lands, and satellite states and exterminated an estimated 6 million (Figure 6-2).

*The function and status of the Chinese throughout Southeast Asia presents an instructive parallel.

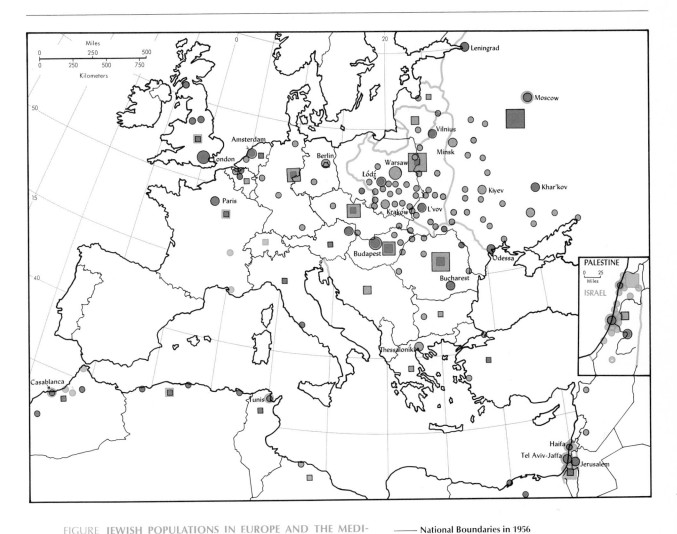

FIGURE **JEWISH POPULATIONS IN EUROPE AND THE MEDI-**
**6-2** **TERRANEAN, 1933 AND 1956**

The changes in the location of the Jewish population
as a result of World War II are startling, especially the
sharp reductions in continental (mostly eastern and
central) Europe, rapid growth in Israel, and slow
growth in northwestern Africa. Based on Sheet 4/X of
*Atlas of Israel,* Department of Surveys, Jerusalem,
1956–1960.

———— National Boundaries in 1956

———— National Boundaries in 1933

| 1933 | 1956 | Number of Jews in Towns and Cities |
|------|------|-----------------------------------|
| ● | ● | 10-50,000 |
| ● | ● | 50-200,000 |
| ● | ● | 200-750,000 |

**Number of Jews outside Towns**
**and Cities Shown**

| | | |
|---|---|---|
| ▪ | ▪ | 10-50,000 |
| ▪ | ▪ | 50-200,000 |
| ■ | ■ | 200-750,000 |
| ■ | ■ | 750-2,000,000 |

Against this European background we must view the Jewish immigration into the United States. Before 1800 only a few thousand, led by the Sephardim, lived in this country. From about 1820 until 1870 the majority of Jewish immigrants came from Germany (the so-called Ashkenazim), bringing the total up to some 200,000. After that time severe persecutions in Russia and in other parts of eastern Europe caused large numbers of Jews to seek refuge in America. This movement continued until shortly after World War I when the United States established a quota system to keep down the influx from eastern Europe. Between 1936 and 1946 the Nazi terror brought about 150,000 Jewish refugees, and later added another 100,000 survivors from concentration camps. Now some 6 million Jews live in this country, the greater part eastern European in origin and about half of them members of synagogues.

Like any other religion, Judaism has its different sects or movements. During the nineteenth century, when emancipation swept through Western countries, many Jews tried to adapt their rites to modern society. This reform included the abolition of many customs so that they could participate in national life like any other citizens. Some Jews were afraid that emancipation would lead to assimilation and thus to loss of identity. There were also those who believed that anti-Semitism always would remain a threat to Judaism. Such feelings led to a political Zionism. The founder of this movement wanted to establish a Jewish state in Argentina, Uganda, or Palestine. The Balfour Declaration of 1917 favored and gave invaluable support to the last project. After many vicissitudes and in face of violent Arab opposition, the state of Israel was proclaimed in 1948.

The ingathering, restricted before, now began. During the 1948 war and later, half a million Moslem natives fled from Palestine, although many others remained as a minority in a Jewish-dominated state. By 1960 there were about 2.5 million Jews in Israel. The establishment of political Zionism caused dissension among the Jews. Some feared that outsiders would identify all Jews with the national state of Israel, thus jeopardizing the position of many who wished to be loyal nationals of their country of residence.

"The Wandering Jew" is an old expression, but still apt if one considers the great shifts of the last century (see Table 6-2). From the large concentration in Europe—chiefly its eastern part—there has been such a great migration across the Atlantic that now half of the world's Jews live in the Americas, 42 percent in the United States alone. After the migrations and massacres, the absolute number of Jews in Europe is down to the level of 1850. The creation of Israel has raised the absolute as well as the relative figures for Asia above those of the nineteenth century.

The spatial shifts have been accompanied by changes in the mode of life. The Jew in eastern Europe lived as a middleman between gentry and peasant, thus usually in a village or small-town environment. In western countries he moved toward the cities, particularly the large ones. Israel is, of course, the exception in that Jews also fill the rural occupations; but here too the cities are the centers of attraction.

## CHRISTIANITY

**The Beginning**   Under the Roman oppression it seemed to the Jews that nothing could save them

**DISTRIBUTION OF JEWS***

| TABLE 6-2 | | 1825 | | 1850 | | 1930 | | 1975 | |
|---|---|---|---|---|---|---|---|---|---|
| | | Millions | Percent | Millions | Percent | Millions | Percent | Millions | Percent |
| | Europe | 2.7 | 83 | 3.9 | 78 | 10.0 | 63 | 3.5 | 24 |
| | Americas | 0.01 | . . . | 0.4 | 8 | 4.7 | 30 | 7.3 | 51 |
| | Asia | 0.3 | 9 | 0.4 | 8 | 0.7 | 4 | 3.1 | 22 |
| | Africa | 0.2 | 7 | 0.3 | 6 | 0.5 | 3 | 0.4 | 2 |
| | Oceania | | | | | 0.03 | | 0.1 | 1 |
| | TOTAL | 3.2 | 100 | 5.0 | 100 | 15.9 | 100 | 14.4 | 100 |

*Based on various sources, of which Lestshinsky, 1930, 1931, is particularly useful for the years before 1930.

but the Messiah, who would restore the rule of God. They differed, however, on how this kingdom-on-earth might come about: by force of arms, or by spiritual regeneration. According to the early accounts, Jesus came from Galilee, on the margin of the old Judaic state, a district which had come under Roman jurisdiction only a few generations before his birth. His teachings contained many elements of Judaic thought, but instead of invoking the authority of old traditions, he explained the meaning of love for God and for one's fellows, and insisted on salvation by faith and on ethical thought and behavior as the road to the supreme kingdom.

The mission of Jesus might have remained a dissenter's movement within Palestine, one of the alternatives to save a sorely tried people. What gave it appeal beyond the homeland was first of all the universal validity of the message, speaking to the downtrodden everywhere. Then the Greek-educated Paul interpreted the originally simple message and gave it an organization by which it could effectively penetrate the Greco-Roman civilization. As the new religion spread along the trade routes of the Roman world, it changed still further, absorbing philosophical ideas, elements of mystic cults, and other popular beliefs. Even so, hostility and active persecution burdened its first 300 years. The conversion of Emperor Constantine established Christianity as the state religion in the early fourth century. This opened the way for militant proselytizing throughout the Roman Empire.

## EASTERN CHRISTIANITY (FIGURE 6-3)

Concerned with our own cultural origins, we usually focus on the western Roman Empire and leave the eastern part a blurred image. Yet during the era of early Christianity, the richer heritage from ancient civilizations and the greater population lay in the countries around the eastern Mediterranean. In comparison, the western European territories that Rome had conquered were mere colonies, semicivilized and soon to be overrun by new bands of barbarians. As the Western Roman Empire disintegrated and the Dark Ages spread over its former realm, the eastern part remained the chief center of Christian-Hellenistic culture, in spite of all spiritual changes and material losses.

In the fourth century there were three patriarchs (highest-ranking prelates) of the church, those of Rome, Antioch, and Alexandria, and soon those of Jerusalem and Constantinople were added. Each had autonomy in his domain. When the seat of the empire was moved to Constantinople (A.D. 330), the see of the bishop of Rome stood like an outpost amidst a rising tide of barbarians. At the same time the Roman bishop gained considerable independence from direct imperial control, while his eastern colleagues, particularly the patriarch of Constantinople, became heavily involved in politics and affairs of the court. The bishop of Rome claimed primacy, but the others challenged his authority. Under the conflicts lay differences in dogma, cultural distinctions, and political considerations. After many centuries of disputes, increasing estrangement between East and West led to the great schism of 1054.

The Eastern, or Orthodox, churches never developed the close-knit unity of the Roman Catholic Church. The latter became a supranational organization under the authority of the Pope; the Orthodox churches remained territorial—later national—organizations, each with considerable autonomy. The Ecumenical Patriarch of Constantinople was, and is, recognized as the spiritual leader, but the final jurisdiction on the matters of doctrine lies with the prelates of all the churches gathered in council. This decentralization is why Orthodox churches have always been closely identified with their own countries. Each has strengthened the national feelings among its followers and has taken part in national politics, sometimes in opposition to the ruler, but more often as a tool in support of the government.

The great Slavic migrations into the Balkan Peninsula began in the third century and lasted for some four hundred years. It became the task of the Byzantine Empire to convert the Slavs to Christianity. Eventually the entire area from Serbia and Macedonia to Bulgaria and Romania became Orthodox, divided into various patriarchates. In the tenth century Eastern Christianity also spread to Russia along the old trade routes across the Black Sea and up the Dnepr River where Scandinavian chiefs held control. With the religion went a form of the Greek alphabet, but the Slavic languages came into use for liturgy and church serv-

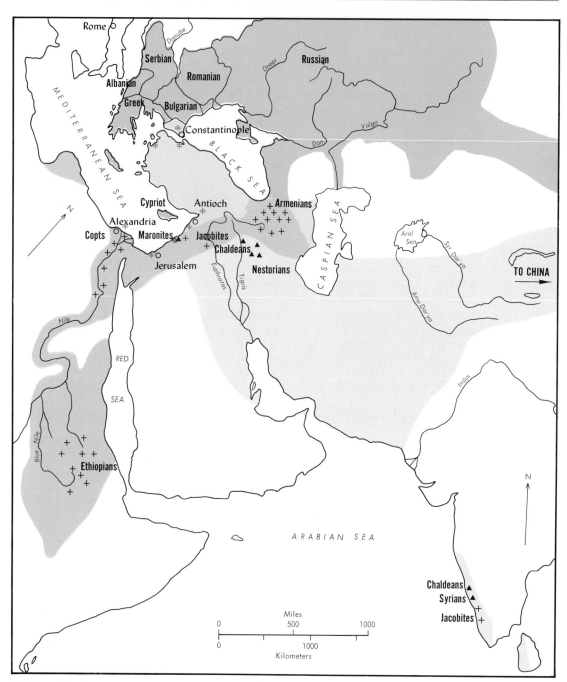

FIGURE **EASTERN CHRISTIANITY**
**6-3**

This map shows the main autonomous churches of
Eastern Orthodoxy and the Christian sects of the Mid-
dle East and India that remain from the time when
Christianity was practiced widely in Asia.

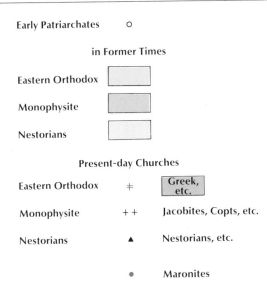

Early Patriarchates ○

in Former Times

Eastern Orthodox

Monophysite

Nestorians

Present-day Churches

Eastern Orthodox ∓ Greek, etc.

Monophysite + + Jacobites, Copts, etc.

Nestorians ▲ Nestorians, etc.

● Maronites

ice. This contrasts with the Latin which Roman Catholicism retained and underscores again the national character of the Eastern churches.

The spread of Islam gravely affected Eastern Christianity. When the Osmanli (Ottoman) Turks took Constantinople in 1453, this spiritual center lost much of its significance. The rise of the Russian Empire made the patriarch of Moscow the most powerful among the prelates, a position he held until the Russian Revolution of 1917. The Soviets separated church from state and proceeded to liquidate religion. Although they reduced the harshness of their control in 1939, pressures and many restrictions remain on religious worship and education. The church is a captive of the government.

Much the same situation, in various degrees of severity, now exists in countries of Orthodox faith which came under Communist control after World War II; Romania, Bulgaria, Yugoslavia, and Albania. The largest Orthodox unit outside the Slavic countries is the independent Church of Greece, still the state church of the country. The immigration from eastern Europe has brought large numbers of Orthodox Christians into the United States. They are split into numerous groups according to national origin.

Although "The Holy Orthodox Catholic Apostolic Eastern Church"—to use for once the official title—is by far the dominant one in influence and number, there are other sects of Eastern

Christianity. Some deserve attention because of their historic or present role in world affairs.

**Schismatic Sects of Eastern Christianity** Heated controversies on matters of doctrine during the fifth and sixth centuries drove several "heretical" groups out of the main church. Among them were the *Monophysites,* so named because they believed that the divine and human in Christ were of one (*monos*) nature (*physis*). To this group belonged the Christians of Egypt, of which small communities remain as the *Coptic* Church. Another survival of the Monophysites is the Ethiopian Orthodox Church, isolated by mountains from conversion to Islam. Both groups, long isolated from the remainder of Christianity, have stagnated.

Another sect is that of the *Maronites* of Lebanon, whose numbers in that country roughly equal that of the Moslems. Since about A.D. 700 they have considered themselves an autonomous nation. At the time of the Crusades they made contacts with Rome and France. This led eventually to the bond of communion with the Roman Catholic Church, although the Maronites retain the Eastern rite. Fanned by conflict between Israel and Arab groups living in Lebanon and by Syrian military activity, smoldering tensions between Lebanese Christians and Moslems burst into open warfare in 1976. This set in motion yet other migrations of the homeless and dispossessed and added yet more instability to life and politics in the Middle East.

The *Nestorians,* named after a heretical bishop of the fifth century, widely diffused their form of Eastern Christianity. In spite of Moslem rule they were numerous in Mesopotamia until the ruthless Mongol invasions of the thirteenth and fourteenth centuries. Refugees reached the mountains of Kurdistan, where some communities still survive. In the seven centuries before the Mongol devastation, the Nestorians were very active as missionaries along the Asian trade routes. All along the caravan trails of inner Asia and into China there were Nestorian congregations, in such famous cities as Tashkent, Samarkand, Kashgar, and Peking. Their church language, Syriac, written in a script similar to the Hebrew alphabet, was derived from the old Semitic Aramaic of Syria and Palestine. Although Nestorianism as a separate religion has disappeared in this realm, it functioned significantly as a cultural intermediary between southwestern and eastern Asia.

Equally important and more lasting was the missionary work of the Nestorians in India. According to Indian tradition, the disciple Saint Thomas brought Christianity to Malabar, on the southwest coast. More likely, the Nestorians introduced Christianity in the sixth century. Hindu influence added some non-Christian features. The "Syrian Christians" concentrate mainly in the present Kerala state, where they form about one-fourth of the population.

The *Armenian* Church prides itself on being the oldest Christian state religion, dating back to A.D. 300, when Saint Gregory converted the ruler of the Armenians. The situation of Armenia, in rugged mountains between the Byzantine and Persian empires, enabled its people to retain a measure of autonomy. To this day their church reflects the spirit of independence. Their stubborn resistance to foreign rule led to severe persecutions by the Turks, culminating in the massacres of 1910 and the subsequent dispersals and deportations. Their homeland straddles the border between northeast Turkey and Soviet Armenia. Numerous Armenians are scattered all over the world, usually engaged in trading, in which they excel. This characteristic, somewhat like that of the Jews and the Chinese, gives evidence, if needed, that not a specific race or a specific religion alone causes national traits, but that such traits develop because of the particular circumstances in which the group finds itself.

## WESTERN CHRISTIANITY (FIGURE 6-4)

Christianity maintained its position in western Europe following the decline of the Roman Empire and through the centuries of the great migrations. The former prestige of the emperor now belonged to the pope, who continued a semblance of law and order through his ecclesiastical organization. In Italy, the Iberian Peninsula, and France the invaders soon joined the Roman Catholic Church (sixth century). When pagan Anglo-Saxons invaded Great Britain, Ireland remained Christian. This "far western" Celtic-Christian culture waxed to a remarkable level during the early Middle Ages.

Conversion of the Germanic and West Slavic tribes beyond the Rhine-Danube frontier took about four centuries, from approximately A.D. 600 onward. This same period saw conversion of the Magyars and those South Slavic groups (Slovenes and Croats) who had settled on the southeast flank of German and Italian territories. The Christian expansion eastward included the Poles, whose pagan ruler in 966 joined the powerful Christian community to fight more effectively against other Slavic and Baltic tribes. East of Poland began the domain of Eastern Christianity. To the north lay Lithuania, which long remained a stronghold of paganism. It joined the Roman Catholic Church in 1386.

Wherever Christianity spread, it took along the Latin language and script, not only for church use but also as the medium for diplomatic intercourse and for the intelligentsia. Equally or more important, it brought along many other aspects of Mediterranean civilization that became diffused among the newly settled peoples, from construction methods and agricultural practices to law and political organization. The monks, a veritable field army of the Church, played a large part in transmitting culture.

While Christianity won northern Europe, it lost most of the Iberian Peninsula to Islam; Moslem rule lasted from 700 until almost 1500, when its last stronghold in the south fell. The momentum of the Christian counterattack led the Portuguese along the coast of Africa and eventually to India, enveloping the "Moor" domain. Spanish and Portuguese discoveries opened Middle and South America to Christianity. They also gained small, and often only temporary, victories among the civilizations of South and East Asia. Only in the pagan Philippines did the work of the Spanish missionaries create a largely Christian society.

In the nineteenth century the Catholic Church became quite active in newly opened-up Africa, and again in Southeast as well as East Asia. In view of current nationalism, often coupled to anti-Western attitudes, it is too early to say whether these gains will hold and, if so, in what form.

**Protestantism** Religious strife in sixteenth-century Europe centered on the issue of authority versus private judgment concerning the meaning

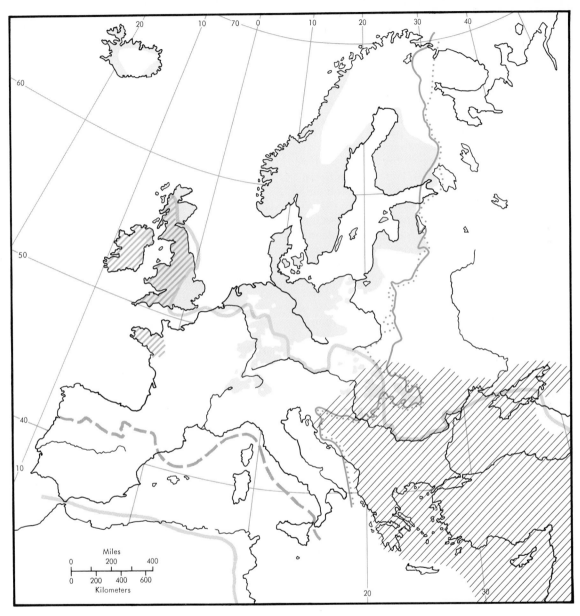

FIGURE **CHRISTIANITY AND ISLAM IN EUROPE**
6-4

///// **Ottoman Empire in 1648**

— — — **Northern Limit of Islam in Western**
**Mediterranean in Tenth Century**

///// **Irish-Celtic Church in Sixth Century**

———— **Boundary of Christianity in Sixth Century**

· · · · · · · **Boundary between Western and Eastern**
**Christianity in 1300**

———— **Boundary between Western and Eastern**
**Christianity in 1960**

▒▒▒ **Protestant Areas about 1700**

of the Scriptures. The way this religious issue was stated, and its acceptance or rejection among different peoples and regions, became intricately bound up with social, economic, and political trends and events. From the twelfth century onward demands for church reform were common in all Roman Catholic countries. However, the Reformation succeeded and maintained itself only in a fairly well-defined part of Europe. This Protestant realm lies almost entirely beyond the Rhine-Danube boundaries of the former Western Roman Empire (Figure 6–4). Were the lands converted to Christianity after the sixth century less firmly anchored than those secured by the old empire? The case of Poland (which remains Catholic) seems to refute this suggestion. But Poland is a special case. It had its religious crisis and might have gone Protestant. Fear of German aggression, which at this time meant German-Lutheran aggression, strengthened the Catholic cause. A similar argument can be made for Ireland because of its antagonism to the English invaders, although its ancient and deep-rooted Catholicism might be sufficient ground in itself.

It has been suggested that the rise of the middle class in northwestern Europe—associated with capitalism, in the sense of private free enterprise—led to Protestantism. If so, why didn't the earlier development of capitalism in northern Italy and in France lead to Protestant victory in those lands? If the answer is that conservative forces in those countries were strong enough to suppress reformation movements (as indeed they were), we are back at the initial query of why Protestantism succeeded in the north but not in the south. We note frequently in history that a new idea is accepted and more fully developed on the periphery of a culture than in its center. Traditions, institutions, and vested interest groups have deeper roots in the core than on the frontier, where culture patterns are less crystallized, more fluid, and thus more open to change. The success of the Reformation in northwestern Europe, beyond the old Roman Empire, conforms to this model.

It has also been argued that physical barriers contributed to the salvation of Protestantism from the onslaught of the Counter Reformation. The English Channel, the marshy delta lands of Holland, and the Swiss Alps indeed gave advantages

to the defense, but they seem secondary to other factors.

The break with Rome led to the establishment of national Protestant churches. The vernacular replaced Latin in the services. There had been earlier translations of the Bible, but now that the Scriptures had become the essence of religious authority for the Protestant, new "approved" renditions were necessary. Every family read or listened to the Bible in its own language, thereby strengthening the influence of standard versions of the various dialects.

Various sects of Protestantism appeared. Luther's creed prevailed in the German-speaking and Scandinavian countries and spread from Sweden into Finland and the Baltic states. Calvinism took root in the Netherlands, Scotland, parts of Switzerland, and among the English Puritans. The Church of England retained a more Catholic character, inherent in the history of that particular schism. Those English who refused to conform split off in various dissenting groups, such as the Baptists, Congregationalists, Quakers, and, at a later time, Methodists.

Protestant insistence on personal salvation tended to favor strenuous morality, austerity, and diligence. Economic success was esteemed, if combined with righteousness. Calvin-inspired groups in Holland, Scotland, England, and overseas in North America strongly held to these values. Without asking which came first, religion or economic milieu, it can be said that the two together produced a remarkable breed of entrepreneurs in agriculture, commerce, and industry. The spirit of free inquiry—though not always observed—and the obsession with material growth stimulated the interest in science and technology which is still very typical of lands with Protestant traditions.

The migration overseas from Britain, the Netherlands, and other northwestern European countries to North America, South Africa, and later Australia and New Zealand gave all these colonies an essentially Protestant character. The only significant exception was the French settlement along the St. Lawrence River, the nucleus of the present French-Canadian Catholic community on the flank of the Anglo-Saxon Protestant realm. Protestant commercial enterprise among the peoples of Africa, Asia, and Latin America gave ini-

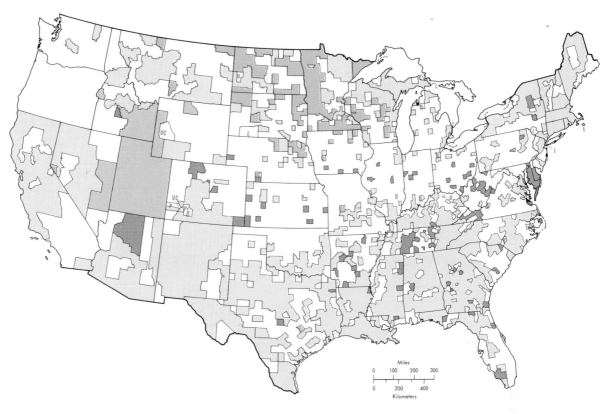

FIGURE
6-5

**UNITED STATES: RELIGIOUS AFFILIATIONS, 1950**

Areas occupied by patterns or letters have at least 50 percent of all reported church memberships in the designated denomination. Data are by counties. Based on a map prepared by John Tremblay for Gaustad, E. S., *Historical Atlas of Religion in America*, New York, 1952. By permission of the author.

|   |   |
|---|---|
| Baptist | |
| Lutheran | |
| Methodist | |
| Mormon | |
| Roman Catholic | |

| D | Disciples of Christ | P | Presbyterian |
|---|---|---|---|
| E | Episcopalian | R | Reformed |
| J | Jewish | U | Unitarian |
| UC | Congregational (United Church) | | |

tially little attention to the spread of religion. Widespread missionary activity began in the nineteenth century. As with similar Roman Catholic efforts, only the future can tell what will remain.

## RELIGIOUS GROUPS IN THE UNITED STATES (FIGURE 6-5)

In the modernized urban-industrial countries, religion has less direct impact on the mode of life than in more traditional societies. The United States conforms to this general rule, but it would be a mistake to underestimate religion as a factor. It is related to economic level, social status, political alignment, and cultural interests. "Religious difference—as distinct from religious feeling *per se*—is a powerful and often highly emotional element in the mind of Americans that works to bind together or separate groups of people and thus to create areal resemblances or contrasts" (Zelinsky, 1961, 166).

The religious composition of the population

reflects origins of immigrants (see Table 6-3). One should beware of placing too much trust in the figures on church membership, however. Data for various denominational groups are not comparable, owing to the variety of definitions of what constitutes membership. For instance, the Roman Catholic Church counts all baptized persons including infants, while most Protestant bodies count only persons who have attained full membership, that is, after confirmation at the age of 13 or older. Obviously, membership ranges from passive adherence to militant participation.

On the average about two-fifths of the adult population attend worship services in a typical week, ranging from three-fifths for Roman Catholics to one-fifth for Jews. The proportions are highest in the Midwest, lowest on the West Coast, highest in rural areas, and lowest in the big cities. Although churchgoing has declined in recent years, the proportion is still substantially above that in most European countries. Decreasing interest in organized religion, however, does not necessarily mean waning belief in religious values.

Fortunately for the national cohesion of the United States, the large denominations are spread all over the country. Jews are almost entirely concentrated in cities; Roman Catholics, Episcopalians, and Unitarians also tend to be urban. In contrast Baptists mainly reside in rural areas, and so do numerous small sects such as Mennonites (including Amish), and various fundamentalist creeds of old Anglo-American stock. This national pattern often has striking local departures as, for example, rural Catholic groups in the Middle West and urban Baptists in California (see Figure 6-5).

Roman Catholics predominate along the Mexican border in Texas, New Mexico, and Arizona, partly because this once was a Spanish-Mexican domain and partly because of recent immigration from Mexico. Louisiana shows its French heritage in the coastal region. Large numbers of Roman Catholics from Ireland and later from central and southern Europe have almost submerged the originally Protestant character of New England. There are Catholic majorities in Massachusetts, Rhode Island, Connecticut, and also upper New England with its many French Canadians. A zone of Catholic concentration reaches through the entire manufacturing belt westward as far as Wisconsin and Illinois. On the other hand, the South—with the exceptions noted—has very few Catholics because it did not attract European immigrants after the Civil War when the North was industrializing. Another part with few Catholics is the intermountain region centering on Utah, where the Church of the Latter-day Saints (Mormons) is without rival. Church membership in all but three counties of Utah is 90 percent or more Mormon. Hawaii, its population very mixed racially and denominationally, is about one-fourth Catholic. In passing, we note that immigration from East Asia has added a significant representation of Buddhism to the United States. Eastern Christianity entered North America with Russian settlement in Alaska and moved southward along the Pacific Coast. Its real growth came in the 1880s and later with immigration from east and southeast Europe, mostly absorbed into industrial districts.

Of the Protestants, Baptists are found mainly in the South, but, in contrast, Lutherans live in the Midwestern farm belt. Both groups are, like all others, well represented on the Pacific Coast, the true melting pot of modern America. Congregational churches still concentrate in New England and are scattered throughout the Middle West. The Protestant denominations least concentrated regionally are the Methodists, Presbyterians, and Episcopalians. Even so, Methodists form a numerous band reaching from the Middle Atlantic states through the Border states and southern part of the Midwest to the Rocky Mountains. The old core of Episcopalians lies in the area from southern New England to Virginia.

In summary we can say that denominations follow a general zoning along east-west lines,

## UNITED STATES CHURCH MEMBERSHIP, 1976

| TABLE 6-3 | | |
|---|---|---|
| Protestant | 72,485,000 |
| Roman Catholic | 48,701,000 |
| Jewish | 6,115,000 |
| Eastern Orthodox | 3,696,000 |
| Old Catholic, Polish National Catholic, Armenian | 849,000 |
| Buddhist | 60,000 |
| Others | 380,000 |
| TOTAL | 132,286,000 |

SOURCE: Yearbook of the American Churches, 1976.

with the exception of the Pacific Coast, where they are quite intermixed. The South, apart from places of Roman heritage, is a Protestant region, mainly of Baptists and Methodists. The religious region remaining most distinct from the others is that of the Church of the Latter-day Saints in the central intermountain area. Religions in the North intermingle greatly, though here also we can observe some specific patterns, such as Jewish concentrations in the large cities, Lutheran and Catholic mixtures in the North Central states, and a strong, even dominant, Catholic element in the East.

## ISLAM

**General Characteristics** Islam means "submission to God." Mohammed, who began his mission about A.D. 600, lived in Mecca, transfer point on the caravan routes from southern Arabia to Syria, site of many shrines of tribal deities. His new religion combined Arab beliefs and customs—such as the practice of polygyny and the veneration of stones—with elements of Judaic and Christian doctrines and ethics. The keystone of the creed was strict monotheism: "There is no God but Allah."

Mohammed admitted that Allah had revealed himself to previous prophets, among them Abraham, Moses, and Jesus, but insisted that he, Mohammed, had received the definitive truth. The prophet wrote down this divine and full truth—in Arabic—as he received it through successive revelations, which he gathered in the Koran. This holy book contains not only religious doctrine and rules of worship but also many pronouncements on worldly matters. Since the Koran was divinely inspired from beginning to end, it is the unalterable fountainhead of Moslem law. Each Moslem must observe the "five pillars" of the faith: repeated saying of the basic creed, frequent prayers, a month of fasting between dawn and dusk, almsgiving, and pilgrimage to Mecca, "if able." Those who perform these tasks faithfully are members in the Moslem community, which knows no bars of color or caste.

There are, of course, many other rules in addition to the five pillars. Some were traditional among many peoples in the Middle East, such as circumcision, and avoidance of the pig. Others were presumably borrowed from Judaism or Christianity, among them prohibition of usury, of gambling, and of showing human images in mosques. The use of alcohol also was forbidden.

As in all religions, at some periods and among some peoples, a number of these rules were not strictly observed, if at all. In contrast to the streaks of puritanism stands sexual latitude, which the Koran allows or at least does not explicitly forbid. Even so, the great majority of Moslems have only one wife, and divorce—available to the husband at his will—is probably no more common than in Western countries. Most Western observers agree, however, that in the world of Islam, esteem for women generally remains at a low level. Perhaps this may be due to socioeconomic conditions rather than to religious precepts.

### SPREAD OF ISLAM

Mohammed found his first followers not in his hometown of Mecca but in the nearby city of Medina, to which he had fled in A.D. 622. The Islamic calendar begins with the year of the flight (*Hegira*). Religious conversion required political control. At the time of Mohammed's death (632) all of Arabia was under his rule. With an amazing burst of expansion the Arab Moslems in less than 100 years conquered lands from the Atlantic Ocean to the borders of India, including North Africa, Egypt, Syria, Mesopotamia, Persia, and most of Spain. In all these countries (except Persia) they overpowered a predominantly Christian population, interspersed with Jewish communities. Because Mohammed had recognized both Christians and Jews as followers of a sacred book, conversion "at sword's point" was not required of them. If they surrendered peaceably but refused conversion, they were allowed to submit under treaty, which gave them protection as noncitizens on payment of a tax. This explains how Christian and Jewish groups survived in Moslem countries. Nevertheless, the powerful factors of economic and social discrimination gradually converted the great mass of population. Moreover, doctrinal disputes caused confusion and dissension among the medieval Christians, giving Islam many wedges for penetration. The simplicity of Islam's basic creed also facilitated its absorption (Figure 6-6).

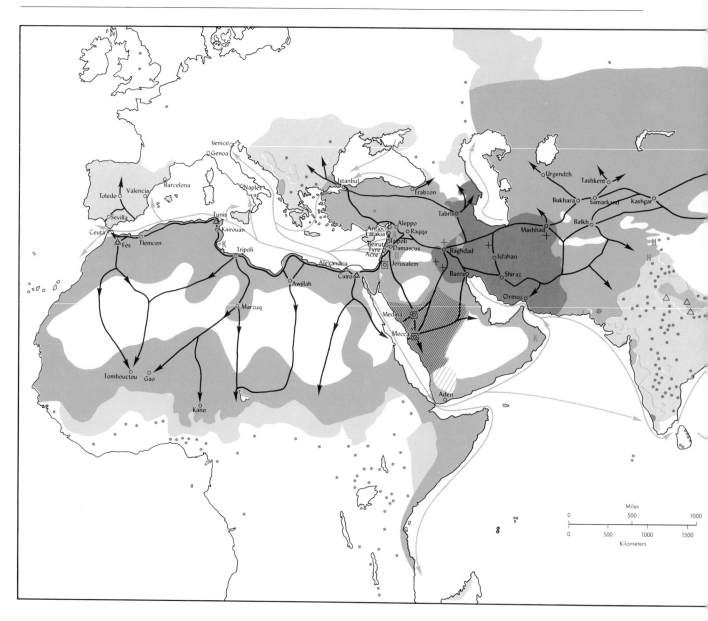

FIGURE **ISLAM**

**6-6**

The main trade routes, as shown on the map, help to explain the diffusion of Islam. Based on many sources, but especially on *Les Musselmans dans le Monde*, Documentation Française, Paris, 1952.

During the following centuries Islam expanded into India, Central Asia, Southeast Asia, the fringes of East Africa, and Africa south of the Sahara Desert. Moslem invaders from Central Asia ruled large territories in northern India from about the eleventh to the eighteenth century and thus laid the foundation for the present Pakistan. In Bangladesh, where Buddhist influence had lin-

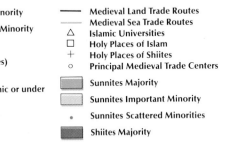

Canton

Malacca

Ternate

Bantam

| | |
|---|---|
| ▨ Shiites Important Minority | ━━ Medieval Land Trade Routes |
| ▨ Ismailites Important Minority | ━━ Medieval Sea Trade Routes |
| ⧅ Zaidites | △ Islamic Universities |
| ▧ Wahhabites (Sunnites) | □ Holy Places of Islam |
| K Kharijites | + Holy Places of Shiites |
| Areas Formerly Islamic or under Islamic Control | ○ Principal Medieval Trade Centers |
| A Alawites | ▨ Sunnites Majority |
| D Druzes | ▨ Sunnites Important Minority |
| H Ahmadiyahs | · Sunnites Scattered Minorities |
| | ▨ Shiites Majority |

gered for quite some time, the tribes or low castes welcomed Islam as an escape from the socio-religious segregation which a then-resurgent Hinduism would have imposed. Figures 6–4 and 6–6 show earlier Islam expansion, such as the push through the Balkans to the very gates of Vienna.

Islam was born in the desert, and the Koran reflects this environment. It is said that this helped its acceptance among peoples of the arid and semiarid belt that stretches from North Africa to the heart of Asia. In support of this argument some writers point out that the isohyet of 20 inches of rainfall coincides with the limits of the main area of Islam. They ignore, however, the fact that more than half of all Moslems live in the humid climates of coastal East Africa and South and Southeast Asia. In view of the total distribution we must reject the suggestion of a sufficient cause-effect relation between climate and the spread of Islam.

The more satisfactory answer lies in another direction, namely, trade routes. The caravan trails led from the Middle East through Central Asia to North China (where there are still a good number of Moslems) as well as across the Sahara to the Sudan. The overseas routes led from Arabia down the east coast of Africa, or to India, and from there through the straits of Malacca to Java and the Spice Islands, and even to China. As was the duty of every Moslem, the traders were missionaries. Even so, the greatest zeal accomplishes little unless circumstances are favorable. For instance, Arab-Moslem traders visited Southeast Asia during the eighth century, but the real impact of Islam did not come in the Malay Archipelago until about 1300, when the Hindu-Buddhist superstructure had begun to disintegrate.

Since the Koran prohibits translation from the original Arabic, Moslems use this language in ritual wherever they live. The prestige of the Arabic language during the early expansion period was such that it replaced the vernacular in several countries of Southwest Asia and North Africa (see Chapter 5). Outside the Arabic-speaking world the youths memorize the ritual passages required for worship. The ritual script, also Arabic, has been adopted in a number of Moslem countries as the alphabet for their own written languages. When Turkey was secularized in the 1920s, the government replaced the Arabic alphabet by the Latin script; Indonesia, Malaya, and some other countries have followed suit.

## DIVERSITY WITHIN ISLAM

As in other religions, the tenets of Islam have been given varied interpretations. When Islam first expanded over the Middle East, Hellenistic philosophy mixed with Arab faith. Scholarship flowered. In comparison Western Christianity looked like a rustic grade school. But in the twelfth century there came a strong reaction against legal and ethical judgments based on reason. The guiding principle became a return to the orthodox faith in the form taught by Mohammed. One example best shows what this meant. There is an Arabic description of the methods of Chinese printing, written in 1307, more than 100 years before Gutenberg "invented" (read "learned of") the process. But Moslems were unwilling to use it. Printing one book might lead eventually to printing the Koran—a sacrilegious act. Whatever additional reasons there may have been, not until 1729 was the first attempt made to print a book in the Islamic world. It led to riots and prohibition of the project. A century passed before the Moslem Arabs established their first press, in Cairo in 1825.

Education without printed books is difficult. Add to this a suspicion of all knowledge that comes from unbelievers, and it is very clear why orthodox Moslems long opposed Western education. Hindus accepted English teaching in mid-nineteenth-century India, but most Moslems continued to reject it for two generations. The Moslems in Indonesia, Malaya, and Mindanao felt the same reluctance to learn from Westerners. To this very day literacy rates for these groups are lower than for their Christian or Hindu neighbors.

This conservative, quasi-medieval outlook hinders the adoption of many aspects of Western life and technology. Now that most Moslem countries are independent again, various sects and movements actively seek ways to give a new interpretation of Islam so it can meet the challenge of today's world. Turkey has gone farthest in this respect; for instance, it has abolished Islamic law and uses instead a legal system derived from western European countries.

Disputes have divided Islam into several sects and subsects. The first and greatest split came over the succession to the caliphate (*caliph* means head of the Moslem community). The *Sunni*, or *Sunnites*, claimed that the caliph should be elected, but the *Shi'ahs*, or *Shi'ites*, insisted that he be a descendant of the prophet. The schism, involving the crucial issue of religious authority, led to diverse interpretations of doctrine. The Sunnites, now by far the larger body, amount to some 500 million people. The Shi'ites number perhaps 50 million, mainly concentrated in Iran and adjacent parts of Iraq, with smaller groups in India, Syria, and Lebanon.

A strongly puritanical movement, called the *Wahhabites*, developed among the Sunni of Arabia early in the eighteenth century. They rejected all intrusions on pure monotheism—such as adoration of saints—and stretched Mohammed's teachings on sobriety to ban the use of tobacco and coffee. The Wahhabite rulers of Saudi Arabia enforce these regulations, as temporary Western residents (mainly of the petroleum companies) well know. Fortunately for Arabs and Westerners alike, air-conditioned cars and homes were beyond Mohammed's vision and its subsequent interpretations.

The Pan-Islam movement of the nineteenth century attempted to unite Islam, especially against Western aggression. It was doomed to failure, if for no other reason than the tide of nationalism. Prolonged conflict with Israel has not brought an outraged Moslem world to unity.

## HINDUISM

**General Character** The complex of rituals and forms of belief prevalent in India is not a religion in the same sense as those we have just sketched. There is no founder, no church establishment, no defined dogma. Hinduism ranges from crude superstition and practice to highly refined philosophy. Therefore, every generalization about Hinduism has its exceptions. To comprehend it is as difficult as to know what "Occidental culture" means, which comprises Abraham Lincoln, Nietzsche, Einstein, as well as both monastic austerity and Madison Avenue antics. In the same way perhaps we should see the Indian ethos as a deeply rooted spiritual culture pattern that in spreading from its core to the many peoples and tribes of the subcontinent has blended with local beliefs and formed new offshoots.

About 1500 B.C. seminomadic cattle herders and plow cultivators of Indo-European speech invaded India from the northwest. As these tribes came into contact with the people of the Indus Valley, they must have taken over much of the culture they found in this more advanced indigenous society. After the tenth century B.C. the center of Aryan power shifted southeastward to the *doab* (interfluve) between the Jumna and Ganges rivers (Figure 6-1). It appears that by this time the Aryans had accepted female deities from Dravidian cults and had abandoned beef eating for the veneration of the cow. From the Jumna-Ganges doab, Hinduism, as elaborated and taught by a hereditary class of Brahman priests, spread eastward down the Ganges and southward into the

peninsula, and grafted itself onto other beliefs and institutions.

For a time the reform movements of Buddhism and Jainism—both around 500 B.C.—gained dominance, at least among the upper classes, but in the end Hinduism virtually absorbed them again, certainly in the homeland. Meanwhile, from the beginning of the Christian era onward, Indian colonists spread into Southeast Asia as far as Java, Celebes, and South Vietnam. Their culture, including Hinduism and later Buddhism, strongly influenced local societies. The heritage persists to this day in mythology, folk culture, and vocabulary, even where the later spread of Islam submerged it. The small island Bali, east of Java, is the only area in southeast Asia where Hinduism still is the predominant religion.

### THE CASTE SYSTEM

Though theories may differ about the beginnings of the Indian caste system, its relationship to the Hindu religion is evident and its impact on social organization is profound. Various criteria define the innumerable caste groups. A Hindu is born into a caste, marries within his caste, worships and works according to the rules of his caste. To understand caste, we must know that the key idea is ritual purity, with its converse, avoidance of pollution. Anything that has to do with destruction of life or with decaying matter is unclean. Thus the people who perform tasks which expose them to pollution are restricted in their contact with those of higher, purer caste groups. Workers with menial occupations—fishermen, butchers, sweepers, garbage haulers, laundrymen, those who crush oilseeds—are necessarily of low caste.

The belief in caste order lies deeply anchored in a metaphysical concept of the universe. The all-embracing order, arranged in a hierarchy, gives all creatures their rank. Man stands at the top level, with the Brahman caste on the highest step. Above and beyond is the final release from earthly existence. Through reincarnation the soul moves into a being, man or beast, high or low on the ladder. The level at which it is reborn depends on conduct during previous existence. This is *karma*, the law of the deed, establishing a strict cause-and-effect relationship between past behavior and present form of life, including caste level. The caste is thus a part of the universal, eternal order. An individual cannot escape it but has the chance to move up in the next existence by earning merit in the present. One can do so in three ways: by following the path of duty according to the usage of one's caste (*dharma*); by one's devotion to the gods; or by pursuing knowledge. The third is the most certain and rapid route to promotion in the next life but also the most difficult, because it requires the arts of asceticism and meditation.

Belief in a universal law of retribution rationally answers the question why one is what one is. At the same time it provides little incentive for material progress beyond the confines of the caste rules. An individual may be virtually fixed in a caste group for the present life, but fortunately there is some mobility for the groups. Collectively they can change their customs (for instance, by rejecting widow marriage, by observing certain food taboos, or by abandoning a defiling occupation), which may result, after some generations of good behavior, in their caste being accepted at a higher level.

The impact of Occidental culture leads Hindus to reconsider the character of their religion as a social force. Plantations, mines, factories, and construction projects bring together workers from different caste groups who must use crowded means of transportation and common eating facilities. Schools and modern forms of mass entertainment no longer can observe the neat rules of segregation.

The lot of the *Harijans,* also called the scheduled or depressed castes, or untouchables, has improved at a very slow pace.* Their members, now about 80 million, had been excluded from ordinary social and religious institutions such as schools and temples. Gandhi championed their cause. The constitution of 1949 outlawed "untouchability" and made discrimination against Harijans a punishable offense. In addition to these scheduled castes there are some 65 million people who belong to the "scheduled tribes." Most of these tribal folk are nominally Hindus, but because they keep to remote areas, neither caste rules nor the new legislation against discrimination greatly affects them.

*Harijan* means "child of God," the term coined by Gandhi to be used instead of "untouchable" and similar pejoratives.

Relaxation of caste rules is more noticeable in the north than in the south, and mainly in the cities. It is doubtful that this in time will result in the disappearance of the caste system. The roots of this tradition are deep and its practice is interwoven with religion. Moreover, the beneficial side to caste must not be overlooked. It is like a cooperative mutual-welfare society, an important feature in an economy where so many people live at bare existence level.

## THE SIKHS

The ideology of the Sikhs, one of many offshoots of the Hindu religion, deserves mention because of its areally distinct pattern. Confronted with Islam, a number of Hindu thinkers attempted to synthesize the two religions. One of them, Nanak, a Hindu native of the Punjab who lived about A.D. 1500, favored monotheism and attacked the veneration of idols and the caste system. His sect later, about 1700, developed into a militant theocracy which waged war against the Moslem Moghul Empire. During this period the Sikhs developed a strong national consciousness (Chapter 7). Now they number about 10 million. The British used them in their army and police forces, for which their long military tradition well suited them. Long hair, carefully wrapped in the turban, and full beard are among their distinguishing features. In their center at Amritsar, the Golden Temple enshrines the sacred book containing the wisdom of their early teachers. Their traditional hostility to Islam made the Sikhs join India at the time of partition in 1947. A number of their shrines now lie within Pakistan. To meet Sikh grievances against their subordinate position among the Hindus, a new state of Punjab was created (see Chapter 7).

## BUDDHISM

**Origin and Development**  According to tradition, Gautama was born in the foothills of Nepal in the late sixth century B.C. and spent most of his life in the middle Ganges region. He became the Buddha, the Enlightened One, when he perceived the path of salvation in the Four Noble Truths: life is full of suffering; the cause of suffering is desire; pain ceases with the end of desire; the way to stop suffering includes the right views and the

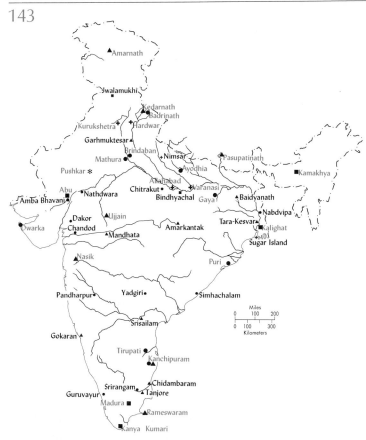

Kedarnath   Centers of National Importance

Amarnath   Centers of Regional Importance

Chief Diety of Pilgrimage Places

⁎  ⁎         Brahma  (Principal of Creation)

·  ●         Vishnu  (Principle of Preservation)

▴  ▲         Shiva  (Principle of Dissolution)

▪  ■         Mother Goddess (Principle of
            Energy)

+  +         Other Principal Places (For Ritual
            Purification by Bathing in Sacred Rivers)

FIGURE   **HINDU PILGRIMAGE PLACES**
6-7

Millions of Hindus make pilgrimages to sacred shrines each year. At places of national renown, such as Varanasi (Banares) and Allahabad, over a million may gather at one time to bathe in the sacred waters of rivers like the Ganges.

The distribution of pilgrimage sites broadly defines the Hindu realm. Pilgrimage fosters a collective Hindu identity which helps to overcome the linguistic diversity and strong regional consciousness of India. Pilgrimage places are intimately related to the daily life of Hindus. At many of them pilgrims seek the help of deities in the solution of personal problems and afflictions. Brahma, Vishnu, Shiva, and the Mother Goddess are the most prominent of the numerous Hindu deities; respectively they symbolize the universal principles of creation, preservation, dissolution, and energy. From data provided by S. M. Bhardwaj.

right conduct—honesty, noninjury of any creature (*ahimsa*), and forgiveness of enemies.

In essence this Buddhist approach was an aid in confronting life's problems calmly. It enables the individual to adjust more easily to our world of finite resources. Ignorance was at the root of desire's evils; knowledge was the cure. This moral road to salvation held no place for worship of deities, blood sacrifices, and caste division. Gautama retained, however, the concept of transmigration of the soul, though in somewhat modified form.

Many of the ethical precepts appealed to the common man, but the full program of self-salvation, with emphasis on meditation, required a special environment. As soon as monastic orders for men and women came into being, the monks became the missionaries of Buddhism. To this day monastic orders maintain such an important position that many lay folk spend at least one year as novice monks or nuns in the religious orders. In some countries this withdraws a substantial fraction of the male population from the economic production process. Since underemployment is common in most of the Buddhist countries, this is no serious problem, though the time may come when society will demand release of this manpower.

In the course of centuries the essentially simple doctrine has been greatly modified. The gods have returned as incarnations of Buddha and are revered in splendid pagodas. Among various sects, two stand out as the main schismatic bodies. The *Theravada,* or southern school—because it is found chiefly in Ceylon and Southeast Asia—emphasizes the road of salvation through the Four Noble Truths. This virtually requires becoming a monk. For this reason the southern branch has been called by its opponents *Hinayana,* meaning the Little or Lesser Vehicle, because only a few can journey to redemption. The other branch is the *Mahayana,* the Greater Vehicle, which has its followers in East Asia. It opens the road to salvation to far greater numbers, because Buddha and many other deities are considered as saviors for all men of true devotion.

### EXPANSION OF BUDDHISM (FIGURE 6–8)

Buddhism made slow headway in India until the conversion of Emperor Ashoka (third century B.C.). As patron of his new faith he supported its spread not only in his own domain but also into southern India and to Ceylon. Alexander the Great's invasion of India introduced Greek art, which strongly influenced the Buddha figure as we know it from sculptures in South Asia and elsewhere. In the first century A.D. Buddhism came into China over the inner Asian trade routes, though it did not become popular there until the fifth century. Chinese missionaries brought the Mahayana form of faith to Korea and Japan. This also radiated southward, with much of Chinese culture, into Tonkin and Annam, the present Vietnam.

The peoples of Mongolia and Tibet also accepted the Mahayana form, but they infused it with other ideas, some perhaps harking back to Nestorian Christianity. Until the Chinese Communist regime took over Tibet, the head of the

priestly hierarchy was the revered Dalai Lama, who was forced into exile in India. Monasteries owned much of the land and monks formed close to one-fourth of the population.

Buddhism spread in the fifth to seventh centuries throughout Southeast Asia as far as Java. Theravada was the dominant creed, with great centers of learning where Indian and Chinese scholars met. Later it lost to Islam its influence in Malaya and the nearby islands, but it has persisted in the greater part of the mainland. Theravada, the state religion in Burma and Thailand, also remained a powerful influence in Cambodia and Laos. In Vietnam the Mahayana branch prevailed although it had no official position. Roman Catholics—many refugees from the north—formed one-fifth of the population of southern Vietnam and held strong positions in the economy until the end of the recent war. The governments of Laos, Cambodia (Khmer Republic), and Vietnam theoretically are still committed to left-wing antireligious doctrines. It remains to be seen whether these societies, so deeply devout in their beliefs and everyday life, will become more secular.

During the seventh century A.D. Buddhism, though it had advanced abroad, began to lose ground at home in India as it was reabsorbed into all-embracing Hinduism. By about A.D. 1200 Buddhism as a distinct creed had almost vanished from the Indian subcontinent. It survives only among the Himalayan mountain folk and on the island of Ceylon (Sri Lanka).

Hīnayāna (Lesser Vehicle)

Southern Buddhism

Mahāyāna (Greater Vehicle)

Northern Buddhism (Lamaism)

Eastern Buddhism (Mixed with Confucianism and Taoism in China, Shintoism in Japan)

Areas Formerly Buddhist

Core Area of Buddhism (Buddha at Kapilavastu 563-483 B.C.)

6th Cent.

Directions and Dates of Spread of Buddhism

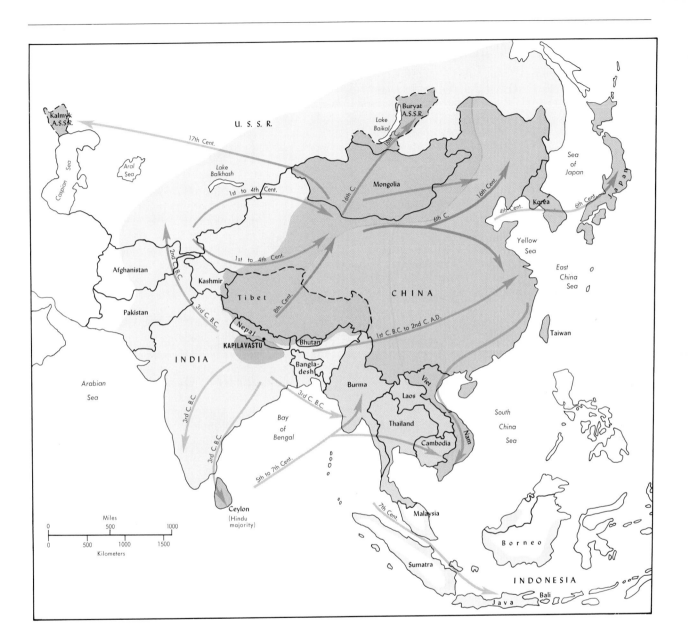

Kalmyk
A.S.S.R.

U. S. S. R.

Buryat
A.S.S.R.

Lake
Baikal

Caspian Sea

Aral
Sea

Lake
Balkhash

17th Cent.

1st to 4th Cent.

Mongolia

16th Cent.

16th Cent.

Sea
of
Japan

2nd C. B.C.

Afghanistan

Kashmir

1st to 4th Cent.

6th C.

4th Cent.

Korea

6th Cent.

Japan

3rd C. B.C.

Tibet

8th Cent.

CHINA

Yellow
Sea

East
China
Sea

Pakistan

Nepal

KAPILAVASTU

Bhutan

1st C. B.C. to 2nd C. A.D.

Taiwan

INDIA

Bangla-
desh

Arabian
Sea

Burma

Viet

South
China
Sea

3rd C. B.C.

Bay
of
Bengal

3rd C. B.C.

Laos

Nam

3rd C. B.C.

Thailand

Cambodia

5th to 7th Cent.

Ceylon
(Hindu
majority)

7th Cent.

Malaysia

Borneo

Miles
0        500        1000

Sumatra

INDONESIA

0    500    1000    1500
Kilometers

Java    Bali

FIGURE  **BUDDHISM**
**6-8**

    Buddhism, although no longer prevailing in the land of
its origin, has spread to other parts of Asia and has become the dominant religion in many countries. This
map is based on a number of sources, but especially
*Grosser historischer Weltatlas,* München, 1957, vol. 3,
183.

## EAST ASIAN RELIGIONS

The very ancient cult of ancestor reverence was once widespread. Later religions largely replaced it though East Asia retained it. This helped to keep the family there as prime unit of social organization, especially in China, where Confucianism is an overlay of moral ideals rather than a kind of worship.

Confucius, who lived about the time of Gautama Buddha, taught ethical precepts based on empirical knowledge. He stressed the reciprocal moral obligations between father and son, ruler and subject: each person must treat others as he wishes them to treat him. He compared the state to the family, acknowledging the ruler as a father to whom filial piety is due but who must equally observe his obligations toward his son. Under the Han dynasty in 136 B.C. Confucianism became the state religion and the source of all education. This led to the examination system for all bureaucratic functions, founded on the Confucian notion that only qualified persons should rule. This system lasted until 1911.

Lao-tse lived at the same time as Confucius. He taught The Way (*Tao*), showing how man must strive to be in harmony with nature, seeking simplicity, tranquility, and spiritual freedom. While Confucius taught a ritualized ethical behavior, Lao-tse was skeptical of ceremony and external authority. He believed that man's conduct should depend on instinct and conscience; life should be inspired by natural goodness. Much Chinese art reflects these values, especially in portraying landscapes which symbolize the mystic interpenetration of quietude in man and nature.

A more popular kind of Taoism also developed, and for some centuries from the fifth onward it became a state cult. As a religion of the masses it degenerated by combining veneration of many gods, from ancestors to emperors, with the use of magic charms and arts of divination—all directed toward the search for longevity and material blessings.

Buddhism in time intermingled with these native ideas and practices to the extent that we are justified in speaking of a Chinese religious ideology. At its best it blends Confucian moral precepts such as the golden rule, Buddhist virtues such as compassion, the Taoist values such as simplicity. Even Christianity—before the communists came into power—fitted into this eclectic thought pattern and made its ethical contributions. The total impression is one of deep concern with life on this earth. In this respect Chinese and Occidental cultures resemble each other, in contrast to the otherworldliness of the Indian ethos. The materialistic ideology of communism is not alien to the Chinese mind. The history of China suggests that its culture modifies and absorbs foreign ideas, as so often has happened, bringing change but not destroying it.

In Korea much the same blend prevails as found in China. In South Korea Christianity has many followers, with an ethnic offshoot in the Chondo-Kyo sect, which opposes foreign influences.

In Japan the ancient native religion is Shinto, a mixture of nature worship and ancestor worship. For a time it was subservient to Buddhism, but the challenge of the Occident in the nineteenth century revived it and resurrected the ancient belief that the emperor is of divine descent. Shintoism became the state religion, a powerful tool for welding the people into a modern nation. After Japan's defeat in 1945, Shinto was disestablished as the state church and the doctrine of divine descent was disavowed. In the postwar period the militant Nichiren Buddhist sect created Soka Gakkai, a lay organization which insists on exclusive observance of its creed. It claims 16 million members—one-sixth of Japan's population—and has as its political arm the Komeito (Clean Government party) with a large representation in parliament. The movement stresses the virtues of the traditional Japanese culture and appeals particularly to the "little man" in the big city, uprooted from his village home, who believes that the new faith and the new party offer solutions to his problems.

## OTHER IDEOLOGIES

In the beginning of this chapter we defined ideology as a system of beliefs, sentiments, and values prevalent in a specific culture. We have reviewed the main religions as influential ideologies and observed the intertwining of religious and secular elements. In "modern" societies other beliefs and feelings often overshadow the role of religion. The consciously secular ideology which now dominates the Soviet Union and China illustrates this, as an extreme case. Fascism and the Nazi dogma were short-lived examples of specific nationalistic ideologies.

Communism, in contrast to these ethnic creeds, has the character of a "universal" ideology, a quasi religion proclaiming its worldwide mission. With its own doctrine, hierarchy, and proselytizing zeal, it tolerates no other ideologies. Nevertheless, as communism encounters peoples of other lands, as different as those of China, Yugoslavia, and the Khmer Republic, its development varies with the new conditions and traditional values. Universal religions in much the same way found, as they spread into different societies, that the teachings of their founders and prophets underwent multiple interpretations, adaptations, and schisms.

## CITATIONS AND FURTHER READINGS

*Atlas of Canada*, Department of Mines and Surveys, Geographic Branch, Ottawa, 1957, 1970. Contains maps of the six leading denominations.

Bhardwaj, S. M. *Hindu Places of Pilgrimage in India: A Study in Cultural Geography*, Berkeley, 1973.

Clark, A. H. "Old World Origins and Religious Adherence in Nova Scotia," *Geographical Review*, 50 (1960): 317–344.

Doeppers, D. "The Evolution of the Geography of Religious Adherence in the Philippines before 1898," *Journal of Historical Geography*, 2 (1976): 95–110.

———"The Philippine Revolution and the Geography of Schism," *Geographical Review*, 66 (1976): 158–177.

Faruqi, I. R. al, and Sopher, D. E. *Historical Atlas of the Religions of the World*, New York and London, 1974.

Fleure, H. S. "The Geographical Distribution of the Major Religions," *Bulletin de la Société Royale de Géographie d'Egypte*, 24 (1951): 1–18.

Gaustad, E. S. *Historical Atlas of Religion in America*, New York, 1962.

Hsu, Shin-Yi. "The Cultural Ecology of the Locust Cult in Traditional China," *Annals of the Association of American Geographers*, 59 (1969): 730–752.

Isaac, E. "Religion, Landscape, and Space," *Landscape*, 9 (1959–1960), no. 2: 14–18.

——— "The Act and the Covenant: The Impact of Religion on the Landscape," *Landscape*, 11 (1961–1962), no. 2: 12–17.

Johnson, H. B. "The Location of Christian Missions in Africa," *Geographical Review*, 57 (1967): 168–202.

Meyer, J. W. "Ethnicity, Theology, and Immigrant Church Expansion," *Geographical Review*, 65 (1975): 180–197.

Paullin, C. O. (ed.). *Atlas of the Historical Geography of the United States*, New York, 1932. For distributions of denominations, see pp. 49–51 and plates 82–88.

Planhol, X. de. *The World of Islam*, Ithaca, N.Y., 1959. First published as *Le Monde islamique: Essai de géographie religieuse*, Paris, 1957.

Schwartzberg, J. E. "The Distribution of Selected Castes in the North Indian Plain," *Geographical Review*, 55 (1965): 477–496.

Shortridge, J. R. "Patterns of Religion in the United States," *Geographical Review*, 66 (1976): 420–434.

Simoons, F. S. *Eat Not This Flesh: Food Avoidances in the Old World,* Madison, Wis., 1961.

Sopher, D. E. *Geography of Religions,* Englewood Cliffs, N.J., 1967.

———— "Pilgrim Circulation in Gujarat," *Geographical Review,* 58 (1968): 392–425.

Tatum, C. E., and Sommers, L. M. "The Spread of the Black Christian Methodist Episcopal Church in the United States, 1870 to 1970," *Journal of Geography,* 74 (1975): 343–357.

Weber, M. *The Protestant Ethic and the Spirit of Capitalism* (translated by T. Parsons), New York, 1930. Originally published in *Archiv für Sozialwissenschaft und Sozialpolitik,* 20–21 (1904–1905).

Zelinsky, W. "An Approach to the Religious Geography of the United States," *Annals of the Association of American Geographers,* 51 (1961): 139–167.

# 7 IDEOLOGIES AND THE POLITICAL ORDER

## THE STATE: TERRITORY AND PEOPLE

The bond between a community and where it lives is an elementary principle of life, observable among animals as well as human beings. People have partitioned the earth into units, from tribal lands to huge sovereign states.* The principles guiding the political organization of space have varied in time and place. Empires and dynasties have gathered under their control lands inhabited by different peoples. Elsewhere and at other times likeness in culture has been the test for delimiting the state.

To survive, any state requires:

... the conviction of integration in the minds of all groups in all areas ..., a feeling, that is, of identification of themselves with the region as a whole and with its organization as a political state. This identification further must be accepted as stronger than any other forms of identification that might lead to conflict: such as identification with a lesser part of the state, a section or a locality; or identification in religious communities overlapping many states; or identification with people of the same language overlapping into another state. (Hartshorne, 1954, 192–193)

**Homogeneity** The sovereign state creates a measure of political homogeneity over its territory, however varied may be the peoples and regions under its rule. The greater the homogeneity, the greater will be the internal strength of the state. This homogeneity has two aspects: *uniformity* and *coherence* (Hartshorne, 1954, 188–189).

*These territorial units are often both "instituted" and "internally perceived" regions (see Chap. 1, pp. 13–16).

Uniformity does not require that the beliefs, customs, rights, and obligations of all citizens be exactly the same. We have only to think of the many religions in the United States, or of the differences in local laws and taxes, to realize that a great deal of diversity in detail can be combined with general rules and standards for the whole. Even so, the sovereign state tends to strive for a high degree of uniformity in those matters vitally affecting its welfare.

Coherence, the second aspect of homogeneity, means a union of parts. The more and stronger the interrelations among the sectors and sections of a state, the firmer the coherence. Barriers of the spirit (different languages, different religions, race prejudice) as well as barriers of nature (seas, mountains, deserts) may form obstacles to coherence. The state makes special efforts to remove such barriers. For instance, Indonesia developed a national language to counteract the linguistic regionalism, and Canada built its first transcontinental railway to bind together its far-flung provinces.

**The National State** Our era regards nationalism as the foremost concept for the organization of sovereign states. According to Hans Kohn, American historian, nationalism is a state of mind which considers the sovereign nation-state as the ideal form of political organization, and nationality as the source of all creative cultural energy and of economic well-being (Kohn, 1944, 16). Nationalism claims the supreme loyalty of all members of the nation, as organized in the state. National spirit, national independence, national economy, national product, international relations, United Nations, all recognize the idea of nationalism as the guiding principle of the state idea. Actually, many states are not nation-states but act as if they were, or strive to become so in the spirit of the nineteenth-century Italian statesman Cavour, who is reputed to have said: "We have created Italy, now we must create Italians."

At present there are some two hundred independent states, most created during the past half century in a headlong rush to freedom from former colonial control. Some are quite small, often islands: 114 report less than 5 million population each and 80 less than 1 million. It is ironic that nationalism fragments the earth into numerous exclusive compartments while the most up-to-date industrial technology and economy need to integrate resources and markets into large territories. Such fragmentation inevitably calls forth counterforces that demand forms of supranational organization.

**What Is a Nation?**  "To be different from others and proud of one's own special features is an essential trait of every human group. No group greatly resents its example being followed, but none likes to follow another's lead. This basic character, inherent to human psychology and sociology, makes every unit of space inhabited by man essentially a human unit. The most stubborn facts are those of the spirit, not those of the physical world" (Gottmann, 1951, 164). This "pooled self-esteem" of the group, whether of a clan of mountaineers in their valley, of a section like "The South," or of a country like France, Gottmann compares with an *icon,* a symbolic image. He uses the word *iconography* to describe "the whole system of symbols in which a people believe." This is another term for what we could call the regional or the national ideology. To quote his statement further:

These symbols are many and varied. A national "iconography" in our sense encompasses the national flag, the proud memories of past history as well as the principles of the prevailing religion, the generally accepted rules of economics, the established social hierarchy, the heroes quoted in the schools, the classic authors. . . . For any group of people, the iconography is the common cherished heritage. (Gottmann, 1952, 516–517)

The French historian Ernest Renan said in 1882: "A nation is a large community, founded on the consciousness of voluntary sacrifices made for the common weal, and on the understanding that this unity of purpose is to continue in the future."

These statements may seem rather vague to one who wants definitions as precise as the formula of a chemical compound. We may well ask whether or not *one* element forms the essential cement, such as a language, a religion, or a well-defined habitat. Inspection of the world's nations, however, shows that while such features, especially language, are important ingredients, they do not in themselves provide the necessary and sufficient bonds for national unity.

**Problems of Heterogeneity**  Ideally, the nation-state is a politically independent group of like-minded people who occupy their own territory. Its areal differences are merely regional variations on the major national theme, giving it the rich expression of diversity-in-unity. Reality seldom measures up to this ideal. Internal friction often occurs. Before illustrating this by a number of case studies, let us single out some major forms of heterogeneity.

*Sectionalism* is an aggravated form of regional consciousness. It need not evolve from contrasts in religion, language, or other cultural traits that usually separate peoples. Sectionalism refers to a strong sentiment of distinctiveness in a segment of the country where tensions arise from divergent social and political norms that restrain individuals from agreeing with the national ideology. A self-assertive section may demand autonomy and, if denied, wish to secede to form its own nation. The American South has been at various points of this regionalism-sectionalism continuum.

A number of states are *polyethnic;* that is, they have several ethnic groups within their borders, each occupying a distinct territory. These groups may vary from large, complex entities—for which the term *nation* is usually reserved—to societies of smaller scope and less elaborate social structure, commonly called *tribes.* Although each of these groups may adhere to the general state idea, their identification ranges from wholehearted support to reluctant participation. Switzerland, the Soviet Union, Belgium, and many postcolonial states belong within this category.

An ethnic group, especially if occupying a border province, may feel strong bonds of unity with like-minded people in an adjacent country. That neighbor may even claim the territory as an unredeemed part (*irredenta*) of its own domain. Cases of this kind abound in recent European history.

A *plural society* within a state presents a different problem. Here various ethnic groups live intermingled throughout the country, often in distinct residential quarters. Each community follows its own life-style and occupies its own niche in the economy—like different organisms living in symbiosis. Societies like this are most common in Africa and in Southeast Asia, but are also present in Trinidad and the Guianas. Chapter 4 briefly sketches such a situation in the Republic of South Africa; we discuss Malaysia later in this present chapter.

The United States is often described as a plural society (see Chapter 4). If you accept this notion, also keep in mind that the structure of this pluralism differs considerably from that prevailing in Southeast Asia and East Africa. Minorities in the United States occupy usually the lower rungs of the economic ladder, while in East Africa and Southeast Asia they stand in the middle or at the top. Furthermore, force of circumstance stripped the largest minority in the United States, the blacks, of most of their heritage. Though some elements of their African culture survived the slave experience, they had to adapt in their own way to the Anglo-American society. Social segregation by race, therefore, and not a distinct culture kept the Afro-American from becoming part of the mainstream of American life.

Smaller racial minorities—native American Indians and Eskimo, and American-born or immigrant Latin Americans—do have their distinct cultures but often face a painful choice between preserving their self-identity and embracing the "American way of life" for its material rewards. Legislation of the 1950s and 1960s backed up the traditional concept of the "melting pot." But even if and when all ethnic communities attain full equality, it is far from certain whether they will totally merge into the preponderant American life-style or still keep and develop their own traditions.

## NATIONALITIES AND NATIONS IN THE EUROPEAN WORLD

For such a small landmass Europe has remarkably many sovereign states. The diversity is even greater than the political map indicates because within the borders of each country are old provinces, regions, *pays*, each with its memories of the past, its claims on the present, its hopes for the future. To grasp the broad pattern of this areal mosaic, we must see it in historical perspective.

Europe is divided into a Mediterranean part, which gave rise to the Greco-Roman civilization, and a northern part, which later received that culture. The contrast between West and East is still more important because the former is rooted in the Latin culture and the latter in the Hellenistic culture of Byzantium. Asian invasions came from the east, sometimes penetrating deep into Europe, and always setting in motion the folk in the path of conquest. As these migrations moved westward, they lost momentum or were successfully repulsed by the people on the Atlantic seaboard. As a result, the eastern part of Europe has a far greater variety of people than its western counterpart.

After the Turkish conquest of Byzantium in 1453 and after subsequent invasions of southeastern Europe, the West moved its center of gravity to the Atlantic Seaboard. It developed a lively maritime traffic which eventually led to overseas colonies, world commerce, and a relatively prosperous economy. The East did not take part in this expansion and remained much longer in a feudal agrarian, economically backward condition.

These differences also affected the degree of national unity attained in parts of Europe. It is no accident that western Europe has few national minorities. First of all, there were not so many residues of foreign invasions. More important, the growth of the middle class fostered national unity and, in alliance with the kings, restricted the power of the local lords. There was mobility of people, exchange of ideas between city and country, integration of the parts under strong central governments. Education spread among the middle class and eventually to the entire population, strengthening the national iconography.

A sharply contrasting situation prevailed in the East, where the feudal agrarian way of life favored self-sufficient regions and discouraged the free movement of persons. It kept manifold peoples in the Russian and Turkish empires segregated from ruling groups. The Hapsburgs created a frontier empire under German-speaking Austrian control. When the Magyars became co-rulers in 1867, this became the Austro-Hungarian Empire, with a multitude of other ethnic groups remaining under their joint domination. Oppression, discrimination, and denial of self-government hardened the personality of each individual locality. What little there was of a middle class consisted of outside elements such as Germans, Jews, or Greeks, a divisive rather than a unifying force.

Up to 1918 one could define fairly accurately the boundary between West and East. It ran through the Gulf of Bothnia to Danzig (now Gdańsk) on the Vistula, then overland to Trieste, and from there south through the Adriatic. To the west lay the Europe of integrated nation-states, to the east the empires of Russia, Austria-Hungary, and Turkey, as well as the eastern fringe of the German Empire, each composed of many peoples (Figure 7-1). The imported ideology of nationalism fired already existing tensions and caused the Turkish Empire to disintegrate even before World War I.

This war broke up the Austro-Hungarian monarchy, cut off parts of the German Empire, wiped out the remains of Turkish control over European peoples, and pushed back the boundaries of Russia. As a result, a new zone appeared, the Danzig-Trieste line its western border, the Leningrad-Odessa line its eastern one. This in-between strip, often called "the shatter belt," held a crazy quilt of communities, plural societies living together within borderlines set up to keep the major nations separate.

It is true that Russia, now the Soviet Union, also contained many nationalities within its boundaries, but each was small compared to the mass of the Russian nation. Among the major policy questions facing this new state with its communist ideology was how to integrate these minorities and, especially, those to the west which were actually part of the shatter belt.

The problem in the shatter belt countries on the western side of the Soviet border was much more complex. After World War I new sovereign states were formed according to the principle of national self-determination, often re-creating states that had existed in the past, such as Poland, Finland, and Hungary. Unlike Western Europe, where state and nation gradually had evolved into the nation-state, Eastern Europe's new political units were superimposed upon a jumble of jealously guarded sentiments which defied neat territorial demarcation. This meant that virtually every new state had to put up with some, if not many, national minorities. In several instances the new states were not satisfied to include their own nationals but wanted to gain valuable territory—an outlet to the sea, a share in river trade, a strategic mountain barrier, or a mining district—regardless of what the inhabitants felt. Such annexations compounded the national diversity. Various treaties were made to protect the minorities and to safeguard their rights. Actually, though, few countries fully observed the rules, once they had gained independence.

In addition to suffering from injustices, most of the shatter belt peasants were poor. Most lived by agriculture, using their traditional methods and equipment, and their local markets. Somewhat better off were the peoples of industrial Upper Silesia, now in Poland, those of the Bohemian-Moravian part of Czechoslovakia, and those of Slovenia in northwest Yugoslavia. Independence came to the shatter belt states, not through internal strength but through the victory of Western Europe and the United States over the central European empires and through the collapse of czarist Russia. Their survival depended on Germany and Russia remaining weak and on Western countries continuing their aid. These conditions prevailed less and less during the interwar years. In the war of 1939–1945, Germany struck first but lost, leaving the field open to the Soviet Union. The latter annexed some borderlands, expanded its power over almost the entire shatter belt (and well into Germany) and controlled the political and economic structure of the countries of Eastern Europe.

After World War II each state tried to adjust to its national boundaries and to solve its minority problems. Cynicism, despair, and opportunism accompanied significant changes in Europe. The Nazis had virtually eliminated the Jews and deci-

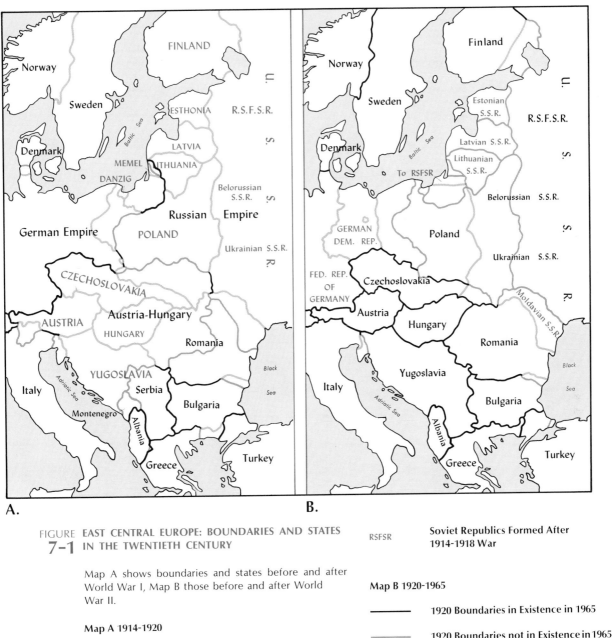

**A.**

**B.**

FIGURE
**7-1**
**EAST CENTRAL EUROPE: BOUNDARIES AND STATES IN THE TWENTIETH CENTURY**

Map A shows boundaries and states before and after World War I, Map B those before and after World War II.

**Map A 1914-1920**

———————— 1914 Boundaries in Existence in 1920

———————— 1914 Boundaries Not in Existence in 1920

···················· New Boundaries 1920

POLAND  States Formed After 1914-1918 War

RSFSR  Soviet Republics Formed After 1914-1918 War

**Map B 1920-1965**

———————— 1920 Boundaries in Existence in 1965

———————— 1920 Boundaries not in Existence in 1965

···················· New Boundaries 1965

GERMAN DEM. REP.  States Formed After 1939-1945 War

Latvian S.S.R.  Soviet Republics Formed After 1939-1945 War

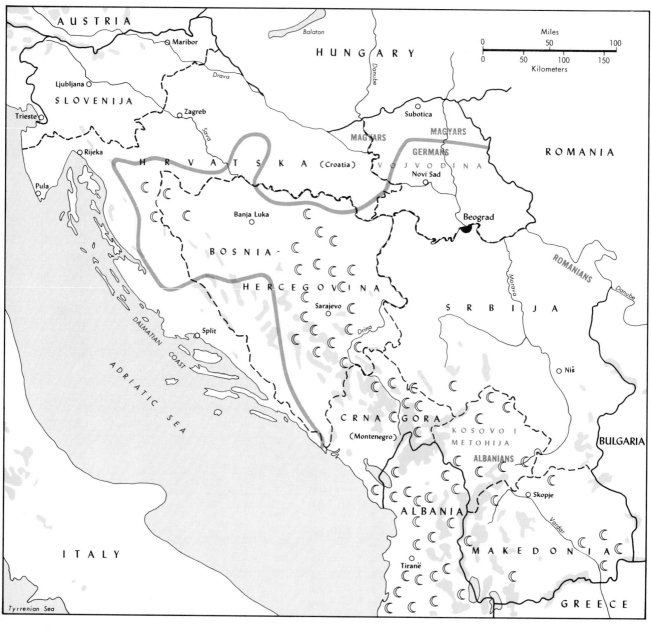

SLOVENIJA    **Republics**

**Autonomous Regions of**
VOJVODINA    **Serbian Republic**

■ Beograd
○ Pula    **Important Towns**

**MAGYARS**    **Linguistic Minorities**

**Boundary between Roman Catholic**
**and Eastern Orthodox Christians**

☾    **Adherents of Islam**

**Land over 5,000 Feet**

155

mated the Gypsies; in turn, the liberated peoples expelled the Germans. Mass transfers of foreign minorities "cleansed" the national territories. Examples are the expulsion of Italians from the Adriatic coast of Yugoslavia and the exchange of populations between Poland and the Soviet Union. Most Finns moved out of the Karelian Isthmus and from other areas lost to the Soviet Union. National groups were exchanged between Bulgaria and Romania and between Hungary and Czechoslovakia (Figure 17–2). At the cost of millions of personal tragedies, each state now has a far greater degree of national uniformity than formerly.

## YUGOSLAVIA, AN EXAMPLE OF A POLYETHNIC STATE

Although ethnic heterogeneity is now more the exception than the rule within eastern European states, Yugoslavia affords a good example of polyethnic problems. The Dinaric Mountains lie parallel to the Adriatic coast. There are large arable plains only in the north of the country on the edge of the Hungarian basin along the Danube and its tributaries. From the Danubian lands the narrow Morava-Vardar corridor leads toward Greece and the Aegean Sea. Dalmatia borders the Adriatic, most of it arid stony hills crowding the sea. Although the majority of Yugoslavians live in the plains, the mountains have been their historical refuge in times of trouble. The Turks never effectively occupied Montenegro, which, with the highlands farther north, also formed a center of resistance to the Germans during World War II.

Of Yugoslavia's 22 million population, almost nine-tenths speak a south (*yugo*) Slavic tongue (Table 7–1). During the Middle Ages the location of the country brought the western part into the Roman Catholic world, while the eastern and southern parts turned toward Byzantine Christianity. Yugoslavia was created after World War I by adding to Serbia (which had won independence from Turkey in the nineteenth century) the South Slavic territories of the Austro-Hungarian monarchy, the independent kingdom of Montenegro, and some border districts of Bulgaria. To weld together the variety of peoples, the Serbs insisted on a centralized state under their control. The other nationalities bitterly opposed the concept and its crude execution. After World War II the state was reconstituted as a federal republic on the Russian model. There are now six constituent republics, each based on a different ethnic group. Within Serbia concentrate the other principal minorities, the Hungarians in Vojvodina and the Albanians in Kosmet—both autonomous districts (Figure 7–2).

The Slovenes live in the Alpine foothills of the northwest (see Table 7–1). For centuries linked to Austria, they are economically the most westernized group in Yugoslavia. They are Roman Catholic and use the Latin script for their language which, in its standard form, differs somewhat from the Serbo-Croatian that most Yugoslavs speak.

The Croats share the Roman Catholic religion and Latin script with the Slovenes, but they have the same standard language as the Serbs. Proud of their central European heritage, the Croats refused to submit to Serbian leadership; they saw them as rude mountaineers tainted with "Eastern" ideas. The Croats live mainly in the plains of the Drava and Sava rivers and in the old province of Dalmatia along the Adriatic. They form at least one-fifth of the population of Bosnia-Hercegovina.

The Serbs are Orthodox in religion and use

### THE POPULATION OF YUGOSLAVIA, 1971

TABLE
7–1

| Ethnic group | Number | Percent |
|---|---|---|
| Nationalities: | | |
| Serbs | 8,143,000 | 40.5 |
| Croats | 4,527,000 | 22.6 |
| Muslims | | |
| (as nationality) | 1,748,000 | 8.6 |
| Slovenes | 1,678,000 | 8.4 |
| Macedonians | 1,195,000 | 5.9 |
| Montenegrins | 509,000 | 2.5 |
| Yugoslavs* | 273,000 | 1.3 |
| Minorities: | | |
| Albanians | 1,310,000 | 6.3 |
| Hungarians | 477,000 | 2.3 |
| Turks | 129,000 | 0.6 |
| Slovaks | 84,000 | 0.4 |
| Gypsies | 78,000 | 0.4 |
| Total population | 20,151,000 | 100.0 |

Based on the 1971 Census of Yugoslavia.
*The word *Yugoslav* was chosen by the number shown to describe their nationality.

the Cyrillic script identical to that of Russia, except for a few letters. In addition to Serbia itself, the Serbs form a majority in the fertile Vojvodina north of the Danube and about two-fifths of the population in Bosnia-Hercegovina. Because of historical traditions the Montenegrins are recognized as a separate nationality, though they are closely related to the Serbs. Slavic groups account for 80 percent of Yugoslavia's population.

Macedonia long was a cradle of conflict among Serbia, Bulgaria, and Greece. Now hardly any Macedonians are left in Greece and very few in Bulgaria. Though there are a number of transitional dialects, the standard version of Macedonian is very close to Bulgarian, and their predominant religion is Orthodox, although some are Muslims. Traditions more than any specific trait keep alive a feeling of nationhood in spite of—or because of?—pressures from all sides. Macedonians fared badly under the old Serbian centralist government, when even the use of their speech in public was forbidden. Now that they form one of the people's republics, the tensions have eased.

Other minorities make up the remainder of Yugoslavia's population, each concentrated in some part of the country. More than a million Albanians, principally Muslims, live in the southwest, most of them in the autonomous Kosmet region. Their language is not Slavic but a vestige of the Illyrian spoken in the peninsula before the Slav invasions. To complicate things more, there are also Muslims of Serbo-Croat speech in Bosnia; and in Vojvodina a half million Magyars and about fifty thousand German-speaking peoples are the remnant of much larger colonies before the last war. To top off the hodgepodge of peoples in Yugoslavia, Slovaks live in the north, Romanians in the very northeast corner, Bulgarians along the east border, and some tens of thousands of Turks and Gypsies throughout the country.

Even the most conscientious territorial partitioner cannot do justice to such a mosaic of groups. Moreover, ethnic differences correspond roughly to levels of living: highest among Slovenes and Croats in the northwest, lowest among Albanians and Macedonians in the southeast. Under President Tito's leadership the age-old rivalries have lessened but not vanished. A crucial test of the republic's coherence may come after he passes from the scene.

## GERMAN EXPANSION AND CONTRACTION

Germany's location between West and East inevitably gave her a special role. On the European plain beyond the ancient Roman Empire lived Germanic tribes, and east of them were Slavs. At the time of Charlemagne (A.D. 800) the boundary between the two ran from about where Lübeck is now, along the middle Elbe and its tributary the Saale, to the Bohemian Forest. Shortly thereafter began the German push eastward (*Drang nach Osten*), a combination of crusade against the pagans, settlement by land-hungry peasants, and expansion of the German feudal system. The domain between the Elbe and the Oder became solidly German. Marshes as well as increasing Polish resistance hampered further advance straight eastward, but was easier northeast along the coast of Prussia and southeast up the Oder into Silesia. The Germans soon outnumbered the Slavic groups that remained in these two wings. In addition, an eastward thrust along the Danube created amidst the Slavs the frontier province of Austria (*Ostmark*, "eastern march"; *Oesterreich*). Germans also spilled across the mountain wall surrounding Bohemia-Moravia, gaining the majority in most of the mountain valleys and establishing substantial communities in the cities of the basin itself (Figure 7-3).

Many Germans migrated beyond these territories, but they had to be content with more modest roles. German merchants and craftsmen formed an important element in many eastern European cities. German gentry owned large estates in the Baltic countries. To demonstrate better farming methods, German peasants were invited to set up agricultural colonies in Russian, Hungarian, and Romanian wastelands or amidst the local folk. Their different language, religion, and socioeconomic status impeded assimilation. German expansionists of the nineteenth and twentieth centuries always considered these settlers in eastern Europe as planters of *Kultur* amidst the barbarians and as the advance guard of the future empire.

The defeat of Germany in World War II wiped out much of 1,000 years of eastward expansion. Virtually all Germans had to leave the lands east of the new Polish frontier along the lower Oder and its tributary the Neisse. The

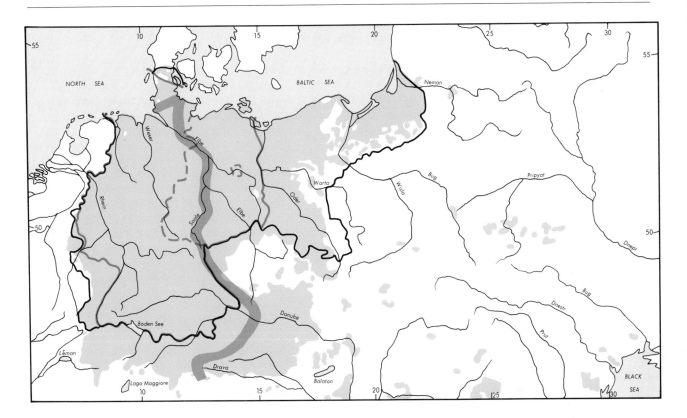

FIGURE
7-3
AREAS OF GERMAN SPEECH IN 1939, AND POLITI-
CAL BOUNDARIES OF GERMANY BEFORE 1918 AND
AFTER 1945

———— Boundary of Germany 1871-1918

———— German Boundary after 1945

- - - - Boundary between East and West Germany after 1945

 Areas of German Speech, 1939

 Eastern Boundary of German Speech ca. 800 A.D.

Miles
0      100      200
100   200   300
Kilometers

Czechoslovaks cleared the Germans out of their country. The remainder of Germany was divided into two republics, the Russians controlling the eastern one, thus extending their hegemony as far as the line Lübeck–Elbe–Saale–Bohemian Forest—roughly the same boundary as that in the ninth century between Germanic and Slavic tribes. Between 1944 and 1950 more than 12 million ethnic Germans moved from eastern Europe to the remaining territories west of the Oder-Neisse boundary. Subsequently nearly 3 million moved from East to West Germany. Once Germany was a buffer between east and west, the heart of a *Mitteleuropa* she hoped to rule someday. Now the buffer zone has shrunk to a line—the "iron curtain."

## WESTERN EUROPE

Most western European states long have had the advantage of substantial national uniformity and coherence. An important cultural division is that between the Romance and the Germanic parts. The two meet in a transition zone which merits closer inspection.

When the Treaty of Verdun (A.D. 843) partitioned Charlemagne's empire between his three grandsons, one received what now is France without its eastern section, another what now is Germany east of the Rhine, the third the Low Countries to central Italy, including eastern France, Switzerland, and Germany west of the Rhine. This middle kingdom soon fell apart under pressures from both sides. But to this very day the belt shows up as a transitional zone in Switzerland, through Alsace-Lorraine and Luxembourg to Belgium. Alsace, originally and today a German-speaking region, came more and more under French cultural influence, though in many ways the Alsatians themselves are neither French nor German. The same can be said of Luxembourg, where both French and a German vernacular are spoken. Switzerland and Belgium deserve special attention because they show different aspects of the polyethnic state.

**Switzerland (Figure 7-4)**  The territory of this federation consists of three landform regions: the parallel limestone ridges of the Jura bordering France; the Swiss plateau to the east, a fertile rolling land which covers only one-third of the country but contains 70 percent of the population; the Alpine area consisting of over half of Switzerland, from Lake Constance (*Bodensee*) to Lake Geneva (*Léman*). Across this high watershed moved medieval trade between north Europe and Italy. In the thirteenth century the main route shifted from the St. Bernard Pass to the St. Gotthard. The German emperors, eager to preserve this access route to Italy, freed the mountaineers on the northern approaches to the pass from feudal control on the condition that they would prevent neighboring lords from gaining possession of it. From this small nucleus of free peasants grew the present confederacy. All groups—whatever their language—entered the union because they adhered to the democratic principles of the original cantons. They wanted no part in the dreams of empire their big neighbors cherished, nor did they wish to dominate their partners in their fledgling commonwealth.

Of Switzerland's 6.4 million population, 72 percent speak as mother tongue one of several German dialects, but they share standard German as the literary language. Along the western border, French is the language of 21 percent. Another 6 percent in the canton of Ticino speak Italian, and 1 percent in part of the eastern canton of Graubünden (Grisons) speak Romansh, a relic of the Latin vernacular. All four languages have equality at the federal level. There is no uniformity of religion: two-fifths have a Catholic heritage, three-fifths Protestant (mainly the Reformed sect). There is some concentration of each faith but also much interpenetration.

In spite of this diversity the Swiss have developed a strong national cohesion. Each cultural group, secure in its right to live according to its own traditions, shares with all the others a common set of national values which evolved—not without trial and error—over six centuries. The formula seems a good one for any composite state. It would be nice if countries were like human individuals. One could call in the doctor, who after making the right diagnosis would prescribe the Swiss cure, which the patient would faithfully follow until complete recovery. Alas, allegory is not reality.

**Belgium (Figure 7-5)**  The Kingdom of Belgium presents an interesting case of changing relationships between two groups long united in one political entity. The people in the northern part speak Flemish. Their dialects merge with those of the Dutch across the border, and the standard language is identical with Dutch. In the south live the Walloons, French-speaking in dialect forms as well as in standard language. The line dividing the two language areas dates back to early medieval times. Originally Flemish was spoken as far west as the Heights of Artois, near Calais in France, but under French pressure it retreated. Today the line starts on the French channel coast at Dunkirk, curves south and east, and enters Belgium near Flemish Kortrijk (*Courtrai*). From this point it runs east through the rolling plain to the south tip of the Netherlands near Maastricht. In Belgium this boundary has remained virtually unmoved since early medieval times; only the capital city of Brussels (*Brussel* in Flemish, *Bruxelles* in French) has

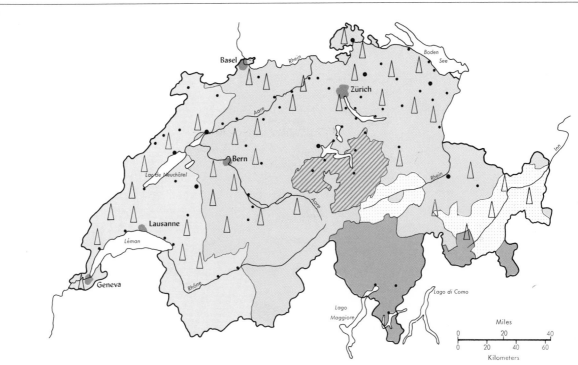

FIGURE **SWITZERLAND**
7-4

This map shows the cantons which formed the original confederation of A.D. 1291 (Obwalden, Nidwalden, Schwyz, Uri). The map does not show the important linguistic and religious minorities present in the main towns.

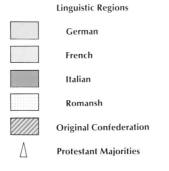

Main Towns

Other Important Settlements

Linguistic Regions

German

French

Italian

Romansh

Original Confederation

Protestant Majorities

changed to an enclave of predominantly French speech.

It is far from clear why and how this boundary came to rest where it is. Apparently the invading Franks retained their Germanic speech in the north and gave it up in the south where they intermingled with the romanized Celts. The presence of sparsely settled, heavy forests at that time across the center of Belgium may have acted as a divider between the two groups. Most of Belgium, together with the Netherlands, formed part of the middle kingdom (A.D. 843), later of the Burgundian domain, and then of the Hapsburg empire.

The wars of the Reformation split the Low Countries. Holland and associated provinces—now the Netherlands—gained their independence from Hapsburg Spain as a Protestant nation. Spain with the help of the Jesuits firmly reestablished Catholicism in the southern part—now Belgium. For more than three centuries Belgium remained subject to foreign rule: Spanish, Austrian, and French. After the Napoleonic Wars the Great Powers united Belgium with the Netherlands to form a barrier against France, but the

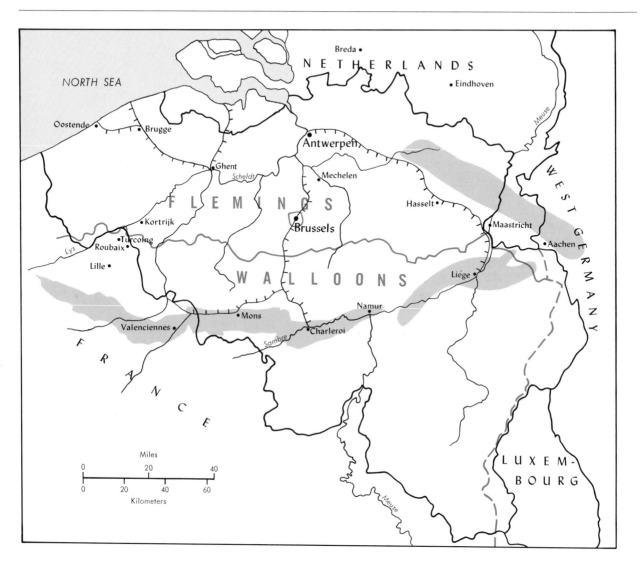

FIGURE **BELGIUM**
7-5

*Internal political problems derive mostly from the antagonisms between French-speaking Walloons and the Flemings.*

| | |
|---|---|
| ——— | **National Boundaries** |
| ⊢⊢⊢ | **Principal Canals** |
| ——— | **French-Flemish Linguistic Boundary** |
| – – – | **French-German Linguistic Boundary** |
| ▨ | **Coalfields** |

two peoples had grown too far apart, and the forced marriage ended in divorce in 1831.

Through the centuries French cultural influence had gained ground, not only among the Walloons but also among the upper-class Flemings. Moreover, the Industrial Revolution mainly benefited the Walloons because the coal mines and associated industries were in the south. French became the language of the government, the army, the court, the universities. Not to speak French meant exclusion from all positions of leadership. The nationalistic spirit of the nineteenth century led the Flemings to insist on equality; this they finally and fully attained after World War I.

The Walloons since then have felt increasingly uncertain about their position in the kingdom. The rate of population growth is higher among the Flemings than the Walloons so that now the former have the majority (55 percent). Other issues crystallize around the linguistic differences. Economically the Flemish north has recently developed faster than the south. The busy ports of Antwerp (*Antwerpen*) and Ghent (*Gent*) and the adjacent new coalfields in Campine (*Kempen*) have stimulated industrial growth, while the south but slowly modernizes its older and out-of-date industrial economy.

In addition, there are sociopolitical conflicts. Although the entire population is nominally Catholic, the Flemings are usually strong supporters of the Church, while the Walloons—like the French—tend to be anticlerical. The Catholic Church strongly supports the Christian-Socialist party, the largest in the country and essentially Flemish. The Socialist party, second in size, is mainly Walloon. The different political attitudes show up on many questions, causing ever sharper antagonisms.

The fact that both France and the Netherlands scrupulously have avoided involvement in the conflict has discouraged any serious thoughts of dissolving the state and joining the parts to neighboring countries. The past cannot be undone. Belgium is neither French nor Dutch. The moderates on both sides agreed in 1970 on a policy of cultural autonomy and economic decentralization instead of the outright federalism that some Flemish and Walloon groups desired. The French-speaking capital city of Brussels—in Flemish territory—was given special status.

## NATIONAL INDEPENDENCE
## AND ECONOMIC INTERDEPENDENCE

In the larger view, the trouble with modern Europe lies not in internal minority problems but in the fragmentation of space among the nation-states themselves. Broadly speaking, the nation-states represent areas of settlement dating back to the Middle Ages; but the technology and economy are of the late twentieth century. Disparities and tensions are everywhere. The coking coal of

the Ruhr is in Germany, the iron ore in France; the port of Trieste is Italian, but its hinterland largely Yugoslav and Austrian; the Rhine and Scheldt rivers flow through several countries but have their North Sea outlets in the Netherlands. Less obvious but even more restricting are the different social and economic systems that have grown up behind the national boundaries, each protecting its own interests and its own culture against outside competition. Many question whether the whole economic thrust of the past two centuries represents unadulterated progress and argue that the cultural and economic costs of international integration may come too high.

Efforts to overcome the throttling effects of fragmentation have been made for some time, for instance, by internationalizing rivers. More recent actions hold great promise for really significant integration. Following World War II and spurred on by the Marshall Plan of massive economic help from the United States, the Europeans began to build supranational institutions. In 1951 six European countries (France, Germany, Italy, Belgium, the Netherlands, Luxembourg) created the European Coal and Steel Community, a federal institution to which the individual states transferred powers over limited fields of activity. In 1958 came the European Economic Community (EEC), called the Common Market, a giant stride toward economic and ultimately political unity (Figure 7-6).

The United Kingdom, torn between its commitments to the Commonwealth, its perceived "special relationship" to the United States, and its connections with the European continent, passed up the initial chance to participate. Attempts to join were turned back in 1963 and in 1968 but succeeded in 1971. Formal membership came in 1973. At the same time Ireland and Denmark, two of Britain's close trading partners, also joined, but Norway rejected membership in a referendum. Negotiations for additional members were under way in 1976. The EEC has special arrangements for countries that were former colonial territories of the European members, especially of France and Britain.

The Common Market thus comprises nine countries with a total population of over 260 million. In the production of goods and services it surpasses the Soviet Union by far and equals the United States. The founding member states com-

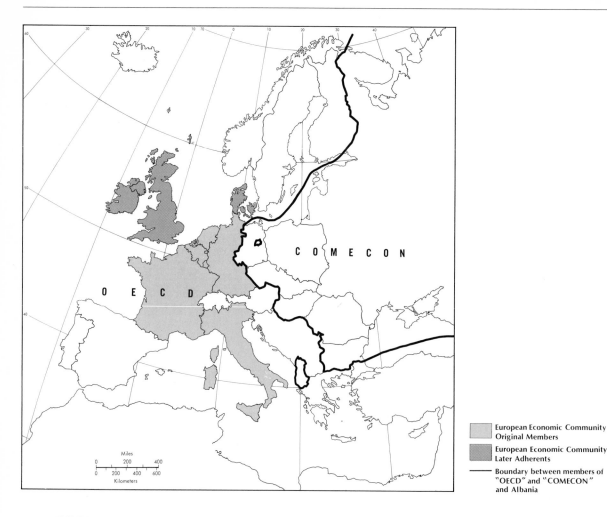

Miles
0    200    400
0  200  400  600
Kilometers

European Economic Community
Original Members

European Economic Community
Later Adherents

Boundary between members of
"OECD" and "COMECON"
and Albania

FIGURE **INTEGRATION IN EUROPE**
7-6

This map shows the situation in 1977. All European countries (except Albania which has strong associations with the People's Republic of China) belong to either the Organization for Economic Cooperation and Development (OECD) or the Council for Mutual Economic Assistance (COMECON). Belgium, Netherlands, and Luxembourg formed a customs union (BENELUX) in 1944. After long negotiation, these countries with France, West Germany, and Italy signed the Treaty of Rome to form the Common Market, or European Economic Community (EEC). The same six countries made up the European Coal and Steel Community (ECSC) and the European Atomic Energy Community (EURATOM). In 1971–1972, the United Kingdom, Denmark, and the Republic of Ireland negotiated membership of the Common Market. OECD countries which

do not belong to the expanded EEC continue to develop special arrangements to maintain their trading links.

mitted themselves to remove customs duties between themselves, establish a common tariff for outsiders, and abolish obstacles to the free movement of persons, services, and capital. Various procedures and agencies were set up to carry out these aims. Although often clumsy and slow-moving, the process of economic integration seems irreversible despite the strains caused by the energy crisis. By 1980 an elected parliament will be meeting, leading inevitably to some form of political union in which each member relinquishes important parts of its sovereignty. Such aims are far beyond a customs union or free trade zone. To harmonize national traditions and institutions posed difficult problems for the six original members. The addition of Britain and other recent members made these issues even more formidable. The challenge is great but so will be the results. After 2,000 years West Europe can even surpass the dreams of Charlemagne and stand among the world powers as an equal of the Soviet Union, the United States, and China.

In eastern Europe the desire for integration led in 1949 to the formation of the COMECON (Council for Mutual Economic Assistance), consisting of the Soviet Union, Poland, East Germany, Czechoslovakia, Hungary, Romania, and Bulgaria. Initially the Soviet Union tried to force the others into accepting a division of tasks in which each satellite country would continue to develop the specialty to which its economy had been geared until then. Such a scheme would have been especially detrimental to the agrarian countries—Hungary, Romania, Bulgaria—which aspired to a more diversified economy. Determined opposition led to more flexible forms of cooperation which take into account the varied needs of all states concerned. Economic integration is being gradually worked out. Because some countries objected, especially independent-minded Romania, the Soviet Union gave up its idea of supranational economic organization. The current program calls for all COMECON countries to participate in opening up mineral deposits and improving transportation, including pipelines. Free convertibility of currencies, though essential for economic integration, does not exist and apparently will not come in the near future.

At this stage we cannot ascertain the final outcome of the European drives toward integration, but one observation must be made. A political boundary is like a bundle of limits to legal, social, and economic systems. Necessarily, boundaries within a bloc such as the Common Market lose several of these functions. On the other hand, where boundaries coincide with the line between opposing ideologies, they form greater barriers than ever. There is no better illustration of this than the ease with which a traveler moves from one EEC country to the next, in contrast to the wall and no-man's-land dividing East and West Germany.

## THE FRANCO-CANADIANS

European settlement overseas generally led to much larger territorial units than the cramped national compartments of the homeland. It also brought about a blending of various immigrant groups. All the more interesting, therefore, is the case of the French-speaking population of Canada (Figure 7-7).

When England acquired Canada from France in 1763, it brought under its rule some 65,000 French who then formed the chief body of European settlers in that colony. About 1830 their number had grown to about 250,000, but Tocqueville described them as "the wreck of an old people lost in the flood of a new nation." Many people, at least British settlers in Canada as well as those in the United States, must have agreed with him. Now those in Canada number over 7 million, close to one-third of the population, and they are as conscious as ever of their collective personality.

That they survive as a separate group is all the more remarkable because no mother country keeps the national ties alive, and no brutal foreign rule welds the bonds of common suffering. The Franco-Canadians share language, religion, and tradition. This might not have prevented their absorption into the English-speaking Canadian majority had they not solidly occupied a territory and made it their genuine homeland. Here in Québec province they form four-fifths of the population. In addition, substantial numbers live in adjacent parts of the Maritime Provinces, where they make up over one-third of the population of New Brunswick, and in Ontario, where they form one-tenth.

Their core land lies along the St. Lawrence. As their numbers grew, they spread up the Saguenay River to Lake St. John, and along the Ottawa River. South and east of the St. Lawrence they moved into the Eastern Townships, where they are now the dominant element. In the eighteenth century the English deported and dispersed a large part of the French settlers from New Brunswick and Nova Scotia (Acadia), but later *Les Acadiens* moved back again. Scattered colonies were also established on the prairies. Many mi-

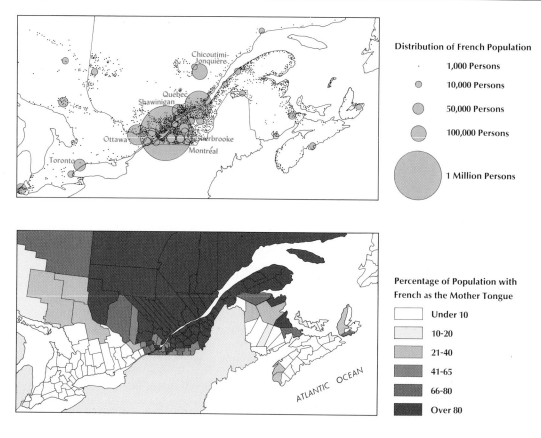

**Distribution of French Population**

·      1,000 Persons

◦      10,000 Persons

○      50,000 Persons

○      100,000 Persons

○      1 Million Persons

**Percentage of Population with French as the Mother Tongue**

☐      Under 10

☐      10-20

☐      21-40

☐      41-65

☐      66-80

☐      Over 80

FIGURE **"LES FRANCO-CANADIENS"**
**7-7**

These maps show two aspects of the French Canadian population: (1) Distribution, using dots and circles to locate them; (2) A percentage of total population, by census divisions. Sources of data: *National Atlas of Canada,* Ottawa, 1957, 1970, and *Census of Canada, 1970.*

grated to the United States, which now has more than 2 million people of Franco-Canadian stock, mostly located in the Northeastern states.

In the seventeenth century and first half of the eighteenth, the French government encouraged farm settlement in the St. Lawrence Valley, chiefly through a quasi-manorial system whereby peasants (*habitants*) farmed the lands granted to noblemen. Most of the peasants as well as coastal fishermen had come from Normandy, Brittany, and other parts of northern France. Only the Catholic French were admitted. Since France

showed little interest in Québec, the provincial governor and the Church shared the responsibility for the welfare of the population.

When England took over Canada, many French aristocrats left the country, and the Church remained as the only source of leadership. The Quebec Act of 1774 guaranteed freedom of worship, language, and customs, the latter as embodied in the local civil law. Whatever feelings of loyalty were left toward France disappeared during the French Revolution when the motherland turned against the Catholic Church. Québec's freedom of religion attracted a number of Catholic refugee priests from France. The Church maintained a strong position, especially through the educational system which, until recently, was managed by mixed committees of clergy and laity. The prominent and well-frequented churches, the processions and other religious festivals show the strong bond between *les Québecois* and their beliefs. They preserved the virtues of their peasant tradition as hardworking, sober, and conservative people. Formerly they had a higher reproduction rate than their English-speaking neighbors and doubled their numbers every generation, thereby keeping pace with the natural growth plus immigration to the rest of Canada. Lately, however, the size of their families has been shrinking until now the birth rate is lower than that of Ontario.

In former times many sons sought new farmland (others became priests or teachers), but now most of them find work in factories and offices. In the past large numbers moved to the textile towns of New England. In recent decades, though, branch factories of various kinds have been established in Québec, using the plentiful local labor supply. Montréal's big business is mainly in the hands of English Canadians or Americans, who also own and manage many industries elsewhere in Québec. Franco-Canadians fill a relatively low proportion of positions in the federal service at any level. Quite understandably, they are unhappy about this state of affairs.

Devotion to their own *genre de vie* joins with dissatisfaction with their role in Canadian life. They assume that "progress" will wipe out their traditional values, and they do not want to sell their heritage. Moreover, they retain a strong sense of "perpetual injury and frustration," from the memories of English misdeeds in Acadia to the feeling that *les Anglais* set the national goals without regard for Franco-Canadian aspirations. Over and over the divergent outlooks have led to crisis. For example, in two world wars Franco-Canadians opposed conscription because they were against involvement in "those English wars." At other times there has been friction because the Franco-Canadians desired constitutional changes which would assure them a stronger position in the federation as a whole while safeguarding their own way of life.

The growth of separatist sentiment coincides with similar feelings in European countries, for example, Scotland and Wales. In 1976 *les Québecois*—at least those who voted in the provincial election—put the party dedicated to the political independence of Québec into power for the first time. *La Partie Québecois* promised a separate referendum on the independence question. This may have helped them win the election although, according to public opinion polls, only 10 to 20 percent favor separation.

## DIVERSITY IN POSTCOLONIAL ASIAN AND AFRICAN STATES

Until after World War II, European powers held huge colonial territories in Asia, Africa, and tropical America. Often these territories consisted of diverse peoples held together by the ruling power. Homogeneous culture areas were carved up with a slice going to each competing colonial state. Economic change, administrative organization, and the trappings of imperial power sometimes forced coherence on different cultures and tribal groups, but these external forces rarely led to the creation of a nation.

Nevertheless, in the postwar world the old colonial lands became independent states. The problems of nation building dominated the early years, often under the leadership of Western-educated elites. It is hardly surprising, therefore, that many new states show great regional diversity, sectionalism, rebellious minorities, plural societies, irredentist claims—if not all of these problems, at least a combination of some of them.

For many of these heterogeneous countries a federation might be a better structure than a unitary state. The ruling group, however, often fears that in a loose federation the centrifugal forces of subnationalism or tribalism would tear the state apart, and thus it prefers to keep centralized control (for example, Indonesia). In other cases the diversity is so obvious that a federation or a confederacy is the only way to launch the new ship of state (as in Nigeria, Malaysia). Many of these new states are still in an experimental phase. Must these countries go through the painful stages that Europe experienced: tribalism, nationalism, and "Balkanization"? Can they find a shortcut to supranational cooperation and political integration? From the many problem areas in the Caribbean, Africa, and Asia, we select two samples: the Indian subcontinent and Nigeria. Then we discuss Malaysia, as an example of the problems of plural societies.

Following a decade of fighting for liberation, Mozambique celebrated independence from five centuries of Portuguese rule on June 25, 1975. The scene is at Maputo (formerly Laurenço Marques), the capital of the new country. (Photograph—United Nations)

## THE INDIAN SUBCONTINENT
## (FIGURES 5-6 AND 7-8)

In an area as large as the Indian subcontinent and with such a long, tempestuous history, we must expect a great variety of races, religions, languages, and social organizations. British rule tolerated particularism and even found it useful for maintaining its hold according to the old Roman maxim of "divide and conquer." On the other hand, it imposed on this land many institutions and a network of transportation which greatly aided in forming the present large states.

In recent times religion has been the chief cause of internal conflict; but in India religion involves a far wider sphere than in Western nations. Being a Hindu (actually a Hindu belonging to a specific caste), or being a Muslim, Sikh, Jain, Parsee, or Christian conditions or even determines one's diet, dress, calendar, holidays, and—more important—education, social status, and economic activities. In short, religion is the main constraint on one's code and mode of life. In Indian politics as well as in the census, the term *community* is often used to express the notion that more than creed distinguishes the various religious groupings.

**The Partition of 1947** When independence loomed ahead, the leaders of the Muslim minority insisted on a territorial partition along communal lines. According to the census of 1941, the population of the entire British Indian Empire was 387 million, of whom 92 million (24 percent) were Muslims. However, only the western borderlands solidly adhered to Islam. In the Punjab there was a gradation from over 90 percent in the west to 30 percent in the east. Eastern Bengal also held a concentration of Muslims, consisting of about three-fourths of the local population. A substantial number lived throughout the rest of the subcontinent.

After long and bitter negotiations, a partition plan was finally agreed upon in 1947. It created the new states of India and Pakistan, the latter split into the West (23 million Muslims, according to the 1941 census) and the East (30 million Muslims). Some 39 million brothers in the faith were to remain in India and some 20 million non-Muslims in Pakistan. Large population transfers took place, partly in panicky flight from bloody riots immediately following partition, partly in more orderly fashion during subsequent years. As a result, the western part became almost entirely Muslim; the east remained more mixed and counted 16 percent Hindu in 1961, with the proportion decreasing slowly as the years passed.

**India's Linguistic Diversity** The sovereign Republic of India is about one-third the size of the United States and has a population of 660 million (1977). During the colonial era the British directly governed the territories and the so-called provinces. In addition, hundreds of princely holdings, ranging in size from mere estates to big countries, all gathered under British suzerainty by treaties, were almost fully autonomous in domestic affairs. Following independence, this archaic structure was streamlined by mergers, a real step forward toward national unity and more efficient administration.

But nationalism can also be a divisive force if it imbues a local people with a consciousness of its own distinct character. While the territorial reorganization was in progress, voices called for a division according to linguistic units. India has over 150 languages—not counting hundreds of dialects—but only a dozen are spoken by sufficiently large numbers to be politically significant (say, about 5 million). To redivide the country along linguistic lines would disrupt many existing economic relationships and, worse, might seriously undermine incipient Indian national unity. Nevertheless, persistent demands compelled the government to accept the linguistic principle as the major criterion in establishing new states.

The state of Andhra was cut from the old province of Madras to give the Telegu-speaking people a unit separate from their Tamil neighbors. Added to Andhra was the Telegu-speaking section carved from the large Deccan region of Hyderabad. The part of Hyderabad where the Kannada live became joined with areas of the same predominant language in southern Bombay province to create the new state Mysore. The remainder of Hyderabad, together with a section of Bombay province, gave the proud Marathis of northwestern Deccan a state of their own. This caused serious conflicts with the Gujarati-speaking group in Bombay city, who control the trade and dislike being dominated by the Marathis. The northern parts of former Bombay province were incorporated into Gujarat State.

Although the Sikhs joined India at the time of the partition, they insisted on their group individuality. In 1961 there were 7.8 million Sikhs in India, 6.8 million concentrated in Punjab state, where they constituted one-third of the population. To gain a more favorable position, they agitated for a territorial revision, ostensibly to create a Punjabi-speaking state, but actually to make a unit in which Sikhs would have the majority. In 1966 the government of India gave in. In the reduced new Punjab state, the Sikhs constitute slightly over half the population. The other part of the former Punjab, now called Haryana, speaks mainly Hindi.

With all this linguistic subnationalism, there is need that one language serve as means of communication for all of India. Hindi, the main language of the north, spoken in various versions by some 280 million, was chosen for this purpose. To effect this decision requires a tremendous educational effort. Resistance in the south against Hindi—which has its own Devangari script—has been so strong that English remains the lingua franca among educated people and serves as the chief vehicle for government affairs and for higher education.

Among the other minorities in India, the 12 million Christians, most of them in the southwestern state of Kerala, are less militant but often important in local political issues and economic affairs. The 2 million Jains, a distinct Hindu sect concentrated in Gujarat and Rajasthan, has considerable influence all through northern India and includes many traders and bankers. The Parsees, followers of the ancient Persian religion of Zoroaster, hold an economic position out of all proportion to their number of a mere 100,000. Most of them live in the Bombay area, among them many powerful industrialists and financiers, such as the Tata family.

**Pakistan and Bangladesh**  The partition into India and Pakistan severed many bonds of interdependence that had developed during British rule. The tragedy was compounded by the politically awkward structure of Pakistan, which consisted of two sections a thousand miles apart, two blocs strikingly different except that their populations had the same creed. Events in 1971 shattered this uneasy union when East Pakistan declared its independence and adopted the name Bangladesh (land of the Bengali). To understand the background of the conflict, we need to know the basic geographic features of the two parts, which now are called Pakistan (formerly West Pakistan) and Bangladesh (East Pakistan).

Pakistan is a semiarid to arid country with 75 million inhabitants. Its core is the densely populated and fairly prosperous western Punjab, where wheat and cotton are produced with canal irrigation. To the northeast lies Kashmir, whence come the rivers, Pakistan's lifeblood. The Northwest Frontier is inherited from the British, together with all its problems of tribal warfare, raids, and doubtful loyalties. In the south lies the dry Sind, where large-scale irrigation works have created a zone of rice and cotton farming.

Bangladesh, in contrast, is a water-soaked delta, intensively cultivated, with rice its main food crop. Only the size of Arkansas, it contains 82 million inhabitants with an average population density of over 1,400 per square mile. It is not surprising that the mass of people live in shocking poverty, always with a food deficit. Jute provides the great cash crop. When the partition of 1947 assigned to India the port-metropolis and jute-processing center of Calcutta, Bangladesh—then East Pakistan—was virtually decapitated. It built some jute mills of its own and developed a seaport at Chittagong, but unfortunately the location was offside the commercial routes.

Associated with the differences in ways of life, each Muslim region has its own culture. The main languages of Pakistan are Punjabi and Sindhi, with Urdu as the lingua franca, whereas Bangladesh speaks Bengali. The peoples of Pakistan have a long tradition of militant Islamism and feel close to other Muslims of the Middle East. They proudly remember their conquest of India under the Moguls and earlier dynasties. The Bengalis have no such traditions and descend mainly from converted lower-caste Hindus. No wonder the idea of Pakistan was not born there but in western India, whence came the driving power to establish the new state.

The disparity between east and west as well as internal dissension within the western part built up tensions which by 1970 could no longer be ignored. To ease the situation, West Pakistan divided into four provinces along linguistic lines, each with home rule. Much more crucial, however, was the bitter discontent in East Pakistan. The Bengalis felt exploited by their western compatriots, who dominated the civil service, the military, industry, and business. Their jute export provided foreign exchange but the funds, as well as foreign aid, were used to develop distant West Pakistan.

To solve the fundamental problem of state organization, the Bengalis formed a national assembly to draw up a new constitution. For the first time, based on the principle of one man one vote, the main East Pakistan party won an absolute majority. West Pakistan, faced with the loss of its privileged position and even with the possibility that East Pakistan might secede, struck with military force and occupied the country. Some 9 million persons, mostly Hindus, fled to India. An underground government proclaimed independence for East Pakistan, naming it Bangladesh. These events gave India the chance to intervene. She defeated West Pakistan's occupation army and supported the independence of Bangladesh. Thus India gained a client state in the east and greatly reduced the danger that the rump state of Pakistan would attack her west flank.

FIGURE **SOUTH ASIA: POLITICAL DIVISIONS**
7-8

Compare this map with Figure 5-6. Note the correspondence of languages and states within India and the lack of correspondence between linguistic and international boundaries. The states and territories of India are named.

**The Kashmir Conflict**  In the western part of the high mountains, reaching from Karakorum across the Himalayas to the edge of Punjab, lies the state of Jammu and Kashmir, as it was officially named in prepartition days. A Hindu prince ruled it then, but three-fourths of his subjects were Muslims. The upper Jhelum Valley, the Vale of Kashmir, formed its core land. Muslim mountain folks lived to the north and west. Mongoloid tribes lightly inhabited the east toward Tibet—Muslim or Buddhist in religion but Tibetan in language. China now controls and occupies part of this area as well as Tibet. In the southern portion of Jammu, Muslims made up a small majority (53 percent in 1947) over Hindus and other communities but now are less than half the population.

At the time Kashmir was partitioned, the Maharajah, faced by communal riots and invasions by Muslim tribesmen, used his princely prerogative to join India. India's claim to this area rests upon this legal fact of accession. She sent troops and Pakistan counterattacked, but when a cease-fire line was finally established in 1949, India held most of the country. Her part contains most of the 5 million inhabitants and virtually all the agricultural lands. The Pakistanis argue that this area should have been joined with their state because it has a Muslim majority and is contiguous to Pakistan. The Indians maintain that most of the Muslims do not want to associate with Pakistan. Only a free plebiscite—to which India had agreed in principle—could prove this contention. Meanwhile she pushed social and economic reforms in an attempt to gain friends and influence.

In late 1965 the tension over Kashmir led to a new armed conflict, which ended under severe diplomatic pressure from the Soviet Union and the United States. No resolution of the dispute is in sight. An independent Kashmir, even supposing that both parties would agree to this, seems hardly viable. Pakistan and India could work together only if both countries were on good terms, a condition that obviously does not exist. The cease-fire line meanwhile remains the boundary.

The loss of Kashmir is far more important to Pakistan than its gain to India. Kashmir forms part of the watershed of the western Punjab and thus controls—at least theoretically—Pakistan's supplies for irrigation and hydroelectric power. In the past most economic relations that Kashmir had with the outside world were through what is now Pakistan. To offset the traditional trade routes, India has built several highways and a railroad joining her with Kashmir.

## NIGERIA (FIGURE 7-9)

The most populous of Africa's fifty states and territories is the Federation of Nigeria with an estimated 84 million inhabitants. In area it surpasses the combined six countries that fringe the Guinea Coast to the west. Its large territory contains a polyethnic conglomerate that the British glued together during their century of colonial rule. Now Nigeria must prove its ability to balance political unity against cultural diversity. Forty-four percent of the population is Muslim, 35 percent Christian, and the remainder belong to various tribal religions. There are an estimated four hundred languages, of which almost fifty have enough standing to be used in radio broadcasting. Nigeria offers a good illustration of the dilemma many African countries face in their attempts to create national coherence among the welter of communities that a former colonial power assembled under its rule.

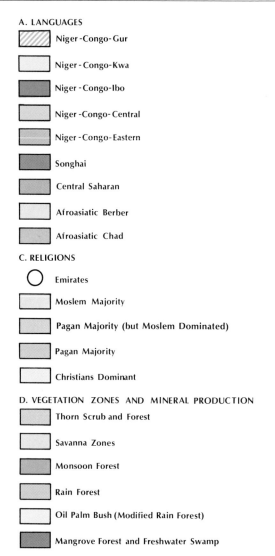

**A. LANGUAGES**

Niger-Congo-Gur

Niger-Congo-Kwa

Niger-Congo-Ibo

Niger-Congo-Central

Niger-Congo-Eastern

Songhai

Central Saharan

Afroasiatic Berber

Afroasiatic Chad

**C. RELIGIONS**

Emirates

Moslem Majority

Pagan Majority (but Moslem Dominated)

Pagan Majority

Christians Dominant

**D. VEGETATION ZONES AND MINERAL PRODUCTION**

Thorn Scrub and Forest

Savanna Zones

Monsoon Forest

Rain Forest

Oil Palm Bush (Modified Rain Forest)

Mangrove Forest and Freshwater Swamp

Nigeria derives its name from the big river that enters the country in the northwest and forms a large delta on the eastern coast. The southern zone, behind the coastal mangrove swamps, carries a dense population which over the years has greatly altered the original tropical forest. In the western part the main language group is the Yoruba, who inhabit large towns that combine the functions of marketplace and residence for the agriculturists. In the east beyond the Niger River live the Ibo and related groups.

## A. LANGUAGES

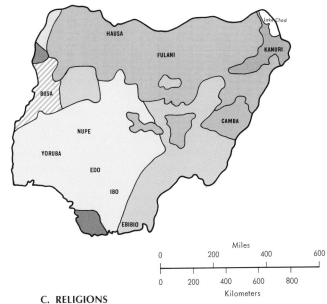

HAUSA
FULANI
KANURI
BUSA
NUPE
CAMBA
YORUBA
EDO
IBO
EBIBIO

## B. STATES, TOWNS, AND COMMUNICATIONS

Sokoto
Kaura Namoda • Katsina • Nguru • Lake Chad
SOKOTO • Kano • KANO • Maiduguri
Zaria • BORNO
KADUNA • BAUCHI
Kaduna • NIGER • Jos
KWARA • PLATEAU
Minna • GONGOLA
OYO • Ilorin • Baro • Benue R.
Oyo • Lokojo • BENUE • Yola
Abeokuta • Ife • ONDO • Makurdi
OGUN • Ibadan • ANAMBARA • Ogoja
LAGOS • Lagos • Benin • CROSS
Bight of Benin • Onitsha • RIVERS
BENDEE • Enugu
IMO • Calabar
RIVERS
Gulf of Guinea • Port Harcourt

Miles
0    200    400    600

0    200    400    600    800
Kilometers

## C. RELIGIONS

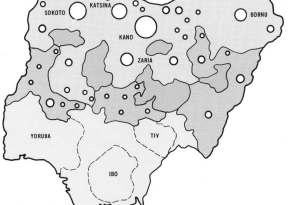

SOKOTO    KATSINA    BORNU
KANO
ZARIA
YORUBA    TIV
IBO

## D. VEGETATION ZONES AND MINERAL PRODUCTION

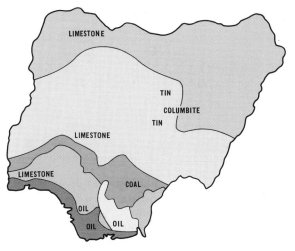

LIMESTONE
TIN
COLUMBITE
TIN
LIMESTONE
LIMESTONE
COAL
OIL
OIL    OIL

FIGURE **NIGERIA**
**7-9**

These maps are based in part of the work of
D. Greenberg, K. M. Buchanan, and J. C. Pugh.

Prior to 1967, Nigeria was divided into four regions:
Northern (four times the area of the others combined), Western, Mid-West, and Eastern. Following the
civil war the country's government was strengthened
at the central level and many new regional administrative units were created.

When the Portuguese arrived on the coast in the latter part of the fifteenth century, they found here well-organized kingdoms and a relatively prosperous population engaged in agriculture and trade, and accomplished in metalworking—including remarkable brass sculpture. Nearly three centuries of slave traffic followed, organized mostly by Europeans and Arabs. During the nineteenth century the British gradually gained control over the coast and ended the slave trade. Christian missionaries followed the flag and established schools. As a result, the great majority of inhabitants in this southern zone are Christians and possess at least an elementary Western form of education.

These peoples, especially the enterprising Ibo, participate actively in supplying world markets with oil palm products, cocoa, rubber, timber, and other export commodities. The Niger delta puts out enough petroleum to place Nigeria among the world's top ten producers. Cities and towns bustle with activity, among them Lagos, the main port and federal capital; Ibadan, the business and university center in the southwestern interior; and Port Harcourt in the delta.

Farther inland in the parklike savanna country lies the sparsely populated area called the "Middle Belt" of Nigeria. For centuries it was desolated by wars and slave raids. The hilly uplands served as refuge to Africans from different tribes who escaped the slave raiders threatening from north and south. In recent times the Jos plateau has gained significance because of large tin deposits.

The northern and drier savanna zone bordering the Sahara Desert has long been in contact with the Mediterranean realm. This is evidenced by the intermingling of Caucasoid and Negroid races, and by the presence of Hamitic languages and of Islam. The Hausa predominate in number, forming the main element in cities such as Kano and Sokoto that developed at the south end of the trans-Saharan caravan routes. Most of the farmers produce grains, cotton, and peanuts, the latter mainly for export.

Hausa kings governed the region until about 1800, when the Fulani gained control. These were nomadic herders who for over three centuries had drifted in among the Hausa. The Fulani replaced the rather lax adherence to Islam by

strict observance in orthodox fashion. As the British extended their rule to this area, they left much power in the hands of the Sultan of Sokoto and the local emirs (Islamic political and religious leaders). Because the Muslims prohibited Christian missions and their schools, there are far fewer Western-educated leaders in the north than in the south.

With the question of independence after World War II, the only hope to maintain Nigeria as one state lay in establishing a federal system. The choice was whether to create a few big subdivisions or to have many, though still manageable, units. Because of their colonial experience, the British saw Nigeria as a threefold division in which the leading peoples were Yoruba, Ibo, and Fulani-Hausa. When Nigeria gained its independence in 1960, this three-region structure (plus Lagos as the federal capital district) was put into effect. The Northern Region included no less than four-fifths of the territory and over half of Nigeria's population, which consisted mostly of Muslim Hausa and, half their number, of Fulani. The Western Region in essence was Yorubaland. The Eastern Region combined the Ibo country with the former kingdom of Benin, west of the Niger. (In the middle sixties the Benin area was split off and given separate regional status.) Because of the multitude of languages, English remained the official vehicle of communication in government, commerce, and higher education. In the north, however, Hausa had long been the lingua franca.

The three-way division soon proved a mistake. The economically advanced and largely Christian south resented the political hegemony of the conservative Muslim north. Numerous minority groups in both regions felt that they had been reduced to second-class citizens. Frustration, dissension, disorder—aggravated by nepotism and corruption—were common.

To a greater extent than any other ethnic group the Ibo had accepted Western values. Many had moved to other parts of the Federation, especially to the north, to exploit new opportunities in civil service and business. Other peoples resented their preeminence in these key positions. In the late 1960s they massacred the Ibo and other eastern "strangers," by the thousands. The Ibo seceded from the Federation and proclaimed Biafra as an independent state. The ensuing civil war lasted more than two years and ended with Biafra's defeat. The union was preserved but at the cost of 2 million deaths, mostly by starvation.

Meanwhile the Federation had been reorganized into twelve instead of three states. Though this arrangement was more realistic than the former, the number could not do justice to Nigeria's heterogeneity. In 1976 the country was reorganized again, this time into nineteen states. The division of northern and central Nigeria weakened the grip the Fulani-Hausa held over this huge area. The creation of new states in the south also freed several minority peoples from Yoruba or Ibo domination. The new structure, though under strong military control, emphasizes the concept of cultural autonomy within "One Nigeria," and gives hope for greater stability in the future.

### PROBLEMS OF PLURAL SOCIETIES

When Europeans first landed on the coasts of eastern Africa and southern Asia, they found there, besides the native peoples, a number of foreign traders—Arab, Indian, or Chinese. The initial phase of European domination was chiefly the struggle to obtain a share or, if possible, a monopoly in the commerce. In the nineteenth century industrialization and urbanization of western Europe created a mass demand for raw materials and food stuffs, such as vegetable oils and fats, tin, and later rubber. In most colonies the native population, living in self-sufficient village communities, proved either unable or unwilling to furnish the wage-labor force for plantations, mines, and port or railroad construction works. Moreover, the emerging urban centers had no native middle class to perform the various services from shopkeeper to artisan and business clerk. Laborers were imported for this from India or China. After serving their contract terms, many started petty businesses of their own. Others came as traders and moneylenders to profit from the expanding economy, continuing their traditional roles, but in larger numbers.

The new economic growth thus was reflected fully in the occupations of the ethnic groups. Indigenous farming people formed the broad base of the social pyramid. Europeans who held executive positions in government and private enterprise were at the top. In the middle, Chinese, Indians, and Arabs served as wage laborers, also increasingly as intermediaries between native mass and ruling group. In this way normal economic competition between big and little business, capital and labor, agrarian producers and city folk was combined with the rivalry among ethnic, cultural, even racial groups. Though all met in the marketplace, each kept to itself, with its own values and standards of conduct. The hierarchy resembled a caste system but without the metaphysical rationale and religious sanction of the Indian system (see Boeke, 1942, and Furnivall, 1939 and 1941).

Inevitably there was friction, but there could be no political struggle as long as the colonial authority held the reins of control. All this changed when colonial rule ended in World War II and afterwards. The plural society had to find a common set of values and a common purpose if the new state were to survive. The indigenous people felt that they were masters of the land and that their culture patterns should prevail. Other groups, including Europeans, opposed a stiff-necked execution of this maxim, for it meant they had to choose between assimilation into the native culture and exclusion through either expulsion or denial of citizenship. At a stage when economic development was crucial, removal of "foreigners" would result in the loss of virtually all entrepreneurs. Moreover, the immigrants from China, India, and Arabia, who considered their own culture far superior to that of the native peoples, found assimilation therefore difficult if not impossible.

The problem of the plural society in the modern state and the attempts to resolve it vary according to the local situation. Kenya and Tanzania (East Africa) pressured Indians and Pakistanis to leave. Indonesia under President Sukarno rejected foreign elements regardless of economic consequences. Its neighbor the Federation of Malaya—now the western wing of the Federation of Malaysia—has faced the problem in a more constructive way. Its official language is Malay, though it contains proportionally much larger minority groups; it has even dared to expand and compound the challenge of a plural society by initiating the formation of the Federation of Malaysia. This instructive example is the subject of the following case study.

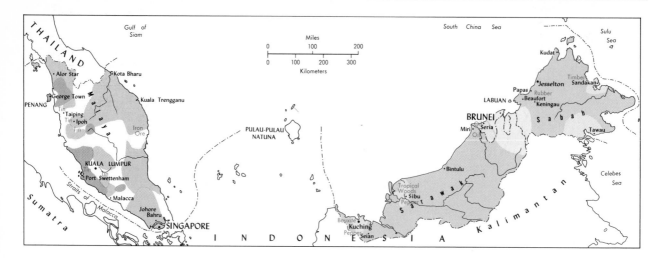

FIGURE **MALAYSIA, SINGAPORE, AND BRUNEI**
7-10

The proportions of ethnic groups are based on separate census data for Singapore, Malaya, and the Borneo territories. The percentages used to show the various groups differ in Malaya and Borneo.

⌁ **Singapore**

KUALA
• LUMPUR **Federation Capital**

• Kuching **Regional Capital**

· Malacca **Other Towns**

▨ **Large Indian Minorities**

▨ **Over 60 Percent Chinese**

▨ **Over 60 Percent Malay**

**In Borneo Only**

▨ **40-60 Percent Malay**

▨ **40-60 Percent Chinese**

▨ **Indigenous Peoples**

## THE FEDERATION OF MALAYSIA

After World War II, Britain resumed control over the Malay Peninsula (Malaya), the offshore island port of Singapore, the two colonies North Borneo and Sarawak (before the war under private British rule), and the protectorate of the sultanate of Brunei. The Federation of Malaya became independent in 1957. Singapore, with its predominantly Chinese population, was excluded from the Federation and became a "self-governing state," sharing the responsibility for its internal security with Britain and Malaya. In 1963 North Borneo (renamed Sabah) and Sarawak joined with Malaya and Singapore in the new Federation of Malaysia, but in 1965 Singapore resumed its separate existence.

Only within the last century has Malaya—now often referred to as West Malaysia—been transformed from a collection of somnolent sultanates, almost smothered in the tropical rain forest, to a well-organized country specializing in tin and rubber production. Singapore's fame is older. After Raffles in 1819 established a free port here on this strategic island, it became the great entrepôt for the trade of Southeast Asia.

The plural society that resulted from economic reorganization is shown in Figure 7-10. The Malays are Muslims. Most of them still live in agrarian villages, grow rice for food, and collect rubber from small groves of trees, for cash. Their culture—like that of so many peoples of Southeast Asia—lacks the competitiveness so conspicuous, for instance, among the Chinese. They show little interest in entrepreneurship. The well-educated prefer positions in government or in the professions, leaving business beyond the village sphere mainly to the immigrant groups.

In contrast to the easygoing Malays, the Chinese are aggressively industrious. Though the majority toil at menial tasks as tin miners, truck farmers, and factory hands, many have risen from coolie to big businessman. It is no exaggeration to say that the Chinese made possible the modern economic development of Malaya and Singapore. At the same time, their presence has largely created the problem of the plural society. The Chinese have remained Chinese, passing their cultural heritage on to the next generation through home training and school education.

The third main population element of Malaya consists of Tamils from southern India who were recruited for labor on the large rubber plantations and on railroad and port construction. Through their labor unions, they have developed a well-trained leadership which gives them greater weight in politics than their numbers might indicate. Also brought in were smaller groups of Pakistanis, Sikhs, and Sinhalese. They too cling to the traditions of their own cultures.

With so many potential sources of friction, the Federation of Malaya survived the first critical years only through moderation and tolerance on the part of all communities. The Malays have the political power, even though they form only half the population, because all adult Malays may vote, whereas various tests of citizenship restrict the ballot of other groups.

Although the Chinese form 37 percent of the population, perhaps not more than one-fifth of these have the right to vote. Islam is the state religion, but other religions have freedom of worship. The language problem is a delicate one. The more extremist Malays insist that theirs be the official language. Private Chinese schools, now under federal control and receiving federal subsidy, must teach Malay in addition to Chinese. But most Chinese consider Malay a peasant tongue unfit for modern society, far less useful than English, which they would prefer as their second—

and also Malaya's official—language. The Malays, their political power backed up if necessary by army and police, can force the issue, but their leaders so far have wisely abstained from such action. After all, the Chinese virtually control finance, commerce, and manufacturing. If driven to despair, they could wreck the economy. Nevertheless, occasional confrontations between Malays and Chinese reveal existing tensions.

Across the causeway from Malaya lies Singapore island with its great port city and a population three-fourths Chinese. It needs Malaya's trade, and Malaya needs the port. But Singapore's Chinese, if added to those of Malaya, would make them equal in number to the Malays and might further increase their economic hold. That is why Singapore was initially excluded from the Federation of Malaya. If left by itself, Singapore might have fallen under Communist control. From this danger came the plan to enlarge the Federation and draw in the Borneo territories as a counterweight to Singapore.

The cultural pluralism of Borneo has a somewhat different hue. As in Malaya and Singapore, the British held the top positions in administration and commerce. There were few plantations and thus no great influx of Indians. Instead of tin there is petroleum, concentrated by an irony of fate in the little sliver of territory that remains of the once mighty sultanate of Brunei. This tiny but rich state has been unwilling to join the Federation of Malaysia.

The Borneo territories export chiefly rubber, petroleum, pepper, coconuts, and timber. The three main ethnic groups are the indigenous pagan people (some converted to Christianity) of the interior, the coastal Malays and other Muslim peoples, and the Chinese. Of the latter about half are farmers, the other half mostly townfolk. Of the Malays only a fraction actually are descendants of the settlers from the homeland in Sumatra; the majority stem from indigenous people who joined Islam and were assimilated into Malay culture. Most of them are farmers and fishermen.

The indigenous folk are the Dayaks, Dusuns, and many other tribes. Most of them live in longhouses and exist by primitive subsistence farming. Where given the opportunity, they show great ability to adjust to modern life, perhaps more so than the coastal Malays. Both Islam and

Sibu, Sarawak, exemplifies the plural economy of the country. The population of this commercial center on the Rejang River, some 80 miles from the sea, consists almost entirely of Chinese. The fronts of the "shop-houses" are closed at night with vertical boards. Note the sign for outboard motors, popular in this tropical-forest environment, where the canoe is the main means of transportation. (A Shell photograph)

Christianity continue to make converts; this, together with the penetration of new ideas from the secular world, erodes the traditional cultures.

The indigenous tribes in the Borneo territories constitute 46 percent of the total population, against 28 percent Malays and other Muslims and 26 percent Chinese. They need protection against Chinese economic exploitation and Malay political dominance. Although the Malays must have hoped to line up the native tribes in a common front against the Chinese, they had little success. The competition for power between Malays and

Chinese may strengthen the position of the indigenous groups.

The Malaysian Federation—actually a confederacy—is an experiment in political and economic integration and as such deserves sympathetic consideration. It has increased the heterogeneity of social units, cultural patterns, and historical traditions. Each group insists on safeguards for its own interests and institutions. For instance, Sarawak and Sabah joined the larger Federation of Malaysia with the assurance that their religious freedom (including Christian missionary activity) would be respected. Singapore meanwhile kept a free hand in pursuing its socialist aims. Apparently its political stance so exasperated the conservative government of Malaya that it expelled Singapore from the Federation.

The Federation of Malaysia lies on the meeting ground of Chinese overseas expansion and Muslim Malay culture. In this larger view the basic questions remain: Will these two groups subordinate their distinct ideologies to a common allegiance? Or will they tear apart in a struggle for supremacy?

## CITATIONS AND FURTHER READINGS

Adejuyigbe, O. "Ethnic Pluralism and Political Stability of Nigeria," in Evenden, L. J., and Cunningham, F. F. (eds.), *Cultural Discord in the Modern World,* Vancouver, 1974, 83-110.

Boeke, J. H. *The Structure of the Netherlands Indian Economy,* New York, 1942.

Broek, J. O. M. "National Character in the Perspective of Cultural Geography," *Annals of the American Academy of Political and Social Science,* 370 (March 1967): 8-15.

Burghart, A. F. "The Bases of Territorial Claims," *Geographical Review,* 63 (1973): 225-245.

Catudal, H. M., Jr. "The Plight of the Lilliputians: An Analysis of Five European Microstates," *Geoforum,* 6 (1975): 187-204.

Clarke, C. G. "Insularity and Identity in the Caribbean," *Geography,* 61 (1976): 8-16.

Dale, E. H. "Some Geographical Aspects of African Land-Locked States," *Annals of the Association of American Geographers,* 58 (1968): 485-505.

Dikshit, R. D. "Geography and Federalism," *Annals of the Association of American Geographers,* 61 (1971): 97-130.

East, W. G., and Spate, O. H. K. (eds.). *The Changing Map of Asia,* New York, 1961.

Fisher, C. A. "The Malaysian Federation, Indonesia and the Philippines: A Study in Political Geography," *Geographical Journal,* 129 (1963): 311-328.

Furnivall, J. S. *Netherland India: A Study in Plural Economy,* London, 1939 and 1944.

———— *Progress and Welfare in Southeast Asia,* New York, 1941.

Gottmann, J. "Geography and International Relations," *World Politics,* 3 (1951): 153-173.

———— "The Political Partitioning of Our World: An Attempt at Analysis," *World Politics,* 4 (1952): 512-519.

Hamdan, G. "The Political Map of the New Africa," *Geographical Review,* 53 (1963): 418-439.

Hartshorne, R. "Political Geography," in James, P. E., and Jones, C. F. (eds.), *American Geography: Inventory and Prospect,* Syracuse, N.Y., 1954.

Knight, D. B. "Racism and Reaction: The Development of a Batswana 'Raison d'Etre' for the Country," in Evenden, L. J., and Cunningham, F. F. (eds.), *Cultural Discord in the Modern World,* Vancouver, 1974, 111-126.

Kohn, H. *The Idea of Nationalism,* New York, 1944.

Kosiński, L. A. "Changes in the Ethnic Structure in East-Central Europe, 1930-1960," *Geographical Review,* 59 (1969): 388-402.

Kristof, L. K. D. "The Nature of Frontiers and Boundaries," *Annals of the Association of American Geographers,* 49 (1959): 269-282.

Mayfield, R. C. "A Geographic Study of the Kashmir Issue," *Geographical Review,* 45 (1955): 181-196.

McColl, R. W. "The Insurgent State: Territorial Bases of Revolution," *Annals of the Association of American Geographers,* 59 (1969): 613-631.

Nystrom, J. W., and Hoffman, G. W. *The Common Market,* 2d ed., New York, 1976.

Pounds, N. J. G. *Divided Germany and Berlin,* Princeton, N.J., 1962.

———— *Poland between East and West,* Princeton, N.J., 1964.

Prescott, J. R. V. *The Evolution of Nigeria's International and Regional Boundaries: 1861–1971,* Vancouver, 1971.

Ratzel, F. "The Territorial Growth of States," *Scottish Geographical Magazine,* 12 (1896): 351–361.

Reitsma, H. J. "Malawi's Problem of Allegiance," *Tijdschrift voor Economische en Sociale Geografie,* 65 (1974): 421–429.

Sabbagh, M. E. "Some Geographical Characteristics of a Plural Society: Apartheid in South Africa," *Geographical Review,* 58 (1968): 1–28.

Sauer, C. O. "The Personality of Mexico," *Geographical Review,* 31 (1941): 352–364.

Soja, E. W. *The Political Organization of Space,* Association of American Geographers, Commission on College Geography, Resource Paper no. 8, Washington, D.C., 1971.

Stanislawski, D. *The Individuality of Portugal: A Study in Historical-Political Geography,* Austin, Tex., 1959.

Stephenson, G. V. "Pakistan: Discontiguity and the Majority Problem," *Geographical Review,* 58 (1968): 195–213.

———— "Cultural Regionalism and the Unitary State Idea in Belgium," *Geographical Review,* 62 (1972): 501–523.

Wikkramatileke, R. "Malaysia: Inherent Disparities and the Quest for Stability and Continued Development," in Edgell, M. C. R., and Farrell, B. H. (eds.), *Themes on Pacific Lands,* Victoria, B.C., 1974, 41–96.

Wilkinson, J. C. "The Oman Question: The Background to the Political Geography of South-East Arabia," *Geographical Journal,* 137 (1971): 361–371.

# 8 CULTURE REALMS

Every individual is distinct and unique. But each of us belongs also willy-nilly to many groups, whether these actually exist as organizational units or are conceived by the social scientist as categories of generalization. In previous chapters we have explored several of these generalizing rubrics—race, language, religion, nationality—and have noted how each acts like a filter projecting a different mosaic on the map.

The question is now whether we can carry spatial generalization one step further by sorting the many diverse segments of the earth into a simple but meaningful framework of broad culture realms. The term *culture realm* signifies a large area where fundamental unity in composition, arrangement, and integration of significant traits distinguishes it culturally from other regions. Because we have not yet discussed economies, forms of settlement, and patterns of population change—all parts of culture in a wider sense—perhaps we should use a more specific term such as sociocultural realm, though the prefix *socio* would add cumber rather than clarity. This chapter is in the nature of a provisional synthesis. Subsequent parts of the book should demonstrate the merit of this tentative regional scheme.

## PROBLEMS OF CLASSIFICATION AND MAPPING

Any division of the earth into regions involves decisions regarding (1) criteria for defining the regions, (2) dateline of the presentation, (3) scale of the investigation, and (4) regional boundaries.

**Criteria** Geographers who want to divide the earth into climatic regions select what seem to them significant measures of universal occurrence (such as precipitation and temperature) and note their spatial variation; they then make a classification of climates, and map their distribution. Can we use this method to distinguish between culture realms? As we proceed, it will become clear that the spatial configuration we seek cannot be defined exactly by selecting a few universal criteria. The traits or complexes that may be good indicators for one culture may be quite different from those characterizing another.

The problem is analogous with that of defining nations: the essence of a nation cannot be found by combining a few cultural variables such as language and religion. A nation derives its distinct nature from a large number of features in their historically grown relationship. In the same way we must understand a culture realm in its totality—its *ensemble*, its *Gestalt*—as a historically evolved individual entity. While this comprehensive view would seem to leave the door wide open for an infinite number of personal intuitive judgments, in practice there is, as we shall see, considerable agreement on the main outlines of the various culture realms.

**Dateline** Cultures are in constant change, and their realms expand and contract. Therefore, a map of culture realms is like a still from a movie, an image true only for a specific cross section through time. Although our primary concern is with the present, it would be a mistake to adopt a "current-affairs" attitude in delimiting the realms. For instance, the fact that the Soviet Union dominates the larger part of Central Europe does not make this area automatically a part of Russian culture. Political control and associated social and economic pressures are powerful levers toward cultural assimilation, but they require a long time span when applied against deeply rooted traditions. A good counterweight against arguments based on the current situation is the historical perspective gained from a knowledge of various culture realms some centuries ago.

**Scale of Study**   If one considers only a part of the earth, such as the Caribbean, West Europe, or the Middle East, one can make fine distinctions based on many culture traits, and produce a map showing many culture areas. For instance, A. L. Kroeber in his study of native Indian cultures of North America distinguished eighty-four culture areas, grouped within ten broad categories (Kroeber, 1939). Such studies, then, are of small areas on a relatively large scale. However, since we aim at a general overview of the earth, our end product is necessarily on a small scale. Inevitably we must neglect details and ignore exceptions. Only the major lineaments will stand out for the very purpose of presenting a simplified, but all the more meaningful, image of the main culture realms.

**Boundaries**   Cultures grade one into another in a vast continuum. The Rio Grande is often quoted as a clear divide between Anglo-America and Latin America, but closer inspection shows even here a transition zone where elements from both realms mingle. Thus, the Rio Grande boundary is a political *line* drawn through a cultural frontier *zone*. Where different cultures have mixed over a long period, as for instance in the African Sudan, the intermediary belt may be quite wide. In such a case one can, of course, designate it as a separate unit, but this necessitates delineating two boundaries instead of one, thus compounding the problem. In some areas where a strong foreign influence is superimposed over the native culture pattern, one can use the technique of presenting both cultures by their respective map symbols. Again, every meeting ground so marked increases the complexity of the map.

When defining periods, a historian has a similar problem. In European history where is the line drawn between "medieval" and "modern"? Should it be at the beginning of the Renaissance in Italy, or at the time of the Great Discoveries, or at the Reformation? For a broad overview one may select an approximate date and even introduce transition periods ("Middle Ages gamma,"

"Modern Period alpha"), but which dates should be assigned to the in-between eras? Whatever the method of division, it is a minor matter compared to the agreement that "medieval" and "modern" are significant historical concepts. In the same way, the geographer finds the heart of the matter in the nature of different culture realms, not in the exact location of their boundaries.

## VARIOUS PROPOSALS FOR CULTURE REALMS

Several writers have suggested a division of the earth into culture realms. Classifications by anthropologists, however, deal mostly with preliterate peoples. Studies by historians—if they include culture realms—rarely reach to the present. Sociologists focus mainly on social phenomena within their own culture sphere and, therefore, on Occidental culture. Few scholars besides geographers have produced maps of culture realms. Among them is Toynbee, though his map and the weight of his work primarily concern the great religions. We will briefly examine his theories and those of some geographers before we present our own design.

**Toynbee's Civilizations**   An important exception to the usual concern of historians is Arnold J. Toynbee's view of the current era. In his majestic *Study of History* he "presents a single continuous argument as to the nature and pattern of the historical experience of the human race since the first appearance of the species of societies called civilizations . . ." (Toynbee, 1947, ix). A small map in the atlas which accompanies the work depicts cartographically the extent of the present "civilizations" (Figure 8-1).

It should be noted that Toynbee does not examine all cultures, but only those on the higher level which have shown an advanced degree of creativity. He discusses each of these civilizations in its genesis, growth, and breakdown, as well as in its relation to other civilizations.

Toynbee distinguishes twenty-six civilizations, including five "arrested" and several "abortive" ones. Of this total, sixteen are now dead, leaving ten survivors. Among the latter he characterizes three as "arrested": Polynesian, Nomad,

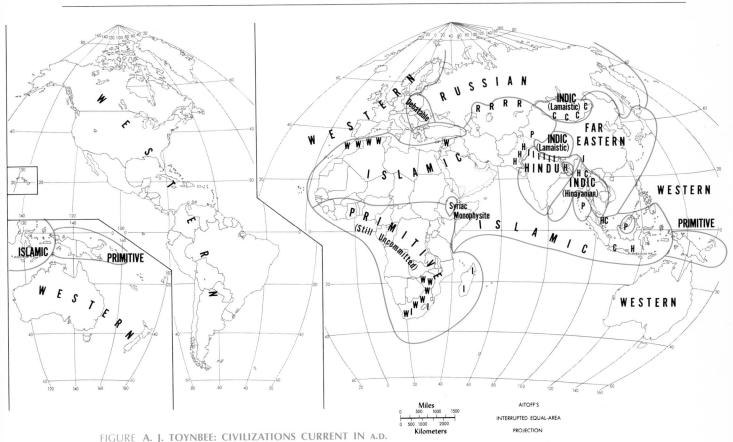

FIGURE
8-1

A. J. TOYNBEE: CIVILIZATIONS CURRENT IN A.D. 1952

Toynbee includes the Pacific Ocean, the Americas, and West Europe in his "Western" civilization. Russian civilization is a distinct unit. Intrusions from other civilizations are shown by initial letters (W—Western, R—Russian, I—Islamic, H—Hindu, C—Chinese). P refers to "Primitive" remnants. After Toynbee, A., and Myers, E. D., *A Study of History,* vol. 12, *Atlas and Gazetteer,* London, 1958.

and Eskimo, each of which, he claims, poured its energy into a determined attempt to meet the "challenge" of a difficult physical environment and suffered the consequences of its overspecialized "response." There is no need to examine here the validity of the thesis. It suffices to note that he lists seven living civilizations: our own Western Society, or Western Christendom; Orthodox Christendom in southeastern Europe; its transformed offshoot in Russia; the Islamic Soci-

ety; the Hindu Society; the main body of the Far Eastern Society in China; its offshoot in Japan.*

**Culture Realms by Geographers** Geographers before and after Toynbee—and in the latter case not necessarily dependent on him—have devised systems of division, without much discussion of the rationale behind their schemes or in reference to other authors. Sociocultural as well as economic features seem to be the criteria employed for most of their maps.

Virtually all distinguish, under whatever name, East Asia (or "Orient"); South Asia ("Hindu" or "Indic"); North Africa together with Southwest Asia ("Islamic," "Dry World"); and Europe–North Asia ("Western World," "Occident"), usually di-

*At various points of the discourse and also on map 4 in the *Atlas* there are references to an Indic Hinayanian Buddhist civilization, or Southern Buddhism.

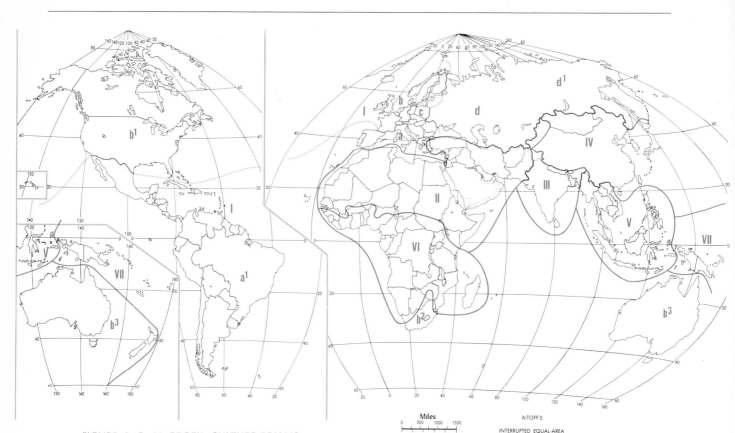

FIGURE J. O. M. BROEK: CULTURE REALMS
8-2

This map was originally designed in 1950. Only the
Occidental realm has been divided into subdivisions. A
similar procedure could be applied to the other
realms.

Miles
0   500   1000   1500
0   500 1000   2000
Kilometers

AITOFF'S
INTERRUPTED EQUAL-AREA
PROJECTION

vided into a western and an eastern part. A few
American publications combine the cultures of
East and South Asia into one realm, and call this
the Oriental world.

There is general agreement that the Americas belong to the Western world. Most authors
make a distinction between Anglo- and Latin
(Ibero-) America. Australia and New Zealand are
usually included in the Occidental realm, but in
some cases are part of a "Pacific" culture area.
Since none of the geographers limit their categories to "civilizations" in Toynbee's sense, they recognize a special culture realm in Central Africa—
an area which Toynbee calls "primitive, still uncommitted"—and some also distinguish Arctic,
Central Asian, and Melanesian cultures.

**A. Major Realms**

I.  Occidental

   **1. Maritime European**

      a. **Mediterranean European**

         $a^1$ **Latin American**

      b. **Northwestern European**

         $b^1$ **Anglo-American**

         $b^2$ **South African**

         $b^3$ **Australian-New Zealand**

   **2. Continental European**

      c. **Central European**

      d. **Russian**

         $d^1$ **North and Central Asian**

II.  **Main Islamic**

III.  **Indic**

IV.  **East Asian**

**B. Minor Realms**

V.  **Southeast Asian**

VI.  **Meso-African**

VII.  **Southern Pacific**

**Map of Culture Realms** The consensus of various geographers on the major culture realms suggests the basic validity of their schemes. While agreeing with the broad alignments, the writers of this book prefer certain details and, therefore, propose the following classification (Figure 8-2).

We distinguish two groups of culture realms. One consists of four major regions (comparable to Toynbee's civilizations). The other has three minor ones. This division ignores some peoples such as the American Indian, Australian aboriginal, Bushman, and Eskimo. Their cultures are so deeply affected by more dominant ones that it does not seem justified to include them as distinct realms in a broad survey. Here follows the list of seven, with alternate names in parentheses:

**A.** Major realms (civilizations)
   **I.**   Occidental (Western; European)
   **II.**  Main Islamic (North African–Southwest Asian; Arab-Persian)
   **III.** Indic (Indian; Hindu)
   **IV.**  East Asian (Sinitic)
**B.** Minor realms
   **V.**   Southeast Asian
   **VI.**  Meso-African (Negro-African)
   **VII.** Southern Pacific*

Each of these realms can be subdivided further. The widespread Occident may serve as an example. Its European cradleland can be divided into (1) Maritime Europe and (2) Continental Eu-

rope. Maritime Europe can be split into a Mediterranean Europe and b Northwestern Europe. Each of these has its overseas expansion wing or wings: $a^1$ Latin America; $b^1$ Anglo-America; $b^2$ South Africa; and $b^3$ Australia and New Zealand. Continental Europe comprises c Central Europe (the shatter belt) and d Russia, with its continental expansion, $d^1$ into Asia (Table 8-1).

## CULTURE REALMS IN THE FIFTEENTH CENTURY

To provide historical perspective on the present scene, it is useful to survey briefly the extent of the main cultures before the European eruptive expansion (Figure 8-3). Even before 1500 the areas of civilization formed a continuum, surrounded by a periphery of simpler, if not primitive, ways of life. In the Old World the belt of civilizations stretched through the middle latitudes from the Atlantic to the Pacific Ocean. Each civilization—Occidental, Islamic, Indic, and Chinese—had its nucleus which was spatially distinct or even far distant from the other centers, but their margins touched and often interpenetrated each other. This zone of civilizations formed the cultural ecumene—not all of the inhabited Old World, but its creative, dynamic core.

The native American civilizations were, of course, remote from those of Eurasia, but within the Americas they too were linked together by marginal zones. Deserts, mountains, and tropical rain forests separated the belt of culture hearths from other favorable but as yet only primitively used habitats. These barriers and the relative youth of Indian civilizations may explain why

*In this list and in Figure 8-2 a Southern Pacific (Melanesian-Polynesian) culture realm is recognized, mainly because of its huge extent.

**SUBDIVISIONS OF THE OCCIDENTAL CULTURE REALM**

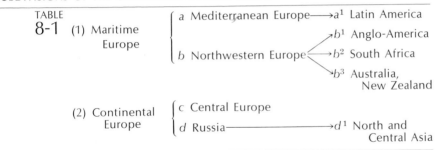

TABLE 8-1

(1) Maritime Europe
   a Mediterranean Europe ⟶ $a^1$ Latin America
   b Northwestern Europe ⟶ $b^1$ Anglo-America
                          ⟶ $b^2$ South Africa
                          ⟶ $b^3$ Australia, New Zealand

(2) Continental Europe
   c Central Europe
   d Russia ⟶ $d^1$ North and Central Asia

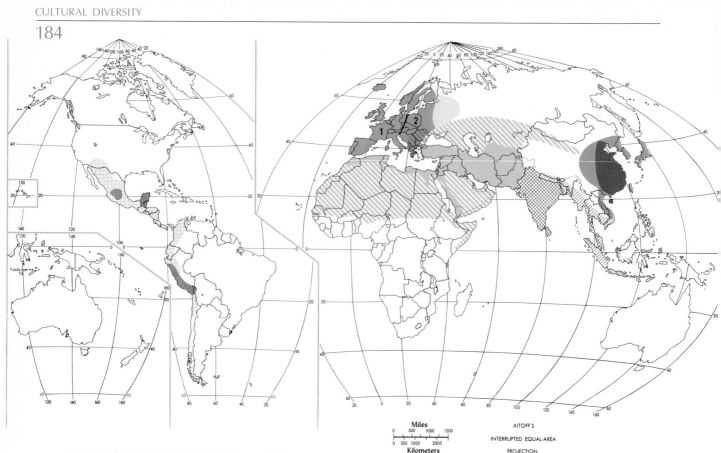

FIGURE
8-3 **CULTURE REALMS ABOUT A.D. 1450**

Based in part on Hettner, A., *Der Gang der Kultur über die Erde,* Leipzig and Berlin, 1929, and Bobek, 1959 and 1962. (See *Further Readings.*)

Occidental Culture Area
    1 Maritime European
    2 Continental European

Margin of Occidental Culture Area

Islamic Culture Area

Margin of Islamic Culture Area

Indic Culture Area

Margin of Indic Culture Area

East Asian Culture Area

Margin of East Asian Culture Area

American Culture Area

Margin of American Culture Area

such vast areas in the Americas remained peripheral in culture until the Europeans arrived.

In the other continents these low-level cultures characteristically occupied lands either far distant from the cultural centers or climatically handicapped. Thus, preliterate tribes lived in most of Africa, Eurasia's taiga and tundra, parts of Southeast Asia, all of Australia, New Zealand, and other islands in the Pacific. To be sure, most of them had received in the course of time a number of culture traits from more advanced peoples, but these were mainly in the material sphere, such as domesticated plants and animals, iron tools, or the wheel. Some areas (Australia, Tasmania, and the south tips of South America and Africa) had received very little.

The civilizations of the cultural ecumene all had their elaborate ethical or religious ideologies: calendars and written languages, and thus historical records; territorial organization in states; a well-developed agriculture and high level of craftsmanship; division of labor, long-distance trade, and cities; and relatively advanced means for controlling the physical environment, such as the use of water and wind for energy production.

In the late fifteenth century the Occidental realm occupied a modest area in the western peninsula of Eurasia. There was a lively trade among the countries on the seaboards of the Mediterranean, North, and Baltic seas, and the Portuguese were groping their way down the west coast of Africa. Five hundred years earlier Norsemen had already crossed the Atlantic by way of Iceland and Greenland, and had reached Newfoundland, but their accounts had not become part of general European knowledge. Central Europe was—and remained for centuries—the arena of struggles between continental empires. On its eastern margin the grand duchy of Muscovy was emerging as an offshoot of Byzantine culture, but had not as yet been assimilated to Europe.

The core lands of the Islamic, Indic, and Chinese realms were in 1500 much the same as now. The Muslim Turks controlled most of the Balkan Peninsula and would continue to threaten Christendom until the end of the seventeenth century, but their conquests in Europe always remained marginal to the central zone of Islam. In most of Southeast Asia, Indic cultural influence prevailed, at least until about 1300. By 1500, though, Islam had superimposed itself upon Hinduism and Buddhism in the island world. Meso-Africa, while in contact with the Arab world in the Sudan and on the east coast, had remained for the greater part beyond the purview of the civilized world.

In the fifteenth century the various Eurasian civilizations appeared as distinct, self-sufficient units, although they were aware of each other's existence through the accounts of sailors, missionaries, ambassadors, and other travelers by land and sea. The Iberian sea voyages and the rediscovery of America marked the beginning of a new era, in which the whole earth was to become an interlocked unit. However European civilization may be judged in the future, one must acknowledge that it linked together all parts of the earth, one of the great achievements in the history of mankind.

# THE OCCIDENTAL CULTURE REALM

## SPREAD OF OCCIDENTAL CULTURE

The expansion of European civilization during the last four centuries took three forms: settlement, colonial rule, and cultural diffusion.

Europeans spread overland and overseas into northern Asia, the Americas, South Africa, Australia, and New Zealand. These settlements were in the mid-latitude climates and to some extent in the tropical highland zones. Equally important, they were in areas of weak, peripheral cultures. Only in Andean America and Meso-America did European settlement displace native peoples in the core areas of other civilizations.

Europeans controlled trade, investment, and strategic colonies by superimposing their administration and business management on peripheral cultures (tropical Africa, Southeast Asia, and America) and on large parts of non-Occidental civilizations (Peru, Mexico, India, Middle East, and to some extent China).

In addition, the Occident even without settlement or political control has affected the entire earth through cultural diffusion. Western goods and technology have dispersed much faster and farther than have Western value systems and institutions. Can a non-Western society accept the former and reject the latter as if the various parts of a culture had no connection? It is not easy to provide a simple yes or no answer. Adoption of Occidental forms of technology and economy will inevitably affect other sectors of life, but the new ideas must be fitted into the indigenous cultural heritage.

Thus, we must not look upon non-Occidental civilizations as obsolescent vehicles, ready to be replaced by a uniform and worldwide standard model of Western design. Instead, they appear as living entities with capacity for adaptation to new circumstances. To be sure, civilizations develop and decay, but none of the present major cultures show clear signs of a swift demise, in spite of what prophets of doom may say. The underlying thought of this chapter—and indeed much of this book—is that different culture realms will continue to exist side by side, though in ever closer association.

## MEDITERRANEAN EUROPE AND LATIN AMERICA

In the late Middle Ages Mediterranean Europe was still the nucleus of Occidental culture. The merchants of Genoa and Venice had built commercial empires extending over the entire midland sea. Together with Italian geographers and navigators, they laid the basis for later oceanic voyages by Portugal and Spain.

The Spanish conquest of Middle and South America destroyed the superstructure of Indian civilizations from Mexico to Peru. It led to demographic collapse, especially in the densely settled parts, so that within a century the indigenous populations had been severely reduced to only a small proportion (say, one-tenth) of what they had been (see Chapter 16). Spanish institutions were imposed wherever feasible. Viceroys administered the colonies by order of the absolute monarch and with help of the army. The Catholic Church converted the Indians and held a close rein on the spiritual life of the entire population. Members of the elite received large land grants including feudal rights over the Indians. Thus army, church, and landed aristocracy became the ruling triad in Spanish America, separated economically and socially from the mass of population.

The Portuguese colonization in Brazil was in many ways similar to the Spanish system. Their domain, however, lacked the precious metals which at an early date drew the Spaniards to the highland civilizations of the interior. In contrast, the Portuguese showed more interest in cultivating export crops, which explains why their settlements remained for a long time in the coastal areas.

Diversity of habitats, peoples, and governments make Latin America less a unit than the name indicates. Within the zone of pre-Columbian civilizations the Indian way of life, including language, social organization, and communal landholding, has survived, at least at the village level, in many regions. English, Dutch, and French incursions into the Caribbean area and the Guianas left their mark in speech, political institutions, style of life, and racial composition. Plantation agriculture on the islands as well as the tropical mainland resulted in large concentrations of Africans. On the other hand, in the so-called "temperate climates" of Argentina, Uruguay, and southern Brazil the population in great majority is of European stock. The permissive attitude of Latins toward intermarriage with nonwhites has led to considerable race mixing. Intermarriage with blacks has produced the widespread *mulatto* type in the Antilles and Brazil. The *mestizo* blend of European and Indian predominates in Mexico and southward through Colombia and Venezuela into most of South America. In many areas the three races are interbred. Only in the central Andean countries are the people more Indian.

Politically fragmented Hispanic America stands in sharp contrast to the two huge units of Anglo-America. The revolt against Spain in the early nineteenth century involved only the Spanish colonial elite. In each population cluster the leading group took over the authority of the Spanish Crown and assumed control over the outlying areas as far as it could maintain effective power. Brazil preserved its unity principally because the Portuguese royal family moved to Brazil during the Napoleonic Wars.

In Europe the many states reflect the mosaic of nations, but this is less true in Spanish America, where the cultural tradition of the elite in one country is much the same as that in the other countries. The cleavage between classes within each country exceeds that between members of the same class in different countries. The spatial variety in culture and economy is thus often more one of regionalism or sectionalism than of nationalism.

The democratic spirit of the French and American revolutions hardly touched Latin America, or did so only recently and in isolated instances. The bulk of the population remains illiterate, poor, and only partly assimilated in the national entity. A wealthy minority of landed aristocracy, allied with the army, still governs most countries and sets the tone in values, customs, and institutions.

## NORTHWESTERN EUROPE AND ITS OVERSEAS WINGS

From 1600 onward northwestern Europe became the veritable dynamo of the Occident. Its inhabitants overtook the Iberians in exploration, trade, and colonization, developed modern capitalism, strengthened the middle class, extended democratic institutions, and turned rational thought into modern science and technology. The diffusion of Occidental culture over the world since 1600 was largely the spread of ideas and things which originated in Northwest Europe. In the vanguard were France, the Netherlands, and Britain, but Scandinavians, Germans, and Swiss also participated in the overseas ventures or were directly affected by the economic and social development generated by the new overseas frontier.

Until World War I northwestern Europe was the main seat of political and economic power. The outcome of World War II made it the chief arena of struggle between the new superpowers of the United States and the Soviet Union. The remarkable reconstruction after that war demonstrated the vitality of the nations of Northwest Europe. The European Economic Community affirms the idea of the fundamental units of Maritime Europe.*

**Anglo-America**   We must not take the term *Anglo-America* too literally. The indigenous peoples still remaining from the Arctic to the Rio Grande, the French Canadians, those of Spanish, Puerto Rican, and Mexican heritage suggest plurality rather than monolithic unity. Yet the term is apt if one considers that the English language and institutions have molded the predominant culture pattern.

Even the most astute observer in 1750 could hardly have foreseen this "Anglo-America," stretching from Atlantic to Pacific, and divided into only two sovereign states. At that time there was only a narrow band of English colonies—which had incorporated the Dutch and Swedish settlements—between the ocean and the Appalachians. Enveloping it in a large arc lay the French empire controlling the St. Lawrence and Great Lakes drainage basin as well as the Ohio-Mississippi valleys. In the far west, Spanish rule extended across the Rio Grande and Colorado rivers into the southern plains and California. Yet, within half a century the French gave up all claims and the British withdrew to Canada. The United States annexed the Spanish territories later, not

*For other characteristics see relevant sections of Chaps. 6 and 7.

because they were important or necessary at that time. To the contrary, this tenuous and neglected extension of the Spanish-Mexican frontier lay on the other side of the continent, separated from them by arid lands and mountains.

Unlike Latin America, North America had no native civilizations whose riches attracted Europeans into the interior. But this also meant that there was no large and settled Indian population to subdue, exploit, and assimilate. Nor was there, as in Latin America, the voice of the Catholic Church, demanding conversion of the heathens as a spiritual task of the conquest. The virtual elimination of the Indians made the greater part of Anglo-America a white man's country, where the settlers themselves had to perform all tasks from the most menial to the most exalted.

The important exception was the subtropical South, where the planters of cash crops came to rely on imported labor from Africa. Here a different way of life developed, with strictly observed caste rules dividing the free whites and the slave blacks. The "cancer of slavery" eventually was removed, though a hundred years thereafter the place of the black in American society, whether in South or North, was still at issue.

The vast domain of the United States with its rich resources and its common market offered great economic opportunities. Moreover, its location between two oceans afforded protection against outside interference during the formative years. These were the necessary conditions that gave rise to paramount world power in the first half of the twentieth century. But the ultimate cause lay in the kind of society that grew up in the new habitat. The immigrants, while turning their backs on Europe, brought along their aspirations for a new freedom as conceived by visionaries in their homeland. On new ground in America, released from the fetters of tradition, the incipient modern ideas received fresh meaning and expression: "industrialism as a technology, capitalism as a way of organizing it, and democracy as a way of running both" (Lerner 1957, 39).

In Canada, with the exception of Québec, the British tradition remains, of course, stronger than in the United States, but such differences are minor compared to the overall similarity between the two Anglo-American subcultures. Canada suffers from two handicaps. One is the division between the English and French, which is far from resolved. The other is the contrast between the narrow strip of effective settlement and the vast wilderness that reaches north from Lake Superior and thus cuts the effective territory of the country in two. Fur hunters, loggers, and miners by their scattered and often ephemeral occupancy created a typical frontier economy in the vastness of boreal forest and tundra. But farm settlement has not followed, as would have happened in more genial climates. At the same time, Occidental intrusions have deeply disturbed the native way of life. Thus, most of Canada lies on the periphery of Occidental culture, an indefinite area between the old which is going and the new which is reluctant to take hold. Alaska has much the same character, though its role in relation to the rest of the United States is far less important than that of the Canadian Northlands to inhabited Canada.

**Other Transoceanic Offspring from Northwest Europe** Australia offers interesting similarities and contrasts to Canada. Here too a narrow populated zone is joined to a vast and virtually uninhabited domain. While Canadians can take some comfort in the thought that beyond its Arctic borders the wilderness continues into the northern regions of the Soviet Union, Australians know that beyond their dry wastelands lie the well-populated Asian countries. And while Canada's location makes it an integral part of the North Atlantic community, Australia's situation destines it to remain a distant and isolated outlier of Occidental culture. Even within the inhabited part, occupancy is patchy and rural settlement spread thinly over large farm units. Over two-thirds of the 12 million people live in cities, and 6 million are concentrated in five of them.

Australia puts considerable efforts into developing its tropical north but has accomplished comparatively little so far. Inhibiting factors are the distance from markets and amenities of living and, especially, the character of the environment, which restricts agriculture. The barren lands and inhospitable coast have been left to aborigines over thousands of years. Indonesian sailors did not settle here, and even the early Malay seafarers searching along the Pacific islands for lands suitable for rice culture bypassed north Australia.

In South Africa, an offshoot of Western cul-

ture faces point-blank on its borders and in its midst the rising consciousness of black Africans, the vast majority practically unassimilated. Antagonisms are compounded by the presence of other ethnic groups, such as Indians and Malays, and by the split between the Afrikaners (Boers) and the English. The size of the European minority (four million), as well as their racially inspired policies, means that the threat of prolonged violence will remain for many years. In Kenya, where statehood came early in the process of African decolonization, the white minority numbered only a few thousand; the transfer of power to the African people came without significant difficulty, once independence seemed certain. In other areas accommodation between blacks and whites has allowed nonviolent transition to black majority rule and the creation of several independent states. The transition is not so easy in Rhodesia, where the European minority numbers a quarter of a million.

In comparison to Australia and South Africa, New Zealand is almost idyllic. In a pleasant climate its immigrants have created an egalitarian and somewhat more comfortable England. The indigenous Maori have been treated quite well since the 1880s and are rapidly increasing; in 1977 they formed a minority of 8 percent. The greatest drawback of this South Pacific outlier of West European civilization is its remoteness—far from other lands and at the very opposite of the earth from what older New Zealanders still regard as "home."

## CONTINENTAL EUROPE AND ITS EASTWARD EXPANSION (FIGURE 8-4)

Inland from Maritime Europe lies the shatter belt of Central Europe. Essentially continental in character, it did not participate in the great adventure of oceanic discovery and expansion, nor in the subsequent economic upsurge of northwestern Europe. It has been the meeting ground of Slavic and Germanic peoples, of Eastern and Western Christendom. It is a transition zone which deserves recognition because it is neither western Europe, nor Russian Europe. Since its composite character has already been discussed in Chapter 7, we turn to Russia to conclude our overview of the Occidental culture realm.

Toynbee classifies Russia as a separate civili-

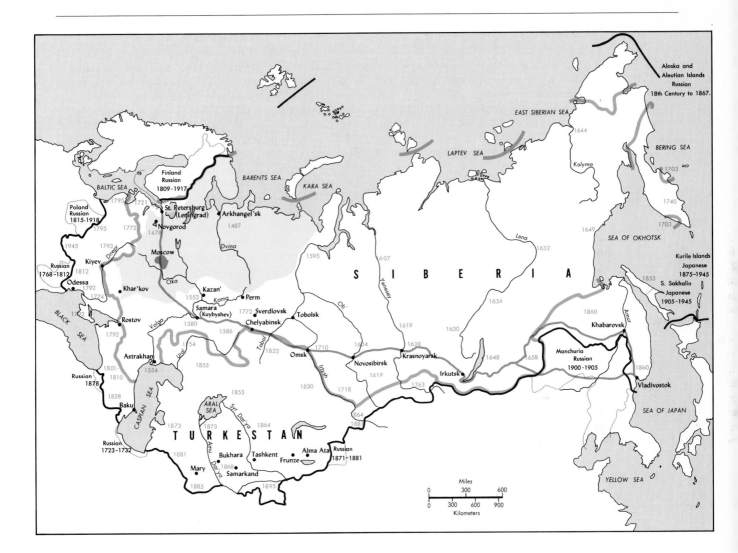

**FIGURE 8-4**

**THE EXPANSION OF RUSSIA**

The dominions of the czars were extended rapidly in the seventeenth century across Siberia to the shores of the Pacific Ocean. Expansion southward into Asia proved more difficult as the Russians encountered the Islamic and Chinese societies.

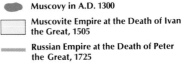

Muscovy in A.D. 1300

Muscovite Empire at the Death of Ivan the Great, 1505

Russian Empire at the Death of Peter the Great, 1725

U.S.S.R., 1965

Other Boundaries

Trans-Siberian Railway, 1891-1901

zation, for he considers Russia a successor to Byzantine-Eastern Christianity, in his view something quite different from Western Christianity. Perhaps his emphasis on religion has made him minimize other features which justify the inclusion of Russia as part—a distinct part—of Occidental civilization.*

The Muscovy of 1500 was still on the fringe of Western culture, a semibarbarous state in spite of its Orthodox Christianity and its linguistic affiliations to other Slavic peoples farther west. But in the following century the process of acculturation to western Europe began, and by 1700 it gained momentum when Czar Peter the Great made a purposeful drive for Westernization.

The Marxist ideology, as developed by Lenin and others, drew its inspiration from West European ideas, even though it changed their ideals. Again, one is reminded of the thesis that innovations often find a better home on the periphery of a culture than in its center. In Russia, untouched by Reformation and French Revolution and virtually without the vested interests and liberal traditions of a middle class, a new type of industrial society replaced at one swoop the semifeudal system. By the nature of its totalitarian regime and doctrine, Soviet Russia is committed to creating a homogeneous society for its multinational population. Harmless diversions such as folk dancing are encouraged, and religions such as Islam are tolerated as long as they do not lead people to "backward nationalism." Nothing must interfere with the progress toward what the Communist party elite sees as the ideal of modernity.

The original Muscovy grew up in the forests on the margin of the Tartar Empire, which controlled the steppe to the south. Russia's initial expansion across the Urals followed the narrow belt of open woods and prairies between the subarctic forests to the north and the deserts to the south. Here the advance was rapid, not only because the environment was favorable but also because the sparse indigenous population, loosely organized in many tribes, offered little resistance. Through this zone was built, at the very end of the nineteenth century, the Trans-Siberian Railroad, the spinal cord of Russian Asia.

*On the relation of Russia to the West see also Kroeber, 1962, 32–33 and 47–54.

The conquest of Turkestan came in the latter half of the nineteenth century, much later than that of Siberia. The Soviet government has made intensive efforts to integrate the Turkic Muslims and to modernize their traditional dual economy of oasis agriculture and nomadic herding.

Between the heartlands of Russia and China lies a wide belt which is peripheral to both cultures. This zone, from the borders of Manchuria to Sinkiang (Chinese Turkestan), is not a cultural unit, being sparsely occupied by peoples of widely divergent languages and traditions. The political boundary between the Soviet Union and the People's Republic of China marks their individual spheres of control—at least in their overt forms—but the line must be understood as the current divide in an unstable power equilibrium. It has shifted widely during recent centuries and may do so again in the future.

## THE MAIN ISLAMIC REALM

Finding a fitting name for this Islamic realm is difficult. In German it is called the *Orient,* a term the English formerly used but now commonly reserve for East Asia. People extend the "Middle East" to suit their own convenience, but stretching it as far west as Morocco and east to Pakistan overstrains its elasticity. The same goes for the French *Levant*—"rising," land of the rising sun—which essentially refers to lands around the eastern Mediterranean. Although less than one-half of all Muslims live in this vast realm, the prevalence of Islam is its chief cultural feature and suggests the name Islamic Realm.

North Africa and Southwest Asia have arid to semiarid climates. Everywhere there is the contrast between pastoral nomad and oasis dweller, between steppe and field. The time is long past when the Middle East comprised the hearths of civilization, but its location always has given it strategic significance either as a bridge or as a barrier between different cultures.

Within the local horizons of Central Europe, the Ottoman sultanate remained the great threat to Christendom until its defeat near Vienna in 1683. At about the same time, the Muslim Mogul Empire reached its greatest extent in India. However, in the broader view, the European expansion overseas and overland had already outflanked Islam. By 1500 the Portuguese had entered the Indian Ocean and begun to disrupt Arab trade routes. From 1600 onward, the Russian Cossacks moved eastward into the Asian interior, reaching the Pacific in 1638. Subsequent West European colonial conquests pushed the rule of Islam back to its core lands in Southwest Asia and North Africa. Even this inner domain of Islam was, for the greater part, swallowed up by the British, French, and Russian empires in the nineteenth and early twentieth centuries, leaving only Afghanistan, Iran, an amputated Turkey, and Arabia as nominally independent buffer states. This historic reminder serves to point up the rapid retreat of Western rule in the middle of the present century when all lands of Islam, with the exception of those in the Soviet Union and China, became independent again.

Under the influence of Occidental ideas the traditional authority of family, clan, and tribe is breaking down. Instead, the nation-state claims the full loyalty of its citizens as individuals. Loyalty implies identification with the goals of the new state, but these goals are as yet often far from clear. In all these lands there is an ancient contrast between the poor, debt-ridden peasants in the countryside and the rich landlords and merchants in the cities. Economic development demands of the upper strata sacrifices they are loath to make and requires the pursuit of productive work many disdain. Thus, social and political instability characterizes the entire zone from Morocco to Pakistan.

In addition there are deep cleavages among the various countries. Turkey and Iran, both non-Arabic and once the seats of great empires, are antagonistic to the Arabs. Pakistan, the other major non-Arab unit, has always been more involved in the affairs of the Indian subcontinent than in the Middle East. European rule, mostly French, has greatly influenced the North African countries of Morocco, Algeria, and Tunisia. And the Arabs of the Middle East still feud among themselves in spite of the ideal of Pan-Arab unity.

In view of this diversity it may seem idle to insist on the fundamental strands of internal unity—the preponderance of Islam, the Arab-Persian roots of culture, and the similarities in mode of life. If this uniformity seems contrived, one may turn the argument to the question of whether a more meaningful classification is feasible by dividing this realm among its neighbors. If this proves invalid, it reaffirms our view that, for both positive and negative reasons, the area is a distinct cultural entity.

In Africa the southern boundary of the realm runs through the zone where Islam impinges upon the tribal and Christian religions of Meso-Africa. For many centuries Caucasoid peoples speaking Hamitic or Semitic languages have penetrated into the Sudan, the highlands, and the coastal areas of East Africa. The limit of their settlement, as shown in Figure 8–2, coincides fairly well with the boundary between the grass and thornbush steppe to the north and the wooded savanna to the south. To be sure, the coastal strip of East Africa, southward as far as Beira in Mozambique, also has many Arabs and Arabic culture traits as a result of long trade contacts with southern Arabia, but on the whole this area may properly be regarded as part of the Meso-African realm.

Since 1973 the role of oil-rich countries in the Middle East has changed significantly. With the price of oil increased fourfold, huge amounts of foreign currency flow into lands like Libya, Saudi Arabia, Iran, Iraq, and Kuwait. This new wealth purchases rapid economic development for the people, creates well-equipped armed forces, and fills what once was a power vacuum in world affairs.

## THE INDIC REALM

Mountain walls and ocean shores make the Indian subcontinent a distinct physical unit. However, the northwestern section has always been in close communication with Central Asia and the Middle East, and it shares many aspects of their life and landscape. This justifies our excluding Pakistan from the Indic culture realm. Even with this restriction, so many diversities and incongruities remain that it may seem rash to assert its individuality. Yet there is truth, however evasive, in this concept.

Religion is doubtless a major force in Indic culture. Deep concern with the fate of the soul has cast its spell over the people for whom ultimate rewards are not in this world but in a better birth in a subsequent incarnation. Monks and other holy men are highly esteemed because they exemplify the ideal conduct through retreat from the ignoble struggle of life.

The individual-spiritual ends are pursued within and through the social organs of extended family, village community, and caste. There is a rift between these primary groupings and the political organization of the state. In the absence of an enduring tradition of imperial government, political rule has been largely of a personal nature, often despotic and always fleeting. Foreign conquerors, entering the subcontinent from Persia or inner Asia, built the larger and more lasting empires, but their successive domains fell apart again as their power waned. At the same time, the weakness of the political and administrative systems prevented the state from interfering substantially with the established social order.

In view of these considerations, it is no wonder that India's impact on other parts of the world has been chiefly of a spiritual nature. Its religions, especially Buddhism, have profoundly influenced the cultures of Central, East, and Southeast Asia. Campaigns of conquest outside India have been rare, and the number of settlers in overseas colonies has been small, if one excludes Indian workers who were recruited for manual labor overseas during the last century.

Because of its religion East Bengal (now Bangladesh), which in other respects is an integral part of the Indic culture realm, was torn off politically and linked with distant Pakistan. In 1971 it broke this tenuous bond and moved into India's sphere of influence. Sri Lanka (Ceylon), always somewhat different from the mainland because of its island nature, has resumed its separate way since British rule ended.

The problems of present-day India are in many ways similar to those of other underdeveloped countries. It has the advantage of a long tradition of civilization and of political unity, frail as it may be, over a vast area. The dense and still rapidly growing population, mainly agrarian and living on the edge of hunger, makes it especially difficult to solve the urgent need for economic growth. If India is to go modern, it must change its social order and reinterpret its ideology. Its

tradition and the legacy of British political thought militate against regimentation. Indira Ghandi's temporary acquisition of power began some speedy economic and social adjustments. Nevertheless, the country seems to prefer gradual advance rather than great leaps forward. One must hope the pace is fast enough to escape from the clutches of poverty.

## THE EAST ASIAN CULTURE REALM

Essentially this is the area of Chinese, or Sinitic, civilization with its variants in Korea and Japan. Although China's physical frame lacks the clear-cut boundaries of the Indian subcontinent, the vast deserts, high plateaus, and rugged mountains of Central Asia have shielded it, more than any other major culture realm, from outside contacts. To be sure, in its formative stage Chinese civilization received much from southwestern Asia, for which the string of inner Asian oases served as relay points; but from then on, its development has been essentially a native growth. By the end of the Han dynasty (206 B.C.–A.D. 214) imperial China covered much the same area as China Proper today. The enduring unity of the country for 2,000 years manifests the fundamental homogeneity and stability of its social order and political institutions. Invasions by pastoral nomads were frequent, but the foreigners ruled "through a state organization originally created by the Chinese and . . . operated through an officialdom which has usually been overwhelmingly Chinese" (Latourette, 1951, 68). And commonly the conquerors adopted the Chinese way of life.

Feelings of cultural superiority create ethnocentric attitudes. Just as the Greeks distinguished between themselves and the barbarians, so the Chinese divided the world into the Middle Country—their own—and the Outside Countries, whose inhabitants were beyond the pale of civilization. This self-satisfaction suffered rude shocks when the Occident at last forced its way into East Asia in the nineteenth century, but now there is good reason to believe that the old chauvinism is emerging in new form.

The Chinese ethos stands in stark contrast to that of India. Whereas the latter is metaphysical, Chinese thought stays close to concrete reality. Rather than religion it emphasizes human relations. Thus the maxims on the organization of society, from family to state, take precedence over the claims of otherworldly religions. Temporal power had divine sanction (the emperor was considered a manifestation of Heaven), but there was never any doubt that the state came first, with religion as its servant. Not the priesthood but the civil service bureaucracy, selected by examinations and promoted by merit ratings, supervised the social order.

It is still too early to tell how much the Communist revolution will actually transform the foundations of Chinese society. Judging by the past, it is likely that the Chinese, while adopting Western things and thoughts, will mold them in their own image, as they have done before with foreign intrusions. If they succeed in modernization, China with one-fifth of the world's population may again become the powerful Middle Kingdom—in their eyes, the pivot of the earth.

To a large degree pride in the homeland explains the posture of the 10 million or more Chinese in Southeast Asia. They are reluctant to conform to local ways of life, which they consider inferior to their own culture. Humiliations in the nineteenth century made some falter in their loyalty. China's rise in stature under the Communist regime gives new confidence and confirms belief. At the same time this makes the possibility more remote than ever that they can be assimilated into other societies.

### JAPAN AND KOREA

While Chinese influence in Japan and Korea has been substantial, these two countries must not be considered mere transplants of Sinitic civilization. Many Japanese words show ancient relationships with Polynesian languages, and the grammar indicates links with the Altaic (North Asian) linguistic family. Much later, in the fourth century A.D., the impact of horse-riding pastoral nomads from northeastern Asia brought about unification of the tribes in southern Japan (the Yamato empire). Direct contacts with China began after A.D. 500. The Japanese incorporated many Chinese words into their vocabulary, modeled their writing system after the Chinese example, and borrowed many other customs and institutions.

In all these culture transfers, Korea by its very position and shape served as the bridge between mainland and islands. It received from northern Asia and China, handed on to Japan, and had its own culture molded in the process. All through Korean history there appear the alternating themes of continental and maritime influences and interests. In Korea the present split between North and South is a sharp reminder of its traditional position as an embattled zone of passage.

The Japanese islands became the home of a tightly organized nation, able to surmount the shock of exposure to Occidental civilization. It purposefully imitated the ways of the intruders, even to building a vast, though short-lived, empire along the rim of the western Pacific. The energetic reconstruction of the economy and the disciplined acceptance of reforms after the war give additional evidence of Japan's social stability. Managerial acumen and industriousness have catapulted this country to the forefront of the world's economic powers. It is unlikely that Japan will ever again rule East Asia. Nevertheless, its ability to fuse Asian and Occidental strains assures its special position in this culture realm.

## THE SOUTHEAST ASIAN CULTURE REALM

In contrast to previously discussed realms, Southeast Asia is not a unit with its own culturally distinct character. Instead, it is an area of transit and transition where different cultures meet and mingle. Its personality is defined in a negative way: neither East Asian nor Indic, neither Islamic nor Occidental, yet containing elements of all. In a sense this condition parallels that of the shatter belt regions between Europe and Soviet Russia and perhaps that of culturally mixed Central Asia.

Southeast Asia includes the Asian mainland east of India and south of China, as well as the entire archipelago. The predominant race is South Mongoloid, and thus more related to the peoples of East than of South Asia. Some ancient customs, such as building houses on stilts, suggest a primeval unity, but this unity has been virtually obliterated by the heavy overlays of subsequent foreign intrusions. The cultural impact of India has been

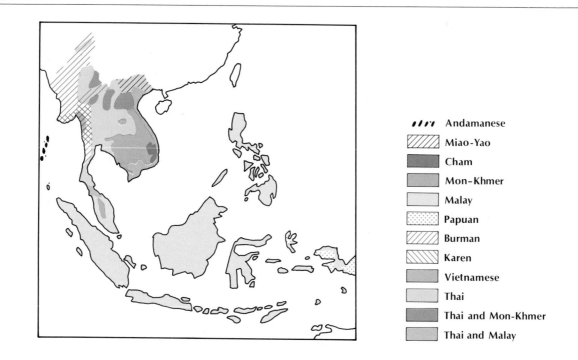

FIGURE **SOUTHEAST ASIA: LANGUAGES**
**8-5**

Based on a map in Broek, J. O. M., "Diversity and Unity in Southeast Asia," *Geographical Review,* 34 (1944):175–195.

strong over most of the area, as evidenced by religion and the arts. Also from early times, commercial and political relations existed with China, but the Chinese made no attempt to civilize the barbarians of the Southern Seas (Nan Yang). Only Tonkin-Annam (Vietnam), for centuries a vassal state on China's southern frontier, was strongly affected by Chinese culture, but without losing its identity. Islam replaced Hinduism and Buddhism in the Malay Peninsula and Islands; but it had not advanced much beyond the limits of Indic influence when the Europeans arrived in the sixteenth century. Thus the pagan population of the Philippines was Christianized and in the course of years became the carrier of that peculiar hybrid culture in which indigenous traits mingle with those from Spain and the United States (Figures 8–5 and 8–6).

The chief nations on the mainland are separated from each other not only by highlands with unassimilated tribes but also by memories of bitter strife and by the different experiences during the centuries of European hegemony. Malaysia, the Philippines, and Indonesia together may be considered as a distinct subunit because of their linguistic affinity. However, most of their languages are mutually incomprehensible. More important, each of these countries has been subject to very different impacts, of which British, American, and Dutch rule were only the last in a succession of foreign influences.

All the countries of Southeast Asia for at least the last 2,000 years have been culturally a low-pressure area. As such, they have been recipients rather than donors of culture. It would be rash to project past performance into the future and declare Southeast Asia a permanent cultural ward of other civilizations. (What Roman could have foreseen the future role of northwestern Europe?) Nevertheless, now that Occidental rule has receded, India and China may well return to their former roles as dynamic culture centers and thus confront this vast area with new challenges.

Southeast Asia's strategic position between the Indian and Pacific oceans, and between the landmasses of Asia and Australia, its sparsely populated sectors, and its rich resources combine to

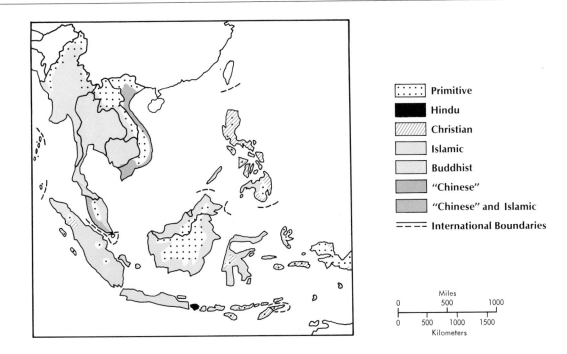

Legend:
- Primitive
- Hindu
- Christian
- Islamic
- Buddhist
- "Chinese"
- "Chinese" and Islamic
- International Boundaries

Miles
0 — 500 — 1000

Kilometers
0 — 500 — 1000 — 1500

FIGURE **SOUTHEAST ASIA: RELIGIONS**
**8-6**

Based on a map in Broek, J. O. M., "Diversity and Unity in Southeast Asia," *Geographical Review,* 34 (1944):175–195.

make it of special interest to many outsiders. In the face of these external relations and potential pressures, the glaring weakness of this realm is its ethnic and political fragmentation—a kind of Asian Balkans. It needs greater units for defense and for internal development. Even its leaders as yet only dimly perceive this long-range self-interest amidst the diversity of memories and aspirations.

## THE MESO-AFRICAN CULTURE REALM

Many scattered peripheral cultures survive— American Indians, Melanesians, Polynesians, Arctic peoples, and others—but Negroid Africa is different, not only because it is such a large unit but also because it has preserved its identity to a much larger degree than most. We could call this

culture realm Central or Middle Africa, but these terms already have other (admittedly vague) geographic meanings. We prefer to avoid "black" or "Negro" with their racial connotations. Therefore we propose "Meso-Africa" as a fresh name, not burdened by political, physiographic, or racial implications.

Physical barriers by land and sea hampered Meso-Africa from communicating with other lands. Practically cut off from Old World regions in ancient and medieval times, it did not share in the development of new thought and technology. Even so, a number of ideas and materials filtered in. The great desert, in spite of its barren width, provided the main passageway for diffusion from north to south, especially in the east where the Nile Valley connects the Mediterranean with the interior.

Hamitic pastoral nomads penetrated into the grasslands of the Sudan and also moved southward over the savanna corridor of the eastern highlands into South Africa. Besides livestock, they doubtless introduced other materials and traits derived from northern Africa. The east coast received impulses from southern Arabia, India,

Kano, northern Nigeria, lies in the zone where Islamic and Meso-African cultures have met for many centuries. The city (population about 250,000) has long been a focus of caravan routes through Sahara and Sudan; now it is an important entre-pôt served by roads and railroads. The Moslem Hausa, of Negroid stock with Caucasoid infusions, form the main population group. The buildings, of unique architecture, have mud walls. (A Shell photograph)

and even the Malay Archipelago. Sailing ships used the monsoons to travel west in one season and return eastward with the reversal of the winds. Arab contacts with Africa's coast may reach back 2,000 years; they became frequent after the seventh century A.D. Islam is strong in the coastal towns, and Swahili, the lingua franca of eastern Africa, contains many Arab words. The peoples

and cultures of Madagascar show so clearly the imprint of Malay settlers (dating back perhaps 1,500 years) that one must assume they also frequented the coast of the mainland. The widespread occurrence of crops from the Malay Archipelago that are grown in tropical Africa supports this view.

The west coast of Africa, in contrast, became exposed to foreign influences much later, when the Portuguese extended their voyages southward. The direct impact of the European, however, was limited until the middle of the nineteenth century to some coastal areas, chiefly along the Guinea coast. Slave trading moved millions across the seas to the Americas, causing severe population losses far inland. But good harbors were few, and the rivers that tumbled over the highland escarpment hindered rather than helped in entering the interior. Tropical rain forest and diseases also discouraged exploration. Thus, until only a century ago the greater part of Meso-Africa remained a blank on the map.

The economic basis of Meso-African culture consisted of crop farming on shifting fields, the hoe as main tool, and of raising cattle, sheep, and goats in regions free from the tsetse fly (see Chapter 9). Although a number of crops and animals came from outside the realm, the upper Niger country appears to be the center where several native African plants were domesticated. West Africa—more specifically the Cameroons—probably was where the Bantu peoples originated. They spread east and southward some two thousand years ago, settling first the savannas and open woodlands and later pushing into the tropical rain forest. In their expansion they either absorbed or obliterated the primitive hunters and gatherers, of whom only scattered remnants survive in the Congo forest and in the Kalahari Desert.

In common with other peripheral cultures, Meso-Africans had animistic religions and no systems of writing. In some respects, however, their level was above that of other nonliterate cultures, owing to the trickle of impulses from civilizations to north and east. The density of population, considerably higher than among Indians of tropical America, reflects their greater diversity of means to cope with the habitat. Among their specialized traits were the art of metalworking, the relatively well-developed (though despotic) tribal organization, a feeling for law, and a fairly keen interest in the acquisition of property. A notable feature of western Meso-Africa was its large towns.

European exploration of "Dark Africa" was swiftly followed by its partition. Since then, as in all colonial countries, there has been humiliation and exploitation of the native peoples, but also much constructive effort. The scourge of slave raiding and trading, already an old one by the time that Europeans began to participate, was abolished and tribal warfare suppressed. Occidental forms of religion, law, education, medicine, agriculture, and production for foreign markets were introduced. Such intrusions deeply affected the traditional ways of life. Moreover, instead of preserving the native cultures, Europeans imposed their own. Thus, when European rule withdrew from Meso-Africa after the middle of the twentieth century, it left behind a multitude of societies which were too much disturbed to return to their native folkways but not transformed enough to possess a new social order.

The change from primitive tribe to modern society, which took some two thousand years in other parts of the world, could hardly have been accomplished here in a hundred years, even though the pace of change has quickened. The crucial issue is now whether or not native-born, Western-educated elites can lead the mass of tribal folk toward a better life in today's world. Closely related to this is the problem of how to create states that are socially coherent and economically viable from colonial conglomerates and strategic slices and slivers. This issue is accentuated in countries where territorial frameworks straddle the ethnic faultline that separates Meso-Africa from the Islamic Realm. Relations between peoples on either side of this line that runs from Senegal on the Atlantic eastward through Mali, Nigeria, Chad, and Sudan, range from uneasy coexistence to open separatist warfare.

Resident groups and temporary immigrants of non-African descent materially take part in future economic development, unless social and political pressures isolate or expel them. Among these groups are European farming and business communities in the eastern highlands from Kenya to Rhodesia, mixed-bloods in Angola and Mozambique, and Indians in the coastal areas of East Africa. Whether their presence assists or impedes economic development is a question. They occupy managerial, administrative, technical, and commercial positions, thus hindering the emergence of native entrepreneurs and administrators who would be more able to adapt foreign imports to local culture. The new African governments themselves bring in experts from Europe, America, the Soviet Union, and China, to do the work they think themselves not yet qualified to do.

These are fateful years in Meso-Africa. The end and outcome of independence cannot be foreseen. Though the wind of change blows strongly, the new countries want to control their own affairs; they are not prepared to do so. Decisions do not lie solely within Meso-Africa. Its economic resources and political weakness inevitably attract influences from abroad, whether these take the form of welcome "foreign aid" or suspect "neocolonialism." Although the legacy of European culture still dominates, one cannot be certain whether Meso-Africa will pattern itself in this Western mold, turn for its inspiration to other cultures, or find strength to develop its own ethos.

## CITATIONS AND FURTHER READINGS

Augelli, J. P. "The Rimland-Mainland Concept of Culture Areas in Middle America," *Annals of the Association of American Geographers*, 52 (1962): 119–129.

——— "The Controversial Image of Latin America: A Geographer's View," *Journal of Geography*, 62 (1963): 103–112.

Bacon, E. "A Preliminary Attempt to Determine the Culture Areas of Asia," *Southwestern Journal of Anthropology*, 2 (1946): 117–132.

Bobek, H. "The Main Stages of Socioeconomic Evolution from a Geographical Point of View," in Wagner, P. L., and Mikesell, M. W. (eds.), *Readings in Cultural Geography*, Chicago, 1962, 218–247. Originally published in *Die Erde: Zeitschrift der Gesellschaft für Erdkunde zu Berlin*, 90 (1959): 259–298. [Map]

Broek, J. O. M. "Diversity and Unity in Southeast Asia," *Geographical Review*, 34 (1944): 175–195.

Cahnman, W. J. "Frontiers between East and West Europe," *Geographical Review*, 39 (1949): 605–624.

Fisher, C. A. *Southeast Asia: A Social, Economic and Political Geography*, London and New York, 1966.

Jackson, W. A. D. *Russo-Chinese Borderlands: Zone of Peaceful Contact or Potential Conflict?* New York, 1962.

Kolb, A. "Die Geographie und die Kulturerdteile," in *Hermann von Wissmann Festschrift*, Tübingen, 1962, 42–49.

Kroeber, A. L. *Cultural and Natural Areas of Native North America*, University of California Publications in American Archaeology and Ethnology, no. 38, Berkeley, Calif., 1939.

——— "Culture Groupings in Southeast Asia," *Southwestern Journal of Anthropology*, 3 (1947): 175–195.

——— *A Roster of Civilizations and Culture*, Viking Fund Publications in Anthropology, no. 33, New York, 1962.

Latourette, K. M. *A Short History of the Far East*, rev. ed., New York, 1951.

Lerner, M. *America as a Civilization*, New York, 1957.

Lomax, A. *Folk Song Styles and Culture*, Washington, D.C., 1968.

Lowenthal, D. *West Indian Societies*, New York, 1971.

McNeill, W. H. *The Rise of the West: A History of the Human Community*, Chicago, 1963.

Nostrand, R. L. "The Hispanic-American Borderland: Delimitation of an American Culture Region," *Annals of the Association of American Geographers*, 60 (1970): 638–661.

Pryce, W. T. R. "Migration and the Evolution of Culture Areas: Cultural and Linguistic Frontiers in North-West Wales, 1750 and 1851," *Transactions of the Institute of British Geographers,* 65 (1975): 79–107.

Smith, H. "Accents of the World's Religions," in Bowman, J. (ed.), *Comparative Religion. The Charles Strong Trust Lectures,* 1961–70, Leiden, 1972, 1–18.

Toynbee, A. J. *A Study of History,* abridged ed. by Somervell, D. C., 2 vols., New York and London, 1947, 1957.

Townsend, A. R., and Taylor, C. C. "Regional Culture and Identity in Industrialized Societies: the Case of North-East England," *Regional Studies,* 9 (1975): 379–393.

Unstead, J. F. *A World Survey from the Human Aspect,* 5th ed., London, 1961.

Vogeler, I. "The Peasant Culture of Appalachia and Its Survival," *Antipode,* 5 (1973), March: 17–24.

Part II presented the social and cultural variety of mankind. We now turn to the analysis of economic differentiation and integration, confident that the reader will not think of "economic systems" and "economic man" in the abstract, but as forms of economy practiced by real people in concrete places. The point gains meaning when we consider the existence of rich and poor peoples. There is no standard remedy for poverty, whether regional, national, or continental; its treatment demands measures that fit the cultural matrix of the particular society.

In line with this thought we will discuss economic activities within the framework of a threefold division of societies: tribal, traditional, and modern. The first part of Chapter 9 presents this idea; the remainder of the chapter then examines the economic life of tribal cultures. Chapter 10 discusses agriculture in traditional and modern societies, and also reviews the plantation, a Western intrusion into other societies. Large-scale manufacturing, so characteristic for the Occidental world, forms the theme for Chapter 11. Part III concludes with an inquiry into the nature of underdeveloped countries and discusses ways of increasing the material welfare of their peoples.

# PART III PATTERNS OF LIVELIHOOD

Flooded rice fields (sawahs) in the highlands of West Java. (Photograph—Koninklijk Instituut voor de Tropen, Amsterdam)

# 9 FORMS OF ECONOMY: GATHERING AND AGRICULTURE IN TRIBAL SOCIETIES

The contrast between rich and poor is the most striking feature in the manifold diversity of mankind. This disparity requires that we try to understand the different forms of economy. The word *economy* as we use it here refers to more than the system of techniques, tools, resources, and organizations by which a society makes a living. We will also evaluate the economic relationships among various parts of the earth; their interdependence becomes vitally meaningful as we move toward the end of this century.

## A THREEFOLD DIVISION OF SOCIETIES

To bring order into our study, it will be most useful first to classify the world's infinite variety of economic pursuits into some broad categories. It will help us if we view economic activity in the context of sociocultural differentiation. It follows naturally that our primary division must be according to the kind of society, and from there we can further subdivide each one into dominant forms of economy.

The marked differences in level of living between the so-called "developed" and "underdeveloped" lands suggest a basic classification into industrial-commercial societies and all others. But the "others" consist of most of the earth's population and range from bands of primitive food collectors to ancient and sophisticated cultures. Evidently we must make some further distinction. We propose, therefore, to divide the underdeveloped world into *tribal* and *traditional* societies and to use the brief term *modern* for the industrial-commercial peoples (Figure 9–1). These labels admittedly are open to question, but so are

others such as "primitive-peasant-urban" or "primitive-intermediate-modern." The terminology, however, is less important than the widespread recognition of three basic types of societies. This tripartite division necessarily is a gross generalization; some segments of modern societies seem quite underdeveloped, and many commercial and even highly industrialized regions exist within tribal and traditional societies. The purpose of the grouping is to clarify our thinking by creating a framework on which to hang much information about the various economies.

These primary categories suggest the general social, economic, and political conditions in which people gain their livelihood. They also imply a progression from small, isolated, culturally homogeneous communities with simple skills toward large, heterogeneous entities that depend on specialized labor and sophisticated technologies for their urban way of life—communities characterized by a high degree of social and spatial mobility.

*Tribal societies,* small in scope and self-contained, base their social relations on kinship or village community. With no state organization, no clearly defined central authority, no social-economic hierarchy, all members hold equal cultivation or grazing rights within their common territory. They use simple tools and cultivate the land extensively, leaving much of it unused or fallow for long periods. Exceptions to this are some tribal peoples with rather intensive forms of agriculture.

Throughout the ages tribal societies learned to live in harmony with the earth, close to the land which provides their primary necessities. Usually they work merely to satisfy short-range needs. There is no specialization beyond the division of labor between the sexes. As a result the small productivity per worker leaves no savings to build up capital. Because the technological level is modest, these communities cannot always cope with difficulties such as extreme drought and diseases of epidemic or endemic nature. The insecurities of life and of making a living demand group solidarity. The members help each other, especially in sharing a fortuitous food surplus. Work and gift exchanges cement social relations and serve to redistribute wealth—such as it is. Rules of custom, sanctified by rituals, prescribe these rights and obligations. Inevitably the population of tribal societies remains quite low.

There are many deviations from such an ideal type of tribal society, and all the more as outside forces intrude. A tribal folk which formerly was isolated cannot maintain its ways of life when outside rulers and powerful economic systems take over. Instead of working for the subsistence of their own community, the people must produce for the benefit of others. They are forced to labor on a plantation, in a factory, on road construction or whatever activity—for strangers who do not understand local traditions or care about conserving the ecological balance. Though local markets may provide a means of exchanging certain products, the strangers handle the processing and the long-distance trade through urban concentrations, which are also foreign creations. When world markets collapse, or the land has been exploited and the supply exhausted, the once self-sufficient tribal society faces disaster.

*Traditional societies* occupy a broad range. Some have relatively simple economies and make a living in ways not much more complicated than those of tribal groups. Others in their technical occupations and social organizations approach the complexity of modern commercial-industrial states. China shows how difficult it is to classify countries during a period of rapid change. An Oriental state that claims to be the model of the Marxist revolution seems hardly to belong in the category of traditional countries. However, its current efforts gain meaning exactly because it strives to transform a traditional society.

The traditional society is prescientific, that is to say, based on attitudes toward knowledge and technology which prevailed before Western science created a new concept of nature and of man's power to manipulate it. In contrast to the tribal form, the traditional society is organized as a state with a hierarchic structure. The ruling class claims rights to the land and exacts tribute or rent—usually in goods and services—from those who work it. This relationship has been called "rent capitalism" (Bobek, 1962). Some writers refer to the societal type as a "peasant society," because the mass of the people are peasants—cultivators of the land, subject to the demands and sanctions of the power-holding stratum (Wolf, 1966).

Production depends largely on the muscles of man and beast, supplemented by water and wind and, increasingly, by modern forms of energy. The zone of traditional societies includes huge areas of extensive land use, especially nomadic herding. However, rural areas which are intensively cultivated have extremely high population densities. Their crop yields are very high per hectare; the labor input in farming is huge, but the output per worker low. In many regions, massive environmental alterations have taken place, especially with the development over centuries of large schemes for irrigation and terracing. Nevertheless, the farming peoples of southern and eastern Asia have struck a rough balance with nature. Even the effects of such events as earthquakes, typhoons, or prolonged drought are rarely long-lived. Some cities of the traditional societies are large, many of them being administrative centers; however, they contain only a small proportion of the total population of a country.

Birth into a specific family, clan, or caste usually determines the status of a person. Wealth rests mainly on owning land which, in turn, gives political power and access to top positions in government. The landlords reside in urban centers and spend their profits either on conspicuous consumption or on investment in more land rather than in industrial or commercial ventures. Often they consider such enterprises below their dignity and leave them to other classes or even to foreign entrepreneurs. Thus, the middle class is apt to be small. The illiterate debt-ridden peasants form an inert mass, living in ignorance and poverty. Normally, birth rates are high and so are death rates. However, the latter have declined sharply in recent years wherever modern notions

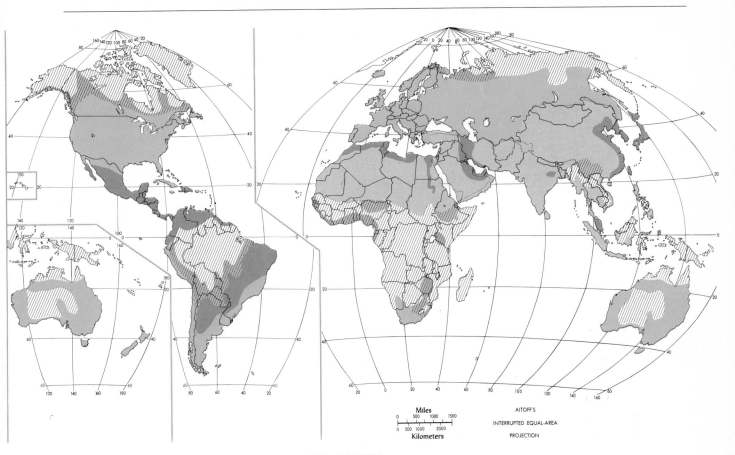

**WORLD: TRIBAL, TRADITIONAL, AND MODERN SOCIETIES**

The threefold division, although tentative, provides a broad perspective on types of economy. The boundary lines are actually zones of contact. Significant areas of mixture are shown; in some cases they indicate two kinds of society living side by side, in others a blending of old and new forms of societal organization.

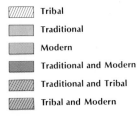

| | |
|---|---|
| ▨ | Tribal |
| ▨ | Traditional |
| ▨ | Modern |
| ▨ | Traditional and Modern |
| ▨ | Traditional and Tribal |
| ▨ | Tribal and Modern |

of public health have penetrated, causing an alarming growth rate of population and a precarious food situation.

Western intrusion added external and distant relationships to the economies of many traditional societies whose trade had been an important but not large part of life. In time the livelihood of millions became connected with the integrated world economy as organized by European and North American powers. Whether American-dominated oil corporations in the Middle East, Dutch plantations in Southeast Asia, British companies in Africa, or Russian state farms in Turkestan—all made inroads upon traditional societies and, for good or ill, started them on the way to modernization.

*Modern societies* intensively use science and technology as developed in the Occidental world over the last 200 years. In some countries, the high output per worker allows a comfortable level of living and substantial savings for new investments. Regions and countries have become integrated systems of diverse services and industry. Agriculture employs only a small fraction of the labor force. Farmers act like businessmen, either as private landowners or as tenants who pay rent in money according to the market price of the land; this freedom contrasts with the life of peasants in a more traditional society. Most people of a modern society live in cities, participating in an intricate network of impersonal relationships and moving easily from place to place. They achieve financial rewards through competence and achievement, though inherited social position may be the key to acquiring the necessary individual qualifications. The vertical scale of status offers considerable opportunity for change. Unless the state bureaucrat takes over his function, the private entrepreneur plays a large role in organizing and directing production. The economy depends highly on import of raw materials from the less developed countries and, in turn, on export of industrial materials and services.

The effect of rampant modern technology on the earth presents a paradox. We often feel that the voracious demand for industrial goods is destroying our habitat by making air unbreathable and water at sea or on land unusable, and by debasing wild plants and animals. As long as technical ability is used merely for profit making and constantly searching for new products, it can be of little help. We must find new ways to channel technology if we would preserve the earth's environments for future generations.

As a society adopts the modern way of life, it first experiences death control, which results in a huge burst of population; then it slowly acquires low birth and death rates and, we hope, will settle into a gradual or almost zero growth.

One needs to sound a note of caution. The ideals of equality are far from realized; the poor still crowd the streets of the richest societies. Obviously the process of modernization has not obliterated all tribal and traditional features in the societies it has touched. Remnants remain even in the hearth of modern industrialism, even in England, where much modern political thought and economic organization first developed. Such vestiges include a "house of lords" (in part still based on inherited titles), a relatively strong class system, and landownership patterns that sometimes seem medieval in their aristocratic brashness. In the United States the political system, especially at the local level, still reflects the rural and small-town dominance set up for the agrarian society of the eighteenth and nineteenth centuries. In the Soviet Union, prerevolutionary cultural ways continue in the class structure and in rural and urban economic traditions. On the other hand, Meso-Africa in its headlong rush toward a new economy is adopting some of the most up-to-date elements of modern societies; there new things exist side by side with traditional and tribal folk forms.

## FORMS OF ECONOMY

We turn first to ways of making a living directly from the land and will later discuss manufacturing and service industries. Each type of society contains various forms of land use which tend to localize in different regions (Table 9-1). Thus we can speak of a winter wheat region, where the predominant agrarian economy is the production of winter wheat. This does not mean that all people in the area are engaged in this activity or that only winter wheat grows here, or that the entire production of winter wheat is concentrated in this place. Instead of distinguishing an agricultural region by its commodity, we may find it more significant to note the methods of production (e.g., irrigation, plow, or hoe tillage) or its purpose (subsistence or commercial). The ideas of Eduard Hahn are of special interest in this connection (Figure 9-2).

Some tribal societies still live by gathering (collecting, hunting, or fishing), but most practice simple forms of agriculture either on temporary clearings or on permanent plots. In traditional societies—as among some tribal folk—the predominant agrarian occupations range from intensive subsistence tillage to nomadic herding. Western large-scale enterprises such as the plantation, livestock ranching, or mechanized commercial farming of tropical crops have invaded and altered other economies (see Chapter 10).

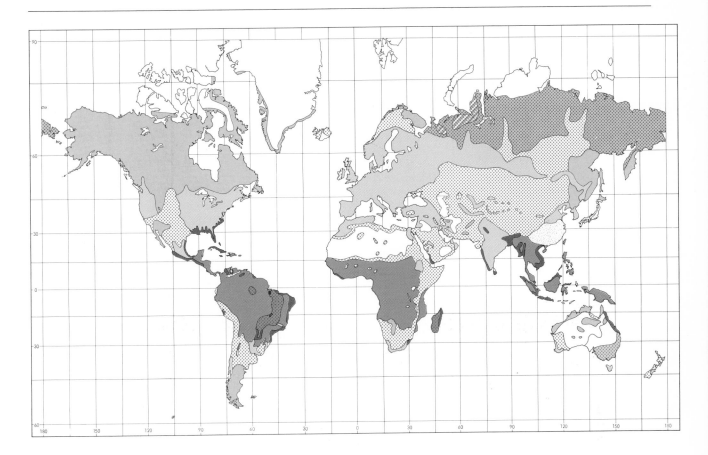

FIGURE
9-2

WORLD: FORMS OF ECONOMY (AFTER E. HAHN, 1892)

up to the present. After Hahn, E., "Die wirtschafts-formen der Erde," *Petermann's Geographische Mitte-ilungen,* 38 (1892): 8-12.

The work of Eduard Hahn (1857–1928) revolutionized thought on agricultural origins and diffusions. He disposed of the traditional notion of three universal stages of economic evolution (hunting—herding—agriculture) and identified types of land use as forms of culture. He viewed hoe agriculture as the oldest form of tillage and plow agriculture (with domesticated animals for draft power) as a later development, originating in Mesopotamia. Intensification of hoe culture led to horticulture, in Hahn's opinion "the highest form of agriculture." He also considered plantation agriculture as a specialized, commercial type of hoe culture. According to him, nomadic herding evolved from plow agriculture as an ecological adaptation to arid lands. Hahn's ideas stimulated a new approach to the understanding of land use, although later research has modified or even disproved some of his hypotheses.

This map, the original form of which was published eighty years ago, has been the model for many others,

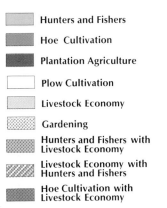

Hunters and Fishers

Hoe Cultivation

Plantation Agriculture

Plow Cultivation

Livestock Economy

Gardening

Hunters and Fishers with Livestock Economy

Livestock Economy with Hunters and Fishers

Hoe Cultivation with Livestock Economy

TABLE
9-1

A. *Tribal societies*

1. Gathering, hunting, and/or fishing
   a. Nonspecialized foraging
   b. Specialized hunting and fishing

2. Reindeer herding

3. Shifting cultivation (swiddens)

4. Cattle herding

5. Tillage of permanent fields

B. *Traditional societies*

1. Intensive cultivation, with plow or hand tools

2. Extensive plow cultivation, supplementary large livestock

3. Nomadic herding

C. *Modern societies*

1. Mixed crop and livestock farming

2. Dairy farming

3. Crop farming
   a. Mediterranean agriculture
   b. Specialized horticulture
   c. Grain farming
   d. Cotton farming

4. Livestock ranching

5. Plantation farming

## COLLECTING, HUNTING, AND FISHING IN TRIBAL SOCIETIES

Human beings for most of their existence lived as predatory creatures. Only some ten thousand years ago they began simple agriculture. Nevertheless, by now almost all have changed to crop growing. Only scattered survivals remain of what once was the universal way of life (Figure 9-3). True, some farming societies still practice food gathering and hunting; and even modern fishing or forestry methods are giant forms of gathering—adjuncts to other well-established ways of production.

## UNSPECIALIZED GATHERING

Remnants of gathering societies may seem insignificant, yet we cannot ignore them. They give us clues how early mankind lived and affected the biophysical environment. The small groups that remain, relics of the oldest ways of life, live in formerly nearly inaccessible areas where they took refuge when peoples of more advanced culture invaded their lands. Recent examples of this in the western parts of the United States are Indian tribes such as the Paiute and Pomo (see Figure 9-3). Such displaced gatherers usually belong to another race than that of the now predominant peoples. This difference partly explains why they cling to their ancient ways. They seem to change slowly, but this is also because they live in isolation on the least desirable lands. Just the same many have picked up some elements of their economy from more traditional or modern neighbors. Each group needed to adapt to its environment to survive, whether in the rain forests of southeast Asia or bleak deserts of Patagonia or the arid lands of the western United States.

The Pueblo Indians raised crops in the desert, though the Indians of the intermontane basins to the north did not do so. In California the gathering and hunting afforded such a good living (always relative, of course) that there may have seemed no need to grow crops. Abundant acorns provided the staple food, supplemented by grass seeds, bulbs, berries, and wild fruits. Shellfish were easily available along the coast, huge flocks of ducks and geese came in the fall to the marshes, and there was always open season to hunt deer, rabbits, ground squirrels, and field mice. Even so, the California Indians might have changed to crop growing had they lived closer to the agricultural cores in Meso-America, or if their population had exceeded the supply of food. At the far tip of South America, and in Australia and Tasmania, isolation certainly was a reason for the backward economy of the gatherers.

These peoples are often called "primitive," a value-loaded term that refers to their technology and organization, not to their intelligence. Gatherers require much forethought and certain specialized skills if they are to subsist on marginal lands. They need to observe, hunt, adjust to extreme circumstances, and fashion tools from

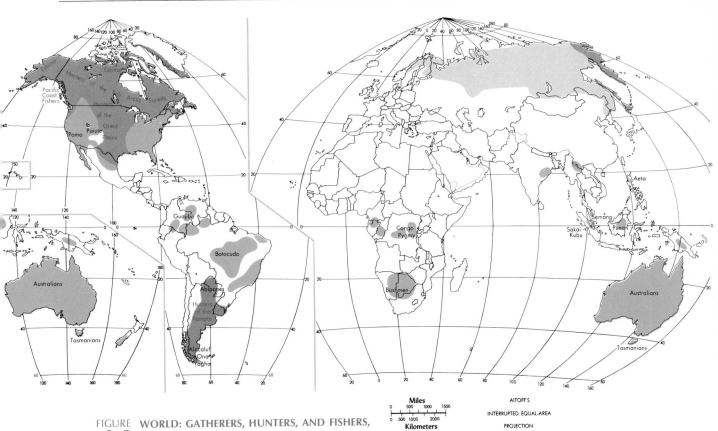

FIGURE **WORLD: GATHERERS, HUNTERS, AND FISHERS,**
**9-3** **ABOUT A.D. 1500**

Miles
0    500   1000   1500
0  500 1000   2000
Kilometers

AITOFF'S

INTERRUPTED EQUAL-AREA

PROJECTION

In the Americas, nonagricultural types of economy prevailed over far wider areas than in the Old World, and many of them were specialized forms of hunting and/or fishing.

**Distribution about A.D. 1500**

Unspecialized Gatherers (with Subsidiary Hunting and/or Fishing)

Specialized Hunters and Fishers

Hunters and Fishers with some Cultivation

Hunters and Fishers with Herding (Mostly Reindeer)

Paiute     Unspecialized Gatherers

Pacific Coast Fishers     Specialized Hunters and Fishers

available materials. They may be intensely concerned with matters we consider unimportant. Certainly they live close to nature and to the world of spirits and of their ancestors. Many tribes, as for example, the Australian aborigines, have an elaborate kinship system and cherish a mythology.

Gathering and hunting imply mobility, but this does not mean that tribal bands are always on the move. A group may camp near a stream or water hole as long as there is good foraging in the environment, or they may change with the seasons to places where the food supply is ready to harvest. Submarginal lands average one to five persons over 20 square kilometers. The population in more congenial regions is considerably higher and needs a smaller territory per person in which to gather and hunt.

Jivaro Indians, upper Amazon Basin, Ecuador. The Jivaros practice some shifting cultivation but do much hunting with long blowpipes and darts tipped with curare—a paralyzing poison extracted from a plant root. They are probably best known for their custom of shrinking the heads of slain enemies. (A Shell photograph)

Whether in camp or village, there usually is a division of labor. The women remain near home base to care for the children, provide meals, and store the surplus. They make cloth from bark, prepare skins and equipment such as nets, baskets, and pottery. They gather food, fiber, and fuel from the vicinity. Meanwhile the men rove at greater distance, also gathering materials, but hunting and fishing, often using tools and methods of remarkable ingenuity, such as the pointed stick, bow and arrow, boomerang, blowgun with poison darts, and various snares and traps.

The dog is the only domestic animal. The common explanation for its domestication presents the early wild dog as a camp follower that was tamed, bred in captivity, then used for hunting purposes. However, the more primitive gatherers and hunters do not use the dog for hunting. Because our own culture is so utility-minded, we assume all peoples at all times had the same motivation. Perhaps the domestication of the dog simply began with young ones being adopted as pets.

## SPECIALIZED HUNTING AND FISHING

Until a century ago these forms of economy were widespread in the Americas. Now they survive— and precariously at that—in areas not occupied by people of Occidental culture. Even where their lands were not taken away or their means of livelihood destroyed, many died from diseases to which they were not immune. The following are several examples of such vanishing societies.

Pacific Coast Fishers   Along the Pacific coast from southern Alaska to Oregon, only vestiges remain of the once flourishing Indian fishing economy. In California too, where Indians came to gather shellfish from the tidal zone and to fish and hunt fowl in estuaries, their way of living has been replaced by urban settlement, motels, and industrialization. Little more than a century ago Indians lived in villages at the foot of the heavily forested coastal mountains, or along the water's edge, or on island chains that dot the glacier-sculpted sounds. The men went out in sturdy boats to exploit the sea and its shores. By far the most important resource was the salmon they caught in rivers and salty inlets. They also hunted seals and sea lions, dolphins and porpoises, and sometimes even harpooned whales in the larger bays and the open sea. Occasional hunting trips on land decidedly were secondary to the fishing activities.

Hunters of the Grasslands   The acquisition of the horse from the Spaniards, some four hundred years ago, revolutionized the way of life for the Indians of the Great Plains. Before that time few Indians lived there or ventured out to hunt in the dry, high lands. On foot they followed the American buffalo (bison), their prime resource for meat, skins, and sinews; they also caught antelope, deer, coyote, jackrabbits, and prairie dogs (actually a kind of squirrel). The horse gave them mobility and changed the Great Plains from a submarginal region into a rich hunting domain. This era of affluent livelihood lasted at most only a century. Then the white man came. Though the Indians fought—the hunters becoming swift cavalry brigades—their defeat was inevitable. The rifle sup-

planted bow and arrow, and it rapidly depleted the buffalo. The Europeans expelled the Indians from their lands and placed them within reservations.

The story of the South American pampas, the great grasslands of Argentina and Uruguay, is similar. The pampas were home for huge numbers of wild creatures, including the rhea (American ostrich) and the guanaco (a species of the American camel related to the llama and the alpaca). To capture them, the Indians used the bola, a throwing device consisting of round stones attached to a bundle of leather thongs which entangled the prey. The coming of the horse, a post-Columbian import from the Old World, transformed radically this simple hunting-collecting economy. A highly mobile society evolved whose ritual life as well as economy revolved around the horse. The new animal not only increased hunting effectiveness greatly but also made its rider a formidable foe of the Spaniard. Not until the latter half of the nineteenth century—after new technologies had greatly enhanced the value of the pampas in European eyes—were the Pampa Indians defeated and replaced by agricultural colonizers, mostly from Spain and Italy.

The Eskimo   The popular image of the Eskimo is mainly derived from their traditional way of life in the Canadian Arctic. Here the seal was the main source of food, clothing, implements, fuel, and light. During the winter the people lived in igloos, houses built of snow blocks on the sea ice; they caught the seal by harpooning it when it came up to the breathing holes in the ice. Hunters traveled over the ice by dog-drawn sleds. In summer they hunted the seal and other sea mammals by boat, the light, skin-covered kayak. In spring many Eskimo groups moved to the tundra, where they caught freshwater fish and birds and collected eggs. When the caribou were plentiful, hunters intercepted them in their annual migrations.

The Eskimo of Greenland have more open water than do their cousins in the Canadian Arctic, and thus depend more on the kayak than the sled. The warming of waters in the Labrador Sea since the early twentieth century has caused seals to move farther north; at the same time cod and other fish came northward, thus providing southern Greenland with a new resource base. Alaska presents another regional variation on the general theme. Because of unstable ice conditions along the north coast, winter settlement on the sea ice was rare. For the western Alaskan groups the main game were the sea lion, fur seal, and especially the walrus. Since the walrus and sea lion do not keep breathing holes open in the ice, they frequent the edge of the open sea.

The Viking settlements in Greenland from the eleventh to the fifteenth century had little impact on the indigenous economy. This land for the last 200 years has been under Danish influence and rule. The government during the present century has used an integrated approach to the problems of social and economic change. While protecting the Eskimo against the disruptive influence of an outside world, it provided them with social services and encouraged them to settle in large villages. It replaced the older mammal-based economy of the north with sheep raising and established a modern fishing industry in the south. Slowly the old order disintegrates under a benign government.

The Canadian government also is taking a heightened interest in the plight of the Indian and the Eskimo in helping them to adapt to new circumstances. Here as elsewhere the rifle has replaced the harpoon, the steel trap, and the bow and arrow. Caribou herds have declined catastrophically, fur-bearing animals such as the arctic fox become scarce. With the depletion of wild animal stock, the future economy is uncertain. The old cultural patterns of collective hunting and sharing have broken down. The coming of the military to build early-warning radar systems in the Arctic gave many jobs to the Eskimo, but spread disease among them and herded them into shanty towns. The Canadian government's interest in Indian and Eskimo welfare resulted in a more deliberate and humane policy, one that is dedicated to preserve vital elements of the indigenous culture.

Seal hunting and whaling during the nineteenth century brought the Eskimo of the Aleutians and coastal Alaska into close contact with outsiders, and thus with alcohol, tuberculosis, and other diseases. By the end of the century the harpoon gun and rifle had seriously depleted whale, walrus, seal, and caribou. Reindeer herding, introduced in the 1890s, failed in the long run. The reindeer joined the wild caribou or were eaten by wolves. In some areas the herds grew too large and overgrazed the pastures. The caribou, however, now again are increasing.

In Canada and Alaska the Eskimo are now involved in a money economy. First it was the pelt trade, then wage labor in fish canneries, in mines, and on defense installations. The Eskimo now tend to concentrate in larger settlements along the coast. Health problems are severe, abetted by poor nutrition, for no well-balanced diet has replaced the former high consumption of animal protein. The Danes consistently have aimed to stabilize the economic conditions of Eskimo communities. American policy, though more haphazard, has tried in recent decades to improve the way of living through education and various welfare measures.

In spite of several programs undertaken by the Canadian and United States governments, the Eskimo and, no less, their Indian neighbors have grown increasingly discontent. They question the dominant role of whites in government and in resource exploitation, and they demand that aboriginal rights to the land and its riches be recognized. Their claims are accentuated by the discovery of the huge petroleum field on the north slope of the Brooks Range in Alaska and by the presence of various mineral deposits in the Canadian Arctic—areas that powerful ice-breaking ships make accessible.

The United States government in 1971 finally settled the century-old land claims in Alaska. Native villages and regional corporations of natives may choose and divide 40 million acres but may not select any of the lands that the Secretary of the Interior set aside for the trans-Alaska oil pipeline; nor may they challenge the drilling for oil on the North Slope and its transportation.

In summary, the Eskimo are forced to adjust to fundamental shifts in the ecological setting as well as in the technical, social, and psychological environment. But, as one observer remarked, "the difficulty is that they are adapting not to the Arctic but to a Temperate Zone way of living. The new people with their new standards have nearly overwhelmed the Eskimos, not in numbers but in wishes and wants" (Hughes, 1965).

**Reindeer Herders of Northern Eurasia**  In contrast to North America the indigenous peoples of the

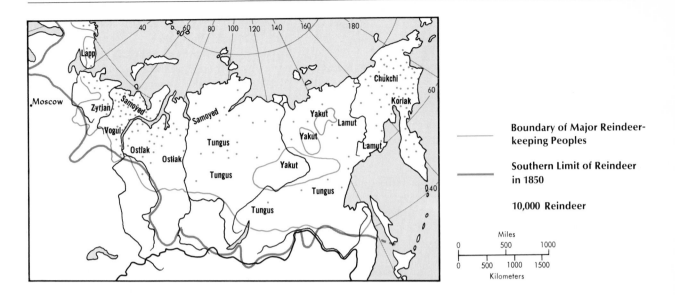

Boundary of Major Reindeer-
keeping Peoples

Southern Limit of Reindeer
in 1850

10,000 Reindeer

Miles
0    500    1000
0    500    1000    1500
Kilometers

FIGURE NORTHERN EURASIA: REINDEER HERDING
9-4

In the last century reindeer herding has, on the whole, receded northward under pressure of more intensive forms of land use. The Yakut enclaves are areas of cattle and horse rearing. After Mirow, N. T., "Notes on the Domestication of Reindeer," *American Anthropologist,* 47 (1945): 393–408 (Map).

Eurasian tundra do not depend on sea mammals. Their main resource is the reindeer, the domesticated variety of the caribou. In winter the herds feed in the subpolar forest, and in summer they pasture on the mosses and grasses of the tundra. The people gain a supplementary food supply from fishing, hunting, and collecting berries and roots.

Perhaps the reindeer was domesticated in the Lake Baikal region of southern Siberia in imitation of the pastoral nomads to the south. Some writers claim its separate domestication among the Lapps after they had had contact with the husbandry of European peoples. It also is possible that prehistoric hunters of the north European plain formed some symbiosis with the reindeer, leading to its domestication. The use of the reindeer differs among various tribes. Milking is practiced mainly by the Tungus and the Lapps. Most tribes use the reindeer for drawing the sledge, but the Tungus ride and pack it. The Chukchi and Koryak consider their large half-wild herds mainly

as a meat reserve on the hoof. All over the region dogs are used to guard the herds (Figure 9-4).

The Russian Cossacks who invaded this domain in the early seventeenth century exacted tribute in furs. In the nineteenth century Russian farm colonists moved into the southern fringes of the taiga and along the Lena River even farther north to its confluence with the Aldan. Mining and lumber enterprises, port and defense installations, as well as political exiles and prisoners from European Russia, all contributed to cultural and economic changes in the Russian northlands. Russia's more northern location as compared to the ecumene of the United States and Canada makes integration of the polar and subpolar zones imperative. It is hard to judge from available Soviet literature exactly how the native peoples of this belt have fared under this expansion.

**Preagricultural Human Impact on the Earth**
It might seem at first thought that these technologies were too weak to make any permanent impact upon the habitat. People lived off the bounty of the land, one might say, and nature quickly replaced the little taken. This image of early humans living in idyllic harmony with their physical milieu has been challenged in recent years. One small band of hunters and gatherers may hardly

disturb the habitat, but the cumulative effect of occupance over thousands of years must have been considerable.

One of the earliest great achievements was to make fire, using it for warmth, cooking, and also as an aid to hunting and perhaps even intentionally as a means of spreading grassland, thus increasing the number of herbivores. In this way extensive areas changed from forest to grassland. Some trees withstand heat better than others or grow much faster and thereby may survive the next fire. Also, the seedlings of some species tolerate glaring sunlight and dried-out topsoil whereas others need shade and moisture. Fire therefore acts as a selector, determining the composition of the forest or making it a grassland with scattered trees of a few or only one species.

In lands with year-round precipitation, the forest—though altered in character—most likely will reestablish itself. In regions with sparse moisture or with a pronounced dry season, the forest vegetation is more vulnerable. Of the world's grasslands in tropics as well as in middle latitudes, a large part may well be a form of man-induced vegetation. It is well known that the extensive grassy uplands of the Middle West, devoid of woody vegetation when the Europeans arrived, now grow trees wherever desired.

Another result of early human predatory activities was the extermination of game animals. Some scientists say climatic changes during the glacial and interglacial periods caused certain species such as the American forms of elephant, camel, horse, and sloth to disappear from what are now the western deserts and steppes of the United States. But there are indications that humans were at least a strong contributing factor. In New Zealand the moa, a gigantic herbivorous running bird, became the prey of the early Polynesians, who arrived there perhaps in the ninth century A.D. Since the hunters were few and had only simple tools, they used fire to capture the moa and in the process changed much forest into grassland (Cumberland, 1962). Also in Europe several game animals vanished in recent prehistoric times, when climatic change could hardly have been the cause. Early humans changed the environment in other ways too. Travel by boat and raft must have spread rodents, insects, parasites, and plants from mainland to offshore islands. De-

struction of vegetation on sloping surfaces may have sped up the natural processes of erosion.

Mankind's role in changing the face of the earth is not merely a modern creation. Although present techniques enable us to bring about spectacular alterations for better or for worse, we cannot ignore how preagricultural peoples over the ages have altered their habitats.

## AGRICULTURE IN TRIBAL SOCIETIES

### MULTIPLE ORIGINS OF AGRICULTURE

Most available evidence points to the Middle East and Nuclear America (Mexico to Peru) as the earliest sites of agriculture. But this does not preclude the possibility that plants and animals were not domesticated even earlier in other parts of the world (see Chapter 3). No doubt several areas contributed to the present assemblage of crops and animals. Most of these regions of origin are tropical or subtropical and have considerable differences in altitude, therefore offering a great variety of environmental niches for species. This gave a wide diversity from which the people selected what best suited their needs.

From these early centers man-altered crops and animals spread to other lands as far as conditions allowed. European colonization around the world resulted in especially rapid transfer of agricultural plants and animals. Today one can hardly imagine the Americas without cattle, horses, sheep, wheat, barley, rice, and other small grains, or think of Eurasia and Africa without maize, manioc, and various kinds of potatoes. Rubber, cinchona (quinine), and cocoa were introduced into tropical Asia and Africa, the main producers now. In turn, such major commodities of tropical America as coffee, bananas, and sugar cane came from the Old World.

### SHIFTING CULTIVATION

Today shifting cultivation, though surviving in remote corners of Europe and East Asia, persists mainly among peoples of tropical lands (Figure 9-5). Perhaps as many as 200 million people, occupying one quarter of the world's land surface, make their living this way. In broad definition, shifting cultivation is "any continuing agriculture system in which impermanent clearings are cropped for shorter periods in years than they are fallowed" (Conklin, 1961, 27). Other terms for shifting cultivation are: bush-fallow, slash-and-burn agriculture, forest-field rotation, and land rotation. All stress some salient aspect of this form of land use. "Burning" is not always a universal feature, and not practiced everywhere; "rotation" and "fallow" are not strictly correct where land is abandoned without plan. Each language has its own term for the cleared plot. Some such terms are now widely used in literature, as, for instance, that for a burned-over field: *swidden* (from early English), *milpa* (Middle America), *roca* (Brazil), *chitemene* (Central Africa), *ladang* (Indonesia), and *caiñgin* (Philippines).

Shifting cultivation does not usually imply that the people move to a new place (Figure 9-6). Each village holds its territory in communal ownership. The use-right on the cleared land belongs to the villager who cultivates it, but actual ownership is not associated with tribal peoples. If the plot is far from the village, the worker may build a temporary shelter near it. Only when the clearings are quite distant may the whole settlement move to a more convenient site. More commonly, a group may split off from the parent village and start anew in virgin territory.

The cultivation cycle runs about as follows: After the men by common consent have selected a site for a swidden, they clear the forest in the dry season with ax or machete. Depending on tools and vegetation cover, they girdle or actually fell big trees and slash smaller woody growth. Cutting down scrub or grass cover requires, of course, less work. Before the rainy season begins, they burn trees and trash.

Each family receives a part of the clearing for its own use. Women do most of the planting, but men usually participate. Cuttings and seeds are planted by dibble (pointed stick) or hoe in the soft top layer of forest earth and wood ash. There is no place for draft animals and plow—even if known—amid the tree stumps. Usually each plot carries many kinds of plants, often growing in tiers, each cared for individually and harvested at the proper time. To a Western observer the swidden may look like chaos; it is actually quite a rational form of intercropping. The dense plant cover, not arranged in rows, protects the soil from erosion, and the association and succession of various crops retard exhaustion of the soil.

The crop complex differs according to the environmental situation, dietary habits, and various cultural factors. Maize and cassava (manioc) are staple crops in America, rice in Southeast Asia, millets and sorghums in Africa; nevertheless, in some places crops introduced from elsewhere have become more important than the indigenous ones. Certainly today all of these crops occur in all continents. Rice of the "upland" or "dry" variety does not need flooding. It is often grown as the single crop on swiddens in Southeast Asia and in West Africa. Also important and widely grown are various root crops and tubers such as yam, sweet potato, arrowroot, and taro. Quite common are sugarcane, plantain (cooking banana), and a multitude of vegetables, among them beans and peas, squash and melon, and the eggplant.

The time span necessary for cultivating the land depends on the fertility of the soil and on the kind of crops. In some areas the plot is used only one year, but more likely two to three years. Besides loss of fertility, the problem is to keep back the forest growth which invades the clearing from every side. When the plot is abandoned, it regenerates under natural vegetation succession. First, light-loving grasses occupy the clearing, but they disappear as shade increases. After some ten to twenty years a good forest of second-growth trees has reestablished itself and the land can be cleared again to begin the new cycle.

Many tribes that practice shifting cultivation have, in addition to the swiddens, small permanent gardens within or near the village. Here grow coconut and other palms and fruit trees, as well as various vegetables and spices. Hunting and gathering from the forest adds sources of sustenance. In the African savanna, where the vegetation cover consists of scrub and grass with scattered trees, shifting cultivation occurs in association with livestock herding (see p. 219).

The usual explanation of why shifting cultivation prevails in the wet tropics stresses low soil fertility. True, constant conditions of heat and moisture intensify processes that deplete plant nutrients. Whereas the natural forest maintains a stable relationship with other components of the

FIGURE **WORLD: FORMS OF LAND USE IN TRIBAL SOCIETIES**
9-5

This is the first of three maps showing forms of land use. The others are for traditional land use (page 226) and modern land use (pages 246–247).

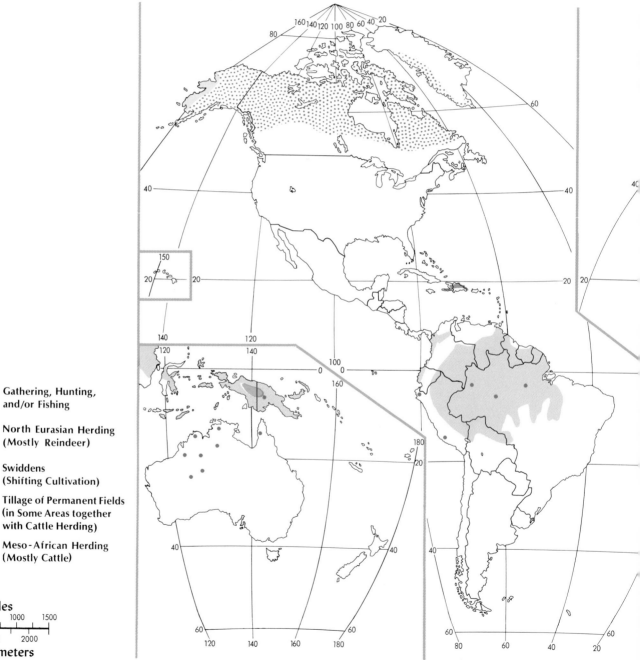

 Gathering, Hunting, and/or Fishing

North Eurasian Herding (Mostly Reindeer)

Swiddens (Shifting Cultivation)

Tillage of Permanent Fields (in Some Areas together with Cattle Herding)

 Meso-African Herding (Mostly Cattle)

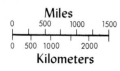

Miles

0   500   1000   1500

0   500  1000        2000

Kilometers

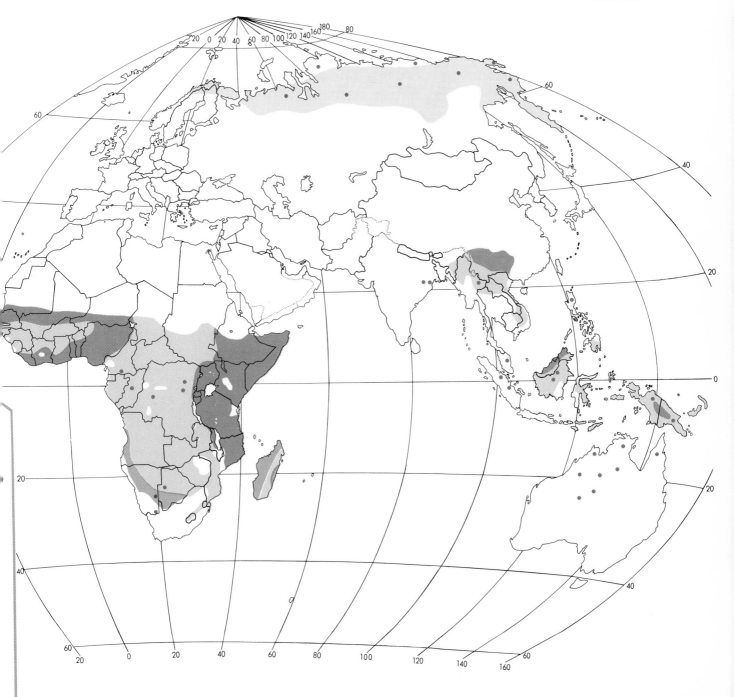

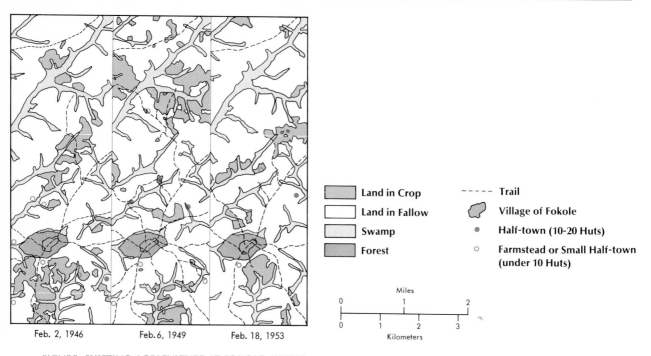

Feb. 2, 1946    Feb. 6, 1949    Feb. 18, 1953

FIGURE **SHIFTING AGRICULTURE AT FOKOLE, LIBERIA**
9-6

The village of Fokole has about 1,000 inhabitants, most of whom engage in shifting agriculture. Dry or upland rice is the main crop. About 2.5 hectares of land are in fallow for each hectare of crop. Notice that by 1953 the farmers had returned to cultivate land that was used in 1946 but fallow in 1949. The area covered by the map accounts for only part of the land used by the people of Fokole. Based on maps prepared by P. W. Porter from air photographs taken on the dates shown.

ecosystem—such as climate, soil, fauna—the shifting cultivator interrupts the closed equilibrium. Crops exhaust the transient availability of the nutrients in the topsoil and, after fertility declines, a new clearing must be made elsewhere.

Technology presents the other side of the argument. In his book *Germania* the Roman author Tacitus described the tribes east of the Rhine. They were shifting cultivators and—contrary to his opinion—worked poor soils. In time, by changing their techniques they became tillers of permanent fields. Without denying that some tropical environments are difficult, we need to emphasize human ability to overcome such handicaps. Relatively few such areas remain in tropical Asia, sug-

gesting that the inhabitants have developed or borrowed effective methods to care for their land. In contrast, peoples similarly located in tropical Africa and, particularly, in South America still cling to primitive ways.

These considerations gain urgency because living conditions deteriorate quickly in areas of shifting cultivation when too many people depend on a limited food supply. This system of farming usually was adequate as long as cultivators and their wants were few. During the twentieth century, with disease control and other changes, population growth has increased at an accelerating rate. At the same time more and more shifting cultivators planted part of their swiddens in commercial crops. For instance, in Indonesia, instead of abandoning a ladang to natural vegetation, it would be planted to rubber seedlings. In Africa it might be oil palms, in Polynesia coconuts, in America coffee. Such tree crops occupy the land a long time and consequently remove it from the food-producing rotation cycle. In theory, one might argue that the sale of these cash crops diminishes the need for homegrown foodstuffs; in practice it does not work that way.

Some agricultural experts today claim that in the tropical rain forest environment the best solution to the problem of land use would be to cultivate food-producing trees rather than the industrial tree crops mentioned here.

Food production by shifting cultivation is not merely a farming method; it is the way of life, closely linked with religious values and rituals. Every critical stage—selecting the site, clearing, planting, and harvesting—needs group action and the approval or appeasement of the spirits. Thus shifting cultivation continues, but more land must be cleared to provide food for more people while the total area available shrinks because of commercial crops. This leads to shorter fallow periods, with the result that the soil fails to regenerate completely. To counter the lower soil fertility, the agriculturists clear larger areas and this further increases the pressure on the land. Frequent fires result in a grass cover and a sod difficult to break with simple tools. Such grasslands in effect must also be subtracted from the arable land. In Africa, however, the use of grass savanna for swiddens is not uncommon; perhaps the African hoe is a better tool to deal with the sod.

External forces also restrict the area available for temporary clearings. Formerly, colonial governments often granted European planters the land rights in "unused" village territories, unaware of how these lands functioned in the native's agricultural cycle. Modern resource management looks with disfavor on the destruction of forest because the trees have economic value and they prevent soil erosion.

There is no simple solution to these problems. One may expect that the growing pressure will gradually force people to more intensive methods of farming, as has happened in the past, but this process will be very slow and more painful than is acceptable in our modern age. Everywhere government agencies, often with aid from advanced countries, are searching for new farming methods to replace shifting cultivations. The schemes must take into account the specific features of each habitat as well as the traditions of the people.

## LIVESTOCK HERDING IN AFRICA

The tropical rain forest is inimical to grazing animals. The inhabitants of the Amazon Basin, the Guinea Coast, the Congo Basin, and the interior of Borneo have only small domestic animals such as poultry, ducks, and pigs. But most tribal societies live in lands that have only seasonal rainfall where the natural vegetation consists of open deciduous forest, but more often of savanna. Although the grasses are usually not very nutritious, they provide extensive grazing for cattle, sheep, and goats. The integration of crops and livestock, which to us seems so obvious as a means to maintain soil fertility, hardly exists in indigenous farming. This separation of livestock and cropping is particularly marked in Meso-Africa, where vast areas of savanna surround the tropical rain forest.

In Africa the blood-sucking tsetse fly largely determines the distribution of livestock (Figure 9–7). Certain of the various species carry the single-celled organism known as trypanosome, which when passed into the blood of humans causes sleeping sickness, and when passed into the blood of domestic animals gives them the nagana disease. The tsetse flourishes in the shady but warm environment of tree and scrub cover, forming discontinuous "fly belts" within Africa south of the Sahara. The tsetse fly doubtless is an important factor in the retardation of this region. Owing to modern drugs, sleeping sickness has ceased to be a main cause of death, but the nagana disease still wastes the cattle. For this reason alone, mixed farming cannot be the substitute for shifting cultivation today in many parts of Meso-Africa.

Livestock husbandry and crop farming, even where they exist side by side, are often practiced by ethnically different groups. The pastoralists, although the minority, dominate the cultivators. They attach great social, even mystical, value to their stock. The more cattle a man has, regardless of its quality, the higher is his status. The animals are not sold for beef and produce very little milk. They are like a bank account, a means of acquiring wives who, in turn, will bear girls who can be married in exchange for more cattle. This value system has affected many cultivator tribes; the men tend the cattle on the natural pastures while the women work the fields. Because of the low carrying capacity of the grasslands (10 or more hectares are needed for one head of cattle), the herds have to range over wide areas. Even so, most pastures in the tsetse-free areas are grossly

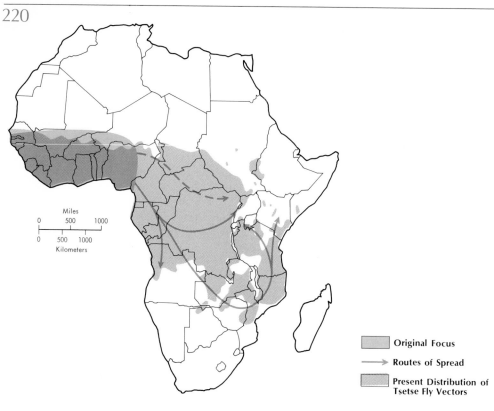

Original Focus

Routes of Spread

Present Distribution of
Tsetse Fly Vectors

FIGURE   **AFRICA: REGIONS INFESTED BY THE TSETSE FLY**
**9-7**

Based on maps in Knight, C. G., "The Ecology of African Sleeping Sickness," *Annals of the Association of
American Geographers*, 61 (1971): 23–44. Sleeping sickness spread from its West African focus to other parts
of Central Africa, becoming prevalent in parts of East
Africa by the early twentieth century. The disease (trypanosomiasis) affects mankind, domestic livestock, and
wild animals; its various forms are transmitted by
about a dozen species of the tsetse fly.

overstocked, causing severe soil erosion. Elimination of scrubland has pushed back the tsetse fly,
but the new expanses of grassland quickly fill
with more of the half-wild cattle instead of serving to produce food crops.

### AGRICULTURE ON PERMANENT FIELDS

In the tropics there are, in addition to shifting
cultivation, three forms of cropping on permanent fields: (1) intensive subsistence tillage,
mainly among more advanced "traditional" societies (Chapter 10) but some in tribal societies;
(2) small-scale plantation farming; (3) crop rotation. We will now examine these forms of land
use insofar as they are employed in tribal societies.

Shifting cultivation in Southeast Asia appears as a marginal and shrinking form of land
use, mainly among forest dwellers in the highland. There are several well-documented cases of
the changeover from swiddens to permanent
fields as, for instance, in the nineteenth century in
Cebu (the Philippines), in the hill lands of Java,
and more recently in central Celebes (Sulawesi).
In the highlands of East Africa the dense population around Lake Victoria and on the slopes of
Kilimanjaro has developed an intensive system of
permanent garden cultivation with plantains,
sweet potatoes, cassava, and maize as food crops,
and cotton or coffee for cash. Some groups even
practice stable feeding of livestock and manuring

Nomads in Chad, north central Africa. As summer rains move across the savanna, cattle-raising tribes migrate with their herds to fresh pastures. The long-time mingling of Negroid and Caucasoid peoples in the Sudan is reflected in their physiques. (Photograph—Koninklijk Instituut voor de Tropen, Amsterdam)

of fields in addition to crop rotation. Among the Hausa of Nigeria, permanent fields are expanding with the aid of various government experimental schemes. In dry Senegal and Mauritania, crops are planted as the annual floods recede from the river and lake shores. Among them are rice, millet, sorghum, and beans, with peanuts as the big cash crop.

In Latin America, although milpa agriculture is common—and not only among Indians—the Andes of Peru and Bolivia stand out as an area of permanent fields, a legacy of the civilization that once flourished here. The Indians of the Andes, though oppressed, form an increasing and integral element of the national economy. Their land utilization is not as intensive as it once was, but in the intermontane basins and valleys, lying well below the cold plateau surface, one can still see carefully terraced plots rising in twenty to fifty or more tiers against seemingly unscalable mountain slopes. The higher terraces are mostly less than 3 meters wide but rise 3 meters above the lower one. Skillfully built rock walls retain the earth layer on each terrace. The lower layer of earth, coarse stones and clay, is covered by a 1-meter top layer of fine soil, carried up by human labor. These "hanging gardens" are irrigated from ditches, fed by highland streams. The land in the valley or basin depends for irrigation on the local river, carefully canalized between stone walls. In this system, the enormous amount of labor input stands in no monetary relation to the produce. It can only be understood as a way of life for people to whom the land is almost sacred.

## CASH-CROP FARMING

Although the tribal societies live primarily by subsistence agriculture, to an increasing extent

A farmer of Nkometou, in the African country of Cameroon, picks pods from a cacao tree, the raw material for manufacturing cocoa and chocolate. (Photograph—United Nations)

they produce commodities for the market. In some cases colonial governments and foreign enterprises pressured them to do this; in other cases they have imitated in their own way the examples of plantation agriculture. Most of these cash crops do not fit into the regular swidden practice. Many are perennial bushes or trees. Their production by native smallholders means the expansion of sedentary field—or "orchard"—agriculture. The need for transportation tends to limit production to areas near the coast, along navigable rivers, and close to the few tentacles of railroads and highways that penetrate the interior.

In Southeast Asia the main commodity is rubber from the *Hevea brasiliensis,* in the 1890s introduced as a plantation crop, but soon planted by native people on abandoned ladangs. The coconut palm of Southeast Asia and the South Pacific, highly valued since ancient times for its many food and household uses, is also grown for export of copra (dried coconut meat).

Within Africa there are many "islands" of commercial production, even though their total surface is small compared to the huge area used for shifting cultivation. The Atlantic side of Africa, closer to the traditional European market than the opposite side, has a far larger share of the market and export agriculture. Senegal and Gambia produce vast amounts of peanuts; Ghana and southwestern Nigeria specialize in cocoa, grown by smallholders. Also for export are the coffee and cocoa of the Ivory Coast, the peanuts and cotton in northern Nigeria, and the oil palm in southeastern Nigeria. In the eastern highlands of Africa as well, smallholders raise coffee and cotton, especially north and west of Lake Victoria.

Although tropical America is an important producer of agricultural commodities for the world market, the Indian tribal societies have virtually no share in it. This lies in the peculiar nature of the socioeconomic stratification in Latin America. Indians who retain their ancestral community bonds—and only they are identified as Indians—remain cultivators of crops for their own use and for a thriving local market system. Outside the home village, Indians work as wage earners, tenants, or sharecroppers. Indian villages sell to the mining centers or nearby towns any surplus production such as corn, wheat, coffee, bananas, vegetables, or the sheep and alpaca wool that are sent down from the central Andes to the coast, even for export.

# CITATIONS AND FURTHER READINGS

## SOCIOECONOMIC CLASSIFICATION

Bobek, H. "The Main Stages in Socioeconomic Evolution from a Geographic Point of View," in Wagner, P. L., and Mikesell, M. W., *Readings in Cultural Geography*, Chicago, 1962, 218–247.

Spencer, J. E., and Horvath, R. J. "How Does an Agricultural Region Originate?" *Annals of the Association of American Geographers*, 53 (1963): 74–92.

———— and Stewart, N. R. "The Nature of Agricultural Systems," *Annals of the Association of American Geographers*, 63 (1973): 529–544.

Wagner, P. L. "On Classifying Economies," in Ginsburg, N. (ed.), *Essays on Geography and Economic Development*, University of Chicago, Department of Geography, Research Paper no. 62, Chicago, 1960, 49–62.

Whittlesey, D. S. "Major Agricultural Regions of the Earth," *Annals of the Association of American Geographers*, 26 (1936): 199–240.

Wolf, E. *Peasants*, Englewood Cliffs, N.J., 1966.

## GATHERING

Cumberland, K. B. "Moas and Men: New Zealand about A.D. 1250," *Geographical Review*, 52 (1962): 151–173.

Curtis, E. S. *The Kwakiutl*, New York, 1919.

Fry, V. K. "Reindeer Ranching in Northern Russia," *Professional Geographer*, 23 (1971): 146–151.

Haines, F. "Where Did the Plains Indians Get Their Horses?" *American Anthropologist*, 40 (1938): 112–117. See also 429–437.

Hughes, C. C. "Under Four Flags: Recent Culture Change among the Eskimos," *Current Anthropology*, 6 (1965): 3–54.

Kroeber, A. L. *Cultural and Natural Areas of Native North America*, University of California Publications in American Archaeology and Ethnology, no. 38, Berkeley, Calif., 1939.

Lewis, O. *The Effects of White Contact upon Blackfoot Culture, with Special Reference to the Fur Trade*, American Ethnological Society, Monograph no. 6 (1942).

Métraux, A. "The Botocudo," *Handbook of South American Indians*, Washington, D.C., 1947, vol. 1, 531–540.

Oakley, K. P. "On Man's Use of Fire, with Comments on Tool-making and Hunting," in *Social Life of Early Man*, Viking Fund Publications in Anthropology, 31 (1961): 176–193.

Sahlins, M. D. "On the Sociology of Primitive Exchange," in Gluckman, M., and Eggan, F. (eds.), *The Relevance of Models for Social Anthropology*, New York, 1965.

Sauer, C. O. "A Geographic Sketch of Early Man in America," *Geographical Review*, 34 (1944): 529–573.

———— "The Agency of Man on the Earth," in Thomas, W. L. (ed.), *Man's Role in Changing the Face of the Earth*, Chicago, 1956, 49–69.

———— "Sedentary and Mobile Bents in Early Societies," *Social Life of Early Man*, Viking Fund Publications in Anthropology, 31 (1961): 256–266.

Sonnenfeld, J. "Changes in Eskimo Hunting Technology: An Introduction to Implement Geography," *Annals of the Association of American Geographers*, 50 (1960): 172–186.

Stewart, O. C. "Fire as the First Great Force Employed by Man," in Thomas, W. L. (ed.), *Man's Role in Changing the Face of the Earth*, Chicago, 1956, 115–133.

## SHIFTING CULTIVATION

Bartlett, H. H. "Fire, Primitive Agriculture, and Grazing in the Tropics," in Thomas, W. L. (ed.), *Man's Role in Changing the Face of the Earth,* Chicago, 1956, 692–720.

Conklin, H. C. *Hanunoo Agriculture: A Report of an Integral System of Shifting Cultivation in the Philippines,* Food and Agriculture Organization, Forestry Development Paper no. 12, Rome, 1957.

———— "The Study of Shifting Agriculture," *Current Anthropology,* 2 (1961): 27–61 (with extensive bibliography).

Denevan, W. M. "Campa Subsistence in the Gran Pajonal, Eastern Peru," *Geographical Review,* 53 (1963): 59–78.

Food and Agriculture Organization. "Shifting Agriculture," *Unasylva,* 2 (1957).

Freeman, J. D. *Iban Agriculture,* Colonial Research Studies, no. 18, London, 1955.

Gourou, P. "The Quality of Land Use of Tropical Cultivators," in Thomas, W. L. (ed.), *Man's Role in Changing the Face of the Earth,* Chicago, 1956, 336–349.

Harris, D. R. "The Ecology of Swidden Cultivation in the Upper Orinoco Rain Forest, Venezuela," *Geographical Review,* 61 (1971): 475–495.

Murdock, G. P. "Staple Subsistence Crops in Africa," *Geographical Review,* 50 (1960): 523–540.

Schlippe, P. de. *Shifting Agriculture in Africa: The Zande System of Agriculture,* London, 1955.

Spencer, J. E. *Shifting Cultivation in Southeastern Asia,* University of California Publications in Geography, no. 19, Berkeley and Los Angeles, 1966.

Vermeer, D. E. "Population Pressure and Crop Rotational Changes among the Tiv of Nigeria," *Annals of the Association of American Geographers,* 60 (1970): 299–314.

Watters, R. F. "The Nature of Shifting Cultivation," *Pacific Viewpoint,* 1 (1960): 59–99.


## TILLAGE ON PERMANENT FIELDS AND CASH-CROP FARMING

Barrau, J. *Polynesian and Micronesian Subsistence Agriculture,* South Pacific Commission, Noumea, 1956.

Benneh, G. "Systems of Agriculture in Tropical Africa," *Economic Geography,* 48 (1972): 244–257.

Chang, Jen-hu. "The Agricultural Potential of the Humid Tropics," *Geographical Review,* 58 (1968): 333–361.

Moodie, D. W., and Kaye, B. "The Northern Limit of Indian Agriculture in North America," *Geographical Review,* 59 (1969): 513–529.

Spencer, J. E., and Hale, G. A. "The Origin, Nature, and Distribution of Agricultural Terracing," *Pacific Viewpoint,* 2 (1961): 1–40.

Uzozie, L. C. "Patterns of Crop Combination in the Three Eastern States of Nigeria," *Journal of Tropical Geography,* 33 (1971): 62–72.

Ward, R. G. "Cash Cropping and the Fijian Village," *Geographical Journal,* 130 (1964): 484–506.

Withington, W. A. "The Major Geographic Regions of Sumatra, Indonesia," *Annals of the Association of American Geographers,* 57 (1967): 534–549.

Wolf, E. *Peasants,* Englewood Cliffs, N.J., 1966.

# 10 TRADITIONAL LAND USE; THE PLANTATION; MODERN AGRICULTURE

## LAND USE IN TRADITIONAL SOCIETIES

The use of land in the Islamic, South Asian, and East Asian civilizations ranges from highly intensive crop tillage on well-watered plains to nomadic herding in arid regions. These societies occupying Asia's rimlands and North Africa have more advanced technology and organization than do tribal societies. Nevertheless, for various reasons their productivity per worker remains low. There are, of course, no clear and firm lines dividing the types of economy. Some of these traditional lands try to adopt the technology of the modern West; on the other hand, some parts of the Occidental world still cling to their ancestral ways of making a living.

The monsoon lands of Asia and parts of the Middle East have some strikingly high densities of agricultural population. The farms in most regions are small, from 1 to 2 hectares (2 to 5 acres), rarely over 5 hectares. Moreover, the holding is often fragmented into several parcels scattered around the village. Draft animals and plow, even if available, cannot be used effectively on the smaller plots. This necessitates labor with hand tools. Although yields per unit area often are very high, they are distressingly scant when measured against productivity per worker. This is the root cause of the low level of living. The amount of food the average farmer produces sustains his family and one to two additional people. In contrast, the American farm family grows enough to support some twenty families. To put it in another way, most traditional societies use more than two-thirds of their labor force in agriculture. Although all are needed at critical phases of production, such as planting and harvesting, there is little work at other times. Thus, the villages hide much unemployment. Where economic conditions are nearly static there are few jobs outside agriculture.

### INTENSIVE CROP TILLAGE

Plow agriculture based on bread grains and herd animals reached its early climax in the river lands of Mesopotamia. From here it diffused to Egypt, the Indus Valley, and the valleys of the Wei Ho and Huang Ho in northern China (Chapter 3). In these arid and semiarid regions evolved techniques of water control, organization of labor, and forms of land use which spread widely into other parts of Asia and North Africa.

A different form of agriculture originated in moist tropical Asia, based on the propagation of root crops and, above all, the growing of rice on flooded fields. Wet rice or sawah* cultivation is one of the truly great inventions of agriculture. Its origin lies in Bengal or one of the other floodplains of mainland Southeast Asia. In vital contrast to the tropical swidden, the sawah is a permanent field not subject to erosion, which can be relied upon to yield good harvests generation after generation. In the course of prehistory the practice of wet rice cultivation moved north and west, where it met and mingled with the Middle Eastern bread grain systems as they spread to east and south. Out of the encounter have come various "crossbreeds" of agriculture: planting of rice, followed by a wheat crop; the use of hoe or spade on small plots side by side with plowing on larger fields; and the raising of root crops on hilly ground next to grain cultivation on level surfaces (Figure 10-1).

*Sawah is the Malay-Indonesian word for a field capable of being flooded for the cultivation of rice. Another term is paddy field, derived from the Malay-Indonesian padi, meaning unhusked rice.

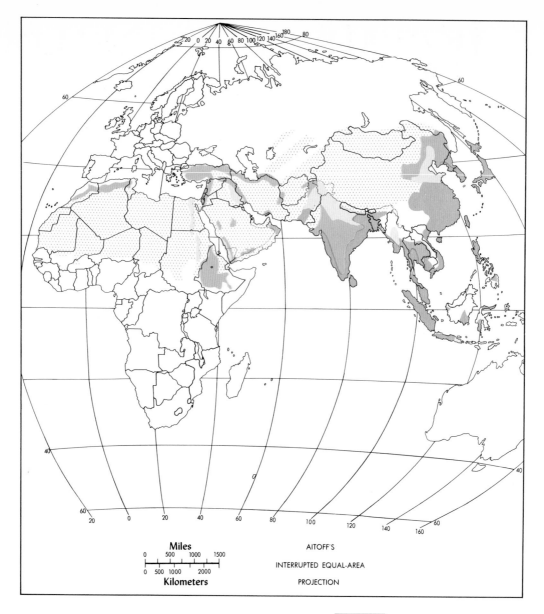

FIGURE **AFRICA AND ASIA: FORMS OF LAND USE IN TRADI-**
**10-1** **TIONAL SOCIETIES**

These are basic land-use categories for the historic traditional societies of the Old World. In many areas, for
example the south-central part of the Soviet Union
and in Japan, traditional practices have given way to
modern agriculture. In other areas, from China and
India to North Africa and the Middle East, the impact
of modern ideas and technology moves farming out of
its traditional molds.

 Intensive Cultivation, with Plow and
Hand Tools: Rice Dominant

Intensive Cultivation, with Plow and
Hand Tools: Other Crops Dominant

 Extensive Plow Cultivation:
Supplementary Large Livestock

 Nomadic Herding

Over centuries, countless individuals with simple tools invested immeasurable time and energy to create a "hydraulic" landscape for growing rice. They built tiers of terraces rising from valley floors and made levees in lowlands against river floods, dug reservoirs, canals, and ditches, fashioned ingenious devices to lift water for irrigation. Today these agricultural villagers widely practice crop rotation and manuring of fields. Where climate permits, they raise two or more crops simultaneously or successively in one year. They do the work and consume the produce. As with the chicken and the egg, it is hard to say whether the rapid increase of population forces intensive cultivation or whether development of productive techniques allows more people to survive. However this may be, constant need restricts the detour of plant foods via large livestock to provide meat and dairy products. Cattle, water buffalo, donkeys, and camels—used mainly as draft or pack animals—graze on poor unplowed land or on harvest stubble. Although milk and its products are widely used in the Middle East and South Asia, its consumption is at a low level. Milk is not part of the traditional diet in East and Southeast Asia. Fowl and pig serve as scavengers around the village and are eaten, unless religious taboos prohibit the pig's presence. Fish provide an important source of animal protein, but simple boats and gear keep down the catch. Lack of good preservation methods restricts fish marketing to coastal areas. Japan, which has rapidly modernized its farming in the twentieth century, is the outstanding exception to these general statements.

Toward the dry interior, land use becomes less intensive, except for oasis culture, and often consists of dry farming of one crop, before giving way to pastoral nomadism. In Southeast Asia the mingling of cultures has caused a mosaic of land use from shifting cultivation to terrace farming.

## MAIN CROPS

Rice, a highly nutritious grain, needs a hot growing season and a great deal of water. It requires much labor to care for the seedlings in the nursery bed, to transplant them to the prepared field, to regulate the flooding of the field and its draining when the grain ripens, and to harvest the crop. Water is the critical element. Fortunately the Asian "wet" monsoon brings rain in the warm season. This provides water for one rice crop and, in a few areas, even for two. More commonly, if the growing season is long enough, a "dry" crop follows the rice harvest on the drained field. Paddy fields must be level. Terracing hillsides requires a tremendous amount of labor. And the soil must not be so porous that it lets the water drain off underground. All this means that only a part of the arable land is suitable for rice. The remainder grows "dry" or "upland" crops, either annuals like maize, tubers, and leafy vegetables or perennials such as fruit, nut, and rubber trees, or tea and coffee bushes.

The other major grain, wheat, though irrigated in some dry climates, is mainly raised in lands of moderate rainfall. It does not do well in moist and hot climates. Moreover, it meets in these areas the cultural preference for rice. However, wheat often is the second field crop (after another "dry" crop or rice), sown in the fall and harvested in spring. In cold-winter climates it is sown in spring and harvested in the summer. Though wheat does not need large amounts of moisture, some other grains such as barley, millet, and sorghum resist drought better. These crops, therefore, characterize lands of low and uncertain rainfall where irrigation is not feasible. The following brief survey of some major regions will help to give us a clearer picture.

## CHINA

Intensity of land use reaches its peak in the humid lowlands of China, Japan, and Korea. The laborious care bestowed on each plot, even each plant, is like that of the painstaking gardener. As Marco Polo said of China as early as the thirteenth century, "no spot on earth is allowed to lie idle that can possibly be cultivated."

Before the Communist regime collectivized agriculture in mainland China, the average farm consisted of about 1 hectare (2 to 3 acres), and contained some six plots scattered around the village. Although the need for land of different quality (e.g., for dry crops and for wet rice) justified some dispersal, an excessive fragmentation resulted from land-tenure customs as well as from land hunger. This made each bit of land, however poorly located, desirable. In the classical Chinese tradition, landownership gave higher prestige than riches gained in trade and manufacturing, and wealthy families and clans left the working of the soil to tenants, who comprised a majority of all farmers.

Much of China is too mountainous or dry for producing crops. Of the total area only "China Proper," about 15 percent, is suitable for farming. The huge cultivable North China plain has a growing season of five to eight months. Rain comes during the summer but varies from year to year, exposing the region to severe drought as well as to devastating floods from the Huang Ho. The South, though it includes the Yangtze Valley, is for the larger part a hilly, even mountainous land. Its growing season extends to the full year in the Szechwan basin of the interior and on the southeastern coast, where the rainy period is longer and heavier.

Farming has adjusted itself to these contrasting ecological conditions. The North grows mainly wheat and cotton, while in the South the dominant crop is rice. The nonirrigable lands in the South produce sweet potatoes, yams and other tubers, maize, peanuts, citrus fruits, tea, and tung (valuable for its oil), also, though less than formerly, mulberry trees to feed silkworms. In the North, oxen are widely used to draw plow and cart; in the South the water buffalo pulls the plow, but often the peasant works his small plot with hand tools. Much of the traditional transportation in the South is by boat over the numerous rivers, canals, and lakes. The Yangtze region forms the transition zone between North and South. Its preferred food crop is rice, but wheat is grown as the second crop on the drained paddy fields.

The peasant who favored the revolution because he longed for an unencumbered farm of his own was led in three stages to living in a commune. The first step, formation of *mutual-aid teams*, brought together a few farm families to pool labor, field animals, and tools, but not the land. Next came the *cooperative*, which managed the land as a unit. The final step established the *commune*, comprising scores of villages and 10,000 or more people, in which everyone became a wage earner, with no other possessions than a few personal belongings (Figure 13-7).

The reforms released large numbers of farm workers who were organized into labor battalions to build dams for new irrigation and hydroelectric projects, construct dikes for flood control, re-

forest hillsides, or work in new factories. The government intensified agricultural research and waged a fight against crop damage by insects, rodents, and diseases. It encouraged the use of commercial fertilizers and improved the means of food distribution. When crops failed to meet expectations, it imported massive amounts of wheat, especially from Canada.

No doubt Chinese farming needed reform. Yields per unit area, while fairly good when compared with those of countries like India and Java, took inordinate amounts of labor, mainly by debt-burdened tenants who paid exorbitant rents to landlords. The trend in modern agriculture is toward larger units that make possible more efficient employment of labor. Such field consolidation, however, is less advantageous in much of southern China because of the terrain and because transplanting rice is best done by hand. It may have been more successful in the plains of northern China, especially in Manchuria, which, because of its recent settlement, already had a more commercial-agricultural structure and larger farms.

## SOUTH ASIA

This realm, stretching from the Himalayan mountain arc in the north to the island of Ceylon in the south, is less than half the size of the United States, but contains over 800 million people, more than two-thirds of them tillers of the soil. Again, as in East Asia, the amount of labor applied to each acre of arable land is prodigious, but crop yields are well below those of China. It is no wonder that the peasants of South Asia are among the poorest.

The tillable land lies mainly in the vast plain at the foot of the mountains, drained by Indus, Ganges, and Brahmaputra, and in the coastal plains and river deltas of the east coast. The peninsula offers only pockets and ribbons of arable land. The length of the growing season presents no problem, but the supply of moisture does. Most of South Asia has a pronounced division into dry and wet (monsoon) seasons. The northwest is virtually rainless, but in parts of northeast Assam the rainfall is the highest recorded anywhere—over 10 meters annually (400 inches)! The monsoon also brings heavy rain to the western rim of the peninsula and to the hills of Ceylon.

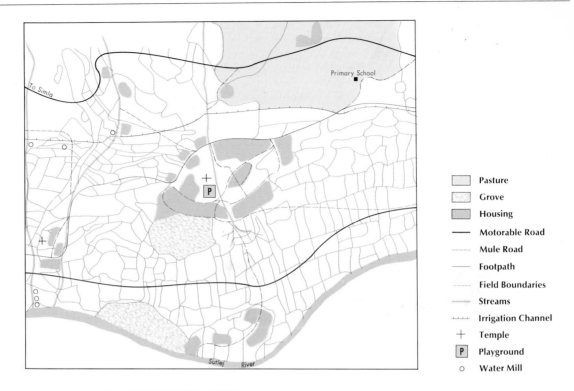

Pasture

Grove

Housing

———— Motorable Road

------ Mule Road

——— Footpath

······ Field Boundaries

～～～ Streams

·–·–· Irrigation Channel

+ Temple

P Playground

○ Water Mill

FIGURE **A VILLAGE IN HIMACHAL PRADESH, INDIA**
**10-2**

Shakrori, a small village of about 350 inhabitants, lies in the foothills of the Himalaya Mountains on the bank of the Sutlej River. The main crops are wheat, rice, and corn. Irrigation water is drawn from the river. The three main groups living in the village are Brahmans, Rajputs, and Lohars (blacksmiths). Other castes represented are Sood (traders), Chamar (a depressed caste of leatherworkers and agricultural laborers), and Kumhar (potters). Based on a sketch in Government of India, "A Village Survey of Shakrori," *Census of India, 1961, 20:* 6 Simla, Himachal Pradesh, 1963.

But most parts have lower and less reliable rainfall. The lower Ganges plain of India and Bangladesh has about 1,500 millimeters (60 inches), ample for wet rice production. It also has very heavy rural population densities. Elsewhere, rain is less than 1,000 millimeters; in the fertile upper Ganges Valley and Punjab, irrigation is necessary for intensive and dependable grain farming (Figure 10-2).

Four-fifths of the arable land is actually cropped; the remainder lies fallow or rarely sown.

Rice occupies one-fourth of the crop area, other grains almost one-half, and fiber and oil crops most of the rest.

In the past few years impressive strides have been made toward self-sufficiency in food grains, mainly through the introduction of new and improved varieties of rice and wheat, "the miracle seeds." The expansion of area in high-yielding varieties has been substantial, which suggests that the South Asian peasant is not as conservative after all as was formerly supposed. It is questionable whether India's dependence on imported grains is ending. She maintains "buffer stocks" lest drought should cause a shortage. The new seeds, however, require concomitant development of the fertilizer industry, control of insect pests, and, above all, commensurate irrigation facilities. Thus, the increase of production per unit area is far from uniform over all of South Asia. High yields are confined largely to the areas of irrigated rice and wheat.

This "green revolution" has generated a lively debate. On the negative side, it tends to exaggerate existing income inequalities, if accompanied by mechanization to increase unemployment; to increase vulnerability to long-range disasters from plant diseases and insects due to standardized crop strains; to increase dependency on chemical inputs based on nonrenewable resources; and to decrease control by peasants over their own lives. More positively, higher yields have led to sustained increases in output, reducing the risk of hunger and mass starvation and lowering dependence on foreign suppliers of grain. If current optimism on the food front is to become a long-term reality, it is vitally necessary to sustain efforts for intensifying agriculture and to continue stress on widespread family-planning programs.

The number of livestock in South Asia is huge. For India alone it is estimated at over 175 million cattle, 53 million water buffalo, 42 million sheep, 65 million goats, and 1.1 million horses. Most Hindus eat no beef, and many Indian Muslims avoid it, although their religion permits it.* Apart from the beef taboo, many Indians are vegetarians. Animals thus contribute mainly milk to the diet, mostly in the form of ghee (clarified butter), but the yield per animal and the average consumption per person are sadly low. Since livestock feed on nonarable or fallow land, supplemented by grain straw, they are generally undernourished. Cattle dung, so badly needed to restore soil fertility, is mainly used for fuel. Oxen and buffalo serve chiefly as draft animals for cart and plow.

Though the South Asian diet is seriously deficient in animal protein, the surrounding seas are exploited very little. The average annual consumption of fish per capita in India is about 2 kilograms (less than 5 pounds) but 9 kilos in Ceylon and over 30 kilos in Burma. In many ways Ceylon presents a less gloomy picture than the mainland. The pressure on the land is not as great—as suggested by the fact that only half of the labor force is employed in agriculture—and there is room for expanding food production. Within India, Bangladesh, and Pakistan there are, of course, also regional differences in economic level. Especially the Punjab, divided between

India and Pakistan, stands out as a relatively prosperous region, thanks to the vast system of canal irrigation the British developed, subsequently expanded by both India and Pakistan. Irrigation canals now also extend into the Rajasthan desert.

New irrigation facilities are the best way to bring more land under cultivation, increase double-cropping, and raise the yield per unit area. Since the possibilities of diverting normal river flow into irrigation canals have been virtually exhausted, the present projects in India and Pakistan call for high dams and large reservoirs to store floodwaters for use in the dry season and, where feasible, to generate electricity (Figure 10-3). Also coming into use more and more are tube wells with diesel or electric pumps to tap the groundwater. In India the irrigated area has doubled since 1950.

Modern technology, however, will accomplish little unless accompanied by transformation of the traditional agrarian way of life. Farm units—2 hectares (5 acres) on the average—are too small and fragmented for efficient production; tenancy, coupled with exorbitant rents, makes farming a constant struggle; thousands of villages are without roads to local markets; many peasants lack cash to buy commercial fertilizer for exhausted soils; malnutrition and disease sap both energy and initiative. And there is, of course, the ever-increasing population which threatens to devour all gains in production.

## SOUTHEAST ASIA

The lands east of India and south of China have been subjected to many foreign influences. The impact has been slight in the less accessible parts, such as the interior highlands of the mainland and the eastern islands of the archipelago. The simple agriculture of these folk societies has been discussed in Chapter 9. Here we turn to the more advanced economies of Southeast Asia. Although included among the traditional societies, they are in many ways marginal to China, India, and the Middle East.

The climate, though tropical, is not uniform over the whole area. There are, of course, differences in temperature between the lowlands and uplands; but more important is the amount of rainfall. Along the equator, including Malaya, Sumatra, West Java, Borneo, and the southern Phil-

*The Hindu taboo on beef eating is not observed strictly, if at all, among depressed castes and tribal groups.

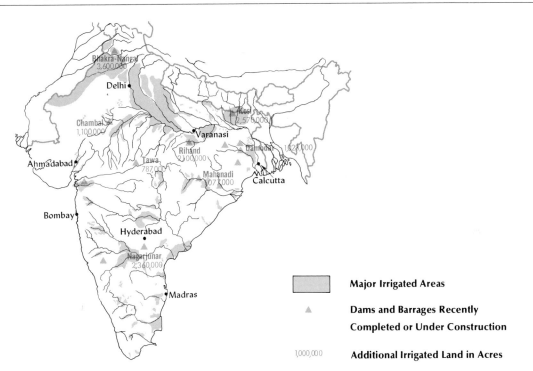

FIGURE **INDIA: IRRIGATION PROJECTS**
**10-3**

Based on information supplied by J. E. Schwartzberg, South Asia Historical Atlas Project, University of Minnesota.

ippines, heavy rain comes in all months. The remainder of the region has a dry season which restricts but does not preclude agriculture. River valleys and deltas receive fresh silt in flood season. Volcanic eruptions in the Philippines and Indonesia have rejuvenated the soil in many areas. The Red River delta of Tongkin (northern Vietnam) has supported a dense population for many centuries, thanks to its intense water management and crop tillage in Chinese fashion, whereas the southern delta of the Mekong is still part of an agricultural frontier. Java, although its density was probably always higher than that of adjacent islands, had only some 5 million people in 1815; the intensification of land use under Dutch rule made it possible to sustain ten times that number by 1940.

The percentage of population engaged in subsistence farming is in general even higher than in East and South Asia—not for the more urban and commercial economy of Malaya. Farming units are about 1 hectare (2 to 3 acres) in the densely populated sections and 2 or more hectares elsewhere. The main food crop is wet rice, grown wherever possible. In the delta lands of the Irawaddy (Burma), Menam Chao Phraya (Thailand), and Mekong (the old Cochin-China in southern Vietnam) the farmers grow only one crop of rice in the rainy season. Yields are rising rapidly where the new rice varieties have been introduced. But their large areas under this monoculture and the relatively sparse population make these three regions the chief exporters of rice, at least under peaceful conditions. Although farming may be called "intensive" in terms of labor applied in raising the crop—certainly so by Western standards—it is a far cry from the "gardening" methods of East Asia.

However, in well-settled parts of the Philippines (central Luzon, Cebu), in Java and Bali, and in most of the Vietnam lowlands, the use of land is more expert. Even in these areas two successive crops of rice are uncommon. In some areas rice is a minor crop, either because there is not enough water to flood the fields or because the soils cannot hold the water on the surface. Such conditions result in a preponderance of dry field crops over rice.

Many farmers produce a small surplus of these food crops that is sold to the cities, or even abroad. In addition to these modest sales there is widespread cultivation of cash crops, mainly in regions with relatively abundant land. For instance, farmers may have a planting of coconut, kapok, or abaca (Manila hemp), a garden of coffee, tea, or pepper, or a field of cassava or maize. Fifty years ago they began to imitate the Western estates in planting *Hevea* rubber trees. In the Federation of Malaysia, the largest natural-rubber producer in the world, 46 percent comes from smallholders; in Indonesia, second in rank, 70 percent, mainly from Sumatra and Borneo. Thailand's rubber plantings are in the wet peninsular part, all on small holdings. Until the rubber boom of the early 1900s, Malaya—the peninsular part of the Malaysian Federation—was a sparsely inhabited country with very little commercial agriculture. There was ample room for rubber planting. This explains why rubber now occupies almost two-thirds of its cultivated area (Figure 10–6). This stands in marked contrast to other Southeast Asian countries, where rubber and other cash crops occupy only a small fraction of the land. In Malaya the position of large-scale plantations, controlling one-third of the planted area, also is exceptionally strong.

Although the population pressure in Southeast Asia is less acute than in China and India, the rapidly growing numbers as well as the desire for economic uplift demand far-reaching reforms. The nature and urgency of the problems vary from country to country. Thailand provides a good example of projects accomplished or planned to expand the arable land. Because the central plain of Thailand does not receive sufficient rainfall to flood paddy fields, additional water from the irregularly flowing Menam Chao Phraya is needed to ensure a good harvest.

After World War II new projects were undertaken with plans to develop the river. The major diversion dam is at Chainat, at the head of the delta; it benefits 400,000 hectares of rice land.

On the Ping River, which enters the plain in the west, a high dam has been built to form a large reservoir. This project has opened up new land below the dam which could not be used before for rice because of excessive flooding; also it will provide part of the Bangkok plain with irrigation for a second rice crop. Similar plans to harness the giant Mekong River of Indochina can benefit several countries. Electric power, irrigation, flood control, and transportation are part of the development scheme which foreign aid is backing.

## EGYPT

Herodotus said, "Egypt is an acquired country, the gift of the Nile." Apart from a few oases, all cultivated land is in a narrow strip astride the Nile and in its delta below Cairo. The gift of the river has more complex origins than Herodotus knew. In southern Sudan, the White Nile spreads out over a vast low plain through reed- and grass-covered marshes. This region, El-Sudd, acts as a regulator so that the flow downstream is quite even. Other sources of Egypt's water supply are the Blue Nile and the Atbara, both rising in the Ethiopian highlands. The floods carry along masses of red silt and arrive in Egypt late in June, reaching their maximum in October, then subsiding quickly. The volume of both White and Blue Nile decreases markedly downstream because of high evaporation in the desert climate (Figure 10–4).

The old method of farming consisted of flooding basins each year to provide water and nutrients for the grain crops. After letting the water stand for a month or two, the peasant planted wheat, barley, and other crops. Following an April harvest, the land lay fallow to await the next flooding. Thus the entire rhythm of life was attuned to the seasonal ups and downs of the river.

About 1820 the Egyptians started to build dams in the river so that water for irrigation would be available beyond the flood season. This so-called "perennial irrigation" did not work well until modern hydraulic technology was introduced about 1890. British engineers built dams with navigation locks and sluice gates at the head of the delta near Cairo and at several points upstream. The main work was at Aswan, some 850 kilometers from the sea, where the Nile flows through a granite outcrop, causing the first of a

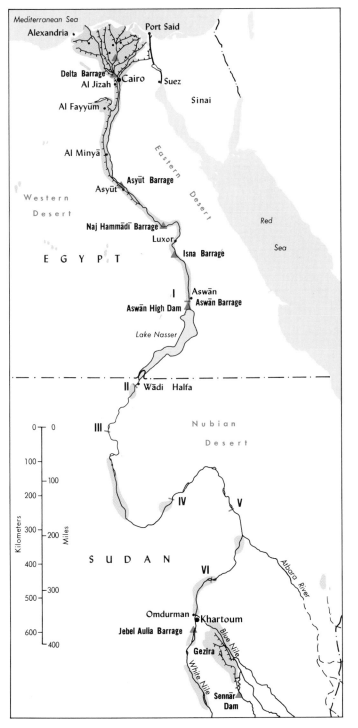

series (counted upstream) of rapids or cataracts. Closing the gates in October or November caught the tail of the flood behind the dam, to be released during the low-water period from February to July.

By 1970 a much higher dam had been built just south of Aswan, with Russian aid. This dam controls the entire river flow and permits over-year storage. This provides a steady supply of irrigation water, even if the requirements in a particular year have exceeded the discharge. The backed-up Nile waters form a narrow lake 600 kilometers long, reaching deep into Sudan. The dam also improves navigation downstream, protects Egypt against destructive floods, and serves to generate large amounts of hydroelectrical power. Downstream, additional land has been reclaimed from desert and from delta marshes. Egyptian pride in this great achievement is tempered by technical problems and the need to supply food to a population that continues to increase at over 2 percent a year.

Perennial irrigation greatly aids production by allowing summer cropping of rice, maize, and, especially, a long staple cotton of high quality—Egypt's main export. Of the bread grains, grown in winter, wheat is most important. Although larger farms more and more employ modern methods of production, most peasants still use the sickle and the archaic wooden plow drawn by ox or water buffalo.

Until recent land reforms, Egypt suffered under a feudal system of huge estates in which most agricultural workers were debt-ridden sharecroppers. Since 1960 there has been considerable progress in redistributing these lands to

| | |
|---|---|
| ▨ | **Irrigated Areas and Oases** |
| ⊢⊢⊢⊢ | **Irrigation Canals** |
| ——— | **Rivers** |
| – – – | **Seasonal Rivers** |
| ·Aswan | **Towns** |
| ●Cairo | **Capital Cities** |
| ▲ | **Dams and Barrages** |
| – II | **Cataracts (I to VI)** |

FIGURE **NILE VALLEY: IRRIGATION**
**10-4**

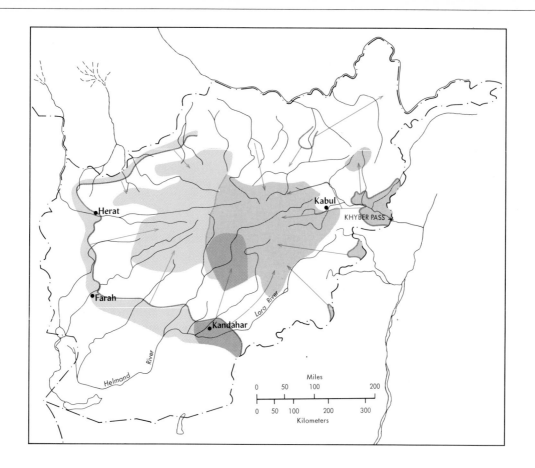

FIGURE **AFGHANISTAN: PASTORAL NOMADISM**
**10-5**

Plateaus and their valleys at elevations between 300 and 1,000 meters surround mountain ranges which rise in the northeast to 7,000 meters in the Hindu Kush. Besides transhumance and local nomadism there are many long-range movements, as this map shows. In winter the nomads live in tents at elevations below 1,000 meters amidst the sedentary peasants and pasture their sheep and goats on hillsides and uncultivated plains. By the end of March they move to encampments on the lower mountain slopes, joined by groups that come across the border from Pakistan. In early June the nomads start out for the upper pastures, as high as 3,000 meters. Here they remain for two or three months and then descend again, arriving at their winter quarters in October or November. Many tribes cover some 1,000 kilometers in these annual migrations; when traveling they drive their flocks at a pace of about 15 kilometers per day. Dromedaries are used as beasts of burden. The pastures of the two main tribal groups are shown on the map. Adapted from a map by K. Ferdinand in Humlum, J., *La Géographie de l'Afghanistan*, Copenhagen, etc., 1959.

—— **Upper Limit of Winter Pastures**

▨ **Pastures of the Southern and Western Tribes**

▨ **Pastures of the Eastern Tribes**

←— **Direction of Movement in the Spring**

smallholders, their lack of capital and experience compensated for by cooperatives. The farms, no larger than 40 hectares, grow mostly cotton, but not enough food for the population, which reaches a density of 1,150 per square kilometer (3,000 per square mile). The cooperative scheme for economic development has been most successful in areas where the government is responsible for the irrigation, the local administration board markets the produce, and the workers enjoy a level of comparative prosperity.

## PASTORAL NOMADISM

In spite of the persistent popular notion, nomadic herding of livestock is not an evolutionary economic stage preceding sedentary farming. In early Middle Eastern agriculture, grain growing and livestock herding were separate yet intertwined activities. The biblical story of the brothers Cain, "tiller of the soil," and Abel, "keeper of sheep," reflects the ancient agricultural dichotomy. Those who left the sown land for the steppe became pastoral nomads, wandering in search of pasture and water for their flocks. Yet the nomad cannot divorce himself from the farmer. He needs flour and dates, tea or coffee, which he obtains in exchange for skins, leather, wool, or cheese. Nomadic herding is a land-extensive form, somewhat similar to the land rotation among shifting cultivators. Since fodder and water must be obtained throughout the year, the herders move seasonally from one grazing ground to another (Figure 10–5).

Nomadic herding has, of course, some traits in common with ranching, especially in the early days of the "cattle kingdom" on the American Great Plains when the herds moved freely over vast areas of unfenced land. But nomadic herding differs fundamentally in that it is a traditional subsistence mode of life for the entire family or clan, while ranching is an Occidental commercial-agricultural enterprise, centered on the ranch establishment.

**Forms of Pastoral Nomadism** The theme of pastoral nomadism has almost endless variations. In eastern Africa we have already met the herder-on-foot, either as full- or part-time cattleman. In the steppes and deserts of North Africa and Asia,

many nomads use horses or camels as trained auxiliaries to guide and guard sheep, goats, and cattle, as well as for travel and transportation of the family. But others use the horse mainly for rounding up cattle, and employ oxcarts for transportation. This fully nomadic existence contrasts with that of the seminomad, who has instead of a tent a house, owns land in an oasis, and only moves for one season with his family to an encampment on fresh pastures. Or one may distinguish between nomadic groups by radius of movement: some groups oscillate only some 50 or so kilometers between regular summer and winter pastures; others cover a much longer circuit with many encampments along the way. The mountains and plains, cool or hot summers, cold or mild winters, grass or scrub vegetation influence the time, direction, and duration of the trek, the kind of animals reared, and the relations to sedentary folk. It is generally true that among full nomads there is no private landownership. A clan or federation of clans considers its grazing lands common property. Individual wealth depends on the number of livestock one owns. But here again, there are many exceptions to the rule, especially where land is scarce.

Distinct from pastoral nomadism is *transhumance;* this term refers to the seasonal movement of livestock, accompanied only by a few shepherds. It is quite common in countries where sedentary agriculture is well established, such as in the European highlands and in the western United States. It is also characteristic where former pastoral nomads have become sedentary keepers of livestock.

**Horse- and Camel-riding Nomads** The horse and dromedary transformed the pastoral nomad from a plodding shepherd into a swift-moving aggressive warrior. As mentioned earlier, the horse was probably domesticated in the open woodlands or steppes of southern Russia or Central Asia and, before it became a riding and pack animal, was used for food or for drawing a light chariot. (Not until the horse collar was invented in the ninth century A.D. could the horse pull heavy loads.) Horse riding may date back to 1800 B.C. in Central Asia; 600 years later it had spread throughout the Middle East.

Although the two-humped or Bactrian

camel had been domesticated earlier (3000–2500 B.C.?), this slow pack and draft animal could not compete with the horse as a means of travel. The one-humped camel, or dromedary—probably domesticated in southern Arabia before 1000 B.C.—provided the desert dweller with a fast-moving mount, one that could endure drought much better than the horse. The dromedary spread gradually through all desert regions, although it appeared in North Africa only in Roman times.

Apart from their value as riding and pack animals, camels and horses have other uses. Various Asian nomads milk the mares, to make *kumyss,* a fermented beverage. Also, they eat horsemeat, which the Arabs do not. Arabs consider the camel a working beast and the horse a nonutilitarian showpiece of the rich—at least until the advent of the Lincoln and Rolls-Royce. Many nomadic groups also milk camels, eat their flesh, manufacture their hide and hair into rugs and clothing, and use the dung as fuel.

The mobility that horse and dromedary gave the nomads overshadowed the domestic advantages. The impact the swift and ruthless marauder made on sedentary peoples continues in their legends from centaur to Hun. These roughriders repeatedly invaded and ruled large parts of the rimlands of Eurasia. The so-called Aryans and many other peoples from inner Asia down to the Moguls pushed into India. The Manchus were but the last of the many nomadic tribes, including Tartars and Mongols, that entered China in spite of the wall; Mongols, Arabs, and Turks penetrated deep into Europe. Some scholars seek to explain these human eruptions by severe drought conditions which prevailed at certain periods in the traditional grazing areas. The evidence is doubtful, and it seems wiser to consider additional factors—social, economic, and political. After all, the steppe and the sown existed side by side for thousands of years in a highly unstable association. A new technique of irrigation would expand agriculture into the desert, but withdrawal of imperial border guards might tempt the nomads to regain former pasturelands.

The caravan trade was another and equally important feature of the dry lands of the Old World. It linked by land the advanced countries of the Middle East, China, and India with each other as well as with their sources of raw materials. This long-distance transportation inevitably had to cross deserts and steppes occupied by nomads, be it Sahara or Sind, Tarim or Gobi. The nomads offered little in trade goods, but controlled the terrain. For long-distance journeys the merchants therefore usually made arrangements with a nomad chief who provided the camels and the escort of drivers, guides, and guards. As on the sea, commerce invited piracy. Safe passage depended on skill as well as luck. For greater security the long-distance caravans were quite large, like ships traveling in convoy, consisting of hundreds and even thousands of laden camels.

**Decline of Nomadism**  The domain of the pastoral nomad has shrunk substantially in the last hundred years. The spread of farming, with or without irrigation, more and more restricts the wide open spaces and, even where they still exist, the closed frontiers deny access to former pasture grounds. Railroad, truck, and plane have severely reduced the income from caravan trade, transport, camel breeding, and pillage. In Saudi Arabia and many other countries government policy aims at settling the nomads, either as farmers or as livestock ranchers, so that they may be absorbed in the nation-state. Others have been attracted to work full or part time in the petroleum fields of Iraq, Arabia, and the Sahara. In Russian Central Asia, where once Kirgiz, Kazakh, and many other nomadic peoples roamed the steppe, the traditional way of life is virtually gone. Instead, the indigenous people now work on collective ranches and farms, in mines, and in manufacturing industries. Almost everywhere the number of nomads decreases, so that even in a desertlike country but a small proportion of the population keep to their ancient ways.

A possible exception is the Mongolian People's Republic, where pastoral nomads make up three-fourths of the population. Only a strong physique can endure the hardships of drought, cold winter, and hot summer under the primitive living conditions of interior Asia's dry lands. The Mongols have long been known as a tough lot, whether as shepherds or warriors. This was the homeland of Genghis Khan and his grandson Kublai Khan; their dynasty ruled much of Asia in the twelfth and thirteenth centuries.

In winter the Mongol nomads stay in the lower parts of the valleys, which afford some protection against the icy blasts. In summer many groups move with their animals to the high valleys and mountain slopes, but others wander down to the steppe in late summer after the rains have revived the cover of short bunchgrass—unless a severe drought has parched the land. Sheep are the prized animals, providing wool for felt making, skins for clothing, mutton and milk for food (sour drink, cheese, and butter). Total livestock in Mongolia number 25 million: in addition to sheep there are large herds of goats, cattle, horses, and camels. The big neighbor the Soviet Union has aided to improve hay production and to build better shelters for the winter.

Socialist principles govern the organization of the state and its economy. Herds formerly belonging to Buddhist monasteries were handed over to collective farms. Many poor shepherds have been drawn into these enterprises. Expansion of dry farming is making inroads on the pastures of the nomad, but most of the land is too dry for crop growing. It is likely that nomadic herding will maintain itself for a long time in this northern outpost.

## THE PLANTATION

It is one thing to speak of "the plantation," but quite another to define it. Everyone agrees that it is a large-scale commercial-agricultural enterprise, but few would consent to the obverse and call every large farm a plantation, such as the big wheat farms in Montana and Kansas, the huge orchards in California, the sugar-beet farms in Colorado or northern France, and the various collectives in the Soviet Union. Some writers distinguish the plantation by its location in the tropics or subtropics—in other words, they use a climatic definition. In this line of thought the large citrus farm in Florida is a plantation, but the complex of vegetable farms under central management in New Jersey is not. Others have sought the answer in the kind of crops grown or in the use of cheap native or imported labor. Still others point out that a plantation combines cultivation with processing the product, giving it the character of an agricultural-industrial business. This disagreement has led to the counsel of despair which bans

the word *plantation* from any serious discussion of agricultural production systems.

Nevertheless, we cannot ignore this widely used term. Most definitions fail to include the sociocultural component that is always present in a typical plantation: it is essentially the intrusion of one society into the land and life of another. "The plantation . . . is a large landed estate, located in an area of open resources (i.e., land-rich and labor-poor), in which social relations between diverse racial and social groups are based upon authority, involving the subordination of resident laborers to a planter for the purpose of producing an agricultural staple which is sold in a world market" (Thompson, 1935, 5).

In the United States the southern plantation was a way of organizing production on land that had been virtually denuded of its indigenous American population and, therefore, was a region of expanding European settlement. Most of such plantations are gone with the wind. The plantation was a frontier institution thrust into a less developed society for economic exploitation. This purpose, rather than migration and settlement, characterized most of the plantations in Asia and Africa. In the last four centuries the plantation has been almost exclusively a form of Occidental expansion into other non-Occidental realms. The main exceptions have been Japanese enterprises in Taiwan and the western Pacific islands and the Chinese concerns in Malaysia and Indonesia. Plantations have been established in tribal societies but also in traditional societies such as India, Ceylon, and Java (Figure 10-6).

### THE PLANTATION IN LATIN AMERICA
By conquest Spain and Portugal foisted onto the southern parts of the New World a system of large landownership, often including seignorial rights over the labor of the resident Indians. Many early Spanish *haciendas* and *estancias de ganado* (cattle ranches) had little direct commercial purpose, but were landed estates to serve the status and comfort of the new aristocracy. The *caballero*—the Spanish landowner on horseback—and the *peon*—the servile Indian on foot—symbolized the dualism of the socioeconomic structure. Even today, in the backcountry at least, the hacienda is more a way of life for the owner and his family than a business.

The Portuguese were on the whole more interested than the Spaniards in obtaining direct profits from their land. Europe had no market for the strange American plants, so sugarcane was brought over to provide a cash crop. The Indians did not know how to cultivate the cane, nor had they any tradition of private landownership and commercial production. Thus, the plantation came into being in the New World. Capital and management were provided by the Portuguese entrepreneur, labor by the Indians (soon to be complemented and then replaced by African slaves), the land taken from the Indian communities and granted by the king. Subsequently other crops were added, such as cotton, tobacco, cacao, coffee, and, much later, bananas. English, Dutch, and French invaded the Iberians' domain and took over or created new plantations in the Caribbean and the Guianas.

Toward the end of the nineteenth century, western Europe and the United States had far surpassed Latin America in commercial-industrial development. The latter was looked upon as a source of raw materials, vegetable as well as mineral. This led to a new cultural intrusion, especially of entrepreneurs from the United States. They furnished capital and management, but used local land and wage labor to produce the needed staple goods, such as bananas and sugar. This stratification of cultures—Indian, traditional Latin, and modern industrial-commercial—occurs over large parts of Middle and South America. It is least prevalent in Argentina, Uruguay, southern Brazil, and Chile; here the Indian element is virtually absent and the modern way of life dominates the cities, leaving the countryside as refuge for the traditional economy. But in rural areas, too, significant social and economic changes are taking place, with the result that the large-scale agricultural enterprises are more like farms than plantations.

In Mexico, land tenure has changed so much in the last fifty years that little is left of the old *latifundium* system (from Latin *latus,* broad, and *fundus,* estate). Before 1910 a small minority of landed aristocrats owned most of the land, which was worked by Indian sharecroppers or debt-bonded tenants. There were sugar and coffee plantations, but most of the private holdings were used for cattle grazing. In the second

half of the nineteenth century Spanish-Mexican landowners in northern Yucatan developed a veritable plantation district, replacing the food-producing maize and livestock economy by henequen, an agave plant yielding hard fiber.

In the Mexican Revolution of 1910–1920 and by subsequent reforms, estate lands were expropriated, reassigned to adjacent Indian *pueblos* (towns) as *ejidos* (common lands), and then parceled out for the use of individual families. These measures eliminated the old landed aristocracy and raised the morale of the peasants, but they also caused a decline in productivity of the land, because the small farms produced less efficiently than the former large-scale enterprises.

The henequen plantations of Yucatan have been transformed, too, but have retained some of the old features. Most Spanish-Mexican landowners still have their allotment of 300 hectares and, highly important, also the fiber-processing plant. Maya Indians now cultivate former sections of the hacienda and bring their bundles of henequen leaves to the *desfibradora* for processing. The former functional unity of landownership and agricultural management has been replaced by a probably unique compromise: an association of communal and private land tenure, both producing the cash crop, which is processed by the private producer.

Puerto Rico offers a good example of the Spanish agrarian system incisively modified by planned evolution rather than revolution. Before 1940 large absentee corporations, mostly American-owned, used the best lands for sugarcane production, and less favorable areas for livestock. The land reform restricted ownership by corporations to 200 hectares and gave the excess to Puerto Rican farmers in private ownership. The companies still operate sugar refineries, but buy most of the cane from the small planters. In contrast, Cuba follows the socialist model of eliminating the latifundia and substituting large-scale state-run farms. It is too early to evaluate the effect on Cuba's economy, but now the term *collective* seems more appropriate than *plantation.*

Elsewhere in Latin America the plantation survives, either as the traditional hacienda with peonage or as the modern estate with wage labor. Among the plantations, several of the Caribbean islands raise sugar or bananas, those in the coastal lowlands (*tierra caliente*) of Central America grow bananas, sugar cane, or cotton, and others in the highlands (*tierra templada*) produce coffee. Estates along the dry Peruvian coast raise sugar and cotton under irrigation. The northeastern coastal region of Brazil has sugar and cacao plantations, but the industry is only a shadow of its golden age in the sixteenth and seventeenth centuries when sugar was king. A plantation boom in coffee started in the 1850s in the southern hill lands of Rio de Janeiro state and then moved to the large expanse of fertile soils in the state of São Paulo and in northwestern Paraná, which is still the main coffee region. As so often with commercial crop production in Brazil, the coffee *fazenda* was, and partly still is, a migratory, speculative enterprise. When the virgin soil is exhausted, the planter moves on to new lands.

## PLANTATIONS IN ASIA AND AFRICA

For ages, spices from India and Indonesia reached Europe by means of various intermediary traders. The discovery of the sea route to the "East Indies" enabled the Europeans to gain control of this trade. There was no need, as in America, to superimpose a new production system on the native forms of economy. Forced deliveries were often demanded, but the actual production of crops was left to the local people. The picture changed in the nineteenth century. In Europe and North America the spreading industrialization needed more raw materials while the rising living standards of the growing population increased the demand for fats and oils, sugar and tobacco, tea and coffee. About the same time two major events in the Western Hemisphere reduced its ability to meet these needs: The abolition of slavery disturbed the labor supply, and the newly won independence of Latin American countries resulted in unstable governments. Many investors and entrepreneurs turned to South and Southeast Asia where colonial governments were expanding and strengthening their rule and where crowded peasants of India, Java, and China served as a large reservoir of docile and industrious labor. In addition, the opening of the Suez Canal in 1869 greatly diminished the handicap of larger distance from Europe than from the "West Indies." After that the trickle of investment to tropical Asia swelled to a stream. Grown on plantations, cane sugar became

a major export commodity of Java and the Philippines, and tea of Assam and Ceylon. Cinchona and *Hevea brasiliensis*, both American plants, were introduced into Southeast Asia, which soon gained virtually a monopoly on the production of quinine and rubber. Coconut and oil palm, sisal, abaca, tobacco, and kapok also became important plantation products.

The case of the Philippines was somewhat different. Here the Spaniards had transplanted their colonial land system from Mexico, especially to the lowlands of Luzon and the Visayan Islands, where they gained effective control. However, most haciendas remained at or near the subsistence level until the end of the nineteenth century, when the Spanish-American War gave the Philippines new overlords. American rule, faced with the Spanish legacy of a severe land tenure problem, discouraged the formation of new large holdings. Moreover, the announced intention to prepare the islands for independence made American investors reluctant to put money into long-term business ventures. Nevertheless, on a considerable number of existing large landholdings in Luzon, Panay, and Negros, sugar production was intensified. Building upon the Spanish tradition, the plantation consists of a number of tenant farms, each producing sugarcane under the direction of the central management, and food crops for family use. The tenants bring the cane to the owner's mill (*central*) for processing.

When the Dutch in Indonesia and the British in Malaya and India began to develop plantations in the mid-nineteenth century, they had to choose whether to locate in densely populated areas where labor was abundant but land scarce, or in sparsely populated sections where large tracts were available but labor was absent. In most cases they took the latter alternative and imported the necessary labor. In this manner evolved the tea plantations in the hills of Assam, of southern India, and of Ceylon. Similarly, the lowlands of the western Malay Peninsula became the site for numerous rubber plantations, using Indians as laborers (Figure 10–6).

The Dutch converted a virtually empty wilderness on the northern coast of Sumatra into a prosperous plantation region. They introduced plants from other lands and, using local and Chinese labor, produced tobacco, oil palm, rubber,

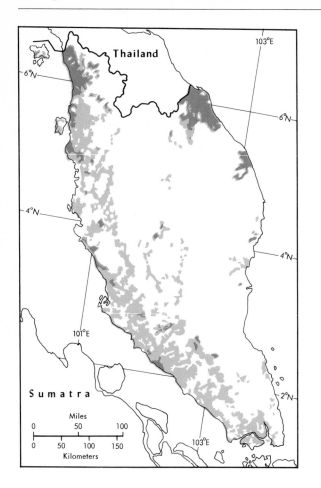

sisal, sugar, and other goods for export. On densely populated Java, where the overriding need was for food, Dutch attempts at integrating sugar growing in rotation with rice were abandoned during World War II.

Europeans did not gain control of most of Africa until late in the nineteenth century. Before that time the Portuguese and Arabs planted sugar and cloves on coastal areas and islands. But in the two decades before World War I there was a rush of soldiers, administrators, and managers to "open up" the new colonial territories. Many plantations were founded producing such crops as oil palm and sisal. The eastern highlands, because of their temperate climate, areas of volcanic soil, and sparse population, attracted European settlers, who acquired medium to large landholdings. Most were farms run by the settler, his family, and some servants. Such foreign expropriation of African land and exploitation of African labor under the plantation system was mostly ended by World War II. Only in South Africa and Rhodesia does the old colonial economy survive, complicated in both countries by the presence of large minorities of European origin. There too the wind of change blows, as elsewhere.

The prospects of the plantation look dim. Desire for national independence and for freedom from foreign interference restricts or even does away with plantations. Cases in point are land reforms in several Latin American countries and the taking over of foreign enterprises in Cuba and Indonesia. The wealthy countries have less need than formerly for some products because substitutes are cheap to manufacture; many derived from petroleum. Moreover, if old plantation lands are developed on Western models with modern technology and organization, they become in character more like the other rapidly spreading big industrial-commercial enterprises.

In retrospect, it is easy to detect faults of the plantation system, especially in ways that land was acquired, politics imposed, and labor treated. Criticism, however, must be tempered with a realization of what was gained, especially for those countries which wish to follow a Western-oriented form of economic development. Some of the infrastructure of modernization was built: roads, railways, ports, towns. Elementary health care began the process of death control. Markets were

FIGURE
10-6
MALAYA: RUBBER- AND RICE-PRODUCING AREAS

Because Malaya some fifty years ago was very sparsely populated, much land was available for rubber planting, first by estates, later also by smallholders. The rice-growing areas indicate the main concentrations of Malay semisubsistence agriculture. Most of the remainder of the Malayan peninsula is dense forest, on mountains and in swamps. Based on a map published by the Superintendent of Maps, Federation of Malaya.

■ Rice
■ Rubber

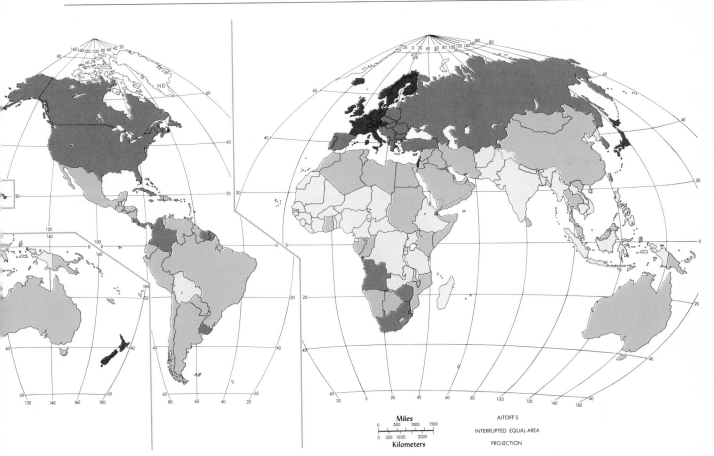

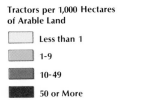

**Tractors per 1,000 Hectares
of Arable Land**

Less than 1

1-9

10-49

50 or More

FIGURE **WORLD: TRACTORS PER 1,000 HECTARES OF**
**10-7** **ARABLE LAND (ABOUT 1975)**

Among the countries with modern farming those that
combine intensive land use with mechanization have
the highest number of tractors per unit of arable land.
In the underdeveloped countries mechanization is
mainly associated with production of commercial field
crops, such as wheat and cotton.

developed for plantation products, and an exchange economy, however unfair its terms of
trade, was established. Scientifically efficient production methods were made available, at least by
example, for the people to emulate in their own
agriculture. Whether or not countries will wish to
convert these to advantage as they proceed with
development using the Western model of economic progress, or whether they will want to
follow some other form of economic change, is of
crucial importance.

# LAND USE IN MODERN
SOCIETIES

In modern societies, agriculture has changed from
a way of life into a specialized industry closely
integrated with other commercial and industrial

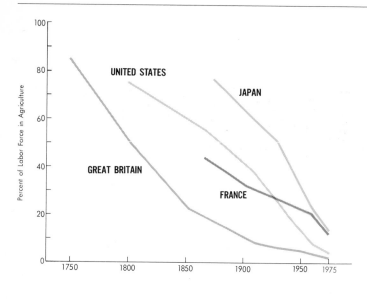

**PERCENTAGE OF LABOR FORCE IN AGRICULTURE IN SELECTED COUNTRIES**

activities. Like other forms of business, it applies science and technology to achieve high productivity per worker (Figure 10-7).

Formerly the farmer himself processed and marketed most of his produce. As much as possible he supplied the needs of his own household from the farm. His wife made bread from wheat or rye harvested from their own land and wove cloth from thread spun from home-grown wool. Today others perform these tasks, while the farmer concentrates on raising whatever brings the most profit in the market.

Now that the output per worker has greatly increased, only a fraction of the national labor force is needed for farming. In Anglo-America, northwestern Europe, Australia, and New Zealand, persons engaged in farming constitute less than 20 percent of all employed—in the United Kingdom only 4 percent, in the United States 5 percent (Figure 10-8). As one goes east and south in Europe the percentages rise, indicating less complete changeover to the modern economy, but they are still low compared to those of traditional agrarian societies.

One should keep in mind that workers outside farming have taken over many tasks formerly done on the farm, such as processing, manufac-

turing, and to some extent transportation and trade. In the United States these various operations—including transportation and wholesale and retail trade in agricultural products—engage over 10 percent of the labor force in addition to the 5 percent who actually farm.

The rise of industrial-commercial agriculture in the Western world has not completely obliterated traditional ways. Some regions have few machines; others retain a feudal land-tenure system. Elsewhere farmers are still intent on supplying the local market. Furthermore, since continuous innovation characterizes modern society, new and improved farming methods constantly develop but take time to spread from their points of origin to other areas (see Figure 2-1).

Rapid and forceful changes create stresses that governments hopefully try to ameliorate. As agriculture seeks to adjust to new technological and commercial patterns, many Western countries subsidize farmers in one way or another. Since farmers, as a carry-over from the traditional way of life, still hold much political power, other elements in society often pay them subsidies in the form of taxes or higher prices. Commercial production has become a total commitment, and the small semisubsistence family farm is fading away. In the United States even farming as a capital-intensive family business seems in danger of being replaced by corporate giants.

## LAND TENURE

Much as agriculture in the modern world differs from the olden days, the ties between farmer and land remain. Thus, the rules controlling ownership of land and the rights of its use are as important as ever. In some countries outdated laws and customs still prevail, in others they have gradually been adapted to new circumstances. Elsewhere revolutionary land reforms have at one stroke abolished the old order. The four main types of land tenure existing today are (1) communal tenure, (2) latifundium or estate, (3) freehold ownership, and (4) tenancy (Fryer, 1965, 83-118).

*Communal tenure*, in a variety of forms, was once widespread among simple agrarian societies. The land was considered to be common property of the community. Each member had the right to work a parcel of land and enjoy its produce for private use. Redistribution of farm plots after a number of years was not uncommon. This system has tended to give way to private ownership, be it as freehold of small farmers or as large holdings of powerful individuals who in one way or another usurped the rights to lands that formerly were held in common.

Though communal tenure is old, variations of it have been adopted in some revolutionary situations during this century: for example, in Mexico the *ejido,* in Israel the *kibbutz,* in eastern Europe and the Soviet Union the *kolkhoz* or collective, in China the *kung-she* or commune. Whether these methods of farm organization can succeed in economically advanced countries is open to question, though in Israel the *kibbutz* seems to be a flourishing institution. In the Soviet Union agriculture has been the least successful branch of the economy, partly because of too much central and regional bureaucratic control, partly because adequate rewards are lacking for better performance. Some socialist countries, such as Poland and Yugoslavia, have largely rejected collective farms and have injected the personal-profit motive into the system, either by reinstating individual ownership of farms or by adding personal inducements to the remaining collective operations.

The *latifundium* also has ancient as well as modern manifestations. Such large estates have existed for centuries throughout the Mediterranean, Middle East, South Asia, and Latin America. The landed aristocracy, basing wealth and power on the control of vast areas, has proved to be long-lived. Even in countries undergoing land reforms it often survived, though in reduced circumstances. In many regions, owners are absentee landlords, renting out land to sharecroppers.

While large estates sometimes disappear in violent popular revolutions and are replaced by small farms operated by the formerly landless peasantry, it is somewhat paradoxical that a country with a soviet political system sets up another form of latifundium in its agricultural frontier regions. In the Soviet Union, virgin lands recently put to the plow in the steppes of Kazakhstan have been divided into large state farms with their managers and laborers operating under central-government control. In present-day China, state farms are numerous in northern Manchuria and on the drier western margins of the agricul-

tural frontier. State farms in the Soviet Union and other Communist countries tend to produce less than their proponents would wish.

In countries where the capitalistic system of private enterprise operates, the number of farms with corporate structure increases. Many corporate crop and livestock farms in western Europe and North America lead in technological and organizational development. Such farms operate purely from the profit motive, and provide the incentives for personal performance that collective and state farms usually lack. The plantation, discussed above, is, in some cases, a variant of the traditional latifundium, with tenants operating parcels; in other cases it is like the corporate farm, employing wage labor.

The *freehold* (especially fee-simple or absolute) ownership of a farm is greatly prized among many peoples. Most freehold farms in continental western Europe are small, the average size about 20 hectares (50 acres). Division of freeholds has often led to uneconomic fragmentation of farm units. Owner-occupied farms are larger in the British Isles, and especially in North America, Australia, and New Zealand. The freehold farm in the Midwest and Great Plains of the United States provided a livelihood for millions of immigrants who came to North America in the latter part of the nineteenth century.

*Farm tenancy* is the legal condition under which a farmer pays the owner for farming the land. Tenancy of many different kinds flourishes in the traditional society, where often it seems to block increased economic efficiency. Sharecropping, an arrangement by which the tenant pays the owner with part of the crop, is common in all continents, but especially in Asia and Latin America. Sharecropping marks backward regions even in otherwise modernized lands, such as parts of the southeastern United States where vestiges of this once widespread system remain. The system is inefficient because it does not give the tenant increased income from improvements he has made. The owner, like the slum landlord in cities, acts as rent collector, not as an improver of the land and its use.

In many modern situations, however, the position of tenancy differs considerably from this. Tenants pay cash for the use of their farms, hold legal contracts that guarantee their rights, receive

Farms in the Northeast Polder of the Zuider Zee reclamation project, the Netherlands. Since 1942, when the 50,000 hectares of this area were pumped dry, carefully planned land development and colonization have created a landscape of medium-sized family farms. The modern prefabricated homes and barns snugly nestle within their tree shelters in a pattern as neat and geometrical as a Mondrian abstraction. (Photograph—Aerofilms, Ltd.)

compensation for improvements they make, and are protected from landlord exploitation. Such legal safeguards in Britain explain why among modernized countries it has the highest rate of farm tenancy. With proper measures tenancy can be efficient and profitable for both tenant and owner.

## TYPES OF MODERN FARMING

In modern societies types of agriculture are identified according to what crops and animals the farmer raises and what the purposes of production are. In Europe there are two very old traditions of farming: in the Mediterranean region, the growing of field and orchard crops tends to be distinct from the raising of livestock; north of the Alps, the basic type is mixed or general farming, featuring integrated production of crops and animals. From these two have evolved various specialized forms (Figures 10–9, 10–12).

**Mixed (Crop and Livestock) Farming**  The historic form of this type of agriculture is described in Chapter 13 (pages 310–316). The essential feature of modern systems of mixed farming lies in cultivating crops partly for sale and partly for fodder to feed farm animals that are sold for meat. Although operators of mixed farms use a wide range of crop and livestock associations, all practice crop rotation—that is, a succession of different crops in a specified order on the same field. In eighteenth-century Europe the introduction of roots and legumes in the cropping cycle made it possible to eliminate the age-old fallowing of land. The higher yield in fodder crops enabled the farmer to keep more livestock, which in turn increased the manure so necessary for maintaining soil fertility. Great progress occurred in the nineteenth century, when rotation practices were scientifically tested and chemical fertilizers developed. This made it possible to bring much marginal land under intensive cultivation.

In essence, rotation crops are selected from three groups of plants: (1) row crops such as corn, potatoes, beets, turnips, and other roots, (2) close-growing grains like wheat, rye, oats, and barley, and (3) sod-forming or rest crops, among them clover, soybeans, and alfalfa (lucerne). A simple rotation cycle would be, for instance, corn—oats—clover, grown in succession over

three years on the same field. Actually most rotation systems involve more crops and stretch over more years, depending on quality of land, market value of crop and livestock products, and also on the farmer's attitude. A sound rotation system will not aim at the highest immediate returns but at satisfactory yields, which at the same time maintain soil fertility.

America's heartland of crop and livestock farming lies in the Corn Belt, a wedgelike zone reaching from central Ohio westward to southern Minnesota and central Nebraska. In Canada the Ontario Peninsula also belongs to this type. In the Old South, the predominant monoculture of tobacco and cotton has given way to a mixed form of agriculture. Traditional cash crops still have a place, but now blend in rotation systems with other land use, especially improved pastures. For example, the Alabama "black belt," once the type area for Southern plantation farming, has become a highly productive beef-cattle region. In the Southern Hemisphere mixed farming is much less developed, and quickly shades over into other forms, principally stock rearing and grain farming.

While ecological conditions affect the crop and animal combinations in these regions, food habits too must be considered. West Europeans eat mainly wheat bread, Central and East Europeans usually rye, although increasingly also wheat. Potatoes have a much larger place in the diet of Europe than of Anglo-America. High consumption of meat in the United States leads farmers to put a greater proportion of their land in fodder crops than do the European farmers, who grow more food crops.

Each subtype of mixed farming covers large areas in the United States, but in Europe the mosaic is on a microscale. Over the ages farmers there have worked out fine adjustments to the variety of ecological conditions. Moreover, transportation in much of Europe was formerly poor and expensive, which promoted local production of as many different foodstuffs as possible.

**Dairy Farming**  Milk and milk products have been part of the Occidental diet for a very long time, but their production on specialized farms is of rather recent date. Dairy farming expanded in response to growing demands from cities for milk, cream, butter, and cheese. Advances in the tech-

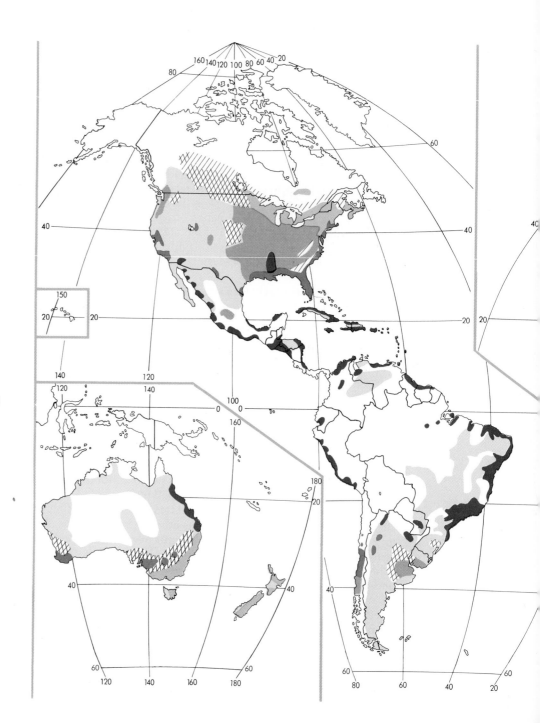

Intensive Crop Farming

Intensive Crop and
Livestock Farming

Dairy Farming

Livestock Ranching

Plantation Farming

**Extensive Crop Farming:
Supplementary Livestock
Husbandry**

Subsistence and
Local Market Type

Commercial Type

Miles

0    500    1000    1500

0    500   1000    2000

Kilometers

AITOFF'S

INTERRUPTED EQUAL-AREA

PROJECTION

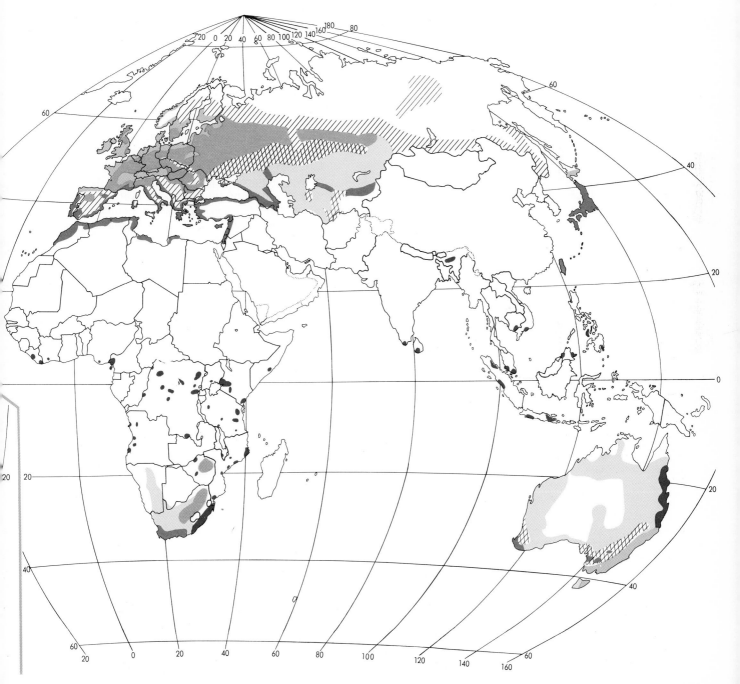

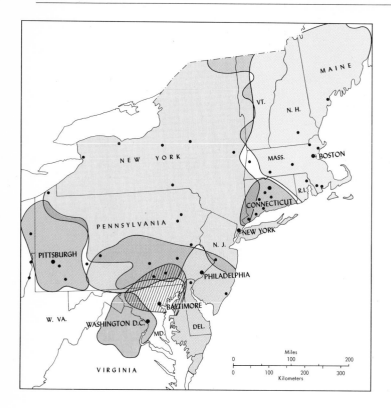

FIGURE
10-10
UNITED STATES: MAJOR MILKSHEDS IN THE NORTHEAST

Seven milksheds are shown, six of them supplying large metropolitan areas (Boston, New York, Philadelphia, Baltimore, Washington, D.C., and Pittsburgh) and one serving the cluster of cities in western Connecticut. In areas where the main markets are close together, there is a considerable overlap of milksheds as in southern Pennsylvania. The smaller dots are medium-sized cities which compete with the larger cities for milk supply. Based on a map in Gottmann, J., *Megalopolis: The Urbanized Northeastern Seaboard of the United States,* New York, 1961, 230.

nologies of preservation and in transportation aided its development.

Because fluid milk is bulky and perishable, it must be produced within reasonable distance from consumption centers. Thus, each urban area has its nearby dairy farms, even though the chief type of agriculture may differ. An instructive case is that of dairying in southern California, which grows apace with rapid urbanization.

Dairy farming as the regionally dominant form occupies two large areas, one in Anglo-America, the other in Europe. Smaller areas exist elsewhere, but only a few (Alps in Europe, New Zealand) can be shown in Figure 10–9. The American dairy zone lies mainly on the northern flank of the vast urban market of the northeastern United States and adjacent Canada. Mixed farming tends to occupy the more favorable lands south of the urban zone. Within the dairy belt the eastern part specializes in fluid milk, which brings a premium price in this highly urbanized section (Figure 10–10). But the western part, especially Wisconsin and Minnesota, produces far more milk than cities can buy. The surplus is converted into less perishable form. Butter, cheese, and other manufactured products have high value per weight and allow transportation over great distances. Canada, apart from the "fluid milksheds" around the cities, exports cheese, butter, and condensed milk to Britain.

Many dairy enterprises resemble crop and livestock farms in raising beef besides producing milk. They often gain additional income by selling calves, hogs (fed on skimmed milk and whey), and also poultry, eggs, and old cows. The larger enterprises, to a greater extent mechanized, have low production costs; in contrast, many small farms hold an economically marginal position. Tenancy is low, because the owner-operator has greater incentive to devote care and demanding labor to the animals.

Agricultural regions as shown on small-scale maps are always gross simplifications. This is particularly true for the zone in Europe commonly designated as the dairy belt. A large-scale view of any section of this belt would show how intermingled it is with districts of mixed farming, specialized horticulture, and transitional forms hard to classify. West European agriculture went through a crisis in the late nineteenth century, when imports of cheap grain from overseas compelled farmers to find more specialized forms of production. Dairying proved to be the answer in parts of the British Isles, in lands around the North and Baltic seas, as well as in interior highlands like Switzerland. Population growth and continuing concentration into urbanized regions increased the market for dairy products.

Denmark pioneered in modern dairy methods and in farmers' cooperatives, now common to this branch of agriculture. Its pasture grazing became secondary to the feeding of cultivated crops, imported corn, and high-protein oil cakes. A cooperative creamery collects the milk and makes it into butter and cheese. To feed his pigs, the farmer buys back the skimmed milk, barley, and imported concentrates. A cooperative bacon factory processes the fattened hogs. This example shows the complexity of production, with the farms in essence converting the plants into milk and meat.

In the Netherlands many polders* along the North Sea have a water table too high to permit crop cultivation. Thus, grazing on permanent pastures is more common there than in Denmark. Holland's bacon production for export is minor, but condensed and powdered milk and cheese are important trade commodities. Other industrial countries in Europe have their own dairy districts, but may import part of their butter and cheese. This is especially true for Great Britain, although much of its land surface is in dairy farms.

New Zealand's dairy industry is concentrated in the North Island, where mild winters and adequate moisture provide year-round grazing on fine improved pastures. Efficient production on large enterprises plus rigid quality standards makes it possible for New Zealand butter and cheese to overcome high labor costs and freight charges to distant markets (Figure 10–11).

**Crop Farming**  In modern societies, crop farming can be classified into a number of different types.

*Mediterranean agriculture* developed in ancient times as an adaptation of Middle Eastern farming to the seasonal rainfall of the Mediterranean. Today cereals—mainly wheat—are planted in the fall, grow slowly in the cool and moist winter, and are harvested in summer. Drought-resistant vines and trees, above all the grape and olive, occupy much of the remaining farmland. The small water volume available in summer restricts irrigation, which is necessary for citrus fruits, introduced from more humid homelands in eastern Asia. Animal husbandry is usually separate from or only loosely associated with the main activity of crop cultivation. Livestock browse on

*A polder is a dike-enclosed area with a controlled groundwater level.

deforested, often badly eroded, uplands during the summer and graze in winter on whatever lowland pastures can be found.

Agriculture in these lands is gradually becoming integrated with the modern commercial economy, though many vestiges of the past remain. Semifeudal latifundia sharply contrast with small semisubsistent peasant plots. Compared to northern Europe, a larger proportion of the population here depends on agriculture.

Raising grapes for wine is widespread. A few districts have become famous for their specialty, among them Malaga wine, Andalusian sherry from Spain, and port from northern Portugal. The irrigated coastal fringes of southeastern Spain are veritable garden spots (*huertas*), where rice fields alternate with almond and citrus orchards, or vegetable plots. Northern Sicily and southern Italy, too, produce citrus fruits. Israel has made the desert bloom, using modern cultivation methods to produce a variety of fruits and early vegetables. The French and Italian *rivieras*, protected by mountains, have diverse production, including flowers for seeds and perfume essences.

A three-storied use of land is not uncommon, with grapevines festooned between olive trees and with vegetables covering the ground. The olive occupies areas unfit for other crops because its long roots tap moisture from deep below the surface and it does fairly well on poor, stony soils. Its main product is the oil, which is used in all kinds of food in place of the butter and lard so common in Europe beyond the Alps. There are few cattle. Goats and sheep provide milk that is made into cheese, but sheep are chiefly kept for wool. Large flocks under the care of a few shepherds move seasonally from winter to summer pastures and back again (*transhumance*).

The broad fertile plain of the Po River in northern Italy, although within the Mediterranean region, forms a transition to the types of land use in transalpine Europe. Irrigated meadows and fodder crops support large herds of dairy and beef cattle. Milk is manufactured into well-known Italian cheeses. While the heavier rainfall and the river plains—so different from southern Italy— explain in part the agricultural features of the Po Plain, the progressive character of its farming owes much to the stimulus of a large market in the industrial centers of this region.

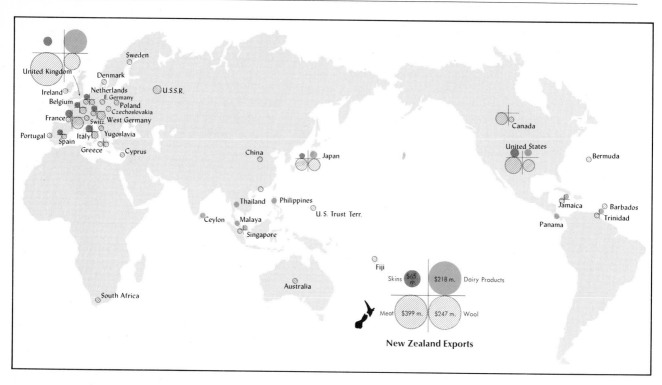

New Zealand Exports

FIGURE **NEW ZEALAND: AGRICULTURAL EXPORTS**
**10-11**

This map shows the principal destinations of four categories of exports from New Zealand for the year 1969. Their total value was U.S. $929 million; all other exports from New Zealand amounted to U.S. $253 million. Data from *United Nations Commodity Trade Statistics, 1969,* Statistical Papers, Series D, vol. 19, no. 1–33, New York, 1970.

**Value of Exports from New Zealand:**
**Millions of U.S. Dollars**

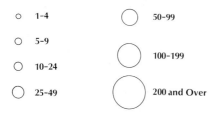

○ 1-4      ○ 50-99

○ 5-9

○ 10-24     ○ 100-199

○ 25-49     ○ 200 and Over

*Specialized horticulture* as a dominant land use is a modern phenomenon in Europe north of the Alps, closely related to the increasing city population with its rising living standards and to the technology of conservation and transportation. The United States with an affluent market of continental size and a great variety of climatic conditions strikingly demonstrates this interplay of various factors. Although most cities have "truck farms"* in their vicinity, they buy the bulk of their fruits and vegetables from specialized, often quite remote districts. Each horticultural area has developed its own organizations and services for harvesting, processing, and marketing, thus uniting agricultural, industrial, and commercial functions into an efficient regional complex.

The three Pacific Coast states produce over half of all fruits and nuts and one-third of all vegetables sold in the United States. California has a huge output and versatility of production.

*The term *truck farming,* used in the United States since the eighteenth century, derives from the French *troquer,* meaning "to exchange."

Old World specialty crops each have found there an ecological niche in climates ranging from cool, foggy summers to blazing desert skies and on soils of great variety. The growing season is long and there is water for irrigation almost everywhere.

Harvesting this diversity of fruits and vegetables requires a large labor force. Migrant workers have been used—and often abused—for a long time: Chinese and Japanese in the nineteenth century, Filipinos and "Okies" before World War II, more recently Puerto Ricans and Mexicans—the latter on special entry permits. Farmers mechanize operations wherever possible, especially on large holdings, many owned by corporations. These large farms often switch from one crop to another, depending on the estimated consumer demand and the prices for particular items. This type of industrial-commercial agriculture is a far cry from the more traditional horticulture of Mediterranean Europe.

Specialized horticulture in favorable districts along the Atlantic and Gulf coasts supplies adjacent city markets. Tobacco grows in the Connecticut Valley and lands to the south, truck crops along the seaboards from New Jersey to Virginia. Citrus and other fruits, vegetables, and sugarcane come from the south coastal region from Florida to Texas. More inland lie peach orchards of South Carolina and Georgia and apple orchards of the Shenandoah and other Appalachian valleys. In the north the frosts of late spring or early fall may easily hurt fruits. Vineyards and orchards in the Great Lakes states therefore seek shores where large bodies of water temper the climate.

Although Europe north of the Alps produces great quantities of vegetables and fruits, political fragmentation has discouraged such large-scale regional specialization. Small gardens are almost everywhere. Each farmer coaxes with intense hand labor as many crops as he can from the land. Fruit still comes from orchards that are part of general or dairy farms. Much trade flows across international boundaries from specialized horticultural districts to urban agglomerations—for instance, from the Netherlands to the Ruhr district. Near the great cities, greenhouses cover extensive areas producing table grapes, tomatoes, other fruits, and vegetables, in virtually perfect ecological conditions. Some districts concentrate on flowers, seeds, or bulbs; others produce hops for use in beer and ale making. Probably the best known horticultural specialty of western Europe is the wine-producing vineyard. Because of climate, soil, and traditional skill some districts have become famous for their red or white premium wines, among them the region near Bordeaux in southwest France, Burgundy and Champagne in the northeast, also the Rhine and Moselle valleys of adjacent Germany.

*Grain farming* is obviously the major element in most types of agriculture; however, in some regions virtually only cereals are grown. This commercial specialization came to the fore when increasing city populations of the Occidental world required ever more bread grains. The pioneer farmer in the Middle West, the Great Plains, the Canadian prairies, Australia, and Argentina responded by making wheat his cash crop. Scarcity of labor as well as the nature of grain cultivation encouraged use of machinery. As more intensive forms of agriculture occupied the humid lands closer to the markets, specialized grain farming became largely restricted to the subhumid lands in more remote locations. The lower yields per acre were countered by increase in farm size, demanding in turn more mechanization of the production. Thus, grain farms are on the average the largest of all crop-growing enterprises and the most mechanized.

Climatic risk presents an ever-present danger. The mean annual precipitation in most wheat regions is between 10 and 25 inches (25 and 62 centimeters), but varies greatly from year to year. When grain prices are high, the farmer expands beyond the safe climatic limits until a series of crop failures beats him back. In the United States the lessons of droughts and dust storms have been taken to heart, but in the Soviet Union the unsuccessful plowing up of the "virgin lands" on the dry margins of Turkestan suggests that each country must learn its own lesson the hard way.

In the Southern Hemisphere grain cropping commonly is associated with livestock grazing, as in the *pampas* of Argentina, where wheat serves both for cattle feed and for export. Wheat, most important agricultural product in international trade, is shipped in huge but varying quantities from modern farming regions of the New World to the Old, especially to China, South Asia, and the Soviet Union (Figure 10–13).

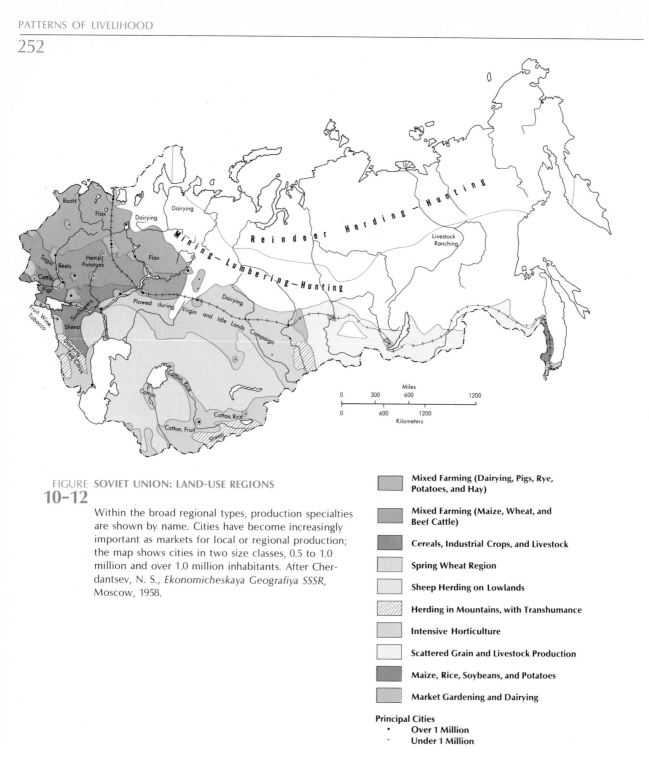

FIGURE **SOVIET UNION: LAND-USE REGIONS**

**10-12**

Within the broad regional types, production specialties are shown by name. Cities have become increasingly important as markets for local or regional production; the map shows cities in two size classes, 0.5 to 1.0 million and over 1.0 million inhabitants. After Cherdantsev, N. S., *Ekonomicheskaya Geografiya SSSR,* Moscow, 1958.

**Mixed Farming (Dairying, Pigs, Rye, Potatoes, and Hay)**

**Mixed Farming (Maize, Wheat, and Beef Cattle)**

**Cereals, Industrial Crops, and Livestock**

**Spring Wheat Region**

**Sheep Herding on Lowlands**

**Herding in Mountains, with Transhumance**

**Intensive Horticulture**

**Scattered Grain and Livestock Production**

**Maize, Rice, Soybeans, and Potatoes**

**Market Gardening and Dairying**

**Principal Cities**
- **Over 1 Million**
- **Under 1 Million**

+++ **Trans-Siberian Railway**

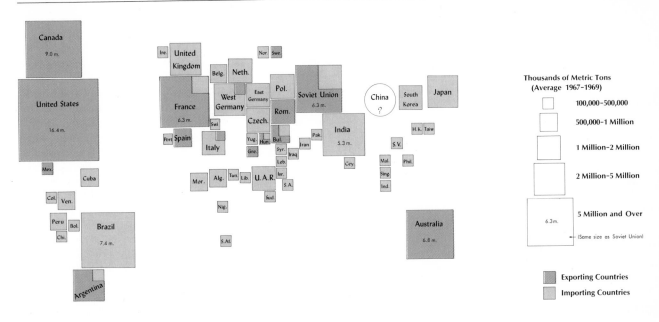

**Thousands of Metric Tons (Average 1967–1969)**

☐ 100,000–500,000

☐ 500,000–1 Million

☐ 1 Million–2 Million

☐ 2 Million–5 Million

☐ 6.3 m. 5 Million and Over

— (Same size as Soviet Union)

■ Exporting Countries

☐ Importing Countries

FIGURE **WORLD: INTERNATIONAL TRADE IN WHEAT**
**10-13**

This cartogram shows the main importers and exporters of wheat. Compiled from data published by the Food and Agriculture Organization of the United Nations.

*Cotton farming* used to be the principal economic activity of the Old South, then called the American Cotton Belt. Sharecroppers worked parcels of plantation holdings with hoe and mule-drawn plow; at harvest time entire families moved between the rows to pick the cotton bolls. The sharecropper lacked the motivation, the knowledge, and the means to break the vicious routine of cotton growing. Monoculture exhausted the land. Production per worker as well as per acre remained low, and poverty was the inevitable lot of most of the population, Negro tenant as well as poor white.

The Old South has greatly changed in recent years. The scourge of the boll weevil in the 1920s, the depression of the 1930s, and subsequent government restrictions on cotton growing, together with mechanization, all brought about diversification in agriculture. Although cotton is still an important crop, it now shares the land with pastures and fodder crops for beef cattle, and with

soybeans, peanuts, vegetables, and fruits. New crops, better methods of tillage, and wide use of fertilizers, all promoted by agricultural experiment stations, have restored soils and stopped erosion. Scarred slopes have been planted to new forest, yielding timber, pulp, resins, and turpentine. The use of machines, including the mechanical cotton picker, compelled the consolidation of small tenant farms. The released human power moved to industrial jobs, or perhaps to welfare rolls, mainly in northern cities.

The only part of the Old South where cotton is still king lies in the rich river-bottom lands of Arkansas and Mississippi; form of enterprise and the remains of a traditional social structure justify including this area among the world's plantation regions. But more cotton is grown now in the southwestern states of Texas and Oklahoma, usually with irrigation.

The only other leading cotton producer among the industrial countries* is the Soviet Union, its chief area in the irrigated river plains east and south of the Aral Sea in Soviet Asia. Almost the entire crop is raised on state farms and collectives.

*Latin American countries, especially Mexico, have rapidly increased cotton production in recent years.

**Livestock Ranching**  Like nomadic herding, livestock ranching depends on extensive grazing, but here the similarity ends. Ranching is a specialized commercial offshoot from European agriculture—either from Mediterranean or from mixed farming—with the operator living in a permanent residence on privately owned property. Although ranching mainly occupies dry lands with short grass or shrub vegetation, it also occurs on more humid grasslands remote from large markets, as in New Zealand and the southern parts of Africa and South America.

Europeans occupied most of the mid-latitude grasslands in the course of the nineteenth century. Initially, lack of transportation prohibited production of beef or mutton; only hides, wool, and tallow had value for export. Herds of livestock grazed on the open range under the care of cowboys, *gauchos,* or *vaqueros.* Overstocking the range was common; herds were exposed to droughts or blizzards. In most countries the clash between advancing farmer and rancher ended in the latter's retreat to sections unsuitable for crop production. The range changed into the ranch, with barbed-wire fenced pastures, provision for water and, where necessary, animal shelter. Fencing not only regulated grazing but also protected the herd against interbreeding with poor strains.

Better means of transportation have made hides and tallow minor products as compared to meat. Nevertheless, livestock ranching remains, on the whole, a marginal agricultural activity. It competes with increasing difficulty against the ever more efficient production in regions of intensive livestock husbandry. The latter areas support also, by far, the larger number of animals, a fact sometimes overlooked because livestock ranching takes in such vast expanses of land. Most ranches in the United States own over 1,000 hectares and many have more than 4,000 hectares. In Australia the holdings are even larger. Ownership by corporations is not uncommon, especially by those operating packing and other processing plants. Ranchers in the United States and Canada often grow supplementary feed on their own irrigated fields or buy it from nearby districts, particularly alfalfa and tops of sugar beets as well as the beet pulp from the sugar-beet factories. In such favorable areas the ranch has virtually become a mixed-farming enterprise. Elsewhere

herdsmen take the livestock in summer to mountain pastures in the public domain. The western rancher usually does not attempt to fatten his cattle, but sends them to feedlots in the Middle West and East.

In Australia, with most of the land arid or semiarid, with sparse population and remote location, conditions favor sheep raising. In the zones of heavier rain, crops supplement range grazing and sheep are produced for wool and meat. Toward the drier interior, the critical factor in determining the carrying capacity is the amount of fodder available during the drought period. Less than 10 hectares of pasture per sheep leads to overgrazing. Stations, as ranches are called here, necessarily cover wide areas, averaging some 8,000 hectares. Although the land itself is cheap, substantial investments are required for fencing the "paddocks" (pastures) and supplying adequate water. On the other hand, supplementary feeding is rare, and the mild weather obviates the need for shelter. In this interior region wool provides the exclusive source of income.

Ranching is also quite important in New Zealand, with emphasis on sheep in the cooler South Island. Irrigation water from the western mountains supplements the moderate rainfall to maintain the rich improved pastures. In addition to wool, lamb provides an important export commodity for the British market.

In Argentina and Uruguay the general farming of the humid pampas shades off into livestock ranching on the drier margins. In Patagonia wool sheep are the principal animals. A mixture of savanna and scrub forest covers the interior of Brazil. This sparsely inhabited country is mainly used for cattle grazing. The herders live a semi-nomadic life around the widely scattered ranch headquarters. The thin scrub cattle are grown for hides, tallow, and the production of salt beef (the poor man's meat), or driven long distances to farms to be fattened before being sent to the city slaughterhouse.

## TRENDS IN MODERN AGRICULTURE

Vast and rapid changes are revolutionizing Occidental twentieth-century agriculture, as we see most clearly in the United States. The farm becomes an industrial enterprise requiring large in-

A combine crew moves across a Nebraska wheat field. These harvesters rent their services to farmers, beginning in the middle of May in Texas and ending up by the end of September at the Canadian border. On a seasonal circuit a crew operating four combines will travel about 5,000 kilometers and harvest 10,000 hectares. (Photograph—U.S. Dept. of Agriculture)

vestment of capital and competent management. Mechanical power replaces manual labor wherever feasible. Machines shake trees, sort fruits, test and pick radishes and cotton, process and pack head lettuce. Airplanes broadcast seed, spray pest- and weed-killing chemicals, spread fertilizer, and frighten away birds. In dairying, all except the cow becomes a fully automated industry.

Mechanization permits, but also requires, mass output of standardized commodities. Production, controlled at every step, ensures high yields of the desired quality. Even in normally humid climates overhead irrigation provides crops with water in the right amount at the right time. Seeds and breeds are created to meet environmental conditions, mechanical handling, or consumers' preferences.

Industrialization of agriculture leads to larger-sized enterprises, either by consolidation of adjacent small farms or by integration of widely scattered holdings. It is not uncommon for cattlemen, grain farmers, or horticulturists to own or rent land in different parts of the country as a hedge against climatic risk or as a means to use their machinery the year round. In addition to this horizontal combination there is increasing vertical integration, forging closer links between farm and market. Besides corporate structure, the expanding practice of contract farming relates orchards to processing plants, hatcheries and dairies to supermarket chains.

Efficient production leads not only to consolidation and integration, but also to concentration on better land. Thus, fewer farmers produce more commodities on fewer farms occupying less area. Land taken out of production is put into forest or used for public and private recreation. New types of economy replace old ones: dairy farming and beef-cattle rearing expand in the South, and diversified agriculture invades the Great Plains.

Modern farmers are into agribusiness. They may reside on their farms or in town, or live "out of a suitcase" while supervising operations on one of their holdings. They follow market trends closely, consult agricultural experts, and read journals reporting the results of the latest research in agronomy and farm management. While this summary represents only a minority of farmers today, it promises to be true for nearly all before the end of the century.

The same general trends can be observed in western Europe. Although this region needs imports, especially of animal fodder, the impressive gains in agricultural output demonstrate what can be accomplished in an area where land use was already at a high level of intensity. The tremendous productivity of North American farming presents the paradox of an embarrassing plenty at home while much of the world goes hungry. Without entering into a discussion of how to deal with this perplexing problem, it is quite clear that in the near future the world's staggering population surge will require all the surplus food the United States, Canada, and a few other countries can spare. At the same time, countries with too many people to feed will undoubtedly try to increase their own food production. While the intensive agriculture developed by traditional societies can support huge populations and can expand into thinly occupied lands, there is a ceiling on what it can do. Perhaps the American and Western European method of applying science and technology—by no means a perfect model and one that threatens an ecological upset—may help to suggest ways toward providing enough for everyone.

## CITATIONS AND FURTHER READINGS

### TRADITIONAL LAND USE

Adams, R. M. *Land behind Baghdad: A History of Settlement on the Diyala Plains,* Chicago, 1965.

Awad, M. "The Assimilation of Nomads in Egypt," *Geographical Review,* 44 (1954): 240–252.

Beardsley, R. K., Hall, J. W., and Ward, R. E. *Village Japan,* Chicago, 1959.

Broek, J. O. M. *Economic Development of the Netherlands Indies,* New York, 1942, reissued in 1971.

Bromley, R. J. "Markets in Developing Countries: A Review," *Geography*, 56 (1971): 124-132.

———, Symanski, R., and Good, C. M. "The Rationale of Periodic Markets," *Annals of the Association of American Geographers*, 65 (1975): 530-537.

Buck, J. L. *Land Utilization in China*, 3 vols., Nanking, 1937.

Clarke, J. I. "Studies of Semi-nomadism in North Africa," *Economic Geography*, 35 (1959): 95-108.

Davies, H. R. J. "Nomadism in the Sudan," *Tijdschrift voor Economische en Sociale Geografie*, 57 (1966): 193-202.

Eyre, J. "Mountain Land Use in Northern Japan," *Geographical Review*, 52 (1962): 236-252.

Fryer, D. W. *Emerging Southeast Asia*, New York, 1970.

Gautier, E. F. *Sahara: The Great Desert*, translated by D. F. Mayhew, London, 1935.

Geertz, C. *Agricultural Involution: The Process of Ecological Change in Indonesia*, Berkeley, Calif., 1963.

Ho, R. "Mixed-farming and Multiple-cropping in Malaya," *Journal of Tropical Geography*, 15 (1961): 46-65.

Horvath, R. J. "Von Thünen's Isolated State and the Area around Addis Ababa, Ethiopia," *Annals of the Association of American Geographers*, 59 (1969): 308-323.

Hsieh Chiao-min. *Taiwan—Ilha Formosa: A Geography in Perspective*, Washington, D.C., 1964.

King, F. H. *Farmers of Forty Centuries*, 2d ed., New York, 1927. [China]

Ladejinski, W. "Agrarian Revolution in Japan," *Foreign Affairs*, 38 (1959): 95-109.

Lambton, A. K. S. *Landlord and Peasant in Persia: A Study of Land Tenure and Land Revenue Administration*, London, 1953.

Matley, I. M. "Transhumance in Bosnia and Herzegovina," *Geographical Review*, 58 (1968): 231-261.

Mikesell, M. W. *Northern Morocco: A Cultural Geography*, University of California Publications in Geography no. 14, Berkeley, 1961.

Murphey, R. "The Decline of North Africa since the Roman Occupation: Climatic or Human?" *Annals of the Association of American Geographers*, 41 (1951): 116-132.

Myrdal, J. *Report from a Chinese Village*, translated by M. Michael, New York, 1965. Describes the impact of the social and political revolution on a village in northern Shensi.

Nath, V. "The Growth of Indian Agriculture: A Regional Analysis," *Geographical Review*, 59 (1969): 348-372.

Pulyarkin, V. A. "Nomadism in the Modern World," *Soviet Geography: Review and Translation*, 13 (1972): 163-176.

Simoons, F. J. "The Antiquity of Dairying in Asia and Africa," *Geographical Review*, 61 (1971): 431-439.

Spate, O. H. K., and Learmonth, A. T. A. *India and Pakistan: A General and Regional Geography*, 3d ed., London and New York, 1967.

Thompson, J. H. "Urban Agriculture in Southern Japan," *Economic Geography*, 33 (1957): 224-237.

Tschudi, A. B. "People's Communes in China," *Norsk Geografisk Tidsskrift*, 27 (1973): 5-37.

UNESCO, "Nomads and Nomadism in the Arid Zone," *International Science Journal*, 11 (1959): 481-585. A symposium of eleven authors.

Wikkramatileke, R., and Singh, K. "Tradition and Change in an Indian Dairying Community in Singapore," *Annals of the Association of American Geographers*, 60 (1970): 717-742.

## PLANTATIONS

Broek, J. O. M. "The Economic Development of the Outer Provinces of the Netherlands Indies," *Geographical Review*, 30 (1940): 190-196.

Chardon, R. E. *Geographic Aspects of Plantation Agriculture in Yucatan*, National Academy of Sciences—National Research Council Publication no. 876, Washington, D.C., 1961.

——— "Hacienda and Ejido in Yucatan: The Example of Santa Ana Cuca," *Annals of the Association of American Geographers*, 53 (1963): 174–193.

Pan American Union, *Plantation Systems of the New World*, Social Science Monographs no. 7, Washington, D.C., 1959.

Thompson, E. T. *The Plantation*, Chicago, 1935.

——— "The Climatic Theory of the Plantation," *Agricultural History*, 15 (1941): 49–60.

Waibel, L. *Probleme der Landwirtschaftsgeographie*, Breslau, 1933.

——— "The Tropical Plantation System," *Scientific Monthly*, 52 (1941): 156–160.

——— "The Climatic Theory of the Plantation: A Critique," *Geographical Review*, 32 (1942): 307–310.

Withington, W. A. "Changes and Trends in Patterns of North Sumatra's Estate Agriculture, 1938–1959," *Tijdschrift voor Economische en Sociale Geographie*, 55 (1964): 8–13.

## MODERN LAND USE

Alexander, J. W. "International Trade: Selected Types of World Regions," *Economic Geography*, 36 (1960): 95–115.

Baker, O. E. "Agricultural Regions of North America," *Economic Geography*, 7 (1931): 109–153; 8 (1932): 325–377.

Calef, W. *Private Grazing and Public Lands: Studies of the Local Management of the Taylor Grazing Act*, Chicago, 1960.

Chisholm, M. *Rural Settlement and Land Use: An Essay in Location*, London, 1961.

Coppock, J. T. *An Agricultural Geography of Great Britain*, London, 1971.

Durand, L., Jr. "The Major Milksheds of the Northeastern Quarter of the United States," *Economic Geography*, 40 (1964): 9–33.

Fisher, J. S. "Negro Farm Ownership in the South," *Annals of the Association of American Geographers*, 63 (1973): 478–489.

Fryer, D. W. *World Economic Development*, New York, 1965.

Gregor, H. F. *Geography of Agriculture: Themes in Research*, Englewood Cliffs, N.J., 1970.

Harris, C. D. "Agricultural Production in the United States: The Past Fifty Years and the Next," *Geographical Review*, 47 (1957): 175–193.

Hart, J. F. "Loss and Abandonment of Cleared Farm Land in the Eastern United States," *Annals of the Association of American Geographers*, 58 (1968): 417–440.

Higbee, E. C. *Farms and Farmers in an Urban Age*, New York, 1963.

Hofmeister, B. "Four Types of Agriculture with Predominant Olive Growing in Southern Spain—a Case Study," *Geoforum*, 8 (1971): 15–30.

Kollmorgen, W. M., and Jenks, G. F. "Suitcase Farming in Sully County, South Dakota," *Annals of the Association of American Geographers*, 48 (1958): 27–40.

Lewis, R. A. "The Irrigation Potential of Soviet Central Asia," *Annals of the Association of American Geographers*, 52 (1962): 99–114.

Lewthwaite, G. R. "Wisconsin and the Waikato: A Comparison of Dairy Farming in the United States and New Zealand," *Annals of the Association of American Geographers*, 54 (1964): 59–87.

——— "Commonwealth and Common Market: The Dilemma of the New Zealand Dairy Industry," *Geographical Review*, 61 (1971): 72–101.

Mather, E. C., and Hart, J. F. "The Geography of Manure," *Land Economics*, 32 (1956): 25–38.

Meinig, D. W. *On the Margins of the Good Earth: The South Australian Wheat Frontier, 1869–1884*, Chicago, 1963.

Melezin, A. "Soviet Regionalization: An Attempt at the Delineation of Socioeconomic Integrated Regions," *Geographical Review,* 58 (1968): 593-621.

Prunty, M. C., and Aiken, C. S. "The Demise of the Piedmont Cotton Region," *Annals of the Association of American Geographers,* 62 (1972): 283-306.

Simpson, E. S. "Milk Production in England and Wales: A Study in the Influence of Collective Marketing," *Geographical Review,* 49 (1959): 95-111.

Stroyev, K. F. "Agriculture in the Nonchernozem Zone of the RSFSR," *Soviet Geography: Review and Translation,* 16 (1975): 186-197.

Symons, L. *Russian Agriculture: a Geographic Survey,* London, 1972.

Thoman, R. S., and Patton, D. J. *Focus on Geographical Activity: A Collection of Original Studies,* New York, 1964.

Wadham, S. M., and Wilson, R. K. *Land Utilization in Australia.* 4th ed., Melbourne, 1964.

Wagret, P. *Polderlands,* London, 1968.

Webb, W. P. *The Great Plains,* Boston, 1931; New York, 1959.

Yates, P. L. *Food, Land and Manpower in Western Europe,* London, 1960.

# 11 INDUSTRIAL COUNTRIES AND REGIONS

Industrialization may be viewed as the process of spreading modern technology outward from its cradle to other lands. In a modern society, manufacturing and its associated operations permeate all of everyday life. To many parts of the third world, however, technology still remains a foreign intrusion amid the ancient ways. Even when a developing country modernizes, it will differ from the others in how it accepts, adapts, or rejects the new within the context of its singular culture. Most countries lie somewhere between the two extremes of complete modernization and preindustrial condition. Useful indicators as to the extent of industrialization include the proportion of industrial workers in the labor force (Figure 12-3), the use of energy per capita (Figure 12-4), the transportation systems (Figure 3-11), and the income or product per capita (Figure 12-2). Supporting evidence can be gleaned from the level of education and the degree to which urbanization prevails along the full range of town and city sizes. In all these indexes the heavily industrialized countries score highly.

The geography of manufacturing is quite complex. Industry comprises many branches, each with its own combination of technique, organization, supply, and market factors. New industries may choose appropriate sites, but older ones often still occupy their original locations, selected under conditions far different from those today. Especially during the nineteenth century industrialists built factories where they wished. Even late in the twentieth century such laissez faire conditions still survive in some countries. At the other end of the scale, a state like the Soviet Union plans its entire economy, including the locations for industries and the types and sizes of the manufacturing plants. In most countries governmental and corporate policies determine the character of industrial development and of economic change. The kinds of industries a nation has reflect its level of income, technological know-how, and degree of contact with other peoples—in short, the nature of its society.

To discuss the geography of manufacturing, we first inquire what factors influence decisions about plant location, and illustrate this by the example of the iron and steel industry in the United States. Then we take an overview of the main industrial regions, followed by a closer look at one region, South Wales.

## FACTORS OF INDUSTRIAL LOCATION

Why is each specific plant located where it is? We can approach answers to this question in many ways, for example, by discussing the decisions made at the board meetings of industrial companies, the wishes of individual executives, the actions of legislatures, the dictates of economic ministries. No doubt by studying these one can gain insight into the factors determining location of industry.

Another approach would be to consider the origins of the raw materials a particular industry needs and the destination of its products, using the transportation system as the key to analyze plant location.

Yet another point of view stresses the technology of the nation and the markets available for industrial products—in other words, the kind of society in which the industry is present. Compare, for example, manufacturing locations in western Europe or the United States in the first phases of industrialization with those in a fully developed industrial-commercial situation. Earlier, the mass production of basic metals and textiles was the main concern. Plant locations were usually tied to a specific advantage, whether a coalfield for power supply, a mine for raw materials, or a port for transportation. Such factories were self-contained and had easily recognizable connections with a few raw materials, power sources, and markets. Today these aspects are often present in countries that are in the initial stages of developing a manufacturing economy.

In an advanced economy, a multitude of different industries provide in great variety for the needs and wants of the consumer. Industries relate in complex ways not only to raw materials, power, and markets but also to each other. The automobile that runs off the assembly line at Gorki, Detroit, Paris, or Coventry represents a final product of many different components made in many different plants, each of which depends in turn on other factories for its supplies. In this situation proximity to key industrial plants often strongly influences where other projects may locate.

As an industrial area expands and intensifies, its locational advantages increase. Transportation improves, and ancillary services, from repair shops to technical consultants, multiply. Its population growth induces the establishment of more and better facilities for education, recreation, and other social services, making life more attractive to both white- and blue-collar workers and their families. Thus, economic and cultural factors improve conditions for still more new enterprises. This cumulative process of location through interaction and interdependence is often called agglomeration or aggregation (Weber, 1929; Ullman, 1956). It largely explains the development of gigantic industrial regions such as the North American manufacturing belt, northwestern Europe, and southern Japan.

## MARKET

As an industrial location factor, the market increases in importance with the degree of economic development and the growth of consumer wealth in a society (Harris, 1954). In countries like India where subsistence farming still predominates, the mass of people are little involved in a monetary economy; big-scale consumer industries are therefore largely missing.

Market influences can be thought of in three ways. First, many industries need to be close to the consumers of their products. People like to eat bread fresh from the bakery; thus, bread factories tend to locate in population centers. Much of the printing industry in the United States is also oriented to local markets. This is especially true for newspaper and job printing, the latter done in thousands of relatively small plants throughout the country (Figure 11-1).

Second, many industries prefer to be located in or near the largest single urbanized region of a country. From these prestige locations, as centers of fashion and arbiters of affairs, whether New York, Paris, or Tokyo, they supply the metropolitan market and also, by using the fine network of transportation facilities that converge on the metropolis, serve other regions. New York, the largest single concentration of manufacturing in the United States, has a great share of the apparel and publishing industries.

Third, industries that provide other industrial plants with components for manufacturing tend to locate near their market. This is the process of agglomeration already noted.

## LABOR

Sometimes industries locate in particular places to take advantage of known qualities in the local labor force. Many important textile districts began with factories established in poor farming areas where labor was cheap. Much of the United States textile industry moved in the early twentieth century from the high-priced labor of New England to the lower-priced labor of the Southeast. The garment industry established itself in New York in the nineteenth century because of both the market and cheap immigrant labor.

Industries choose places where the people have specific industrial traditions. The Lyon district of southeastern France once was the center of European silk weaving. When synthetic fibers came to the fore, it was feared that Lyon's textile industry would collapse. In fact, the district remains a leading textile center because the local expertise of entrepreneurs and operatives attracted the new fiber industries. In the United States the electronic-

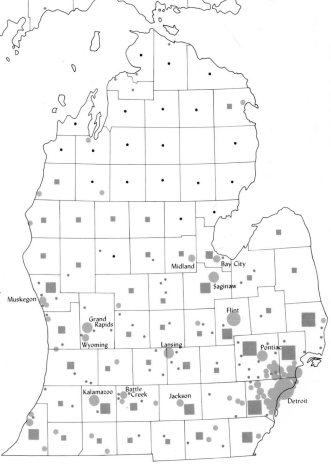

FIGURE **MICHIGAN: EMPLOYMENT IN THE PRINTING AND**
**11-1** **AUTOMOTIVE INDUSTRIES, 1960, BY COUNTIES**

These two maps show the contrast between a service industry located according to the distribution of population and a manufacturing industry located according to the forces of industrial agglomeration. The shades within the circles show the percentages of employees in the printing and automotive industries. The frequency diagrams indicate that most counties have a small proportion of their work force in printing, but that a few counties have high percentages in the automotive industry and many have very low percentages or none. Based on data in U.S. Bureau of the Census, *Census of Population, 1960.*

| Number Employed in Manufacturing | Places with 2,500 or More Inhabitants | Remainder of County |
|---|---|---|
| 250 - 1,000 | | |
| 1,000 - 5,000 | | |
| 5,000 - 10,000 | | |
| 10,000 - 25,000 | | |
| 25,000 - 50,000 | | |
| 229,000 | | |

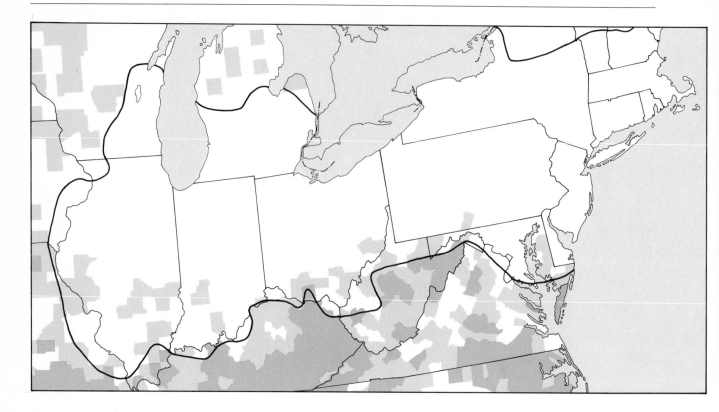

FIGURE **NORTHEASTERN UNITED STATES: FAMILY INCOME**
**11-2** BELOW $3,000, 1959

Many counties to the south of the main North American industrial region, especially in Kentucky and West Virginia, have income levels well below those of the manufacturing belt. Based on the map *Families with Incomes under $3,000 in 1959, by Counties of the United States,* prepared by the Geography Division, U.S. Bureau of the Census, Washington, D.C., 1960.

**Percent of Families with Incomes below**
**3,000 Dollars in 1959 by County**

Under 35 Percent

35-50 Percent

Over 50 Percent

———— Industrial Region Boundary

computer industry concentrates where it can recruit highly skilled personnel from universities. Its main focal points are in New York, New England, and California, with a subsidiary area in Minneapolis-St. Paul.

Government policies concerned with employment often affect industrial location. Regions depressed by technological change (coal-mining areas of Appalachia) or loss of market (shipbuilding in Britain) can present social and political problems unattractive to new industries. In such cases, the people unable to help themselves need government assistance for retraining workers, for tax allowances, low-interest loans, and other inducements to new enterprises. Such schemes sometimes are initiated to integrate low-income rural areas with the industrial economy. Most notable of these government-sponsored projects was the development of the Tennessee Valley in the 1930s. In recent years Appalachia has received

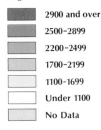

**Regional Income Per Capita, 1970, in U.S. Dollars**

- 2900 and over
- 2500–2899
- 2200–2499
- 1700–2199
- 1100–1699
- Under 1100
- No Data

**Regional Trends (EEC only) 1970–1975**

+ Rise Two Percent or More Per Year
− Fall Two Percent or More Per Year

(1000) Gross National Product Per Capita, 1974

——— National Boundary
—·—·— Regional Boundary

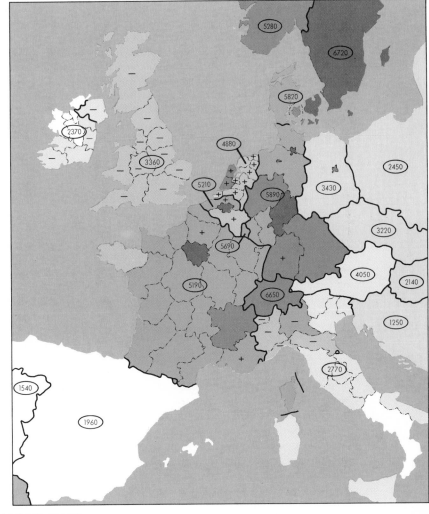

FIGURE
**11-3**  **WESTERN EUROPE: INCOME PER CAPITA**

The enlarged European Economic Community has created a Regional Development Fund to solve the problems created by economic imbalances within the Community. This map shows, for EEC members, national and regional per capita incomes. Regional data for Norway, Sweden, Switzerland, Spain, and Portugal are not shown. Missing from the map are Greece (national income per capita, $1,970), Finland ($3,580), and Iceland ($3,460). Based on information in *Statesman's Yearbook, 1976–1977*, London, 1976.

substantial government aid. In western Europe, too, governments have taken steps to spur the development of backward regions such as southern Italy, northern Norway, and western France (Figures 11-2 and 11-3). The case of South Wales, as an example of British "development areas," will be discussed later.

**POWER**

The use of large amounts of energy is, of course, the essential feature of modern manufacturing. As a determinant of location, however, power has declined in significance. In the early stages of industrialization, factories located mainly where power was available. At first many small waterwheels produced the needed mechanical energy. Early New England industries were housed in the old mill by the stream, and many still maintain these initial sites (with buildings and operations much expanded). A variant of the waterwheel was the windmill, used for pumping as well as milling. In the seventeenth and eighteenth centuries over a thousand windmills powered the industries of Amsterdam along the river Zaan, just north of the port.

When coal supplanted waterpower, the new "mills" located on or close to coalfields, unless they could receive coal cheaply by river, canal, or sea. As steam-powered railroad nets developed, coal could be sent over greater distances to other locations, thereby spreading the impact of manufacturing. In iron and steel making, coal in the form of coke was used to smelt the iron ore in blast furnaces. So much coke was needed that proximity to the source of metallurgical coal was commonly the decisive locational factor.

Steam engines no longer supply power directly to industry. But they still provide the principal means of converting fuels like coal, oil, natural gas, and even nuclear energy into electricity, now the chief power source for industry. Electricity is transported much more easily than mechanical steam power. However, it loses considerable voltage over long distances. With the growth of transmission networks and the construction of strategically placed power stations, most heavily populated regions of developed countries do have access to electricity in industrial quantities. If newly industrializing countries follow Western leads, they will give high priority to creating an electrical power network.

For most industries, energy is now only a small fraction of the production cost. They can, therefore, locate according to market, labor, raw materials, or other conditions. Nevertheless, certain industries need very large amounts of power to refine metals or produce chemicals. They tend to gather near sources of abundant energy, mainly the big hydroelectric power stations. In turn they attract clusters of fabricating plants. In this way many once remote uplands have received a share of modern industry, among them the Alpine and Scandinavian highlands in Europe and various mountain regions in the United States and Canada.

## RAW MATERIALS

Metallic ores and similar raw materials (salt, sulfur) are very bulky. Rather than transporting them over long distances the ores are concentrated, if at all feasible, near their source to rid them of the weight that would have to be removed anyway at the end of the haul. Thus, raw materials having a high weight-loss ratio tend to be processed where they are extracted.

The United States copper industry illustrates this principle. Many American copper ores contain only 1 percent copper. Initial concentration is done at the mines in Montana, Utah, Nevada, Arizona, and New Mexico. It removes 97 tons of waste material for every 100 tons of ore. The next stage, smelting, eliminates almost all the remaining impurities. Since relatively little weight is lost in the reduction of concentrate to blister copper, the copper smelters are not bound to the mineheads. Nevertheless, most of them are in the mining areas. The smelters in Tacoma, Washington, and in the New York City area rely upon imported concentrates. Blister copper, no longer an orelike raw material, has a relatively low weight-loss ratio. It needs large quantities of electrical power to refine it, a process which yields in addition to the pure copper also small amounts of valuable impurities such as gold, silver, and zinc. These refineries locate either where much electrical power is available or where the pure copper will be used. The refineries in New Jersey that handle domestic as well as imported blister copper show the influence of the market factor.

A similar case concerns the low-grade iron ore of the Lake Superior region. In northern Minnesota, iron ore with only about 30 percent iron content, known as taconite, is refined near the mines into high-grade iron-ore pellets with about 65 percent iron content. These can then be shipped economically via the Great Lakes system of waterways to the iron and steel centers in the heart of the American industrial belt.

## TRANSPORTATION

The problem of locating a factory resolves into the question how best to overcome distance separating markets, raw materials, power, labor, and

In the eighteenth century at the start of the Industrial Revolution, the new machines were driven by waterpower. This picture shows an old water mill in upland Yorkshire, a row of workers' cottages, and the owner's house. Later, a steam engine powered by coal led to the expansion of the factory. Stone walls enclose the open fields in this region. (Photograph—Aerofilms, Ltd.)

other elements of the production process. Means of transportation and communication are therefore the vital links of the modern economy, whether tankers, trains, trucking fleets, transmission and pipelines, or telephones. For this reason economists, geographers, and others have singled out transportation to develop a general theory of industrial location. It is useful in two ways: as a generalized explanation of the many forces that determine industrial location; and as a set of hypotheses that can be applied when investigating single places. A German economist in the early twentieth century, A. Weber, first refined such a theory (Weber, 1929). While he recognized the variation in labor cost and the attractive force of industrial agglomeration, he assumed that weight and distance determined transportation costs and that these costs were decisive in the selection of industrial locations.

Transportation prices include (1) terminal costs incurred on entering or leaving a particular system, (2) increasing costs with greater distance carried, and (3) decreasing rates per mile for longer hauls. Costs vary, of course, for different transportation systems. At present (and the di-

FIGURE DISTANCE AND COSTS FOR DIFFERENT TRANSPOR-
11-4 TATION

FIGURE TRANSPORTATION COSTS TO AND FROM A TRANS-
11-5 SHIPMENT POINT

Total costs for locations A, B, and C are the same; for
A and C, q + r; for B, q + q.

verse carriers change their relative costs over time) trucks have the lowest terminal costs and ships the highest. Rates per mile are cheapest for short hauls by trucks, for medium distances by train, and for long distances by ship or barge (Figure 11–4) (Alonso, 1964, 79–106).

In a simple problem of location involving only one kind of carrier we can see that the total transportation costs are at a minimum at either end of the haul; in other words, the optimum plant location in this respect is at the source of materials or at the market, but not at any point between them.

However, suppose that A to B is over water and B to C over land (Figure 11–5). Now B becomes a necessary transshipment point. Thus there are now no extra costs of locating the industrial plant at B. This simple fact helps to explain why so many industries are located at ports. A multitude of examples illustrate this condition. Grain is shipped by Great Lakes freighter from the West to Buffalo, where it is milled at lake side; the flour is distributed by rail. In northwestern Europe many large oil refineries lie at tidewater, where supertankers can unload petroleum from the Middle East and elsewhere; the refined products are distributed by coastal tanker, pipeline, rail tank car, and truck.

This generalizing approach also offers valuable insights when applied to weight-reducing industries (e.g., ore processing). Other industries yield goods that gain weight, having used ubiquitous materials like water and air in their production (e.g., the soft-drinks industry).

PERSONAL FACTORS

There remain personal elements in the locating and success of a new enterprise. Amenities of climate or culture, or family traditions may be decisive in the choice. The skill of a particular entrepreneur may build an industrial empire where others failed. The Ruhr region in western Germany, with many advantages for industrial development since the mid-nineteenth century—coal and other raw materials, a fine water-transportation system, and a large supply of experienced labor—also has benefited from the managerial élan of industrial wizards like Krupp and Thyssen who helped bring the Ruhr to its industrial dominance.

## LEGACY OF THE PAST

Many industrial plants are located where they are because of decisions made in the past under conditions that no longer have relevance. We have seen how many waterpower sites lost their hold on industry with the introduction of the steam engine, and how in turn electricity freed many industries to seek any convenient site. Yet a number of industries have remained at formerly favored sites. With the ubiquity of electricity and better transportation many industries are "footloose" in the sense that they are not tied to any specific locations. Old sites may therefore be just as good as others. This "historical momentum" or "geographical inertia," as it is variously called, gives the world's industrial regions a complexity that can be understood only by reference to the past.

## THE UNITED STATES IRON AND STEEL INDUSTRY

Modern society relies on steel as the basic material for industrial goods, consumer items, and construction. In the United States over 2 million workers are employed in iron and steel mills. Since the country is a leading industrial power, it has a large iron and steel industry, with an annual capacity of about 150 million tons. But the total capacity is rarely used, and annual production is usually in excess of 100 million tons. Total output has risen more slowly than world production so that the American share has declined from over one-half in the 1940s to less than a quarter in the 1970s. In contrast, Japan, the Soviet Union, and Western Europe all increased their share.

The main production centers lie in three clusters: (1) along the rivers that run through or connect with the Pennsylvania and West Virginia parts of the Appalachian coalfield; (2) on the southern shores of the Great Lakes; and (3) on the Middle Atlantic Seaboard. Important centers in each of these groups are Pittsburgh and Youngstown; Chicago-Gary, Detroit, Cleveland, and Buffalo; and Baltimore and Philadelphia (Figure 11–6).

### STEEL TECHNOLOGY

The purpose of the iron and steel industry is to remove impurities from iron ores and scrap iron and to produce steel, which is purified iron with a small proportion of carbon in it. These operations require heavy capital investment and huge quantities of raw materials including iron ore, coal, limestone, scrap iron, hot air, oxygen, and cold water. The plants and stockpiles need ample tracts of land, transportation facilities with big capacities for assembling materials, and a great deal of managerial and operative labor.

The technology is complex. Most steelworks produce pig (crude) iron in blast furnaces. These furnaces are very expensive to build and operate, but once lit, and with proper materials and management, they can turn out pig iron on a continuous basis. Many modern blast furnaces are 40 meters high and over 10 meters in diameter. Machines charge the furnaces, usually automatically, with iron ore, limestone, and metallurgical coke. The key feature of the process is that the enormous heat created in the furnace is recycled to produce a hot-air blast. The operation produces pig iron, which has a high carbon content. The physical and chemical reactions in the furnace have removed most of the impurities. New methods using cheap electrical power or raw materials of exceptionally high quality do not as yet rival the blast furnace in the mass production of pig iron.

Pig iron needs further refining. This is done by four different methods: (1) in open-hearth furnaces—first developed by Siemens in England in the mid-nineteenth century—in which hot air and gases treat the impurities and slowly remove them (three-fourths of American steel is produced this way); (2) in LD converters—called after the towns of Linz and Donawitz in Austria, where they were developed in the 1940s—which blow oxygen and lime through a lance into the molten pig iron (one-sixth of American steel); (3) in electric arc furnaces, which are particularly good at producing high-quality alloy steels (one-tenth); and (4) in Bessemer converters—first used in England in the 1850s—in which a hot-air blast burns the carbon out of the pig iron (1 percent).

Each of these processes has advantages and disadvantages for different types of iron ores. For example, many iron ores contain small percentages of phosphorus, which must be removed from the pig iron before steel of reasonable quality can

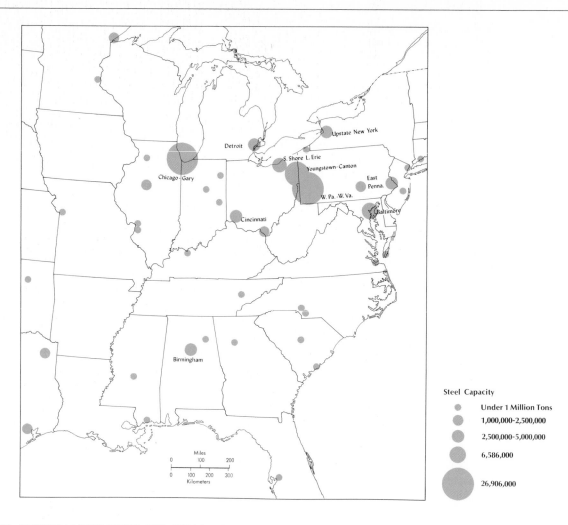

Steel Capacity

- Under 1 Million Tons
- 1,000,000–2,500,000
- 2,500,000–5,000,000
- 6,586,000
- 26,906,000

FIGURE **EASTERN UNITED STATES AND CANADA: STEEL PRO-**
**11-6** **DUCTION CAPACITY, 1970**

There are also large steel plants at Pueblo, Colorado; Geneva, Utah; and Fontana, California; and smaller plants at Seattle, Portland, San Francisco, and Los Angeles.

be made. The Gilchrist-Thomas process—developed in Wales in the 1860s—utilizes limestone linings in open-hearth Siemens furnaces; during the refining stage the phosphorus combines with the lime. In this way phosphoric ores like those of Lorraine became usable for steelmaking.

The largest areas of modern plants are not occupied by blast and steel furnaces, but by roll-ing mills, pipe mills, and similar installations that form raw steel into a series of primary shapes. Most of these were first designed in the United States. The continuous-strip mill, nearly one kilometer long, produces sheet steel for purposes from automobile bodies to cans. With the growth of consumer industries requiring such materials, many iron and steel centers throughout the industrialized world have set up strip mills.

The enormous expense of building these installations prevents quick shifts to new methods; also it tends toward maintaining plants that were constructed to use raw materials which since have been exhausted or replaced by better sources. Thus the iron and steel industry more than any other is likely to persist at outdated locations.

## SHIFTS IN LOCATION

In the early nineteenth century blast furnaces were set up in eastern Pennsylvania, near supplies of anthracite valuable for smelting. After the Civil War and the discovery of great seams of high-quality metallurgical coal in western Pennsylvania, a large industry developed around Pittsburgh. Toward the end of the century vast newly discovered bodies of iron ore were tapped, especially along the Mesabi Range of northern Minnesota. Boats transported the ore from Lake Superior to the south shore of Lake Erie, whence the railroads carried it to Pittsburgh. The open-hearth method provided the best method of refining the Mesabi ores with their relatively high-iron and low-phosphorus content.

By the first decade of the twentieth century Pittsburgh and nearby centers completely dominated the industry. Coal still determined the location, for it required more coal than ore to make a ton of steel. Materials could still be assembled at lowest cost in western Pennsylvania. Investments in plants already there militated against developing new projects in different places.

Gradually other locational influences made themselves felt. The Midwest became a huge market for steel. Improvements in technology somewhat reduced the amount of coal needed for refining. The Lake Superior mining district increased its lead in iron-ore output. These factors led to building new iron and steel plants at the southern end of Lake Michigan and along the south shore of Lake Erie. These two regions in time surpassed Pittsburgh in capacity and production.

By the 1930s and even more after World War II, locational advantages moved back toward the East Coast. Overseas iron-ore fields in Canada, Venezuela, and elsewhere began delivering high-quality ores at cheap prices to eastern tidewater ports. This led to the building of a virtually new plant near Baltimore and of a massive integrated iron and steel plant on the Delaware River upstream from Philadelphia. Coal comes to these locations by rail and water from West Virginia via Norfolk.

In California shipbuilding created a new market during World War II. After the war, consumer industries developed, giving rise to the use of scrap and imported ores, mostly refined by a direct process. In Texas the steel industry is expanding also to serve the local market. It uses local ores and hydrocarbon fuels provided by the gas and oil industries.

It is clear from this overview that the location of the United States iron and steel industry reflects a historical process. The fact that the industry has been established at different locations at different times shows the impact of changing technology, markets, sources of fuels, and raw materials. Other industrial countries which have experienced analogous changes show a similar diversity of location.

# MAIN INDUSTRIAL REGIONS

Industrial plants, although each may manufacture a different product, tend to cluster. Thus, even within the most industrialized countries some regions stand out in their industrial aggregation compared to others, where the economy, though quite mechanized, does not primarily depend on manufacturing. The following section outlines the major industrial regions.

## NORTH AMERICA'S CHIEF MANUFACTURING BELT

Over two-thirds of all persons employed in manufacturing in the United States, and about the same proportion in Canada, live in the industrial heart of Anglo-America (Figure 11–7).

Foremost among the subregions within this vast area is the New York metropolitan region with over 50,000 large and small industrial plants. New York offers the greatest single market for all kinds of consumer goods, from telephones and bread to women's clothing and office equipment. Its large pool of skilled and unskilled workers results chiefly from its historic position as the principal port of entry. On its excellent harbor converge networks of rail, highway, water, and air transportation. New York is headquarters of the managerial class and the organization man; it is the center of international finance and business.

Three great industrial wings spread from

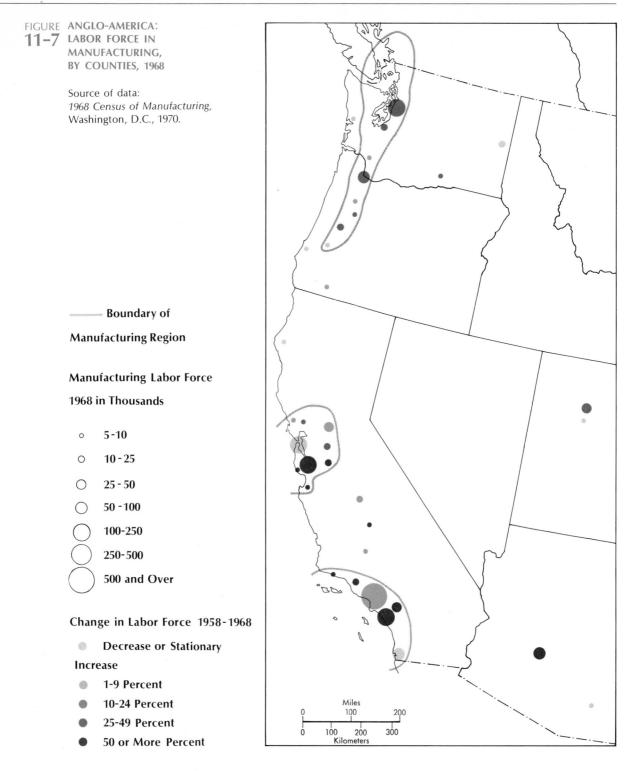

FIGURE
11-7 ANGLO-AMERICA:
LABOR FORCE IN
MANUFACTURING,
BY COUNTIES, 1968

Source of data:
*1968 Census of Manufacturing,*
Washington, D.C., 1970.

—— Boundary of

**Manufacturing Region**

**Manufacturing Labor Force**

**1968 in Thousands**

- 5-10
- 10-25
- 25-50
- 50-100
- 100-250
- 250-500
- 500 and Over

**Change in Labor Force 1958-1968**

**Decrease or Stationary**

**Increase**

- 1-9 Percent
- 10-24 Percent
- 25-49 Percent
- 50 or More Percent

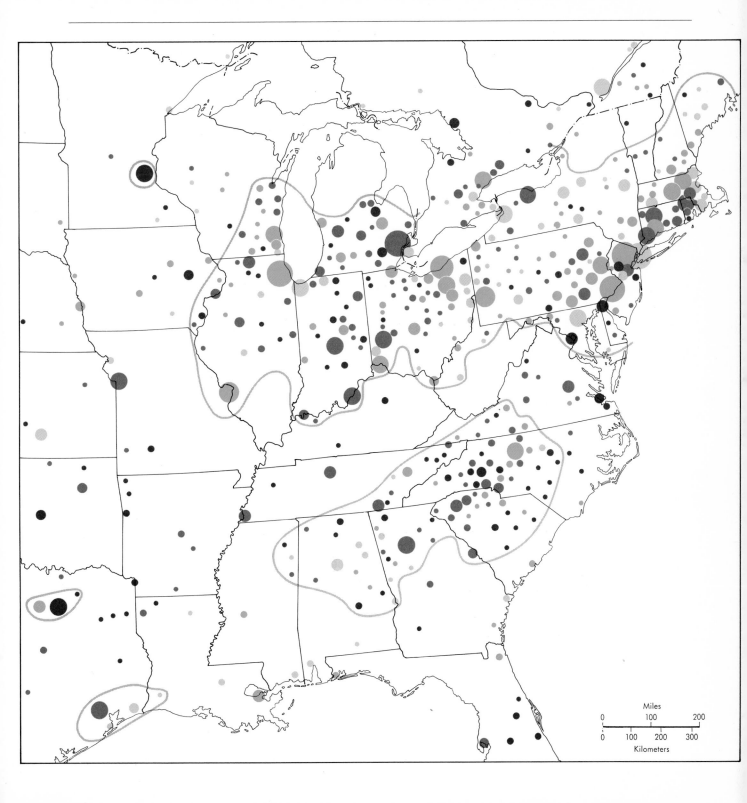

Miles
0   100   200
0   100   200   300
Kilometers

FIGURE
**11–8**
**SOUTHERN NEW ENGLAND: INDUSTRIAL
ESTABLISHMENTS, 1968**

This map shows the number of manufacturing establishments with more than 20 employees in all towns
with more than 450 total manufacturing employees in
Connecticut, Massachusetts, and Rhode Island. In 1968
there were 7,702 such establishments in the three
states, and a further 11,793 with 20 or less employees
each. Source of data: *1968 U.S. Census of Manufacturing,* Washington, D.C., 1970.

Number of Manufacturing Establishments
with Over Twenty Employees in Towns
Over 2,500 Persons

Less than 10
10-24
25-49
50-99
100-250
650

New York, their economic life intimately bound
with the city. New England is the country's oldest
manufacturing district (Figure 11–8). In early days
machines were brought over from England and set
up in factories at many small waterpower sites.
These sites lost their locational advantage to the
coast when steam power based on shipped-in
coal came into general use.

The Middle Atlantic states include the industrial complexes of Philadelphia and Baltimore.
Like New York, this Middle Atlantic agglomeration of industrial cities controls a large market and
has a series of fine ports that connect with other
parts of the country by road and rail.

In central New York State numerous industrial cities developed along the Erie Canal—dug in 1825 through the only low level connection between the East Coast and the interior. In 1857 the first railroad was built along this same route between Albany on the Hudson River and Buffalo on Lake Erie. The Buffalo area between the Great Lakes shipping lanes and the canal and railway to the Atlantic coast gave rise to industries associated with transportation and those depending on the massive power produced by the Niagara Falls.

The Middle West includes large industrial cities like Pittsburgh, Cleveland, Detroit, Chicago, and a host of smaller manufacturing towns. The origin of this present core of the industrial belt goes back to the second half of the nineteenth century when the Great Lakes, the Ohio and Mississippi rivers, and the spreading rails were links between the Atlantic Seaboard and the developing interior. As the national rail system became centered on the Middle West, its increasing efficiency helped strengthen the region's industrial agglomerations during the twentieth century. At the same time, mass production and mass consumption of industrial goods became part of the American economy.

The Ontario Peninsula contains a large proportion of Canada's industries. Its industrial cities extend from Toronto westward. This Canadian manufacturing region, smaller in scale though similar to the industrial Midwest, developed for the same reasons.

In recent decades many of the manufacturing belt's older industries—such as metal production—have stagnated or even declined. Conversely, new consumer-oriented enterprises tend to locate at or beyond the margins of the nineteenth-century belt as, for example, in central New York State, southwestern Ohio, and Wisconsin (Figure 11-7).

## OTHER INDUSTRIAL
## DISTRICTS OF ANGLO-AMERICA

Although the main manufacturing belt remains the heartland of American industry, a number of other regions have industrialized since the 1940s, some of them extremely fast. The industrialization in the southeastern states started with the processing of cotton, timber, and tobacco, but its main incentive to growth was not the availability of raw materials but rather the existence of a large pool of labor willing to work for relatively low wage rates. In Texas, industrial cities grew rapidly in the 1960s. Petrochemical plants relate to nearby oil and gas fields, while the federal aerospace industry (including the NASA center at Houston) owes much to the influence that a succession of powerful Texas politicians have had in Washington. On the West Coast industrial regions have grown up in and around Los Angeles and San Francisco. Both have been fueled by the explosive growth of California's population. A much smaller industrial region lies along Puget Sound and in northwestern Oregon.

Lastly, some important industrial cities have isolated locations: Montreal on the St. Lawrence is the largest manufacturing center of Canada and is its main port; Minneapolis–St. Paul (the Twin Cities) have diversified industries as befits a metropolitan center with such a large tributary area; Kansas City and Denver perform a similar function for their hinterlands.

## WESTERN AND CENTRAL EUROPE

The content and intensity of Europe's industrial regions differ from those of North America. An imaginary line connecting Londonderry in Northern Ireland with Bergen (Norway), Stockholm, Warsaw, Budapest, Rome, Barcelona, Bilbao (Spain), and back to Londonderry takes in the broad industrial region of western and central Europe. Within this we can identify a number of industrial concentrations (Figure 11-9).

Most manufacturing cities in Great Britain lie in the center and south (Figure 11-10). London, with one-quarter of Britain's population, is the largest single market and industrial agglomeration of Europe. Other industrial regions like the Midlands, southeast Lancashire, and central Scotland, were the first homes of the Industrial Revolution.

In continental western Europe the most concentrated and diversified industrial area on earth spreads from northern France across Belgium and the southern Netherlands into West Germany (Figure 11-11). The highest density falls within the circle from Amsterdam to Boulogne (France), Cambrai, Köln (Cologne), Hamm (Ruhr), and back to Amsterdam. On its south and east side lie the heavy industries related to the coalfields, above all the Ruhr district. On its west side are the port cities of Antwerp, Rotterdam,

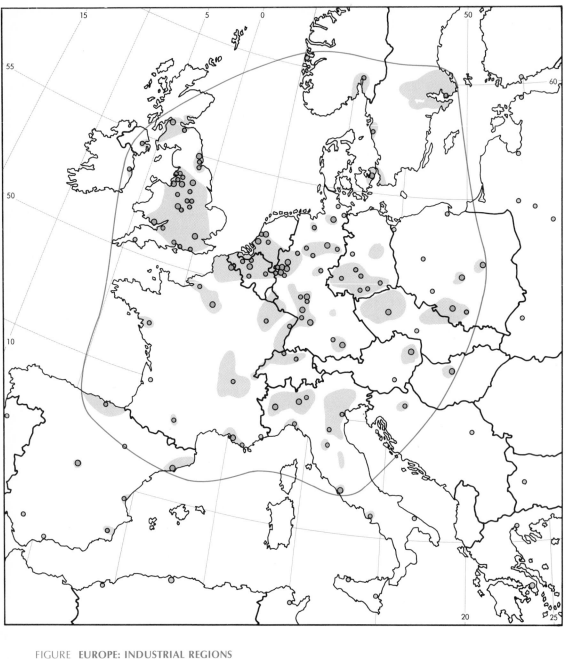

FIGURE  **EUROPE: INDUSTRIAL REGIONS**
**11-9**

Miles
0        250              500

0        400              800
Kilometers

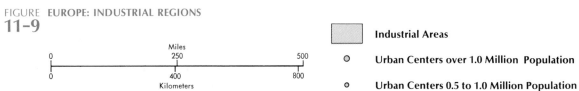

▦  **Industrial Areas**

◉  **Urban Centers over 1.0 Million Population**

∘  **Urban Centers 0.5 to 1.0 Million Population**

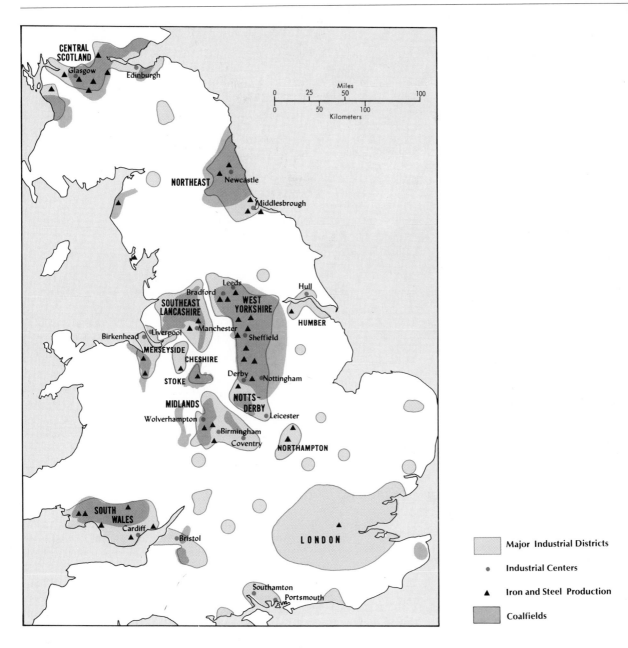

**Major Industrial Districts**

● **Industrial Centers**

▲ **Iron and Steel Production**

**Coalfields**

FIGURE **GREAT BRITAIN: INDUSTRIAL DISTRICTS**
**11–10**

and Amsterdam, connected with their hinterland by the Rhine and canals, and by railroads and superhighways. Between coast and coal mines lie many other industrial centers such as Lille, Brussels, and Eindhoven.

Other important industrial districts are close by: Paris metropolitan region, nerve center and biggest single industrial market of France; heavy concentrations from Lorraine-Luxembourg to the Saar district of West Germany; and the upper

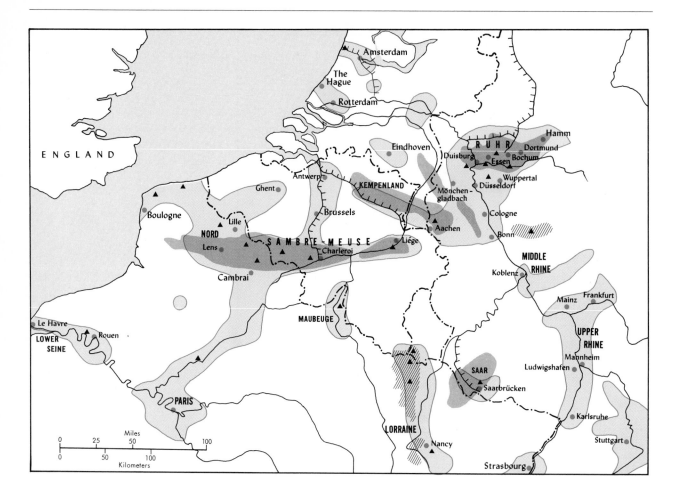

Major Industrial Districts

Industrial Centers

Ironfields

Coalfields

▲ Iron and Steel Production

Rhine Basin with its many large cities, including Frankfurt am Main and Stuttgart.

These industrial regions of northwestern Europe possess distinct advantages. They have capital for industrial expansion, substantial resources of coal, iron ore, chemicals, and newly discovered natural gas and oil—also a superb location for river and sea communications. Moreover, the population has a tradition of technical skill and economic organization that has built up vast markets at home and overseas.

Outside this core are smaller industrial concentrations, many of them, like central Sweden, Switzerland, and northern Italy, highly significant in relation to the individual countries. In central Europe industrial cities extend from the borders of East and West Germany to Bohemia in Czechoslovakia, and include Berlin, Leipzig, and Prague. Silesia is Poland's equivalent of the Ruhr. Lastly, many of Europe's industrial cities lie outside the districts described above, including Barcelona and Lyon as well as most capitals of Scandinavian and eastern European countries.

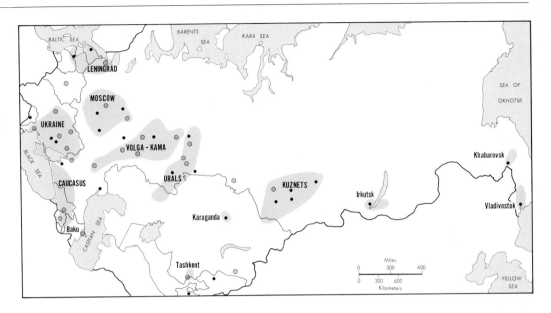

FIGURE **SOVIET UNION: INDUSTRIAL DISTRICTS**
**11-12**

## THE SOVIET UNION

Industrial regions in the Soviet Union are easier to define than those in western Europe. The reason is that the industrial expansion, which began on a large scale in the 1920s, produced mainly basic materials like metals rather than consumer goods (Figure 11-12). This means that raw materials, more than the market, determine where industries locate. The principal exception to this is the Moscow region, which has one-fourth of the Soviet Union's industrial output. Moscow's central location and the presence of the government have favored the growth of a wide variety of industries. Leningrad, too, lies far from raw materials, but access to the sea and a skilled work force have made it a center of shipbuilding and precision engineering.

The Soviet Union's main center of heavy industry is in the Ukraine, based on a large population, massive resources of coal, iron and manga-nese ores, waterpower, and an industrial buildup that began late in the nineteenth century.

The Ural Mountains, containing a variety of metal ores equal to any on earth, early attracted smelting and fabrication works. The great expansion came during World War II, when the Axis forces occupied the Ukraine and threatened Moscow and Leningrad. New resources such as the Volga-Urals oil field and even the distant Karaganda coal basin added fresh impetus to the industrial growth of the southern Urals.

The existence of an industrial region in the Kuznetsk Basin of Siberia, 2,200 kilometers east of the Urals, illustrates the impact of Soviet planning on the location of industry. The area has enormous resources, especially in coal, iron ore, and potential hydroelectric power. The Kuznetsk Basin (Kuzbas) was planned in the 1930s as the power-house for Central Asia and received further stimulus for rapid expansion from migrations eastward from European parts of the Soviet Union during and after World War II.

## EAST AND SOUTH ASIA

After a beginning in the late nineteenth century, Japan industrialized rapidly in the 1950s and 1960s, and by 1970 was the third largest industrial power,

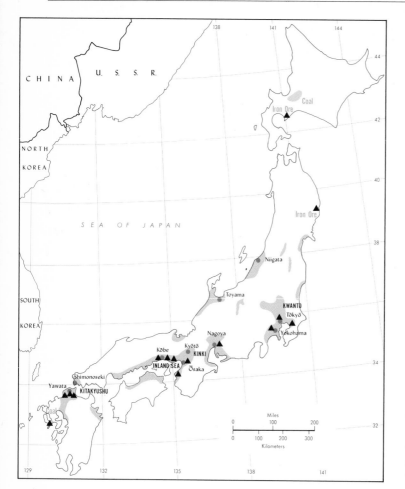

Kyushu and Shikoku. Tokyo, together with Yoko-hama, has a great variety of establishments; Osaka and Kobe put more emphasis on heavy industries. Nagoya is a textile center. The coalfields of northern Kyushu have most of the iron and steel production (Figure 11-13).

Someday China may develop an enormous industrial capacity commensurate with its vast population. Plans once envisaged widespread development of basic industries, particularly metals, but this appears to have given way to large-scale industrial plants gathered around a few cities such as Peking, Shanghai, Tientsin, Chungking, Chengtu, Wuhan, and Sian.

As yet Manchuria contains China's one full-fledged industrial region. The initial development of Manchuria, which was an almost empty frontier land early in this century, began with Western capital and direction. Industrialization developed rapidly, the impetus given by the Japanese, who occupied Manchuria between the two world wars. Now that Manchuria is incorporated into the People's Republic of China, it supplies iron, steel, chemicals, and other basic industrial products for the growing needs of the country as a whole.

Important factors in developing this region were the existence of large reserves of coal and iron ore, and the availability of land- and water-transportation systems. Nearby were millions of unemployed or partly employed peasant laborers in the farms, villages, and towns of the North China Plain. The story of the peopling of Manchuria is that of the largest human migration of this century. Million after million of migrant laborers traveled northeast by train, road, and ship to work in mine, in factory, or on farm, especially in and around the great industrial agglomerations.

In India, abundant coal, iron, manganese, and waterpower of the extensive Chota Nagpur plateau, west of the Ganges Delta, support several large iron- and steelworks. Also in this modest-scale "Ruhr" region are plants for metal fabrication, cement, and fertilizer. Important industrial cities outside this area are Calcutta in eastern India, Bombay in the north, and Madras and Bangalore in the south.

## OTHER INDUSTRIAL CENTERS

In some modern countries with but relatively

FIGURE **JAPAN: INDUSTRIAL DISTRICTS**
**11-13**

The main industrial areas are the Kwanto Plain, the Kinki Plain, the shores of the Inland Sea, and Kitakyushu.

behind the United States and the Soviet Union. To pay for huge quantities of imported raw materials, she developed a massive exporting industry, aimed particularly at markets in the United States.

The manufacturing districts of Japan form a belt from Tokyo southwestward on the main island of Honshu and on the two smaller islands of

An iron and steel plant near Dortmund, in the Ruhr industrial region of West Germany. Modern power-based industries often pollute water and air, damage agricultural land, destroy scenery, and create other serious problems. The spread of the urban industrial network with its transportation facilities consumes space at a high rate. (Photograph—United Nations)

small populations, industrial regions are evident, as in Australia and South Africa. Some of the Latin American countries—especially Brazil, Argentina, and Mexico—have begun to industrialize, mainly within or near their metropolitan centers, such as São Paulo, Buenos Aires, and Mexico City.

## AN INDUSTRIAL REGION: SOUTH WALES

Several early developed coalfields, once among the foremost producers of fuel, iron, and steel, fell into hard times when they failed to adjust to new conditions. The Sambre-Meuse region of Belgium, the industrial area of western Pennsylvania and eastern Ohio, and South Wales belong to this group. South Wales is a good example of attempted reconstruction after a period of severe depression.

Short valleys run southward through the southern edge of the Welsh uplands and cut through the oval-shaped coalfield. Its varied layers of rock, including the coal strata, lie like a pile of

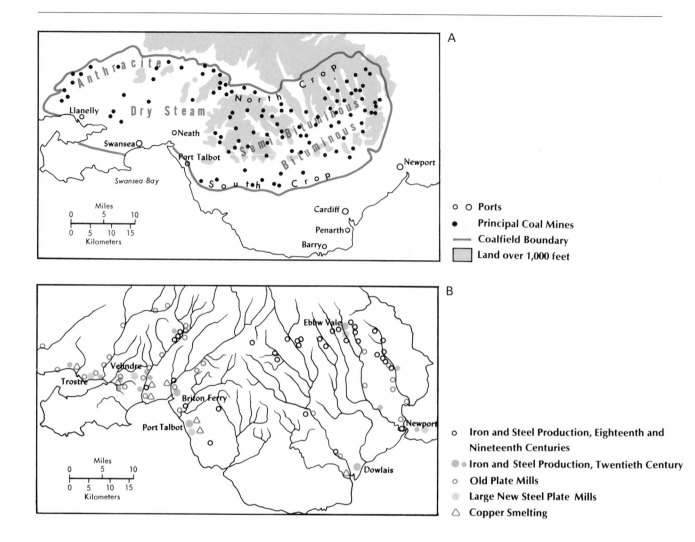

A

Miles
0 5 10
0 5 10 15
Kilometers

o o Ports
● Principal Coal Mines
— Coalfield Boundary
Land over 1,000 feet

B

Miles
0 5 10
0 5 10 15
Kilometers

o Iron and Steel Production, Eighteenth and
Nineteenth Centuries
● Iron and Steel Production, Twentieth Century
o Old Plate Mills
Large New Steel Plate Mills
△ Copper Smelting

broken plates (Figure 11-14A). The field is famous for its high-quality coals. In the southeast medium-quality coal is mined for gas making and for steam raising at electrical power plants. The center of the field contains higher-carbon coal that was used in the past to power most of the world's steamships; now it is mainly used in metal making. The almost pure carbon anthracite of the northwest serves for cement making and central heating. In the "north crop," where the valleys run through gently sloping coal seams, mining has been relatively easy; along the "south crop" mining poses a greater problem because the seams run into the ground at a steep angle.

## THE RISE OF INDUSTRY

Mining started around Swansea Bay before the Industrial Revolution, with the coal shipped across the sea to Bristol and other places. During the eighteenth century metal industries, especially ironworking, gathered in valleys and along the coast. Canals were dug to provide cheap transportation from pit to port. In the nineteenth century railways joined the mines to newly built harbor docks. Markets for Welsh coal expanded with increasing metal production, factories run by steam, railway and steamship traffic, and domestic use. By the 1880s production had expanded to 25 million tons annually. The landscape had changed

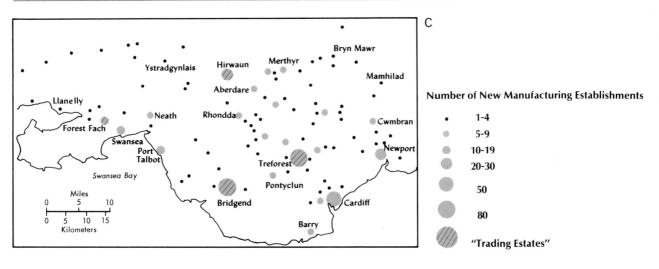

C

**Number of New Manufacturing Establishments**

- 1-4
- 5-9
- 10-19
- 20-30
- 50
- 80
- "Trading Estates"

FIGURE **SOUTH WALES**

**11-14**

Based on a number of sources, especially Davies, M., *Wales in Maps*, Cardiff, 1959.

A. The Coalfield. Most of the coal has been mined in the narrow valleys in the eastern half of the field.

B. Metal industries. Metal manufacturing has migrated from the coal valleys toward the coast. The Dowlais plant near Cardiff is named after an old blast furnace in a valley near Merthyr.

C. Industrial Reconstruction, 1934-1959. The largest groupings of new factories are on the coastal plain.

to an intensely industrial scene, with pitheads, railways, slag heaps, and tiers of dark row houses built of stone.

The mines and factories were manned by a rapidly increasing population. Migrants came from other parts of Wales, from nearby English counties, and even from overseas. In spite of unhealthful living conditions this population had a very high natural increase and lived in relative affluence much of the time. The immigrants changed the population from a Welsh-speaking community with local origins to an English-speaking group who, nevertheless, became closely identified with Welsh nationality. The greatest growth in population came in the last half of the nineteenth century; for example, between 1851 and 1921 Rhondda's population rose from 2,000 to 163,000, and that of Cardiff from 18,000 to 200,000.

**REGRESSION**

During World War I, Wales lost its export markets for coal. Other disasters followed: ships changed their power from Welsh coal to oil; free trade broke down in the 1920s; the general world depression of the 1930s aggravated conditions. In 1913 coal production was 57 million tons, two-thirds of which was exported. Since then it has declined until it now appears to have stabilized at 10 million to 15 million tons each year. The number of miners has dropped from 270,000 in 1913 to fewer than 50,000 in recent years. The basic-metals industry of the region was hit severely. Life in the coalfield communities became hard. Mineowners, unable to rationalize production methods or plan long-term investments, faced frequent strikes, or they used lockouts. Miners by the tens of thousands moved to coastal ports, sought work in other industrial regions, or migrated overseas. Many who remained were unemployed.

**INDUSTRIAL RECONSTRUCTION**

The national government took the lead, as early as 1934, to halt the decline. It encouraged new industries and the refurbishing of old ones. For instance, the government assisted in rebuilding the old metalworks at Ebbw Vale into a large integrated iron and steel plant. A number of "trading estates" (industrial parks with many small to medium-sized factories) were set up and attracted scores of industrial operations making a wide variety of products. At the same time steps were taken to increase wages, rehabilitate housing, and improve social services. After World War II the coal industry was nationalized and its production and plans were vested in the National Coal Board. Uneconomic pits along the north crop of the field were closed, and new deep shafts were sunk along the south crop. Thus, the focus of coal production shifted to an arc stretching eastward from Neath. This new industrial variety has helped to reduce unemployment to well below 5 percent of the work force. Between 1945 and 1970 over 100,000 new jobs were created. Out-migration is now a mere trickle (Figure 11-14C).

### PRESENT INDUSTRIAL PATTERN

Metals, the foremost industry of South Wales, run the full range from iron and steel production to aluminum and copper refining (Figure 11-14B). In the west the port city of Swansea lies near high-quality coal; the town and its environs provide a reservoir of skillful workers. The port has oil, chemical engineering, and metallurgical works and lies between the steel-rolling plants and the plating factories. Coated with tin to make tin-plate, steel sheeting serves to make cans, car radiators, oil barrels, and other containers for materials that need protection from corrosion. The tin-plating industry has been modernized: a few large plants now do the work formerly carried on in scores of small mills. The steelworks at Port Talbot, much expanded since 1945 and now one of the largest in Europe, provide sheet steel.

Other metal industries include refining nickel, titanium, copper, and duralumin.

To the east the coastal cities of Cardiff and Newport dominate with their iron and steel production and numerous metal-fabrication plants. Many people still live in those coal valleys where modern offspring remain of the once important iron industry, as at Ebbw Vale. The Cardiff urban area grew from a small market town in 1800 to become the national capital of Wales. Its rise paralleled the growth of coal mining and manufacturing; it has become an important industrial center.

Economic renewal and social improvement have changed the way of life in South Wales. The job now is farther from home than formerly. Instead of a walk down the valley side to the pithead, many now take a bus or go by car or cycle to a plant some miles away. Most new industries have located not in the coal valleys but where the valleys enter the coastal plain.

The occupations now represent the diversity to be expected for a balanced industrial region. Coal miners number less than 50,000, while the people employed in metal industries, some 100,000, make up less than one-fourth of the labor force. Another one-fourth engage in light manufacturing; the remaining one-half serve in occupations from retailing to the professions.

Other old Industrial Revolution centers in Europe have experienced similar government-stimulated revivals. In these also, the general welfare of the people has much improved as economic horizons have lifted. Levels of living remain, however, below national averages. Other regions, especially great metropolitan centers of affairs like Paris, London, Rotterdam, and the Rhine-Ruhr cities of West Germany, forge further ahead with their manifold present-day advantages.

## CITATIONS AND FURTHER READINGS

Allen, G. C. *Japan's Economic Expansion*, London and Fairlawn, N.J., 1965.

Alonso, W. "Location Theory," in Friedman, J., and Alonso, W. (eds.), *Regional Development and Planning*, Cambridge, Mass., 1964.

Berman, M. "The Location of the Diamond-Cutting Industry," *Annals of the Association of American Geographers*, 61 (1971): 316-328.

Chapman, K. "Agglomeration and Linkage in the United Kingdom Petro-Chemical Industry," *Transactions of the Institute of British Geographers*, 60 (1973), November, 33-68.

———— "Corporate Systems in the United Kingdom Petrochemical Industry," *Annals of the Association of American Geographers*, 64 (1974): 126-137.

Darkoh, M. B. K. "The Distribution of Manufacturing in Ghana. A Case Study of Industrial Location in a Developing Country," *Scottish Geographical Magazine*, 87 (1971): 38-57.

De Geer, S. "The American Manufacturing Belt," *Geografiska Annaler*, 9 (1927): 233-359.

Estall, R. C., and Buchanan, R. O. *Industrial Activity and Economic Geography: A Study of the Forces behind the Geographical Location of Productive Activity in Manufacturing Industry*, New York, 1961.

Fleming, D. K. "Coastal Steelworks in the Common Market Countries," *Geographical Review*, 57 (1967): 48-72.

Foust, J. B. "Ubiquitous Manufacturing," *Annals of the Association of American Geographers*, 65 (1975): 13-17.

Fuchs, V. R. *Changes in the Location of Manufacturing in the United States since 1929*, New Haven, Conn., 1962.

Gibson, L. J. "An Analysis of the Location of Instrument Manufacturing in the United States," *Annals of the Association of American Geographers*, 60 (1970): 352-367.

Grotewold, A. "The Growth of Industrial Core Areas and Patterns of World Trade," *Annals of the Association of American Geographers*, 61 (1971): 361-370.

Harris, C. D. "The Market as a Factor in the Localization of Industry in the United States," *Annals of the Association of American Geographers*, 44 (1954): 315-348.

Hartshorne, R. "Location Factors in the Iron and Steel Industry," *Economic Geography*, 4 (1928): 241-252.

Humphrys, G. *Industrial Britain: South Wales*, Newton Abbot, Devon, 1972.

Khrushchev, A. T. "The Formation of the Industrial Complex of the Kursk Magnetic Anomaly," *Soviet Geography: Review and Translation*, 16 (1975): 239-249.

Lewis, E. D. *The Rhondda Valleys: A Study in Industrial Development, 1800 to the Present Day*, London, 1959.

Li Choh-ming (ed.). *Industrial Development in Communist China*, New York, 1964.

Logan, M. I. "Locational Behavior of Manufacturing Firms in Urban Areas," *Annals of the Association of American Geographers*, 56 (1966): 451-466.

Lonsdale, R. E., and Thompson, J. H. "A Map of the U.S.S.R.'s Manufacturing," *Economic Geography*, 36 (1960): 36-52.

McCarty, H. H. *The Geographical Basis of American Economic Life*, New York, 1940 (reissued in 1971).

Pounds, N. J. G. "Historical Geography of the Iron and Steel Industry of France," *Annals of the Association of American Geographers*, 47 (1957): 3-14.

———— "The Spread of Mining in the Coal Basin of Upper Silesia and Northern Moravia," *Annals of the Association of American Geographers*, 48 (1958): 149-163.

Pred, A. "Manufacturing in the American Mercantile City: 1800-1840," *Annals of the Association of American Geographers*, 56 (1966): 307-338.

Privalovskaya, G. A. "The Physical Factor in the System of Conditions Determining the Location of Industrial Production in the U.S.S.R.," *Soviet Geography: Review and Translation,* 16 (1975): 279–290.

Rodgers, A. "The Locational Dynamics of Soviet Industry," *Annals of the Association of American Geographers,* 64 (1974): 226–240.

Smith, D. M. *Industrial Location. An Economic Geographical Analysis,* New York, 1971.

Ullman, E. L. "The Role of Transportation and the Bases of Interaction," in Thomas, W. L. (ed.), *Man's Role in Changing the Face of the Earth,* Chicago, 1956, 862–88a.

—— "Regional Development and the Geography of Concentration," *Papers and Proceedings of the Regional Science Association,* 4 (1958): 179–198.

[Weber, A.] Friedrich, C. J. (ed.). *Alfred Weber's Theory of the Location of Industry,* Chicago, 1929.

Zimmermann, E. W. *World Resources and Industries,* 2d ed., New York, 1951.

# 12 THE RICH AND THE POOR

At several points we have discussed instances of technical breakthrough, such as harnessing plant and animal energy, which brought about the agricultural revolution, and using mineral fuel, which heralded the Industrial Revolution. Some societies quickly adopted new energy sources, others were slow to accept, or even remained ignorant of them. As a result there always have been haves and have-nots.

There are, nevertheless, important differences between the present and olden times. Western society during the past two centuries, and especially the last generation, has integrated the world economy, binding together the fortunes of rich and poor nations, for better or for worse. It is said that as the West developed, it "underdeveloped" the third world through economic exploitation* (Blaut, 1975). Even if that is too narrow a view, it has some truth in it. Dozens of states, formerly colonial territories but now politically free, remain economically dependent on the modern West.

Peoples have become more aware of their own condition compared to that of others, and strive consciously to improve their well-being. This has changed the facts of inequality and dependence into the problems of development. This chapter surveys the areal differentiation in level of living, relates these to other spatial variables, and reviews the ways and means of economic progress.

*Teilhard de Chardin used the term *third world* to distinguish those lands and peoples not part of the liberal democratic West (United States, Canada, Western Europe, etc.: the "first world") or part of the socialist West (Eastern Europe, the Soviet Union, etc.: the "second world").

## DEVELOPED AND UNDERDEVELOPED COUNTRIES

### THE ROLE OF ENERGY

Energy is the capability to do work. The geographer James Fairgrieve observed that "in its widest sense on its material side history is the story of Man's increasing control over energy." The story, as unfolded since the beginning of agriculture, divides into two main periods: before and after the Industrial Revolution.

For centuries people everywhere relied on muscle strength, their own and that of domestic animals. To some extent controlled fire released energy from wood. Wind and water propelled sailing ships and powered mills. All these forms of energy, from plants that sustain life to air and water, depend ultimately on current receipts of solar heat and light.

The second part of the story opens with the advances in science and technology in Europe that made possible massive uses of new power sources: coal, petroleum, and natural gas. These are stored-up supplies of solar energy that in one way or another had escaped the normal cycle of life and decay. They gave a tremendous boost to human ability to produce, transport, and communicate. These fossil fuels, virtually nonrenewable, eventually will be exhausted.

The central concern of ordinary people in preindustrial societies was to grow enough food and fodder to furnish energy for man and beast so that they could work to replace what had been consumed. Thus a virtually closed, self-perpetuating food-cycle economy operated at a low level of input and output. Physical drudgery was rewarded with inevitable scarcity. Admittedly this exaggerates the picture. Civilizations could not have risen without some surplus beyond hand-to-mouth existence. But as long as animate energy provided the chief source of power, surplus remained necessarily small, gained by squeezing the population masses, whether humbler citizens, slaves, or colonies.

In contrast, modern inanimate sources of energy produce a surplus more easily and much larger in relation to the input of human work. People direct and manage the forces rather than furnish the energy themselves. Increasingly complex and versatile resource-converting techniques transform inorganic and organic substances into goods to satisfy human wants. Space-adjusting techniques, from telephone to elevator, shorten effective distance and permit intensified use of space (Ackerman, 1958). Information storage and retrieval complement the human brain.

The development of such an economy in the nineteenth and twentieth centuries vastly enhanced the productivity per worker in those regions where it became the way of life. It promised an abundance of food and other essentials and produced all kinds of commodities to support the good life for everyone. The idea that the modern mass consumption eventually could spread to all peoples everywhere was commonplace in the 1950s and 1960s. But the dream fades. Particularly in underdeveloped countries, but also among commercial-industrial societies, people recognize that there can be—and must be—values other than material consumerism. With massive increases of population, especially in the third world, production of adequate supplies of food and other essentials is uncertain, and must take precedence over the making and buying of the huge quantities of goods that give higher levels of comfort. Realization grows that the resources used for energy production and for other industries are finite and, as time passes, become scarce and cost more. Many believe that the material standards of living in modern mass-consumption societies are unlikely to rise much more and, what is more important, cannot be transferred as models to other peoples. In addition, there are limits to the capacity of the earth to absorb the shocking effects of industry on our environment. Increasingly modern societies spend their wealth counteracting the pollution caused by their industrial economy.

De Souza and Porter (1974, 3–4) redefine the goals of development to include adequate diet, medical care, work, education, and housing; control of disease and of production in the long-term interest of the habitat; and an egalitarian political and social milieu. They argue that if technological diffusion and integration of global economy fail to include these humane considerations the result instead of leading to development may only compound the problems of underdevelopment. Precisely because twentieth-century economic forces form a worldwide complex, modern countries to achieve the above objectives must reevaluate and reorder their attitudes toward the processes of development. Resource exhaustion and environmental difficulties may force the wealthier countries to make considerable changes in their policies and in their methods of production (Schumacher, 1973).

## THE MEANING OF "UNDERDEVELOPED"

The Western world of a generation ago referred to peoples with less advanced economies in simple blunt words: primitive, backward, colonial. New terms have replaced the old, terms ranging from undeveloped, underdeveloped, and less developed to emergent and developing. At least the switch in terminology indicates greater courtesy, at best more understanding, even though clumsily expressed. The people so designated may not share these judgments. American Indians and Appalachian mountain folk do not necessarily consider themselves underdeveloped. They live another kind of life because their values differ from the standards prevailing elsewhere in the United States. What is true for these groups applies with even greater force to peoples beyond the realm of Occidental culture. Though many of them profess desire for material progress, they may cherish some of their values above all, and settle for less money and more bliss. In the familiar words of Henry Thoreau: "If a man does not keep pace with his companions, perhaps it is because he hears a different drummer." Thus, although levels of material welfare may be good measures for developed countries, they must be used with caution when applied to the third world.

Another warning concerns the use of the words *emerging* and *developing*. If these euphemistic terms suggest that all poor nations are now catching up with the rich, nothing could be further from the truth. In many countries economic development proceeds at a snail's pace when compared to the continuing advance of others. Thus, the differences between the top and bottom of the scale become greater as time passes. Moreover, we cannot presume that all countries are on the same scale; some emulate economic development as structured in the West, others do not.

When speaking of developed and underdeveloped countries, one has in mind political entities formed by sovereign states and dependencies. These units indeed we will consider in the following pages. One can, of course, also make a close-up of each country to inspect regional differences in levels of living (Figure 12-1). Even the rich United States has its poverty pockets, the United Kingdom its depressed areas, France its *zones critiques*. In turn, states classified as underdeveloped may have their places of plenty. Brazil shows great internal contrasts between the relatively wealthy southern portion and the poverty-stricken or undeveloped and empty remainder.

## THE SYMPTOMS OF UNDERDEVELOPMENT

To classify all countries into categories according to their economic level requires worldwide statistical data. Unfortunately, essential facts are scarce for many underdeveloped countries, and even those reported for developed countries are open to different interpretations. The systems of accounting in most socialist countries make comparisons with other states difficult. Data available are usually those useful for measuring the economies of modern countries; they may be inadequate measures of third-world economies and tend to set up the modern states as ideals to be emulated. Each criterion of the following list can help us to judge levels of economic well-being. Although there are few data available for some of them, this is less serious than it might seem. Rather than being an independent variable, each factor represents one aspect of an interlocked economic structure. Thus the known values of some measures can provide clues to the others.

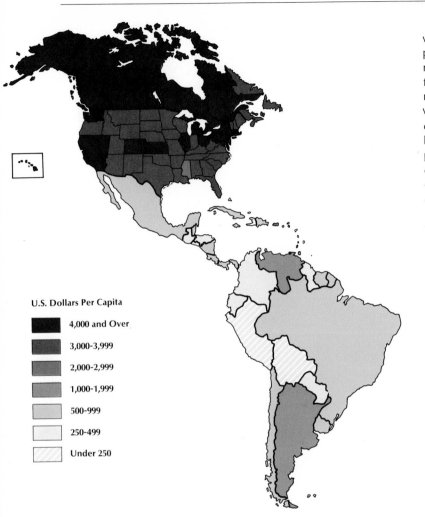

**U.S. Dollars Per Capita**

- 4,000 and Over
- 3,000-3,999
- 2,000-2,999
- 1,000-1,999
- 500-999
- 250-499
- Under 250

FIGURE
**12-1**

**THE AMERICAS: INCOME PER CAPITA, ABOUT 1975**

For Canada and the United States the data refer to personal income per capita and are given by provinces or states. For other countries the figures refer to national income per capita. Based on data in various yearbooks and statistical abstracts.

Measures of economic development and under-development are:

1. Income or national product per capita
2. Occupational structure of the population
3. Use of (commercial) power per capita
4. Degree of commercialization of agriculture
5. Amount of domestic savings (including taxes) to be used as investment capital
6. Amount of income spent on food
7. Productivity per worker

Economic structures affect social conditions, and vice versa. We could draw up a list of social criteria, from the availability of education, health care, and an adequate diet, to sanitation, mortality characteristics, and class structure. These factors would tend to vary with the economic data. If there is not enough surplus to pay for education, the people remain illiterate, and the prevailing ignorance bears upon the productivity of labor and many other aspects of life. Birth rates usually are high; death rates, formerly high, are declining, mainly owing to external aid. Most of the population is rural. The number of business and professional people, civil servants, and technicians is small. Where an indigenous people lack this middle class, foreigners often perform the services, thus giving rise to a dual or plural society, laying the basis for tensions between the different groups.

## THREE MAJOR CRITERIA

To judge the level of economic development, we will use the three yardsticks at the top of the list of measures.

1. Gross domestic product is essentially the aggregate production of all resident producers. It differs from the gross national product, which also includes net income received from abroad. These measures can be refined in various ways: for instance, by allowing for capital consumption and depreciation, yielding the net product. Instead of using production data, one can also consider the distributive shares as they show up in income. National income, then, represents by and large the sum of incomes accruing within a year to people normally resident in the country. A weak-

ness is that the total does not measure the distribution of income among a population.

The most commonly used criteria are the gross domestic product (GDP) and gross national product (GNP), because production statistics are more readily available than those on income. The product per capita is obtained by dividing the total product by the number of inhabitants. For the purpose of worldwide comparison, these values are expressed in the currency of a single country, usually United States dollars. This raises further questions, not only of the correct conversion rate, but also of adjustments to account for different purchasing power of the monetary unit. One should, therefore, treat with caution the figures on national income, national product, and domestic product, and not attach too great significance to small differences between countries. Figure 12-2 presents the world distribution of gross national product per capita.*

2. Another valuable yardstick to measure the economy is the proportion of the labor force employed in agriculture and related primary occupations or, conversely, those in secondary and tertiary forms of economic activity (Figure 12-3). As noted earlier, it is in the nature of underdeveloped countries that agricultural production demands the service of most of the labor force. In many of these countries over half the working population are so engaged. One should remember, however, that this agricultural activity involves more than cultivating fields and tending animals. These workers also process the output, often transport and market it, build their homes, and make their tools. Employment in agriculture, therefore, has a different meaning here from that in advanced societies. For this very reason the measure significantly indicates the degree of labor division and thereby shows the general character of the economy.

3. The third important criterion is the per capita use of commercial energy (Figure 12-4). Excluded from the data are noncommercial

*For explanation of fundamental concepts and definitions of terms, see United Nations *Yearbook of National Accounts Statistics,* 1957–; shorter definitions appear in the United Nations *Statistical Yearbook* at the end of the relevant tables.

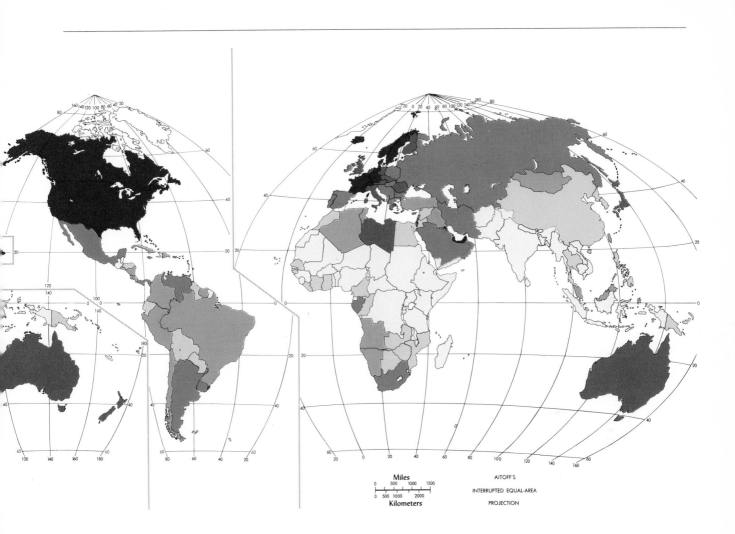

## U.S. Dollars per Capita

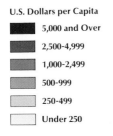

5,000 and Over

2,500-4,999

1,000-2,499

500-999

250-499

Under 250

FIGURE **WORLD: GROSS NATIONAL PRODUCT PER CAPITA**
**12-2**

All currencies are expressed in United States dollars. Data for countries of the communist block and for certain Asian and African countries are estimates. Source of data: Population Reference Bureau, *World Population Data Sheet, 1976,* Washington, D.C., 1976.

sources, such as windmills on farms, wood and agricultural wastes for domestic heating and cooking, and the muscle power of man and animal. The resulting figures underestimate total energy use, especially in underdeveloped countries, but bring out all the more sharply the contrasts between preindustrial and industrial modes of life.

When comparing industrial countries, a point to bear in mind is that differences in temperature affect the share of energy used for heating. This may explain minor differences between countries in cold and mild climates. Apart from such reservations, the commercial power consumption per head indicates fairly well the level of economic activity.

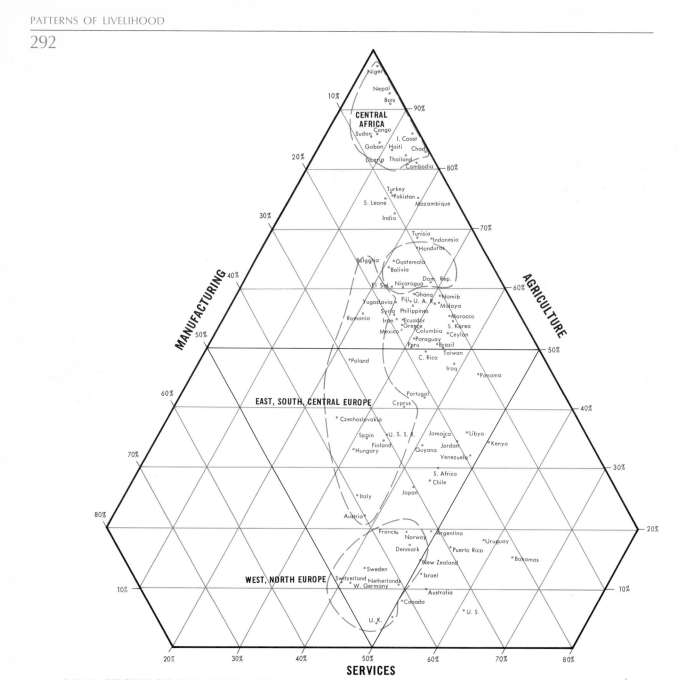

FIGURE **PERCENTAGES OF WORKING POPULATION IN**
**12-3** **AGRICULTURE, MANUFACTURING, AND SERVICES**
**IN SELECTED COUNTRIES**

This triangular coordinate graph repays careful study. The total working population of each country has been allotted to three categories: agriculture (including fishing and forestry), manufacturing (including mining and construction), and services (including transportation and utilities). For example, the position of the dot for the United States results from 61 percent in services, 33 percent in manufacturing, and 6 percent in agriculture. Data are from the late 1960s as given in various United Nations publications.

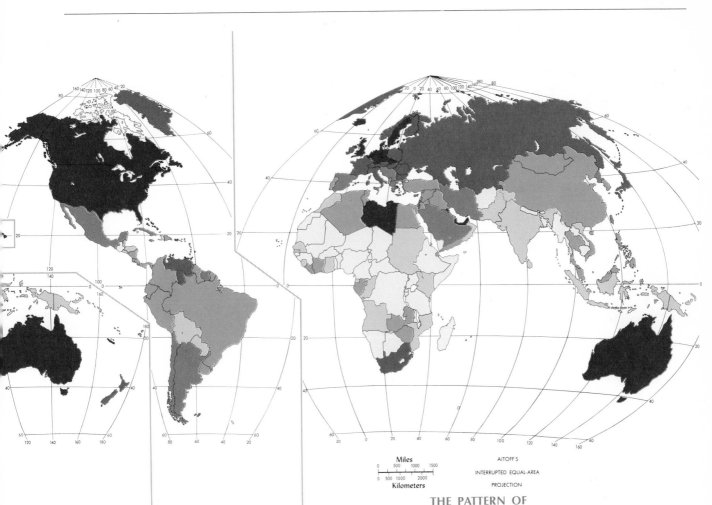

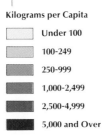

**Kilograms per Capita**

| | |
|---|---|
| | Under 100 |
| | 100-249 |
| | 250-999 |
| | 1,000-2,499 |
| | 2,500-4,999 |
| | 5,000 and Over |

FIGURE **WORLD: ENERGY CONSUMPTION PER CAPITA**
**12-4**

Consumption of energy from coal, lignite, petroleum products, natural gas, hydroelectricity, and nuclear electricity has been converted into kilograms of coal equivalent. Source of data: *United Nations Statistical Yearbook, 1975*, New York, 1976, table 138.

Miles
0 500 1000 1500

Kilometers
0 500 1000 2000

AITOFF'S

INTERRUPTED EQUAL-AREA

PROJECTION

## THE PATTERN OF ECONOMIC DEVELOPMENT

To gain an overview, one may consolidate the distributional patterns formed by specific criteria into one generalized map (Figure 12-5). This involves some arbitrary decisions where countries fall into different categories for specific measures—but these cases are not many. They could be minimized by setting up more classes, but this would defeat the purpose of this presentation. The map divides the countries of the world into three main classes: (1) developed, (2) intermediate, and (3) underdeveloped, with the latter subdivided into (a) an upper and (b) a lower group.

1. The developed class comprises most of Europe, the Soviet Union, and the overseas extensions of Occidental culture in Anglo-America,

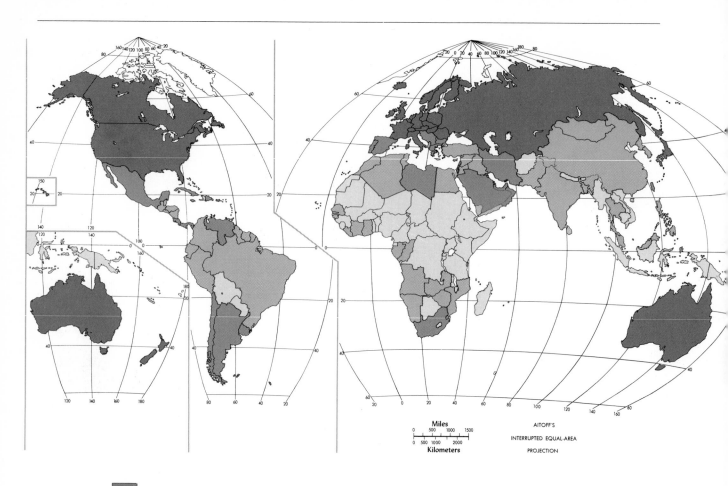

Developed

Intermediate

Underdeveloped, Upper Group

Underdeveloped, Lower Group

Miles
0  500  1000  1500

0  500  1000  2000
Kilometers

AITOFF'S

INTERRUPTED EQUAL-AREA

PROJECTION

FIGURE **WORLD: ECONOMIC DEVELOPMENT AND UNDER-**
**12–5 DEVELOPMENT**

Australia, and New Zealand. Israel shows up as an outlier in the Middle East. Japan is the only non-Occidental country in this category. All rank high in per capita GNP, use of commercial energy, and service and/or manufacturing employment. The developed countries total about 1 billion in population, or about 23 percent of the world's inhabitants.

2. The countries at the intermediate level include some at the southern fringes of indus-

trial-commercial Europe. Several oil-producing countries with high income per capita race toward the developed state; in the meantime they fall in this category. Examples are Saudi Arabia, Libya, Iran, and Venezuela. In Asia, Taiwan, Hong Kong, and Singapore can be included, as can the three southernmost countries in Latin America, as well as Mexico and some other states in and around the Caribbean. In Africa, only South Africa qualifies from the regions south of the Sahara; to the north the countries bordering the Mediterranean may soon be included in this category. In many intermediate countries the masses remain poor, the growing wealth being shared among relatively large middle and upper classes. The population of the intermediate class adds up to about 420 million, or 10 percent of the world total.

3. The remaining two-thirds of the earth's

inhabitants live in countries we may call under-developed. Broadly speaking, they form the lands of the traditional and tribal societies, with the exceptions noted above. Their great range of conditions warrants dividing them into two groups, although the lack of reliable data makes this a hazardous undertaking. Group A countries have a considerable degree of commercial-industrial development, or some degree of political or social organization which allows for some success in economic planning; group B have little of these.

Most East and South Asian states would be in group B if rated only on GNP per capita, but other factors bring them into group A. North Africa and much of the Middle East, as well as the greater part of tropical America, also rank in group A. Some countries in Meso-Africa and Southeast Asia can also be placed in group A, although they are not far above those in group B.

## CAUSES OF
## ECONOMIC UNDERDEVELOPMENT

It is easier to recognize symptoms of underdevelopment than to understand causes. Yet all too commonly casual observers, their convictions inversely related to their knowledge, point to a single mainspring as the force that determines a country's economic position.

1. Some people consider racial differences adequate for explaining variety in economic levels. After what has been said in Chapter 4, there is no need to stress again that scientific evidence does not prove some biological groupings inferior or superior. However, we must recognize that beliefs and social attitudes toward race contribute to economic differentiation. Many groups or whole societies are debarred from access to the means of advancement because their "race" marks them as not belonging to the privileged ingroup. In turn, less advanced societies may reject ideas from a group that differs racially from their own, for fear of losing their identity.

2. The doctrine of environmental determinism proclaims that man is a product of his biophysical environment. As with racism, one must reject such single-minded explanations. This does not mean one can dismiss the factors of "natural environment" as irrelevant to economic development. Quite to the contrary, there is great need for further study of the manifold and subtle forms of interplay between society and habitat. Attention should be paid to moisture supplies, soil conditions, potential photosynthesis, and climatic variability, as well as control of disease in humans, plants, and animals. Only by examining specific situations can we escape the fog of meaningless generalities about man-nature relationships.

Aside from climate and related features there are the highly important mineral resources that supply raw materials and energy for the industrial economy. To possess abundant natural assets of this kind obviously is an advantage, but the fact is that no country can claim self-sufficiency in this respect. The more industrialized an economy, the more energy and raw materials it needs, and the more it depends on foreign sources. Nevertheless, despite historically low prices for primary products, some underdeveloped countries have derived benefits from investing the income in enterprises that push the economy upward, such as education, land reform, or public utilities.

But proper use of the profits depends on many other factors. To make a comparative study of Venezuela, Libya, Saudi Arabia, Kuwait, Iraq, and Brunei—all countries with large incomes from petroleum—would give an instructive picture of the variant role natural resources play in economic development. It is also worth noting that some countries without substantial mineral wealth have achieved much in the modern world; witness Japan, the Netherlands, and Switzerland. Evidently mineral resources can be a great asset, but are not by themselves the touchstone to success in the modern world.

Instead of seeking the ultimate cause of stagnation in some internal condition, one can look for it among external influences. Two of these outside forces deserve inspection.

3. Many underdeveloped countries blame their poverty on that favorite scapegoat—colonial rule. One must agree, rapacious exploitation by powerful foreigners often has actually diminished, if not destroyed, native wealth, morale, even a whole way of life. Although peoples of other cultures and other times, from Babylonian and Aztec armies to Arab slave traders and Chinese merchants, have abused their power, Western civilization carries the more recent guilt of such behavior. But there is also a more positive

The Asian Highway System which runs east from Turkey and Iraq to connect with Singapore and Indonesia includes over 55,000 kilometers of roads serving communities with over 800 million people. Beginning in 1958, international agencies and individual governments developed the project. It took more than two decades to complete construction of the section through Afghanistan, over the Khyber Pass (pictured here), and across into Pakistan and India (see page 302). (Photograph— United Nations)

side to many encounters between different peoples. In other words, colonial rule has been an agent for cultural transmission, often with deleterious effects, it is true, but also sometimes of advantage to the colonized society.

4. Isolation from main avenues of traffic tends to have a retarding influence. Backwoods are backward. On several occasions we have noted the effect of marginal as well as central

location. Shifts in trade routes and innovations in transportation change the pattern of accessibility. One might conclude that in the modern world there are no remote places anymore. But isolation always has been a relative condition, and so it is today. All places are accessible, but some are more so than others. However, favorable situation alone does not provide the magic key that opens the door to progress. Japan comes to mind, a country in a rather marginal location when it began its rise to industrial prominence.

Isolation may also result from a country's self-imposed wish to avoid foreign contacts. Seclusion has been a significant theme in periods of East Asian and Russian history. It crops up in other areas too, though less consistently and in different forms. Harsh foreign domination may lead to intense distrust of outsiders and their ideas; or a blind devotion to a national or religious ideology may also isolate a people. Attempts at autarchy (economic self-sufficiency), either combined with an ideology or strictly as an economic policy, tend to separate a country from others. While there is merit in the desire to protect a way of life, barring the door to outside influences very likely prevents the sharing of beneficial knowledge and of any widespread economic advancement.

The lesson to be learned from this brief review of various alleged causes for economic underdevelopment is at first sight a negative one; no single factor, whether racism, resources, foreign domination, or relative location, can be the ultimate and universal cause of stagnation—or of progress. By freeing ourselves from these dogmatic assertions, we gain a vantage point that permits a broader view of the complex reality of rich and poor countries. Today's challenge of making the best use of the physical environment is not so much technological as economic and political. But in turn, economic handicaps and political hurdles form part of the wider field of sociocultural forces.

## PATHS TOWARD ECONOMIC PROGRESS

### THE IDEA OF PROGRESS

Yearning for the good life must be as old as Homo sapiens. Philosophers of ancient civilizations in China, India, and the Mediterranean world created visionary models of the ideal society. The spiritual ferment in West European thought expressed itself in numerous social designs, from Sir Thomas More's *Utopia* (1516) onward. But the ideal commonwealth usually was envisaged as a static state of moral paradise. The idea of progress, especially material progress of the entire national economy, came to the fore in eighteenth-century France and Britain. It found its most influential expression in Adam Smith's treatise *The Wealth of Nations* (1776).

The Western notion of progress spread around the world. All peoples, or certainly their leaders, now profess a desire for economic development. But it cannot be attained by merely importing the mechanical trappings. First and foremost, social and political transformation must break "the cake of custom" that stifles the traditional and, even more, the folk societies. New attitudes that permit and even encourage innovations must replace value systems hostile to change. Institutions from family to school and church need to drop old tasks and assume new responsibilities. But the will to change is not enough. What is needed is the power to carry out the will. Whether by evolution or revolution, by capitalist or socialist methods or a mixture of both, the forces of reform must control the national economy before real progress becomes possible.

Assuming that the will and the power to change are there, how does one break the vicious circle of poverty and stagnation? In essence the recipe is simple: Instead of producing merely to replace consumed goods and services, all possible resources must be devoted to efforts that promote growth toward valid socioeconomic goals. As noted before, low labor productivity is the universal hallmark of underdeveloped countries. Raising the worker's productivity requires a more advanced technology or, as economists put it, more capital goods. How can this capital be obtained? It must either be imported or squeezed from domestic sources.

### EXTERNAL SOURCES OF CAPITAL

In colonial countries the government of the metropolitan power or its private citizens provided most of the capital goods. They spent large sums on railroads, ports, other public works, agricultural experiment stations, hospitals and, to a lesser extent, on schools and public health. While part of the money came from profits made in the colony and was spent primarily for the benefit of the foreign investors, nevertheless it created in the favored areas the rudimentary underpinnings—the "infrastructure"—for a modernized economy.

This form of capital import largely ended when colonialism collapsed in the middle of the twentieth century. Unstable political conditions and restrictive economic measures in many newly independent countries have discouraged the private investor. Governments of affluent countries to some extent have restored the flow of capital through outright financial grants, development loans, and investments. However, political rather than economic considerations often have determined the direction of the flow, its volume, and its use. Since World War II the United States has spent some $60 billion in foreign aid, excluding military assistance. In recent years congressional appropriations for this purpose have dwindled to well below the international goal for foreign assistance set by the United Nations: 1 percent of the GNP of each advanced country.

We should keep in mind that much of the aid money consists of loans. As the debt piles up, an underdeveloped country must set aside for debt service an increasingly greater part of the funds received, leaving little for genuine development. Moreover, the donor countries usually tie much of their aid to the condition that the recipients purchase equipment from them. Because of this, the country receiving the loan or grant cannot shop around for lower prices. Much of the benefit of foreign assistance thus returns to the advanced country as a disguised subsidy to its manufacturers.

It is generally acknowledged that sound development is better served by trade than aid. In fact, less developed areas do pay for most imports of capital goods by exporting raw materials such as coffee, rubber, palm oil, metal ores, or petroleum. But it is in the nature of underdeveloped economies that these surpluses are small in proportion to the population.* Moreover, colonial

investments concentrated on one or a few commodities that a dependency seemed best able to produce; this resulted in a lopsided export package. To rely on a single export commodity is always hazardous, and even more so today because of the competition with synthetic rubber, fibers, drugs, dyes, and the many substitutes for metals and woods available in industrial countries. To make matters worse, prices for basic foodstuffs and raw materials have suffered a relative decline when compared to the prices for services and manufactured goods. Thus, an agricultural and mining country gets fewer machines and less structural steel than twenty years ago for the same volume of exports.

A further problem arises when developing countries start producing manufactured goods in modern factories. Often the home market is not large enough to provide a solid base for industrialization. Efforts to expand sales through export frequently fail because of high tariffs, quota systems, and other discriminatory barriers. There may be difficulty because of poor-quality products. To improve this situation, a number of advanced countries have agreed to facilitate imports from underdeveloped countries. In view of rising protectionism, it remains to be seen whether the promise will be more than a kind gesture.

## INTERNAL SOURCES OF CAPITAL

The conclusion is inescapable that the underdeveloped country must find within itself the greater part of the capital needed to become modern. It must save part of its current production to invest in growth-promoting activities, techniques, and equipment. How this can be done depends on the given situation in each state. To achieve this is much more difficult in a full-blown subsistence-farming economy than in one that has already a substantial commercial component. And it is harder in a country with great population pressure than in one with a more favorable ratio between the people and material resources (Figure 12–6).

As noted earlier, agrarian communities at near-subsistence level have much hidden unemployment. This surplus labor must be led into productive work. If there is no capital to provide them jobs, they can work with shovels and baskets to create capital, such as roads, dikes, and dams. As services and industries expand, they

*Exceptions are mainly the large petroleum exports from some countries.

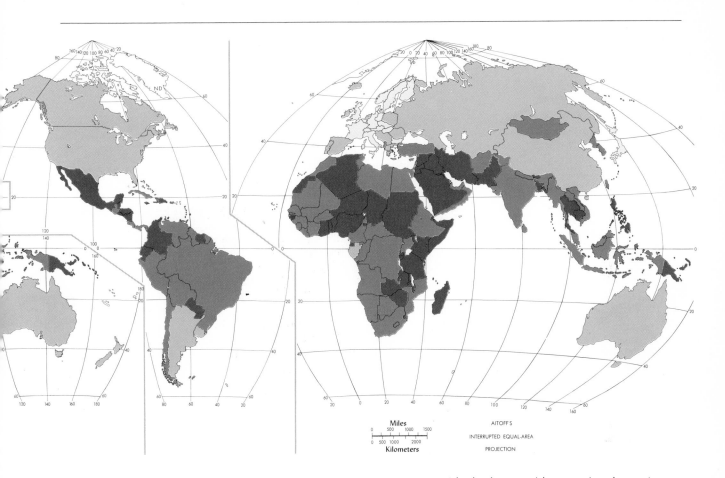

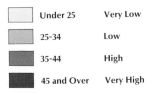

| | Under 25 | Very Low |
| | 25-34 | Low |
| | 35-44 | High |
| | 45 and Over | Very High |

FIGURE **WORLD: PERCENT OF POPULATION UNDER FIFTEEN**
**12-6** YEARS OF AGE

In the developing countries, problems of raising the level of living are compounded by the large proportions of the total population who depend on the remaining portions for the necessities of life. Children under the age of fifteen constitute nearly one-half of the population in many countries of Africa, Latin America and Asia; in most European countries they are only one-fourth of the population. Source of data: Population Reference Bureau, *World Population Data Sheet, 1976*, Washington, D.C., 1976.

provide the farmer with a growing domestic market. With the cash received—or with credit on anticipated sales—he can buy better seeds, tools, fertilizers, and insecticides, in short, increase his own productivity. Little plots can be consolidated into larger farms, thus further increasing the productivity of labor. Countries blessed with reserves of arable land, like those in most of Latin America, Meso-Africa, and Southeast Asia, should use them to create cooperative farms of a size adequate for commercial production instead of permitting the spread of small homesteads which merely extend the poverty of subsistence.

Many other factors contribute to higher productivity per worker, though in the end most depend on access to capital goods. Highly important among them is education in the broadest sense of the word. It must prepare workers to use new techniques and, above all, it must open their minds to new ideas (Figures 12-7 and 12-8).

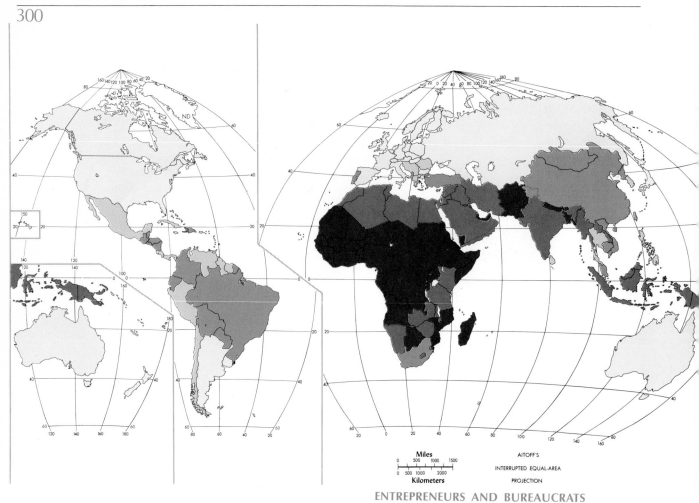

Miles
0   500   1000   1500

0  500 1000      2000
Kilometers

AITOFF'S

INTERRUPTED EQUAL-AREA

PROJECTION

**Percentage Illiterate**

Under 10

10-25

25-50

50-75

Over 75

FIGURE **WORLD: ILLITERACY**
**12-7**

Percentage of population aged fifteen and over who cannot read and write. Illiteracy and economic under-development are highly correlated. Source of data: UNESCO *Statistical Yearbook 1974,* New York, 1975, tables 1.3 and 1.4.

## ENTREPRENEURS AND BUREAUCRATS

Many writers stress the role of the *entrepreneur,* the person who organizes and directs business, who will risk new ventures to make large profits. As technical and commercial innovators such people are considered the dynamic element in a free market economy. Many agrarian societies, especially in Southeast Asia and Meso-Africa, had little tradition of this type of business leadership. Outsiders filled the entrepreneurial positions as the incipient capitalistic order developed: Westerners and, mainly at the lower socioeconomic levels, immigrants from the Middle East, India, and China. However, a society will not develop a market economy very far if it does not fill the slots of manager, merchant, and banker from its own ranks. Unfortunately, an energetic and imaginative class of entrepreneurs does not appear over-

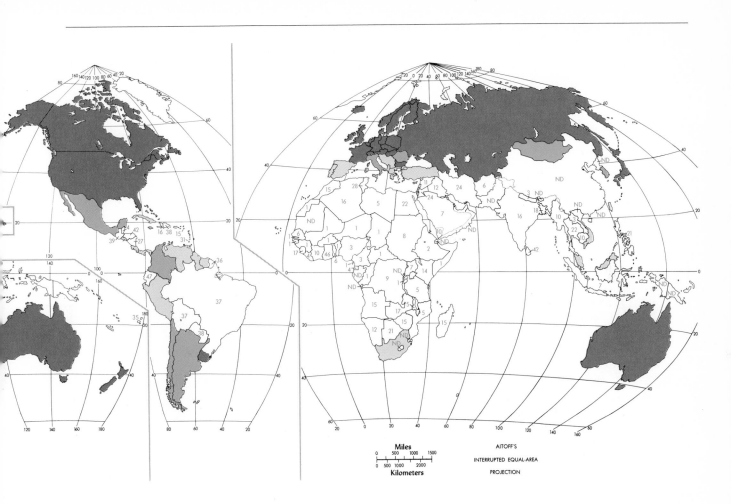

**Under Fifty Copies per 1,000 Inhabitants
Shown by Figures**

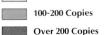 50-99 Copies

100-200 Copies

Over 200 Copies

FIGURE **WORLD: DAILY NEWSPAPERS, NUMBER OF COPIES**
**12-8** **PER 1,000 INHABITANTS**

In the underdeveloped parts of the world, there is
higher newspaper circulation in Latin America than in
Meso-Africa and South and East Asia. The size of a
daily newspaper may range from a single sheet to fifty
or more pages, depending on the country. Source of
data: United Nations *Statistical Yearbook 1974,* New
York, 1975, table 209.

night. Such skill grows slowly in response to
changing social values and economic institutions.

In many third-world countries, large migrations to the main cities are creating a class of
people who live by their wits, "on the street," in
small individual or family enterprises, usually of a
service nature. The "official" economy, whether
capitalistic or socialistic in structure (or both),
exists alongside them and, as it expands, draws
on them for its work force (see Chapter 17,
page 438).

In principle, socialism in the communist
state opposes private property and private capital,
replacing the market mechanism by allocating
capital according to a national development plan.
The government acts as manager of the "one-firm
state." Entrepreneurs are replaced by government
officials and bureaucrats who seek success or power

A camel train crosses the main route of the Asian Highway in Iran between Tabriz and Teheran. See Page 296. (Photograph—United Nations)

in the hierarchies of industrial management, government ministry, or political party. But under the most rigid and authoritarian regimes economic development for the masses has come as slowly and painfully as under market systems based on entrepreneurs. It is doubtful that either of the opposing Western political-economic theories, capitalistic or socialistic, can bulldoze a country into economic well-being. In modern countries the most successful economies are those that combine public control of development while at the same time allowing considerable play for market forces. Perhaps it is this pragmatic, nondoctrinaire view that augurs best for presently underdeveloped countries. Each society seeking progress must decide what combination of private and government enterprise suits its own situation best.

Many underdeveloped countries give the state far-reaching control over the economy, partly because they believe that conscious collective effort at self-improvement is more likely to be successful. Yet, the signal progress made in countries like Puerto Rico, Taiwan, and the Federation of Malaysia indicates that private enterprise can be an effective partner in economic and social betterment.

### THE WIDENING GAP
Will all peoples eventually reach the same level of affluence that now characterizes advanced nations? The experience of the 1960s points in the opposite direction. During that decade the gap between haves and have-nots widened. The average annual income per capita increased $650 in

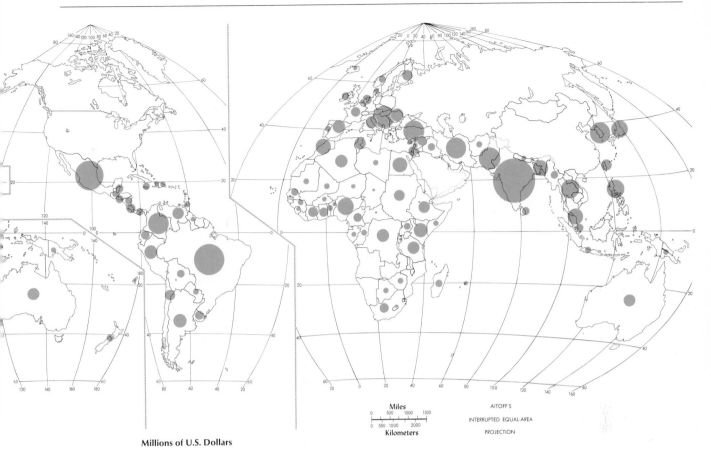

Millions of U.S. Dollars

| · | Under 10 |
| · | 10 |
| ● | 50 |
| ● | 100 |
| ⬤ | 500 |
| ⬤ | 1,000 |
| ⬤ | 5,000 |

FIGURE **WORLD BANK LOANS AND CREDITS, 1945–1976**
12-9

Following World War II and in subsequent decades, huge amounts of foreign aid (economic, technical, military) have been given away by the United States. Other countries also began to provide aid of varying kinds. The World Bank is an international organization supported by members of the United Nations that provides loans and credits to countries with development and reconstruction needs. Source of data: World Bank, *Annual Report, 1976*, Washington, D.C., 1976, 14–15.

the developed countries but only $40 in the underdeveloped ones. Furthermore, the share of world exports for the latter fell from 21.3 percent in 1960 to 17.6 percent in 1970. Clearly, while the advanced countries forged ahead, the disadvantaged ones were left farther and farther behind.

Gunnar Myrdal, the Swedish social scientist, stresses the mechanism of accumulation of advantage or, as he calls it, circular causation. He points out that a change normally "does not call forth contradicting forces but, instead, supporting changes, which move the system in the same direction but much further. Because of such circular causation a social process tends to become cumulative and often gathers speed at an accelerated rate" (Myrdal, 1957, 13). For example, private capital for new plants is much easier to obtain for an area that already has proved its worth for manufacturing than for one where modern industry is a pioneering venture. Entrepreneurs of modernized countries know how to take advantage of new opportunities, while the less experienced native businessleaders of a less developed country may have to retreat in the face of stiff competition. Expressed in familiar terms, the rich get richer and the poor get poorer. Even as the poor inch forward, they see the distance widen between themselves and the rich, who move ahead at a fast clip.

In Myrdal's view the increasing inequalities between nations result from "the cumulative tendency inherent in the unhampered play of the market forces." The theoretical solution might be the presence of "a world state which could interfere in the interest of equality of opportunity." The reader who is aware of the stubborn problems that depress areas within national states—in spite of all government proddings and a constant gentle rain of favors—may well be skeptical of this answer. Myrdal realizes that there exists at present no basis of "mutual human solidarity" on which a world state necessarily must rest. In his opinion the best hope lies in expanding intergovernmental organizations that initiate and strengthen international economic integration and promote equality. These "are ideals which no country and, indeed, no responsible human being can ever afford to give up." To which he adds wryly: "If for no other reason, we need them to console our international conscience" (Myrdal, 1957, 64–66).

Among obstacles to advancement, one looms at present larger than any other: the rapidly increasing population. A nation may show commendable growth of its national product, but if this gain merely equals that in population, no economic progress results. Underdeveloped countries in particular suffer under the burden of accelerated population increase—another instance of circular causation ("the rich get richer, and the poor get children . . .").

Other and perhaps even more fateful problems crowd in when one contemplates the future impact of modern technology. Few think the earth has enough resources to provide more than 4 billion people with material comforts equaling those now prevailing in developed countries—and by the year 2000 there may be over 6 billion! It is doubtful whether the biophysical environment can survive if the pressures so evident today in modern societies spread to all parts of the earth. It is estimated that each American generates fifty times as much waste as one individual in a preindustrial society. If the entire world population were to consume so recklessly, the pollution of our planet would be beyond imagination. An approach toward material equality for all peoples is likely to be reached only through a redistribution of income, with the rich sacrificing their wealth and wasteful ways, to bring up the third world to humanly tolerable levels of living without destroying our entire ecological system. These topics of population growth and of man's use and abuse of the environment receive special attention in Part V of this volume.

## CITATIONS AND FURTHER READINGS

Ackerman, E. A. *Geography as a Fundamental Research Discipline,* University of Chicago, Department of Geography, Research Paper no. 53, Chicago, 1958.

Blaut, J. M. "Imperialism: The Marxist Theory and Its Evolution," *Antipode,* 7 (1975): 1–19.

Boserup, E. *The Conditions of Agricultural Growth: The Economics of Agrarian Change under Population Pressure,* Chicago, 1965.

Boulding, K. E. *The Meaning of the 20th Century,* New York, 1964.

Brookfield, M. C. *Interdependent Development,* London, 1975.

Brutzkus, E. "Centralized versus Decentralized Pattern of Urbanization in Developing Countries," *Tijdschrift voor Economische en Sociale Geografie,* 64 (1973): 11–23.

Conkling, E. C., and McConnell, J. E. "A Co-operative Approach to Problems of Trade and Development. The Central American Experience," *Tijdschrift voor Economische en Sociale Geografie,* 64 (1973): 363–377.

Connell, J. "The Evolution of Tanzanian Rural Development," *Journal of Tropical Geography,* 38 (1974): 7–18.

Darkoh, M. B. K. "Industrial Strategy and Rural Development in Africa with Special Reference to Ghana: a Review of Current Trends and Suggestions for a Plan of Action," *Geoforum,* 16 (1973): 7–24.

Dean, V. M. *The Nature of the Non-western World,* New York, 1962.

De Souza, A. R., and Porter, P. W. *The Underdevelopment and Modernization of the Third World,* Washington, D.C., 1974.

Dickson, K. B. "Background to the Problem of Economic Development in Northern Ghana," *Annals of the Association of American Geographers,* 58 (1968): 686–697.

Ginsburg, N. S. *Atlas of Economic Development,* Chicago, 1961.

Goulet, D. *The Cruel Choice,* New York, 1971.

Gourou, P. *The Tropical World,* translated by E. D. Laborde, 2d ed., New York, 1962.

Hartshorn, T. A. "The Spatial Structure of Socioeconomic Development in the Southeast, 1950–1960," *Geographical Review,* 61 (1971): 265–283.

Heilbroner, R. L. *The Great Ascent,* New York, 1963.

Hodder, B. W. *Economic Development in the Tropics,* London, 1968.

Hoffman, G. W. "The Problem of the Underdeveloped Regions in Southeast Europe: A Comparative Analysis of Romania, Yugoslavia, and Greece," *Annals of the Association of American Geographers,* 57 (1967): 637–666.

King, R. "Land Reform: Some General and Theoretical Considerations," *Norsk Geografisk Tidsskrift,* 25 (1971): 85–97.

Kuznets, S. *Modern Economic Growth. Rate, Structure, and Spread,* New Haven and London, 1966.

Mabogunje, A. L. "Manufacturing and the Geography of Development in Tropical Africa," *Economic Geography,* 49 (1973): 1–20.

———— "Geography and the Problems of the Third World," *International Social Science Journal,* 27 (1975): 288–302.

Myrdal, G. *Rich Lands and Poor,* New York, 1957.

Peppelenbosch, P. G. N., and Tempelman, G. J. "Tourism and the Developing Countries," *Tijdschrift voor Economische en Sociale Geografie,* 64 (1973): 52–58.

Richardson, H. W., and Richardson, M. "The Relevance of Growth Center Strategies to Latin America," *Economic Geography,* 51 (1975): 163–178.

Santos, M. "Space and Domination—A Marxist Approach," *International Social Science Journal,* 27 (1975): 346–363.

Schumacher, E. F. *Small Is Beautiful; Economics as If People Really Mattered,* New York, 1973.

Smith, D. M. "Mapping Human Well-Being," *International Social Science Journal,* 27 (1975): 364–371.

Susman, P. "Cuban Development: from Dualism to Integration," *Antipode* 6 (1974), December, 10–29.

Ward, B. *The Rich Nations and the Poor Nations,* New York, 1962.

The word *settlement* indicates to the geographer all man-made facilities resulting from the process of settling, including the establishments that shelter people and their possessions, the roads that connect, and the fences that part them. The functions and forms of settlement express cultural differences.

Buildings and property lines remain long after the people who made them. Thus the study of settlements has a strong historical component. It views the present as an amalgam of old and recent forms, reflecting different phases of social organization and technical skill, or even a succession of cultures.

But settlement geography also relates immediately to the future, because it points up shortcomings of our present environment. The needs of a society in rapid transition strain the shell of wood, brick, steel, concrete, and asphalt that former generations have left behind. Changes in technology, economy, and social organization demand modification in the nature and arrangement of buildings, roads, and open spaces. Every citizen has a direct stake in creating surroundings that promote the quality of life.

Geographers usually classify settlements into rural and urban, but recognize that the distinction often blurs, particularly in modern societies. Chapter 13 deals with agricultural occupance forms. Chapter 14 discusses the nature of cities in different culture realms and their distribution in different eras and regions. Chapter 15 analyzes the metropolis, the environment of modern man, full of baffling problems.

# PART IV
# SETTLEMENTS

**A** lively scene in Sandaga Market in Dakar, the capital city of Senegal. (Photograph—United Nations)

# 13 FARM AND VILLAGE

The medieval burgher was well aware of the political, social, and economic factors that set him apart from the folk beyond the city gates. The view from the ramparts simply confirmed what he knew about the proper functions of town and country in the scheme of things: here the towers of cathedral and city hall, the market square with its guild houses, the busy streets lined by the homes of merchant and craftsman; across the moat the open fields, the river meadows and woodlots, the villages or single farmsteads here and there.

Today the resident of that same European city also observes how his way of life differs from that of the farmer, but the differences are in degree, instead of sharp contrast. Means of transportation and communication have spread an essentially urban culture all over the land. The once marked division between opposing landscapes, too, has blurred into a broad transition zone. The urban fringe that looks like a rural scene actually contains the dispersed residences of people who work in the city or perform urban tasks in their rustic homes. In other words, the countryside surrounding the city, though deceptively rural in appearance with farmsteads, lanes, fields, and woodlots reflecting former uses, now has decidedly urban associations.

In this chapter on farm and village we first look at various geographic aspects of rural settlement proper —that is, occupance patterns created by primary production, principally agriculture. Then we sample the problems of settlement study in western Europe, eastern North America, East Asia, and Southeast Asia.

## GEOGRAPHIC APPROACHES TO RURAL SETTLEMENT

### DISTRIBUTION

The first thing the geographer wants to know about agrarian settlements is their distribution. The three aspects of distribution are (1) dispersion, (2) density, and (3) pattern. Dispersed living on isolated farmsteads is typical for North America and other European-colonized lands, but in many parts of the world the village predominates.

Closer inspection of villages reveals various degrees of dispersion. In some the buildings are grouped together to form a "compact" village;* in others a looser sprawl of buildings surrounds a dense core—the "nucleated" village; still others are a swarm of buildings without a core—the "agglomerated" village. Many regions have only one characteristic form of dispersion; others are a mixture, e.g., Utah with its older Mormon villages and the later spread of isolated farms.

The density of settlement results mainly from how intensely the land is used. The widely spaced farmsteads in Montana differ from the relatively close ones in New Jersey; they contrast decidedly with those in Java's countryside, where there is a village every kilometer or so.

Settlement pattern denotes the arrangement of the units according to natural or artificial features such as streams, spring lines, ridges, canals, and roads. A geometric pattern results

*The communal longhouse can be considered an extreme form of compactness, a village under one roof in which each family occupies a one-room unit.

where a central authority determines division of land and layout of roads before allowing settlement. The Romans established a regular system of land division (centuriation) in colonizing parts of their empire. The United States Land Survey, begun in 1785, divided the unoccupied lands of the western territories into a grid system. The Dutch laid out their newly reclaimed lands in meticulous detail before permitting the farmers to move in.

Under changing conditions of land use, any settlement plan, however well drafted for the needs of the time, becomes inadequate. This leads to a new pattern of use that may show only faintly the former divisions. In many instances in the United States new technologies in farming and transportation have drastically altered the original lattice design.

### FIELD SYSTEMS

To understand rural settlements, we need to analyze the spatial relationships between dwellings and farmland. In the United States the typical farmstead stands on the farm property, commonly a single tract of land. In some parts of Europe and over much of Asia and Africa, however, the people usually live in villages, with their lands in the surrounding area, each farmer with his holding, usually in scattered plots or strips. Such a settlement reveals ancient forms of social organization. On large-scale plantations or collective farms the labor force may live in compact settlements.

### STRUCTURE OF VILLAGE AND FARMSTEAD

Villages in different parts of the world display a fascinating variety of traditional forms. A closeup (large-scale) view of village or farmstead reveals its ground plan, typical construction materials, architectural style, and other features of cultural significance. For instance, in East Africa a circle of beehive-shaped huts around the cattle corral (*kraal*) is a common type. Some districts in China and Japan have the grid pattern. In Europe linear villages, often with an open central space, string along river dikes or roads. Other villages, however, have irregular forms, with narrow lanes winding between dwellings and walled compounds or barnyards.

No less interesting are the buildings themselves, whether grouped in a village or isolated on a farm. Worthy of attention are American farmsteads in their regional variety. In Europe the types are highly localized, so that on a day's drive one may discover several. In some the dwelling, with its characteristic floor plan, stands apart from the barn, stable, and other buildings, similar to American practice. Elsewhere the house, animal shelter, storage space, and workshop are under one roof.

The farmstead may be a two- or even three-storied building, take the shape of a T, an L, a U; or the units may fully enclose a courtyard with only a broad gateway giving access. Often such a courtyard has in the middle a large manure pile, mark of the skillful farmer.

Beyond the Occidental culture realm, the villages and house types—to us exotic—merely represent other solutions to the universal problem of constructing establishments that best serve social and economic needs in a specific physical environment (Figure 13-1).

To analyze and explain our observations may not be easy. As with most cultural phenomena, cause-and-effect relationships in settlement patterns are complex; the simple answer that points toward one single force is always suspect. "Occupance patterns sum up . . . the nature of man's rapport with the earth . . ." (Kniffen, 1965, 552). It follows that any interpretation must consider both physical and cultural factors. The examples of rural settlements to be discussed in this chapter amply demonstrate how involved such a study can be.

## WESTERN EUROPE

The peoples that lived in England, northern France, the Low Countries, and Germany during the Middle Ages practiced varied kinds of crop and livestock farming. Most of these lands were covered with broadleaf deciduous forests, interspersed with conifer stands on sandy soils and mountain slopes. Thus, agriculture essentially was an adaptation to forest environment. Earlier inhabitants had already cleared fertile, well-drained, easily tilled soils such as the gently rolling loess lands that stretch through northern France, the southern Low Countries, and central Germany; here crop growing predominated. Stock raising

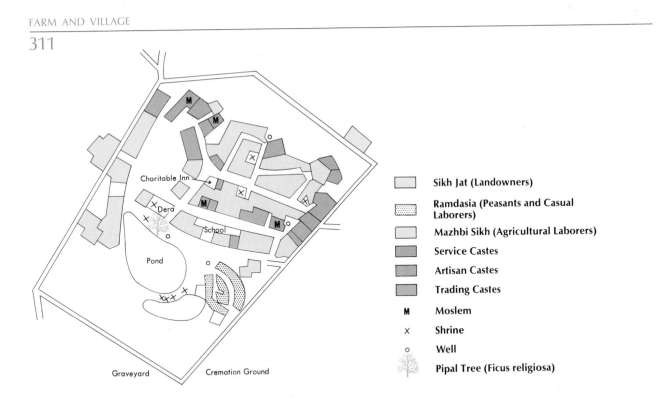

Legend:

- Sikh Jat (Landowners)
- Ramdasia (Peasants and Casual Laborers)
- Mazhbi Sikh (Agricultural Laborers)
- Service Castes
- Artisan Castes
- Trading Castes
- **M** Moslem
- x Shrine
- o Well
- Pipal Tree (Ficus religiosa)

FIGURE **INDIA: A VILLAGE IN PUNJAB**
**13-1**

The 1,000 inhabitants of Kunran village belong to several castes. Most numerous are the Sikh Jat (seventy-six households), Ramdasia (twenty-seven households), and Mazhbi Sikh (twelve households). Other casts represented include Tarkhan (carpenter), Bazigar (acrobat), Jhiwar (water carrier), Sunar (goldsmith), Nai (barber), and Bania (shopkeeper). Among the villagers are thirty Moslems, including those of Mirasi (drummer) and Teli (oil presser) castes. Note the peripheral location of the service castes. The map is based on a sketch in Census of India, "Kunran: A Village in Sangru District in Punjab," *Village Survey Monographs of Punjab*, no. 36, *Census of India, 1961*, vol. 13, part 6, Chandigarh, 1963.

held first place in marshy river bottoms and coastlands, as well as on cool, rainy uplands. In fertile areas villages of substantial size were surrounded by a broad expanse of cropland. In pastoral areas small villages, often no more than hamlets, had a modest "home field" or "infield" for crops and a wide "outfield" for grazing, or perhaps occasional cropping.

## ANCIENT FORMS IN LOWER SAXONY

In northwestern Germany and eastern Netherlands the region called Lower Saxony lay somewhat between those lands that were dominantly arable and those of purely pastoral character. Once these plains were covered with forests or with vast moors. Ribbons of alluvial river land cut through the plain, where a sparse population lived in forest clearings. Perhaps no more than a dozen dwellings stood in an irregular and loose cluster, sometimes around a central green (Figure 13-2). Each house sheltered a family and its harvest and livestock, although in later times the space became compartmentalized for different uses.

The cropland (*esch*) lay nearby on higher, well-drained land; whether it consisted of one or more fields cannot be answered in general terms, because conditions varied in time and in space. Under the one-field system, rye was grown year in, year out. More commonly, from the ninth or tenth century onward, the cropland was divided into two or three fields. A full member of the

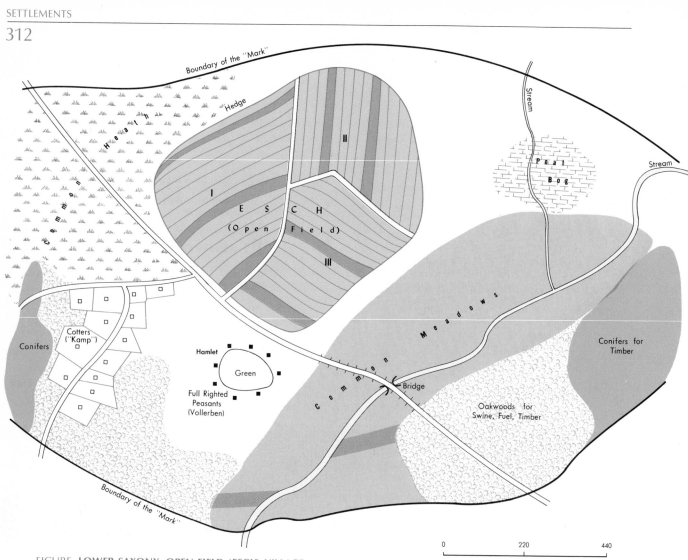

FIGURE **LOWER SAXONY: OPEN FIELD (*ESCH*) VILLAGE**
**13-2**

This generalized diagram portrays the situation in the Middle Ages. The darker strips in the three fields of the *esch* belong to one full-righted peasant. The common meadows often were, at least in part, subdivided into privately owned lots, of which two are shown in the sketch. The entire land area belonging to the community was called the "mark."

community held equal shares in each field, which was laid out in long strips to facilitate plowing. (A similar practice in England gave rise to the measure of the furlong, 220 yards, the length of a furrow.) In the three-field system the usual rotation of crops consisted of a spring sowing of barley or oats, a fall sowing of rye or wheat, and then a year of fallow.

Most communities used the meadows along small streams to cut hay as precious winter fodder or to pasture their livestock. The villagers held these areas either in common or in private parcels, but they all shared the surrounding forest for

Laxton, England. The medieval open fields of this village escaped enclosure, and are now preserved as a historic monument. Although the old narrow strips have been consolidated to create more workable plots, and some of the old common lands are hedged, the layout of the fields and the typically straggling English village are clearly visible. The light patch in center background is the South Field. Between it and the village runs a stream (left to right), bordered by meadows. The East Field lies in the left foreground. (Photograph—Aerofilms, Ltd.)

pasture, timber, and fuel. During the Middle Ages the forests deteriorated from overgrazing and burning and became the heathlands which today are typical local landscape features. With the change came a shift from cattle to sheep because sheep are better browsers.

Another reason why livestock raising was important is that the leached sandy soils depended heavily on the availability of manure. The number of livestock a village could maintain was of crucial importance, quite apart from their value for meat, milk, wool, and hides. Stubble grazing after harvest provided the field with animal fertilizer. When the animals were kept in the barn, soil was dug from the forest floor and brought in to enrich with the manure before it was spread over the fields. Removing forest soil brought the surface closer to the groundwater level, which further encouraged the growth of heather instead of trees. This practice of mixing heath sod with manure to increase the organic content of the soil continued in this area from late medieval times until the last century. The process raised the level of the fields so that now the *esch* is a gently rising mound in the landscape.

This form of agriculture demanded community cooperation. Farmers owning individual strips in an arable field had to agree on the crop rotation plan and on the proper time for plowing, sowing, and harvesting. They helped each other in harvesting and in repairing the fence that enclosed the large field. Only a few tracks led to the *esch,* and to reach almost any strip required crossing another man's property.

Villagers with full community rights (in German, *Vollerben*) and those without (cottagers or cotters) might be permitted to clear a forest patch and build a home. In this way a number of new farmsteads, each located on its compact enclosed property (called *kamp*) gradually spread around the *esch* village.

Though the feudal system made little impact in Lower Saxony, it dominated other parts of western Europe. Often the nobility acquired property rights over village lands and reduced the peasants to servile status. Such a feudal unit was known as the manor. Village and manor might coincide, or there might be two or more manors in one village. Serf or hired labor worked the home farms of the lord's *demesne* (domain) where stood his house or castle. Arrangement and use of arable fields, pastures, and woodland, however, was much the same as in communities of free farmers.

During the seventeenth and eighteenth centuries better rotation systems, including clovers and a variety of root crops, were introduced. They made the fallow field unnecessary and provided fodder for more livestock which, in turn, increased the supply of manure. These advances, first introduced on large estates in Holland and England, eventually also reached Lower Saxony.

The landscape of Lower Saxony has greatly changed during the last hundred years. Chemical fertilizer enabled the farmers to convert heathlands into productive pastures and arable fields. To feed the growing cities and to compete with cheap grains from America, they switched to fodder crops, dairy cattle, poultry, and hogs. More efficient production demanded that scattered small holdings be consolidated into larger units; in many communities this was carried out by voluntary exchange. It has encouraged living on the farm instead of in the village. Nevertheless, in spite of all changes, the region retains a character singularly its own.

## LINEAR VILLAGES

A very different settlement form developed from about A.D. 1200 as marshes were reclaimed along sea and river. The land of each farmer stretched from the dike, where his home and other buildings stood, into the marsh as one long, narrow lot. This type of village in much of the Netherlands and northern Germany still consists of a long row of houses along the dike road. In the mountains of central Germany we find a similar arrangement (Figure 13–3). The farmsteads lie on the valley floor and the holdings run from the meadows along the river, via cropland on cleared higher ground, into the forested steep slopes (*Waldhufendorf*—Figure 13–3).

## GERMAN SETTLEMENTS EAST OF THE ELBE

German expansion eastward across the Elbe and Saale rivers into Slavic lands began around A.D. 900 and gained full momentum toward 1200. The Slavs practiced a simple agriculture, depending mainly on cattle raising. The village farmsteads formed an enclosure, roughly a circular open space, for the livestock. Around the village lay the croplands. Germans moving into these territories often retained the original layout of the village but added new fields according to the strip system. One can still see many of these *Rundling* (round-shaped) villages in central Germany (Figure 13–3).

Where the Germans settled unoccupied lands, they carefully planned their new colonies. Often the clustered village and open-field system followed the familiar pattern from the homeland. Other designs were the *Strassendorf* (street vil-

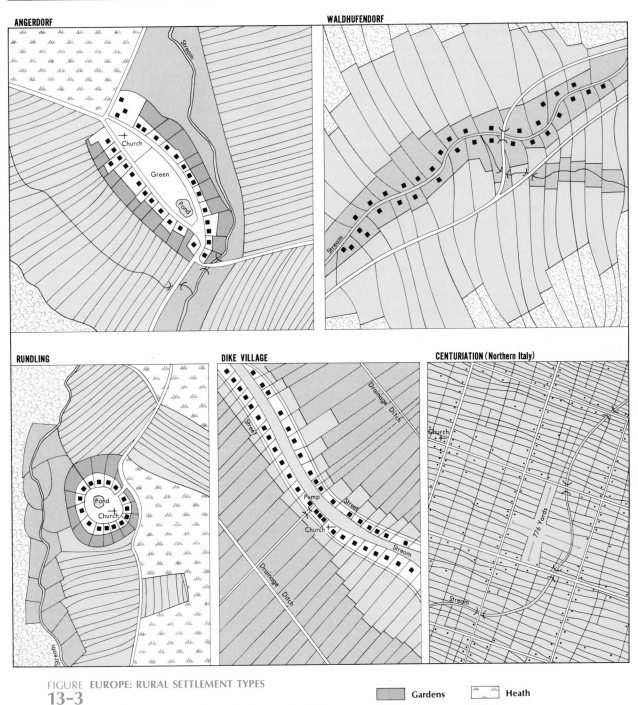

ANGERDORF

WALDHUFENDORF

RUNDLING

DIKE VILLAGE

CENTURIATION (Northern Italy)

FIGURE
13-3
EUROPE: RURAL SETTLEMENT TYPES

These diagrams are on the scale of approximately
1:10,000, except for the centuriation sample, which is
about 1:33,000.

| | | |
|---|---|---|
| ■ Gardens | ■ Heath | |
| ■ Arable | ■ Woods | |
| ■ Meadow | ■ · Farm House | |

lage) with farmsteads on both sides of a road, and the *Angerdorf*, farmsteads around an almond-shaped common (*Anger*) with its church and pond. The arable land surrounding the village was usually divided into three blocks, each with individual holdings distributed in long narrow strips (Figure 13-3).

The feudal lords who conquered the Slavic lands received grants commensurate with their status and service. They expanded their holdings when peasants in distress abandoned their land or offered it in return for protection. In this way many estates grew up between the villages of free farmers. As expanding western European cities needed grains for bread, the landholders of northern Germany converted their lands into large enterprises, using their serfs for labor. Although hereditary serfdom was abolished early in the nineteenth century, estates remained dominant here until the end of World War II, when East Germany and Poland broke up the large holdings.

## ENGLISH AND OTHER LANDHOLDINGS

Similar large estates developed in England during the fifteenth century, but here sheep raising for profit gave the impetus. By legal means or simple theft the gentry acquired peasant lands, and enclosed the open fields and pastures, thus creating privately owned holdings. The tenants, who did the work, lived in hamlets or on dispersed farmsteads.

We have purposely emphasized the European types of settlement because they contrast sharply with those of the United States and Canada. The trend in modern times is toward locating farmsteads on the property instead of in a village. Numerous factors contributed to this: the removal of feudal restrictions, loosening of community bonds, allocation of communal village lands to private owners, consolidation of lands, the urge for efficient farm management, and the facility of transportation.

# ANGLO-AMERICA

Early European colonists to America brought along notions of farming, land tenure, field patterns, and housing as practiced in their home-

lands. Although climate and vegetation of the Atlantic Seaboard were on the whole remarkably similar to western Europe's, the challenge of organizing the new territory was entirely different. This inevitably led to modifications of traditional ways and created a distinctly American imprint on the landscape.

Four separate settlement patterns evolved along the Atlantic Seaboard: (1) French in Acadia (Nova Scotia) and along the St. Lawrence river; (2) English in New England; (3) ethnically mixed colonists in the Middle Atlantic states from lower New York to southeastern Pennsylvania; (4) English in the South, from Maryland to Georgia. The occupance forms of these four source areas spread inland, some to a limited extent, others eventually as far as the Pacific coast.

Even in the early years these four main settlement patterns were not sharply separated. Pioneers moving through the Appalachian valleys and across the ranges later brought about a further meeting and mingling of traits. The farmer from the eastern woodlands coming to the dry, treeless plains found new problems requiring different modes of settlement.

The Land Ordinance of 1785 and the Homestead Act of 1862 also profoundly affected the layout of rural settlement. Changes in agricultural practices and in building materials and methods of construction, all called for modifications of the original patterns. Nevertheless, their impact is clear, especially in the east; settlement forms today can be understood only as descendants from earlier models.

## FRENCH LONG-LOT FARMS

The kings of France in the seventeenth century, to stimulate colonization along the St. Lawrence River, awarded land grants with feudal privileges (*seigneuries*) to their noblemen and to the Church. Each tract had frontage of a kilometer or more on the river or its tributaries and stretched a distance inland, sometimes a hundred kilometers or more. The *seigneurs* parceled out their properties in parallel strips to settlers (*habitants*) so that each would have access to the river, which at that time was virtually the only transportation route.

Soon the French tradition of equal inheritance rights among the sons led to subdivision of each farm. Roads at right angles to the river were

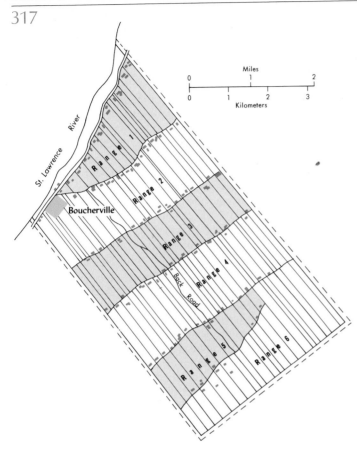

## NEW ENGLAND

To explain why agricultural settlements in New England had compact form, scholars emphasize different reasons. Some see the village as an obvious transfer of the rural parish from the home country, though without the lord of the manor; others stress the need for defense against the Indians. A third group claims the main reason why early colonists built their dwellings in clusters was the social organization of their closely knit religious communities (Brown, 1948; Scofield, 1938; Trewartha, 1946). In spite of European background, Indian danger, and government pressure, early colonists outside New England rarely settled in villages. This fact lends credence to the argument that the seventeenth-century rural New Englander consciously chose the compact settlement as best suited to fulfill his religious, educational, and other social needs.

Early agrarian colonies in New England were group efforts in land development. The Crown had granted extensive lands to trading companies which, in turn, gave out tracts ("towns" or "townships") of 6 to 16 kilometers square to groups of men called "proprietors" for the purpose of establishing a "plantation"—that is, a planting or colony of immigrants.

Each settler received a home lot in the village, ranging from 0.25 hectare in some places to 2 hectares in others, but also varying within each village according to the owner's status. These lots accommodated at least the farmstead, including a kitchen garden, while the larger ones afforded space for an arable field. The degree of village compactness depended, of course, on the size of the home lots. The center of the village was the green or common, flanked by the meetinghouse or church, the burying ground, the school, and the homes of distinguished residents.

Around the village were fields, pastures, and woodlands. The planting grounds usually were laid out in two or three blocks, in locations best suited for crops. Every family received several strips in each block to ensure an equitable share in the different types of land. A fence around the large planting fields kept out animals and relieved the individual farmer from the need to enclose his

FIGURE **QUEBEC: LONG LOTS IN THE SEIGNEURY OF**
**13-4** **BOUCHERVILLE**

Beyond the first range of lots, parallel roads were the starting lines for new ranges of lots as settlement proceeded. A road at right angles to the river, called the "back road," linked the successive ranges with the river. From Tompkins, G. S., and Hills, T. L., *A Regional Geography of North America*, Toronto, 1962.

built to reach inland properties. In this way the long-lot farm developed and still characterizes the zone between Montreal and Quebec (Figure 13-4). Instead of the manor village so typical for large parts of feudal France (and initially promoted by officials in Lower Canada), each settler built his farmstead on his land strip close to river or road. The resulting pattern resembled beads on a string. French farms in Louisiana and along the Great Lakes (Detroit) and the Mississippi (Kaskas-

property. All original settlers held the woodlands and pastures in common, though they often divided the hay meadows into private parcels.

From the beginning there was an uneasy balance between the social advantages of village life and the economic disadvantages of scattered farm plots (Trewartha, 1946). As the population grew in the village, new fields had to be cleared; these were necessarily farther from the center and more difficult to farm. The receding danger of Indian attacks encouraged establishment of isolated farmsteads. Because the farm tracts were designed in long, narrow strips at right angles to a road, the new colonists tended to build their homes along such a road. The resulting row settlement was reminiscent of the European street village (*Strassendorf*) (Figure 13-5b).

Where there was little planning the farmsteads lay dispersed throughout the town area. Although church and school lots were provided near the center of each township section, they no longer formed the village nucleus, and the traditional common was omitted. The landscape of modern New England still shows the difference between the layout of the old seventeenth-century villages, even where they have changed into urban centers, and of the later settlements which grew from individual farms (Scofield, 1933).

### MORMON VILLAGES

The Church of the Latter-day Saints did not follow the settlement patterns that characterized the South and Middle Atlantic colonies. To keep the relation close between community and Church, the Mormons centered in villages while they were in Missouri and Illinois. By the time they occupied Utah in the middle of the nineteenth century, their church leaders had carefully planned a form of colonization that would best serve the material and spiritual needs of the people. Their design of Salt Lake City became the model for all Mormon agrarian colonies.

Each village was divided into square blocks of about 4 acres, providing four home plots large enough to accommodate the various farm buildings, a kitchen garden, and an orchard. Sites were reserved for churches and schools (Figure 13-5e). Irrigation ditches and shade trees lined the wide streets. Each villager had several fields—rectangular where feasible. To equalize the distance, each

had a small plot near the village and the larger fields farther out. This plan worked as long as the economy remained subsistence farming, but when it changed to commercial production and the society became more individualistic, the fragmentation of holdings proved a serious drawback to efficiency. Many farmers moved out of the old villages onto their land, but still they had to contend with scattered fields which often were too small for modern techniques. Though Salt Lake City retains its spacious core, much of the original pattern has been changed to accommodate business and automobile traffic.

### THE MIDDLE COLONIES

Colonization in the Middle Atlantic area differed markedly from that in New England. Compact rural settlement was the exception rather than the rule even though public officials and private landowners allowed it, often encouraged it, and sometimes even demanded it. Two reasons are usually advanced for the early prevalence of dispersed occupance. First, land development here from the beginning had a pronounced commercial character. Land companies or individuals who had been awarded vast tracts sold them to settlers as compact freeholds. Second, the colonists who did come, singly or in small family groups and from many countries, lacked the homogeneity that characterized early New England. Besides the English, there were Dutch and Walloons settling along the Hudson, Swedes on the Delaware, Scotch-Irish and Germans in southeastern Pennsylvania. The immigrants found land prices low enough to acquire good-sized farms of 50 to 100 hectares. Under these circumstances the obvious choice was to live on the farm.

### THE SOUTH

Initially the Virginia Company established the early colonists in fortified villages. After 1624, when Virginia became a Crown colony, settlers had the opportunity to acquire private holdings, to which they moved their residence. Some religious groups formed compact clusters; and the trustees of the charity colonies in Georgia insisted that their semimilitary frontier settlements be organized in villages. Nevertheless, a dispersed pattern of occupance soon prevailed throughout the South.

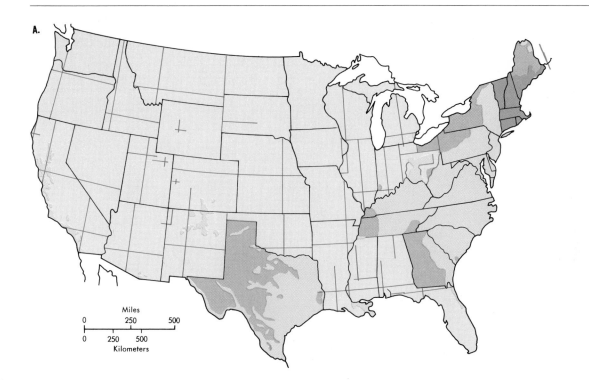

**A.**

Miles
0    250    500

0    250    500
Kilometers

FIGURE **AMERICAN SETTLEMENT FORMS (SEE NEXT PAGES)**
**13-5**

A. United States: Land Survey Systems. From Marschner, F. J., *Land Use and Its Patterns in the United States,* U.S. Department of Agriculture Handbook No. 153, Washington, D.C., 1959, page 20.

B. Springfield, Massachusetts, 1640. From Reps, J. W., *The Making of Urban America,* Princeton, N.J., 1965, page 121.

**Federal Rectangular Survey**

☐ **Areas Covered by Township and Range Systems**

╂ **Principal Meridians and Base Lines**

**Other Land Division Systems**

☐ **Unregulated**

▨ **Independent Rectangular Divisions (States and Land Companies)**

▨ **New England Towns**

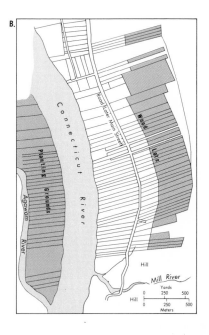

**B.**

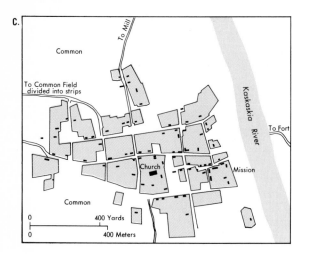

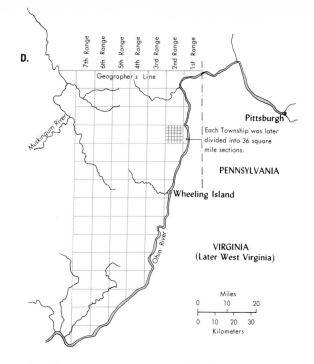

C. Kaskaskia, Illinois. Eighteenth-century French settlement in the Mississippi Valley. The fields adjacent to the village were laid out in strips. From Reps, J. W., *The Making of Urban America,* Princeton, N.J., 1965, page 74.

E. Mormon Village. Escalante, Utah, like all Mormon villages, was laid out in square blocks, each divided into four home lots. The map shows the settlement in the 1960s. Houses are black dots, barns are orange dots. The shaded area is wooded. Based on United States Geological Survey 1:24,000 Topographic Sheet, Escalante, Utah.

D. 1786 Plat: Geographer's Line. Following the enactment of the Land Ordinance of 1785, Thomas Hutchins (the Geographer to the United States) began the survey of the "Seven Ranges" at the point where the Ohio River intersected the western boundary of Pennsylvania. Based on a map in Paullin, C. O., and Wright, J. K. (eds.), *Atlas of the Historical Geography of the United States,* Washington, D.C., 1932, plate 41.

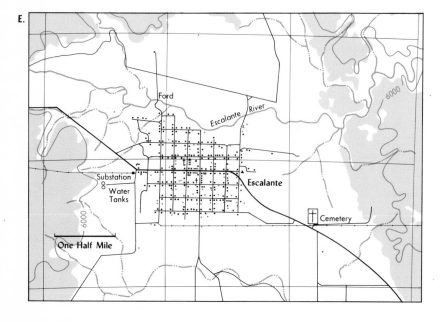

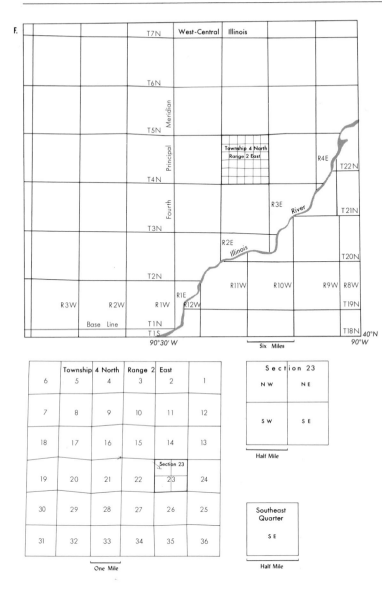

F. West-Central Illinois. The set of four diagrams illustrates the basic system of the Federal Rectangular Survey, from Base Line and Principal Meridian, to Township and Range, and Section and Quarter Section.

Most of the Southern farmers produced commercial export crops. Cultivation of tobacco, the main crop in Maryland, Virginia, and North Carolina, spread slowly inland from the coast. Rice and indigo became important in South Carolina and Georgia. Overseas markets made it necessary to site the holdings along rivers. The farms remained relatively modest in size as long as labor was scarce—mostly European indentured workers. When large numbers of Negro slaves were imported, beginning about 1700, many farms developed into the classic Southern plantation (Figure 13-6a).

Near the planter's comfortable home—rarely as large and opulent as shown in novels and movies—were the slave houses, commonly in a compact rectangle. There were also various service buildings including sheds for tools and food storage, barns for draft animals, smokehouses, salt houses, houses for baking, quarters for weaving and spinning, a cotton gin or rice mill, and a blacksmith shop. Virtually all plantation wants were satisfied by and within the establishment, doing away with the need for local market towns.

Though the plantation buildings formed a cluster, their function and structure differed from that in compact village settlements elsewhere. The large fields around the plantation allowed efficient employment and supervision of the labor gangs. Prunty, whose study of the Southern plantation we follow here, found that "in general, half or slightly more of the cropland was devoted to specialty staple crops and the remainder to plantation foodstuffs and feeds for livestock" (Prunty, 1955, 465).

Abolition of slavery led to an entirely new occupance pattern. The plantation owner divided his holdings into units of 10 to 20 hectares, to be worked by sharecroppers or tenants. Instead of the agglomeration of dwellings around the plantation headquarters, the house sites became dispersed, each operator living on the land he worked.

Farm mechanization created a new occupance pattern on many old plantation holdings (Figure 13-6b). Because the poor sharecropper or tenant could not afford to buy machinery, the landowner controlled the cultivating power. And because small plots were inefficient to cultivate

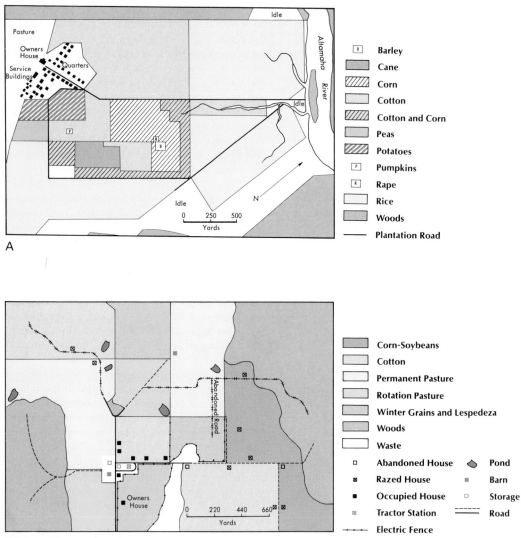

Barley
Cane
Corn
Cotton
Cotton and Corn
Peas
Potatoes
Pumpkins
Rape
Rice
Woods
Plantation Road

Corn-Soybeans
Cotton
Permanent Pasture
Rotation Pasture
Winter Grains and Lespedeza
Woods
Waste
Abandoned House          Pond
Razed House              Barn
Occupied House           Storage
Tractor Station          Road
Electric Fence

FIGURE  **THE SOUTHERN PLANTATION (AFTER PRUNTY, 1955)**
**13-6**

A. HOPETON PLANTATION, GEORGIA, IN 1827

B. NEOPLANTATION TYPE, 1950s

and harvest, mechanization made it necessary to consolidate the fields. "The functional focus of the neo-plantation is the tractor station . . . which also shelters harvesting, cultivating, and accessory machinery, spare parts, repair tools, and fuel. . . . The tractor station is always located close to the manager's or owner's residence, a locational factor suggesting the intimate interrelationship of centralized management and cultivating power" (Prunty, 1955, 485).

Such a "neoplantation" (or large-scale farm)

changed with the decline of cotton in the South, the rise of livestock ranching, and the movement into villages and towns. New techniques greatly reduced the labor force; houses decreased in number in the countryside. Those houses remaining have often been relocated to make room for large fields and now stand along the all-weather roads or in loose settlements. Prunty sees this transformation of the rural settlement pattern as advantageous to the people because the closer grouping of houses in a compact village provides the amenities of life more economically.

In the Old South small farms far outnumbered the plantations. Their owners produced mostly grain and livestock for their own use, with at best a little tobacco as cash crop. At first they lived between the riverine plantation belts, then moved gradually into the piedmont and beyond into the Appalachian ridge and valley country. Here they joined with the southward thrust of Germans and Scotch-Irish from Pennsylvania. The folkways of the Appalachian region still give evidence of these origins and diffusions.

## SYSTEMS OF LAND DIVISION

During colonial times in New England and through much of the Middle Atlantic and the South, parcels of land were defined by "metes and bounds." Starting and ending at a given point, property lines were described by direction and distance of each segment between two points, often using landmarks such as conspicuous trees, rocks, or river shores. As settlement increased and moved inland, the lack of a fixed land allocation policy led to uncertainty of titles and frequently to boundary disputes.

Following independence, the original states ceded to the federal government all claims to land north of the Ohio and east of the Mississippi. Thomas Jefferson, as chairman of a congressional committee charged with the task of devising a uniform method of land division for the Northwest Territory, proposed that it be divided into square blocks of 10 by 10 miles, each "hundred" to be subdivided into lots of 1 square mile. Jefferson may have been inspired by the Roman system of land division in square blocks (each called a *centuria*), or he may have drawn his idea from information held by the committee on the rectangular system used in Holland for reclaimed land.

When Congress in 1785 passed the Land Ordinance, it accepted the proposal of grid lines to be laid out on the cardinal points of the compass, but it substituted for the "hundreds" a system more like that of New England: 6- by 6-mile townships, divided into thirty-six sections of 1 square mile each. That year, a line was surveyed westward from a point of origin where the Ohio River intersects the western boundary of Pennsylvania (Figure 13-5D). From this line surveyors laid out the first "Seven Ranges" of townships. As surveying extended farther into Ohio, the procedure was gradually modified; by the time the Indiana border was crossed, it had become the form used later for all lands to the west. The primary operation was to survey a "base line" and a "principal meridian," the intersection of which served as the point of origin for dividing and numbering townships and sections (Figure 13-5F). As time went on, new base lines and meridians were set up until the Pacific Coast was reached.

Parts of the West settled by the Spanish, French, and English during the colonial era retained their metes and bounds divisions, as in southern California, New Mexico, and some places along the Mississippi. These areas became embedded in the federal rectangular surveys. Texas remained completely outside the federal system, though vast lands were surveyed in rectilineal fashion (Figure 13-5A).

## AMERICAN HOUSE TYPES

European geographers devote much attention to typology of folk housing because the traditional home in each agrarian landscape provides significant clues to cultural dispersions. In comparison, North America appears as a land of relatively recent Occidental settlement, with mobility of inhabitants, with variety of habits, and with spreading standardization modified only by fleeting fashions.

For these reasons American geographers on the whole have paid little attention to regional differences in rural house types. Nevertheless there are significant exceptions. Kniffen in particular vigorously has maintained that the study of American rural dwellings is a fundamental and rewarding segment of geographic inquiry, not only in itself but also because it sheds light on other cultural origins and continuities. The fol-

A West-African house type. This model village near Tamala, northeastern Ghana, follows the building tradition of the large Dagomba tribe that inhabits this area. (A Shell photograph)

lowing paragraphs present in general some of his findings on folk housing in the eastern part of the country (Kniffen, 1965; Kniffen and Glassie, 1966).

Four source areas of rural settlement patterns on the Atlantic Seaboard had quite distinct house types. The early French used two modes of wood construction. In one they made walls of closely set upright posts or square timbers either sunk in the ground or placed on sills, filling the spaces between with clay, mortar, or other materials. Kniffen saw this as "a method of construction which was very old and largely vestigial in western Europe [and which] experienced a brief rejuvenation in timber-rich America." The other

mode, which soon became the dominant one (where not replaced by stone), consisted of horizontal logs above each other—not notched at the corners like the "American" log house but slotted or tenoned into vertical posts at the corners and often also into intermediate ones. This method, still used in Quebec and neighboring areas of the United States, "permits the utilization of short logs and at the same time puts no restrictions on the size of the building" (Kniffen and Glassie, 1966, 51).

Frame construction dominated in New England. Initially the settlers followed the European tradition of building a heavy frame of vertical, horizontal, and diagonal timbers and filling the interstices with various materials (half timbering), but soon they used the abundant wood to cover the frame with horizontal sidings of clapboards (weatherboarding). This evolved into a two-room deep, two-story high, rectangular building with gabled roof and one chimney in the middle or two at the ends. Modifications in architecture followed the fashion of the day.

"Balloon framing" (lighter timbers nailed together) prevailed only after 1850. The frame house replaced the log cabin which, if built at all, served merely as provisional shelter. This type of building spread from New England toward the Great Lakes and beyond, its particular form "at any specific point on the westward trek [following] the principle of Dominance of Contemporary Fashion" (Kniffen, 1965, 558, 560). The New England barn, a frame structure with pitched roof and with walls of upright boards, changed little as it moved west.

The Middle Atlantic area, centering on southeastern Pennsylvania, contributed important elements to the landscape. One of these was the house of horizontal logs notched at the corners. It is thought that the log cabin came from the Swedish settlements on the Delaware in the 1630s. Evidence, however, proves that the English settlers did not adopt the Swedish log construction, but Germans, arriving later, used the plan and it soon was taken over by the Scotch-Irish (Kniffen and Glassie, 1966, 56–59). This prototype of the American log cabin was of one room with a chimney at the end. The nature of notched log construction put limitations on enlarging the dwelling. It required either putting a story on top or extending the size by adding a second log room at the chimney end of the first cabin, resulting in a central-chimney house.

Another and more common procedure was to build two separate log cabins, with gable facing gable, and to roof over the intervening space, like a breezeway. This produced the so-called "dog-trot" or "two-pens-and-a-passage" house. As affluence increased, the log houses were sided with weatherboards. Later frame houses followed the same pattern, enlarged with porches and other appendages. But all reveal their ancestral origin: gables to the end, a depth of only one room, a length of at least two rooms, and usually a height

of two stories. This narrow "I" house, as Kniffen called it, spread from Pennsylvania into the Appalachian valleys and through the entire upland South. It also diffused westward into Ohio, central Indiana, and southern Illinois, forming a distinct contrast to the New England type in the northern parts of these states.

The original barn of the Pennsylvania Dutch (actually German), also built of logs, often resembled the dogtrot house. The planked floor between the two pens—right behind the wide doorway—served for threshing. Kniffen considered this structure the forerunner of the great Pennsylvania forebay barn, located (with its waterwheel) on a stream.

The tidewater South also had a traditional house type which extended from lower Chesapeake Bay all along the coast to the Mississippi. Although half-timbering was common in the early days, frame construction soon became the mode. The basic form, that of the English cottage, was one room deep, two rooms in length, usually $1\frac{1}{2}$ stories high, and with steep roof and exterior end chimneys. Later it became common to add a front porch and a rear shed for a kitchen with its own chimney. During the last third of the eighteenth century "the cottage was raised as much as a full story on brick foundations or piers" (Kniffen, 1965, 565).

As the settlers moved across the continent, they carried along their traditions and house types. Inevitably their cultures mixed together. In many a western town, a single street may have half a dozen or more architectural types, the people living in the houses being of varied backgrounds. The spread of housing styles can be more easily followed in rural areas away from the traffic of today's living.

## VILLAGE AND HOUSE TYPES IN EAST ASIA

### CHINA

Since early times the characteristic Chinese landscape has presented a clear contrast between the city (seat of the district or provincial administration) and the countryside with its closely knit agrarian villages (Figure 13–7). Dispersed farm-

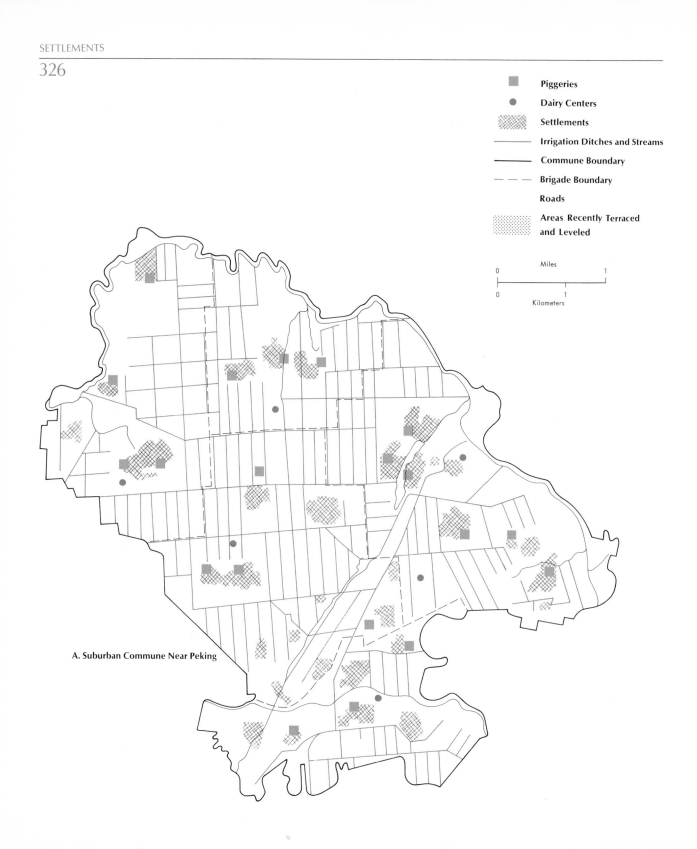

Piggeries

Dairy Centers

Settlements

Irrigation Ditches and Streams

Commune Boundary

Brigade Boundary

Roads

Areas Recently Terraced
and Leveled

Miles

0                                    1

0                1

Kilometers

A. Suburban Commune Near Peking

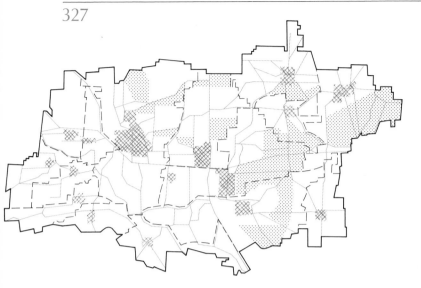

**B. Commune in Shensi Near Sian**

FIGURE **CHINA: TWO AGRICULTURAL COMMUNES (AFTER**
**13-7** **BUCHANAN)**

These two diagrams are based on maps in Buchanan, 1969, 146 and 151. In modern China transformation of the traditional peasant society is accomplished through the commune, which integrates "not only various types of agricultural economy but the whole of rural life; it is the basic cell in the economic and social organism" (Buchanan, K., *The Transformation of the Chinese Earth*, London, 1969, 141).

The work of the suburban commune near Peking (A) is divided between fifty-five production teams grouped in five production brigades. Each brigade area includes a number of villages. The commune has a population of 25,000 and is located some 20 kilometers east of Peking (see Figure 16-3). Production is diversified to meet the varied needs of the capital. Increased irrigation has led to greater intensity of production.

The commune near Sian (B) is in the rolling loess terrain south of the city (see Figure 16-3). Much land has been terraced or leveled and now supports grain cultivation. The zone along a stream, on the west side, is intensively cultivated. Each of the production brigades corresponds to a village in the settlement pattern. The total population is 16,000.

steads do occur, but mainly in dissected uplands where arable land is scarce and fragmented. The larger villages often have a rough grid plan, in former times surrounded by a mud wall. Many villages, however, consist of a double row of houses stretched along a road or levee. The house is usually constructed by raising four corner posts as roof supports and by filling in the walls with tamped earth, sun-dried adobe, or half-fired bricks (Spencer, 1947). This very old building method may have originated in the Middle East. It is well suited to the dry alluvial plains of north China, where timber is scarce.

The Chinese carried this tradition into the subtropical regions they colonized, adopting there the indigenous way of using bamboo wattle and plaster for walls. In northern China the mud walls are left bare, the building and land blending in an all-pervading yellow. In central China an outer layer of mud plaster is often applied; in south China and Szechwan whitewashing is common. The gray tiled or thatched roof slopes down on both sides of a straight ridgepole. The curved roof of tile seems to be a rather late modification, possibly developed in the south. The door is always placed in one of the walls parallel to the ridgeline. The more affluent farmer builds his home on an earth platform or on a raised foundation with wooden floor; the peasant usually has but a dirt-packed floor.

The Chinese, who highly prize privacy in family life, traditionally arranged the components of their homestead around a central courtyard. Many peasants did with less than that, from a single-storied rectangular to an L- or U-shaped dwelling.

JAPAN

Most lowland farmers in Japan live in hamlets or small villages, but in northern Honshu and especially Hokkaido, where farms are larger, dispersed farmsteads are common. The latter also prevail in mountainous regions (Trewartha, 1945, 151–192). The villages may be fairly compact and arranged in a grid of streets and lanes. In the alluvial lowlands they stand on slight elevations amid the paddy fields. Because dry sites are frequently old beach ridges, river levees, volcano margins, or terraces, many villages string out in linear form.

We find a particularly interesting type in the

plains of the Kinki district of southern Japan between Kyoto, Nara, and Osaka (Hall, 1931, 1932). The rural population lives in small villages spaced no more than 1 kilometer apart. The distinctive feature is that each settlement is a rectangular arrangement, probably derived from an old Chinese field system. Around this checkerboard village is a rectangular wall or hedge and moat. Although changed conditions have caused walls and many moats to disappear, the ancient design still is clear. Each farmstead within the village stands as a secluded unit, with the dwelling and various service sheds facing an inner yard. "One sees only continuous lines of walls and closed gates on either side of the narrow street. One receives a peculiar impression of deadness in such settlements, broken only by the voices which can be heard beyond the walls or by a fleeting glance of some individual disappearing through a neighbor's gate" (Hall, 1931, 102).

The light construction of the Japanese house reveals its tropical origin. The use of stilts instead of a continuous foundation gives a clue to ancient cultural ties with Southeast Asia. This traditional home, admirably suited to the long hot and humid summer, provides little comfort during the winter, which is quite marked in southern Honshu and downright cold in the northern parts of the country. Four corner posts resting on stones support the steep-pitched thatched or tiled gable roof. There is no chimney. The floor, on stilts, is up to 1 meter above ground. The walls, placed well under the overhanging eaves, are simply screens between vertical posts and made of mud plaster except on the sunny side of the house; there they are light wooden sliding panels with set-in translucent paper or glass panes. Instead of painting the exterior wood surfaces, the Japanese let them weather to natural grayish tints.

The farmhouse, usually of one story, contains three or more rooms in a rectangular floor plan, with the kitchen at a slightly lower level and under a separate roof. Movable partitions and absence of special furniture make for versatile use of the room space. Charcoal braziers take the place of stoves and fireplaces. The uncluttered interior of the house with its rectilinear lines expresses the artistic quality as well as the economy and simplicity of Japanese traditional life. We

cannot do justice in this general description to the regional variety of Japanese farmhouses (so well described by Nishi, 1967).

## THE STILT HOUSE IN SOUTHEAST ASIA

Houses built above the ground on piles or posts occur in widely separated parts of the world, but nowhere do they characterize such a vast area as in Southeast Asia. They extend from Assam and lower Burma eastwards to the Philippines and Moluccas, suggesting that there must be an ancient unity in this culture realm which in so many other ways is highly diverse (Chapter 8).

Most writers try to explain this mode of construction by pointing to some utilitarian motive. For instance, pile dwellings built out into lake or sea facilitate fishing and, at the same time, give protection against human or animal intruders. On land the space under the house can shelter livestock and fuel, or provide a pleasant workplace shaded from the sun. Most often, the stilt house is considered an adaptation to the humid, warm climate.

None of these reasons explains its widespread presence on well-drained land, in subhumid areas, and on cool mountains. As so often with culture traits, the reason for building on stilts is no longer a rational one; it has become a deeply ingrained custom. Probably its origin lies back among Neolithic peoples of mainland Southeast Asia, including what now is southern China. Perhaps earlier than 2000 B.C. they began migrations east into the island world and north along the China coast toward Japan. In the archipelago these peoples usually are identified as Malaysians or as Indonesians.

The dwellings in Southeast Asia are often more primitive than in Japan. The floors usually are much higher, from 1 to 5 meters above ground. The walls consist of split and plaited bamboo or other fibers, rarely of plaster or wood. Palm thatch usually covers the steep roof. The one-family house now prevails, but in remote parts throughout the mainland and archipelago the communal longhouses point toward a tradition of clan life under one roof (Figure 13–8).

Some areas in Southeast Asia have houses

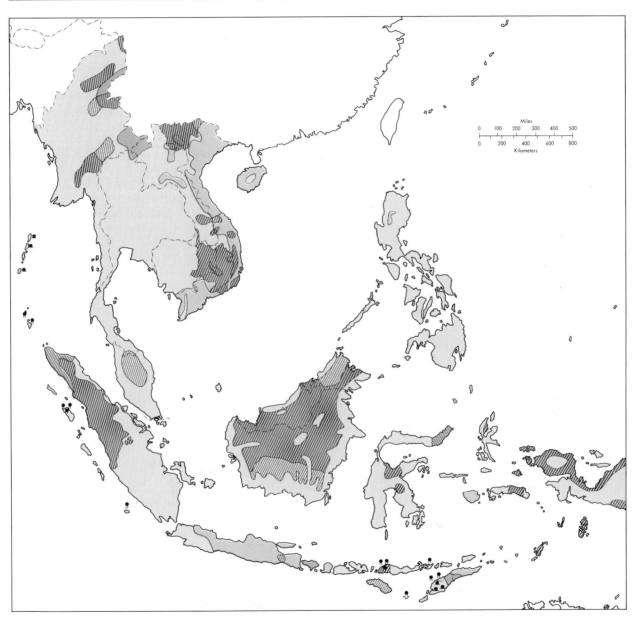

FIGURE SOUTHEAST ASIA: HOUSE TYPES
13-8

🮲 Round Houses on Stilts

🮲 Round Houses on the Ground

Houses on Stilts

Houses on the Ground

Houses on Stilts and on the Ground

Communal Dwelling Houses

Communal and Single Family Houses

Communal Dwelling Houses used in
Former Times

built upon the ground. These indicate the influence of Chinese culture. Long ago the Tonkinese of Indochina took over building traditions and other customs from their Chinese neighbors to the north and carried them along as they migrated southward. There they mixed with earlier peoples and became the Vietnamese. When the French colonists brought them as laborers into the Mekong delta region, the Vietnamese retained their ancient customs, which included building houses in Chinese fashion.

The Javanese too usually build houses on the ground but use shorter supports. It is not clear whether this results from Indian contacts or from scarcity of timber on their densely populated island. However, their granaries for very practical reasons are always built on stilts.

In some remote areas of the archipelago—for instance, on Timor and nearby islands—dwellings also are built on the ground. In other places the folk construct round instead of rectangular houses; these are either on poles or on the ground. All these places are in peripheral locations, suggesting vestiges of an older culture stratum, perhaps of the Australoid peoples who lived there before the seafaring Malaysian invaders took away all lands they found suitable for cultivating rice.

Settlement forms in other parts of the world also pose many intriguing questions. Whether in Southeast Asia or Africa, the United States or Germany, house types tell a fascinating story. The geographer finds significant features in their diffusion and present distribution that help to explain the character of places, not only as they are now but also within the meaningful context of their past.

## CITATIONS AND FURTHER READINGS

Aalen, F. H. A. "Vernacular Architecture of the British Isles," *Yearbook of the Association of Pacific Coast Geographers,* 35 (1973): 27-48.

Brown, R. H. *Historical Geography of the United States,* New York, 1948.

Buchanan, K. *The Transformation of the Chinese Earth,* London, 1969.

Clout, H. D. "Agricultural Plot Consolidation in the Auvergne Region of Central France," *Norsk Geografisk Tidsskrift,* 28 (1974): 181-194.

Darby, H. C. "The Clearing of Woodland in Europe," in Thomas, W. L. (ed.), *Man's Role in Changing the Face of the Earth,* Chicago, 1956, 183-216.

Demangeon, A. "The Origins and Causes of Settlement Types," in Wagner, P. L., and Mikesell, M. W. (eds.), *Readings in Cultural Geography,* Chicago, 1962, 506-516, translated from "La Géographie de l'habitat rurale," *Annales de Géographie,* 36 (1927): 1-23, 97-114.

De Young, J. E. *Village Life in Modern Thailand,* Berkeley, Calif., and Los Angeles, Calif., 1955.

Dickinson, R. E. "Rural Settlements in the German Lands," *Annals of the Association of American Geographers,* 39 (1949): 239-263.

Dodgshon, R. A. "Towards an Understanding and Definition of Runrig: the Evidence for Roxburghshire and Berwickshire," *Transactions of the Institute of British Geographers,* 64 (1975): March, 15-33.

Dussart, F. (ed.). *L'habitat et les paysages ruraux d'Europe,* Les Congrès et Colloques de l'Université de Liège, vol. 58, Liège, 1971.

Evans, E. E. "The Ecology of Peasant Life in Western Europe," in Thomas, W. L. (ed.), *Man's Role in Changing the Face of the Earth,* Chicago, 1956, 217-239.

Francaviglia, R. V. "Mormon Central-Hall Houses in the American West," *Annals of the Association of American Geographers,* 61 (1971): 65-71.

Hall, R. B. "Some Rural Settlement Forms in Japan," *Geographical Review,* 21 (1931): 93-123.

———— "The Yamato Basin, Japan," *Annals of the Association of American Geographers,* 22 (1932): 211-230.

Harris, R. C. *The Seigneurial System in Early Canada. A Geographical Study,* Madison, 1966.

Hart, J. F. *The Look of the Land,* Englewood Cliffs, N.J., 1975.

Hickey, G. C. *Village in Vietnam,* New Haven, Conn., 1964.

Hudson, J. C. "A Location Theory for Rural Settlement," *Annals of the Association of American Geographers,* 59 (1969): 365–381.

Hunter, J. M. "The Social Roots of Dispersed Settlement in Northern Ghana," *Annals of the Association of American Geographers,* 57 (1967): 339–349.

Jackson, R. H., and Layton, R. L. "The Mormon Village: Analysis of a Settlement Type," *Professional Geographer,* 28 (1976): 136–141.

Johnson, H. B. "Rational and Ecological Aspects of the Quarter Section: An Example from Minnesota," *Geographical Review,* 47 (1957): 330–348.

Johnson, J. H. "Studies of Irish Rural Settlement," *Geographical Review,* 48 (1958): 554–565.

Kniffen, F. "The American Covered Bridge," *Geographical Review,* 41 (1951): 114–123.

———— "Folk Housing: Key to Diffusion," *Annals of the Association of American Geographers,* 55 (1965): 549–577.

———— and Glassie, H. "Building in Wood in the Eastern United States: A Time-Place Perspective," *Geographical Review,* 56 (1966): 40–66.

Kovalev, S. A. "Transformations of Rural Settlements in the Soviet Union," *Geoforum,* 9 (1972): 33–45.

Langtvet, O. "The Farm-Seter System in Ausdal, Norway. An Analysis of Change," *Norsk Geografisk Tidsskrift,* 28 (1974): 167–180.

Loeb, E. M., and Broek, J. O. M. "Social Organization and the Long House in Southeast Asia," *American Anthropologist,* 49 (1947): 414–425.

McIntire, E. G. "Changing Patterns of Hopi Indian Settlement," *Annals of the Association of American Geographers,* 61 (1971): 510–521.

Meitzen, A. *Siedlung und Agrarwesen der Westgermanen und Ostgermanen, der Kelten, Römer, Finnen und Slawen,* 3 vols. and atlas, Berlin, 1895.

National Academy of Sciences—National Research Council. *Rural Settlement Patterns in the United States, as illustrated on 100 Topographic Quadrangle Maps,* Publication no. 380, Washington, D.C., 1956.

Nelson, L. *The Mormon Village. A Pattern and Technique of Land Settlement,* Salt Lake City, 1952.

Nishi, M. "Regional Variations in Japanese Farmhouses," *Annals of the Association of American Geographers,* 57 (1967): 239–266.

Pattison, W. D. *Beginnings of the American Rectangular Land Survey System, 1784–1800,* University of Chicago, Department of Geography Research Paper no. 50, Chicago, 1957.

Pfeifer, G. "The Quality of Peasant Living in Central Europe," in Thomas, W. L., Jr. (ed.), *Man's Role in Changing the Face of the Earth,* Chicago, 1956, 240–277.

Prunty, M., Jr. "The Renaissance of the Southern Plantation," *Geographical Review,* 45 (1955): 459–491.

Rapoport, A. *House Form and Culture,* Englewood Cliffs, N.J., 1969.

Scofield, E. "The Origin of Settlement Patterns in Rural New England," *Geographical Review,* 28 (1938): 652–663.

Smith, E. G. "Fragmented Farms in the United States," *Annals of the Association of American Geographers,* 65 (1975): 58–70.

Spencer, J. E. "The Houses of the Chinese," *Geographical Review,* 37 (1947): 254–273.

Szulc, H. "The Development of the Agricultural Landscape of Poland," *Geographia Polonica,* 22 (1972): 85–103.

Trewartha, G. T. "The Unincorporated Hamlet," *Annals of the Association of American Geographers,* 33 (1943): 32–81.

_____ Japan: *A Physical, Cultural and Regional Geography*, Madison, Wisconsin, 1945.

_____ "Types of Rural Settlement in Colonial America," *Geographical Review*, 36 (1946): 568–596.

_____ "Some Regional Characteristics of American Farmsteads," *Annals of the Association of American Geographers*, 38 (1948): 169–225.

Zelinsky, W. "The New England Connecting Barn," *Geographical Review*, 48 (1958): 540–553.

# 14 TOWNS AND CITIES

The city of today contrasts sharply with settlements of the past. The physical and social complexity of the modern metropolis almost defies analysis. Virtually no one seems engaged in providing the few biological necessities of life. Everyone appears to be a small cog in an intricate machine. To classify city workers, census bureaus use detailed lists of jobs that sometimes run to thousands of items. Most people earn a living by continually interchanging goods, skills, and thoughts. Moreover, to accomplish their own tasks and to use the labor of others, modern citizens need not be tied to any one part of town, nor to any particular town. They may reside in one place, work in another, attend school, relax, or vacation in still others.

An increasing part of the earth's inhabitants reside in urban settlements ranging from the small market village to the great metropolis. Over one-third of humanity now dwell in cities and towns, a proportion that increases as people forsake traditional rural ways and as nations modernize their societies. In many countries more than half the population reside in such urban places (Figure 14-1).

From a geographical point of view, this chapter describes towns and cities as distinctive kinds of places which share some general and almost universal characteristics through time and space, but also possess individual, unique features that vary through the ages and from culture to culture. First we note how the concepts of site and situation relate to growth of towns and cities; then we trace the spread of cities from their origin and note differences that developed between various culture realms. Finally we discuss the number of inhabitants and the internal structure, functions, and spatial arrangement of urban places. The next chapter considers trends in city life and especially how the metropolitan region emerges as the dominant type of areal organization in modern society.

## SITE AND SITUATION

*Site* plays a considerable part in shaping the growth of urban places. At the center of modern Paris a small island in the Seine River marks the original settlement, a defensive refuge in time of trouble, a bridge point during peaceful conditions. Close to the heart of Athens rises a distinctive, steep-sided, flat-topped hill, the site first chosen as a natural fortress, later used for a group of temples. Venice too was built for defence, on a waterlogged group of islands, a refuge from mainland marauders to the west. Today this historic city, half in the water, half out, attracts so many visitors that its main business has become tourism. The builders of towns have selected many kinds of sites—islands, hills, gaps between hills, flatland next to deep water, springs—all with qualities to exploit with advantage.

Though all cities have sites, the key to their character and growth is not so much site as *situation,* or *relative location.* Paris lay at the focal point of land- and water-transportation routes; it was also near the center of the emerging nation-state of France. Athens grew because it was the chief town of an important city-state and, in addition, possessed a strategic location relative to the seaways of the eastern Mediterranean. Venice flourished because it had the advantage of both site and situation at the head of the Adriatic Sea, the deepest penetration of the Mediterranean into the landmass of Europe, where land routes converged from west, north, and east.

As towns grow, they often acquire new

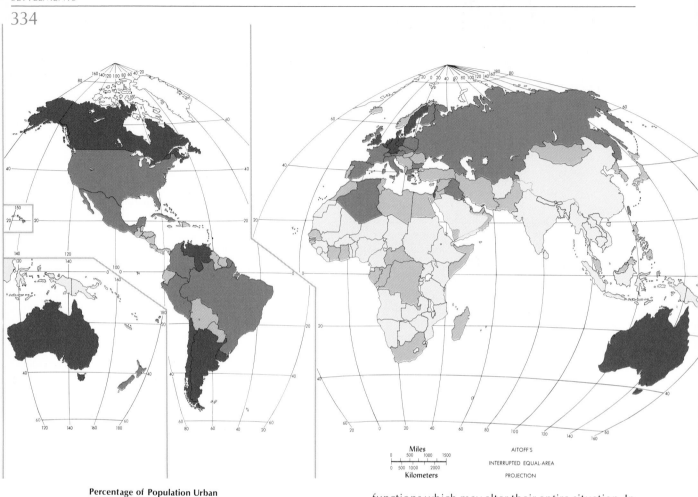

**Percentage of Population Urban**

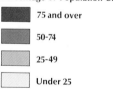

| | |
|---|---|
| ■ | 75 and over |
| ■ | 50-74 |
| ■ | 25-49 |
| □ | Under 25 |

FIGURE **WORLD URBANIZATION OF NATIONAL**
**14-1** **POPULATIONS**

Based on national definitions of "urban population."
These vary greatly between countries: They include,
for example, localities with more than 5,000 inhabitants in Ghana, municipalities with more than 10,000
inhabitants in Greece, places with over 1,000 inhabitants in Australia, and incorporated places with more
than 2,500 inhabitants in the United States. Much of
the data are from Population Reference Bureau, *World
Population Data Sheet, 1976,* Washington D.C., 1976.

functions which may alter their entire situation. In
the recent past, industrialization has reshaped
many places. Numerous towns and cities retain a
distinct core from former times when functions
and life differed. Often civic pride cherishes historic areas like Boston Common, the "old town"
of many European cities, the baroque center of
Warsaw, the ruins of ancient Rome. A case study
of an American city will illustrate more fully these
ideas of site and situation.

## SITE AND SITUATION AT
## PITTSBURGH (FIGURE 14-2)

French and British colonial powers in the middle
eighteenth century both perceived the great strategic value of a small point of land between the
Allegheny and Monongahela rivers where they
join to become the Ohio. They were engaged at

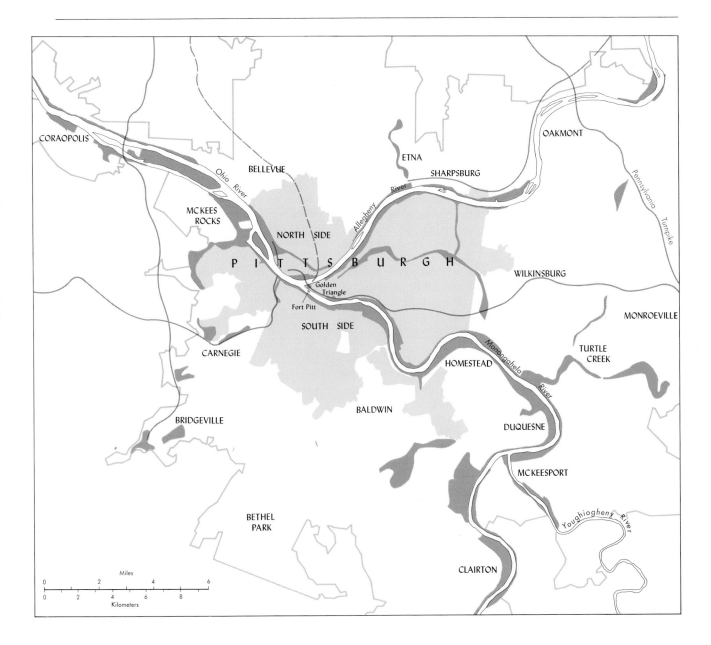

FIGURE
14-2 **PITTSBURGH, PENNSYLVANIA**

The rivers are slightly over 700 feet above sea level.
Iron and steel plants crowd the narrow valleys. The
land away from the rivers is dissected plateau country,
mostly 300 to 500 feet above water level. Low density
residential housing has spread beyond the limits of the
urbanized area.

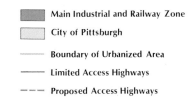

Main Industrial and Railway Zone

City of Pittsburgh

Boundary of Urbanized Area

Limited Access Highways

Proposed Access Highways

the time in imperial rivalry for the North American interior. To protect their fur traders in the Ohio frontier, the French built Fort Duquesne at the confluence of the two rivers, a site easy to defend. This location proved superb for strategic as well as economic purposes because in those days rivers were the main highways.

France lost its North American possessions in the war of 1756–1763 to the British, who themselves set up Fort Pitt on the same site the French had used. Mostly because of its situation astride the head of the Ohio—the one important water route from Pennsylvania to the west—the town of Pittsburgh grew there in the nineteenth century as the Middle West became settled. The population rose from 2,000 in 1800 to 140,000 in 1870.

Fame came to Pittsburgh during the second half of the nineteenth century when its iron and steel industries were established. By then coal resources in the Appalachian Plateau were being discovered and vigorously exploited. Pittsburgh's location—on the waterway system that drained much of the coalfield near the center of the developing manufacturing belt—meant it was the best place to assemble the raw materials for iron and steel production, and a place as good as any other for distributing steel to market. By the first decade of the twentieth century Pittsburgh led by far in iron and steel production. By 1920 the population of its metropolitan area had grown to 1,750,000.

Though Pittsburgh's situation was close to ideal for a great industrial city, its site proved a handicap. Steel mills and blast furnaces operate best on large areas of flat land at water level. Pittsburgh, limited by steep-sided valleys, had little such land. Mills crowded the narrow ledges along the river. The business district centered in the place now known as the Golden Triangle just upstream from the site of the forts. As the city spread along the valleys and up on the plateau, the riverboats and railways still served as principal means of transportation; this made it increasingly difficult to link various parts of the industrial metropolis. The valleys trapped fumes from iron and steel plants. A pall of smoke often covered the low-lying city center. Not until the 1950s, when strict smoke-abatement ordinances were enforced, did the smog disappear.

Today with many competitors in steel production, and steel no longer commanding the heights of the national economy, Pittsburgh nevertheless retains a vital locational advantage—its central position in the United States manufacturing belt. At the same time its situation has diminished in importance with the decline of river transport, with the drop in the ratio of iron ore to coal weight in steel production, and with the rise of the more distant orefields in Minnesota, Canada, and elsewhere.

Twentieth-century living adapts to the rough terrain of Pittsburgh's environs. Widespread use of cars and trucks enables the metropolis to extend over valleys and plateaus many miles in all directions. The tourist appreciates the dramatic site of the central core with its reconstructed Golden Triangle. A sports complex on the North Side, across the Allegheny River, attracts tens of thousands to frequent major sporting events. Industrial and business services find Pittsburgh a convenient location. Though production of industrial materials remains basic to the city's economy, diversification is the trend, a development related to Pittsburgh's accessibility to the populous northeast of the United States.

## THE ORIGIN AND SPREAD OF CITIES

Cities as we know them came into existence at a particular place and time: the Middle East during the fourth millennium B.C. Since then urban ways have spread to many regions. Civilization—from the Latin *civilis* (citizen)—as expressed in urbanism has developed through long periods of time. As conditions changed, new forms emerged and older ones were discarded or became less important. Historical events like the Industrial Revolution added to the wealth of experience that is absorbed but modified to accommodate the new. The modern city as a way of life is a mixture of inheritance, present endeavor, and hopes for the future.

From earliest times cities have shown three fundamental characteristics: *centrality, symbol, and welfare*. These three features complement one another. In a particular historical period or in a specific region one may predominate; however, the others will always be in the background wait-

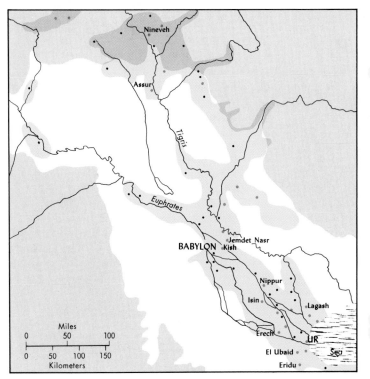

FIGURE
14-3 MESOPOTAMIA: ANCIENT CITIES

Many of these places had been agricultural villages long before they became cities.

- **Urban Places by 3000 B.C.**
- **Urban Places by 2000 B.C.**

 **Approximate Extent of Cultivated Land**

**Land over 1,000 Feet**

ing, as it were, to assert themselves as conditions change.

*Centrality* has two facets. In the wider view the city serves as focus for the surrounding area, the node of circulation, the receiver and sender of goods, and the provider of services. In the city itself, centrality refers to the way various urban activities relate to the center. Both of these aspects of centrality are best explained by the principles of least effort and the division of labor. Centrality

means the efficient location of cities and, within each, the coming together of all functions within the urban core.

A city is the created *symbol* of a society's purposeful integration. Its overall design and the nature of its buildings can show the mission and the power, even the mystery, of the state. Thus, a number of societies have their old walled inner cities: the Kremlin in Moscow, the Forbidden City in Peking, the palace-temple-fortress complex in ancient Middle Eastern cities, the brooding castle and towering church of medieval Europe. All these, with vistas and lines of approach, stress seclusion and aloofness to impress the citizens with the ministry of the rulers and what they represent, rather than the circulation and accessibility so typical of the city as central place. Modern capital cities like Brazilia, and city halls, opera houses, and other public buildings, represent the continued relevance of the symbol idea.

The city also expresses *social welfare*. From this viewpoint a city is a collectivity of effort and behavior designed by its inhabitants to enhance the quality of their lives. Ideally the many parts of the city or city region with their different communities support one another. Competition is replaced by cooperation. Because each group contributes to the common good, each merits the attention of the rest. City life and functions break down when exploitation or discrimination neglects or threatens any sizable segment of the population.

### THE FIRST CITIES

In Chapter 3 we discussed how the development of agriculture permitted increased control over food supplies. In the Middle East lie the Old World beginnings of seed farming and animal herding, of floodplain irrigation—especially along the Tigris and Euphrates—of more efficient storage facilities, and of metalworking to fashion better arms and tools. The peoples of the region created institutions and organizations to meet the ever-growing complexities of life.

About 3500 B.C. in lower Mesopotamia small farm villages became towns with sizable populations (Figure 14-3). They provided services and goods other than food. Each town formed a community, giving its inhabitants the advantages of a richer and safer life. Economic and social relations between urban place and country brought a new kind of areal organization into being. A network of trade developed between towns and with more distant regions.

These urban features did not necessarily originate in cities. Rather, it appears that cities emerged when distinct traits that had evolved in isolation from each other were joined. Some writers refer to this as "the urban implosion," a centripetal coming together of traits within a container (Mumford, 1961, 34). The situation of the Middle East favored this process. As Sjoberg puts it: "The region was a crossroads that facilitated repeated contacts among peoples of divergent cultures for thousands of years. The resulting mixture of alien and indigenous crafts and skills must have made its own contribution to the evolution of the first true cities out of the villages of lower Mesopotamia" (Sjoberg, 1965, 56). Of course, the earliest cities like Ur, Erech, and Lagash could not have emerged without a surplus of food above what the farmers needed. This surplus, however, was not the cause but only a necessary condition for urban life.

Soon the Sumerian townspeople developed methods of writing and record keeping; they invented systems of measuring and reckoning. A class of writers and clerks sprang up. Trade increased, especially in woods and metals. Craftsmen and merchants became important. Armies were formed to guard traders, farms, and granaries as well as to protect the elite and the city against capture and sack. A division of labor is one of the distinctive features of early cities.

Each activity had its own location in its city, its own buildings, its corps of workers. Though the individual towns of Sumer varied in complexity, they shared many similarities. In each there emerged the temple, palace, and fortress center and also areas for granary, market, and crafts. From their dominating home and power base the rulers could oversee and direct the lives of the people. Some of the Sumerian towns had large tiered "towers of Babel" (ziggurats) with a road or walkway in spiral fashion running up the outside. These religious monuments were symbols to remind both town and country folk how important the city and its institutions were to them.

The Mesopotamian plain had a common culture including language, religion, economy, social organization, and technology. Individual cities, however, were independent. The accepted political norm for a city-state consisted of a town with its surrounding farm and wasteland.* Each urban center controlled the economic and social organization of its own tributary area. Considered as a group, the towns were evenly spaced—at distances of about 15 kilometers over the cultivated river plains.

At the end of the third millennium B.C. many towns based on the Mesopotamian model appeared around the eastern Mediterranean, first at Ugarit and Byblos, later at Tyre and Sidon, and on the island of Crete at Knossos and Phaistos. About 2500 B.C. cities evolved in the Indus Valley and also in China, where Anyang was built soon after 2000 B.C. in the Huang Ho valley. Scholars argue whether the city of these eastern regions developed independently; the preponderance of evidence implies diffusion from Mesopotamia, with unique cultural contributions from the regions concerned.

Still later cities grew up around other parts of the Mediterranean, throughout Persia and Central Asia, and in the Ganges Valley of northern India. Many of these places show connections with and direct influence from the Middle East and the eastern Mediterranean. In Egypt cities were few. They served as administrative centers, but unlike the cities of Sumer they failed to develop the central functions of trade and other activities. Most were occupied for relatively short periods and reflected the character of Egypt's court civilization. Tombs for the pharaohs and their families and servants, built as cities of the dead—necropolises—were usually abandoned after the burials. In their design Egyptian towns served as religious symbols.

## CITIES IN CLASSICAL TIMES

The spread of cities westward in the Mediterranean and to Europe is associated with the seafaring Phoenicians and Greeks. As traders and colonizers they linked barbarian Europe with the civilized Middle East. By the second half of the first millennium B.C. the Greeks had achieved a dominant position by their skillful use of sea

*"Political" derives from the Greek word *polis*, "city-state."

Four thousand years ago Mesopotamia was the most densely settled region on earth. Arbela (Erbil) was one of its earliest cities. The mound in the center consists of the flattened remains of many generations of buildings in the ancient city. Around it are built-up areas of a later date. (Photograph—Aerofilms, Ltd.)

power and by actual military victory over the Middle Eastern empires. Fighting between the city-states delayed formation of a Greek League, but they united to defeat the Persian forces. In 334 B.C. Alexander the Great began his campaign against Persia and during the eleven years before he died carried Hellenistic culture into Central Asia and far into the Indian subcontinent.

The Romans inherited Greek culture and an urbanized Mediterranean basin. In turn they carried the city way of life inland and northward into Europe. Like Babylonians and Persians before them, the Romans consciously created a spatial hierarchy of towns to control large areas, thus establishing the city as central place. Rome stood at the head, the imperial capital and largest city of all. At the second level were the provincial capitals and, below these, third and fourth orders of towns, each administering its own area and each subordinate to the next higher authority. Beyond this strict system lay the defense settlements—quite numerous along the Rhine-Danube frontier—and also some specialized market and manufacturing centers, located mainly in the eastern Mediterranean.

While the Romans built hundreds of cities large and small, Rome itself remained the greatest. Its population varied from time to time, but during the second century of the Christian Era it probably had as many as half a million. The empire had few large cities in the West, the most important being settlements along the Mediterranean. There were many in the East, however, including Athens, Alexandria, Antioch, Constantinople, Ctesiphon, and Seleucia.

## CITIES OF MEDIEVAL EUROPE

After Roman authority collapsed in the western empire, administrative activities and long-distance trading ceased there or became less important, and city life declined. Arabs attacked from the south, Vikings from the north, and nomadic horsemen from the eastern steppes. But many cities survived these disruptions, and their way of life continued under the rule of lords and kings and the ecclesiastical hierarchy. Their residences and palaces occupied the sites of former Roman authority. At times the thread of city life became thin, and where it broke, a local, enclosed rural life resumed dominance.

Gradually, from the ninth century onward, trade revived and towns awakened. During this long period lands were colonized, the Islamic threat was turned back, the Vikings and mounted nomads were contained or absorbed. In southern Europe the city reappeared as a flourishing institution, notably at Venice and Genoa and in the merchant centers of northern Italy. Similar developments took place around the shores of the "narrow seas" between the British Isles and the

Low Countries, and into the Baltic, where seamen and artisans combined their skills to increase trade and manufacturing. Soon Ghent, Bruges, Antwerp, and London rivaled Italian cities in size. In late medieval Europe more than 100 cities thrived, most of them concentrated in several regions. Some became large, for example, the French capital Paris; sea and river port cities like Bristol and Köln (Cologne); centers on land routes such as Salzburg, Augsburg, and Nürnburg; the imperial capitals of Vienna and Prague.

Now once again cities dotted Europe, though the number in any one region varied greatly and though they contained a low proportion of the total population. Their character, whether commercial, religious, or administrative, reflected their diverse functions. Where commerce became the prime force, in the zone between the North Sea and Italy, the central market square served as heart of the city's structure. The accumulation of wealth and its expenditure on public buildings such as city halls, churches, and universities made many late medieval towns into symbols of civic pride. Merchants of various north European cities and towns formed the Hanseatic League to gain safety and privileges and power, a confederation that lasted until the seventeenth century. With the perfection of the sailing ship their exploits took them into ever farther seas and in contact with a wide world to be explored.

In late medieval times the city-state again dominated life and political organization as it had before in ancient Greece and in Sumer. On the margins of a commercial region, towns developed of a more colonial, military, or administrative character with garrison buildings and fortresses. Often outsiders built them, as the English did after their conquest of Wales, and the Germans in their penetration of east central Europe.

Medieval towns became partly independent political entities amid the rural feudal society which opposed them. They represented political forces that modified the social order, usually in alliance with the king, whose powers waxed as those of the feudal nobility waned. Royal decree granted charters to the cities to give them a measure of self-government. This alliance between town and crown greatly stimulated the development of modern Western society. In a perceptive article that compares the city in Europe with that in China as a center of change, Murphey argued: "The cities of western Europe have been, at least since the high Middle Ages, centers of intellectual ferment; of economic change; and thus, in time, of opposition to the central authority. They became rebels in nearly every aspect of their institutional life. It was trade (and to a somewhat lesser extent specialized manufacturing) which made them strong enough to maintain their challenge to the established order" (Murphey, 1954, 350).

## DEVELOPMENTS IN
## OTHER CULTURAL REGIONS

Wherever the city remained closely associated with the countryside, as in lands outside western Europe, it did not tend to become a stronghold for political radicals. More often than not it was dedicated to maintaining the status quo. This was especially true in China, as Murphey pointed out: "In China, while the peasant and the countryside were in some respects like the West, the cities' role was fundamentally different. Chinese cities were administrative centers. With few exceptions this function dominated their lives whatever their other bases in trade and manufacturing. Their remarkably consistent, uniform plan, square or rectangular walls surrounding a great cross with gates at each of the four arms, suggests their common administrative creation and their continued expression of this function" (Murphey, 1954, 353) (Figure 14–4). In this sense, we could also draw a parallel between China and the ancient Roman Empire.

In the eastern Mediterranean the city continued its importance during the Dark Ages of western Europe. The Byzantine Empire, with Constantinople its chief city, preserved the ancient heritage. The Arabs in North Africa and in the Middle East carried on this classical civilization and adopted the city as a dominant settlement form. They made Cairo, Alexandria, and Baghdad great centers of Arab culture. A little later they gave rebirth to city life in Seville, Cordoba, Tunis, and Palermo in the western Mediterranean. Arab civilization kept its strong position until the Turks overran it at the end of the Middle Ages. Before then few cities of Christendom—among them Paris and Venice—rivaled Arab cities in size and sophistication.

In India first under the Hindus and later under the Buddhist kings and emperors of two millennia ago, the need for administrative centers stimulated city growth in the Ganges Valley. Social and commercial functions were relatively minor. Indeed, Alexander's conquests may have introduced them when he brought in elements of Greek culture—even built wholly new towns. After the thirteenth century A.D., when Islam dominated society, city life in South Asia became increasingly diverse and complex. In Central Asia the cities along the great trade routes connecting China and the West remained strongly commercial. Many of them, such as Samarkand, Bukhara, and Tashkent, despite the turmoil of invasion, plunder, and cultural clash, grew at times rich and opulent.

Trading towns also developed along sea routes that linked South and East Asia with the Arab world and ultimately with Europe and the Mediterranean. Urban settlements came to life wherever ships stopped along the western coasts of India, on the Arabian littoral, and at the eastern entrances to the Indian Ocean. Thus, even before the modern era cities formed an important element in the fabric of settlement throughout China, India, Central Asia, the Middle East, North Africa, and much of Europe. It is true that in all these regions the rural population still heavily outnumbered urban dwellers. Yet the city, because of its regional administrative power, commerce, and defensive advantage, not only had become firmly entrenched but also had importance far in excess of its share of population.

## URBANIZATION IN
## PRE-COLUMBIAN AMERICA

In the Americas, especially around the Caribbean Sea and in the northern Andes region, towns and some cities were common even while Europe was experiencing its Dark Ages. Empires rose and fell as they competed in warfare, took slaves, exacted tribute, engaged in trade, developed handicrafts, and raised their crops. The Inca Empire became the most powerful state of all because its economy was based on intensive agriculture, terracing, fertilization, and irrigation from mountain streams. Among many crops the peasants grew corn, beans, and sweet potato. This organized agriculture doubtless provided the food surplus to sustain pre-Columbian cities.

**PEKING**

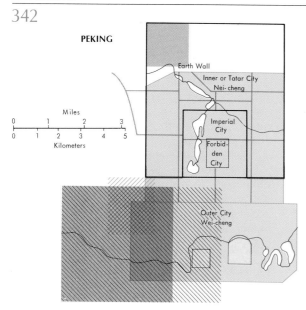

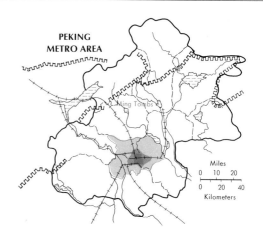

PEKING
METRO AREA

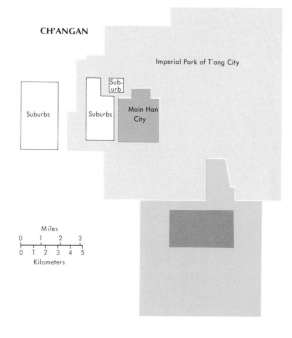

CH'ANGAN

FIGURE
14-4 **PEKING AND CH'ANGAN, CHINA**

A city of importance has occupied the site of Peking since the end of the second millennium B.C. New, planned cities were built by successive dynasties; all were walled and rectangular, often partly overlapping in area. Ch'angan, located in the core area of earliest Chinese civilization near the confluence of the Huang and Wei rivers, became the magnificent capital of the T'ang Dynasty and was the model for the later planning of Peking.

Modern Peking, now once again the capital of China, extends beyond the fifteenth-century walls that bounded the chief city of the Yuan Dynasty. The metropolitan area has a population of between eight and ten million.

The Inca Empire of over 2 million square kilometers reached from Colombia-Ecuador to Chile. The ruler was thought to be divine, a descendant of the sun god. A hierarchy of priests, nobles, peasants, armies, and slaves carried out his absolute will, built roads, fortresses, and remarkable monuments. When Pizarro and his men in 1524 explored the Pacific coast south of Panama, they hurried back to tell the king of Spain of their discovery, especially of the gold. Pizarro came back with the authority and means to conquer and exploit the wealth of the Inca Empire. This he did. Today we may visit the extensive ruins of Chan Chan, coastal capital of Peru, and see what is left of Cuzco, Machu Picchu, and other highland centers.

Before the European invaders came, there existed settlements in Yucatan, Guatemala, and central Mexico that had some features similar to those of Old World cities. For the time being, we

**PEKING**

CHI (1030–221 B.C.) Capital of Yen Kingdom (Chou Dynasty)

YENKING (70 B.C.–220 A.D.) (Han Dynasty)

YUCHOW (118–906) Residence of Military Governors (T'ang Dynasty)

NANKING (937–1013) Southern Capital of Liao Dynasty and YENKING 1013–1153 (Sung Dynasty)

CHUNG-TU (1153–1264) Central Capital of Chin Dynasty

TATU OR CAMBALUC (1267–1367) Capital City with Imperial City and Forbidden City (Yuan Dynasty)

PEKING (1421 to Present) Northern Capital of Ming Dynasty with Inner Tatar City and Outer City

Main Parks of Modern City

Main Streets of Cambaluc

Streams and Lakes of Cambaluc

**PEKING METRO AREA**

Walled City

Modern Built-up Area

Inner Suburbs, Including Farmland

Far Suburbs, Including Satellite Towns

Metropolitan Area Boundary

Great Wall

Reservoirs

**CH'ANGAN**

Capital City of Han Dynasty

Capital City of T'ang Dynasty, Began by Siu Dynasty A.D. 582

City of Ming and Ching Dynasties, Also Modern Sian, on the Site of the Palace and Administrative Inner Cities of the T'ang Capital

must assume that they developed independently. Evidence seems slowly building to the conclusion that there were fleeting connections in ancient times between the urbanized Mediterranean and Middle America.

After a late start the archaeological record is gradually being filled in. The physical remains of the Mayan civilization show many ceremonial temples and other structures surrounded by densely settled farming areas. They also indicate some division of labor among masons, metalworkers, scribes, and priests; but the closely packed towns so characteristic of Old World urbanism do not appear. Instead, the loose aggregations possess both rural and urban features.

In central Mexico a similar development took place, perhaps derived from Mayan examples. Near modern Mexico City the site of Teotihuacan reveals a settlement large enough to contain at least 100,000 people. The city—if we may call it that—was widely spread and had a basic grid street pattern and many ceremonial buildings. No doubt many of its inhabitants farmed the land full time or, more probably, part time.

## CITIES IN THE MODERN ERA

When Europeans left their homelands for colonies and empires in far parts of the world, they built towns where there were none or converted the settlements of other people to their own uses, primarily trade and defense. In the Orient they placed their fort overlooking the trading town, often a coastal port. In Asia, Africa, and Latin America many a town has a long European tradition added to that of the indigenous groups. Around the eastern and western exits from the Indian Ocean and along the coasts of India, the Arab element was strong. The older parts of towns from Mombasa and Dar-es-Salaam to Goa and Malacca show their variegated past in the cosmopolitan air of their temples, mosques, and churches, palaces, castles, and homes, markets, bazaars, and business quarters (Figure 14-5).

As Europeans took firm political control in foreign areas, many towns became their administrative centers. This was especially true in India's subcontinent, where the apparatus of British imperial rule attached military and administrative

FIGURE
14-5

IBADAN, NIGERIA

The Yoruba people of southwestern Nigeria have a long tradition of urban life, towns having an important role in their culture. Ibadan has a large and densely settled old core where most of the city's inhabitants live. Attached to this area, but partly within the ruined town walls, are administrative, governmental, residential, and commercial zones begun during the colonial era. The total population is over half a million. After Mitchell, J. C., "Yoruba Towns," in Barbour, K. M., and Prothero R. M. (eds.), *Essays on African Population*, London, 1961, 279–302.

| | Yoruba Old City |
| --- | --- |
| ∿∿∿∿ | City Walls (Now Ruined) |
| | Recent Built-up Area |
| | Administrative, Government, Military, Mission, School, and Commercial Areas |

quarters to the already mixed heritage. In other cases, the colonizers founded new cities the better to serve their imperial purposes. Among these cities were Calcutta at the head of the Bay of Bengal, Saigon in southern Vietnam, and Batavia (now Djakarta) in Indonesia. The cities in the

New World, built by the Spanish and Portuguese, developed strong administrative functions, reflecting the centralized nature of imperial rule. In North America during the colonial era the main towns all were ports: Charleston, Baltimore, Philadelphia, New York, Boston, Salem, Québec, and Montréal. With the exception of Québec, their administrative element was less evident than in the Spanish cities.

Overseas enterprise brought rapid growth to many of Europe's port cities like Seville, Lisbon, Bordeaux, Bristol, Liverpool, and Amsterdam. When these cities combined port with capital, as in the case of London, they became particularly large. Their only rivals were inland capitals of centralized states. Paris was among the big ones, like London having over half a million inhabitants by the end of the seventeenth century. Madrid, chosen in the sixteenth century as capital of Spain because of its central location, grew within a few decades from a small town to a large city. In central and eastern Europe the disparity between capitals and other towns was also marked, partly because the lesser towns had little long-distance trade. Within their regions Moscow, Kiev, and Prague were unequaled in size. In all these cases we see the development of "primate cities," a term Mark Jefferson introduced (Jefferson, 1939).

The importance of the big cities should not make us overlook local centers and humbler market towns. In Europe and its overseas extensions, especially in North America, the small town represents a vital link in the settlement hierarchy between rural places and greater cities. As the economy became more commercialized and the mass of population wealthier, small towns increased in number and became more secure as functional bases. In many regions clearly marked levels of cities emerged with time; towns of the same size offered similar services for their well-defined tributary areas. In most of these instances, whether in Europe or North America, widely spread urban systems performed economic, administrative, religious, and other activities that became structured in hierarchical order and in spatial pattern.

## THE INDUSTRIAL CITY
Machine-driven large-scale manufacturing added a new dimension to the urban life of the Occi-

Edinburgh, the capital of Scotland. A lake bed, now drained and occupied by railway stations and tracks, separates the old city from the Georgian "New Town" which was laid out on the gridiron plan in the late eighteenth century. The picturesque old city is tightly built on a narrow ridge between Holyrood palace (left background of picture) and the Castle (not shown, to the right). Salisbury Crag rises in the distance. Famous Princes Street, the elegant promenade facing the ravine and the medieval city, forms the inner edge of the New Town. (Photograph—Aerofilms and Aero Pictorial Ltd.)

dental world. The process set in at different times in different countries. In Britain industrial centers like Birmingham, Manchester, and Sheffield already had become sizable towns by the early nineteenth century.

At that time coal was king, commanding the location of industry. Towns on or near coalfields became surrounded by mine shafts, slag heaps, mills, factories, railroads, and—amid these—row upon row of grimy workers' houses. As these towns merged, they formed industrial agglomerations, notably on the coalfields of central and northern England, Sambre-Meuse, and the Ruhr. In most of these regions a town hierarchy already existed; now a clutter of new urban features was superimposed upon it. These manufacturing districts lacked the marked nuclear form so typical of the historic city. Instead, they presented a haphazard conglomeration of industrial, commercial, and residential units, enclosing surviving fragments of the former rural landscape.

Some already existing large towns—most notably the great capitals—added an industrial component to their functions. They grew to be chief markets of their countries, the centers of transportation systems. Capitals such as London, Paris, Brussels, Berlin, Budapest and Moscow became as well the largest single industrial cities. In North America a similar process concentrated manufacturing in major cities, including the ports of New York, Philadelphia, and Montréal, and also on the coalfields and transportation points such as Pittsburgh and Chicago.

Industrial cities outside Europe and North America were mainly developed with Western capital. A number of port towns which European maritime connections had expanded in Asia and in Latin America now added manufacturing industries, using local materials and labor. Largest of these were Shanghai, Bombay, Calcutta, and Buenos Aires. The Japanese, inspired by Western example, expanded their own industry. Their southern port cities—Yokohama-Tokyo and Kobe-Osaka—became centers for diversified industry. The coal mines of Kyushu attracted iron- and steelmaking. Age-old agrarian economies changed with the impact of this foreign influence and the challenge of world markets.

## THE SERVICE CENTER

With industrialism came an ever-increasing complexity of organization in commerce, banking, transportation, communication, and government services. As living standards rose, more people became a market for goods and services. Before, they had to be content with the bare necessities of life, and only a few could afford luxuries. The modern city offers in enormous quantities a wide range of products from foods and automobiles to entertainment and fashions. These services offered to the ordinary individual were so many that they provided employment, even rivaling manufacturing. In some countries the service centers contribute a share even greater than that of industry to the national wealth. In the United States such services utilized 61 percent of the nonagricultural labor force in 1970 as compared with 48 percent in 1940 and 26 percent in 1900.

On the whole, today the services are provided for urban populations. Small towns, even the market centers in purely rural areas, look to larger towns for certain needs; these in turn depend on larger cities for specialized services. This hierarchy is a marked feature of the urban structure in modernized countries. As one proceeds up through the different size levels from town to city, the quantity and variety of available goods and services increase.

# FOUR FACETS OF CONTEMPORARY CITIES

## NUMBERS OF INHABITANTS

In our statistically minded age, lists of the world's great cities, with population numbers attached, attract much interest (see Table 15–1). Often signs along the highways announce a town's name and population. In most encyclopedias the first piece of information given about a place is its number of inhabitants.

In a general way the terms indicating places suggest their size: hamlet (from the old Germanic *ham* for a group of buildings) and village (from Latin *villa*, meaning a dwelling in the country) imply rural settlements. Town (from Germanic *tun*, an enclosed area) usually connotes a smaller urban center than city (French *cité* from Latin *civitas*). Metropolis literally means mother city (from the Greek *meter* and *polis*) and suggests an important central city. Megalopolis (the Greek *megale* means great) is a good label for the modern giant-city complex. There is no general agreement, however, on the size limits that mark town from city and city from metropolis.

Regardless of whether an urban place is a town or large city, how shall we calculate its population? Who will be included and who left out? The answers involve more than a simple counting of heads; they are important for city planning, providing various services, redrawing boundaries, and including or excluding individual towns from certain political status.

What is "New York"? Its population? In 1973, according to the U.S. Bureau of the Census, New York City— consisting of Manhattan, Bronx, Kings, Queens, and Richmond counties—had in round figures 7.6 million inhabitants. But this is only the central part of the massive concentration. The New York Standard Metropolitan Statistical Area (SMSA), which includes a further four counties, numbers 9.7 million. However, this wider region does not take in the nearby constellations of central cities and suburbs in New Jersey, Long Island, and Connecticut. These cover Newark SMSA and Nassau and Suffolk SMSA, each with over 2 million inhabitants, and add eleven more counties. The total population of this vast urbanized region was 17.3 million in 1973.

Obviously there are many ways of defining a city. At one extreme is Manhattan Island, nerve center of the city region and a great employer of people. At the other extreme and beyond the definitions given above, New York forms but a part of Megalopolis, the urbanized seaboard of the northeast United States. Which definition to use must be a matter of informed choice depending on one's aims.

For comparing urban places within a single country, one can use a standard definition based on groupings of local government units that conform to certain criteria. The U.S. Bureau of the Census defines "urbanized area" as a contiguous built-up area with a certain population density. The SMSA concept has less use for comparative purposes, partly because it is based on the county—which rarely coincides with the settlement concentrations—and partly because townships instead of counties are used in New England, where the urban mesh is closer than in other parts of the country. On the other hand the SMSA makes it easier to note the variables from one census to another.

Comparisons between different countries become even more difficult because their statistical areas and governmental units are organized on another basis. The character of urban and rural settlement varies greatly. Density criteria used in the United States may not apply at all to other lands.

Unless the data for defining the population of an individual town are explicitly stated, it is impossible to determine accurately what percentage of a country's inhabitants are urban. Though most countries have a legal definition as to what constitutes an urban place, each has its own meaning and it may not agree with that of others. In the United States the census classifies as "urban" all incorporated places with 2,500 or more inhabitants; those in unincorporated territory and in incorporated places below 2,500 are "rural."

England considers as "urban" all places with the governmental status of boroughs and urban districts, regardless of the population number. In Japan all municipalities with over 30,000 are "urban." Figure 14-1 is based on such statistics with varying national definitions of "urban." It might be possible to make a map showing the proportion of national populations living in settlements above a specific size level, but this also would have its drawbacks. Many countries have large agricultural villages with thousands of inhabitants, while many modernized societies have places that number as few as 100, yet properly could be called urban.

Population counts are far from accurate in some lands. Moreover, rapid urbanization and high internal migrations may quickly make an accurate census out of date. Administrative units often publish information that fails to reflect the actual extent of urban places. This holds true not only for large cities which straddle many political units but also for small urban centers that may not have any political status. Finally, political boundaries once defined are slow to change and usually lag behind the socioeconomic realities of a settlement complex.

The proportion of people living in towns of different sizes varies from country to country. In modernized states towns grow in most of the size classes. Disregarding problems of boundary definition, we note that in the United States since 1900 the proportion of population living in size classes above 5,000 has increased but that below 5,000 has decreased. According to the 1970 census, cities with over 100,000 inhabitants represent 28 percent of the population; 69 percent live in the SMSAs. In England and Wales even greater proportions live in cities and over half in urban areas with more than 100,000.

At the other end of the scale are countries like India, where four-fifths of the people live in places with less than 5,000. A further 10 percent are in centers with between 5,000 and 20,000, though many of these are actually farm villages. Only 8 percent dwell in cities numbering over 100,000.

Similar differences between highly urbanized and newly urbanizing countries become evident if towns are ranked by size and plotted on a graph. Figure 14-6 compares the United States and India in this respect. The deeper curve of the

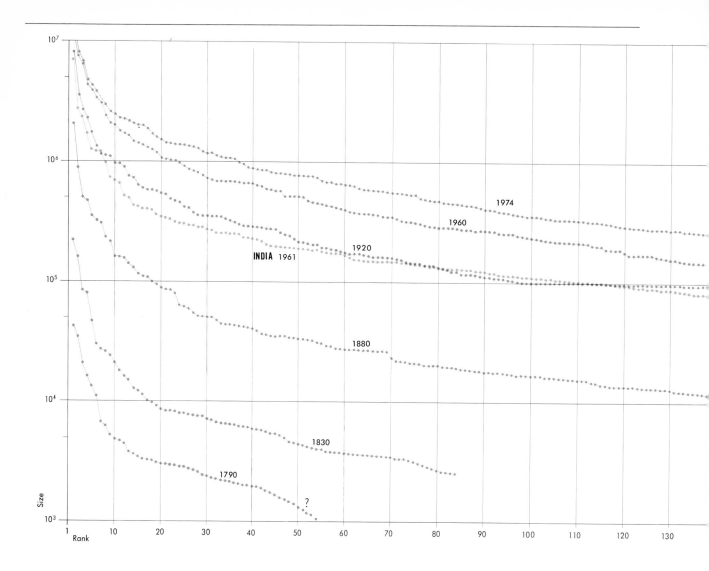

FIGURE **UNITED STATES AND INDIA: RANKS AND SIZES OF**
**14-6** CITIES

On this graph the 140 largest cities of the United
States (1790 to 1970) and the 140 largest cities of India
(1961) are ranked by population size and plotted by
semilogarithmic scale. Data for the United States supplied by J. R. Borchert and F. Lukermann. Data for
India from *Census of India, 1961,* Paper 1 of *Final Pop-*
*ulation Totals,* 1962.

Indian line indicates the relative lack of middle-
sized cities. The decreasing depth of the United
States curve since 1790, during the process of
urbanization, illustrates the same point. When the
automobile replaced the horse and buggy, the
need dwindled for a local town in favor of the
larger center with greater facilities and wider
choice of goods and services.

INTERNAL STRUCTURE OF TOWNS
Each city is an individual place with its own site
and situation, its own population, its own history

A.

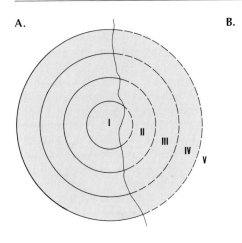

B.

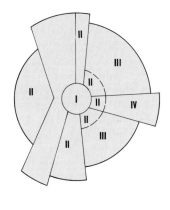

C.

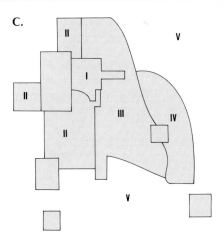

FIGURE **THEORIES OF URBAN STRUCTURE AND GROWTH**
**14-7**

**A. CONCENTRIC**
After a map by Burgess in Park, R. E., Burgess, E. W., and Mackenzie, R. D. (eds.), *The City,* Chicago, 1925. The diagram refers to Chicago in the 1920s.

**B. SECTOR**
After Hoyt, H., *The Structure and Growth of Residential Neighborhoods in American Cities,* Washington, D.C., 1939.

**C. MULTIPLE NUCLEI**
After Harris, C. D., and Ullman, E. L., "The Nature of Cities," *Annals of the American Academy of Political and Social Science,* 242 (1945): 7–17.

I  Central Business District
II  Low-class Residential
III  Medium-class Residential
IV  High-class Residential
V  Commuters' Zone

of development and change, and its own activities. These express themselves in the internal physical structure, comprising road and street pattern, and in the location as well as the nature of different kinds of facilities: retail stores, wholesale warehouses, industrial plants, offices, residences, railroads, airports, parks. But each place, unique in itself, also possesses certain broad elements that repeat themselves from town to town.

To generalize about these common elements, we use three well-known theories; each

illustrates an important feature (Figure 14–7). The *concentric ring* model emphasizes the central zone and how distance from it influences land use and social use of space. The *sector* thesis also considers the city core but in terms of transportation avenues that lead to and from it. The *multiple nuclei* model shows the relationship of the different parts of the city to each other and to the city center.

Small towns—many of them "central places" or, in older terminology, "market towns"—have a distinctive feature in common: the business district. Here most citizens work, providing services for country and town dwellers. Closely packed shops and offices, mutually interdependent, offer economy of movement to the served and servers alike. The amount of floor space is increased by having a greater area of buildings in relation to the lot size than in other parts of town.

The larger the town, the more complex its internal structure. After studying many European and American cases, Dickinson made a basic division into four zones. The *central zone* is "the hub of the city and includes the older town and its pre-modern extensions." Roads and railways converge on it, causing traffic congestion. Competition for land leads to a heavily built-up condition that gradually expands into the area around it. The central zone "includes the retail, wholesale, administrative, commercial, and business districts; markets, hotels, residential enclaves for both the elite and the poor; and large public buildings that cater for the community as a whole" (Dickinson, 1964, 163). Buildings in this zone quickly become obsolete, at times necessitating reconstruction and rearrangement of uses. Detailed study reveals that the population constantly is changing. On working days people fill the zone, but at night and on the weekend it becomes almost empty except for hotel and entertainment areas.

The *middle zone* developed mostly in the late nineteenth and early twentieth centuries. Its row houses, tenements, and frame houses contain dense populations. Mixed with housing are small industrial plants, shopping areas, schools, churches, wasteland, and derelict buildings. Industrial districts flank the main transportation lines of land and water. Actually, the middle zone is a conglomerate of diverse land uses. It contains many blighted neighborhoods and it houses most of the low-income groups. These so-called "gray areas" present a major problem in urban reconstruction.

The *outer zone* was first settled by wealthy people in the late nineteenth century. The spread of mass transportation since World War I has built it up fully. Wider-spaced residences keep these districts at a much lower density than those in the inner zone. Parks, shopping areas, and newer industrial plants interrupt the housing areas.

The *urban fringe* beyond the outer zone spreads into the countryside along highways and commuter rail lines. New housing often congregates around old villages or market towns. Open lands and woodlots still remain among the newly built-up areas.

The establishment of a factory or a supermarket complex can trigger settlement in an open area. Real estate developments convert the countryside into urban sprawl and commuter housing. Changing social needs and ease of transportation are breaking down the old rural-urban distinctions. The population in rural areas of some Western countries grows faster than that in cities. Obviously the Dickinson four-zone model remains general in its application to specific cases.

In the United States, for example, most cities have a basic grid plan with straight streets intersecting each other at right angles. As the city grew, the grid was superimposed upon the old highways, often paralleled by railways which still form main industrial axis lines to the center. The American city in sheer areal size and extended suburban fringe usually exceeds its European counterpart.

Cities on the European continent show many distinctive features. The medieval heart, often with narrow and winding streets, is contained within a ring road (French *boulevard,* related to bulwark; German *Ringstrasse*), once the site of the old wall or fortifications, now dismantled (Figure 14–8). The city outside this core was created in the nineteenth and twentieth centuries. Railway stations and industrial areas that developed along existing roads on the edge of the old town, together with the ring road, determined the later transportation net, giving the whole a radial-concentric pattern.

Because few British towns had walls, they lack the well-defined structure found in so many continental cities. In the modern age expanding cities in Britain engulf the dense settlement of towns and villages from the past. This gives many urbanized areas multiple nuclei.

In Western Europe the private car is virtually a universal possession. Widely spread suburbs of the American type are unusual, however, and may never become common. Land is too precious. Governmental planning agencies generally hold strict control of the expansion within an already heavy mesh of settlement.

Cities in other cultural regions often differ radically from their Western counterparts. Other values and other ways of living give towns other roles. In Asia and Africa—and to a lesser extent in Latin America—city populations remain poor and the masses lack permanent, well-paying jobs. Many come from rural areas and lack the skills to cope with the city. Their poor quarters consist of shacks huddled together wherever there is space, usually at the outskirts or in the densely populated center. Third world cities especially face overwhelming problems; national and local governments lack the resources to care for their exploding populations. Under such conditions transportation systems, even by bus, may be too expensive to use. Markets spread throughout the city instead of being concentrated in distinctive shopping districts. The residential districts of the more affluent are usually in distinct sectors, often within walls to keep out the poor.

**FIGURE 14-8**  **PARIS: CENTRAL AREA**

The modern metropolis extends far beyond the border
of the map. See also Figure 15–9.

| | | | |
|---|---|---|---|
| Cité | Industrial Zone | Walls and Fortifications |
| Administration | Open Spaces | Inner Boulevard |
| Zone des Affaires | Area Served by Metro System | Railroad Terminals |
| Quartier Latin | Bridge | |

During the colonial era, Europeans directed their business, governmental, and military operations from the main towns. The newly independent national states have inherited these capitals and large cities, complete with central business districts, government quarters, military "cantonments," and "civil lines" where Europeans lived. The needs of the new nation may not fit this colonial urban structure. The inflow of folk moving in from the countryside increases tensions between the indigenous rural tradition and the discipline of modern city life. It will take time before these strains will ease and the city be fashioned to express more truly the culture of the emerging nation.

## URBAN FUNCTIONS

The idea that the city performs certain functions is the essence of its definition. Whatever is done in a city relates it to the surrounding area and to other urban settlements in the same web. Saying "this city does this (or that)" reduces the complex of activities, buildings, and people with all their interrelationships, to a single term. Pittsburgh is a "steel town," Minneapolis the "mill city," Antwerp a port, Peking the capital of China. Although rather more inclusive in its connotation, "market town" indicates the same directness of purpose.

Central places provide services for the surrounding country (tributary area or hinterland), but specialized towns provide for wider regions. A city may manufacture goods or offer services to a whole nation. Some cities proudly announce that they are the "such and such" capital. Washington is the nation's capital; Chicago the railroad hub; Detroit the center of the automotive industry; Hibbing, Minnesota, the iron-ore capital.

A number of geographers have proposed methods for classifying cities by their functions, especially by concentrating on activities that dominate and distinguish one town from another. Harris, in his classification of American cities, used various statistical criteria to define such types as manufacturing, wholesale, retail, transportation, and diversified. He then placed each city, according to its employment structure, into the proper category indicating its function (Harris, 1943).

The idea that single city functions are re-

sponsible for the life of the community derives from the analogy that cities are organs of the national body and that each performs its own distinctive task. This notion became fashionable some decades ago when many social scientists used analogies from biological sciences to describe and explain the phenomena that interested them.

More recently a theory prevailed, based on concepts from physics, that cities are centers of gravity, exerting attraction on people and things in the surrounding field. In reality, of course, cities do not actually "do" anything, though writers today constantly use simple functional terms to describe them. The danger of labeling cities by a single function is that this obscures the multifunctional character of most of them.

Certain classifications try to take into account both multiplicity and specialization of activities (Webb, 1959). Two basic urban types emerge from these discussions. One type is the town which to a high degree maintains its association with a particular piece of local territory. It funnels goods and services from the outside world to its hinterland and from it also collects and sends out regional products. Whether large or small, this is the typical central place or market town.

The other urban type is that which offers some special services or goods. Usually such a town can be identified by the large proportion of its work force engaged in a certain activity. For example, a single firm may dominate urban employment in a small town that concentrates on mining, on food processing, or on being a railroad division point. Large towns may also specialize, particularly as manufacturing centers. Other cities may be centers for insurance interests, public administration, or higher education. In fact, most cities have a specialized activity plus the general function of central place—a characteristic particularly evident within the great industrial belts of Europe and North America. Certain functions develop strongly during the change to modernization when better transportation systems link up with the settlement fabric.

## SPATIAL ARRANGEMENT

The above statement that central places serve their surrounding areas needs closer inspection. It

353

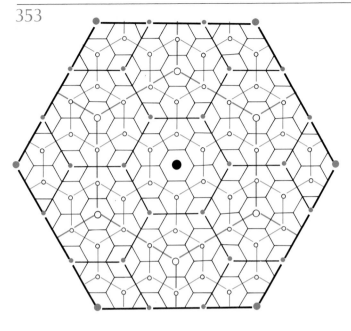

FIGURE **CENTRAL-PLACE SYSTEM**
**14-9**

The basis of the system is the small market town, represented by the small open circles. Six of these surround each higher order center, and so on up to the regional capital, represented by the black dot. After Christaller, W., *Diezentralen Orte in Süddeutschland,* Jena, 1933. English translation by C. Baskin, New York, 1966.

points up some general principles that affect the nature and spacing of urban settlements. The theoretical concept of a spatial hierarchy of central places, formulated by Walter Christaller in 1933, has since been developed in a multitude of studies, especially in Sweden and the United States (Figure 14-9). The analysis of spatial arrangement applies particularly to the city as an economic entity because, as already noted, centrality is based on the principle of least effort. Therefore, most studies of central places deal with the economic determinants of city size and spacing.

People tend to spend as little time and effort as possible in using urban services. Usually they obtain what they need from the nearest center. Naturally their wants, and the time and distance they will travel to satisfy them, vary widely. They expect to find a grocery shop and

drugstore in every neighborhood but travel willingly a long distance for help from a medical specialist.

We can presume that each service needs a minimum number of customers to maintain itself. This minimum level is called the threshold. The thresholds are low for services of common requirement and convenience, such as food stores and gasoline stations. They are much higher for more specialized services such as a hospital, a stock brokerage, or a junior college.

If only thresholds mattered, services of various kinds might lie widely scattered, each in the center of its customer circle. But this is not so, for a number of reasons. First, services must be accessible and, thus, located on roads, railways, and other means of transportation. Second, transients as well as residents use the services, reinforcing the factor of accessibility. Third, mutual advantage draws services together because each unit benefits from the customers who are attracted by the interdependence and diversity in one location. As a result, services agglomerate at specific locations, forming clusters of different sizes. The smallest centers are closely spaced and have only a few facilities, with very low thresholds. Larger centers are farther apart and offer services with higher thresholds, as well as more of those at the lower end of the scale. In this way a hierarchy of service centers emerges. "Centers of each higher order group perform all the functions of lower order centers plus a group of central functions that differentiates them from and sets them above the lower order. A consequence is a 'nesting' pattern of lower order trade areas within the trade area of higher order centers, plus a hierarchy of routes joining the centers" (Berry and Pred, 1961, 4).

Many regions have been studied to discover whether or not an urban hierarchy exists. Most research has been done on small towns where the issues involved are clearer and where urban functions serve the immediate surroundings. The same notions of spatial arrangement also apply to large cities and extensive regions. The centrality of Paris and of Madrid relative to their national territories obviously stimulated their growth. Chicago's raison d'être and its rise to urban dominance are a response to its site as well as its relative location on the south shore of Lake Michigan, which

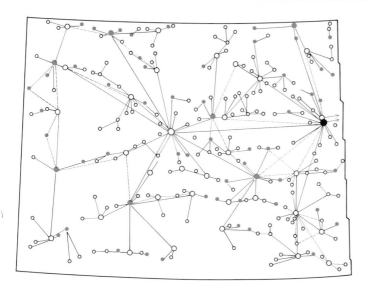

| Level in Hierarchy | Population (Range) | Services (Range) |
|---|---|---|
| ● Provincial City | 24,355 | |
| ○ City | 7,458 | 156 |
| ● Greater Town | 670-1,938 | 37-78 |
| ○ Town | 218-728 | 13-45 |
| • Village | 60-388 | 8-29 |
| ○ Hamlet | 3-196 | 2-13 |

FIGURE
**14-10** SOUTHWESTERN SASKATCHEWAN: CENTRAL-PLACE SYSTEM

The "provincial city" is Moose Jaw; the "city" is Swift Current. The dashed lines indicate partial service function. Based on Royal Commission on Agriculture and Rural Life, Service Centers, Report no. 12, Regina, 1957, and on a map in Lukermann, F. E., "The Role of Theory in Geographical Enquiry," *Professional Geographer*, 13.2 (1961): 1-6.

reaches deeply into the interior of the United States. Early road and rail routes were forced to go around the lake. With the lake waterway they converged on Chicago, bringing industrial and other materials from local and world ports. Later taking advantage of Chicago's centrality, air lines and highways joined with the railroads to make Chicago the chief transportation hub of the country.

Centrality influences the size and distribution of cities according to density of population and to the technical and economic level of society. For example, many eastern areas in the United States were settled when riverboat and horse-drawn wagon provided the main means of transportation, apart from foot travel. When railroads added new lines of long-distance travel, the horse and buggy continued to serve in the interstices. Most of the Midwest and the Great Plains were

settled during this stage of technology. Central places had to be relatively close together so farmers could journey to town and home again the same day. Figure 14–10 shows a part of the Canadian prairie province of Saskatchewan that was settled during the railroad and horse-wagon era. In those days rails crossed the land at regular intervals so that no farming district was more than a day's journey away, under normal weather conditions. Service centers of different sizes strung along the railways still form an areal hierarchy of towns.

Few regions have a pattern as regular as that on the prairies. The heavily populated manufacturing parts of eastern North America and western Europe show a very different picture. Factors such as sources of power, raw materials, and sale of specialized goods over a widespread market determine location of industries. Manufacturing towns, therefore, do not adhere to the principles that govern the central-place arrangement. Neither do resort, mining, and garrison towns, or any other urban places related to particular advantages of site. Nevertheless, they usually include the functions of central places by serving their own populations rather than those outside.

It becomes clear, then, that the use of the

central-place model has limitations. Theorists in the field recognize the plan as a gross oversimplification, an attempt to ignore some important variables to permit the influence of others to be better understood. It assumes a market in which buyers and sellers have an essentially free economy. Such conditions do not apply to much of the world—historically or today. Such a model does not fit feudal societies, those centrally planned, nor even the mixed economy of our own. Moreover, the model does not show the lay of the land, the climatic differences, distribution and density of population, location of earlier settlements, or communication lines. These and other variables of real "filled" space are omitted. The sheer logic of the central-place model clarifies thought and provides a means to understand a part of reality. Nevertheless, it is not in itself the end of geographic inquiry.

Transportation and communication serve as vital forces in developing and operating a network of central places. Within our time, automobiles and trucks have increased the efficiency of road transportation; telephone, radio, and television expand communication by electronic means. These radical changes upset the balance of area and distance on which the former central-place system depended. Many small services cannot compete with those in larger towns that offer greater variety and quantity. Relics of once-thriving small villages and hamlets dot the North American Midwest. In contrast, many a small town and village of southern New England has been revitalized by close contact with the expanding orbit of the Atlantic seaboard Megalopolis: they become residences for commuters and weekend or summer homes for vacationers.

Thus, late-twentieth-century man with his greatly increased mobility has altered the spatial relationships that were forged between settlements of a different transportation age. Some central places waste away. Others come to life. More tenuous associations replace the old strong ones between a particular piece of rural territory and a specific town. In the United States and in other countries with well-developed commercial economies and good communication systems, towns no longer have exclusive tributary areas. Urban places are used by people from near and far. Individuals no longer live out their lives in a single urban context. How far this process of spatial disassociation will go, time alone can tell.

## CITATIONS AND FURTHER READINGS

Adams, J. S. "Residential Structure of Midwestern Cities," *Annals of the Association of American Geographers,* 60 (1970): 37–62.

Adams, R. M. *The Evolution of Urban Society: Early Mesopotamia and Pre-Hispanic Mexico,* Chicago, 1966.

Armen, G. "A Classification of Cities and City Regions in England and Wales, 1966," *Regional Studies,* 6 (1972): 149–182.

Aurousseau, M. "The Distribution of Population: A Constructive Problem," *Geographical Review,* 11 (1921): 563–593.

Berry, B. J. L. *Geography of Market Centers and Retail Distribution,* Englewood Cliffs, N.J., 1967.

———— and Pred, A. *Central Place Studies: A Bibliography of Theory and Applications,* Regional Science Research Institute, Bibliography Series no. 1, Philadelphia, 1961.

Borchert, J. R., and Adams, R. B. *Trade Centers and Trade Areas of the Upper Midwest,* Upper Midwest Economic Study, Urban Report no. 3, Minneapolis, 1963.

Bourne, L. S. "Urban Systems in Australia and Canada: Comparative Notes and Research Questions," *Australian Geographical Studies,* 12 (1974): 152–172.

Braidwood, R. J., and Willey, G. (eds). *Courses toward Urban Life,* Viking Fund Publications in Anthropology, no. 32, Chicago, 1962.

Briggs, A. *Victorian Cities,* London, 1963.

Brush, J. E. "Spatial Patterns of Population in Indian Cities," *Geographical Review,* 58 (1968): 362–391.

———— and Bracey, H. E. "Rural Service Centers in Southwestern Wisconsin and Southern England," *Geographical Review,* 45 (1955): 559–569.

Burghardt, A. F. "A Hypothesis about Gateway Cities," *Annals of the Association of American Geographers,* 61 (1971): 269–285.

Chang, Sen-dou. "Some Observations on the Morphology of Chinese Walled Cities," *Annals of the Association of American Geographers,* 60 (1970): 63–91.

Christaller, W. *Die zentralen Orte in Süddeutschland,* Jena, 1933. English translation by C. Baskin, New York, 1966.

"Cities," *Scientific American,* 213 (Sept., 1965).

Davies, W. K. D. "The Morphology of Central Places: A Case Study," *Annals of the Association of American Geographers,* 58 (1968): 91–110.

Dickinson, R. E. *City and Region: A Geographical Interpretation,* London, 1964.

Gallion, A. B., and Eisner, S. *The Urban Pattern: City Planning and Design,* Princeton, N.J., 1963.

Gottmann, J. "Why the Skyscraper?" *Geographical Review,* 56 (1966): 190–212.

Green, C. M. *The Rise of Urban America,* London, 1966.

Gutkind, E. A. *Revolution in Environment,* London, 1946.

Hamm, M. F. (ed.). *The City in Russian History,* Lexington, Ky., 1976.

Hammond, M. *The City in the Ancient World,* Cambridge, Mass., 1972.

Hardoy, J. *Urban Planning in Pre-Columbian America,* London, 1968.

Harris, C. D. "A Functional Classification of Cities in the United States," *Geographical Review,* 33 (1943): 86–99.

———— and Ullman, E. L. "The Nature of Cities," *Annals of the American Academy of Political and Social Science,* 242 (1945): 7–17.

Holzner, L. "World Regions in Urban Geography," *Annals of the Association of American Geographers,* 57 (1967): 704–712.

Isard, W. *Location and Space-Economy: A General Theory Relating to Industrial Location, Market Areas, Land Use, Trade and Urban Structure,* New York, 1956.

Jackson, J. C. "The Structure and Function of Small Malaysian Towns," *Transactions of the Institute of British Geographers,* 61 (March, 1974): 65–80.

Jefferson, M. "The Law of the Primate City," *Geographical Review,* 29 (1939): 226–232.

Johnston, R. J. "Towards a General Model of Intra-Urban Residential Patterns: Some Cross-Cultural Observations," *Progress in Geography, International Reviews of Current Research,* 4 (1972): 83–124.

Jones, E. *Towns and Cities,* New York, 1966.

Lapidus, I. M. (ed.). *Middle Eastern Cities: Ancient, Islamic, and Contemporary Middle Eastern Urbanism, a Symposium,* Berkeley, Calif., 1969.

Lewis, P. F. "Small Town in Pennsylvania," *Annals of the Association of American Geographers,* 62 (1972): 323–351.

Marshall, J. U. "City Size, Economic Diversity, and Functional Type: the Canadian Case," *Economic Geography,* 51 (1975): 37–49.

Mumford, L. "The Natural History of Urbanization," in Thomas, W. L. (ed.), *Man's Role in Changing the Face of the Earth,* Chicago, 1956, 385–400.

———— *The City in History,* New York, 1961.

Murphey, R. "The City as a Center of Change: Western Europe and China," *Annals of the Association of American Geographers,* 44 (1954): 349-362.

Nelson, H. J. "A Service Classification of American Cities," *Economic Geography,* 31 (1955): 189-210.

Park, R. E., Burgess, E. W., and Mackenzie, R. D. (eds.). *The City,* Chicago, 1925.

Pillsbury, R. "The Urban Street Pattern as a Culture Indicator: Pennsylvania, 1682-1815," *Annals of the Association of American Geographers,* 60 (1970): 428-446.

Pirenne, H. *Medieval Cities,* New York, 1925, and later (paperback) editions.

Pounds, N. J. G. "The Urbanization of the Classical World," *Annals of the Association of American Geographers,* 59 (1969): 135-157.

Pred, A. *The External Relations of Cities during "Industrial Revolution," with a Case Study of Göteborg, Sweden, 1868-1890,* University of Chicago, Department of Geography Research Paper no. 76, Chicago, 1962.

—— "Intermetropolitan Location of American Manufacturing," *Annals of the Association of American Geographers,* 54 (1964): 165-180.

Preston, R. E. "The Structure of Central Place Systems," *Economic Geography,* 47 (1971): 136-155.

Reps, J. W. *The Making of Urban America,* Princeton, N.J., 1965.

Sjoberg, G. *The Pre-industrial City, Past and Present,* New York, 1960.

—— "The Origin and Evolution of Cities," *Scientific American,* 213 (Sept., 1965): 54-63.

Stanislawski, D. "The Origin and Spread of the Grid-Pattern Town," *Geographical Review,* 36 (1946): 105-120.

—— "Early Spanish Townplanning in the New World," *Geographical Review,* 37 (1947): 94-105.

Stewart, C. T. "The Size and Spacing of Cities," *Geographical Review,* 48 (1958): 222-245.

Ullman, E. L., Dacey, M. F., and Brodsky, H. *The Economic Base of American Cities,* Seattle, 1969.

Vance, J. E. "Land Assignment in the Precapitalist, Capitalist and Postcapitalist City," *Economic Geography,* 47 (1971): 101-120.

Webb, J. W. "Basic Concepts in the Analysis of Small Urban Centers in Minnesota," *Annals of the Association of American Geographers,* 49 (1959): 55-72.

Weber, A. F. *The Growth of Cities in the Nineteenth Century: A Study in Statistics,* New York, 1899; Ithaca, New York, 1963.

Wheatley, P. "Archaeology and the Chinese City," *World Archaeology,* 2 (1970): 159-185.

—— *The Pivot of the Four Quarters, A Preliminary Enquiry into the Origins and Character of the Ancient Chinese City,* Edinburgh, Scotland, 1971.

Wycherley, R. E. *How the Greeks Built Cities,* London, 1962.

# 15 EMERGING URBAN PATTERNS

In the twentieth century, Western cities have exploded into the countryside. Old cultural patterns that separated town and country have collapsed. In most of heavily populated Europe and North America this metropolitan way of life spreads over wide areas, perhaps because people knowingly flee from the machine-age city in search of a better life, but probably because there are few alternatives to buying a home in a new housing development. The suburban dormitory, with its miles of new and aging housing and its road and rail links to city workplaces, is the twentieth century's contribution to mass settlement in the modernized Western world. Many people move beyond the suburbs to the "real country," bringing old villages and small towns, as well as farming areas, into the orbit of large cities. Jobs, stores, and schools follow, creating a diffused urbanism in which the various components of the city are separated by discontinuities such as lakes, woods, and fields.

## THE DISTRIBUTION OF LARGE METROPOLISES

The Scotsman Patrick Geddes was one of the first to perceive the new scale of modern cities (Geddes, 1915). In the British Isles, he identified several broad urban regions (many with multiple nuclei) and, looking abroad, saw similar clusters in the Ruhr, around Paris, and Chicago, and along the northeastern seaboard of the United States.

Official governmental definitions usually claim areas smaller in extent than the facts warrant. The main statistical unit used for large cities in the United States is the Standard Metropolitan Statistical Area, based on counties. However, counties are sometimes too large or their boundaries too arbitrary to provide an adequate basis for defining the regions of smaller cities. At the other end of the size scale, the city region of New York, which obviously takes in parts of New Jersey and Connecticut, has an SMSA that excludes nearby Jersey City and Newark, but includes Rockland and Westchester counties—farther from the center, but in New York State.

In England, the official definition includes only continuous built-up areas, much smaller than Geddes's far-ranging "city regions and town aggregates." The London city region, broadly defined as including populations within 60 kilometers from its center, increased between 1951 and 1969 from 11.7 million to 13.0 million. In contrast, over the same period the area officially designated as Greater London actually declined from 8.2 million to 7.7 million. A reasonable forecast for 1981 is 7.0 million for Greater London and 14.2 for the larger region. By that time, however, it is likely that the London city region may need to be defined as covering the whole of southeastern England, with a predicted population of 20.1 million.

The International Urban Research Group (IUR) at Berkeley, California, developed a definition of urbanized regions suitable for application to most countries. Metropolitan regions of the world were defined as urban areas with at least 100,000 population, with over 50,000 in a central city. Administrative areas outside the central city were included if contiguous to the central city or to other areas that also met one of the following conditions: (1) two-thirds of the population in nonagricultural occupations *or* (2) population density at least half that of the central city, or at least twice that of the next ring of administrative areas at a greater distance from the central city. Figure 15–1 shows the world pattern of large metropolitan areas and is based on data modified

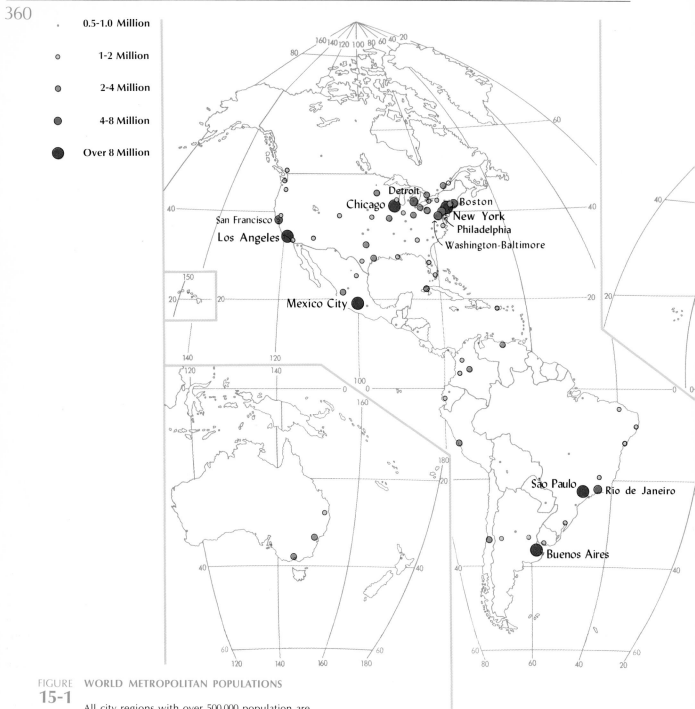

0.5-1.0 Million

1-2 Million

2-4 Million

4-8 Million

Over 8 Million

Detroit

Chicago

Boston

San Francisco

New York

Los Angeles

Philadelphia

Washington-Baltimore

Mexico City

São Paulo

Rio de Janeiro

Buenos Aires

FIGURE    WORLD METROPOLITAN POPULATIONS
15-1
All city regions with over 500,000 population are
shown. Those with over 4 million inhabitants are
named. In many instances populations of adjacent cities have been combined; for example, western Connecticut, Randstad Holland, Ruhr-Rhine.

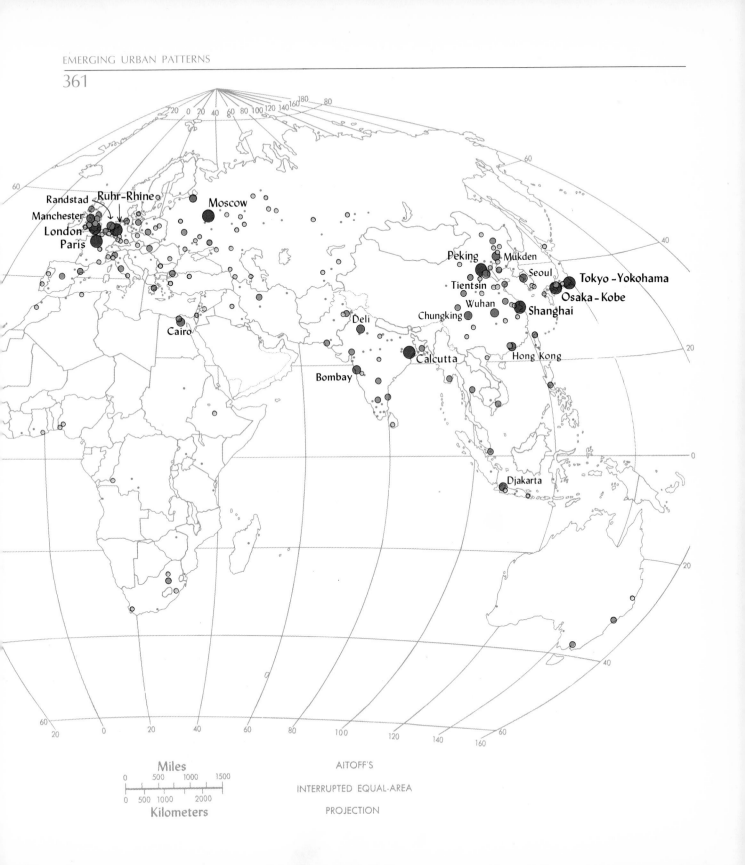

Randstad
Ruhr-Rhine
Manchester
London
Paris
Moscow
Cairo

Peking
Mukden
Tientsin
Seoul
Tokyo - Yokohama
Osaka - Kobe
Shanghai
Wuhan
Chungking
Deli
Calcutta
Bombay
Hong Kong

Djakarta

Miles
0    500   1000   1500
0   500  1000        2000
Kilometers

AITOFF'S

INTERRUPTED EQUAL-AREA

PROJECTION

**CITY REGIONS WITH 2.5 MILLION INHABITANTS OR MORE, AND THEIR NEIGHBORS WITH OVER HALF A MILLION INHABITANTS, 1975**

| TABLE 15-1 City region | Population, millions | Associated cities[a] |
|---|---|---|
| **Africa** | | |
| Cairo | 6.7 | Alexandria |
| Alexandria | 2.5 | Cairo |
| **Asia** | | |
| Tokyo-Yokohama | 17.0 | Shizuoka-Shimizu, Nagoya, Gifu-Ichinomiya; Osaka-Kobe, Kyoto |
| Shanghai | 10.0 | Soochow, Wuhsi |
| Osaka-Kobe | 9.5 | See Tokyo-Yokohama |
| Peking | 8.5 | Tientsin |
| Calcutta | 8.0 | Howrah |
| Bombay | 5.5 | Poona |
| Seoul | 5.0 | |
| Djakarta | 5.0 | |
| Tientsin | 4.7 | Peking |
| Wuhan | 4.4 | |
| Hong Kong | 4.3 | |
| Manila | 4.3 | |
| Lüta-Lüshun | 4.1 | |
| Shenyang (Mukden) | 4.0 | Fushun |
| Teheran | 4.0 | |
| Karachi | 4.0 | |
| Chunching | 3.6 | |
| Delhi | 3.5 | |
| Haerphin | 2.9 | |
| T'aiyüan | 2.8 | Yu-tzu |
| Madras | 2.8 | |
| Bangkok | 2.5 | |
| Canton | 2.5 | |
| Nagoya | 2.5 | See Tokyo-Yokohama |
| Taipei | 2.5 | |
| **Europe (including the Soviet Union)** | | |
| London | 13.5 | Birmingham, Coventry, Stoke, Nottingham, Manchester, Merseyside, West Riding, Teesside, Tyneside, Edinburgh, Clydeside, Bristol, South Wales, Portsmouth-Southampton |
| Paris | 10.0 | |
| Moscow | 9.0 | |
| Inner Ruhr | 6.8 | Rhine-Ruhr cities,[b] Mainz, Frankfurt am Main, Mannheim-Ludwigshafen, Karlsruhe, Stuttgart, Nürnberg, München, Randstad Holland, Liège, Ghent, Brussels, Lille, Antwerp, Charleroi |
| Randstad Holland[c] | 4.4 | See Inner Ruhr |
| Leningrad | 4.2 | |

| TABLE 15-1 City region | Population, millions | Associated cities[a] |
|---|---|---|
| Berlin (E.-W.) | 4.0 | Hamburg, Hannover, Bremen, Braunschweig, Magdeburg, Halle, Leipzig, Dresden, Karl-Marx-Stadt, Prague |
| Manchester | 3.8 | See London |
| Silesia[d] | 3.5 | Kraków |
| Madrid | 3.2 | |
| Birmingham | 3.1 | See London |
| Rome | 3.0 | |
| Warsaw | 2.8 | |
| Istanbul | 2.8 | |
| Hamburg | 2.5 | See Berlin |
| Milan | 2.5 | Turin, Genoa |
| Athens | 2.5 | |
| **North America** | | |
| New York[e] | 18.5 | Megalopolis[f] |
| Los Angeles | 10.0 | San Diego |
| Chicago | 7.5 | Milwaukee, Gary |
| San Francisco | 6.0 | Sacramento |
| Philadelphia | 5.7 | See New York |
| Detroit | 4.8 | Toledo, Cleveland, Akron, Youngstown, Pittsburgh |
| Boston | 3.7 | See New York |
| Cleveland | 3.3 | See Detroit |
| Washington | 3.2 | See New York |
| Toronto | 3.2 | Hamilton, Buffalo, Rochester, Syracuse |
| Pittsburgh | 2.9 | See Detroit |
| Montreal | 2.8 | Ottawa |
| St. Louis | 2.4 | |
| **Middle America** | | |
| Mexico City | 12.0 | |
| **South America** | | |
| Buenos Aires | 9.5 | |
| São Paulo | 9.0 | |
| Rio de Janeiro | 7.5 | |
| Lima-Callao | 3.5 | |
| Santiago | 3.1 | Valparaiso |
| Bogota | 3.0 | |
| **Oceania** | | |
| Sydney | 2.9 | |
| Melbourne | 2.7 | |

[a]An "associated city" is within 160 kilometers of another city in the same cluster, and at least one "associated city" is within 150 kilometers of the main city region.
[b]Rhine-Ruhr cities—Inner Ruhr, Düsseldorf, Wuppertal, Krefeld, Mönchen-Gladbach, Köln (Cologne), Bonn.
[c]Randstad Holland—Rotterdam, Amsterdam, Haarlem, 's Gravenhage (The Hague), Utrecht.
[d]Silesia—Katowice, Zabrze, Bytom, Gliwice, Chorzow, Sosnowiec.
[e]Including northeastern New Jersey and southwestern Connecticut.
[f]Megalopolis—Boston-Lowell, Worcester, Providence, Lawrence, Springfield-Holyoke-Chicopee, Hartford, New Haven, Bridgeport, Albany-Schenectady-Troy, Allentown-Bethlehem-Easton, Scranton-Wilkes-Barre, New York-northeastern New Jersey, Philadelphia, Baltimore, Washington.

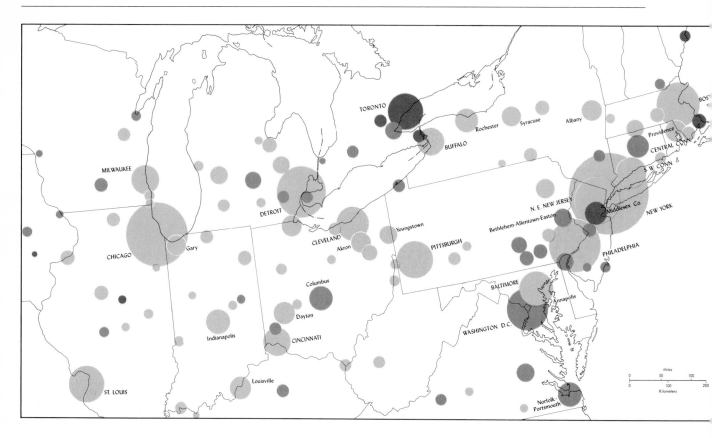

FIGURE **EASTERN NORTH AMERICA: LARGE AND MEDIUM-**
**15–2** SIZED CITIES, 1975

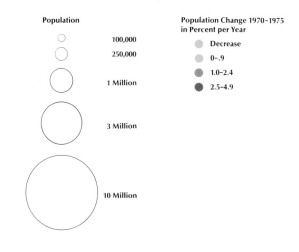

**Population**

○ 100,000

○ 250,000

○ 1 Million

○ 3 Million

○ 10 Million

**Population Change 1970–1975
in Percent per Year**

● Decrease

● 0–.9

● 1.0–2.4

● 2.5–4.9

from IUR calculations. Table 15–1 lists all city regions with over 2.5 million inhabitants, plus moderately large cities no more than 160 kilometers distant from them. At the present time 80 kilometers seems the limit of intensive influence of major urban centers. Map and table show that the main groups of adjacent metropolitan areas are in North America, Europe, and Japan.

## NORTH AMERICA

Many city groupings are coalescing to form regional clusters, centered around two or more large cities. In North America, the peripheral expansion of large cities has been phenomenal since World War II. The urbanized northeastern Atlantic Seaboard—Megalopolis*—is the largest aggregation of

*To Jean Gottmann the term has two meanings: first, a general connotation of "great city" (used earlier by Geddes and Mumford); second, as "the great *city of ideas* that predetermines and commands the material world in which we live, and this greater city of ideas [is] called Megalopolis" (Gottmann, 1961, 772).

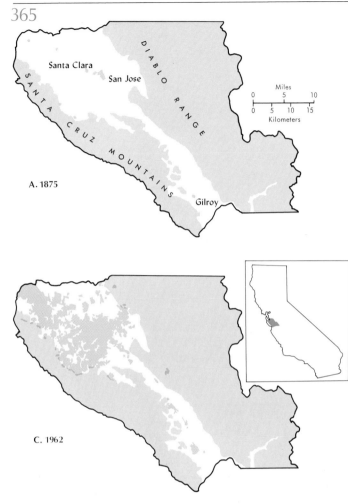

FIGURE SANTA CLARA VALLEY, CALIFORNIA: SETTLEMENT
15-3 CHANGES

This valley lies directly south of San Francisco Bay. In 1875 it was entirely agricultural, with San Jose as the local metropolis. By 1939 the northwestern part of the valley included some suburban outliers of San Francisco. By the 1960s the northern section had become part of the urbanized Bay Region. Based on data in Broek, J. O. M., *The Santa Clara Valley, California: A Study in Landscape Changes,* Utrecht, 1932, and White, C. L., "Sequent Occupance in the Santa Clara Valley, California," *Journal of the Graduate Research Center,* Dallas, 34 (1965): 1.

city regions in the world. By 1970 it contained over 40 million people. To the west another group of growing city regions extends from Pittsburgh to Cleveland and on to Detroit and the car-manufacturing towns of Michigan; these have about 15 million inhabitants. Still farther west begins the Chicago-Milwaukee complex with 11 million inhabitants, now extending around the south end of Lake Michigan. These Midwestern city regions, with others like those of southwestern Ohio (3 million) and upstate New York-Toronto (5 million), may well fuse together with Megalopolis before the end of the twentieth century (Figure 15-2).

In the western United States are two large and rapidly growing city regions. The more phenomenal is in southern California, largely a twentieth-century creation, with its main center at Los Angeles, but extending south to San Diego. Between 1950 and 1960 this widely spread urban belt increased in population by almost two-thirds, and by 1970 had reached 13 million inhabitants. The San Francisco Bay group grew almost as fast, with over 6 million by 1970 (Figure 15-3). A third but smaller concentration extends along Puget Sound from Vancouver, British Columbia, to Tacoma, Washington.

## EUROPE

Urbanized Europe differs in several respects from urbanized North America. The long-distance interaction of people, goods, and services, so common in North America, is less apparent in Europe.

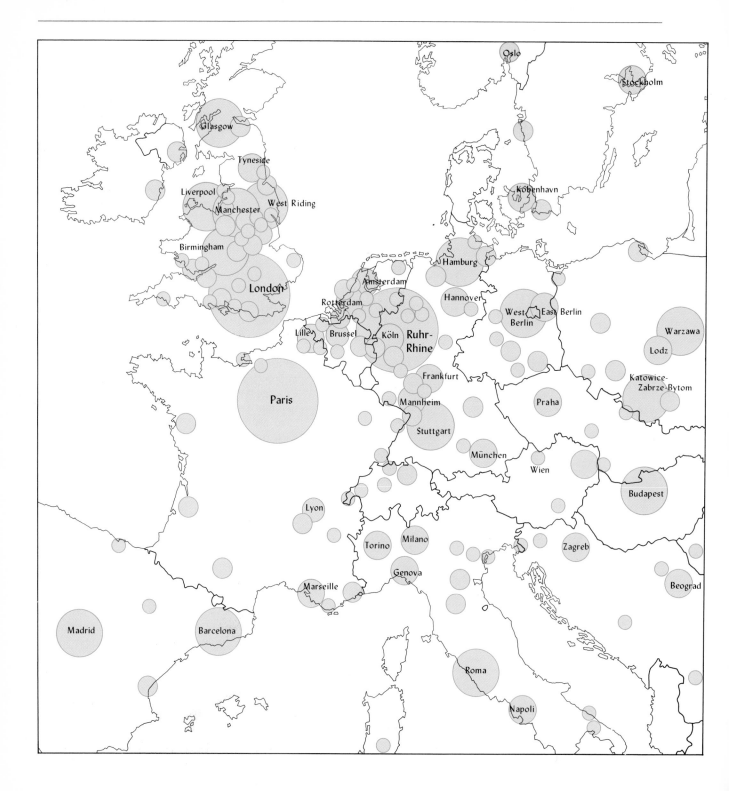

FIGURE **WESTERN AND CENTRAL EUROPE: LARGE CITIES**
**15-4**

Many small and middle-sized cities have been omitted. The dateline is about 1975.

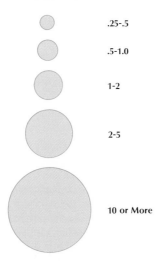

**Population in Millions**

.25-.5

.5-1.0

1-2

2-5

10 or More

The greater age of the European city gives it a more distinctive personality, which one hesitates to disregard by identifying multicity agglomerations. Furthermore, many large cities are adjacent to international boundaries; to join them may imply bonds that do not actually exist.

With these reservations in mind, we can outline groupings of large cities in Europe (Figure 15-4). London, with over 13 million inhabitants living in or near it, is the largest single metropolis of the continent. Heavily settled land stretches in all directions, especially along the coasts and toward the northwest, where Birmingham lies only 160 kilometers away. Not far north of Birmingham, industrial agglomerations are but a short distance from each other: included are southern Lancashire, West Riding, Tyneside, and Clydeside. In America such city regions would be brought under one heading, but in Britain we recognize five: London and southeast England, Bristol and south Wales, central Scotland, the industrial Midlands and north, and Tyneside-Teesside.

Across the English Channel and the North Sea a great complex of cities stretches from the coastal and tidal river ports to the upper Rhine Basin and Bavaria. The international borders of France, the Benelux countries, and West Germany run between many cities in the northern part of this grouping. As economic integration proceeds and nationalism slowly declines, linkages increase between these cities. With urbanized Britain added, this dynamic and diversified region becomes comparable to the North American megalopolis.

In the Low Countries the main city regions lie close together. Largest in the Netherlands are Rotterdam, Amsterdam, and The Hague, with short distances to many other towns including Utrecht. By the end of this century the urbanized region of the western Netherlands, already called *Randstad* (ring-city), will form one interconnected system with individual towns separated from each other by carefully preserved greenbelts. A similar development typifies Belgium, where Brussels, Antwerp, Ghent, and Liège are the main foci of urbanization. These urbanized sections, unlike their Netherlands counterparts, extend across the borders into France to join with Lille and nearby industrial towns, and into Germany to link up with Aachen and the Ruhr-Rhine cities.

The Ruhr-Rhine complex of cities is unique in that it has so many nuclei. No part dominates, although Düsseldorf is the "headquarters" city, Essen the center for heavy industry, and Köln (Cologne) a metropolis with diversified industry. The Rhine and its tributaries connect these industrial cities with others, including Frankfurt am Main and Stuttgart, München (Munich) and others beyond.

Paris, expanding northwestward along the Seine River, lies some distance from the other major cities of France, and therefore might appear isolated. However, a network of road, water, and rail routes connects it with the urbanized peripheral regions.

The borders between West Germany, East Germany, and Czechoslovakia intervene between groups of city regions that reach from Hamburg in the northwest, through Berlin in central Germany, to Leipzig in Saxony, and Prague in Bohemia. Like the Ruhr-Rhine cities, this varied group grows slowly, reflecting the virtually stable populations of the two Germanys.

In Silesia the coalfield-industrial towns form a closely knit complex with Katowice the dominant center. Elsewhere in Europe city regions are comparatively isolated. While Madrid, Athens, Budapest, Bucuresti, and Barcelona each have their share of satellite towns, in none of these has an urbanized region developed. In northern Italy, however, Turin and Milan are the main centers of a growing urbanized area that includes many small and medium-sized towns.

### JAPAN

Outside North America and Europe, groupings of city regions are rare, although some very large individual cities have grown rapidly in recent decades. The main exception to this is Japan, where northern Kyushu and the densely populated southern half of Honshu include a number of closely connected thriving centers. In the last two decades industrialization and commercialization have swelled in-migration from the country and smaller towns. The largest conurbations, Tokyo-Yokohama and Osaka-Kobe, are joined by high-speed rail service—the famous Tokaido express. The industrial centers at the strait where Honshu and Kyushu come together form another growth point.

### SOVIET UNION

Groupings of city regions are conspicuously absent in the Soviet Union. Like all great cities, Moscow and Leningrad have their satellite settlements. Elsewhere, except for the Donets industrial region, there are no urban areas with many more than a million inhabitants. One reason for this lack of concentration is the large size of the populated territory in the Soviet Union. Another has to do with government policy: Successive groups of national planners have consciously tried to develop the Soviet economy on a regional basis. Thus, while many cities number between 100,000 and 1 million, there are no dominant groupings among them. Furthermore, many sectors of the Soviet economy remain only partly developed. Surprisingly many people still work in agriculture; if farming had been modernized, they long since would have swelled the number of city dwellers. By restricting service and consumer industries, the Soviet authorities provided an effective brake to the growth of metropolises and, incidentally, to the wealth and diversity that go with them.

### OTHER REGIONS

Elsewhere in the underdeveloped and partly developed regions of the world, industrialization lies like a thin veneer over rural ways of life. Large cities are few, mostly associated with administration and other governmental functions, or they result from Western-oriented commercial operations. When they are the main trading ports, their population includes a high proportion of their country's industry. They lack, nevertheless, the broad range of metropolitan activities and the diversity of occupations associated with great cities in North America, Europe, and Japan. Recent growth of cities in underdeveloped countries is discussed in Chapter 17.

## THE QUALITIES AND PROBLEMS OF METROPOLITAN LIFE

### THE INDIVIDUAL AND THE SYSTEM

It is paradoxical that great cities of the modern industrial countries, where increasing numbers live and newcomers arrive each day, are said to lack the graces of life, or even that they strangle the more valuable aspects of civilization. A national commission set up in the 1930s to investigate conditions in Britain's industrial cities reported "a vast—and many would add alarming—growth of population in London and Southeastern England largely at the expense of the rest of the country." London had absorbed, between 1931 and 1939, one-third of the national population growth. The results were "overcrowding, an increase in land values, the absorption of open spaces, smoke and noise and desolation, traffic congestion and long daily journeys, damage to health and national income from loss of vitality and waste of working hours in sickness and travelling, and the burdens of palliative services" (Barlow, 1940).

In a contemporary work Lewis Mumford added to the catalog of woes (Mumford, 1938). A polemical but scholarly writer on the quality of city life, Mumford in 1961 repeated his criticisms. He sees parallels between the modern city and ancient Rome. "They have come back today: the arena, the tall tenement, the mass contests and exhibitions, the football matches, the international beauty contests, the striptease made ubiquitous by advertisement, the constant titillation of the senses by sex, liquor and violence—all in true Roman style. So too, the multiplication of bathrooms and the overexpenditure on broadly paved motor roads, and above all, the massive collective concentration on glib ephemeralities of all kinds performed with supreme technical audacity . . ." (Mumford 1961, 242).

In the years since Mumford assailed the general metropolitan life-style, other problems have come to the fore. The poor have concentrated in the large cities, especially the blacks who occupy the ghettos. Millions depend on welfare checks from city, state, and federal sources. Crime has increased so that living in a city means constant danger. Freeways have replaced much housing and have brought more cars into the inner city, which chokes in bad air and other wastes. Whites have fled to the suburbs, leaving the impoverished city to cope with all these troubles and to educate an increasingly segregated population.

Many observers believe that only a change in basic political and social values can save the city. Nevertheless, more people than ever are choosing to settle in or near cities despite the seemingly incurable problems. The very large Western cities attract with completeness, variety, and range of choices. They are the centers of affairs. If there is much to spend money on, wages and salaries are higher than in smaller places. The variety of life in a great city can satisfy everyone (Hall, 1963, 38). Even Mumford had to admit: "At present the world-cities . . . contain many of the best elements of man's heritage" (Mumford, 1938, 230). No one gives total criticism or approbation of city life. Though all applaud the diversity of the metropolis, many agree with Mumford that modern elements in its way of life too often lack "the human scale." This condition finds expression in the changing patterns of living. While the population of the inner city decreases, that of the formerly stagnant or declining rural areas increases.

The modern metropolis offers an experience unique in human history. Most of its citizens share more or less in its many facets, though each leads an individual life. Whereas a village or small town presents personal associations near at hand, uncomplicated by spatial discontinuities, the city has become a phenomenon of quite a different scale. City dwellers have diffuse spatial associations; in the course of a single day they may meet and speak to a hundred people—many of them strangers or mere acquaintances—travel many miles from one part of the city region to another, and develop a feeling of rootlessness that persists after they return home from work.

It is useful to think of a large city as a functioning whole, a system with interlocking parts, a complex with a "nodal" unity. Actually, most city folk conduct their daily business and even live through their entire lives without ever acquiring this holistic sense of their urban environment. They consider a city region a series of places—neighborhoods, districts, areas—some known intimately, others only in passing, many not at all.

In the United States the federal government has linked major cities with superhighways, and created new road systems within the cities themselves. These changes inevitably affect the use of adjacent land. The federal government also has sponsored or supported schemes of "urban renewal"—physical reconstruction in and around the city center within national guidelines. However, there never has been a clear mandate for the large-scale rectification of land use within the cities. Little comprehensive planning has been done on a regional basis. The American genius excels in wholesale attack on a specific problem or a related group of problems, but fails to coordinate the different programs. Many argue that this is only proper, that too much government control would destroy the laissez faire political and social system they believe in. They admit that problems exist but maintain that individuals or groups should gradually solve them. Others insist that the political system is mixed—laissez faire *and* planned—and that both public and private elements should work at, even compete in, shaping the environment.

Concerning the cities of the United States Eastern Seaboard, Gottmann writes: "Laissez faire or interference? The present period, with its great momentum of change, has had to ask [the question] again to cope with the remarkable concentration of population and activities in Megalopolis, where cities have been breaking out of old bounds. But the purpose . . . here is not to defend labor against employers, nor to call public authorities to limit the freedom of action of private business. For quite some time governments have been exerting their rights to interfere in these areas. Rather it is a call for the reform of the

A squatter settlement on a hillside in Bogota, Colombia. Huge migrations to third world capital cities and a high natural increase among the migrants create housing problems that are only solved by human ingenuity. Tens of millions live in the squatter settlements of Latin America, Africa, and Asia. (Photograph—United Nations). In Montreal, the apartment complex "Habitat 67" perhaps foreshadows future life in the modern metropolis. Housing, streets, walks, parks, and parking all blend into a pleasing environment. Habitat 67 was designed by Moshe Safdia for the World's Fair of 1967. (Photograph—United Nations/M. Tzovaras)

governmental structure, with a view toward securing better coordination and more far-sighted policies in a period of rapid change" (Gottmann, 1961, 744).

In western Europe both local and national governments have been granted wider powers to deal with the problems of large conurbations. In Britain, for example, no land can be developed or building altered unless the proposed change conforms to detailed zoning ordinances (development plans) laboriously worked out between planning agencies of local and national governments. Under this system the government holds considerable control of land use. Town planning in western Europe gives attention to detail unmatched in the

United States; streets and roads are architecturally tidy, advertising is muted, new development minutely regulated. Until recently, though, the big problems associated with metropolitan aggregations were attacked only in piecemeal fashion. Now at last, rapidly compounding problems are being met by comprehensive programs for redistributing population, locating industry, and coordinating and improving transportation systems. The basic political problem in European as in American planning is to achieve a balance between governmental control and private action, and to allow the people themselves in whatever community a part in making decisions.

## METROPOLITAN MIGRATIONS

Individual mobility characterizes metropolitan life. Migrants from other countries, from rural areas, from small towns and different city regions, commuters between residence and work, all combine to create a society on the move. Foreign settlers always have been attracted to large cities. Though fewer enter the United States than formerly, most locate in such places. Immigrants in Europe also tend to concentrate in cities. In France, Algerians and others go to Paris and Marseille. In West Germany the mass of Italian, Greek, Turkish, and other immigrant workers locate in industrial centers like the Ruhr, Frankfurt am Main, and Köln. In Britain the influx of West Indians, Pakistanis, and Indians settled especially in London and Birmingham.

In both North America and western Europe many migrants come to cities from small towns. Rural migrants also make up a sizable number; as the years pass, however, they form a decreasing proportion of the population. Migration between city regions provides an increasingly important component. With higher job mobility and ease of transportation, large cities continually exchange some of their populations. Of course, with each pair of cities exchanging people, one of them has a net gain—as from eastern to western cities in the United States and Canada. Proper interest in net migration should not make us forget the gross migration volume, which involves far more people.

Most people reside a good part of their lives in one city region, though they may move to another location, perhaps in the same neighbor-

hood, but very often from central areas to the suburbs. Such moves may occur more than once as family income rises and more expensive housing becomes possible. In contrast, other groups are drawn toward the city center. Many of these are single people who work there, or retired and elderly folk. Others are minority groups who for reasons of poverty or discrimination cannot follow the mass exodus to more spacious suburban living.

To the knowledgeable, residents identify themselves by where they live, whether in a new suburb marked only by a real-estate signboard, in an area of recent housing around an older settlement, or in the city center. Naturally, they have the closest place associations with those buildings, streets, and organizations that have become familiar over a length of time. The difficult living conditions in slum districts are mitigated by numerous close contacts with relatives and longtime friends. In spite of these community sentiments, the handling of public affairs is usually left to the distant city authorities. Yet the city neighborhood offers the average citizen an opportunity to participate directly in city government. John Dewey took a strong stand in this matter: "Unless local community life can be restored, the public cannot adequately resolve its most urgent problem: to find and identify itself. Democracy must begin at home and its home is the neighbourly community" (as quoted in Dickinson, 1964, 573).

## METROPOLITAN PROBLEMS AND PLANNING

Individuals and families living in the city face daily problems they are powerless to solve. They cannot cope with the repair of decaying buildings, the disposal of wastes, abatement of smoke and noise, raising school standards, provision of welfare to the poor and the old. Even if they live in the suburbs, there are dissatisfactions and tensions. The husband or wife expends much time and energy commuting to work, while the spouse is alone much of the day without meaningful participation in affairs of the community.

The responsibility to keep up and improve cities falls to local, state, and national governments. They in turn engage professional city and regional planners who are supposed to understand future as well as present needs. Many countries grant power to local and other levels of government to shape the physical and, to a certain extent, the social nature of cities. This century has seen the rapid growth of interest in urban matters. Despite this, the nation, the city, and its communities still are ill-equipped to solve the burgeoning metropolitan problems. So far, theoretical discussions and many practical plans provide no agreed formula for urban design.

Though countries vary in the degree of government control, all modern ones already show the effects of planning on population distribution, transportation systems, patterns of land use, and reconstruction of urban areas.

The ebb and flow of residential migrations, coupled with expanding nonresidential land uses, lead inexorably to depopulation of the old city core. This area of population loss expands and eventually engulfs old suburbs built decades before. Near the heart of the city some islands of minority groups increase, and new housing schemes may bring population gains to small areas; but these only tend to emphasize the more general decrease. In London the region of depopulation spread from its seventeenth-century heart to an area covering 10 square kilometers in the 1890s, 200 in the 1920s, 900 in the 1950s, and over 1,200 in the early 1970s. The same process is at work in other European and American cities. Peak populations pass outward from the old city, each peak lower in density per unit area as its distance from the center increases.

In response to the suburban trend, many jobs have moved out into newly built-up areas. Shopping facilities, office blocks, medical clinics, educational institutions, and industrial plants often draw their employees and clientele from locations well outside the old city. These developments add crosstown streams to the traffic focusing on the center.

## COMMUTING: AUTOS OR MASS TRANSIT

Jobs slowly follow the outward flow of population to the residential suburbs. The old city center, sometimes refurbished with new buildings and facilities, remains the chief employer. The journey to work—even early in this century—had become a common aspect of metropolitan life. Today hundreds of thousands travel each morning into lower Manhattan, central London, and inner Paris—and leave in the late afternoon. The daily tide comes and goes by commuter trains above and below ground level, by bus systems, by fleets of private cars and, in some countries, by bicycle.

In America, and to a growing extent in Europe, the private car provides the main means of personal transportation, permitting further diffusion of residence out in the suburban periphery. In North America new highways run to, through, and around most cities. The new freeways, built on the assumption that Americans like to go to work by car (some assert that this journey is the modern citizen's last resort of individualism), seem a massive rescue operation to maintain vital links between the more and more widely spaced home and job locations.

The new roads are good and wide, and travel is usually fast. Unfortunately, they do not lead to the car commuters' destinations—shops, offices, factories—packed closely together downtown. Freeways bring more cars into the traffic congestion of the center where parking is expensive or impossible. Space-eating parking lots destroy the attractions of city and suburb alike. Workers feel lucky if their jobs are in the suburbs where there is more space.

Car commuting in the United States brought the decline of public mass transportation. Only in New York, Chicago, and Philadelphia do subway and rail bring most workers to their jobs. Few other cities have managed to maintain even skeleton rail commuter systems. But now road congestion and the cost of fuel and of car ownership have brought reassessment by commuters and by city, state, and national governments. With federal government aid, metropolitan areas are rebuilding mass-transit facilities, in some cases from a very small base. The most revolutionary of these are in Washington, D.C., and in the San Francisco area. BART (Bay Area Rapid Transit) runs high-speed computer-controlled trains on 75 miles of track, with relatively long distances between stations in outlying areas and short distances between stations in city centers.

The prohibitive cost of building a rail transportation system causes many cities to maintain or develop bus lines. Attempts to increase bus ridership face difficulties and setbacks but, with new equipment and expanded routes to systems charging no fares, they are becoming moderately successful. Revolutionary personalized transit systems that use separated tracks and guideways

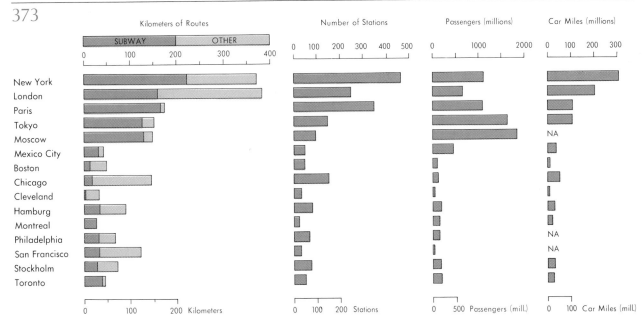

FIGURE **METROPOLITAN SUBWAY SYSTEMS**
15-5

Data are from *The New York Times,* March 18, 1976, 45.

still are in the experimental phase. Though some form of mass transit must come to most large American cities, when and what it will be are not clear. Certainly people do not seem to want new freeways to cover more and more of their cities (Figure 15–5).

While it may be an exercise in practical persuasion to get commuters to use old or new public facilities, the problem of traffic congestion in the city core remains. Experiments to bar private cars from main shopping streets in America and Europe have met with mixed results. More radical proposals are to tax cars that use central areas or to ban them entirely from wide sections of the city.

## SUBURBANIZATION

Around most American cities each new suburb cuts into sparsely occupied territory. At first there are few schools, churches, or other social services and only a makeshift shopping and business area. With not many jobs nearby, the working population mostly commutes to the central city. As time passes, families earn higher incomes, acquire a

second car, and develop new interests. Enterprising groups emerge to diversify the economic livelihood of the place, and a sense of community awakens among the people. The more attractive the location, the sooner business firms and real estate companies move in.

In the initial state the population grows rapidly. Even when house construction ends and some apartment buildings have risen, the population continues to increase rapidly because the suburbanites are mostly young married adults with many births and few deaths. The numerous children require large expenses for education. But as time passes, the schools become half used, even empty. The grown children leave for college, take jobs elsewhere, and settle in newer communities: "eventually out-migration begins as the now grown children of the original in-migrants leave; as the population grows older, the death rate increases and the number of births drops; depopulation begins when the net out-migration becomes greater than the declining natural increase; a new dimension may be added when deaths exceed births and natural decrease is added to net out-migration" (Webb, 1963, 142). Figure 15–6 shows part of this sequence of events at Dagenham, an

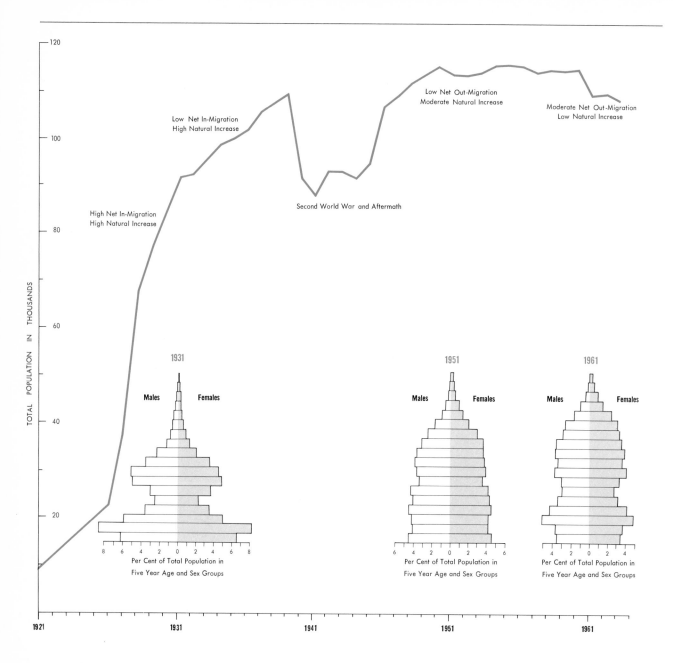

TOTAL POPULATION IN THOUSANDS

High Net In-Migration
High Natural Increase

Low Net In-Migration
High Natural Increase

Second World War and Aftermath

Low Net Out-Migration
Moderate Natural Increase

Moderate Net Out-Migration
Low Natural Increase

1931

Males    Females

Per Cent of Total Population in
Five Year Age and Sex Groups

1951

Males    Females

Per Cent of Total Population in
Five Year Age and Sex Groups

1961

Males    Females

Per Cent of Total Population in
Five Year Age and Sex Groups

FIGURE **DAGENHAM, ENGLAND: POPULATION COMPOSI-**
**15-6** **TION, 1931–1961**

The population of this industrial-residential suburb in
east London rose sharply in the late 1920s and early
1930s. After the interruption caused by World War II
and its aftermath, a peak population was reached in
1955, when a slow decline began. The age and sex dia-

grams show a change from a population of young
adults and children (1931) to one with a large proportion of middle aged (1961). Data are from census reports and annual statistical reviews published by the
General Register Office, London.

industrial-residential suburb to the east of the center of London.

For various reasons many large companies in the United States construct entire suburbs, each development usually within a limited price range. This, plus the general desire to live with one's own kind, tends to segregate suburban populations into districts identifiable by income levels. The zoning determines the size of the lot, the number of dwelling units in a building, and the use of the land. Other restrictions and practices make many suburbs into white reservations.

Governments in western Europe regulate to a far greater extent the building of new suburbs; they rapidly provide schools, sewer lines, social services, and utilities. Suburbs develop in an already densely settled rural and small-town landscape. Income segregation is less apparent. Many suburbs are extensions of older heterogeneous settlement and begin life already with a sense of place.

Beyond the middle-class suburbs lies the "real country," but even this has become part of the metropolitan complex. People with enough money and personal mobility can live in pleasant rural surroundings far beyond the built-up edge of the city. They may have in addition an apartment or a house in town. The "stockbroker belts" around major financial capitals may be more than 80 kilometers from the city center.

At such distances the land area per person can be very large. The amount increases geometrically in successive concentric belts of city-oriented settlement. With greater efficiency and speed of transportation, people of middle income find formerly exclusive "exurbanite" zones within their means for settlement. As a result, many growing but disconnected commuting populations live in residential settlements quite far from some of the largest cities in North America and western Europe.

The United States census of 1970 revealed how suburbanization has affected the distribution of population in this country. During the 1960s the population living in metropolitan areas grew by 20 million, or 16.6 percent. But the central cities increased only 3.2 million, or 5 percent. In contrast, the metropolitan population outside the central cities—the suburbs, for short—grew by 6.8 million, or 28 percent. To put it in another way, the population of the central cities in 1970 accounted for 64 million, or 31 percent, of the national total. That for the suburbs was 76 million, or 38 percent. The remainder—63 million or 31 percent—reside in nonmetropolitan areas. Clearly in this threefold division, the suburbs hold the plurality of the nation's inhabitants.

## QUARTER AND GHETTO

Throughout urban history, residential segregation of ethnic groups has been a frequent phenomenon. Cities of the Middle East in particular contained many culturally diverse groups, each residing in its own district; this situation still exists to some extent or lingers on in the old designation of Arab, Armenian, Christian, and Jewish quarters. Trading towns in South and Southeast Asia also had their urban subsystems for Indians, Malays, Chinese, Armenians, and, later, Europeans. In Europe the word *ghetto* came into use for the enclave where Jews were compelled by law to reside. Now this term is often applied to any urban space that a minority group occupies, even if the settlement results from social or economic pressures rather than from legal constraints.

Quarter or ghetto may be caused either by coercive segregation or by voluntary congregation. Usually it is a product of both forces. Dissimilarities in life-styles lie at its root. In the United States, for example, many immigrants at first were looked down on, even rejected, because of alien behavior. At the same time they found comfort and convenience by living among their compatriots. The stronger the cohesion within an ethnic group and the greater its social distance from the majority, the longer it took to be assimilated and to break free from residential segregation.

The Chinese in North America are a good example of enduring segregation. "Chinatown" is a way of life within a bounded habitat including schools, temples, clubs, banks, and other institutions that express and support the solidarity of the ethnic community. It seems unlikely that the Chinese could maintain their cultural heritage if they lived dispersed. Thus, to preserve its identity a distinct subculture or counterculture may need its own territory for mutual interaction, its own social space—its "turf."

## THE BLACK GHETTO

Segregated black residential areas result, as other quarters do, from the influences of both internal and external pressures. Nevertheless, the black ghetto deserves special attention because of its magnitude and because of the issues it poses for American society. To survey its formation, spread, and structure is difficult, partly because geographers have studied the subject only in recent years and partly because the forces affecting the ghetto change rapidly. Regarding the last point, until the 1950s legal barriers such as race-restrictive covenants were powerful means to seal off white neighborhoods against black encroachment. Now legal obstacles have been removed but the ghetto persists. The explanation must be sought in a shifting aggregate of social, cultural, and economic factors.

Among the current pressures that maintain the ghetto are the old prejudices of the whites, operating largely through the business practices of realtors, banks, savings and loan associations, and insurance companies which carry out—and profit from—what they consider to be the will of the majority. There are signs among whites of increasing racial tolerance, but such changes still make little real impact on residential patterns.

Among the internal forces that favor segregation are: refuge from the outside world, proximity of relatives and friends, presence of churches, schools, clubs, and other social institutions—in short, the congruence of habitat and life-style. These benefits, however, must be measured against the inadequacy of public services, and the prevalence of crime, vandalism, and rundown housing. The balance sheet will not look the same to all blacks.

Another, more activist, motive for congregation has come to the fore since the middle sixties: the ghetto as the basis for political power, a race-conscious bastion that would be lost if blacks were dispersed among whites. Political power can be a lever for communal responsibility and economic uplift. Whites still control most business enterprises and jobs in the ghetto. Most housing still belongs to white absentee landlords. To change this situation, many believe, requires black solidarity.

The antebellum South had little or no spatial segregation of the races (see Chapter 4). The Jim Crow laws passed during the Reconstruction period introduced physical separation. The North had few blacks until World War I, when the halt of European immigration and the need for labor in war industries drew large numbers from the rural South. At first the blacks moved mainly to cities on the Atlantic Seaboard from Baltimore to New York, but later the mainstream shifted inland to the Great Lakes cities, above all Chicago, Detroit, and Cleveland. World War II added currents of black migration to the West Coast metropolitan areas. In recent decades the economic upswing in the South has attracted large numbers of rural blacks to cities there. Since the middle sixties these new opportunities, measured against deteriorating conditions in northern ghettos, have slowed down the outflow from the South.

Ghetto formation in Northern cities began quite inconspicuously after 1900, often as shack towns along industrial railroads near the center. By 1920 the fast-growing urban black population expanded into the old housing areas that white immigrants were abandoning. On the whole, Jewish neighborhoods offered less resistance to the invasion than those occupied by Catholic east and south Europeans. The first to move into white neighborhoods were the middle-class blacks. As the remaining whites became alarmed and fled, increasing numbers of vacancies pressed down rents, giving poorer blacks the chance to obtain housing.

In most cities the ghetto expanded from its old core as one continuous zone or sector, often alongside railroads and in industrial areas. But in a number of cities two or more spatially separated concentrations of black population developed.

As more and more whites moved from the central city to the suburbs, better middle-class housing opened to those blacks who could afford the higher rent. On the other hand, much housing occupied by poor blacks was torn down to make way for freeways or urban renewal. Construction of low-cost homes to replace those destroyed lagged far behind the need. Altogether, while the middle-class black in recent years profited from access to a wider range of job opportunities and better housing, the unskilled low-income group remained in the ghetto core and experienced little if any improvement.

Blacks form an ever larger proportion of the

population in the central cities as a result of white migration to the suburbs and of black immigration plus natural growth. In 1970, when blacks constituted 11 percent of the national population, they accounted for 23 percent of the population in the nation's central cities, an increase of five percentage points over 1960.* In four cities

*These figures refer to central cities of the sixty-seven metropolitan areas with 500,000 or more people in 1970.

(Washington, D.C.; Newark, N.J.; Gary, Ind.; and Atlanta, Ga.) the percentage in 1970 was over 50; in another seven it was between 40 and 50 percent (Table 15-2A). Ballot power has already put a number of blacks in elective posts in central cities and in state and national legislatures, and more will certainly follow as the share of blacks increases in the 1970s (Figure 15-7).

A very different situation exists in the metropolitan areas outside the central cities—called,

### BLACKS IN CENTRAL CITIES AND METROPOLITAN AREAS OF THE UNITED STATES, 1970

TABLE 15-2   **A**   Proportion of blacks in total population of central cities and their metropolitan areas (for cities 40 percent or more black)

| City | Percent of city population | Percent of metropolitan population | City | Percent of city population | Percent of metropolitan population |
|---|---|---|---|---|---|
| Washington, D.C. | 71 | 25 | Detroit | 44 | 18 |
| Newark | 54 | 19 | Wilmington, Del. | 44 | 12 |
| Gary, Ind. | 53 | 18 | Birmingham | 42 | 30 |
| Atlanta | 51 | 22 | Richmond | 42 | 25 |
| Baltimore | 46 | 24 | St. Louis | 41 | 16 |
| New Orleans | 45 | 31 | | | |

**B**   Distribution of metropolitan blacks between central city and suburbs (for the 25 largest Standard Metropolitan Statistical Areas)

| City | Percent in central city | Percent in suburbs | City | Percent in central city | Percent in suburbs |
|---|---|---|---|---|---|
| Milwaukee | 98.7 | 1.3 | Philadelphia | 77.4 | 22.6 |
| Minneapolis–St. Paul | 93.0 | 7.0 | Washington, D.C. | 76.4 | 23.6 |
| Seattle | 91.0 | 9.0 | Anaheim–Garden Grove, Calif. | 69.4 | 30.6 |
| Chicago | 89.6 | 10.4 | Pittsburgh | 68.8 | 31.2 |
| New York | 88.5 | 11.5 | Los Angeles–Long Beach | 68.5 | 31.5 |
| Detroit | 87.2 | 12.8 | St. Louis | 67.1 | 32.9 |
| Buffalo | 86.7 | 13.3 | San Francisco–Oakland | 66.9 | 33.1 |
| Cleveland | 86.5 | 13.5 | Patterson-Clifton-Passaic, N.J. | 65.3 | 34.7 |
| Baltimore | 85.7 | 14.3 | Newark | 59.6 | 40.4 |
| San Diego | 85.4 | 14.6 | Miami | 40.1 | 59.9 |
| Dallas | 84.6 | 15.4 | | | |
| Houston | 82.6 | 17.4 | | | |
| Boston | 82.4 | 17.6 | | | |
| Atlanta | 82.1 | 17.9 | | | |
| Cincinnati | 82.1 | 17.9 | | | |

SOURCE: U.S. Census, 1970.

FIGURE
15-7
**NEW YORK: RACIAL SEGREGATION, 1970**

From maps published in March 1972 by the *New York Times*, based on data from the 1970 United States Census. Between 1960 and 1970 almost one million whites left New York City, mostly for the suburbs of Megalopolis; during the same period nearly half a million blacks and members of other minority races moved in. The result was increased segregation of the metropolitan population. These maps show the degree of segregation in New York City in 1970: at that date the city had 6 million whites and almost 2 million nonwhites. Comparison of 1960 with 1970 data shows that most white residential areas decreased in population density while most black residential areas increased in density.

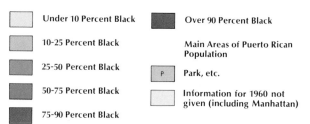

Under 10 Percent Black

10-25 Percent Black

25-50 Percent Black

50-75 Percent Black

75-90 Percent Black

Over 90 Percent Black

**Main Areas of Puerto Rican Population**

P  Park, etc.

Information for 1960 not given (including Manhattan)

for short, the suburbs, although some are actually satellite cities. In the 1960s over 760,000 blacks moved to the nation's suburbs, but this number was very small compared to the 12.5 million whites who did so. As a result, the black share in the total suburban population barely changed: from 4.2 percent in 1960 to 4.5 in 1970. On a nationwide basis, 58 percent of whites in metropolitan areas lived outside the central cities, versus 16 percent of the blacks. The latter figure does not necessarily mean integration beyond the ghetto. Some suburbs with heavy black concentration merely are extensions of ghettos as they spill across city boundaries; others developed near industrial sites or grew from incipient black neighborhoods in small towns.

There are, of course, suburbs with racially mixed populations. Experience in the central city shows that such mixed composition often characterizes the transitional stage to black or mostly black residency. This will not necessarily happen in suburbs where local jobs are scarce and transportation to the central city is expensive. White communities which so far have used restrictive zoning to bar blacks and poor whites with whom they felt they could not integrate are now under pressure from central cities and state and federal governments to drop their restrictive zoning and to accept low and moderate income housing. The metropolitan area in Dayton, Ohio, undertook an interesting venture. The planning commission assigned each segment of the area a quota in the construction of subsidized housing. This dispersed a substantial number of blacks over the entire urban territory and opened the way for those who desire better living conditions. Though militants opposed dilution of both political power and antipoverty funds, the plan was acceptable to many whites, above all to those who lived in the path of an expanding black community.

Cities all across the United States are now facing the fact that blacks and other minorities feel a burgeoning sense of pride in their unique heritage. Whether or not they become an integrated part of a community depends on many variables, such as historical circumstance, conditions in the central city and out in the suburbs, but most of all on the educational qualifications to compete with and meet others on an equal basis.

If the present black ghetto is the territorial expression of a community with its own life-style rather than an involuntary spatial confinement, it will continue for many years as a distinct part of American urban life. Not all blacks now live in ghettos, and it seems likely that increasing numbers will follow their example. Even so, groups of blacks in many cities may prefer to live in their own quarters. If this is true, one must hope that such purposeful congregation of Afro-Americans will be a transitional stage in which the transformation will take place from an existence in anger, frustration, and insecurity to a self-confident and economically strong group, ready to meet and mingle with the other components of the American nation, each respecting the other for its contributions to a rich and varied cultural life.

## THE GRAY ZONE AND URBAN RENEWAL

The "gray zone" is that belt around the center of the Occidental city occupied by immigrant and minority groups and by transitory populations. Some of these districts have very dense settlement, with wide areas of multistoried tenements. When the old buildings are torn down, nonresidential land uses often replace them, such as business structures and new inner-city highway networks. Industry and services of many kinds favor locations around the central core: warehousing, trucking, parking, printing, and certain kinds of retailing. Older nonresidential enterprises such as railroad terminals, classification yards, and factories interrupt the zones of residential land use.

Many living in this transitional zone of "social deterioration" (as it was classed by Park, Burgess, and Mackenzie, 1925) are long-term residents. Also living close to the city core are many transients, including young single persons who stay from a few weeks or months to a few years, working in offices, banks, stores, or other business.

The large metropolitan university in American cities forms a distinctive human and physical complex. Founded in the nineteenth century on the then outskirts of the city, it now finds itself surrounded by the urban gray zone. Often students in great numbers occupy lower-quality residential areas surrounding the universities. Some American campuses draw over 50,000 people

Some of the more than 2 million inhabitants of modern Naples, Italy, crowd into the streets of its ancient city. (Photograph—United Nations)

daily—students, faculty, and office staff—and their traffic patterns rival those of a medium-sized city. Some universities provide special housing for the students, but in many big cities the majority have apartments, or rooms nearby, or are commuters. Faculty members sometimes appropriate the better residential areas near the university, or join the flight to the suburbs.

The fabric of cities needs constant repair. Completion of some single great renewal project does not mean that all is finished, but that efforts must shift to another area. Time moves on, buildings deteriorate, slums expand, business and industrial areas become outdated, streets need widening or replacement.

Many American cities (and European ones

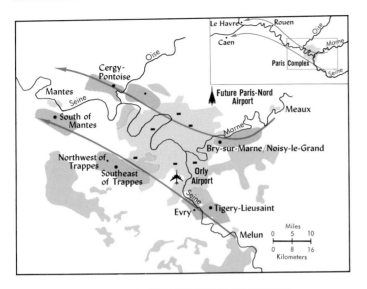

FIGURE
15-8
**GROWTH AXES FOR THE PARIS REGION**

The salient features of the "master plan" for the Paris region, proposed in 1965, are large new urban zones as a counter to the monolithic nature of metropolitan Paris; new cities in these urban zones; the reconstruction of urban areas in Paris; and the guiding of growth along axes toward the sea parallel to the Seine River. Based on a map in Ambassade de France, France: *Town and Country Planning,* New York, 1965.

- New Urban Zones
- Existing Urban Complex
- Forests
- • · New Cities
- - Urban Centers to Be Renovated

too) let things slide during the 1930s and 1940s. By the 1950s they faced a crisis which only massive expenditure of public funds could solve. The federal government stepped in and formed the Urban Renewal Administration.

Beginning about 1950, enormous sums were spent on lifting the once familiar face of "downtown" and the gray zone around it. Projects have cleared areas by the square mile, especially in the older sections of eastern cities like New York, Philadelphia, Boston, and Washington. Block on block of slums fell and in their stead rose massive apartment houses. New skyscraper offices re-

placed outworn buildings on the margins of the business districts. After the dust settled and the newly minted parts of the city appeared, it became clear that even the largest rebuilding programs are no panacea for metropolitan ills. Relocating slum tenants in a relatively short time is exceedingly difficult, and has been less than successful in many cases. Often people find no adequate new jobs for the ones they held in torndown neighborhoods.

Social dislocation, critics claim, vitiates much of the urban renewal program. Viable communities have been destroyed by renewal projects. It is said that instead of creating so many hundred or thousand housing units, adequate enough in themselves, efforts should concentrate on creating a community spirit. According to many experts, the vital theme of urban renewal should be to plan or reconstruct neighborhoods.

As renewal projects in specific locations are put into action, other areas deteriorate. In some cities the amount of inadequate housing increases during the time span of renovation programs. Keeping the city in efficient running order and making it a proud and pleasant place to live in cannot be left to random repair. Commonsense management with planning for the future is essential for changing times. To be effective physically and socially, renewal must be a continuous process, metropolitan in its scope (Glazer, 1965, 204).

## REGIONAL PLANNING AND NEW TOWNS
In the three decades since the end of World War II, the idea of comprehensive city planning has advanced far in western Europe. In 1945 the countries—victors and vanquished alike—were in a parlous state, their economies in disarray, cities in ruins, populations dislocated. A surge in planning accompanied postwar recovery. Far-reaching plans emerged for London, Paris, the Ruhr-Rhine, and Holland's Randstad (Figure 15–8). These plans provided for the preservation of greenbelts, controlled expansion of suburbs, slum clearance, and house building, and for redistribution of central-city inhabitants into new towns and new growth points. The impetus for these policies came from various sources.

Britain has already put into practice a number of new concepts. London had become too crowded, its suburbs formless, its center con-

FIGURE
**15-9**

**SOUTHEAST ENGLAND: PLANNED POPULATION RE-DISTRIBUTION**

This map shows the program of planned population migrations to "new towns" and "expanded towns." The zone between the outer limit of the greenbelt and the main built-up area of London is almost all part of the greenbelt, and is not available for any extensive building. Recent developments, based on the proposals by the Southeast Joint Planning Team (*Strategic Plan for the Southeast,* London, 1970), include a start to the development of the "new city" of Milton Keynes and the "expanded cities" of Peterborough and Northampton.

--- Boundary of Southeastern England

Built-up Areas in 1958

Land Over 400 Feet

**Existing Programs**

Outer Limits of Green Belt (Approved and Proposed)

(125) Existing New Towns (With Target Populations in Thousands)

(50) Expanding Towns (With Target Expansions in Thousands)

(200) Developing New Towns (With Target Populations in Thousands)

**Other Proposed Programs (From the Southeast Study)**

New Cities (150,000-250,000)

Big New Expansions (50,000-100,000)

Other Expansions (30,000 and Over)

gested, its quality of life deteriorated. During World War II plans were made for the peace to come. Among many prescriptions for the country's ills was the Greater London Plan (1944), which accepted the conclusions of the Barlow report (see above, page 368). The plan proposed that suburban house construction be restricted, that a greenbelt of open country be maintained around the built-up area, and that a number of new towns be placed beyond the greenbelt some 30 to 50 kilometers from the center of London. Each new town would be self-contained, with its own manufacturing industries and peopled by families from central London. The towns were to be on the "garden city" model, advocated in the nineteenth and early twentieth centuries by Ebenezer Howard. During the interwar era an example had been built, Welwyn Garden City, a private venture, 30 kilometers north of London.

Eight sites were selected (Figure 15-9), and with detailed meticulous plans complete, building got under way in the late 1940s. A public corporation developed each town, constructing houses, factories, neighborhoods, local shopping centers, business areas, social facilities, and schools. By 1962 the combined population of the new towns had reached 265,000, and they were attracting visitors from all over the world. With this experience, Britain began to build other towns in the industrial northern regions.

In retrospect, the original plans and their execution seemed somewhat doctrinaire. Controls relaxed, but other problems arose. Despite restrictions, an enormous number of people moved into the outer ring beyond the greenbelt; many towns up to 40 miles from the center of London expanded to double their number of inhabitants. The original population ceilings for the new towns became unrealistic.

Even in the mass, people are unpredictable. For example, fertility changes its pattern from time to time, confounding all estimates. The birth rate in England rose during the 1950s and early 1960s. At the same time immigration from overseas increased. Not only were the new towns permitted to admit more than first planned, but a number of selected old towns in southeastern England also experienced planned expansion. Even these failed to solve the problem of redistributing people and jobs. "Industry has grown rapidly in the New Towns partly as a reflection of the rapid growth in the southeast as a whole; people, especially skilled workers, have come to the New Towns not only from London but from the rest of Britain; the rise in the birth rate is causing unexpected growth in the New Towns and in London where it creates a new and a continuing overspill problem. Thus the problem of the growth of London, which the overspill policy was designed to solve once for all, has been exported to the New Towns and the ring of countryside within which they lie" (Hall, 1966, 51).

These issues, plus a heightened sense of urgency, led to larger proposals for the near future, including planned new cities with a third of a million or more inhabitants and radical expansion of many older towns and cities (Figure 15-9). Their economic base will be diverse, concentrating more than the older "new" towns on service activities. Among the large cities now being built is Milton Keynes (near Bletchley), headquarters of Britain's Open University, which has over 100,000 students, who take their course work at home. The main change in policy concerns not only size, but also distance. The new designs envisage the whole of southeastern England as an interlinked system of settlement focusing on London.

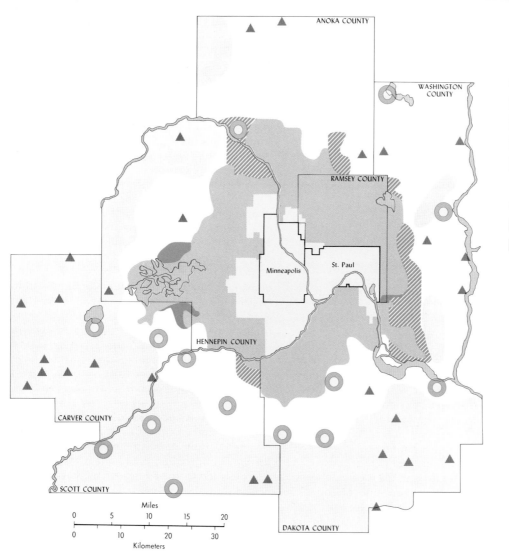

**Urban Service Area**

☐ Fully Developed Area

▨ Planned Urbanization, 1975

■ Additions, 1976-1980

▧ Additions, 1981-1990

◎ Freestanding Growth Center

**Rural Service Area**

☐ General Rural Use Region

☐ Commercial Agricultural Region

▲ Rural Center

FIGURE **MINNEAPOLIS-ST. PAUL METROPOLITAN AREA: EX-**
**15-10** **PECTED GROWTH PATTERNS**

The "development framework plan" for the Twin Cities metropolitan area was prepared and published by the Metropolitan Council. The Council is appointed by the governor of the state to represent community areas of the seven-county metropolitan area. With the passage of time the Council has been granted increasing powers to develop guidelines for planning and to review plans prepared by municipalities.

Three settlement policies guide the Council's framework: (1) to contain urban sprawl by limiting the ex-

pansion of the built-up area of the Twin Cities and by providing for the growth of "freestanding growth centers" beyond the limits of metropolitan expansion; (2) to revitalize the central cities by rehabilitating and constructing upper- and middle-income housing; (3) to provide housing opportunities for low-income groups in suburban areas and thus reduce the concentration of the poor in the inner cities. Based on a map in Metropolitan Council, *Development Framework* (and Appendix), September 1975.

The "new town" idea has spread to other European countries, sometimes in its garden city form, but more often modified to suit the settlement structure and the way of life of particular countries. An interesting variant in Britain is the very concentrated new town at Cumbernauld in Scotland. Another is the "new town in town," that is, the redevelopment of a substantial inner part of a metropolis according to an overall design to provide a partially self-contained community. Examples of this latter innovation are La Défense development in Paris and the Barbican scheme on the north edge of the old City of London.

## GOVERNMENTAL STRUCTURE

The proliferation of governmental units seems at times to be the most intractable of urban problems. In the United States, traditions of local autonomy have resulted in scores (in some city regions, hundreds) of different governmental units, often created for specific purposes (e.g., airports, schools, parks, highways, hospitals). Among the scattered welter of responsibilities, problems grow which, because no one deals with them comprehensively, remain nobody's problem, and thus go unsolved until disaster comes near. Then crash programs must be initiated, with new governmental units to administer them.

Some feel that the only solution is to establish a new order of government with total dissolution of the old, replacing local autonomy with metropolitan or regional control. But there are two reasons why such a radical cure will not do. Past experience shows that the best forms of government blend old ideas with the new. As Chinitz argues: "A community that waits for a whole new order to replace the old, and does not confront the challenge of reconciling the new with the old, runs a serious risk of waiting in vain" (Chinitz, 1965, 138). Further, there is no agreed solution either to metropolitan government or to the application of new technologies to metropolitan problems. It would be foolhardy to go to the extreme and establish a government that might be entirely unsuitable. Informed observers see no immediate solution. Chinitz proposes ". . . that the new order will not be implemented efficiently by private choice, that it cannot be implemented by the substitution of one giant local government where many existed before, and that a way must yet be found to inject a large measure of regional planning and decision" (Chinitz, 1965, 138–139).

Metropolitan governments, whether fragmented or unified, with or without planning machinery, face many issues, a number of which have been discussed in the foregoing pages. The greatest success in solving them has gone to those city regions that have an adequate and continuing metropolitan planning organization, with enough political power to convert its proposals into action. One may feel helpless to solve a problem, but by working with a community of citizens, one can translate this concern into accomplishment. An inspiring example is Stockholm, Sweden, where a city planning agency has operated since the seventeenth century. G. Sidenbladh (1965) has described its forward-looking planning policies and achievements. Other imaginative developments in metropolitan planning are those of Toronto and the Twin Cities (Figure 15-10).

## CITATIONS AND FURTHER READINGS

Abler, A. (ed.). *A Comparative Atlas of America's Great Cities*, Minneapolis, 1977.

Abromisov, P., et al. *Construction and Reconstruction of Towns 1945-1957*, 3 vols., the first two in English and Russian, Moscow, 1958.

Barlow, A. M. (chairman). *Report of Royal Commission on the Distribution of the Industrial Population*, London, 1940.

Borchert, J. R. "American Metropolitan Evolution," *Geographical Review*, 57 (1967): 301-332.

———— "America's Changing Metropolitan Regions," *Annals of the Association of American Geographers*, 62 (1972): 352-373.

Breese, G. *Urbanization in Newly Developing Countries,* Englewood Cliffs, N.J., 1966.

——— (ed.). *The City in Newly Developing Countries: Readings on Urbanism and Urbaniza-tion,* Englewood Cliffs, N.J., 1969.

Brooks, E., Herbert, D. T., and Peach, G. C. K. "Spatial and Social Constraints in the Inner City," *Geographical Journal,* 141 (1975): 355–379.

Chinitz, B. "New York: A Metropolitan Region," *Scientific American,* 213 (Sept., 1965): 134–148.

Coppock, J. T., and Prince, H. C. (eds.). *Greater London,* London, 1964.

Cox, K. R. *Conflict, Power and Politics in the City: a Geographic View,* New York, 1973.

Dickinson, R. E. *City and Region,* London, 1964.

Dwyer, D. J. (ed.). *The City in the Third World,* London and Basingstoke, 1974.

*Ekistics, Reviews on the Problems and Science of Human Settlements,* (monthly), Athens Center of Ekistics of the Athens Technological Institute, Athens, Greece, 1955–.

Forman, R. E. *Black Ghettos, White Ghettos, and Slums,* Englewood Cliffs, N.J., 1971.

Gad, G. "'Crowding' and 'Pathologies': Some Critical Remarks," *Canadian Geographer,* 17 (1973): 373–390.

Geddes, P. *Cities in Evolution,* London, 1915; New York, 1968.

——— *Patrick Geddes: Spokesman for Man and the Environment,* a selection, edited and with an introduction by M. Stalley, New Brunswick, N.J., 1972.

Glazer, N. "The Renewal of Cities," *Scientific American,* 213 (Sept., 1965): 195–204.

Gottmann, J. *Megalopolis: The Urbanized Northeastern Seaboard of the United States,* New York, 1961.

Gravier, J-F. *Paris et le désert français,* Paris, 1958.

Groves, P. A., and Muller, E. K. "The Evolution of Black Residential Areas in Late Nineteenth-Century Cities," *Journal of Historical Geography,* 1 (1975): 169–191.

Hall, P. *London 2000,* London, 1963.

——— *The World Cities,* New York, 1966.

——— "The Containment of Urban England," *Geographical Journal,* 140 (1974): 386–408.

Härö, A. S. "Area Cartogram of the SMSA Population of the United States," *Annals of the Association of American Geographers,* 58 (1968): 452–460.

Harries, K. D. "Ethnic Variations in Los Angeles Business Patterns," *Annals of the Association of American Geographers,* 61 (1971): 736–743.

Harris, C. D. *Cities of the Soviet Union: Studies of Their Functions, Size, Density, and Growth,* Association of American Geographers Monograph Series, no. 5, Chicago, 1970.

——— "Urbanization and Population Growth in the Soviet Union," *Geographical Review,* 61 (1971): 102–124.

Hartshorn, T. A. "Inner City Residential Structure and Decline," *Annals of the Association of American Geographers,* 61 (1971): 72–96.

Harvey, D. *Social Justice and the City,* London, 1973.

Horvath, R. J. "Machine Space," *Geographical Review,* 64 (1974): 167–188.

Howard, E. (F. J. Osborn (ed.) with introduction by L. Mumford). *Garden Cities of Tomorrow,* London, 1946, 1965 (originally published 1898).

International Urban Research. *The World's Metropolitan Areas,* Berkeley and Los Angeles, Calif., 1959.

Jones, P. N. "Colored Minorities in Birmingham, England," *Annals of the Association of American Geographers,* 66 (1976): 89–103.

Lewis, R. A., and Rowland, R. H. "Urbanization in Russia and the USSR: 1897–1966," *Annals of the Association of American Geographers,* 59 (1969): 776–796.

Merlin, P. *New Towns. Regional Planning and Development,* London, 1971.

Morrill, R. L. "The Negro Ghetto: Problems and Alternatives," *Geographical Review,* 55 (1965): 339–361.

Mumford, L. *The Culture of Cities,* New York, 1938.

——— *The City in History,* New York, 1961.

——— Open University. *The New Town Idea,* Milton Keynes, 1973.

——— *The City as a Social System,* Milton Keynes, 1973.

——— *The Spread of Cities,* Milton Keynes, 1973.

Park, R. E., Burgess, E. W., and Mackenzie, R. D. *The City,* Chicago, 1925.

Pokshishevsky, V. V. "Urbanization in the USSR," *Geoforum,* 9 (1972): 23–32.

Pred, A. "Intermetropolitan Location of American Manufacturing," *Annals of the Association of American Geographers,* 54 (1964): 165–180.

——— "Urbanisation, Domestic Planning Problems and Swedish Geographic Research," *Progress in Geography, International Reviews of Current Research,* 5 (1973): 1–76.

Robson, B. T. *Urban Analysis: A Study in City Structure,* Cambridge, England, 1969.

Rose, H. M. *Social Processes in the City: Race and Urban Residential Choice,* Association of American Geographers, Commission on College Geography, Resource Paper no. 6, Washington, D.C., 1969.

——— "The Development of an Urban Subsystem: The Case of the Negro Ghetto," *Annals of the Association of American Geographers,* 60 (1970): 1–17.

——— *The Black Ghetto: A Spatial Behavioral Perspective,* New York, 1971.

——— (ed.). "Contributions to an Understanding of Black America," *Economic Geography,* 48 (1972), no. 1. A symposium.

Senior, D. (ed.). *The Regional City: An Anglo-American Discussion of Metropolitan Planning,* Chicago, 1966.

Sidenbladh, G. "Stockholm, a Planned City," *Scientific American,* 213 (Sept., 1965): 107–118.

Southeast Joint Planning Team. *Strategic Plan for the Southeast,* London, 1970.

Swatridge, L. A. *The Bosnywash Metropolis: A Region of Great Cities,* Toronto, 1971.

Turner, R. (ed.). *India's Urban Future,* Berkeley and Los Angeles, Calif., 1962.

Ward, D. "The Emergence of Central Immigrant Ghettoes in American Cities: 1840–1920," *Annals of the Association of American Geographers,* 58 (1968): 343–359.

——— *Cities and Immigrants: A Geography of Change in Nineteenth Century America,* New York, 1971.

Webb, J. W. "The Natural and Migrational Components of Population Changes in England and Wales, 1921–1931," *Economic Geography,* 39 (1963): 130–148.

Winsemius, J. "Randstad Holland," *Tijdschrift voor Economische en Sociale Geografie,* 51 (1960): 188–199.

Yeates, M. H., and Garner, B. J. *The North American City,* New York, 1971.

Everybody talks about the population problem. Like the weather, it differs from place to place. Unlike the weather, something can be done about it. Birth and death are not mere biologic facts; their incidence reflects cultural values and economic conditions. That is why this discussion of the dynamic aspects of population is placed at the end of this volume, after the reader has become acquainted with the differentiation in culture realms, in developed and underdeveloped countries, in countryside and metropolis.

Part V opens with an analysis of the changing patterns of fertility and mortality, and the resulting natural growth, pointing up the tremendous increases we must expect in Asia, Africa, and most of Latin America. The subsequent chapter surveys the different forms of spatial mobility, from the great transoceanic migrations in the past to current population movements within national borders. Chapter 18 considers the problems of rapid population growth. Though securing an adequate food supply is doubtless the fundamental and urgent issue, overcrowding the earth's habitable space raises other and equally serious questions concerning the quality of human life. The latter topic is more fully discussed in the last chapter.

# PART V
# POPULATION CHANGE

**A** crowd on the waterfront in Bombay, India. (Photograph—Karl Potter)

# 16 THE DIFFERENTIAL GROWTH OF POPULATION

Our age is one of great happenings, swift changes, and perplexing problems. Among them is the rapid growth of world population, which doubled between 1900 and 1965, and may double again between 1970 and 2010. This view of the earth as a whole, while important, hides significant variations between the parts. The merit of the geographic approach to the study of population lies in its emphasis on regional differences. Seen in this way, the much-quoted worldwide explosion of population divides into a succession of bursts happening at different places at different times. This place-and-time perspective enables us to comprehend current growth patterns and from this vantage point to view the prospects.

## POPULATION GROWTH IN THE PAST

Archaeological evidence suggests that at the end of the last glaciation (about 10,000 B.C.) people lived as roaming gatherers, sparsely scattered over the earth. As they wandered through changing environments and improved their means of acquiring food, their numbers gradually increased. By about 8000 B.C. there may have been some 10 million people, widely dispersed throughout the world. At that time came a great population increase in consequence of the invention and spread of agriculture, which could support many more than subsistence gathering.

At the opening of the Christian Era the earth's population added up to some 280 million, which means that the annual growth rate (compounded annually) had averaged only 0.06 percent over the previous eighty centuries. These estimates and the more reliable figures for recent times form the basis for Figure 16-1 and Table 16-1. Modern annual growth rates are phenomenal when compared to those of the past. They rose from 0.3 percent between 1650 and 1750 to just under 1.9 percent today.

### PREHISTORIC TO ANCIENT TIMES

The rimlands of Asia and Nuclear America were the important centers of early farming. These agricultural communities supported two or more persons per square kilometer, a density many times that possible for gatherers. But the farmers were forced to migrate at irregular intervals, because of soil exhaustion or because their numbers had increased above the carrying capacity of the land.

After 4000 B.C. the rise of city-centered societies, linked with advances in farming, led to a fairly continuous zone of increasing population density stretching from the Mediterranean Sea across southwestern Asia into India and, by way of the Central Asian oases, to China. However, shifting political power, warfare, and other calamities caused temporal and regional variations in growth. Where and when a strongly centralized empire enforced peace, the population presumably grew rapidly: e.g., during the Persian Empire (550–425 B.C.), the Periclean Age in Athens (fifth century B.C.), the rule of Ashoka in India (third century B.C.), the Augustan Age of the Roman Empire (first century A.D.), and the Han dynasty in China (202 B.C.–A.D. 220).

Other parts of the earth were but thinly occupied. Pastoral nomadism, particularly in its primitive form, permitted only small bands to roam the vast steppelands of Asia and North Africa. In Europe north of the Alps, until the expansion of the Roman Empire, the tribes practiced a simple agriculture which at best could support only moderate numbers. In the margins of the

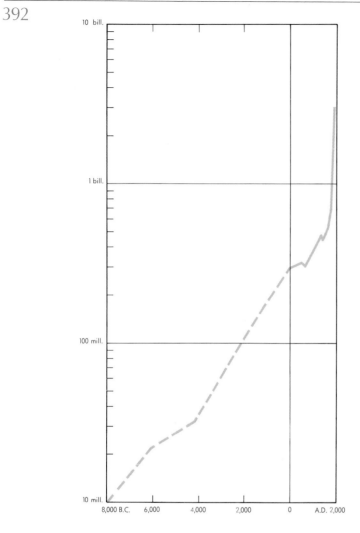

FIGURE **WORLD: POPULATION GROWTH FROM 8000** B.C.
**16-1**

This graph has a vertical logarithmic scale.

obscure in meaning. For other regions no early population data are available, although sometimes inferences can be made from archaeological evidence, size of armies, tax lists, and contemporary writings.

The Roman Empire in A.D. 14 totaled about 70 million people, which increased but slightly during the two succeeding centuries (some scholars advocate higher figures). Administrators of the Han dynasty carried out two censuses for China; they yield estimates of 70 million for A.D. 2 and 60 million for A.D. 156. Ancient India left no enumerations, but it is believed that there were from 100 million to 140 million during the reign of Ashoka, and about 70 million by A.D. 1. By adding modest numbers for Africa south of the Sahara, northern Europe, central and northern Asia, Oceania, and the Americas, we arrive at a total of about 280 million for A.D. 1.

## ANCIENT TO MODERN TIMES

The earth's population doubled during the first sixteen centuries of the Christian Era, but the growth was neither steady nor evenly distributed. The fall of the Roman Empire led to the wholesale depopulation of some frontier regions in Europe. On the other hand, the Mediterranean lands were generally able to absorb the barbarian invaders. During the Dark Ages from the seventh to the tenth century, Europe was periodically ravaged by famines and plagues. The Arabs invaded from the south, Vikings from the north, and mounted nomads from the east (Table 16–2).

In the tenth century began a long period of land colonization and a gradual revival of city life. For about three centuries the population increased, then leveled off as farmlands approached their limits of sustenance. In 1346 came another cycle of misery and death from the plague; in some regions the black death took one-half of the population. Recovery was hampered by the Hundred Years' War between France and England.

The sixteenth century, on the whole, was a period of growth by which the population attained, then surpassed, the level of 1340. There followed new losses, as in Germany during the Thirty Years' War (1618 to 1648), and during occasional outbreaks of bubonic plague. Nevertheless, Europe remained at about the 100 million mark throughout most of the seventeenth century.

world where knowledge of farming had not yet penetrated, populations remained scanty.

Reasonably accurate estimates of some populations can be made for the time around the beginning of the Christian Era, when enumerations were conducted in various countries. However, these sources are difficult to interpret. Roman censuses counted only citizens (perhaps only males); Chinese records may not have been complete; those of ancient American empires are

Southwest Asia and North Africa also lost population during medieval times. Mounted nomads invaded from Central Asia and Crusaders from western Europe, leading to slaughter, destruction, or neglect of irrigation systems. Epidemics of the plague and other diseases decimated the survivors. Not until the nineteenth century did these lands begin to regain their ancient population levels.

Fluctuations also characterized the population history of China, India, and other Asian countries. Numbers increased during periods of peace and order, when water control works expanded and food production rose. In turn, times

**WORLD POPULATION FROM 8000 B.C. TO THE PRESENT**

TABLE
16-1

| Date | Population, millions | | Average annual increase | | Number of generations |
|------|---------------------|---|---|---|---------------|
| | | | Millions | Percent* | |
| 8000 B.C. | 10 | | | | |
| | | Invention of agriculture, development of trade | 0.036 | 0.06 | 266 |
| A.D. 1 | 280 | | | | |
| | | Varied conditions in densely populated regions | 0.150 | 0.04 | 55 |
| 1650 | 520 | | | | |
| | | More peaceful conditions | 1.8 | 0.3 | |
| 1750 | 730 | | | | |
| | | Beginning of social and economic revolutions | 3.5 | 0.4 | |
| 1800 | 890 | | | | |
| | | Rapid growth of worldwide trading system | 5.3 | 0.5 | |
| 1850 | 1,170 | | | | |
| | | Spread of economic growth within European culture area | 8.7 | 0.7 | |
| 1900 | 1,670 | | | | |
| | | Continued economic growth and World War I | 10.1 | 0.7 | 13 |
| 1920 | 1,970 | | | | |
| | | Growth and depression, the loaded pause | 21.8 | 0.8 | |
| 1940 | 2,340 | | | | |
| | | World War II and its aftermath | 24.7 | 0.6 | |
| 1950 | 2,500 | | | | |
| | | Spread of economic and social development | 60.6† | 1.9† | |
| 1965 | 3,310 | | | | |
| | | Increasing political tensions and economic uncertainty | | | |
| 1975 | 4,150 | | 84.0† | 2.0† | |

*Rates of increase compounded annually.
†Amounts and rates of increase affected by improved collection of data.
SOURCE: Carr-Saunders (1936, 42); Clark (1968, 104); *World Population Estimates* (1976); authors' own unpublished estimates.

# THE POPULATION OF EUROPE: ANCIENT TO MODERN TIMES (MILLIONS)

**TABLE 16-2**

| Region | A.D. 1 | 600 | 1000 | 1200 | 1340* | 1500 | 1650 | 1800 | 1975 | |
|---|---|---|---|---|---|---|---|---|---|---|
| Greece and | 3.0 | 1.2 | 5.0 | 4.0 | 2.0 | 1.5 | 6.0 | 8.5 | 9.0 | Greece |
| Balkans | 2.0 | 1.8 | | | 2.0 | 3.0 | | | 32.5 | Bulgaria, Yugoslavia, Albania |
| Iberia | 6.0 | 3.6 | 7.0 | 8.0 | 9.5 | 8.3 | 6.3 | 13.4 | 44.1 | Spain, Portugal |
| Gaul | 6.6 | 3.0 | | | | | | | 53.0 | France |
| France-Lowlands | | | 7.0 | 12.0 | 30.0 | 16.0 | 22.1 | 33.2 | 23.9 | Belgium, Netherlands |
| Italy | 14.0 | 4.0 | 5.0 | 7.8 | 9.3 | 10.0 | 11.0 | 19.0 | 56.0 | Italy |
| | | | | | | | | | 6.5 | Switzerland |
| Germany and | 3.5 | 2.1 | 4.0 | 8.0 | 14.0 | 11.0 | 12.0 | 23.0 | 87.0 | Germany, Austria |
| Scandinavia | | | | | 0.6 | 0.5 | 1.0 | 1.8 | 22.2 | Scandinavia, Finland |
| Great Britain | 0.4 | 0.8 | 1.7 | 2.8 | 5.3 | 4.0 | 6.2 | 10.7 | 54.7 | Great Britain |
| Ireland | | | | | | | 1.6 | 5.2 | 4.6 | Ireland |
| Poland, etc. | | | 1.0 | 1.4 | 1.8 | 3.5 | 5.0 | 8.0 | 48.8 | Poland, Czechoslovakia |
| Russia | 4.0 | 2.8 | 7.5 | 6.0 | 8.0 | 6.0 | 14.5 | 40.0 | 254.3 | Soviet Union |
| Hungary | | | 1.0 | 1.5 | 2.0 | 4.0 | 2.5 | 5.0 | 31.6 | Hungary, Romania |
| TOTAL | 39.5 | 19.3 | 39.2 | 51.5 | 84.5 | 67.8 | 90.0 | 172.8 | 728.5 | |

*An estimate of Europe's population in 1400 is 40.7 million, a reduction of the 1340 estimate by 40 percent resulting from the black death, a form of plague.
SOURCES: Russell (1958, 148); Clark (1968, 64); authors' own unpublished estimates.

of internal disorder had the opposite effect. At the beginning of the modern period, China's population may have been in the order of 150 million, that of the Indian subcontinent 100 million.

Estimates for the population of the Americas for just before the coming of the Europeans in the late fifteenth century are based mainly on early Spanish reports, which are fragmentary and open to different interpretations. Recent studies suggest a population of up to or even more than 100 million, living mostly in the regions of Mexican and Andean civilizations (Borah and Cook, 1963). Spanish conquests extinguished these empires and brought on an unprecedented demographic collapse. The rapid spread of European diseases decimated the Americans, who had no biological defenses; military ruthlessness and economic destruction also dislocated them. By 1650 the population of the Americas had been reduced to less than 15 million. These critical events determined basic world patterns for centuries to come. They help explain why America became more European than Asia or Africa did. Indirectly

they caused most of the African slave trade, with the consequent disruption of African societies, for the surviving Indian populations were unable to fulfill the Europeans' needs for plantation labor. The pre-Columbian Indian population in North America—in the sense of present Anglo-America —was as high as 7 to 10 million. Here too, European intrusion led to a drastic reduction in numbers.

## FROM THE SEVENTEENTH TO THE TWENTIETH CENTURY

Table 16-3 offers a comparison of the populations of the continents at various dates from 1650 to 1970 and gives average annual growth rates, calculated on a compounded basis. Nearer our own times, estimates can be made with greater accuracy. Census enumeration and collection of birth and death data started in northern Europe in the eighteenth century. During the nineteenth century most modernizing countries adopted these procedures. By now nearly all countries have begun them, especially since first the League of Nations, then the United Nations, provided assistance in collecting the data. Carr-Saunders (1936), Wilcox (1940), and Clark (1968) sifted available evidence on regional populations up to about 1900; Clark's estimates have been used for Table 16–3, modified to include the Asian part of the present-day Soviet Union in the European totals.

The European Culture Realm (Figure 16–2) Two outstanding new departures mark the population geography of the earth since 1650: a sharp acceleration in growth rates, and large-scale long-distance migrations. The latter (discussed in the next chapter) were mainly by Europeans or at their instigation, especially the transportation of Africans as slaves to the Americas.

Adding the populations of the Americas, Soviet Asia, and Oceania to those of Europe gives an approximate figure for the European culture area (Table 16–3). Since 1650 its population has multiplied elevenfold. By contrast, Africa and Asia combined have multiplied only sixfold. In the Americas the sustained high rates resulted partly from continual immigration. The second half of the nineteenth century especially witnessed great numerical advances among European populations. This growth slackened in the twentieth century during wars and economic depression,

**THE POPULATIONS OF THE CONTINENTS, 1650–1970 (MILLIONS)**

TABLE
16–3

| Date | Africa | Asia (excl. U.S.S.R.) | Europe (incl. U.S.S.R.) | North America | Middle and South America | Oceania | European culture area* |
|------|--------|------|------|------|------|------|------|
| 1650 | 100 | 306 | 96 | ? | ? | 2 | |
| 1700 | 98 | 416 | 112 | 1 | 12 | 2 | 127 |
| 1750 | 95 | 478 | 136 | 2 | 13 | 2 | 153 |
| 1800 | 90 | 584 | 179 | 6 | 19 | 2 | 206 |
| 1850 | 100 | 741 | 274 | 26 | 33 | 2 | 335 |
| 1900 | 122 | 985 | 411 | 81 | 63 | 6 | 561 |
| 1920 | 140 | 1,124 | 487 | 117 | 91 | 9 | 704 |
| 1930 | 157 | 1,202 | 532 | 135 | 109 | 10 | 786 |
| 1940 | 176 | 1,303 | 573 | 146 | 131 | 11 | 861 |
| 1950 | 207 | 1,370 | 594 | 167 | 162 | 13 | 936 |
| 1960 | 254 | 1,679 | 641 | 199 | 206 | 16 | 1,062 |
| 1970 | 344 | 2,056 | 705 | 233 | 283 | 19 | 1,240 |

Percentage change (compounded annually)

| | Africa | Asia (excl. U.S.S.R.) | Europe (incl. U.S.S.R.) | North America | Middle and South America | Oceania | European culture area* |
|------|--------|------|------|------|------|------|------|
| 1650–1700 | −0.04 | 0.5 | 0.3 | ? | ? | 0.0 | |
| 1700–1750 | −0.06 | 0.4 | 0.4 | 1.5 | 0.1 | 0.0 | 0.4 |
| 1750–1800 | −0.1 | 0.4 | 0.6 | 4.0 | 0.7 | 0.0 | 0.6 |
| 1800–1850 | 0.2 | 0.4 | 0.8 | 3.0 | 1.0 | 0.0 | 0.9 |
| 1850–1900 | 0.4 | 0.6 | 0.9 | 2.3 | 1.6 | 2.2 | 1.0 |
| 1900–1920 | 0.7 | 0.6 | 0.7 | 1.8 | 1.9 | 2.1 | 1.1 |
| 1920–1930 | 1.0 | 0.6 | 0.9 | 1.5 | 1.8 | 1.1 | 1.1 |
| 1930–1940 | 1.1 | 0.7 | 0.8 | 0.7 | 1.8 | 1.0 | 1.0 |
| 1940–1950 | 1.5† | 0.4 | 0.3 | 1.4 | 2.1 | 1.7 | 0.8 |
| 1950–1960 | 2.5† | 2.0† | 0.8 | 1.8 | 2.4† | 2.1 | 1.3† |
| 1960–1970 | 3.1† | 2.1† | 1.0 | 1.7† | 3.2† | 1.8 | 1.5† |

*After 1650. The European culture area includes American Indian and other indigenous populations.
†Rates of increase affected by improved collection of population data.
SOURCE: Carr-Saunders (1936); Clark (1968, 59–122); World Population Estimates (1976).

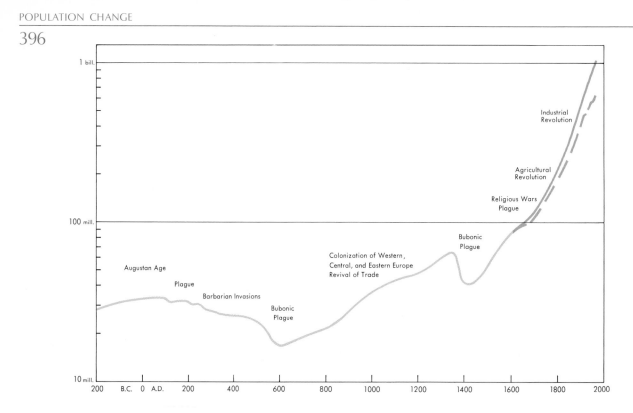

FIGURE **THE POPULATION OF EUROPE AND THE EUROPEAN**
**16-2** **CULTURE AREA SINCE ANCIENT TIMES**

After A.D. 1600 the dashed line shows the growth of Europe's population, the solid line that of Europe plus the Americas, Russian Asia, and Oceania. The vertical scale is logarithmic.

and only after 1945 resumed higher rates, though with variations between different parts of the Occidental realm.

**Asia and Africa** Asia's population increased more than fourfold from the mid-seventeenth century to the mid-twentieth. By 1975, Asia had about 2,400 million—well over half the world's total. In China the founding of the Manchu dynasty (1644–1912) initiated a long period of prosperity and colonization, which led to the tripling of the population between 1650 and 1850. But thereafter the growth rate slowed as floods, famines, epidemics, and warfare brought higher mortality. After 1950 the march of population resumed with only minor interruptions. Estimates of the late

1970s give a total approaching 1 billion for China and 110 million for Japan.

South Asia (India–Pakistan–Bangladesh–Sri Lanka) underwent a more gradual growth from the seventeenth through the nineteenth century, rising to 255 million in 1871. The rate of growth accelerated during the late nineteenth and early twentieth centuries, checked only once by the severe influenza epidemic after World War I. By 1977 South Asia's population had reached 850 million.

In both Southwest and Southeast Asia, growth patterns varied from one oasis, delta land, or island to another. On the whole, they saw only slight increases until the late nineteenth century, when the rates became more rapid, often exceeding those of East or South Asia. On the island of Java, however, swift increases began in the nineteenth century as the Dutch developed the economy. From an estimated 5 million in the first decade of the 1800s it grew to 30 million in 1905. In 1931 Java numbered 41.7 million, in 1970 some

An East African farmer and his wife and five children have a hard time making a living. (Photograph—United Nations)

70 million—all these people, chiefly rural, in an area no larger than the state of New York.

North Africa and the southern two-thirds of the continent differed in demographic trends. In North Africa, growth changed from slow to rapid toward the end of the nineteenth century. South of the Sahara the ravages of the slave trade caused an actual population decline until about 1800. It has been calculated that slaving operations eliminated as many as 50 million Africans, the greater part by death in warfare and from maltreatment before they reached the embarkation ports (Davidson, 1961). In the nineteenth century the population recovered slowly, and in the present century grew at a faster pace. By the 1960s several Meso-African countries were increasing at a very high rate and continued to do so in the 1970s.

## BIRTH AND DEATH RATES

Natural growth is the positive difference between births and deaths. To compare among nations the fertility and mortality (the incidence of births and deaths), we need some simple yardsticks. The *crude birth rate* compares the number of live births in a given year to the total population and is usually expressed in numbers per 1,000; for example, in 1975 the rate for the United States was 14 and for Mexico 46 per 1,000. The *crude death rate* compares the number of deaths to the total population in a given year; in the United States in 1975 it was 9 and in Mexico 8 per 1,000. The *natural increase rate* for the United States in 1975 was 5, and for Mexico 38 per 1,000.

## THE DEMOGRAPHIC TRANSFORMATION

Analysis of population data for the Occidental culture area reveals that economic development was accompanied by a demographic progression through different phases of birth-death relationships. Taking western Europe as an example, the first stage was before 1800 when high birth rates and high death rates resulted in static or, at most, slightly increasing numbers. After 1800 the second stage began, when mortality dropped slowly but steadily as the economy expanded and simple health measures found acceptance. Since fertility at first maintained a relatively high level, the growing excess of births over deaths led to a sharp increase in numbers (Figure 16–3).

The third stage opened when the idea of family limitation began to spread. The need for many births dwindled as more children survived, and as income from child labor decreased. More important, old traditions weakened: A large family came to be felt as an obstacle toward achieving individual aspirations. Effective contraceptives, a product of modern technology, provided the means to limit family size. As birth rates dropped, at first slowly, then more rapidly, the growth curve flattened out. The demographic transformation ended with the fourth stage: a much higher number of people than at the start, with birth and death rates at low levels.

Observation of these changes in Europe has led to formulation of the hypothesis that all societies of the world will pass through the same demographic transformation as they shift from traditional to modern ways. But this hypothesis, as the word implies, is only a supposition. Is the European experience a reliable guide for predicting what will happen in other culture realms? Their death rates have dropped more quickly than in Europe—in numerous cases they are at very low levels—their birth rates may, or may not, decline as rapidly. Depending on these trends, the resulting population increments will differ considerably.

One might ask: Since the death rate in a number of underdeveloped countries has fallen much faster than in Europe, why cannot a break-through to a low fertility level be achieved just as rapidly? The answer is that everyone wants to avoid death, but that the personal decisions regarding family size are governed by a host of social and economic factors. These can change only gradually. Nevertheless, here lies an intriguing and significant issue: Must family planning wait until a society is economically modernized? Or can it be successfully injected at an early stage? As yet there is no clear answer.

## POPULATION PROJECTIONS

Crude birth and death rates relate fertility and mortality to total population numbers. They are not, however, by themselves accurate predictors of future populations. In western Europe birth rates were so low in the 1930s that demographers then forecast the decline of many national populations. By 1975 many of the same countries still had birth rates as low as those of the 1930s; however, there is no talk now of imminent population decline. Why is this? Because the crude birth rate fails to consider the age and sex structure of the population. Populations that pass through the demographic transformation develop variable numbers in different age groups (see the age and sex diagram for Sweden, Figure 16–15). For such countries we need more sophisticated measures of fertility.

A population with an abnormally large proportion of women of childbearing age has a relatively high crude birth rate, even if family size is small. Conversely, a relatively small number of potential mothers means low birth rates, even if family size is large. The *gross reproduction ratio*, which relates the number of potential mothers to the number of female children they bear, gives an estimate of the potential size of the next generation. While the precise method of this ratio's calculation need not concern us here, the ratio would be 1.00 if the average 1,000 women between 15 and 45 had 1,000 female children.

However, some girls die young, and there are varying rates of marriage and motherhood among adult females. We obtain a more exact

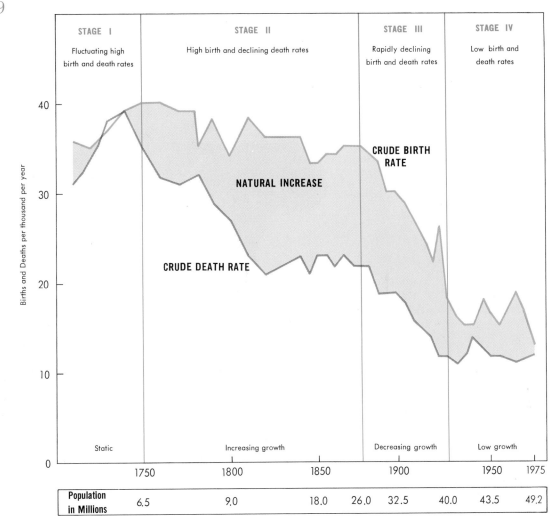

| STAGE I | STAGE II | STAGE III | STAGE IV |
|---|---|---|---|
| Fluctuating high birth and death rates | High birth and declining death rates | Rapidly declining birth and death rates | Low birth and death rates |

NATURAL INCREASE

CRUDE BIRTH RATE

CRUDE DEATH RATE

Births and Deaths per thousand per year

| Static | Increasing growth | Decreasing growth | Low growth |

| Population in Millions | 6.5 | 9.0 | 18.0 | 26.0 | 32.5 | 40.0 | 43.5 | 49.2 |
|---|---|---|---|---|---|---|---|---|

FIGURE 16-3 THE DEMOGRAPHIC TRANSFORMATION IN ENGLAND AND WALES

Huge population increase occurs when the death rate falls and the birth rate remains high. The length of time high increase continues and the amount of increase per year depend on economic and social conditions in individual countries.

ratio by taking account of expected deaths among girls between birth and marriage and of expected marriage rates. This is the *net reproduction ratio,* which being more precise is a better predictor of population. A net reproduction ratio of 2.00 would mean that, other things being equal, the next generation of mothers (or parents) would number twice that of the present generation; a ratio of 0.50 would mean halving the parental population in the next generation. In the United States the net reproduction ratio was below unity in the 1930s, rose rapidly in the late 1940s to a peak in the 1950s, then declined in the 1960s and early 1970s. Thus, the low crude birth rates in many

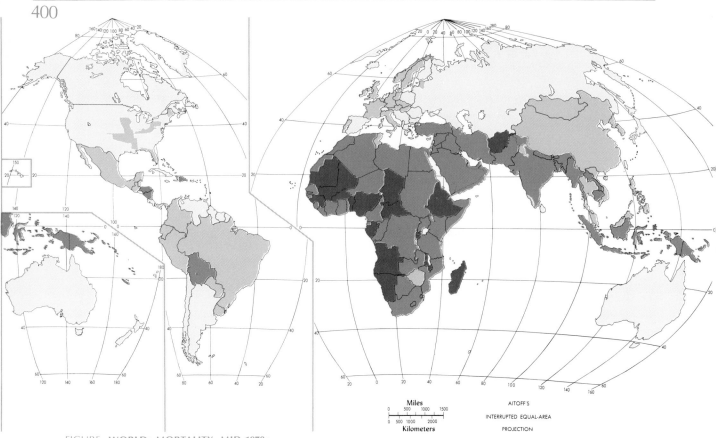

Miles
0  500  1000  1500

Kilometers
0  500 1000  2000

AITOFF'S

INTERRUPTED EQUAL-AREA

PROJECTION

FIGURE  **WORLD: MORTALITY, MID-1970s**
16-4

A generation ago only economically advanced countries had low death rates. After World War II death control spread to most countries of Asia, Africa, and Latin America; in those regions death rates as low as those of Europe and North America are now quite common. Sources of data: *Population Index;* United Nations *Demographic Yearbook;* Population Reference Bureau, *World Population Data Sheet 1976,* Washington, D.C., 1976; Environmental Fund, *World Population Estimates, 1976,* Washington, D.C., 1976.

economically advanced countries result from many factors, among which the number of parents relative to the total population is important.*

Figure 16–7 shows for a number of countries the divergence between crude birth rates and net reproduction rates. Some of the figures must be regarded as only provisional, since the raw statistics on which they are based are incomplete. Most countries are now collecting and publishing vital data of this kind, permitting more accurate statements and predictions than before.

### MORTALITY IN THE TWENTIETH CENTURY

To comprehend the population changes now in progress, we must look more closely at recent death and birth rates in various regions. The maps

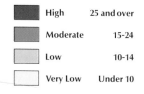

**Crude Death Rates, Mid-1970s**
**(per Thousand)**

| | | |
|---|---|---|
| ■ | High | 25 and over |
| ▨ | Moderate | 15-24 |
| ▢ | Low | 10-14 |
| □ | Very Low | Under 10 |

*The net reproduction ratio can be further refined by taking into account the relative number of potential mothers by single or five-year age groups.

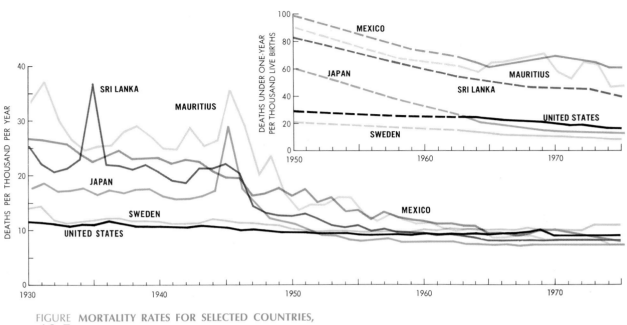

FIGURE MORTALITY RATES FOR SELECTED COUNTRIES,
16-5 1930-1975

depicting the distribution of these indexes in the mid-1970s (Figures 16-4 and 16-6) provide instructive comparisons. Table 16-4 presents the current demographic situation in some fifty countries.

Until recently, the prevalence of death marked all but the most modernized societies. Only forty years ago a list of national death rates clearly showed the distinction between developed and underdeveloped countries. For many in the poverty-stricken lands, poor diet and constant exposure to disease led to general debilitation and early death; famine, epidemic, and natural disaster occasionally carried away large numbers. The impact of calamity varied widely. In countries with relatively low death rates (below 15 per 1,000), the worldwide swine influenza epidemic of 1918 brought only a slight rise in mortality. Sweden, for example, that year had 18 deaths per 1,000 instead of the then normal rate of 14 per 1,000. In contrast, mortality in India rose from the level of about 30 per 1,000 to 85 in 1918.

In the 1930s average life expectancy at birth was only 27 years in India, 33 in Mexico, and 36 in Chile, mostly because so many children died in infancy. In some countries the *infant mortality*

*rate* (the annual number of deaths among infants under one year per 1,000 live births) was as high as 250. In economically advanced countries, however, life expectancy at birth was more than 60 years and the infant mortality rate in most cases below 50 (Figure 16-5).

By 1970 much had changed (Figure 16-4). Most regions have seen the spread of death control through the reduction of disease and rapid mobilization of assistance to disaster areas. Crude death rates in many countries of Asia, Latin America, and east and south Europe sank to the Anglo-American and West European level, or even lower. In some cases death retreated with dramatic suddenness. In Sri Lanka (Ceylon) the widespread application of insecticides brought virtually instant suppression of malaria and fly-borne diseases. The crude death rate per 1,000 tumbled from 20 in 1946 to 13 in 1948, and 9 in 1951. In the island of Mauritius the rate dropped in one decade from 27 to 10 per 1,000 (Figures 16-5 and 16-10).

These events and their consequences stand in vivid contrast to the European experience. Mortality reduction in Europe and also in Anglo-America closely coincided with the gradually ris-

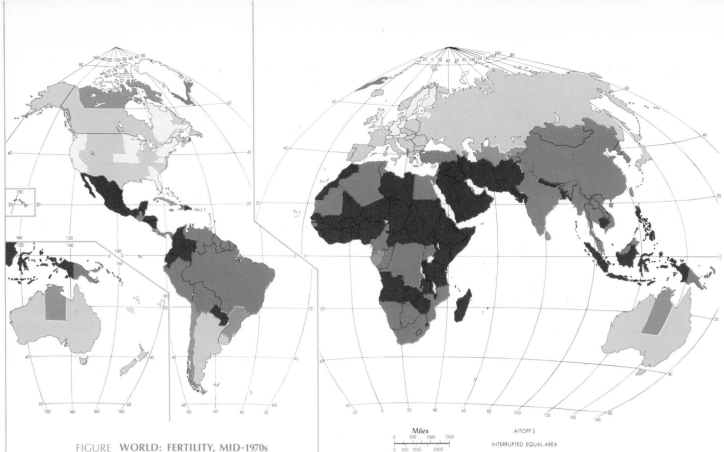

Miles
0   500  1000  1500
0  500 1000  2000
Kilometers

AITOFF'S
INTERRUPTED EQUAL-AREA
PROJECTION

FIGURE **WORLD: FERTILITY, MID-1970s**
16-6

Unlike the map of mortality, the world fertility pattern remains much the same as it was before World War II. The lowest birth rates are in central Europe, the highest in tropical Africa and America and in some countries in southern Asia. Sources of data: See Figure 16-4.

**Crude Birth Rates, Mid-1970s**
**(per Thousand)**

| | | |
|---|---|---|
| ■ | Very High | 45 and over |
| ■ | High | 35-44 |
| ■ | Moderate | 25-34 |
| ■ | Low | 15-24 |
| □ | Very Low | Under 15 |

ing domestic levels of living. The countries now experiencing this sudden death control owe it mostly to external aid. It has come with such a rush that quite often the ensuing population explosion finds the economy unprepared to meet the situation, with the result that the people—

more people—continue to live as marginally as before.

**FERTILITY IN THE TWENTIETH CENTURY**

In the 1930s low fertility was confined to western Europe, Anglo-America, and Australia–New Zealand. Only in small measure was it a response to the depressed economic conditions of that decade; low rates had already appeared in these countries in the 1920s. Moderate rates prevailed in southern Latin America, central and southern Europe, and Japan. Elsewhere high, or very high, fertility was common, with some parts of Asia and Africa recording crude birth rates of 50 or more per 1,000.

In the mid-1970s tropical America, Africa, and Asia maintained their high fertility. A number of countries, formerly with very high birth rates, have experienced some reductions so that now they are merely high on the list; among them are Indonesia, India, and Brazil. A few small countries with formerly high fertility now have low birth rates, such as Puerto Rico, Hong Kong, Taiwan, and the former British West Indies. Others now

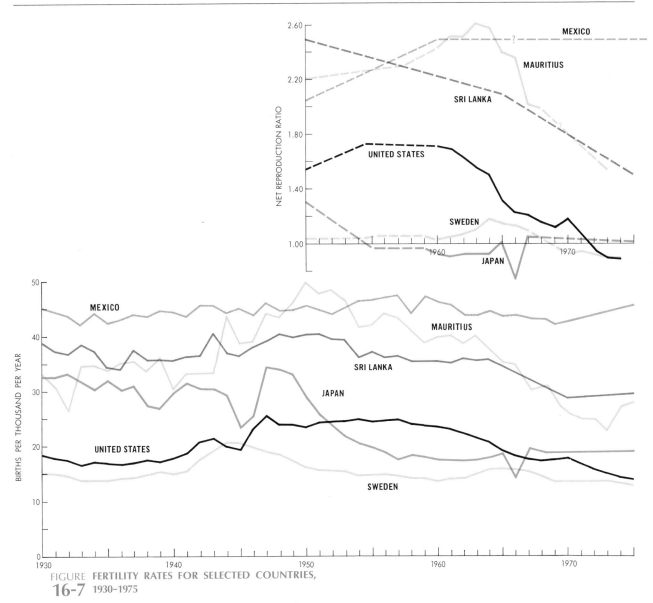

FIGURE FERTILITY RATES FOR SELECTED COUNTRIES,
16-7 1930-1975

have moderate rates, most notably mainland China, but also Sri Lanka (Ceylon), Korea, Costa Rica, Cuba, and Chile (Figure 16-6).

Some countries with moderate birth rates a generation ago have dropped to low rates, for example, Japan, the Soviet Union, the socialist republics of Central Europe, and the Mediterranean countries of Greece, Italy, Spain, and Portugal. Lastly, the increasingly affluent modern countries showed small gains in fertility after World War II. This rise, higher and more persistent in Canada, Australia, and New Zealand than in the United States and western Europe, was apparently a temporary phenomenon. Fertility in these regions is now back to levels as low as or lower than in the 1930s (Figure 16-7).

High birth rates are bound to fall for the simple reason that, in the long run, death control is impossible without birth control. The big question, however, is when and how much fertility

In many countries birth rates remain very high and population increases rapidly. This may bring food shortages, inadequate housing, poor facilities for education, and heavy underemployment. Though birth control is a universal concern, its use spreads but slowly. In the fields outside Lashkargar, Afghanistan, a midwife-nurse in a nomad's tent interviews Kuchi women. (Photograph—United Nations)

will decline in the countries where it is still high. Usually a small "elite" minority already practices family limitation, while the remainder of the society retains traditional attitudes. The masses probably will change their values if the modern way of life takes hold. But the process may be very slow, in part because high fertility puts a brake on economic advance. The governments of a number of countries now realize the adverse effect of unbridled population growth.

The two largest groupings of mankind, India with 650 million and China with about 950 million population, now engage in birth-control propaganda. So far the results have been quite different, owing mainly to their divergent ideologies and political institutions: China's more authoritarian regime evidently has succeeded in reducing fertility to moderate levels; India's birth rate remains high despite the government's recent attempts to interfere in private lives. Evidently attempts at persuasion do not always cause peoples to reduce their fertility rapidly.

## THE CURRENT DEMOGRAPHIC SITUATION

The relation of fertility level to mortality level defines each country's position in the demographic transformation (Table 16–4 and Figure 16–8). The regional differentiation in the mid-1970s can be summed up as follows:

1. Low fertility (crude birth rate under 25 per 1,000) and low mortality (crude death rate below 15 per 1,000) characterized Europe, Anglo-

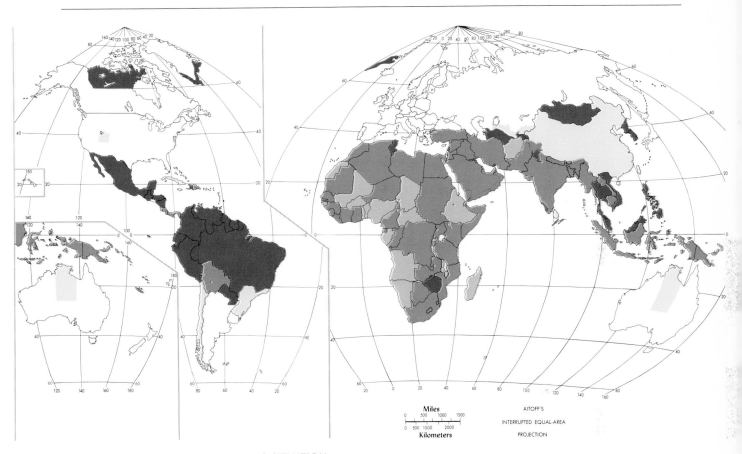

FIGURE WORLD: DEMOGRAPHIC SITUATION
16-8 IN THE MID-1970s

This map analyzes rates of natural increase by classifying countries according to their combination of crude birth and death rates.

**Rates per Thousand**

| | High Birth Rates | Over 35 |
|---|---|---|
| | High Death Rates | Over 25 |
| | High Birth Rates | Over 35 |
| | Moderate Death Rates | 15-25 |
| | High Birth Rates | Over 35 |
| | Low Death Rates | Under 15 |
| | Moderate Birth Rates | 25-35 |
| | Low Death Rates | Under 15 |
| | Low Birth Rates | Under 25 |
| | Low Death Rates | Under 15 |

America, the Soviet Union, Australia and New Zealand, and also Japan and southern Latin America. Natural increases in these regions were low to moderate. A few countries had stationary populations.

2. Moderate fertility (25–35 per 1,000) and low mortality occurred in mainland China, many of the Caribbean islands, Costa Rica, Chile, Sri Lanka, Israel, and some Pacific islands, yielding increases from moderate to high.

3. High fertility (35–45 per 1,000) or very high fertility (over 45 per 1,000) together with low mortality or very low mortality (under 10 per 1,000) prevailed over almost all of Latin America and in southeast and eastern Asia (excluding China), as well as in a few countries in Africa. Under these conditions natural increase was very high.

TABLE
16-4

| Country | Population mid-1976, millions* | Crude rates per thousand | | Annual increase percent‡ | Urban population, percent§ | Population under 15 percent† | Gross national product per capita |
|---|---|---|---|---|---|---|---|
| | | Births† | Deaths† | | | | |
| Very high population increase (3.0 percent per year or more) | | | | | | | |
| Pakistan | 74.2 | 51 | 18 | 3.6 | 26 | 45 | 130 |
| Philippines | 45.9 | 45 | 12 | 3.3 | 32 | 47 | 310 |
| Thailand | 42.7 | 43 | 10 | 3.1 | 13 | 43 | 300 |
| Iran | 36.0 | 45 | 17 | 3.1 | 43 | 46 | 1,060 |
| Colombia | 26.6 | 45 | 11 | 3.2 | 64 | 47 | 510 |
| South Africa | 25.9 | 40 | 17 | 3.1 | 48 | | 1,200 |
| Sudan | 18.9 | 50 | 18 | 3.0 | 13 | 47 | 150 |
| Morocco | 18.0 | 50 | 16 | 3.4 | 37 | 46 | 430 |
| North Korea | 17.0 | 39 | 11 | 3.2 | 38 | | 390 |
| Algeria | 16.2 | 39 | 17 | 3.3 | 50 | 47 | 650 |
| Peru | 16.0 | 42 | 11 | 3.0 | 60 | 45 | 710 |
| Tanzania | 16.0 | 47 | 22 | 3.0 | 7 | 44 | 140 |
| Kenya | 14.1 | 48 | 18 | 3.7 | 10 | 46 | 200 |
| Venezuela | 13.3 | 41 | 8 | 3.4 | 75 | 46 | 1,710 |
| Uganda | 11.9 | 43 | 18 | 3.3 | 8 | 44 | 160 |
| Iraq | 11.4 | 49 | 15 | 3.4 | 61 | 45 | 970 |
| Ghana | 10.3 | 47 | 18 | 3.0 | 29 | 47 | 350 |

Also: Khmer Republic (Cambodia) (population 8.7 million in 1976), Dominican Republic 5.1, Ecuador 7.3, Rhodesia 6.6, Syria 7.6, Saudi Arabia 9.2, Zambia 5.1, and sixteen other states and territories with less than 5.0 million population.

| High population increase (2.0–2.9 percent per year) | | | | | | | |
|---|---|---|---|---|---|---|---|
| China | 964.4 | 33 | 9 | 2.4 | 23 | | 300 |
| India | 652.7 | 43 | 17 | 2.6 | 20 | 42 | 130 |
| Indonesia | 143.4 | 48 | 19 | 2.3 | 18 | 44 | 150 |
| Brazil | 113.0 | 38 | 10 | 2.9 | 58 | 43 | 900 |
| Nigeria | 83.8 | 50 | 25 | 2.5 | 16 | 43 | 240 |
| Mexico | 60.5 | 46 | 8 | 2.2 | 61 | 46 | 1,000 |
| Bangladesh | 82.9 | 46 | 17 | 2.7 | 9 | | 100 |
| Vietnam | 46.6 | 40 | 12 | 2.8 | 23 | | 150 |
| Turkey | 41.3 | 40 | 15 | 2.3 | 39 | 42 | 690 |
| Egypt | 37.9 | 44 | 16 | 2.3 | 43 | 43 | 280 |
| South Korea | 37.1 | 31 | 11 | 2.2 | 41 | 33 | 470 |
| Burma | 31.9 | 40 | 17 | 2.4 | 19 | 40 | 90 |
| Ethiopia | 29.9 | 46 | 25 | 2.6 | 11 | 44 | 90 |
| Zaïre | 25.6 | 44 | 23 | 2.8 | 25 | 42 | 150 |
| Afghanistan | 19.7 | 51 | 27 | 2.5 | 15 | | 100 |
| Taiwan | 16.4 | 23 | 5 | 2.0 | 63 | 43 | 720 |
| Sri Lanka (Ceylon) | 14.0 | 30 | 8 | 2.0 | 22 | 41 | 230 |
| Nepal | 12.9 | 45 | 23 | 2.3 | 4 | 40 | 110 |
| Malaysia | 12.7 | 38 | 11 | 2.7 | 27 | 44 | 660 |

Also: Bolivia (population 5.6 million in 1976), Cameroon 6.6, Haiti 5.2, Guatemala 6.2, Malagasy Republic 7.7, Malawi 5.1, Mali 5.8, Ivory Coast 5.0, Tunisia 5.9, Upper Volta 6.1, Yemen 6.8, and thirty-five other states and territories with less than 5.0 million population.

TABLE
16-4

| Country | Population mid-1976 millions* | Crude rates per thousand | | Annual increase percent‡ | Urban population, percent§ | Population under 15 percent† | Gross national product per capita |
|---|---|---|---|---|---|---|---|
| | | Births† | Deaths† | | | | |
| Moderate population increase (1.0–1.9 percent per year) | | | | | | | |
| Soviet Union | 256.8 | 18 | 9 | 1.0 | 60 | 28 | 2,300 |
| United States | 222.2 | 14 | 9 | 1.3 | 74 | 29 | 6,640 |
| Japan | 112.2 | 19 | 7 | 1.1 | 72 | 24 | 3,880 |
| Spain | 36.0 | 19 | 8 | 1.1 | 61 | 28 | 1,960 |
| Argentina | 26.3 | 23 | 9 | 1.4 | 81 | 30 | 1,900 |
| Canada | 23.1 | 16 | 7 | 1.3 | 76 | 30 | 6,080 |
| Romania | 21.5 | 20 | 9 | 1.0 | 42 | 26 | 2,000 |
| Australia | 13.7 | 18 | 9 | 1.4 | 86 | 29 | 4,760 |
| Chile | 10.8 | 26 | 9 | 1.7 | 76 | 39 | 820 |

Also: Angola (population 6.6 million in 1976), Cuba 9.4, and eleven other countries and territories with less than 5.0 million population.

| | | | | Low population increase (0.1–0.9 percent per year) | | | |
|---|---|---|---|---|---|---|---|
| Italy | 56.2 | 16 | 10 | 0.7 | 53 | 24 | 2,770 |
| France | 53.3 | 15 | 10 | 0.7 | 70 | 25 | 5,190 |
| Poland | 34.4 | 18 | 8 | 0.9 | 55 | 28 | 2,450 |
| Yugoslavia | 21.5 | 18 | 8 | 0.9 | 39 | 28 | 1,250 |
| Czechoslovakia | 14.9 | 20 | 12 | 0.5 | 56 | 24 | 3,220 |
| Netherlands | 13.8 | 14 | 8 | 0.9 | 77 | 27 | 4,880 |
| Hungary | 10.6 | 18 | 12 | 0.3 | 49 | 21 | 2,140 |

Also: Belgium (population 9.8 million in 1971), Bulgaria 8.8, Denmark 5.1, Greece 9.0, Portugal 8.5, Sweden 8.2, Switzerland 6.5, and seven other countries with less than 5.0 million population.

| | | | | Stationary population | | | |
|---|---|---|---|---|---|---|---|
| West Germany | 62.1 | 10 | 12 | 0.2 | 88 | 25 | 5,890 |
| United Kingdom | 56.1 | 13 | 12 | 0.5 | 76 | 24 | 3,360 |
| East Germany | 16.8 | 10 | 13 | 0.0 | 75 | 24 | 3,430 |

Also: Austria (population 7.5 million in 1976) and Barbados and Malta.

*Based on estimates by the U.S. Bureau of the Census.
†Latest available year.
‡Annual rate of population growth, composed of births minus deaths modified by net migration and expressed as a percentage of total population.
§Percentage of population living in urban areas as defined in each country.
SOURCES: *Population Index*, various issues; United Nations, *Monthly Bulletin of Statistics*, various issues; Population Reference Bureau, *World Population Data Sheet*, 1976; The Environmental Fund, *World Population Estimates*, 1976; *World Book Atlas: Population, Per Capita Product, and Growth Rates*, 1975.

4. High or very high fertility joined with moderate mortality (15–25 per 1,000) in most of Africa, much of the Middle East, South Asia, and in some countries of Southeast Asia. In most of these, death rates were declining; this trend, if high fertility continues, will lead to greater natural growth in the years ahead.

5. High mortality (over 25 per 1,000) offsetting high fertility (over 35 per 1,000) persisted in a few African countries and in Afghanistan.

## PATTERNS OF GROWTH

In the 1920s and 1930s mankind experienced increases on the average of just under 1 percent a year. The annual gain was less than 1 percent in most western countries and in Meso-Africa. Moderate natural increases of from 1 to 2 percent a year occurred in the rest of the world, with those of the Soviet Union, Middle America, and some Andean countries on the higher side.

Following World War II the global rate of increase quickened, reaching over 2 percent annually in the early 1960s. In the 1970s the growth rate slackened a little, to just under 2 percent (see Table 16–1). Recent rates of increase may be affected by improved collection of population data. The pattern has changed much from a generation ago. Lower natural increases (under 1 percent per year) occur now in Europe, Anglo-America, and the Soviet Union, and moderate increases from 1 to 2 percent in China, Japan, southern Latin America, Australia, and New Zealand. High natural increase (2 to 3 percent) prevails in Meso-Africa, in most of South and Southeast Asia, and in Korea, the Caribbean, and a few Latin American countries, including Brazil. Very high increases (over 3 percent) are characteristic for North Africa, some countries of Meso-Africa, most of the Middle East, most Latin America countries, and some Asian lands including Pakistan, Thailand, and the Philippines.

## THE PROSPECT

The key to reducing rates of increase lies in stabilizing death rates and further cutting birth rates. The rapid diffusion of medical technology should stabilize death rates at a low level in all countries within the next decade or two. In some countries crude death rates are already rising slowly as those saved from early death grow to middle and old age.

Birth rates may be expected to drop, but the important question is whether they will go to low levels (as in Europe and Japan) or only moderate levels. Obviously, this will make quite a difference in the national increments. At any rate, it is clear that Africa, the rimlands of Asia, and the greater part of Latin America—in short, the underdeveloped countries—pose enormous problems not only to themselves but to the human community

## FORECAST OF POPULATION INCREASE, 1975–2000 (IN MILLIONS)

| TABLE 16-5 | Population | | Increases, 1975–2000 | |
|---|---|---|---|---|
| | 1975 | 2000 | Absolute | Percent |
| Anglo-America | 242 | 295 | 53 | 22 |
| Europe | 474 | 540 | 66 | 14 |
| Soviet Union | 254 | 314 | 60 | 24 |
| Oceania | 21 | 33 | 12 | 57 |
| SUBTOTAL | 991 | 1,182 | 191 | 19 |
| Latin America | 328 | 610 | 282 | 86 |
| Asia | 2,407 | 3,800 | 1,393 | 58 |
| Africa | 420 | 830 | 410 | 98 |
| SUBTOTAL | 3,155 | 5,240 | 2,085 | 66 |
| WORLD TOTAL | 4,146 | 6,422 | 2,276 | 55 |

Based on United Nations medium variant projections as estimated for 1975 populations but modified for undercounting in certain populations. Similar estimates made for 1970 yielded a world total of 6,513 million for the year 2000.

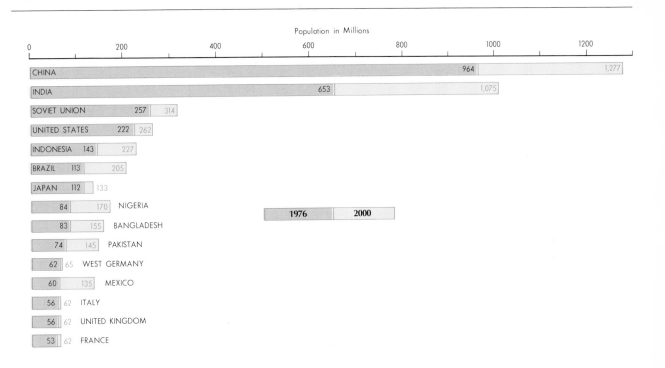

Population in Millions

| | | | | | | |
|0|200|400|600|800|1000|1200|

CHINA 964 1,277

INDIA 653 1,075

SOVIET UNION 257 314

UNITED STATES 222 262

INDONESIA 143 227

BRAZIL 113 205

JAPAN 112 133

84 170 NIGERIA

83 155 BANGLADESH

74 145 PAKISTAN

62 65 WEST GERMANY

60 135 MEXICO

56 62 ITALY

56 62 UNITED KINGDOM

53 62 FRANCE

1976 2000

FIGURE **THE FIFTEEN LARGEST NATIONAL POPULATIONS,**
**16-9** 1976 AND 2000

The figures for populations are in millions. The 1976 data are based on *1976 World Population Estimates,* Environmental Fund, Washington, D.C., 1976. Data for the year 2000 are based on United Nations "medium variant" projections, as applied to 1976 estimates.

as a whole. In these realms massive increases will inevitably occur, even if fertility were to lessen in the near future.

Table 16-5 presents the population in 1975 and a forecast for the year 2000 based on present trends. The figures, given by broad realms, are arranged in such fashion that the top four comprise fairly well the developed countries and the bottom group the underdeveloped countries. The prospect is appalling for those in poverty and for those in richer lands who value human dignity. In the span of twenty-five years the world population is expected to increase by 55 percent, but the now underdeveloped parts will grow 66 percent. In contrast, the regions with modern economy will increase only 14 percent. To put it in another

way, the underdeveloped countries, which now constitute 70 percent of the world population, will in the year 2000 contain 81 percent of a world population over one-half larger than that in 1975. While Latin America and Africa are due to have the greatest percentage increases, Asia will face by far the largest absolute gains.

Population predictions are always hazardous. They necessarily are based on certain assumptions which in the course of time may prove wrong. The predictions for the year 1970 made some thirty years ago have turned out to be much too low. Projections for the year 2000 have been reduced in the past decade; those presented in Table 16-5 may turn out to be still too high. We humans differ from other species; we observe, reflect, decide, and act. The prospect of a tidal flood of additional human beings in the next generation may bring about a drop in birth rates sooner than now foreseen. Some forecasts, anticipating these further declines in fertility rates, arrive at totals substantially lower than the projection in Table 16-5, based on present trends. Even those lower figures—which may well prove to be more accurate—present a formidable challenge to the coming generations (Figure 16-9).

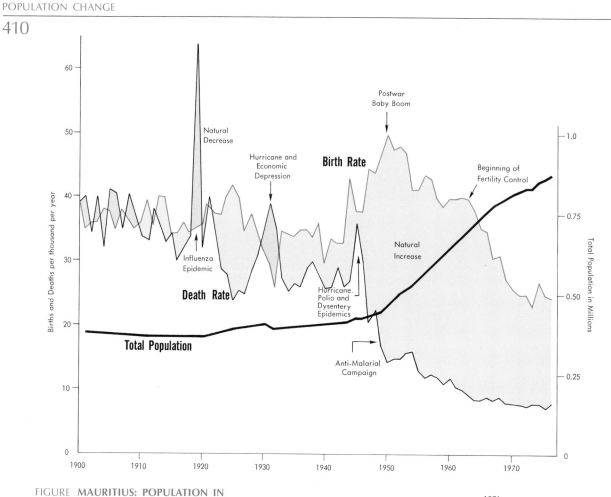

FIGURE  **MAURITIUS: POPULATION IN**
**16-10** **THE TWENTIETH CENTURY**

Mauritius, a small island in the Indian Ocean with three-quarters of a million inhabitants, has excellent population records going back to the nineteenth century. These records permit detailed analysis of fertility and mortality in relation to social and economic conditions and catastrophes both before and after the coming of modern means of death control. In the age and sex pyramids of this and following illustrations, the economically productive age groups (15–64) are shown in gray, the economically dependent age groups (0–14 and 65 and over) in green. Based on materials in Population Reference Bureau, "The Story of Mauritius," *Population Bulletin* 18(1962): 93–115.

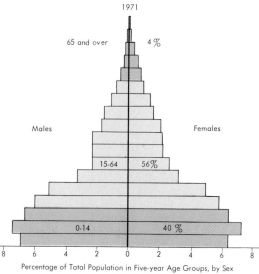

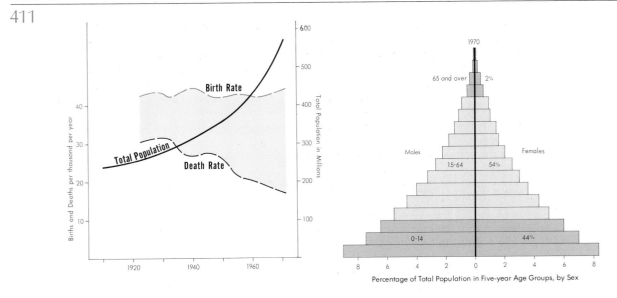

FIGURE **INDIA: POPULATION IN THE TWENTIETH CENTURY**
16-11

## CASE STUDIES IN POPULATION GEOGRAPHY

The following thumbnail sketches show the diversity of recent population changes and the distinctive problems they pose. The order is not arbitrary. Starting with the area where the issue is most acute, we end with a country that has achieved a balance between quantity of people and quality of living.

### INDIA, BANGLADESH, AND PAKISTAN
The fateful race between population and subsistence, which Malthus observed in Europe around 1800, now can be seen in its most dramatic form in the arena of the Indian subcontinent. An already crowded land with a venerable civilization is experiencing a population surge of such magnitude that catastrophe threatens before the end of this century (Figure 16–11).

South Asia's population growth in the past was slow and sporadic. Famine took terrific toll whenever the monsoon failed to bring rain. In 1866 in Bengal and Orissa 1 million died of hunger, in 1869 in Rajputana 1.5 million, in 1876–1878 in peninsular India 5 million, in 1943 in Bengal 1.5 million. The influenza epidemic of 1918 carried away 15 million or more, some 5 percent of the population.

From 1921 to 1951 growth on the whole was larger and steadier, amounting to 1 percent or more per year (Table 16–6). Although this rate of increase was not exorbitant, it added in three decades 131 million to an already dense and largely agrarian population. There were, of course, regional differences. Bangladesh, formerly called East Pakistan, hardly grew at all between 1941 and 1951 because of community strife, recurring famines, and emigration. The name Pakistan applies only to the former West Pakistan.

The decade 1951–1961 brought an unprecedented increase of over 2 percent per year to all South Asia, and during the 1970s the rate became even higher. The reason is a classic example of the uneven diffusion of Occidental culture traits: Western medical technology and disaster relief cut down mortality, but Western notions of family size hardly made a dent on a social system that encourages copious fertility. Though death rates dropped from over 40 to about 18 per 1,000, birth rates are still over 40 per 1,000—in Pakistan even higher at over 50 per 1,000. Since India's mortality rates are twice as large as in neighboring Sri Lanka, further reduction is quite possible, unless countered by a declining level of living.

The Indian Republic in its first Five-year Plan (1951-1956) recognized the need for family limitation as a condition of economic progress, but actually little was accomplished until the 1960s. Although the initial results of the program seemed impressive, they were mainly achieved among those amenable to family planning. Many obstacles to further substantial reduction of fertility remain. To reach most of the population, medical and social workers need to visit 550,000 villages. Communication by other means is difficult because the people are largely illiterate and many villages lack even one radio. Unlike vaccination against a disease, even a simple and cheap means of birth control must overcome widespread reluctance if not resistance.

Declining fertility commonly goes together with increasing urbanization. There are, indeed, signs in India that city people are beginning to limit their families. And the relative number of people living in towns, though small, is rising. This trend, hopeful as it is, will take a very long time to translate itself into a significant decline in fertility. By 1970, less than 10 percent of India's married couples engaged in family planning. The more authoritarian political regime under the leadership of Indira Ghandi tried to speed up fertility control.

*If* the present course of growth continues, India's population will double to 1.35 billion by 2000, Pakistan will double to 150 million by 1995, and Bangladesh to 165 million by 2000. There is always that "if." It is possible that attitudes and motivation will change, which, together with some simple device, would turn the population tide, and thus accelerate economic progress. But what if modernization comes too slowly? Malthus erred on Europe's future; one can only hope that his theory will prove wrong also for the Indian subcontinent.

### MEXICO (FIGURE 16-12)

Mexican cultural roots reach back to both Old

## INDIA, BANGLADESH, AND PAKISTAN: POPULATION GROWTH, 1921-1971, IN MILLIONS

TABLE
16-6

| Decade | Total | India* | Bangladesh (East Pakistan) | Pakistan |
|---|---|---|---|---|
| 1921 | 302.6 m. | | | |
| 1921-1931 | 35.6 m. | | | |
| | 11.7 % | | | |
| 1931 | 338.2 m. | 278.0 m. | 60.2 m. | |
| 1931-1941 | 51.0 m. | 41.1 m. | 9.9 m. | |
| | 15.1 % | 15.0 % | 16.4 % | |
| 1941 | 389.2 m. | 319.1 m. | 41.8 m. | 28.3 m. |
| 1941-1951 | 48.2 m. | 42.5 m. | 5.5 m. | 0.2 m. |
| | 12.4 % | 13.3 % | 19.5 % | 0.5 % |
| 1951 | 437.4 m. | 361.6 m. | 42.0 m. | 33.8 m. |
| 1951-1961 | 95.6 m. | 77.6 m. | 8.9 m. | 9.1 m. |
| | 21.8 % | 21.5 % | 21.2 % | 26.8 % |
| 1961 | 533.0 m. | 439.2 m. | 50.9 m. | 42.9 m. |
| 1961-1971 | 178.1 m. | 130.3 m. | 25.7 m. | 22.1 m. |
| | 33.4 % † | 29.7 % | 50.5 % | 51.3 % |
| 1971 | 731.1 m. | 569.5 m. | 76.6 m. | 65.0 m. |

*Includes Jammu and Kashmir territory, disputed by Pakistan.

†1976 population estimates: India 652.7 million, Bangladesh 82.9 million, Pakistan 74.2 million. These numbers are higher than expected because of improved data collection.

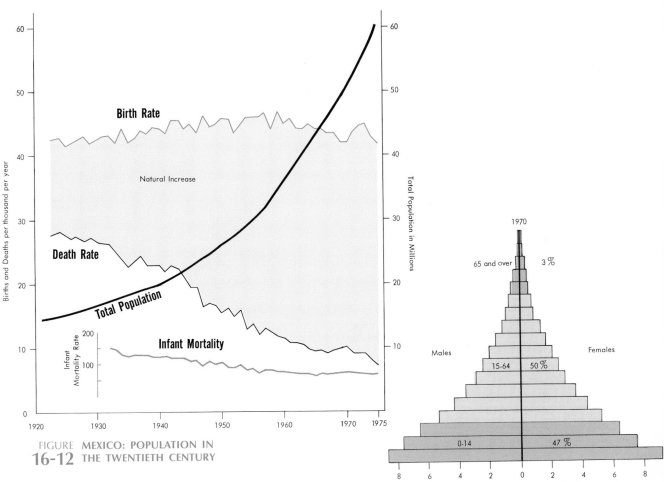

60

50

40

30

20

10

0

Births and Deaths per thousand per year

Total Population in Millions

60

50

40

30

20

10

Birth Rate

Natural Increase

Death Rate

Total Population

Infant Mortality

200

100

Infant Mortality Rate

1920    1930    1940    1950    1960    1970    1975

FIGURE 16-12   MEXICO: POPULATION IN THE TWENTIETH CENTURY

1970

65 and over    3%

Males                          Females

15-64    50%

0-14    47%

8    6    4    2    0    2    4    6    8

Percentage of Total Population in Five-year Age Groups, by Sex

and New World origins; Meso-American and Spanish elements continue side by side, exemplifying the many paradoxes of life. Though the revolution of 1910–1911 turned Mexico toward twentieth-century social and political values, much remains that is traditional. The national spirit and the institutions it has created are tempered by localism and disregard for the law. The urban exchange economy contrasts with that of the countryside, where illiterate peasants still live in subsistence villages. Church and state conflicts, and capitalist versus socialist debates, further reveal the diversities and contradictions in Mexico.

Against this background one must view the population explosion and the economic change which are bringing a new nation into being. Reli-

able statistics date only from 1930. They show a continuous decline in the death rate from just below 30 to about 10 per 1,000. This results from free medical care for the poor, better public health and sanitation, improved diet, and decreased violence. Infant mortality dropped from about 140 per 1,000 in 1930 to about 60 in the 1970s. Life expectancy in the early part of the century was less than thirty years, now it is over sixty years.

Fertility remains high. In the 1960s the crude birth rate was at about 45 per 1,000; the most recent statistics show similar rates. Mexicans marry at an early age and have large families. Births out of wedlock are also common. While the growing middle class does have a slightly lower fertility rate than the lower-income groups, it is unlikely that birth rates will drop substantially within the next decade. The cult of motherhood and that of the virile and courageous male—*machismo*—are powerful stimuli to produce children and are not likely to fade away soon.

The gap between births and deaths remains enormous and results in prodigious population increments. From a total of 14 million in 1920 the number climbed to 20 million in 1940 and leaped to 60 million by 1976. Natural increase rose steadily as the numbers went up: 1.7 percent annually in the 1920s, 2.7 percent in the 1940s, and between 3.0 and 3.5 percent in the 1950s. In the 1970s the high natural increases were partly offset by emigration to the United States. But such emigration is unlikely to continue at a high rate.

Mexico will reach a population of 100 million by the 1990s unless fertility declines. The onrush of births has produced a population heavy with dependents. Well over half of all Mexicans are under twenty years of age. Compared with the United States, a relatively small proportion of the citizens must provide for the young.

Fortunately, economic growth has accompanied the population explosion. The gross national product grew by 61 percent in the 1950s, and the average income per capita reached $1,000 in 1974. The returns from the economic renewal, however, are spread unevenly; urban dwellers, and especially the upper classes, take the lion's share. In 1963, 4.8 percent of all Mexican families received two-fifths of the national income.

Much remains to be done if the economic advance is to maintain its impetus. Each year one-third of a million new jobs must be created. The capital needed to carry development forward will be huge. Housing, education, and social services must be expanded. The rural folk, once numerically dominant in their mostly subsistence way of life, are crowding into the larger cities, settling into spreading makeshift quarters near the center or on the outskirts. Whether in city slum or in the countryside, the poor must obtain a more equitable share in the benefits of progress. Life in the smaller towns and cities should be made more attractive to encourage industrial decentralization. All in all, these objectives in the face of a fast-rising population are herculean tasks. The government now actively promotes family planning

through mass advertising campaigns. As a recent study concludes: "Mexico has acquired a sense of nationality, purpose and dignity. Greater maturity and a sense of accomplishment have given Mexico greater confidence in its own strength and an appreciation of its own culture . . . the situation is hopeful for a free . . . well-fed and well-housed people" (Brand, 1966, 150, 152).

## CHINA

What is the population of China? No one knows, not even the government in Peking. Estimates for 1970 by qualified observers range from 750 to 870 million.* Predictions for 1980 run from 887 to 1,060 million. Which of these figures is correct is less important than the magnitude revealed and the social, economic, and political problems implied, not only for the government and people of China but also for the rest of mankind.

China's population was already well over 400 million by the middle of the nineteenth century, having doubled in less than 100 years. Despite increased intensity of cultivation and the use of higher yielding plants and varieties, the rise in population lowered the level of living for the masses. China had no parallel to the technological breakthrough of the Western Industrial Revolution. Rising numbers meant, by the opening of the twentieth century, a precarious life for most. One may infer that the population fluctuated during the following decades as epidemics, floods, crop failures, or civil war and foreign invasion brought catastrophe from time to time in different regions.

Following the establishment of the People's Republic in 1949, firm control of national life on Marxist principles led to more settled—though regimented—conditions. In the first twenty years the party leadership showed an ambivalent attitude toward the relationship between economic development and population numbers. According to Marx, human misery did not result from excessive population growth but from a defective production system, a view underscored by Lenin's

*Orleans: 753 million; United Nations ("medium variant"): 760 million; U.S. Department of State: 815 million; U.S. Bureau of the Census (preferred projection): 871 million. An estimate for 1976 of 964 million, based as a careful analysis of available evidence, has been used in this book (estimate prepared by the U.S. Census).

remark that population growth was a sign of national vigor. The results of the Census of 1953—the first modern one organized in China—raised questions about population policy. It revealed a population on China's mainland of 583 million, a figure—even if not quite accurate—far higher than expected by either Chinese or outsiders. In the next few years the party leadership moved gradually toward encouragement of planned parenthood. To remain true to Marxist doctrine, the reasons given were that early marriage was undesirable and that contraception would protect the health of mothers and children and would allow mothers more time to work. Twice the growing birth control campaign suffered setbacks when ideological crosscurrents ignored the realities of population pressure: first during the "Great Leap Forward" around 1960, and again in the "Cultural Revolution" of 1966 to 1969. But in the 1970s family limitation appeared to be a widely accepted part of the new way of life.

As elsewhere, effective birth control is not merely a matter of clinics and devices, but rests first and foremost on motivation among potential parents. In traditional China the family was the unit, and its perpetuation a moral precept; moreover, sons were valuable as old age insurance. In Communist China loyalty was shifted from the family to the nationalist leadership. In communal life old people do not depend anymore on their children for support. The revolution also changed the role of women; from child bearers and dutiful wives they became workers in fields and factories. Already in 1950 a law had been passed setting the minimum marriage age for women at 18, for men at 20. But soon thereafter the party actually discouraged marriage before the late twenties and urged couples to have only a few children. Such changes in social values do not take hold overnight but, since the Revolution, a propaganda-saturated generation seems to conform to the new standards of conduct.

What has been the result so far of China's population policy? The answer can be no more than a reasonable guess. We may assume that in the first half of the twentieth century the birth rate was near 45 per 1,000 while the death rate, though fluctuating from year to year, averaged about 35 per 1,000. Since 1950 both fertility and mortality have declined substantially. The death rate first began to drop as the government initiated public health campaigns by urging the people to improve environmental sanitation and personal hygiene and to exterminate mosquitoes, flies, and rats. Improvement in medical facilities and expansion of personnel followed. These measures reduced the incidence of infectious and epidemic diseases and thus, especially, infant mortality. Although the ill-fated "Great Leap Forward," aggravated by natural calamities and crop failures, interrupted the downward curve from 1959 to 1962, it appears that by the mid-1970s mortality was down to about 10 per 1,000—a great gain but similar to the experience of many other underdeveloped countries.

The birth rate went down too, but later and at first slower than the death rate. The result was that natural growth may have reached an annual rate of 2 percent in some years. As the idea of planned parenthood spread, the birth rate dropped more rapidly and may have reached the low 30s per 1,000 in the mid-1970s. If this estimate is true, the decline in fertility in little more than twenty years is substantial. When matched with a death rate of about 10, these figures would indicate a current rate of increase of slightly over 2 percent per annum.*

It is commonly thought that urbanization is a potent force in bringing about the demographic transition. While this may be true in many societies, it seems to be a minor factor in China. Although the country always has had many cities, some quite large, they contained only a small part of the total population, and this is true to this very day. Current reports give estimates of the proportion of urban population varying from 14 to 20 percent of the total. Since the Revolution, the flow to the cities has sometimes swollen, sometimes reversed itself, depending on the trial-and-error approaches of party policy. During most of the 1950s urban immigration was large, partly because of industrialization in the cities, partly because collectivization and later communalization of farming created a surplus of labor in rural areas. The government took a dim view of the massive influx on both pragmatic and ideological grounds: There were not enough jobs, homes, and

*Some scholars believe the birth rate to be in the low 20s per 1,000. If so, the rate of increase would be about 1 percent a year.

other facilities to sustain all newcomers. The urban increases conflicted with plans to uplift the rural masses by decentralizing industrial production, and by enlisting the rural population in the task of narrowing the technological gap between town and country (Orleans, 1971, 29). The government, therefore, has restricted urban population, even by forcible transfers to rural areas, particularly of professionals, technicians, and young intellectuals. Although shifts in policy have at times allowed a surge to the cities, it appears that on the whole the government has been successful in controlling urban growth.

Rural development aimed to improve agriculture and its supporting industries, such as those for fertilizer and agricultural equipment. Food production was stepped up—not without severe reverses—through draining marshes, terracing slopes, building irrigation canals, and other re-

lated activities (Orleans, 1971, 34). Nevertheless, China supplements her food production by large imports of wheat (up to 6 million tons a year recently, mainly from Canada and Australia). However, this import may be, in part at least, a substitute for the higher-priced rice and other foodstuffs China exports. Despite the success in reducing the population growth, massive numbers of additional mouths to be fed in the near future—and fed better—burden the Chinese leadership with a problem of grave concern (Figure 16-13).

## JAPAN (FIGURE 16-14)

Just a century ago Japan started its headlong rush from medieval feudalism into modern industrial capitalism. Its culture today contains an incongruous fusion of Oriental base and Occidental superstructure. That is why superficial similarities with Britain—insular location on the continental periphery, and rapid rise to commercial-industrial hegemony—are misleading. And the transformation of this "Oriental" country can not serve as a reliable guideline to anticipate similar changes in other rimlands of Asia. Nevertheless, Japan's population history makes a fascinating story of what can happen when East and West meet.

Around 1600 the Japanese, living in an island empire a bit smaller than California, numbered approximately 18 million. This represents a much higher density than that of any European country at that time. During the Tokugawa period (1615–1868), the feudal military dictatorship firmly maintained order, furthered land colonization, and built in strict isolation a cohesive nation. The population grew to between 28 and 30 million, then stagnated at that level until the middle of the nineteenth century. Famine, disease, and natural disaster sporadically took away large numbers. But voluntary population control became a necessity in Japan's closed, self-sufficient economy. Infanticide and abortion were widely practiced, at least during periods of hardship.

The modernization after 1868 had to rely on a very limited natural resource base that resembled Italy's more than Britain's. Japan's greatest asset was its dense population, steeped in the traditional ethos of corporate duties rather than individual rights, willing to sacrifice comfort and even life for the future of the commonweal, and

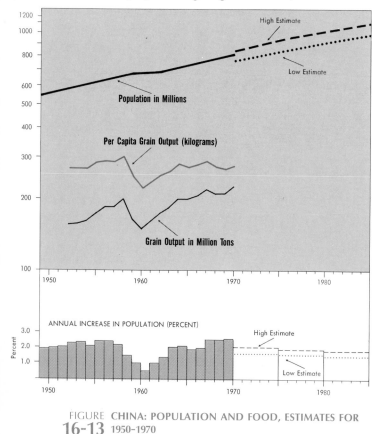

FIGURE 16-13 CHINA: POPULATION AND FOOD, ESTIMATES FOR 1950-1970

Source of Data: U.S. Department of State.

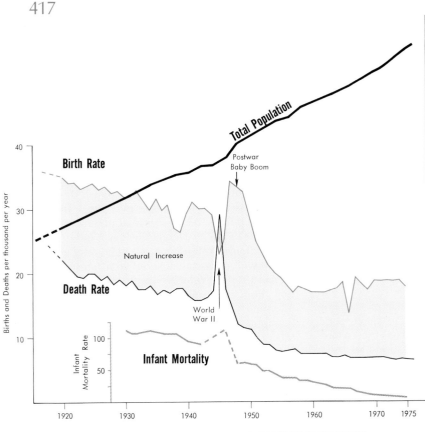

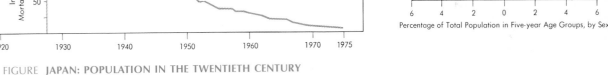

FIGURE **JAPAN: POPULATION IN THE TWENTIETH CENTURY**
**16-14**

easily regimented into a docile work force for giant industrial firms.

The years until 1900 were the period of economic takeoff. By that date the population had risen to about 44 million, but the incomplete vital statistics of the time prevent analysis of the changes in the relation of births to deaths. What shifts there were occurred mainly in cities, because modernization had not yet affected the villages where three-fourths of the people lived. Birth rates may have risen as preventive population checks receded; death rates may have increased under poor sanitary conditions and long working hours in the industrial towns.

The years from 1900 until 1920, although a period of rapid industrialization and urbanization, brought no significant change in fertility and mortality trends; both appear to have been higher in 1920 than in 1900. A substantial migra-

tion from country to city, however, caused a population decline in remote mountain districts.

Industrialization and expansion of cities into great conurbations grew apace after 1920, but new vital trends did not appear until late in that decade: birth rates as well as death rates began to drop very gradually. Since this happened simultaneously, the rate of increase remained about the same (12 to 14 per 1,000) during most of the thirties.

Japan's leaders of that time, desiring a large population growth for their expansionist aims, forebade all birth-control propaganda. Although this policy did not appreciably boost the birth rate, it may have retarded a steeper decline. Altogether, reduction of fertility came very slowly as compared to that in Western industrialized countries between 1920 and 1940.

Japan's defeat in the Pacific war forced the

ruined country to absorb 2 to 3 million returnees from overseas in addition to the 3 million military personnel. New marriages and the reunion of families shot the birth rate up to 34.3 per 1,000 in 1947, while at the same time health measures which the American occupation forces had introduced brought the death rate down to 14.6, and even lower in subsequent years. The result was an unprecedented population increase of 20 per 1,000, or 2 percent, per year. In light of the precarious economic situation, with the island empire shorn of all overseas territories, it is no wonder that the Japanese realized they had to limit their numbers. What is surprising, however, was the speed at which fertility plunged. In 1951 the birth rate sank under the previous low (1939) of 26.6 per 1,000, and in the next ten years it fell below 17. The recent slight upward curve reflects the marriages of the large postwar baby crop. The drop in the birth rate in 1966 shows the persistence of old folk beliefs. Girls born in this Year of the Fire Horse would, according to tradition, make poor wives and perhaps be unmarriageable. More births and delayed birth registrations in 1967 compensated for the reduction.

The precipitous drop in fertility may at first sight seem to be the cure for all countries suffering from severe population pressure. Further consideration shows, however, that Japan's case is likely to remain unique. First of all, Japan with its well-established industrial and urban economy was a developed, not an underdeveloped country. With widespread literacy and cultural homogeneity, the people were able to understand the serious situation and to agree on this way out of the dilemma. Moreover, control of family size had been common during the Tokugawa period, and some of its practices had persisted within living memory. The latter circumstance explains why there was wide social acceptance of the provisions of the Eugenic Protection Act of 1948. This law sanctioned sterilization and abortion to prevent the birth of abnormal children or to protect the health of mothers. Also, and this is especially significant, it allowed termination of pregnancy for economic reasons. Abortions reached over a million a year in the middle 1950s, but this method of birth control has become less common with the spread of contraception.

Because fertility dropped so rapidly, Japan's

age-sex pyramid has taken on a peculiar form; its base, consisting of the age groups under fifteen years, is narrower than the lower middle part comprising the ages fifteen through thirty-four. Since mortality has also declined, Japan's population still grows at an annual rate of about 10 per 1,000. This means that the country must provide for 1 million more each year.

## SWEDEN (FIGURE 16-15)

We conclude this series of close-ups with a look at a thoroughly "modern" country which has passed through the demographic transformation. Sweden, with an area a little over twice that of Minnesota, has a relatively small population, 8.1 million in 1971. The average density is only 22 per square kilometer. But most of the country is cold upland with poor soil, covered with forest. Good farmland is limited to the southern part. Agricultural production and its potential, however, are only a minor factor in Sweden's ability to support its population. The nation prospers by exporting iron ore, timber, and manufactured goods, from ships and cars to roller bearings and plywood, and by performing various services in international trade.

It was not always that way, and the vital statistics—recorded over a long time—reflect the changes in society and economy. Figure 16-15 shows the march of birth and death rates since the middle of the eighteenth century. In the early 1800s sporadic peaks of high mortality during hardship years disappeared, as the Swedes insured themselves against famine by improving farming, developing better means of food distribution, and avoiding war. As the nineteenth century wore on, the death rate declined because preventive and remedial medicine and hygiene gradually became available to the mass of the population. Infant mortality fell and life expectancy increased. In this century improved medical care and diet have helped further to lower the death rate to the present 10 per 1,000.

Beginning in the late nineteenth century, fertility also fell. Parents (using methods of birth control with the approval of church and state) limited their families, and this allowed them and their children a higher level of well-being. By the 1930s the crude birth rate was below 15 per 1,000. The net reproduction rate (p. 399), which had

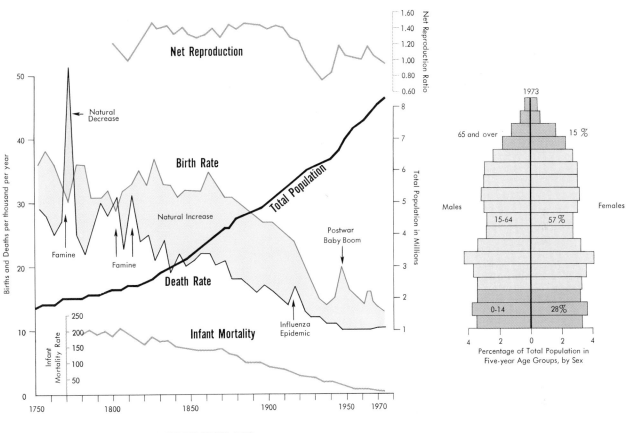

FIGURE
16-15
SWEDEN: POPULATION SINCE 1750

fallen below 1.00 in 1926, continued its downward trend to a low of 0.74 in 1935 during the depression years. Concern with the very real possibility of depopulation led to propaganda for larger families and government aid to parents with small children.

These measures and the economic upswing raised the birth rate to over 20 per 1,000 in the late 1940s. In the late 1950s and early 1960s it dropped again, in part because there were fewer potential parents, the result of few births in the 1920s and 1930s. From 1942 to about 1970 the net reproduction ratio was slightly above replacement level, even though in the 1960s the crude birth rate was as low as or lower than in the 1930s. Since 1970 the net ratio has stood at about 0.90.

To measure actual fertility, one must take into account the sex and age structure of the population. In Sweden the age classes are almost of equal size, resulting in a diagram quite different from the "pyramid" of countries in the early stage of the demographic transformation. In this situation the crude birth rate does not truly reflect fertility level.

The control of birth and death has caused radical changes in Sweden's population. In the nineteenth century, despite substantial emigration, the number rose steeply. By 1930 the population was nearly stationary; since then, natural increase has been modest, and probably will continue that way. Sweden now attracts a small but continuous flow of immigrants, mainly from Finland.

The Swedes enjoy a level of living comparable to that of Americans. The population is highly skilled. Capital is available for investment in industry, commerce, education, and welfare, leading

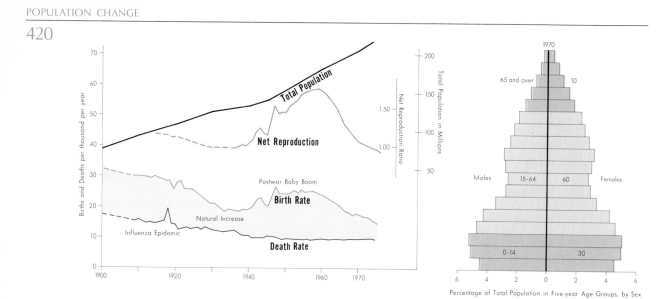

UNITED STATES: POPULATION IN
**16-16** THE TWENTIETH CENTURY

to further advances. The proceeds of the economy are widely distributed throughout Swedish society; there are few conspicuously rich or poor people. Since the population grows only slowly, the economic expansion makes possible a further rise in material well-being.

## FUTURE GROWTH OF UNITED STATES POPULATION

Zero population growth (ZPG) became a rallying point in the late 1960s for Americans concerned about the prospect of continuing population increase in a world of finite resources and a society of doubtful capability to provide for basic human needs. We leave to Chapters 18 and 19 the discussion of the implications of these issues, the question still must be answered: "How might population stability be achieved?" Are people to be dragooned into having only enough children to replace each parental generation? Or, is it enough to hope that individuals of their own free choice will have small families? Beneath these questions, with both social and political implications, lie demographic issues that must be clarified if ZPG or population stability slogans are to be translated either into a national policy or into a reasoned argument for prospective parents.

The present population structure in the United States can be understood only if we study its development during the twentieth century. That structure will powerfully influence any predictions and attempts to control future demographic changes. During and following World War I the United States underwent major population changes. Birth rates fell steeply and, since death rates continued to decrease, though very slowly, the gap between fertility and mortality narrowed, resulting in lower population increments than before. At the same time immigration declined drastically. During the 1930s many years showed a growth of less than 1 percent. Fertility rates dropped more sharply than crude birth rates; in fact, for the first time in American history reproduction fell below replacement levels (Figure 16–16).

Following World War II and until the 1960s, the growth of population quickened to a relatively high rate of 2 percent or more in most years. Immigration revived as the country took in millions in the aftermath of the war. While the death rate continued its slow decline and then stabilized at a low level, the birth rate and the replacement rate rose. Men and women married at younger ages, mothers had their first child at a lower age than before, and three or four children to a family became normal. These

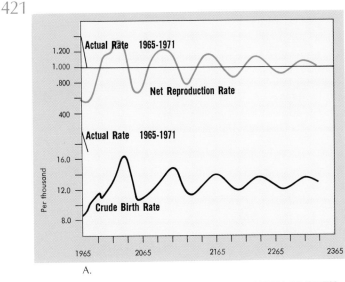

A.

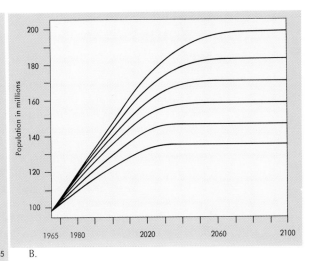

B.

FIGURE **UNITED STATES AND ZERO POPULATION GROWTH**
**16-17**

Sources of Graphs A and B: Population Reference Bureau, *Population Bulletin*, 27 (1971) No. 1: 28 (After Frejka, T., "Reflections on the Demographic Conditions Needed to Establish a United States Stationary Population Growth," *Population Studies*, 22 (1968): 379–397.

**UNITED STATES: PROJECTIONS OF POPULATION, 1980–2020 IN THOUSANDS (INCLUDING ARMED FORCES ABROAD)**

TABLE
16-7

| Year | (1) | (2) | (3) |
|------|-----|-----|-----|
| 1980 | 232,412 | 227,510 | 225,510 |
| 1990 | 266,319 | 254,720 | 247,726 |
| 2000 | 300,789 | 280,740 | 266,281 |
| 2010 | 341,033 | 307,436 | 283,711 |
| 2020 | 385,959 | 335,869 | 299,177 |

(1) Assuming a return to the moderately high fertility levels of the early to mid-1960s (2.77 children per woman in the 15–44 age group).
(2) Assuming a return to the fertility level of 1968 (2.45 children per woman in the childbearing age group).
(3) Assuming that fertility rates move from 2.19 in 1970 toward replacement level (2.10 children per woman in the childbearing age group) during the 1970s.
(All projections include net immigration of 400,000 per year.)
SOURCE: *Population Bulletin*, 27 (1971), no. 1, pp. 14–17, based on U.S. Bureau of Census calculations.

higher rates were achieved with stable or declining numbers of women in the childbearing years.

In the 1960s another important shift took place. As the children of the postwar baby boom reached maturity, fertility levels began to decline. Despite increasing numbers of women in the childbearing age group, crude birth rates also went down. By the mid-1970s these rates had reached 14 per 1,000, and fertility was well below replacement levels.

In population forecasts the chief reason for uncertainty is lack of knowledge about the average *completed* family size of future, and even present, parental generations (Table 16-7). The age structure of the American population is uneven, resulting mainly from the swings in fertility in past decades, as just described. Figure 16–17 shows that achieving a stationary population immediately would require a massive reduction in crude birth rates and fertility rates, followed by wide oscillating changes in these rates for almost four centuries. The age structure momentum of population growth can be demonstrated in another way (Figure 16–17B). Although fertility rates have fallen below replacement levels, a stationary figure cannot be reached until well into the twenty-first century (Frejka, 1968). By that time the United States would have a total population of about 300 million.

## CITATIONS AND
## FURTHER READINGS

Barbour, K. M., and Prothero, R. M. (eds.), *Essays on African Population,* London, 1961.

Beaujeu-Garnier, J. *A Geography of Population,* London, 1966.

Borah, W., and Cook, S. F. "The Aboriginal Population of Central Mexico on the Eve of the Spanish Conquest," *Ibero-Americana,* 45 (1963).

Brand, D. D. *Mexico, Land of Sunshine and Shadow,* Princeton, N.J., 1966.

Bruk, S. I. "Population of the USSR—Changes in Its Demographic, Social, and Ethnic Structure," *Geoforum,* 9 (1972): 7–21.

Carr-Saunders, A. M. *World Population: Past Growth and Present Trends,* London, 1936, 1966.

Chung, R. "Space-Time Diffusion of the Transition Model: The Twentieth Century Patterns," in Demko, Rose, and Schnell, op. cit., 220–239.

Cipolla, C. *The Economic History of World Population,* Harmondsworth, England, 1962.

Clark, C. *Population Growth and Land Use,* London, 1968.

Clarke, J. I. *Population Geography,* 2d ed., Oxford, 1972.

Cook, S. F., and Borah, W. *Essays in Population History: Mexico and the Caribbean,* vol. 1, Berkeley and Los Angeles, Calif., 1971.

Davidson, B. *Black Mother: The Years of the African Slave Trade,* Boston, 1961.

Demko, G. J., Rose, H. M., and Schnell, G. A. *Population Geography: A Reader,* New York, 1970.

Dobyns, H. F. "Estimating Aboriginal American Population: An Appraisal of Techniques with a New Hemisphere Estimate," *Current Anthropology,* 7 (1966): 395–449.

Drake, M. *Population in Industrialization,* London, 1969.

Frejka, T. "Reflections on the Demographic Conditions Needed to Establish a United States Stationary Population Growth," *Population Studies,* 22 (1968): 379–397.

Glass, D. V., and Eversley, D. E. C. (eds.). *Population in History: Essays in Historical Demography,* Chicago, 1965.

Griffin, P. F. (ed.). *Geography of Population* (1970 Yearbook of the National Council for Geographic Education), Palo Alto, Calif., 1969.

Hollingsworth, T. H. *Historical Demography,* London, 1969.

Keyfitz, N., and Flieger, W. *World Population: An Analysis of Vital Data,* Chicago, 1968.

Kosiński, L. A. *The Population of Europe: A Geographic Perspective,* London, 1970.

Milbank Memorial Fund. *Components of Population Change in Latin America,* New York, 1965.

Murphey, R. "The Population of China: An Historical and Contemporary Analysis," *Geography of Population* (1970 Yearbook of the National Council for Geographic Education), Palo Alto, Calif., 1969, 117–134.

Murray, M. A. "The Geography of Death in the United States and the United Kingdom," *Annals of the Association of American Geographers,* 57 (1967): 301–314.

Orleans, L. A. "China: Population in the People's Republic," *Population Bulletin,* 27 (1971), no. 6.

Piotrow, P. T. (ed.). *Population and Family Planning in the People's Republic of China,* Washington, D.C., 1971.

Population Reference Bureau. *Population Bulletin,* Washington, D.C. (six issues yearly); studies of a general nature on demographic topics and also issues dealing with specific countries.

———— World Population Data Sheet, 1971 and 1972.

Russell, J. C. "Late Ancient and Medieval Population," *Transactions of the American Philosophical Society,* Philadelphia, new series 48 (1958), part 3.

Sánchez-Albornoz, N. *The Population of Latin America: A History,* Berkeley, 1974.

Sauvy, A. *Fertility and Survival: Population Problems from Malthus to Mao Tse-Tung,* New York, 1961.

Smith, C. T. "Depopulation of the Central Andes in the 16th Century," *Current Anthropology,* 11 (1970): 453–464.

Spengler, J. J. *Population and America's Future,* San Francisco, 1975.

Spooner, B. (ed.). *Population Growth: Anthropological Implications,* Cambridge, Mass., and London, 1972.

Stamp, L. D. *The Geography of Life and Death,* London, 1964.

Thompson, W. S., and Lewis, D. T. *Population Problems,* 5th ed., New York, 1965.

Tranter, N. *Population since the Industrial Revolution. The Case of England and Wales,* London, 1973.

United Nations *Demographic Yearbook,* New York, 1949 to date.

———— *Statistical Yearbook,* New York, 1949 to date.

U.S. Bureau of the Census. *Historical Statistics of the United States: Colonial Times to 1957: A Statistical Abstract Supplement,* Washington, D.C., 1960.

Wilcox, W. F. *Studies in American Demography,* New York, 1940.

Witthauer, K. "Die Bevölkerung der Erde: Verteilung und Dynamik," *Petermann's Geographische Mitteilungen,* supplement 265, 1958.

Wrigley, E. A. *Population and History,* New York, 1969.

Zelinsky, W. *A Bibliographic Guide to Population Geography,* University of Chicago Department of Geography, Research Paper no. 80, Chicago, 1962.

———— *A Prologue to Population Geography,* Englewood Cliffs, N.J., 1966.

———— Kosiński, L., and Prothero, R. M. (eds.). *Geography and a Crowding World,* New York, 1970.

# 17 POPULATION MIGRATIONS

## INTRODUCTION

### MOBILITY

Life is movement. The distribution of population at a given moment is like a still from a motion picture. Were a population dot map of the United States suddenly to spring to life, it would show a kaleidoscopic array of moving particles: short-distance shuttles everywhere, longer-distance oscillations between cities, a diffuse but steady convergence on metropolitan areas, broad pulsating streams from one region to another, and small currents and countercurrents across all borders.

The mobility of organisms, including man, so impressed Friedrich Ratzel (1844–1904), one of the founders of modern human geography, that he visualized geography as essentially a *Bewegungslehre*—a science of movement, of circulation. In man's association with the earth the time span is long, but the usable space limited. From this relationship Ratzel inferred that human groups must have traversed the more accessible parts of the earth over and over again, mixing biologic features and diffusing culture traits.

Spatial mobility takes many forms. Some of these have already been mentioned in previous chapters: nomadism, transhumance, commuting, and recreational travel. The first two are decreasing in significance, the latter two increasing. Another form is the flow of transient laborers who leave home to live a season or even a few years in another place. These temporary moves are commonly called labor migrations. Strictly speaking, the term *migration* should be reserved for the movement of persons from one place to another for the purpose of permanent settlement. However, the movement of workers—and also of refugees—intended as a temporary shift may well result in permanent change of residence. Hence,

the line between migration proper and some other forms of mobility cannot be drawn sharply.

Migration may be compared with the phenomenon of flow. It goes from a source to a destination; it follows a route over shorter or longer distance; it has a certain composition, volume, speed, and duration. All these components can be expressed, in principle at least, in quantitative form.

### "PUSH" AND "PULL"

Less measurable are cause and effect of migration. In general, it is useful to think of the place of out-migration as exerting pressure or "push," while the area of in-migration attracts or "pulls." Both push and pull are made up of a number of forces and counterforces. The individual migrant, where free to make the decision, weighs the advantages and the drawbacks of staying put, and compares them with the hopes and fears of building a new life in another suburb, town, or country. He may also consider a choice between several places. The way he perceives the situation—that is, his "perceptual environment"—may differ markedly from the "operational environment" (Chapter 2). For instance, the government expert in Djakarta notes population pressure on Java and settlement opportunities in Borneo, but the Javanese peasant does not ascribe his meager existence to population pressure and has not heard about Borneo. Even if he has, he most likely rejects the thought of exchanging his beloved village for the dreaded pioneer life on another island.

We tend to assign simple causes to the aggregate of individual decisions which express themselves in migration currents. Theoretically one can distinguish various categories of determinants: natural catastrophes (earthquake, crop failure); man-made disasters (war, revolution); economic factors (unemployment or, more general, population pressure); sociocultural forces (the quest for spiritual freedom, the attraction of a mild climate or of urban amenities). But quite often these causes mingle. Drought is a natural event, but the subsequent famine may result from human failure to take the proper preventive action. Or population pressure may be the underlying reason, and crop failure merely the trigger that sets off the outflow of people. Antagonism toward some ethnic group and the wish to oust it may rest on—or at least be reinforced by—envy of its economic superiority. Conversely, an oppressed social group may seek a new home because it expects a better economic life there. The complexity of factors obstructs exact measurement of each variable and limits the validity of broad generalizations about why migrations occur.

## THEORETICAL APPROACHES

Movements within one country usually reflect the relatively untrammeled interplay of economic factors. Hence, quantitative studies that aim at theoretical constrictions find internal migrations a more rewarding subject than international migrations. As early as the 1880s the British scholar E. G. Ravenstein analyzed population movements within England. Among the "laws" he formulated, the one best known states that the number of migrants decreases as distance increases.

The Swedish geographer T. Hägerstrand developed quite sophisticated theoretical models to account for population movements. Several American geographers now also engage in this line of research. Some use gravity models to describe and predict movements between areas in terms of mass (population), distance, and relations between the two. Even these few components are not easy to define or simple to relate. "Population" hides important qualitative differences and regional variations; "distance" can be measured in various ways. The formula to express interaction is not simply Newton's law, but requires manipulation to fit the empirical data (for a brief overview of the methodology and pertinent literature see Haggett, 1965, 33–40). More recently Wilbur Zelinsky has advanced a "hypothesis of

the mobility transition." He suggests that the stages of the modernization process underlying the demographic transformation (Chapter 16) also express themselves in patterned regularities in the growth and character of mobility (Zelinsky, 1971). Wolpert developed a framework useful for considering residential migrational behavior of individuals and families in modern Western society (Wolpert, 1965; Pryor, 1976) (See Figure 17-1).

## EFFECTS OF MIGRATION

To give a systematic overview of the consequences of migration would lead too far afield, but to suggest some lines of inquiry may be useful. There is, in the first case, the effect of migration on the places of ingress and egress. It raises such questions as these: Has emigration solved, or at least lessened, population pressure in the country or origin (e.g., Ireland)? Has the eviction of an ethnic group harmed or benefited the remaining society (e.g., expulsion of Jews and Moors from Spain)? What does an immigrant group contribute to the culture or economy of the receiving place (e.g., Germans in Brazil, Chinese in Southeast Asia, Indians in Fiji)?

Another set of questions assesses the effect of migration on the migrant. Who moves and who stays home? In other words, what is the selective process of migration? How far must the migrant travel? And does he move in stages, using intervening opportunities? Where does he settle, and why there? How does he adjust to the new physical and social environment? What functions in society does he perform? Does he maintain close ties with the homeland? Although the answers to some of these questions may lie beyond the competence of geographers, they interest us insofar as they help us to understand the character of a place and its relations with other places.

## INTERNATIONAL AND INTERNAL MIGRATIONS

The distinction between intracountry and intercountry movements reflects the compartmentalization of the modern world into sovereign states. Statistical data adhere to this division because they are derived from national records, which strictly distinguish between the two forms. This duality has merits, but also shortcomings. Boundary changes make time-sequence comparisons

Awareness Space

☐ Indirect Contact Space

▨ Aspiration Space

▨ Activity Space

▨ Search Space

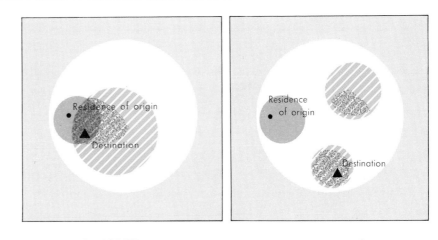

FIGURE **SPATIAL RELOCATION: THE DECISION TO MIGRATE**
**17-1**

According to R. J. Pryor, migration involves the displacement of an individual's (and family's) reciprocal movement cycle (commuting to work or school, trips for shopping, recreation, etc.). Displacement can be partial, as shown in diagram "A," or total, as shown in "B."

*Activity space* contains the reciprocal movement cycle and is the area with which an individual is familiar through regular direct physical contact. *Awareness space* includes activity space but also includes areas perceived as a result of indirect information inputs. *Aspiration space* is that part of awareness space that is perceived to have potentially satisfying usefulness. *Search space* is that part of aspiration space in which a search is made for a new residential location. See Pryor, R. J. "Conceptualizing Migration Behavior," in Kosinski, L. A., and Webb, J. W. (eds.), *Population at Microscale*, Hamilton, New Zealand, 1976, 108.

difficult as, for instance, regarding the outflow from Poland—once carved up among the surrounding empires, reborn in 1919, and subsequently changed in extent during and after World War II.

For migrations in earlier periods, when state territories were ill-defined or nonexistent, the distinction between internal and international movements becomes impossible, even meaningless. In such cases it may be more proper to separate the migrations into those over short and long distance. But even under modern circumstances

distance can be an important variable. Of course, the notion of what is near and what is far changes with improvements in transportation. Fifty years ago the countryman who found a factory job in the city 50 kilometers away would have moved there permanently; his grandson in similar circumstances may commute between his rural home and his work.

Often the distinction between long- and short-distance migration runs counter to that between international and internal migrations. For instance, moving from Quebec to Maine, or from Bangladesh to Bengal (India) is by definition international, though it involves only a short distance. On the other hand, moving from Maine to California or from the Ukraine to the Lena basin is an internal transfer, but much farther than many international migrations.

In spite of the limitations, we classify migrations in this chapter primarily according to their international or internal character. Not only are the statistics poured in this mold but, more important, the move from one country to another usually involves a greater switch in sociocultural environment than one within the national borders.

## INTERNATIONAL MIGRATIONS

The following examples illustrate (1) voluntary migrations, (2) forced migrations, and (3) labor movements. After what has been said before, we

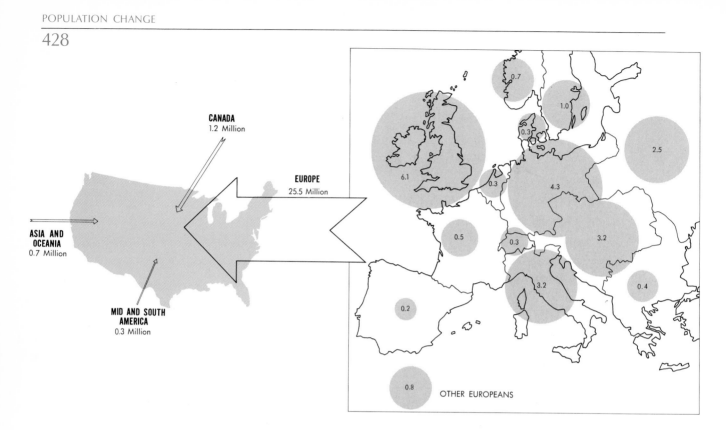

FIGURE
17-2
UNITED STATES: IMMIGRANTS, 1831–1910

Between 1831 and 1910, 27.7 million persons emigrated to the United States. All except 2.2 million (who arrived from Oceania, Asia, and other parts of the Americas) came from Europe. The circles on the map of Europe are proportional in area to the number of emigrants to the United States.

hardly need to point out that the categories are not sharply defined and may overlap.

### EMIGRATION FROM EUROPE

One of the great events of modern history is certainly that of Europeans settling in newly discovered lands. Various estimates place the number who went overseas between 1500 and 1970 at 63 to 75 million. If one subtracts those who returned to Europe, the net number who permanently settled abroad may be put at 50 million or more. Of these, 37 million found a home in the United States. The remainder went to other parts of the Americas, Australia, New Zealand, and South Africa.

Until well into the nineteenth century the outflow of Europeans was a mere trickle, bringing to the Americas somewhat over 2 million people in three centuries. The British Isles, by far the main source in this early period, sent about 1,750,000 migrants overseas, mainly to North America. From Spain a few hundred thousand crossed to its American empire, from France perhaps 25,000 to Quebec and a few thousand to its Caribbean possessions. Over 100,000 migrants left Germany, the only country without colonies to participate significantly in the early settlement of North America.

If these figures seem surprisingly small, it should be remembered that slaves imported from Africa largely filled the labor demand in commercial agriculture. As estimated, by 1800 at least 15 million Africans had been shipped to the Americas, six times as many as the total number of European migrants of that date. Only a fraction of the Africans—perhaps a million—came to what is now the United States.

Mass emigration from Europe began in the

1830s. From an annual outflow of over 100,000 in that decade it rose to 1,500,000 per year before World War I. The sources of the flow also changed. At first the countries of origin were chiefly in western Europe but, in the course of time, the headwaters of the migration streams reached farther and farther back into south and east Europe. After World War I emigration resumed, but at a lower level. The Soviet regime in Russia soon closed the door to emigrants, a policy extended after World War II to its satellites in east Europe.

**ORIGINS OF UNITED STATES IMMIGRANTS FROM EUROPE BY TOP-RANKING COUNTRIES, 1821-1970 (NUMBERS OF IMMIGRANTS PER DECADE IN THOUSANDS)**

TABLE
17-1

| Period | Total from Europe | Percent of all immigrants | Top-ranking countries of origin |
|---|---|---|---|
| 1821–1830 | 144 | 70 | Ireland 51, Great Britain 25, Germany 7 |
| 1831–1840 | 599 | 83 | Ireland 207, Germany 152, Great Britain 76 |
| 1841–1850 | 1,713 | 93 | Ireland 781, Germany 435, Great Britain 267 |
| 1851–1860 | 2,453 | 94 | Germany 952, Ireland 914, Great Britain 424 |
| 1861–1870 | 2,065 | 89 | Germany 787, Great Britain 607, Ireland 436, Norway 72 |
| 1871–1880 | 2,272 | 81 | Germany 718, Great Britain 548, Ireland 437, Sweden 116 |
| 1881–1890 | 4,737 | 90 | Germany 1,453, Great Britain 807, Ireland 655, Sweden 392 |
| 1891–1900 | 3,559 | 96 | Italy 652, Austria-Hungary 593, Russia 505, Germany 505 |
| 1901–1910 | 8,136 | 92 | Austria-Hungary 2,145, Italy 2,046, Russia 1,597, Great Britain 526 |
| 1911–1920 | 4,337 | 75 | Italy 1,110, Russia 921, Austria-Hungary 900, Greece 184 |
| 1921–1930* | 2,478 | 60 | Northwest Europe 871, south Europe 565, central Europe 535, Germany-Austria 445 |
| 1931–1940* | 348 | 66 | Germany-Austria 118, northwest Europe 84, south Europe 83, central Europe 62 |
| 1941–1950* | 622 | 60 | Northwest Europe 263, Germany-Austria 252, south Europe 77, central Europe 29 |
| 1951–1960* | 1,318 | 53 | Germany-Austria 545, northwest Europe 447, south Europe 261, central Europe 65 |
| 1961–1970* | 1,134 | 35 | South Europe 421, northwest Europe 397, Germany-Austria 211, central Europe 93 |

*The postwar boundary changes make strict comparison with previous decades impossible. Northwest Europe includes the British Isles, Scandinavia, Low Countries, France, Switzerland; south Europe: Italy, Greece, Spain, Portugal. Central Europe comprises Lithuania, Latvia, Estonia, Poland, Czechoslovakia, Hungary, and the countries of the Balkan Peninsula, except Greece. The Soviet Union is excluded (immigration 62,000 in 1920-1930, less than 1,000 in later decades). SOURCE: U.S. Bureau of the Census.

## IMMIGRATION INTO THE UNITED STATES

The influx into the United States reflected the European outflow until restrictions were put into effect in the 1920s (Table 17-1). As western Europe became a better place to live in, economically and socially as well as politically, the lure of America faded. Immigration from western Europe was supplemented and soon surpassed by waves of the poor or oppressed from underdeveloped parts of Europe who had become aware of the opportunities that beckoned overseas (Figure 17-2).

Until 1890 the largest contingents came from the British Isles and Germany, joined by Scandinavians in the 1860s. Small numbers from Italy and the multinational Russian and Austro-Hungarian empires began to arrive in the late 1870s and gained dominance in the 1890s. In the decade 1901-1910, when newcomers averaged 800,000 per year, no less than 71 percent of them came from east and south Europe. Many Americans, alarmed by this drastic shift in ethnic composition, favored restrictive measures. The Act of 1882, which had curbed the growing stream of Chinese into California, offered a precedent. In 1921 and 1924 Congress passed immigration laws in order "to maintain the cultural and racial ho-mogeneity of the United States by the admission of immigrants in proportions corresponding to the composition in the present population." The national origins provision of the 1924 act, which became effective July 1, 1929, prescribed that the quota should be determined on the basis of the national origin of the total white population as enumerated in the 1920 census. The total annual quota was set at about 154,000, in addition to nonquota immigrants. No provision was made for entry of blacks from Africa, who constituted the largest block of immigrants until the early nineteenth century.

Economic depression in the 1930s reduced immigration, and war in the 1940s further disrupted the flow pattern. Since 1945, net immigration (the balance between inflow and outflow) has remained relatively low, fluctuating between 250,000 and 350,000 per year. Immigration now accounts for only a small part of the population growth of the United States (Table 17-2).

In summary, from the 1920s to the late 1960s immigration into the United States from Europe no longer reflected population pressures. The process was selective, favoring that part of Europe with the least need for emigration. Of the annual

## COMPONENTS OF UNITED STATES POPULATION GROWTH, 1870-1970 (THOUSANDS)

TABLE
17-2

| Period | Population | | | Natural increase | | Net immigration | |
|---|---|---|---|---|---|---|---|
| | Beginning of period | End of period | Incre-ment | Number | Percent of increment | Number | Percent of increment |
| 1870-1880 | 39,818 | 50,156 | 10,337 | 8,063 | 78.0 | 2,274 | 22.0 |
| 1880-1890 | 50,156 | 62,948 | 12,794 | 8,302 | 64.9 | 4,490 | 35.1 |
| 1890-1900 | 62,948 | 75,995 | 13,047 | 10,516 | 80.6 | 2,531 | 19.4 |
| 1900-1910 | 75,995 | 91,972 | 15,978 | 10,689 | 66.9 | 5,289 | 33.1 |
| 1910-1920 | 91,972 | 105,711 | 13,738 | 10,537 | 76.7 | 3,201 | 23.3 |
| 1920-1930 | 105,711 | 122,775 | 17,064 | 13,974 | 81.9 | 3,089 | 18.1 |
| 1930-1940 | 122,775 | 131,669 | 8,894 | 8,787 | 98.8 | 1,067 | 1.2 |
| 1940-1950* | 131,669 | 150,697 | 19,028 | 18,153 | 95.4 | 875 | 4.6 |
| 1950-1960† | 151,326 | 179,323 | 27,997 | 25,337 | 90.5 | 2,660 | 9.5 |
| 1960-1970† | 179,323 | 203,212 | 23,889 | 20,607 | 86.3 | 3,282 | 13.7 |

*Excludes Alaska and Hawaii.
†Includes Alaska and Hawaii. Not including "illegal" immigrants present at the beginning and end of the period. In comparing Tables 17-1 and 17-2, it should be kept in mind that Table 17-2, aside from slightly different dates, presents *net* immigration from *all* countries.
SOURCE: Population Reference Bureau.

quota total, 72 percent was allotted to Great Britain, Ireland, and Germany. More than half of their options were never used.

In 1965 Congress drastically altered the immigration policy, which became fully effective in 1968. It abolished the former national origin quotas and instead allocated 170,000 immigrant visas a year to the Eastern and 120,000 to the Western Hemisphere. Although in principle the act accords equal treatment to all applicants, it facilitates immigration by close relatives of American citizens and seeks to attract professional and other workers who can contribute to the American economy.

As a result, there has been a marked shift in the origin of immigrants. Canada, Great Britain, and Germany have dropped from their former top-ranking positions. Now the largest contingent comes from Latin America, mainly Mexico, followed by Cuba, Jamaica, the Dominican Republic, and other Middle American countries. Puerto Rico is not included because its special relation to the United States gives its citizens free access. The large in- and outflow of Puerto Ricans leaves on balance some 1.5 million in this country.

Europe comes second, with Italy in the lead. Immigration from Asia is especially noteworthy. While from 1961 to 1965 only 108,000 came from Asian countries, the number rose in 1966–1970 to 323,000, including 86,000 Filipinos, 76,000 Chinese (from Taiwan and Hong Kong), 28,000 Indians, and 26,000 Koreans. Many of them are professional and technical workers—an Asian brain drain. In contrast, Japanese migration remains small because Japan's economy has generated sufficient demand to keep its skilled workers home.

To the official immigrants in the United States should be added the large number of illegal entrants—foreign migrants and their children who somehow have managed to circumvent the immigration laws. They numbered some 8 million by 1976, most of them living in large cities, especially along the east coast Megalopolis. It is said New York City alone has over 1 million "illegals." For much of this century Mexico has been the traditional source for these illegal immigrants, but now many also come from the Caribbean Islands, with large contingents from Haiti and the Dominican Republic. Illegals live under the threat of deportation; thus they conceal their existence from the immigration authorities by not sending their children to school and by not using medical and other social services. Living in such huge numbers in the cores of the largest cities, increasingly they threaten disruption of the social order by undermining the precarious economic position of the poor citizenry who are legally present.

## FORCED MIGRATIONS

The international migrations described in the previous section were classed as "voluntary," not because pressures to move were absent but because, by and large, the migrants on their own account decided to leave their country and settle elsewhere. The present section deals with migrations resulting from coercion by higher authority or by other powerful groups. The historical record of population movements is punctuated by such human crises, among them the Diaspora of the Jews, the expulsion of the Huguenots from France, and the deportation of American Indians from their tribal territories. Arab and European slave hauling from Africa over many centuries was selective removal rather than wholesale evacuation, but such inhuman acts are no less tragic than the cataclysmic deportations of entire ethnic or religious groups.

**Europe** The power of modern governments, together with means of mass transportation, makes possible massive transfers undreamed of in former times. The evidence lies in the events in mid-twentieth century Europe, when some 45 million people were uprooted within a dozen years. The currents and countercurrents of exchange, deportation, expulsion, evacuation, and flight are too complex to describe here (Kulischer, 1953; Proudfoot, 1956). Only some major categories can be mentioned. The Nazis gathered up the Jews, first in Germany, later in occupied territories, and murdered most of them—close to 6 million. To secure an adequate labor force for its war production, Germany took in 8 million laborers from conquered lands and transferred another 4 million from one country to another. Most of those who survived the hardships of slave labor returned to their homes after the war. Other forced mass movements involved the hapless Estonians, Lat-

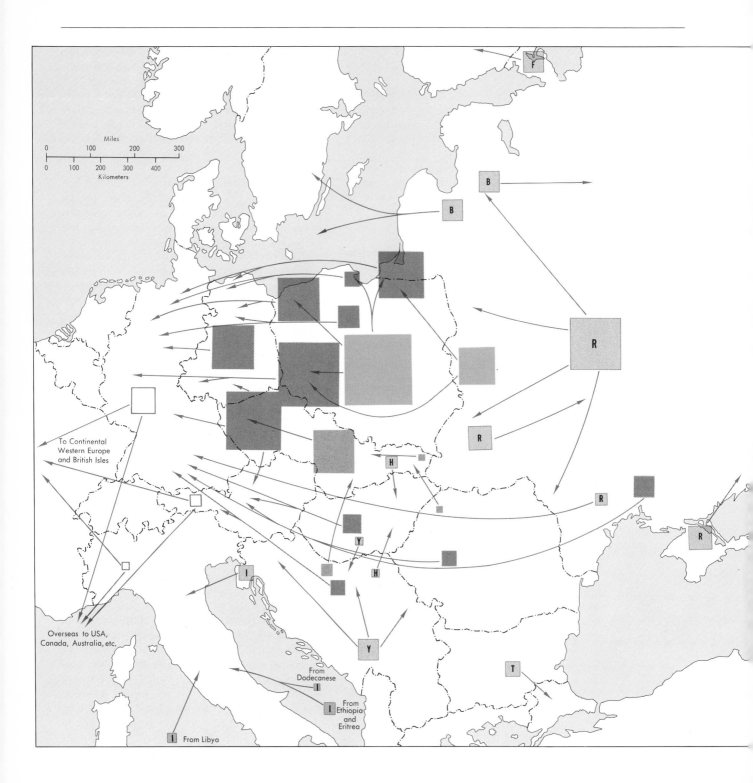

Miles
0    100    200    300

Kilometers
0    100    200    300    400

B

B

R

R

R

R

H

H

Y

Y

To Continental
Western Europe
and British Isles

Overseas to USA,
Canada, Australia, etc.

I

I

From
Dodecanese

I    From
Ethiopia
and
Eritrea

I    From Libya

T

F

FIGURE
17-3

**EUROPE: MIGRATIONS, 1944–1951**

In the aftermath of World War II, mass movements occurred in central Europe. Expulsion of German citizens and ethnic Germans from eastern Europe, Italians and Hungarians from some southeastern European countries, and Poles from the Soviet Union was followed by streams of Slavic peoples moving in a generally western direction. The Russians removed from the Crimea were mainly Tatars. Many Balts fled to the West, others were deported to Siberia. Finns left the territory annexed by the Soviet Union. Many Turks in Bulgaria were repatriated.

**Number of Migrants**

| | |
|---|---|
| ☐ | 25,000 |
| ☐ | 125,000 |
| ☐ | 500,000 |
| ☐ | 2,000,000 |

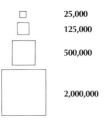

| | |
|---|---|
| ☐ | Displaced Persons Resettled, to 1951 |
| ■ | Germans and German-speaking |
| ▨ | Czechoslovaks |
| ▨ | Poles |
| F | Finns |
| R | Russians, etc. |
| B | Baltic Peoples |
| H | Hungarians |
| T | Turks |
| Y | Yugoslavs |
| I | Italians |

vians, and Lithuanians, caught between the war machines and political designs of Hitler and Stalin. The Balkan countries also experienced various transfers of ethnic groups. Within the Soviet Union at least 1.5 million refugees from eastern Poland were relocated in the Urals and Soviet Asia; hundreds of thousands of Volga Germans (suspected of disloyalty to the Soviet state) were moved to Siberia (Figure 17–3).

The retreat of the German armies from Russia put ethnic Germans to flight from all over eastern Europe. Following the war's end, massive evacuations of Germans took place from Czechoslovakia (2.7 million) and from the territory east of the Oder-Neisse (6.5 million). In addition, over 3 million Germans escaped from Soviet-occupied East Germany to West Germany. Altogether, Hitler's dream of empire caused, as a direct or indirect consequence, at least 15 million ethnic and Reich Germans to lose their homes. As the Germans withdrew, peoples of Slavic speech, mainly Poles, moved westward. Already before the war many Germans had left agrarian east Germany for jobs in Berlin and the western industrial districts. Their places were filled by poor Poles and Slovaks who came chiefly for seasonal labor, but often stayed for long periods or for good. Hence, it has been argued that the sudden westward shift of Slavs after the war was a completion of an already existing trend.

**Israel** The establishment of a national home for Jewish people in Palestine is so closely linked to coercion in other countries that the immigration into this area is best included under the heading of forced migrations. Moreover, the creation of Israel led to an involuntary outflow of Arabs.

In 1882 some 24,000 Jews lived in Palestine among the largely Arab population. By 1919 natural growth and a small influx had raised their number to somewhat over 70,000. While the British controlled Palestine under international agreement from 1919 to 1948, 430,000 Jewish immigrants arrived, 90 percent from Europe. These, together with natural growth, brought the total Jewish population in Palestine to 650,000 in May 1948.

The United Nations' approval of the partition of Palestine in the fall of 1947 led to clashes between Arabs and Jews, which grew into open warfare between the state of Israel, proclaimed in May 1948, and the neighboring Arab states. In the struggle some 700,000 Arabs fled from the territory of the new state. These Palestinian refugees, now doubled in number, still live largely in "temporary" camps, close to Israel's borders, in Gaza, Jordan, Syria, and Lebanon.

In accordance with the policy of gathering in the exiles, the Law of Return gives every Jew the right to settle in Israel. Moreover, the new state, surrounded by enemies, needs people. The size of the country compares with that of New Jersey, but much of it has an arid climate. The truly remarkable resource development demonstrates what a people with vision, zeal—and generous external financial support—can accomplish in a habitat commonly perceived as "desert." Among its many problems is that of building one nation from the diverse cultural strains of Jews now assembled within Israel's borders.

The registration of November 1948 showed 873,000 citizens, of whom 717,000 were Jews and 156,000 (18 percent) non-Jews, mainly Muslim Arabs. Of the Jews 35 percent were native-born (chiefly of European parentage), 55 percent immigrants of "Western" origin, and only 10 percent immigrants of "Oriental" origin.*

By 1976 the total population of Israel had grown to 3.5 million, of whom 88 percent were Jews. Two-thirds of their increase between 1948 and 1972 was due to immigration. To absorb such a high ratio of newcomers in a short time would strain the social and economic framework of any country. In Israel a shift in the origin of immigrants aggravated the problem. After 1950 more Oriental Jews came than European. The new arrivals, from Algeria to Iran and from Egypt to Yemen, were generally illiterate and poor. More important, they brought along the languages, customs, and economic modes of life of the traditional societies whence they came. In almost all respects there was a broad cultural gap between these newcomers and the Western Jews who had

developed the industrial-urban society of Israel. Moreover, the former grew at a faster pace because their families were twice as large as those of the Western Jews. As a consequence, in 1972 the Sephardim constituted somewhat over half of the Jewish population. The effort and cost of absorbing the new immigrants (housing, education, job training, health care, and so on), together with high defense expenditures, impede the country's economic development.

The precarious position of the estimated 100,000 Sephardim who still live outside Israel in North Africa and the Middle East marks them as potential immigrants, which would further enlarge the Oriental majority. Greater inflow of Western Jews to Israel would balance this trend. Few of the 7.3 million Jews in Anglo-America and Europe west of the Iron Curtain show interest at present in moving to the land of their forefathers. The Israeli victory in the Six-Day War of 1967, however, stirred a number to resettle in Israel. From 1967 to 1971 some 34,000 United States and Canadian Jews entered the country with the intention of permanent settlement. Although a third of them left again, this immigration exceeded that in previous years and continued for some time.

A general bar against emigration did not permit the 2.8 million Ashkenazic Jews still behind the Iron Curtain, chiefly in the Soviet Union, to leave. Agitation by militant Jews, however, caused the Soviet government in 1971 to relax the rule sufficiently to allow 13,000 Jews to move to Israel. Tens of thousands followed, but many still are waiting for permission to go. Latin America is the only other remaining source of Western Jewry, but it does not seem that a substantial number of the 800,000 who live there are interested in emigrating to Israel.

The case of Israel strikingly demonstrates how difficult the process of integration can be, even where the national ideology favors it and the government is firmly committed to carrying out the task. The Israeli citizens of Oriental origin are in virtually all respects worse off than their "European" compatriots. They occupy the lower rungs of the economic ladder, have lower incomes, lower literacy rates, and higher crime rates. Yet the diverse peoples must fuse into one nation and—if the present rate of development is to be maintained—they must fit into the Occidental

*The term *Western* corresponds closely to Ashkenazic Jews, or Ashkenazim, those of north European origin whose common language was Yiddish. The "Oriental" Jews are virtually all Sephardic Jews, or Sephardim, who lived for centuries among the Arabs of Spain (until the expulsion in 1492), North Africa, and the Middle East and who, for the greater part, spoke Arabic (see Chapter 6).

pattern conceived by the founding generation. If this fails, the ingathering of exiles may well result in an Israel very different from that envisioned when the Law of Return was proclaimed.

**South and East Asia**   The partition of the British Indian Empire into independent states, in August 1947, set off mass migrations on a scale that rivaled and perhaps surpassed those of Europe. Thousands were killed in communal riots, and millions fled in panic across the newly established borders between India and Pakistan. By March 1948, some 6.5 million Muslims had sought refuge in West Pakistan, and 6 million Hindus and Sikhs had left it.

A little later in East Pakistan (now Bangladesh) Muslim outbursts drove out 3.5 million Hindus. The reaction in West Bengal sent a counterwave of Muslims fleeing to East Pakistan. Altogether these violent displacements involved at least 17 million people. Another massive upheaval took place in 1971 when some 9 million East Pakistanis fled after armed forces from West Pakistan occupied their homeland. However, most of these refugees returned after Bangladesh was established as an independent state.

At the close of World War II, 5.5 million Japanese were repatriated from former Japanese-held territories. In turn Japan sent home 1.1 million persons, chiefly Koreans, who had been working in the mines and factories.

Indochina too provides examples of mass movements. After the French were defeated and Vietnam was divided in 1954, some 2 million people, mostly Catholics, fled to the South. Twenty years later in 1974, when the Vietnam war ended, over 100,000 Vietnamese, chiefly officials and their families, hurriedly left South Vietnam; most migrated to the United States, but some went to Canada and France.

## INTERNATIONAL LABOR MOVEMENTS

**General Considerations**   Shortage of labor in one country and a surplus in others set strong currents of people into motion. If the distance is great, transportation costly, and the home situation repellent, the migrant packs up without hope or intention to return. However, when distance becomes a minor matter and ties with the homeland are strong—or if the receiving country discour-

ages permanent settlement—the worker departs for a limited stay ranging from a season of road construction or farm work to a few years of mine or factory employment. Or he may merely be a daily commuter with his home on one side of the border and his job in the industrial district on the other. Hence, the number of foreign workers who live temporarily at the place of employment increases in comparison to those who migrate for the purpose of permanent settlement. This greater mobility causes an extraordinarily complex pattern of oscillations. New workers stream to areas of labor shortage, brushing past compatriots on the way home after their stint abroad. But not all go home; a number prefer the life abroad, assimilate into the foreign society, and become permanent residents; or they may move on to another country.

At the same time the nation that takes in unskilled aliens at the bottom of the labor pool may lose its top specialists to a more advanced country, temporarily or for good (e.g., the brain drain from Great Britain). To catch in statistical form this anthill-like to-and-fro travel is a complex task.

**Labor Movements in Europe**   In Europe the tragic forced transfers of people during and after World War II were succeeded by broad currents of workers who freely sought better opportunities (Figure 17–4). Europe's general economic upswing during the 1950s and 1960s was especially steep in its commercial-industrial core. It soon attracted labor from the southern periphery where underemployment and lower wages prevail, as in Italy, Spain, Ireland, Greece, Turkey, Yugoslavia, and Portugal. Workers from the eastern European countries did not participate in these movements, not because they were better off but because their governments virtually prohibited emigration.

France attracted its labor supply mainly from Spain, Italy, and North Africa; West Germany also from these same countries as well as from southeast Europe. The number of foreign workers in Britain equaled that of France or West Germany, but many came from Ireland, some to live permanently, as did those from Commonwealth countries, especially the West Indies and Pakistan. Almost all migrant workers in Switzerland were Italian; they formed nearly one-third of the Swiss

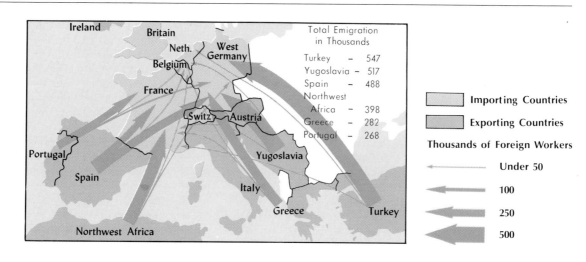

Total Emigration
in Thousands

Turkey        —  547
Yugoslavia  —  517
Spain          —  488
Northwest
  Africa      —  398
Greece        —  282
Portugal      —  268

Importing Countries

Exporting Countries

**Thousands of Foreign Workers**

Under 50

100

250

500

FIGURE
**17-4**

EUROPE: MAJOR SOURCES OF FOREIGN LABOR

The widths of the arrows show the major flows of workers to Europe's industrial countries. The data are for 1972, prior to the difficulties that followed the economic crisis of late 1973. Since then many workers have returned to their home countries. Some other countries have numerous migrant workers: Switzerland, 917,000 in 1970; Sweden, 388,000; and United Kingdom, 1,443,000. Data for the map are from Henze, H., "Social Policy of the European Economic Community for Migrant Workers," *Migration News,* 22 (1973): 3–10.

labor force, a proportion higher than in any other country.

Since then the areas supplying migrant workers have expanded. Take West Germany again as an example: Until the early 1950s over four-fifths of all sojourners were Italian. To fill increasing labor demands, West Germany attracted growing numbers of Spaniards and Greeks and in the 1960s Yugoslavs and Turks as well.

Most of the migrants are unskilled or semi-skilled. They fill whatever less desirable jobs the local people vacate as they move up the social ladder by qualifying as technicians or foremen in industry or by taking positions in the expanding service sector. For instance, West Germany in the middle sixties had 84 percent of its foreign employees in mining, industry, and construction. However, the import of aliens does not cut costs. Because the national unions want no competition from sweated labor, the migrants receive the pre-

vailing wages. They send home a substantial part of their pay—which unfavorably affects the balance of payments of the employer country. The entrepreneur, who usually foots the transportation bill, finds that it takes some weeks before the newcomers can adjust to the new environment and their tasks. Moreover, these foreign workers have a much higher rate of turnover than the local ones; many return home after a short stay.

From the business point of view it would be advantageous to induce the foreigners to remain, have their families come over, and settle down as permanent residents. However, this raises questions of assimilation and integration which the European nations have not yet solved. The Common Market countries have pledged to remove all barriers to free circulation of workers and to give domestic and foreign labor equal treatment. To implement these principles takes time. Moreover, with the exception of Italy, the big labor reservoirs lie outside the Common Market. Further, Switzerland, a substantial importer of labor, is not a member of this group. The Swiss have already severely restricted the influx of foreign workers because the immigration from Italy brought unfavorable social repercussions. Several countries welcome temporary workers, but do not wish to admit their families. If the time away from home is relatively long, this breakup of family life may have harmful consequences.

The sending countries, too, have mixed feelings about labor migration. The remittance of earnings is a very welcome addition to the national income. The skills most of the returnees have gained aid the developing economy. Precisely for this reason these countries do not wish to see the industrial lands to the north permanently cream off their energetic young people. Furthermore, as the economic expansion ended in the 1970s, unemployed foreign labor was expelled or voluntarily returned home. This led to new questions about the rights of these workers who helped a country in time of need but had no say in the system's economic policy.

In summary, Europe's new labor mobility—outside the Soviet sphere—brings benefits as well as problems. Although a portion of the migratory workers may settle for good in the new land, the far greater part considers the time abroad a temporary expedient. Governments of sending and receiving countries alike favor temporary movements over permanent mass migrations. International treaties and domestic laws, taking cognizance of this new phenomenon, must provide rules that protect the migrants and their families, and at the same time serve the interests of the diverse national economies.

**Labor Movements in Africa** Migratory labor commonly occurs in traditional and tribal societies whenever Occidental enterprises settle amid villages geared to subsistence agriculture. The foreign entrepreneur needs labor; the workers, after initial indifference or reluctance, accept the chance to earn cash, but do not want to give up the relationship with their village, clan, or tribe. Thus they travel between two modes of life at intervals of a few months to several years. At mine or plantation, as employees of Western business, they participate in the money economy; in their own community they share as part-time villagers in the social system, including the rights and obligations of kinship and land cultivation. This compromise between the old and the new, the indigenous and the alien worlds, takes on many forms in Latin America, South and Southeast Asia, and Africa.

Africa illustrates especially well the various facets of current labor movements. European entry into interior Africa in the latter part of the nineteenth century brought discoveries of rich mineral deposits: diamonds in Orange Free State, Transvaal, South-West Africa, and later Tanzania; gold at the fabulous Witwatersrand; copper, uranium, zinc, lead, chrome, asbestos, and other metals in Katanga, southern Zaïre, Zambia, and Rhodesia (Zimbabwe). The tribesman within his self-sufficient economy had no incentive to perform wage labor for European enterprises. Since slavery had been abolished—at least by law—the British used taxation as indirect coercion. The taxes had to be paid in money; this forced many Africans to work awhile at the mines. A second stage was to recruit labor, still practiced to some extent, particularly for the Rand gold mines, which employ some 300,000 workers. In most areas the economic incentives to seek employment are now sufficiently strong to ensure adequate labor through voluntary migration, in some cases assisted by free transportation and accommodations along the way.

Since the mining areas lack an adequate local labor force, most of the workers must come from other parts of the same country or from adjoining territories, a number even from quite distant countries. South Africa brings migrants from its own Bantu reservations, but also from Botswana, Lesotho, and Mozambique. Zambia, which in addition to its mines has many tobacco farms, depends for over half of its labor needs on external sources, mainly Malawi and Mozambique.

Although the African laborer supposedly is free to accept or decline work in European enterprises run by whites, it would be naïve to think that there is no coercion. During the initial period working conditions, wages, housing, and other social provisions left much to be desired. Governments gradually issued rules to protect workers, and regulated, by international conventions, the traffic of migratory workers across borders. In the course of time these measures have done away with the worst features of labor migrations. Nevertheless, serious problems remain and they go well beyond the welfare of the migratory worker.

First and foremost the native peasant in south and south central Africa produces foodstuffs for his own use. He obtains cash mainly through wage labor away from his village. As need for money increases, so does mobility. Going off to work is now generally accepted as part of normal young male behavior. But his tribal village remains his home. Hence arises the singular assumption that the black African is a transient in urban areas. In several southern African countries this attitude is reflected in the legal position of the blacks: they belong in a tribal area; they sojourn in a European town only as employees. In consequence, few if any urban areas provide African families with adequate permanent residence. This impedes the adjustment to city life and reinforces the pull of the tribal areas (Mitchell, 1961, 236–239).

As population increases and standards of living rise, the tribal lands fill to capacity. Many Africans, whether they—and the Europeans—like it or not, must find a more viable niche in town. This requires, however, a more stable economic basis, including a broader range of urban employ-

ment than is now available in the mining towns. It also demands that the Africans develop more specialized interests and skills. Obviously such a socioeconomic transformation is a slow and often painful process.

## INTERNAL MIGRATIONS

We have already considered in other contexts some forms of internal mobility: frontier settlement and, for modern societies, the flow toward metropolitan areas and the journey to work. In this section we call attention to rural-to-urban migrants in the underdeveloped countries and to interregional migrations within China, the Soviet Union, and the United States.

### MIGRATIONS TO THIRD WORLD CITIES

Third world cities before World War II held one-third of all town dwellers. This proportion increased rapidly to 44 percent by 1960 and to some 52 percent by 1976, 843 million as compared to the 770 million in more developed countries (Table 17-3). By A.D. 2000 they may contain two-thirds of the world's city population.

These urbanizing regions increase mostly from migrations and from children born into migrants' families, once they arrive in the cities (Table 17-4). The numbers involved are unprecedented. In the one year of 1973, Saõ Paulo's population increased by half a million—70 percent of them migrants. A thousand arrive each day by bus, train, or truck from elsewhere in Saõ Paulo State, from impoverished northeastern Brazil and from the nearby province of Minas Gerais. Very large third world cities—for example, Rio de Janeiro (Brazil), Calcutta (India), Djakarta (Indonesia), Lagos (Nigeria)—receive migrants from most parts of the country; regional and local centers draw from more restricted fields. Most migrants settle in burgeoning squatter areas on the outskirts or in densely packed inner-city housing. There they find a way to make a living—or hope to.

Urbanization in the modernized West accompanied the long march to industrialism. Now Europe and North America are heavily urbanized, the majority of their people living in large cities. But urbanization takes forms other than those

**THIRD WORLD POPULATIONS AND URBAN DEVELOPMENT, 1976**

TABLE 17-3

| Region | Total population, millions | Urban population, millions |
|---|---|---|
| Northern Africa | 99 | 37 |
| Western Africa | 138 | 24 |
| Eastern Africa | 119 | 14 |
| Middle Africa | 47 | 10 |
| Southern Africa | 29 | 13 |
| AFRICA TOTAL | 432 | 98 |
| Southwestern Asia | 90 | 37 |
| Southern Asia | 894 | 179 |
| Southeastern Asia | 338 | 68 |
| Eastern Asia* | 1,041 | 291 |
| ASIA* TOTAL | 2,363 | 575 |
| Middle America | 108 | 56 |
| South America† | 194 | 114 |
| AMERICAS† TOTAL | 302 | 170 |
| THIRD WORLD TOTAL | 3,097 | 843 |
| REST OF THE WORLD‡ TOTAL | 1,150 | 770 |

*Not including Japan.
†Not including Argentina and Uruguay.
‡North America, Europe, U.S.S.R., Oceania, Japan, Argentina, Uruguay.
SOURCE: Environmental Fund, *World Population Estimates*, 1976; Population Reference Bureau, *World Population Data Sheet*, 1976.

## ESTIMATES OF MIGRANTS AS A PERCENTAGE OF RECENT POPULATION INCREASES

TABLE
17-4

| City | Period | Total population increase (thousands) | Migrants as a percentage of total population increase |
|------|--------|---------------------------------------|------------------------------------------------------|
| Abidjan | 1955–63 | 129 | 76 |
| Bogota | 1956–66 | 930 | 33 |
| Bombay | 1951–61 | 1,207 | 52 |
| Caracas | 1960–66 | 501 | 50 |
| Djakarta | 1961–68 | 1,528 | 59 |
| Istanbul | 1960–65 | 428 | 65 |
| Lagos | 1952–62 | 393 | 75 |
| Nairobi | 1961–69 | 162 | 50 |
| São Paulo | 1960–67 | 2,543 | 68 |
| Seoul | 1955–65 | 1,697 | 63 |
| Taipei | 1960–67 | 326 | 43 |

SOURCE: De Souza and Porter, (1974, 55). Based on data from International Bank for Reconstruction and Development.

## FORMAL AND INFORMAL URBAN ECONOMIC SECTORS

TABLE
17-5

| Formal sector | Informal sector |
|---------------|-----------------|
| Difficult to enter | Easy to enter |
| Often uses foreign resources | Relies on indigenous resources |
| Corporate ownership | Family ownership |
| Operations large-scale | Operations small-scale |
| Regular wages | Irregular income |
| Capital-intensive and imported technology | Labor-intensive and adaptive technology |
| Formal skills needed through educational system | Skills needed acquired outside the formal school system |
| Markets protected through tariffs, quotas, and licenses | Markets unregulated and competitive |

SOURCE: McGee (1976, 13) from a publication of the International Labor Organization.

associated with industry. In many regions of pre-modern Europe, the number dwelling in town approached that of the countryside. In the third world, especially in Asia, older indigenous city hierarchies existed before the colonial period added its accretions and before the current surge to urban living, which began after World War II.

Industrialization or modernization, at best, only partially explains third world urban expansion. Few move to the city because they have regular jobs with some large-scale corporation, whether sponsored by government or private enterprise. Most leave the poverty and drudgery of their rural homes with hopes of finding work in the "informal" economy of the city, not in the "formal" sector (McGee, 1976). Third world governments and planners must struggle to determine how far the lives of the new city dwellers can be improved by encouraging survival through individual (or family) irregular work, as against the creation of jobs in modern economic installations (Table 17-5).

In a city in the Philippines, the government has built low-income apartments to house squatter families. (Photograph—United Nations)

## CHINA

From the dawn of Chinese civilization in the lands along the Huang Ho, gradual expansion southward has been a persistent theme of Chinese history. On the north flank the attitude long remained defensive: The Great Wall was the divide between agrarian China and pastoral nomadism. In time, nevertheless, small numbers of Chinese farmers gradually moved beyond the wall into the coastal margin of Manchuria, even though the Manchu emperors of China opposed this trespass onto the grazing lands of their compatriots.

Around 1900 an entirely new situation was created when the Russians completed the Trans-Siberian Railway with its branch line through Manchuria to Port Arthur. Now it became possible for them to use the fertile soils for commercial agriculture and to exploit the mineral wealth of the region. Although in the subsequent fifty years Manchuria became a "cradle of conflict" between Russia, China, and Japan, the imperial shifts of fortune hardly affected the basic trend of development; capital investment created a demand for wage labor, and North China, especially the northern provinces of Hopeh and Shantung, was the obvious reservoir. Initially the migratory movement was mainly agrarian and seasonal, and the net permanent immigration small. As the economy of Manchuria expanded, more and more Chinese settled there on farms and in cities. In the late 1920s when the Chinese government concentrated on building strength in Manchuria against possible aggression, the influx of Chinese reached 1 million per year. In 1931 Japanese occupation stopped the tide, but later immigration resumed as Japanese industrialists in the puppet state of Manchukuo needed labor for their expanding mineral and industrial production.

There are no exact figures available on Manchuria's annual number of migratory workers, permanent settlers, and returnees, nor on the composition, origin, and destination of the population movement. But the vast wave of immigration is suggested by these figures: In 1900 the population of Manchuria was estimated at 10 million, consisting of Chinese in the very south and Manchu nomads elsewhere. In 1910 the number of inhabitants was 20 million, mainly Chinese; in 1940 it had more than doubled to 45 million, 95 percent of them Chinese.

After World War II China incorporated Manchuria as its new Northeastern Region (Shenyang) consisting of the provinces of Liaoning, Kirin (Chilin), and Heilungkiang. Industrial development in the People's Republic of China mainly centers in this region, which must have attracted many workers from other parts of China. The region's mid-1970s population was about 100 million, mostly living along the north-south axis from Harbin via Shenyang (Mukden) to Talien (Dairen).

The confrontation of China with Russia across their lengthy common border, a fact of long standing, has recently taken on an increasingly ominous character. Both the Soviet Union and the People's Republic strive to remove uncommitted indigenous tribes from the border zone, replacing them by ethnic Russians and Chinese. Transportation development and land reclamation in (Chinese) Inner Mongolia and Sinkiang serve strategic as well as economic objectives. The population transfers associated with this frontier settlement involve substantial numbers of Chinese. According to estimates of Western scholars, the number of ethnic Chinese in Sinkiang had risen from about 200,000 in 1949 to 2.5 million in 1965 in a province with a population of roughly 7 million.

The large population increase of mainland China may well cause its leaders to speculate on outlets beyond the present borders. The Soviet Far East and eastern Siberia adjacent to China are sparsely populated lands, rich in mineral resources and capable of further agricultural development in spite of the harsh climate. They may well become a new cradle of conflict.

## SOVIET UNION

In the middle of the sixteenth century, while western Europe was turning toward the ocean, Muscovy began its expansion east across the Ural Mountains. Advancing by rivers and across portages, Cossacks and traders swiftly traversed Siberia and reached the Sea of Okhotsk in 1647 (Figure 8-4). Although the conquest yielded great profits in furs and gold, the Russian colonists by 1800 still numbered fewer than 600,000.

The flow increased in the first half of the nineteenth century, in part through large deportations from Russia proper. After serfdom had been abolished in 1861, many peasants moved into western Siberia, mainly to the open woods and grasslands south of the boreal forest. The building of the Trans-Siberian Railway during the last decade of the nineteenth century brought greater mobility and economic opportunity. The influx became a mass migration. An estimated total of 7 million Russians moved east across the Urals between 1801 and 1914, two-thirds of them in the last two decades of that period. World War I and the revolution stemmed this flow.

In the mid-1920s the Soviet government undertook to develop its Asian frontier in conjunction with the overall planning of the Soviet economy. In contrast to czarist days, industrial growth received the emphasis. Migration was directed toward the new mining and manufacturing centers in the Kuznetsk Basin, the Far East, and Central Asia, instead of western South Siberia. Between 1926 and the German invasion of 1941, some 6 million people were transferred from Soviet Europe to Soviet Asia. To these must be added unrevealed but vast numbers of "politically abnormal" citizens and other delinquents who, in the old Russian tradition, were sent to labor camps in the least attractive parts of Siberia, to work in mines, in forests, and on railroad and road construction. During the war millions of refugees and deportees were resettled across the Urals. The exploitation of the "virgin lands" brought a new wave to Kazakhstan in the 1950s.

Immigration since 1926, combined with a moderately high natural growth, has greatly increased the population of Russia beyond the Urals.

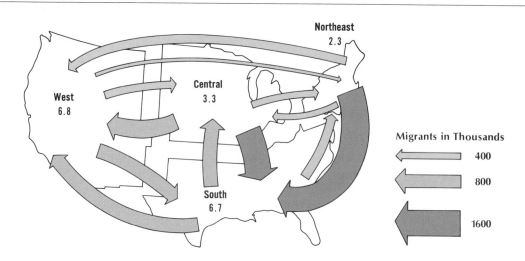

FIGURE **UNITED STATES: INTERREGIONAL MIGRATION,**
**17-5** 1970-1975

Flow-line widths are proportional to the number of
interregional migrants. Based on data in U.S. Bureau of
the Census, *Statistical Abstract of the United States,*
1976, 97th edition, Washington, D.C., 1976.

In 1926 the area contained 27 million; it is estimated that fifty years later the number had more
than doubled. However, of this growth Central
Asia has gained far more than Siberia, which now
has a labor shortage that impedes the development of its rich resources. The shift from agricultural to industrial development caused the urban
population to rise much faster than the rural population.

Soviet colonization policy has deeply affected the ethnic composition. Even in districts
where indigenous peoples are still in the majority—chiefly in Central Asia—economic and political leadership is in the hands of the immigrants.
The Russian cultural impact is profound.

### UNITED STATES

In modern societies to be "on the go" is the norm.
People travel incessantly. A home is often a mere
base for daily, even hourly, forays to work, shop,
study, play, socialize, eat, worship. Although
some people stay put in one residence for a life-
time, that is unusual. Most people change their
homes a number of times—at college age, on
marriage, for other adult occasions, and then on

retirement. According to recent U.S. Census data,
each year 18 percent of Americans one year old
and over move to a new address. About 12 percent of the population move within counties; the
6 percent who cross county lines are about
equally divided between those who take a new
home within the state and those who go to a
different state. This order reminds one of Ravenstein's dictum that migration volume relates inversely to distance. Most leave the countryside
and small towns for the cities, or they change
residence within metropolitan areas.

The movement between states, or more
broadly between regions, deserves special attention (Figure 17-5). Though people move in large
numbers from many states, their goals are concentrated in a few. During the 1950s the North
Central region and the South experienced net
out-migration, but in the 1960s the South—after
many decades of outflow—registered a net gain in
migration, mainly because of Florida's attraction
for whites from northern states. Florida in the
1960s was one of the few states in the country that
gained more population from net in-migration
(1.3 million) than from natural growth (0.5 million). In the same decade the North Central region continued to be an area of net out-migration. However, in most of its states natural growth
more than offset loss through migration. The exceptions were North Dakota and South Dakota,
which declined in population. Outside the North

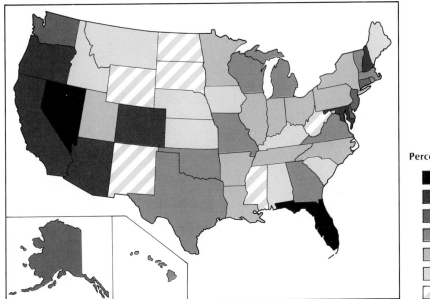

Percentage of the 1960 Population

■ + 20.0 and Over

■ + 10.0 to +19.9

■ + 5.0 to + 9.9

■ 0.0 to + 4.9

■ 0.0 to − 4.9

■ − 5.0 to − 9.9

▨ −10.0 to −14.9

FIGURE
**17-6** **UNITED STATES: NET MIGRATION BY STATES,** 1960-1970

Net migration is the difference between in-migration and out-migration. In the 1960s, net out-migration characterized parts of the South, the Midwest, the northern Great Plains, and the northern Rocky Mountain states; net in-migration was evident in Megalopolis, Florida, Colorado, Texas, and the West. The District of Columbia had 13 percent net out-migration.
Source of data: U.S. Bureau of the Census, *Statistical Abstract of the United States, 1971,* 92nd edition, Washington, D.C., 1971, 11.

Central region absolute loss also occurred in West Virginia and the District of Columbia (Figure 17–6).

The West (comprising the Mountain and Pacific states) continued during the 1960s to be the main region of attraction, although the pace of influx slackened compared to the 1950s. Most of the migrants moved, as before, to the southern part—California, Nevada, and Arizona. Nevada topped the nation in rate of growth (71 percent in the 1960s); it was the only state in the West that grew more by net in-migration (144,000) than by natural increase (60,000). California, as in the 1950s, led all other states in absolute increase (4.2

million); slightly less than half of this figure was due to net immigration. This state illustrates particularly well the slower growth that prevailed in recent years, as compared with the 1950s; its net in-migration in the 1960s was 1 million less than that of the 1950s, and its total population increased by 27 percent as against 48.5 percent in the previous decade. The other fast-growing state in the West was Arizona, but here too the rate of increase in the 1960s (36 percent) was smaller than that in the 1950s (74 percent); almost half of the increment between 1960 and 1970 resulted from net immigration (Figure 17–7).

The growth in the West underscores the common observation that the westward movement continues, though the frontier vanished long ago. But there is also substantial concentration on the Atlantic Seaboard and the Gulf Coast, such as in Megalopolis, Florida, and Texas. Altogether, the United States population is growing faster on the periphery than in the center.

Concerning migrations within the United States today, two conditions stand out. First, young people in their late teens and early twenties make up some of the most mobile segments

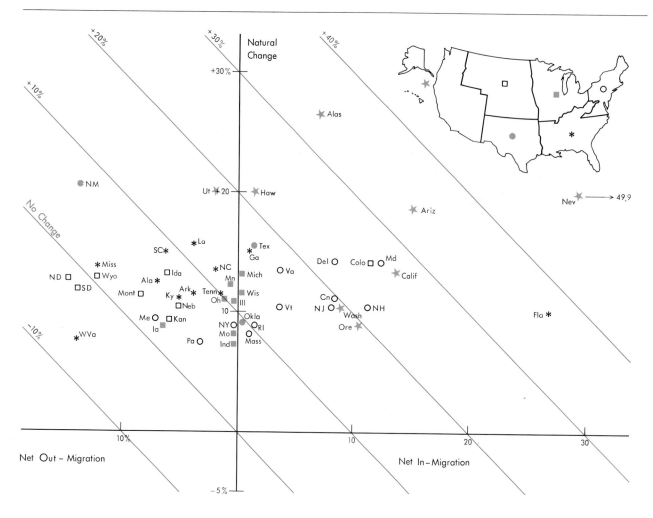

FIGURE **UNITED STATES: COMPONENTS OF POPULATION**
**17-7** **CHANGE, BY STATES, 1960-1970**

This graph shows for each state (1) natural change on the vertical axis, (2) net migrational change on the horizontal axis, (3) resultant population change on the diagonal axis, between 1960 and 1970, expressed as a percentage of the 1960 population. The states are distinguished by regional symbols. Source of data: Same as for Figure 19-5.

of the population. Second, the outflow of blacks from the South has greatly changed their distribution. In 1950 only one-third of them lived outside the South; now one-half do.

## CONCLUSION

To make a living, people do not move to empty lands; they move toward better opportunities. This point needs emphasis because it is a common error to translate the unique experience of the nineteenth-century agricultural frontier into our present situation.

445

The "better opportunities" are not necessarily of an economic nature. The Afro-American leaves the South to escape a caste society; the Muslim Indian flees because he fears Hindu domination; the Middle Westerner seeks the more attractive climate of California or Arizona; rural youth everywhere are attracted by the excitement of the big city.

The time of free international migration is past. The few countries that admit substantial numbers of people carefully screen them on their alleged merits. Even if racial discrimination were unknown, hardly a state in the world would throw its doors open to illiterate and unskilled masses. Yet mass migration would be necessary to give even temporary relief to the mounting pressures in South and East Asia. For example, India's population grows 15 million per year. If only half were to depart for other countries, 20,000 per day would have to leave India's ports. Quite apart from the question of where they would go, the sheer logistics of transportation staggers the imagination. Asia's population increases by 50 million annually; it took Europe over a century to send that many people abroad. Obviously migration offers no cure for dense and rapidly growing populations. Instead, each country must solve its dilemma by internal development, international trade, and widespread effective birth control.

The end of the great intercontinental migrations does not mean less mobility. On the contrary, Europe and North America show how ease of movement allows people to take advantage of economic and other opportunities. Whether or not the third world countries will also develop forms of mass transportation and individual mobility as they change their ways of living will become clearer as the twentieth century moves toward its close.

## CITATIONS AND FURTHER READINGS

Bedford, R. D. "Models and Migration in a Melanesian Archipelago," *New Zealand Geographer,* 30 (1974): 129–150.

Bohning, W. R. *The Migration of Workers in the United Kingdom and the European Community,* London, 1972.

Cummings, F. H. "Internal Migration and Regional Development Planning: Thailand, the Philippines, Indonesia," *Journal of Tropical Geography,* 41 (1975): 16–27.

De Sousa, A. R., and Porter, P. W. *The Underdevelopment and Modernization of the Third World,* AAC Commission on College Geography, Resource Paper No. 28, Washington, D.C., 1974.

Dominedo, F. M. "How Migration Affects the Country of Immigration," *Migration,* 2, 2 (1962): 49–60.

Freeman, T. W. "Population and Emigration," in *Pre-famine Ireland: A study in Historical Geography,* Manchester, England, 1957.

Haggett, P. *Locational Analysis in Human Geography,* New York, 1965.

Hannerberg, D., Hägerstrand, T., and Odeving, B. (eds.). "Migrations in Sweden: A Symposium," *Lund Studies in Geography, Series B, Human Geography,* 13 (1957).

Iwanicka-Lyra, E. "Changes in the Character of Migration Movements from Rural to Urban Areas in Poland," *Geographia Polonica,* 24 (1972): 71–80.

Jones, H. R. "Modern Emigration from Malta," *Transactions of the Institute of British Geographers,* 60 (Nov. 1973): 101–119.

Kindleberger, C. P. "Mass Migration, Then and Now," *Foreign Affairs,* 43, 4 (1965): 647–658.

Klaassen, L. H., and Drewe, P. *Migration Policy in Europe. A Comparative Study,* Farnborough, Hants, and Lexington, Mass., 1973.

Kosiński, L. A., and Prothero, R. M. (eds.). *People on the Move. Studies on Internal Migration,* London, 1975.

Kulischer, E. M. *The Displacement of Population in Europe,* Montreal, 1953.

Lowenthal, D., and Comitas, L. "Emigration and Depopulation: Some Neglected Aspects of Population Geography," *Geographical Review,* 52 (1962): 195–210.

McGee, T. G. "The Persistence of the Proto-Proletariat: Occupational Structures and Planning of the Future of Third World Cities," *Progress in Geography, International Reviews of Current Research,* 9 (1976): 1–38.

Mikesell, M. W. "Comparative Studies in Frontier History," *Annals of the Association of American Geographers,* 50 (1960): 62–74.

Mitchell, J. C. "Wage Labour and African Population Movements in Central Africa," in Barbour, K. M., and Prothero, R. M. (eds.). *Essays on African Population,* London, 1961, 193–248.

Ng, R. C. Y. "Recent Internal Population Movement in Thailand," *Annals of the Association of American Geographers,* 59 (1969): 710–730.

Proudfoot, M. J. *European Refugees, 1939–1952: A Study in Forced Population Movement,* Evanston, Ill., 1956.

Pryor, R. J. "Conceptualizing Migration Behavior," in Kosinski, L. A., and Webb, J. W. (eds.), *Population at Microscale,* IAU Commission on Population Geography, New Zealand Geographical Society, Hamilton, New Zealand, 1976, 105–119.

Ravenstein, E. G. "The Laws of Migration," *Journal of the Royal Statistical Society,* 48 (1885): 167–235; 52 (1889): 241–305.

Rodgers, A. "Migration and Industrial Development: The Southern Italian Experience," *Economic Geography,* 46 (1970): 112–135.

Roseman, C. C. "Migration as a Spatial and Temporal Process," *Annals of the Association of American Geographers,* 61 (1971): 589–598.

Rowland, D. T. "Maori Migration to Auckland," *New Zealand Geographer,* 27 (1971): 21–37.

Safran, N. *Israel Today: A Profile,* The Foreign Policy Association, New York, Headline Series no. 170, 1965.

Simmons, J. W. "Changing Residence in the City: A Review of Intraurban Mobility," *Geographical Review,* 58 (1968): 622–651.

Sternlieb, G., and Hughes, J. W. (eds.). *Post-Industrial America: Metropolitan Decline and Interregional Job Shifts,* New Brunswick, N J., 1975.

Sternstein, L. "Migration and Development in Thailand," *Geographical Review,* 66 (1976): 401–419.

Stouffer, S. A. "Intervening Opportunities: A Theory Relating Mobility and Distance," *American Sociological Review,* 5 (1940): 845–867.

Sundquist, J. L. *Dispersing Population. What America Can Learn from Europe,* Washington, D.C., 1975.

United Nations, Department of Social Affairs. *Analytical Bibliography of International Migration Statistics, 1925–1950,* New York, 1955.

Wolpert, J. "Behavioral Aspects of the Decision to Migrate," *Papers, Regional Science Association,* 15 (1965): 159–169.

Zelinsky, W. "The Hypothesis of the Mobility Transition," *Geographical Review,* 61 (1971): 219–249.

# 18 PROBLEMS OF POPULATION GROWTH

## CONTROVERSIAL VIEWS

All organisms must adapt to their environment or perish. Mankind faces this curious paradox: As we create more and more of our environment, we become increasingly vulnerable to catastrophe. For example, unlocking nuclear energy promises enormous benefits if wisely used but, if uncontrolled, it threatens to kill us all. Another instance—the theme of this chapter—is the antithesis between the modern means to assure a long and healthful life and the danger that mankind will be smothered by its own numbers.

Population growth and its implications have been discussed since ancient times. Plato stressed quality, not numbers, and actually estimated the optimum population size of his ideal city-state. Aristotle expressed concern with more materialistic aspects of excessive population growth, and advocated birth control to prevent poverty. On the other hand, Roman authors favored large and increasing numbers to provide manpower for the expanding empire. These two opposing philosophies cropped up in later times, but not until 1800 did the relation between population growth and welfare become a major controversy.

## POPULATION THEORIES

The idea of human progress came to the fore late in the eighteenth century. Thomas R. Malthus (1766–1834) took issue with the social philosophers who thought that rational man could rapidly perfect his existence through social reforms. In his famous *Essay on the Principle of Population* (1798), he declared population growth the prime and inevitable cause of poverty. He pointed out the conflict between two immutable processes: (1) "the passion between the sexes" which would double the population in one generation, or about twenty-five years, and (2) the much slower expansion of food production. Actually he stated that population, when unchecked, tends to increase in a geometrical ratio (1 – 2 – 4 – 8 – 16 – etc.) while "subsistence" (a term he used alternately with "food") can increase only in an arithmetical ratio (1 – 2 – 3 – 4 – etc.). One may assume that Malthus intended the comparison of the ratios merely to demonstrate in theory the race between the hare of reproduction and the tortoise of food production.

The pressure of population on subsistence made death the chief brake on population growth. Famine, disease, and war were the main "positive checks" that kept a population down to its food supply. In addition, "preventive" or "prudential checks," such as sexual continence and postponement of marriage, operated to reduce the birth rate. However, these preventive measures never would be sufficiently strong to eliminate the pressure of population on subsistence. Consequently, Malthus considered social reforms and emigration mere palliatives bringing only temporary relief from the struggle for existence.

The second edition of the *Essay* (1803), virtually a new and much longer book, was based on extensive study, including much travel in Europe. Although he did not alter his basic position, Malthus recognized that newly settled lands such as the United States could expand food production rapidly, and even double it in twenty-five years. He also observed that "in modern Europe the positive checks to population prevail less and the preventive checks more than in past times," meaning that he assessed correctly, for that region, the relation between population and food. His reasoning can be applied to other traditional societies at various times, including today. But Malthus was wrong in declaring his propositions to be laws, universally valid for all times and places. His own observations should have alerted him to the significance of cultural difference and cultural change, but he insisted that they were only minor deviations from inexorable laws.

Karl H. Marx (1818–1883) held a view diametrically opposed to that of Malthus. He asserted that the laboring masses were the foundation of society and the ultimate source of wealth; thus, society could only benefit by an increase in numbers. Marx believed that imperfections in the capitalistic system caused the poverty of the masses. He advocated a socialistic society with full employment and balanced use of natural resources, thus leading to rising welfare for increasing numbers.

Experience has repudiated the sweeping statements of both Malthus and Marx. Modern "capitalistic" countries show population and prosperity increasing concurrently, as fast as, if not faster than, in a "socialistic" society like the Soviet Union. In spite of official adherence to the Marxist doctrine, birth control is widely practiced in both the Soviet Union and the People's Republic of China. Nevertheless, Marx's point—contrary to Malthus's—that political and economic reforms can raise levels of living is certainly valid (Figure 18–1).

Although Malthus and Marx failed to discover universal laws and cures, others keep on trying. Some say that population density surpassing its optimum reduces fecundity (the physiological capacity to reproduce). Well-documented studies of animal behavior under increasing density conditions point in that direction, but transferring such conclusions to man is dangerous. More important, demographic data do not support the hypothesis.

Conservationists initially, later economists and social scientists, painted a picture gloomier than that of Malthus in his first essay. Claiming that modern man destroys his habitat, they saw future generations as caught in the vise of growing numbers and diminishing resources (Meadows et al., 1972). Population control, wise management of resources, restriction of environmental pollution, plus new international political structures to ensure success in these endeavors—all these and more are needed to bring some sort of reasonable balance between mankind and the planet where we live.

Experience shows that human affairs do have multiple causes. Geographers are aware of this because of their interest in the diversity of cultures and the diversity of habitats. By knowing these we can better understand the vital relationships between the peoples of the earth and the habitats they occupy.

Usually the discussion of population growth centers on how many people the earth can feed. However, even if this problem were solved, the more important issue would remain—the quality of human life. "The revolution of rising expectations" expresses the idea that people all over the world no longer are willing to live by bread or rice alone. Taking into account higher living standards—a cultural concept—greatly complicates the calculations regarding the potential number of people which parts of the earth may support.

## POPULATION PRESSURE

It is easy to talk about population pressure but hard to define it. Like the concept of density, it seems to have been derived from physics. Knowing the density of a gas at a given temperature is sufficient to make accurate statements about some of its other properties. But can the same be said of population density? Take, for example, the mathematical density of a region, that is, the average number of inhabitants per specified unit of area, usually a square kilometer or mile. It is a common notion—perhaps as a carry-over from the days when agriculture was the mainstay of life— that "teeming millions" crowded in space spell poverty. The facts quickly disprove this naïve notion. The northeastern United States has a higher average income per capita than the Great Plains. In Central Africa the people are poor, in Australia well off, though both lands are sparsely settled. The Netherlands, one of the most densely populated countries in the world, ranks among the more prosperous nations.

If mathematical (or crude) density is inadequate to measure the pressure of population on land, are there better yardsticks? Among those proposed is the physiological or nutritional density, that is, the number of inhabitants per unit of agricultural land. The calculation may be based on

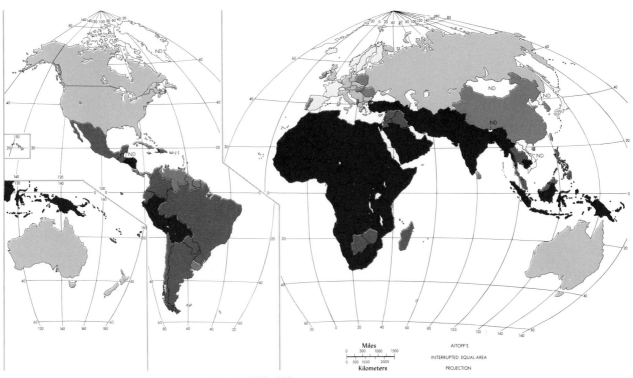

FIGURE **WORLD: INFANT MORTALITY, ABOUT 1975**
**18-1**

Rates of infant mortality reflect the general welfare of populations, that is, the degree to which adequate medical care, food, and other necessities are available or are made available to the whole population. The lowest proportions of infant deaths are in northern Europe, where the philosophy of social welfare is most highly developed. The remainder of Europe, North America, and other modernized countries such as Japan have low rates, usually below 25 per 1,000 population. High infant mortality, often over 100 per 1,000 (a statistic which means that one in ten babies dies before reaching its first birthday), characterizes Africa, Asia, and Latin America. The map is based on data published in Population Reference Bureau, *World Population Data Sheet of 1976*, Washington, D.C., 1976, for which estimates were made for many countries in Asia, Africa, and Latin America where accurate information is lacking.

**Number of Deaths Under 1 year per 1,000 Births**

cultivated (or arable) land only, or may include permanent pastures (Table 18–1). These figures, though quite interesting in themselves, do not tell much about population pressure. It will be noted that physiological densities in East Asia, the Caribbean, and western Europe are of the same order of magnitude, yet the Europeans so far have more success in their struggle for life than do the inhabitants of these other areas. The measure would have validity only if all nations had similar agricultural economies, and each were self-sufficient in food production.

The term *carrying capacity of the land* has a broader connotation because it recognizes other resources than agriculture. Still, it is too restrictive: its focus remains on the relationship, or potential relationship, between the environmental content of an area and its population. As we seek to use the term, its definition continues to recede. To know its meaning for a region, we must know if the area has to be self-sufficient. A farming economy in a region with few outside contacts must supply the population with almost all needs from the local territory. A country embedded in a mesh of trading relationships has to be considered in the context of the spatial organization of the exchange systems to which it belongs. It is hardly meaningful to speak of the "carrying capacity" of Singapore Island, of Hong Kong, or of the Netherlands.

Higher productivity per worker is a key factor in raising levels of living. It is related not only to the level of technology but also to social, economic, and political organization. Resources obviously are important too, but as pointed out before, they are cultural achievements and are thus intricately linked to the society that exploits them. All these factors are interrelated; they are causes, but also consequences. How do population numbers fit into this complex? For one type of society, a fast rate of population growth may stimulate, for another it may seriously impede economic development.

These considerations suggest the difficulty of precisely defining population pressure. Yet there is no denying it exists, and in many countries presents a problem of growing urgency. It shows most clearly where people live close to the level of bare subsistence. When food consumption per capita goes down while the number of people goes up, it is reasonable to blame severe population pressure. Such conclusions may not fit more economically advanced societies. In the 1930s the United States, like many other countries, experienced a severe economic depression. Many blamed population pressure, or "overpopulation," for the distress. Yet the 130 million at that time were only a few million more than in prosperous 1928, and far fewer than at present, when living standards are much higher.

*Level of living* relates to existing conditions, *standard of living* to the cultural image of what the level ought to be (the norm). This distinction

## MAN-LAND RATIOS FOR SELECTED COUNTRIES

TABLE
18-1

| Country | Persons per square kilometer | Persons per square kilometer of arable land* | Persons per square kilometer of agricultural land† | Agricultural workers‡ per square kilometer of agricultural land |
|---|---|---|---|---|
| Australia | 2 | 28 | 32 | 0.1 |
| Argentina | 10 | 77 | 14 | 1.0 |
| Soviet Union | 12 | 112 | 43 | 6.7 |
| United States | 24 | 124 | 51 | 0.9 |
| Mexico | 31 | 243 | 56 | 8.0 |
| Egypt | 43 | 1,392 | 1,392 | 224 |
| Nigeria | 101 | 423 | 193 | 72 |
| Poland | 112 | 230 | 180 | 25 |
| Philippines | 154 | 458 | 315 | 59 |
| Italy | 188 | 364 | 270 | 27 |
| India | 202 | 401 | 370 | 63 |
| United Kingdom | 237 | 775 | 291 | 5 |
| Japan | 302 | 2,005 | 1,701 | 192 |
| Netherlands | 341 | 1,462 | 590 | 19 |
| Puerto Rico | 345 | 1,182 | 489 | 30 |

*Arable land includes land under crops (double-cropped areas are counted only once), temporary meadows for mowing or pasture, land under market and kitchen gardens (including cultivation under glass), and land under fruit trees, vines, shrubs, and rubber plantations.
†Agricultural land includes arable land as defined above, plus permanent meadows and pastures.
‡Agricultural workers are those "economically active in agriculture" as defined in Food and Agriculture Organization, *Production Yearbook 1970.*
SOURCE: United Nations *Demographic Yearbook 1970* and Food and Agriculture Organization, *Production Yearbook 1970.* The data as reported refer to different years, mostly within the period 1967–1970.

Old and new methods of cultivation in Rajasthan, western India. The ragged and undersized grain crop in the foreground contrasts sharply with the tall and grain-rich field in the background which has benefited from chemical fertilizers. By improving farming methods, India could greatly increase her food production. (Photograph—Press Information Bureau, Government of India)

helps to understand the true nature of population pressure in many underdeveloped countries. Even if their production of the bare necessities of life keeps up with population growth, awareness that other peoples live at higher levels makes them want the same and creates a sense of deprivation. To alleviate these feelings requires greater production per capita, well above mere provision of food. But if fast population growth absorbs the gains in production, it dashes all hopes for a more comfortable life. Such frustrations easily lead to social unrest, even to war.

In passing we referred to "overpopulation."

Some people are quick to use this term to explain poverty in crowded countries. The population expert is more reluctant. Before we can speak of overpopulation or underpopulation, we must decide what the optimum number is for the country at a given time. The French demographer Sauvy neatly summed up the relativity of the concept when he defined optimum population as "that which best assures the realization of a predetermined objective" (Sauvy, 1952, vol. 2, 221).

The difficulties of defining optimum population have led others to propose that attention be turned to another measure—the optimum *rate* of growth. This provides a more practical and useful tool because it relates annual population increase to index figures for production, capital formation, consumption, or facilities such as housing, schools, and other social services. This procedure allows a clearer view of what is optimal population growth, because it links it to the immediate objectives of progress. Nevertheless, there remains the arguable assumption that in each country the "national goals" are agreed upon by the entire population.

## NUTRITION

As an average American, one spends less than one-sixth of one's disposable income on food, and for this modest part of one's money obtains not only an ample amount, but a rich variety. In contrast, people in India on the average devote over three-fifths of their wretchedly low income to purchase food and cannot afford much else than a daily ration of cereals and pulses. Other nations lie somewhere between these poles of abundance and poverty, the largest number by far crowded on the lower end of the scale.

Through the process of photosynthesis, plants transform sunlight, water, carbon dioxde, and minerals into organic materials containing in various proportions carbohydrates, proteins, and fats. Animals convert plants into proteins and fats. Because they eat vegetable matter that man cannot digest, they broaden his food supply. If animals eat plants that man can use directly, he may forego the consumption of the carbohydrates to gain the greater nutritive value of animal protein, even though it contains only a fraction, say one-seventh, of the energy originally in the plants. Obviously, this conversion of energy is not efficient. It explains—apart from cultural food avoidances—why densely populated, poor countries do not take the detour of producing meat, but rely mainly on direct consumption of vegetable matter.

The human diet contains carbohydrates, proteins, fats, minerals, and vitamins. Each food yields a certain number of calories per gram when digestion changes it into energy. Amount of adequate food intake varies with conditions. In year-round warm climates a person requires fewer calories than in the mid-latitudes, other things being equal. Small persons need fewer calories than large ones. These differences must be kept in mind when comparing the average caloric intake in Anglo-America with that in Indonesia or Ecuador.

Within a given population, individual food requirements also differ markedly, depending on activity, sex, and age. For example, the Food and Nutrition Board of the National Research Council recommends the following daily quantities of calories: children of 4 to 6 years, 1,600 calories; men of 25, 3,200 calories; men of 45, 2,900 calories. The figures for comparable classes of females are substantially lower. Of course, a man in a sedentary job needs far fewer calories than a farmer or miner. This differentiation must be taken into account when comparing national nutrition data. A young population largely employed in physical labor eats more—or should eat more—than one with a high proportion of white-collar workers and elderly citizens.

In most parts of the world people consume enough food for basic energy needs. But often the quality of intake is inadequate even where the quantity is sufficient. In such cases the stomach is filled, but "hidden hunger" for proteins, minerals, or vitamins remains. This is malnutrition. The body tissues do not receive the elements necessary to function properly, and this inevitably leads to various diseases. Malnutrition also causes apathy. In turn, apathy reduces the worker's productivity and thus tends to make a vicious circle of poverty and malnutrition.

The sad thing is that most countries with low food quantity also have low quality (Figure 18-2). Grains, roots, and tubers, which are rather easy to produce, contain principally starches—carbohydrates that fuel the body. In contrast, the foodstuffs that contain protective elements—meat, fat, vegetables, fruits—are on the whole much more expensive. Hence, in poor countries many people are not only "on the eternal compulsory fast" (as Gandhi said of India's masses), but in addition suffer from malnutrition. Unfortunately, reliable data are lacking for many of the less developed countries. Among those reporting to the United Nations, the following five are at the bottom, each with a daily food supply of less than 2,000 calories per capita: Bolivia, Ecuador, El Salvador, Somalia, and Indonesia.

Unequal population growth intensifies inequalities of nutrition. By and large, the nutritional have-nots yearly add the greatest number of mouths. In many of these countries food production is slipping behind population growth. However, increasing dependence on food import is not necessarily a sign of deteriorating condi-

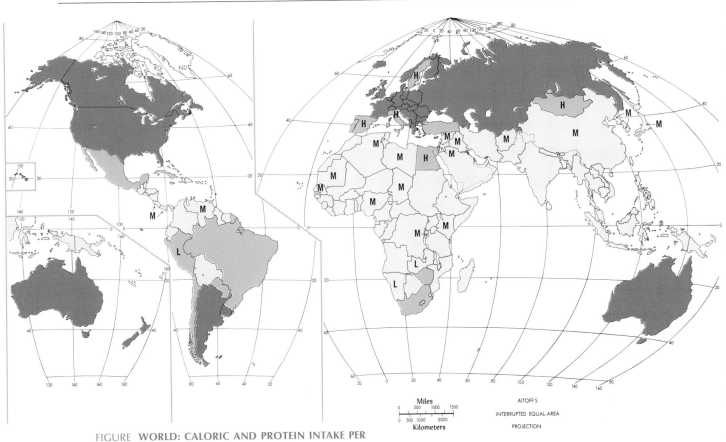

FIGURE **WORLD: CALORIC AND PROTEIN INTAKE PER**
**18-2** CAPITA

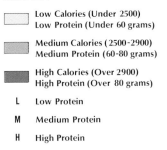

| | Low Calories (Under 2500) Low Protein (Under 60 grams) |
| | Medium Calories (2500-2900) Medium Protein (60-80 grams) |
| | High Calories (Over 2900) High Protein (Over 80 grams) |
| L | Low Protein |
| M | Medium Protein |
| H | High Protein |

While in a few countries the diet has improved during the past two decades, in most the food intake remains much the same. In the underdeveloped countries, population increases have offset the greater production of basic foods. Developed countries maintained their already rich and diverse diets.

Nutritional levels are shown by calories and grams of protein per capita per day. Data are from United Nations, *Statistical Yearbook*, 1974, New York, 1975, table 137.

tions. After all, developed countries buy food with money earned through specialty production or services. But many underdeveloped countries do not have the money to buy food in foreign markets for their hungry people. On the other side, the countries that were the first to have the most—Anglo-America, western Europe, Australia, and New Zealand—show a marked increase of food output. Some, especially the United States, could yield far more if there were no ceiling purposely placed on production.

## MALNUTRITION AND DISEASE

Malnutrition has its own disease patterns. Moreover, gross deficiencies in diet are likely to lower resistance to other diseases. Among the disorders that malnutrition causes, we note first of all those due to protein deficiencies. Most underdeveloped countries in the tropics and subtropics have a

## PLAGUE (Occurrences 1900-1952)

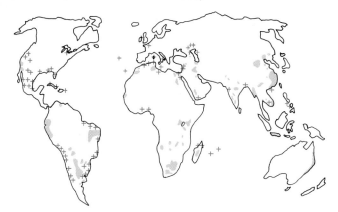

## CHOLERA

Last Epidemic in Americas 1911
Last Epidemic in Europe 1923
Persistent Outbreaks 1946
1931 1939
Egypt 1947
1919
Endemic Area
1940
1946
1946
1935

## YELLOW FEVER (Endemic Areas According to World Health Organization)

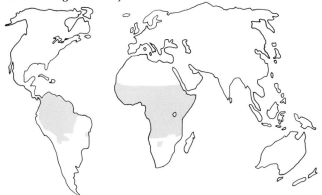

## YAWS (Including Pinta and Bejel)

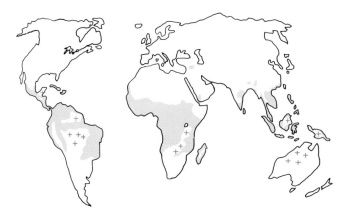

## HOOKWORM

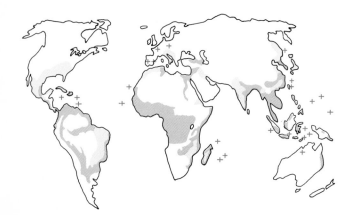

## VITAMIN DEFICIENCY DISEASE (Rickets-D, Beri-beri - B, Scurvy - C, etc.)

FIGURE
**18-3**

**WORLD: DISEASES**

The shaded parts are major areas of occurrence; the crosses indicate minor areas. On the cholera map the arrows show the spread of the disease during the epidemics identified by date. Source: J. May, *Atlas of Distribution of Diseases,* American Geographical Society, New York, 1956, Seventeen plates reprinted from *Geographical Review,* 1950–1955.

high incidence of nutritional edemas and *kwashiorkor.* The latter is the most severe and widespread nutritional disease. It is caused by lack of protein and is commonly found among young children. Their growth after weaning is retarded; abdomen, face, and extremities swell with fluid, the hair loses color and curl. Among Africans it becomes silky and reddish—hence the name of the disease, literally meaning "the little red boy." Only twenty years ago it was discovered that many ailments which had been described in medical journals under various names all were what now is called kwashiorkor. The victims all have a diet consisting mainly of sweet potato, yam, cassava, or banana, with almost no meat or fish or dairy foods.

Goiter is caused by insufficient intake of iodine. The Great Lakes region of the United States, which has very little iodine content in its drinking water and food, has been called "the goiter belt." Actually, the zone stretches westward along the United States–Canadian border to the Columbia River; also Switzerland, interior China, and southern Brazil are well known for the prevalence of goiter. The use of iodized table salt is an effective preventive. Coastal regions where seafood is easily available have a low incidence of goiter.

The distribution of vitamin deficiencies of one kind or another shows high correlation with that of low incomes (Figure 18–3). Each region has its own type of vitamin deficiency diseases, depending on what particular foods are not available or too expensive. In West Africa the scarcity of niacin (a B vitamin) in the local food supply causes widespread pellagra. In Pakistan and north India the lack of vitamin D and vitamin B is responsible for much rickets and pellagra, respectively. South Indians, on the other hand, get little

vitamin C, resulting in scurvy, and little vitamin A, resulting in night blindness. In the rice-eating countries of southeastern Asia, consumption of polished rice results in beriberi, because the vitamin $B_1$ has been discarded with the husk.

These examples suggest the seriousness of nutrition problems in much of the world. It is said sometimes that the advanced countries could produce enough food to avert famine everywhere, at least for the next ten or twenty years. However, if true, this could only refer to the provision of cereals. It might ease undernutrition, but could not significantly alleviate malnutrition.

## INFECTIOUS DISEASES

Mankind is part of a complex food system. We eat plants and animals while, in turn, invading microorganisms exploit our bodies for their own existence. Some are harmless, others cause severe damage. An infectious disease, then, is a disease caused by the entrance, growth, and multiplication of a foreign organism within the body.

Infectious diseases illustrate well the process of interaction between different orders of phenomena. There is first of all the human being as host—never as a mere organism but as a member of a culture, with all that this implies. Then there are the pathogens (disease-causing organisms), each with its own life requirements and often traveling via intermediate hosts (vectors) from one human or animal to another. And finally there is the physical environment with its specific climate, soil, and water supply (the latter two resources often changed by man, with unforeseen biological consequences), favoring or restricting certain life forms.

Many diseases are *endemic*—that is to say, a state of equilibrium exists between man and microorganism whereby the latter is widespread in a community without causing extensive death. For instance, venereal diseases such as gonorrhea and syphilis may be regarded as endemic in the United States and western Europe. An *epidemic* is a sudden and virulent outbreak; if it becomes worldwide, as influenza (now called swine flu because swine were discovered to be vectors) did after World War I, it is called *pandemic.* Diseases to which Europeans had developed considerable

456

immunity, such as smallpox and measles, spread like wildfire among the American Indians and the island peoples of the Pacific after they had been "discovered."

Diseases that rely on indirect methods of transmission do not move so easily, since they need suitable intermediate hosts. A good example is the African sleeping sickness, which is restricted to the range of the tsetse fly vectors. But malaria occurs widely because the approximately 35 species of *Anopheles* mosquitoes that can act as vectors of plasmodia—the disease-causing protozoa—live in tropical climates as well as in climates with fairly warm summers.

During the last thirty years sulfa drugs and antibiotics have greatly diminished the fatal effects of many bacterial diseases: tuberculosis, pneumonia, typhoid fever, bacterial dysentery, rheumatic fever, syphilis, yaws, and cholera. Some virus diseases also have declined because of immunization by vaccination (smallpox, polio). Others are controlled by eradication of mosquito vectors as well as by vaccination (e.g., yellow fever). Viruses of the influenza group and the common cold still enter the human body freely. In some parts of the world, diseases caused by parasitic worms (hookworm, trichina worm, flukes) have been virtually eradicated, while elsewhere they debilitate and kill large numbers.

Our interest is not in the medical aspects of disease control, but in the areal differentiation of this control, and how it affects population growth. In modern societies of the Western world the death rate declined gradually as medical knowledge advanced, public health expanded, and notions of sanitary conduct spread among the population. The introduction of sulfa drugs in the 1930s and of antibiotics in the 1940s only depressed further an already low mortality. Death now for the greater part is caused by accidents and by disorders that result from structural changes or damage in the body, such as cancer, and malfunctioning of the circulatory system, particularly the heart.

The course of events was very different in the underdeveloped countries. By the 1930s modern medical science and public health, although present in only rudimental form, had somewhat lowered the death rate, but progress had been slow. It seemed then that—apart from vaccination for a few diseases—great advances would depend on the cooperation of the local people in accepting public and private cleanliness. It was realized, of course, that this would take much time. Asking people to observe the hygienic rules of Western medicine is asking them to change their customary way of life. Moreover, sanitary conduct usually requires money, even if only for soap or sandals, which may mean sacrificing food or other immediate necessities for an uncertain future benefit.

Wonder drugs and insect sprays, developed shortly before and during World War II, opened new perspectives on the control of infectious diseases in underdeveloped lands. DDT and other insecticides can be applied over wide areas without the active participation of the local populace. As for the drugs, they are essentially curative in character. The person who feels ill is much more willing to submit to an injection or take a dose than one who is told that a shot will prevent future sickness. Since the results are readily apparent, news of the miracle drug spreads quickly and people flock to the clinics. The new confidence soon extends to preventive inoculations, which further reduce death from infectious diseases.

This happened in the underdeveloped countries after World War II, although not everywhere to the same degree. What took the Western countries a century to accomplish in the fight against death can now be done elsewhere in one generation or less. However, if birth rates remain high and food production fails to increase rapidly, the retreat of death simply will mean that more people will live out their longer lives in misery.

## FUTURE FOOD SUPPLY

Most of the present 4,200 million people are poorly nourished. By about the year 2000 the earth is expected to carry over 6,000 million. How can they be fed? Will their diet be better than that of today? Essentially there are two ways to make this possible, given our current technology: expand the area under cultivation, or wrest higher yields from lands now in use. Actually it is not an "either-or" choice. Let us first consider the possibilities of "horizontal" expansion.

## MORE FOOD FROM MORE LAND?

Some 1,424 million hectares are now in cropland and orchards, and 3,001 million in permanent meadows and pastures. Together they form what we shall call agricultural land: 4,425 million hectares, constituting 33.5 percent of the land surface, excluding Antarctica.

If the population were to double in thirty-five years and it had to be fed at present levels of consumption by expanding the agricultural land area, another 4,425 million hectares would need to be added to the area now in use. Thus, in 2010 there should be 8,850 million hectares, or 67 percent of the land surface, in crops or permanent pasture. Improving the diet would certainly require still more agricultural land, perhaps another 5 to 10 percent of the land surface, raising the total to 72 or 77 percent. But where is this new agricultural land to be found?

Many geographers have tried to answer this question. Since there is no reliable inventory of the earth's resources, calculations must be based on rough estimates of regional environmental qualities such as temperature, precipitation, soil, and slope conditions.* Furthermore, one must make assumptions regarding the future state of agricultural technology and the price levels. To illustrate, the frontier moves poleward as quick-ripening crops develop, and desertward with new drought-resistant crops. But how far such expansion actually will reach depends on the financial returns to the farmer. Evidently, estimates of potential agricultural land will differ widely, depending on the assumptions. The calculations of various experts, referring mainly to the total of arable land available, range from 4,450 million to 7,000 million hectares, the highest figure representing 52 percent of the land surface.

In terms of climate about 25 percent of the land surface is too cold for agriculture as now practiced; it comprises the ice caps, the tundra, and the subpolar forest zone. Arid climates cover some 18 percent, semiarid climates another 20 percent of the land surface. Expansion of agriculture in these dry lands is possible through irrigation and better use of the steppelands, although

enormous capital investment would be required to overcome nature's obstacles. Tropical rainy climates extend over 10 percent of the earth. The possibilities of expanding agriculture in this zone are hotly debated. Its sparse use so far suggests the manifold difficulties people face in such an environment. These areas with climates unfavorable to agriculture add up to 73 percent of the land surface. Most of the present agricultural production is concentrated in the remaining 27 percent. What lands are not yet in use here are marginal in quality or worse. Mountains and hills have steep slopes and stony soils, which discourage food production. Part of the more favorable terrain suffers from infertile soils or poor drainage. Drought in semiarid North Africa and dust storms in Soviet Central Asia sharply remind us of the limits of easier farming. Growing cities, roads, parks, and other forms of nonagricultural occupance utilize ever more space, usually in the fertile plains. One must conclude that expansion of farmland, while feasible in some areas, offers no solution for the food needs of the next generation.

## HIGHER PRODUCTIVITY PER UNIT AREA

Instead of basing our hope on agricultural ventures in unfamiliar climate and terrain, we can turn with more confidence to lands of proved value. We have already seen (Chapter 10) what strides modern agriculture has made in the industrial countries. The accomplishments so far are only the beginning of a new era. For instance, the recent breakthrough in the knowledge of the gene structure opens up vistas of plant and animal breeding far beyond present methods. But speculation aside concerning the future, it is clear that widespread adoption of modern farming methods would increase the world's food production tremendously, even without adding more land to that now in use.

The late L. Dudley Stamp, an outstanding British geographer and expert on land utilization, suggested that in regard to land productivity, northwest Europe is a better model for imitation than the United States. Indeed, if greater food production per hectare is the objective, agriculture as practiced in Denmark, for instance, is best. In northwest Europe approximately 0.4 hectare (1 acre) of cultivated land yields enough food to

*Much more exact information is now being gathered with satellite-borne sensors (Earth Resources Technology Satellites—ERTS).

feed one person. Stamp points out that by this standard the really "underdeveloped" countries are Anglo-America, southern South America, Australia, New Zealand, and also the Soviet Union (Stamp, 1952). To support his view he quotes yields in Denmark, the Netherlands, Belgium, England, and West Germany, which are indeed far above those of the United States and similar countries. His argument might be countered by observing that the higher level of living in Anglo-America, or Australia, has been reached by great productivity per worker rather than per unit area, a goal to which other countries should aspire instead of wresting the last bushel of wheat from a hectare.

Somewhere between the divergent objectives of productivity-per-hectare and productivity-per-worker must lie a feasible compromise. Recent increases in American yields per hectare resulting from more fertilizer and improved plants and animals show what can be done in a country where the main objective is high income per worker. On the other hand, Danish or English farmers are hardly peasants tending their fields with backbreaking labor to feed their poverty-stricken families. They combine a high degree of mechanization with high hectare yields and enjoy a fairly good income. These considerations lead to the conclusion that the mid-latitudes offer far greater capability of supporting more people than do the uncertain riches of the tropics (Figure 18-4).

Stamp's estimate that 0.4 hectare of improved farmland can support one human being translates into surprisingly large potentials for what he calls the "underdeveloped countries." According to his standard, the arable land currently in use in the United States could support some 500 million, Canada 100 million, Argentina 75 million, Australia 70 million, and the Soviet Union 560 million, a total of 1,305 million people versus a present population in these countries of about 520 million. Whether these figures need correction or even are desirable objectives is not at issue here.

Higher crop yields are also feasible in the underdeveloped countries. The great increase in agricultural production per unit of land was achieved in Europe and Japan as their economy changed to the industrial-commercial type.

Owing to the recently developed "miracle" wheat and rice varieties, significant gains in food production are possible. Nevertheless the green revolution is not a matter of miracle seeds alone. It also needs changes in land tenure, marketing and credit facilities, also in manufacturing, use of fertilizers, and construction of new transportation and storage facilities. In short, science and technology hold promise of more food, but the fulfillment depends on whether or not the costs of the green revolution can be minimized. Current difficulties include: greater income inequality, because only richer farmers can afford the new inputs; uniformity rather than diversity of crops, leading to potential disaster from diseases and pests; a rise in unemployment where mechanization occurs; and growing dependence on increasingly expensive fertilizers and scarcer energy. There is no time to lose. The years before A.D. 2000 will be the critical period in the race between population and food.

### THE SEAS

There are other ways to improve and increase the food supply. The urgent need for more animal protein calls attention to the promise of the sea. So far the sea has retained the nature of a hunting and gathering ground. With better knowledge of the regional ecology, it should be possible to manipulate the oceans as farmers do their environments: select the best habitat for each useful fish species, breed better strains, weed out harmful interlopers, provide more plankton for feeding, and so on.

But all this must wait until the intensive oceanographic research, now getting under way, can lay a sound foundation for the agriculture of the sea. In the meantime the technology of large-scale fishing becomes so efficient that it threatens to destroy a rich resource before it can be developed as an enduring crop. Naturally, the industrial nations are the ones with the means to build the ocean-going fleets. The countries that most need the animal protein lack the capital and know-how for bringing in the big catch (Figure 18-5).

## BEYOND FOOD

The overriding concern with questions of subsist-

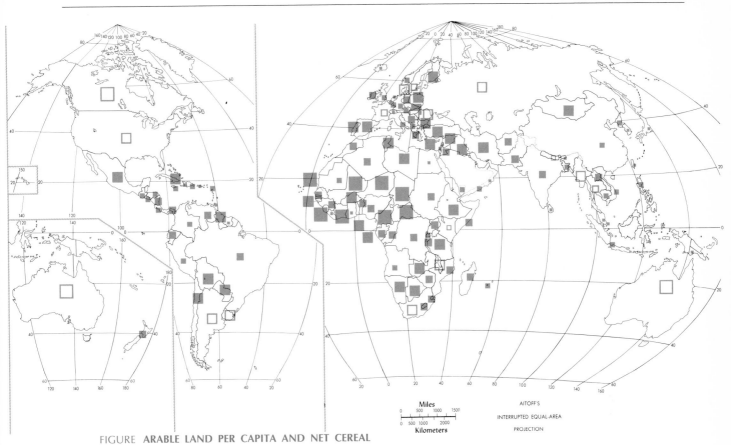

FIGURE 18-4 ARABLE LAND PER CAPITA AND NET CEREAL IMPORTERS, EARLY 1970s

Source of data: United Nations, *FAO Production Year-book, 1974*, Volume 28-1, New York, 1975, table 1.

**Hectares per Capita**

- Under .1
- .1-.2
- .2-.4
- .4-1.0
- Over 1.0

- Net Importer of Cereal Grains
- Net Exporter of Cereal Grains

ence almost makes one forget that for all of us to be truly human we need more than food. To insist on quality is as important today as in the time of Plato. Seen in this light, population pressures may—and do—exist in countries with ample food supply. Some writers who argue that the United States has a population problem point to the insufficiency of schools and hospitals, the scarcity of community recreation facilities, the traffic congestion and the pollution of soil, water, and air. There can be no doubt that the rapid population growth of recent years, coupled with rising standards among all groups, puts heavy pressure on community facilities and on the habitat. Especially noticeable is the strain in metropolitan areas where tensions and troubles seem much more than the temporary maladjustments of an era of swift change.

In densely populated—overdeveloped?—

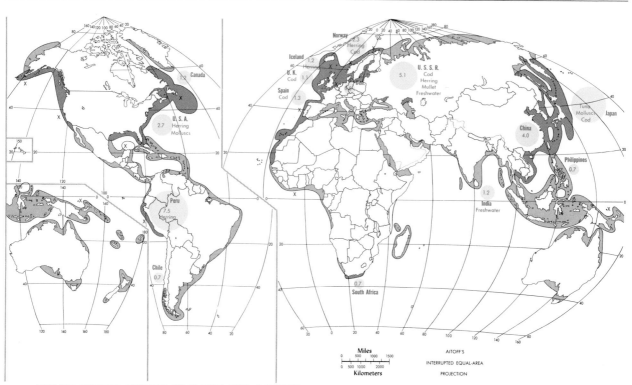

## FIGURE 18-5  WORLD: FISHING GROUNDS AND CATCHES

This map distinguishes between the heavily fished commercial grounds, where huge catches of single species are usual, and other waters, which are exploited to a lesser extent, often for many species. The circles show tonnages landed in the principal fishing countries, from which boats and factory ships often operate at long distances. The main species landed are also shown. The dateline is the mid-1960s.

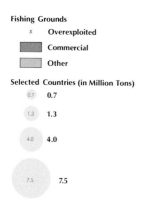

Fishing Grounds

x    Overexploited

    Commercial

    Other

Selected Countries (in Million Tons)

0.7   **0.7**

1.3   **1.3**

4.0   **4.0**

7.5    **7.5**

West Europe the crisis of space shortage is already at hand. Cities, because of higher living standards, expand faster than their populations. For instance, Amsterdam's population increased between 1930 and 1960 by 20 percent, but its built-up area more than doubled. Plans for 1980 foresee a ten-year increase of 7.5 percent, but another doubling of the built-up area. In addition, new industrial plants and expansion of port facilities eat up vast tracts of farmland. As demands for water increase, it becomes short in supply, even in an amphibious province like Holland, partly because cities and industries pollute the streams, partly because seawater penetrates inland as it replaces the drawn-off fresh groundwater.

Open spaces for recreation within reasonable distance from urban areas are getting scarce; hordes of visitors trample the reality as well as the illusion of being "in nature." It has been calculated that the magnificent beaches along the Dutch coast afford each citizen only 2 centimeters. Quite apart from recreational space, the general absence of "elbow room" affects people in many

A swimming pool in Tokyo, Japan. In a relatively wealthy country like Japan, population increase may mean overcrowding of beaches, parks, and pools as well as a shortage of adequate schools, housing, and other facilities necessary to a metropolitan society. (Photograph—United Nations)

subtle ways. If it is hard to define economic population pressure, it is even harder to know what constitutes its psychic counterpart. Biologists have observed stress syndromes as they appear in animal populations when their density becomes too high. This suggests the possibility of pathological behavior in equivalent human situations. At any rate, crowding demands discipline which, if not voluntarily adhered to, must be maintained by regimentation, easily subverted into authoritarianism.

It becomes more and more difficult to be quietly alone. Not all societies equally appreciate the privilege of solitude, even if they can afford it. Nevertheless, the individual in the modern world finds the lack of privacy a frustrating experience that signifies a flaw in our ability to create good environments. Our growing impact on the biophysical world poses such a serious challenge to the quality of life that it deserves closer examination. The following chapter is devoted to this issue.

## CITATIONS AND FURTHER READINGS

Brooke, C. "Types of Food Shortages in Tanzania," *Geographical Review,* 57 (1967): 333–357.
Buchanan, K. "The White North and the Population Explosion," *Antipode,* 5 (Dec., 1973): 7–15.
Chakravarti, A. K. "Foodgrain Sufficiency Patterns in India," *Geographical Review,* 60 (1970): 208–228.

————— "Green Revolution in India," *Annals of the Association of American Geographers,* 63 (1973): 319–330.

————— "Regional Preference for Food: Some Aspects of Food Habit Patterns in India," *Canadian Geographer,* 18 (1974): 395–410.

Coull, J. R. "The Big Fish Pond: a Perspective on the Contemporary Situation in the World's Fisheries," *Area,* 7 (1975): 103–107.

Deshler, W. "Livestock Trypanosomiasis and Human Settlement in Northeastern Uganda," *Geographical Review,* 50 (1960): 541–554.

Duncan, O. D. (ed.). *The Study of Population: An Inventory and Appraisal,* Chicago, 1959, 621–648.

Food and Agriculture Organization. *State of Food and Agriculture* (annual), Rome, 1948–.

Grigg, D. B. "Population Pressure and Agricultural Change," *Progress in Geography, International Reviews of Current Research,* 8 (1976): 133–176.

Horst, O. H. "The Specter of Death in a Guatemalan Highland Community," *Geographical Review,* 57 (1967): 151–167.

Howe, G. M. *National Atlas of Disease Mortality in the United Kingdom,* New York, 1963.

————— *Man, Environment, and Disease in Britain; a Medical Geography of Britain through the Ages,* New York, 1972.

Hunter, J. M. "Population Pressure in a Part of the West African Savanna: A Study of Nangodi, Northeast Ghana," *Annals of the Association of American Geographers,* 57 (1967): 101–114.

Johnson, B. L. C. "Recent Developments in Rice Breeding and Some Implications for Tropical Asia," *Geography,* 57 (1972): 307–320.

Kariel, H. C. "A Proposed Classification of Diet," *Annals of the Association of American Geographers,* 56 (1966): 68–79.

King, R. "Geographical Perspectives on the Green Revolution. Review Article," *Tijdschrift voor Economische en Sociale Geografie,* 64 (1973): 237–244.

Knight, C. G. "The Ecology of African Sleeping Sickness," *Annals of the Association of American Geographers,* 61 (1971): 23–44.

————— and Wilcox, R. P. *Triumph or Triage: The World Food Problem in Geographic Perspective,* Resource Papers for College Geography, Association of American Geographers, Washington, D.C., 1976.

Learmonth, A. T. A. "Ecological Medical Geography," *Progress in Geography, International Reviews of Current Research,* 7 (1975): 201–226.

McGlashan, N. D. (ed.). *Medical Geography: Techniques and Field Studies,* London, 1972.

May, J. M. "Medical Geography: Its Methods and Objectives," *Geographical Review,* 40 (1950): 9–41.

————— *The Ecology of Malnutrition in the Far and Near East: Food Resources, Habits, and Deficiencies,* New York, 1961.

————— *Studies in Disease Ecology,* New York, 1961.

Meadows, D. H., Meadows, D. L., Randers, J., and Behrens, W. W., III. *The Limits to Growth,* New York, 1972.

Prothero, R. M. *Migrants and Malaria,* London, 1965.

Roundy, R. W. "Altitudinal Mobility and Disease Hazards for Ethiopian Populations," *Economic Geography,* 52 (1976): 103–115.

Simmons, J. S. *Global Epidemiology: A Geography of Disease and Sanitation,* 3 vols., Philadelphia, 1944–1954.

Simoons, F. J. *Eat Not This Flesh: Food Avoidances in the Old World,* Madison, Wis., 1961.

Stamp, L. D. "The Measurement of Land Resources," *Geographical Review,* 48 (1958): 1–15.

————— *Some Aspects of Medical Geography,* New York, 1964.

# 19 WHAT MAN HAS WROUGHT

## IS DOOMSDAY NEAR?

Wastes from factories, homes, and feedlots convert our rivers and lakes into sewers. Automobile fumes and smokestack belchings befoul the air. The noise of pavement breakers, trucks, and jets assaults the ear. Oil spills from tankers and offshore wells besmirch beaches, bays, and seas. Ravenous coal-stripping machines gouge the land, leaving behind bleak barrens. National parks choke on traffic and litter. The sea around us carries the flotsam of a plastic civilization. These vistas come to mind when we think of the environmental blight which "advanced" societies inflict upon "The Good Earth."

The relationship between mankind and the planet is by tradition one of geography's main concerns (Chapter 2). Anxiety about the irresponsible way the earth is despoiled has recently propelled the issue into popular interest. Geographers find this gratifying, though they see efforts to save the environment complicated—often counteracted—by indecisive government, powerful private organizations, and careless individuals. In the flood of words that mix emotions, polemics, and politics with objective analysis, it is virtually impossible for the people to disentangle fact from conjecture, knowledge from propaganda.

This much seems clear; modern science and technology have tremendously increased productivity per worker and thus income per capita. This affluence creates ever greater demands for the comforts and conveniences that technology can provide. The spiraling interaction between technology and wealth leads to an accelerated rate of consumption and consequently to ever larger waste accumulation. Also, it stimulates urbanization as more and more people move from agriculture and industry into service occupations. High consumption by itself tends to disrupt and deplete the biophysical environment, and its damaging effects are multiplied in urban areas. There pressures on the habitat join with breakdowns and shortages in the built environment, all of which are aggravated by a concentration of social ills (Table 19–1).

Before succumbing to despair, let us note some more hopeful events. In London, under certain atmospheric conditions, the soft coal soot and smoke from countless chimneys remained trapped over the city, producing the notorious "pea soup" fog. The suspicion that this yellow shroud killed people became a certainty when in 1952 the number of deaths during a four-day period of thick fog shot up to 4,000 above normal. After much public discussion, Parliament in 1956 passed the Clean Air Act. Since then some 5 million homes and other buildings have switched to smokeless solid fuel, gas, or electricity. The results have been spectacular: no dense fog has been reported in London since 1964. The soot spewed into that city's air—156,000 metric tonnes annually—has been reduced by 80 percent, and sulfur dioxide concentration by 40 percent. Winter visibility has increased threefold. The number of bird species present has more than doubled over the past ten years.

San Diego Bay, a crescent-shaped basin 25 kilometers long and 0.5 to 4 kilometers wide, became a murky cesspool in the 1950s because of sewage and industrial discharges from the city, its suburbs, the naval installations, and factories, including tuna canneries and a kelp-processing plant. Phytoplankton—the saltwater equivalent of freshwater algae—proliferated on the phosphates and nitrates supplied by the sewage. Oxygen content of the water diminished as it was consumed by the decomposition of wastes and dead phytoplankton. Worse, fecal contamination became so severe that beaches had to be closed.

As so often, attempts at improvement met with public apathy and even opposition until voters at last in 1960 approved the necessary bond issue. The cleanup system began operating in 1965. Its main features are a primary sewage treatment plant on the ocean shore, with pipes that carry the effluent several kilometers out to sea. Almost immediately the water color changed from reddish-brown to its former sparkling blue as the phytoplankton disappeared. Within a year, fish—from sole and salmon to barracuda—were swarming back into the bay. Density of disease-causing bacteria has decreased to safe levels so the beaches again are open for swimming. To cite these cases is not to claim that all environmental troubles can be fixed easily or permanently. They do suggest, however, that the decline in quality of our habitat is not an irreversible process.

## HISTORICAL PERSPECTIVE

In the last decade all that has been said about human destruction of our environment leaves the impression that this is a recent phenomenon. Though modern technology disturbs the web of life more deeply than ever before, we must remember that Homo sapiens has always tried to manipulate the surroundings to his advantage, usually without concern for widespread repercussions on the landscape.

### CHANGES IN PALEOLITHIC TIMES

When mankind began to fashion tools, make fire, and develop social organizations (Chapter 3), these abilities made possible adaptation to a great diversity of habitats. Humans thus spread over much of the earth's surface. In most places this life became so interwoven with the local biotic

**MISUSE OF RESOURCES**

TABLE
19-1

| Resources | Nature of disruption | | Sector of disruption |
|-----------|---------------------|---|---------------------|
| Biophysical environment | Depletion | | Fossil fuels and/or minerals<br>Water supply<br>Soil<br>Agricultural land<br>Forest<br>Recreational space<br>Wildlife |
| | Pollution | | Air<br>Water<br>Soil |
| Built environment | Breakdowns | | Transportation<br>Waste disposal<br>Visual order |
| | Shortages | | Housing<br>Community facilities |
| People | Individual wastage | | Education<br>Employment |
| | Social failure | | Civil order<br>Crime<br>Health<br>Nutrition<br>Narcotics and alcohol |

Adapted from *The California Tomorrow Plan* (1971).

The Via delle Botteghe Oscura in Rome, Italy, jammed with traffic. Many of the world's great cities have difficulty in accommodating ever-increasing numbers of automobiles with all their accompanying problems, such as air pollution and the consumption of valuable land for highways, streets, and parking facilities. (Photograph—United Nations)

community that its imprint remained hardly visible. Nevertheless, in the long run—and that means during most of the life-span of Homo sapiens—the cumulative impact left its mark, in the refuse dumps (kitchen middens) of the settlements, in the cave paintings, and, in a major way, through destruction of forests by fire (Chapter 9).

While modifications of the tropical rain forest may have been limited to the sunlit shores of river and sea where human bands roamed, in the seasonally wet and dry outer tropics and in the middle latitudes the use of fire gradually transformed forested plains into park lands, even

grasslands (Sauer, 1950; Stewart, 1956). In turn, such environmental disturbances must have affected the animal populations. The extermination of the New Zealand moa by Polynesian hunters has already been mentioned (page 214). Although the population must have been small, their hunting zeal and use of fire destroyed much of the forest mantle and led to the extinction of several animal species—all in no more than five or six centuries.

Could prehistoric hunters also be responsible for the decline and even demise during the late Pleistocene of numerous species of large herbivores—mammoth, giant bison, ancient forms of horse and camel—and their ecologically dependent carnivores and scavengers, such as the saber-toothed tiger and now extinct kinds of wolf? Many writers usually cite changes in climate and consequently in vegetation as sufficient causes for these events. But others (Sauer, 1944;

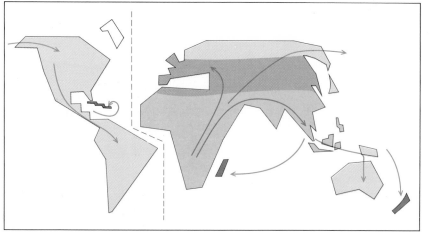

**Period of Major Extinction**

More than 40,000 Years

8,000-13,000 Years

400-4,000 Years

→ Direction of Human Migration

FIGURE
**19-1**   PREHISTORIC MAN AND MAMMAL EXTINCTION

According to some scholars, each major wave of late Pleistocene extinction of large animals coincided with the arrival of prehistoric hunters. The sequence began with (1) Africa and southern Eurasia, continuing to (2) New Guinea and Australia, (3) Northern Eurasia and northern North America, (4) Southeastern United States, (5) South America, (6) West Indies, and (7) Madagascar and New Zealand. The colors on the map represent approximate times of extinction of species, among which were mammoth, mastodon, woolly rhinoceros, giant marsupials, moa, horse (in America), and various species of deer. After Martin, P. S., "Prehistoric Overkill," in Martin, P. S., and Wright, H. E., Jr. (eds.), *Pleistocene Extinctions: The Search for a Cause,* New Haven, Conn., 1967, 75–120. Reprinted in abridged form in Detwyler, T. R. (ed.), *Man's Impact on the Environment,* New York, 1971, 612–624.

Martin, 1967) have argued persuasively that human beings, though few in number, may well over a long time span have been the main destructive agent (Figure 19-1). Martin observes: "The thought that prehistoric hunters ten to fifteen thousand years ago (and in Africa over forty thousand years ago) exterminated far more animals than has modern man with modern weapons and advanced technology is certainly provocative and perhaps deeply disturbing." Deeply disturbing, one presumes, because it suggests that even early human hunters had the capacity to specialize with devastating environmental effects.

## PLANT AND ANIMAL DOMESTICATION

During paleolithic times, human beings caused so few environmental changes that in effect they lived in the ecological niches nature provided. In contrast, neolithic peoples by selecting and protecting useful animals and plants began to create their own niches, thereby starting to dominate their biotic community. The clearings made for crops attracted wild plants that thrived in open sunlit places. Some of these weeds the neolithic farmer recognized as valuable and therefore worthy to propagate. Rye and oats may have been adopted in this manner. Thus, "domestication was a process, not an event" (Anderson, 1956).

As agriculture spread from its early centers to different climates and soils, the domesticates had to adapt or be abandoned in favor of plants or animals better fitted to the new environment. Of course, these modifications led to other changes in the local ecosystem, down to the microlevel of soil bacteria and viruses. In general, human interference replaced the equilibrium of complex natural biological communities with the inherent instability of specialized—and thus simpler—agricultural ecosystems. The impact differed, depending on the form of agriculture. Swidden farming (Chapter 9) disturbed nature far less than single-crop cultivation on fields. Nevertheless, since farming began about 12,000 years ago, its cumulative effect has profoundly altered the biotic world (Figure 19-2).

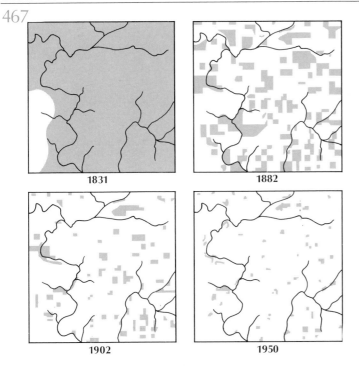

1831

1882

1902

1950

FIGURE
19-2

REDUCTION IN WOODLAND IN CADIZ TOWNSHIP,
GREEN COUNTY, WISCONSIN

Changes in the wooded area of Cadiz Township during
the period of European settlement. The township is 6
miles on a side and is drained by the Pecatonica River.
The maps show the original forest cover and the land
remaining in or reverting to forest in 1882, 1902, and
1950. After map by J. T. Curtis in "The Modification of
Mid-Latitude Grasslands and Forests by Man," in
Thomas, W. L. (ed.), *Man's Role in Changing the Face
of the Earth*, Chicago, 1956, 721–736.

## LAND DETERIORATION
## IN ANCIENT CIVILIZATIONS

The early civilizations evolved on the river plains
in the valleys of the Nile, Euphrates-Tigris, Indus,
and Huang Ho. For over 5,000 years Lower Egypt
and the North China Plain have maintained the
capacity to support large populations. In contrast,
deserts now prevail in the middle Indus Valley
and in Mesopotamia, where once masterful wa-
terworks provided the lifeblood for thriving cultures. It would be unwise to assign a single cause
to such a complex event as the decline of a civili-

zation. However, in arid climates where human
life so directly depends on water, the failure of
irrigation and drainage systems must have been a
prime factor. We take the case of Mesopotamia as
an example (Jacobsen and Adams, 1958).

While irrigation may make "the desert blos-
som like the rose," it also carries risks of ruining
the land unless proper techniques maintain water
supply as well as drainage. Salts dissolved in irrigation water concentrate in the soil as evaporation occurs and plants absorb moisture and tran-
spire. Heavy salt accumulation in the root zone is
detrimental to plants and to the soil itself. Sodium
compounds in particular tend to break down the
soil particles which on absorbing water may form
an impervious gelatinous mass that makes it difficult for plants to take in water and nutrients.
Also silica, iron, and lime deposits in the subsoil
may cement together to form impermeable layers,
commonly called hardpan. With poor drainage
the soil becomes waterlogged, or capillary action
brings toxic alkali concentrations to the surface.
Clearly, proper drainage must balance irrigation,
allowing surplus water to move downward and
away, flushing out excess salts. The irrigation
farmer in ancient times must have been concerned, just as he is today, with these man-
induced processes.

It appears that the land of Sumer, in what
was then Lower Mesopotamia (since then the
coastline has moved far southward into the Persian Gulf), began to be affected by excess salt
about 2400 B.C. Temple records and archaeological
fieldwork indicate gradual abandonment of cropland, the replacement of wheat by more salt-tol-
erant barley, and a general drop in fertility, causing yields to decline by two-thirds between 2400
and 1700 B.C. If these interpretations of the data
are correct, salinization may have contributed
substantially to the shift of political power from
Ur upstream to Babylon.

Silt accumulation in canals occurs in many
irrigation areas. Recent archaeological research in
middle Mesopotamia suggests that the decline in
central authority burdened the local peasants
with a responsibility for silt removal which they
were unable to meet. During most of Mesopotamia's ancient history—say, from 4000 to 300
B.C.—settlements adhered to the main water
courses. Irrigation water drawn from the rivers at

flood stage reached the fields through short canals. The silting problem must have been a minor matter compared to social and political upheavals which interrupted the economy. However, after about 300 B.C. canals were extended all through the alluvium, often involving engineering works of large scope, ordered by the rulers and executed by forced labor of countless peasants. The resulting expansion of arable land could feed an ever larger population which, not without setbacks, seems to have reached its maximum in the sixth century A.D. From then on decline set in. As central authority weakened, the network of canals was neglected, including the coordinated mass effort of removing silt. As the water supply to the fields diminished, they had to be abandoned. By the twelfth century most of Mesopotamia had reverted to a sparsely inhabited steppe and desert country. The invasion of the Mongols in the next century may have been the final blow; certainly it was not the cause of Mesopotamia's decay.

Environmental change in ancient civilizations was not limited to the creation of artificial oases. Livestock grazing and browsing must have affected the plant life of grasslands and woods. It often has been observed that wide areas of low rainfall in the Old World are virtually bare of vegetation, in contrast to climatically analogous areas in the New World which usually have some plant cover. Possibly livestock pasturing over thousands of years, especially of sheep and goats, has caused the difference.

## DEFORESTATION: THE CASE OF THE CEDARS OF LEBANON

Anyone who has flown over the lands surrounding the Mediterranean Sea must have noted the succession of almost barren mountains, even in parts where rainfall would seem adequate for forest growth. Historical evidence supports the suspicion that deforestation and consequent accelerated erosion have degraded the ancient forest mantle into a ragged cover of scrub. A classic and well-documented example is the fate of the renowned cedars of Lebanon (Mikesell, 1969).

The Lebanon Range, rising steeply from the eastern shore of the Mediterranean to about 3,000 meters, receives on its seaward slope an average annual precipitation of at least 700 millimeters and locally as much as 950 millimeters. Once a

forest of cedars interspersed with firs covered this west slope from about 1,300 to 3,300 meters altitude. Below this zone grew oaks and above it junipers. Early historical records sing the praise of the tall, straight cedar, its durability for construction of palaces, temples, and ships, its beauty and fragrance for paneling and coffins, its resin and oil for mummification and enbalming. Treeless Egypt in particular prized this wood and obtained it from the Phoenicians, either as tribute or in trade, throughout the third and second millennia B.C. and later. Mesopotamian rulers, too, valued the cedar above any timber available in the Zagros Mountains and imported it in spite of the long and difficult overland and river route. The Old Testament tells how Solomon used the cedars of Lebanon to build his temple about 950 B.C. Greeks and Romans also were eager to obtain the stately tree. It is no wonder that by the beginning of the Christian Era the cedar forest in the more accessible areas had been depleted.

In the Middle Ages the Christian Maronites and the Druze sect of Shi'ite Muslims who occupied the highlands made further inroads on the remaining stands of cedar and even more on the oak, pine, and juniper forests, cutting them for timber and charcoal or clearing them for crops and pasturing of livestock. This form of land use prevailed until about 1900, when the oppressive rule of the Turks caused many Lebanese to emigrate. As the mountain folk gave up their homesteads, the surrounding vegetation invaded the abandoned crop terraces. Today amidst the scrub forest only a dozen small and scattered stands of cedar remain of what once was "the glory of Lebanon."

## INTERCONTINENTAL TRANSFER OF PLANTS AND ANIMALS

While the spread of people in any era meant that they carried along some other forms of life—microorganisms, lice—the most rapid and far-reaching transfer of fauna and flora occurred during the post-Columbian period. As in earlier times, many dispersals were by accident, others on purpose. Paramount in economic importance were, of course, the exchanges of domesticated animals and plants between the Old and the New Worlds (Chapter 3). Most crops depend so completely on human care for their survival and propagation that they remained associated with settlements wherever they were taken. Some domestic animals show similar dependence, including the sheep, chicken, dog, even the cat, however much it likes to walk alone. Other animals, once having escaped captivity, can fend for themselves where no predator threatens their existence, for example, the donkey (burro), horse, and goat. The latter has become the ecologically dominant species on many small islands.

Besides domesticates introduced for economic reasons, numerous birds and ornamental plants were imported for pleasure or sentiment. Wild animals too were transferred, often with unexpected, even disastrous, results. If the Australians had known what was in store for them, they would not have tried for seventy years to import the rabbit and coax it into reproduction. Because the rabbit had no natural enemies in its new habitat, it proliferated quickly. Its destruction of the vegetation cover in many areas led to serious soil erosion. In hopes of controlling the pest, the fox was introduced but, finding easier prey among the indigenous species, it ignored the rabbit. After various other attempts at control had failed, myxoma virus was deliberately brought in. It eliminated over 90 percent of the rabbits. By the 1960s, however, a strain of rabbit had developed immunity to the virus, and the problem has revived.

Biological control of the prickly pear cactus seems to have met with success. This plant, because it served as food for the dye-producing cochineal insect, was transplanted from America to various overseas countries. Arid regions of Australia offered the plant such ideal conditions that it spread as a massive cover over large parts of Queensland and New South Wales. After several fruitless attempts at eradication, the cactoblastis, an Argentinian moth, was brought over in 1925. In eight years it eliminated the cactus from 10 million hectares. Now small populations of plant and moth survive in balanced numbers.

A mixed blessing resulted when the mongoose was taken from India to Jamaica to kill the rats that took a heavy toll of the sugarcane. The little alien so successfully reduced the rat population that it turned for food to other small ground animals. Now the mongoose is considered a pest in the West Indies. Opinions differ as to the mer-

its of the English sparrow and the European starling, both brought to North America—the latter as recently as 1890—and today spread widely over the continent.

A curious and spurious belief in the salubrious effect of the eucalyptus was in part responsible for extensive plantings of several species of this Australian tree genus in California more than 100 years ago (Thompson, 1970). Before the connection between mosquito and malaria was understood, it was thought that miasma—vapors rising from the ground—caused the disease, as the name mal-aria (bad air) indicates. The eucalyptus supposedly absorbed or neutralized these noxious gases—this "air pollution," we would say today. Perhaps the medicinal aroma of the leaves bolstered this notion. Indirectly the eucalyptus may have reduced malaria to some extent because it withdraws much moisture from the ground, thereby reducing the surface water mosquitoes need for breeding. By the time the true cause of malaria was revealed in the 1890s, the eucalyptus—also because it resists drought and grows rapidly—had become a familiar part of the California landscape.

### RESOURCE DEGRADATION IN MEXICO

Indigenous milpa agriculture and imported Spanish modes of land use have destroyed in Mexico wide areas of natural vegetation, causing severe erosion. Maize, the paramount crop, quickly exhausts the soil. The Indians, using the ancient slash-and-burn (milpa) method, shifted plots every two or three years. As the population of the pre-Spanish empires increased, they expanded the milpa clearings, often to steep slopes and cropped them more frequently. In flat Yucatan—the Maya realm—the soil consists of only a thin layer of decomposed limestone, highly prone to exhaustion by intensive milpa use. This may help to explain the ups and downs in Maya culture as periods of abundance and population growth alternated with decreasing soil productivity, population pressure, starvation, and migration to other sites (Simpson, 1967).

On top of native impact came Spanish exploitation. The conquerors brought along their livestock, crops, and the plow. The plow, much more effective than the Indian planting stick in breaking up the root mat that binds the soil together, caused gully erosion. The Spaniards found Mexico well suited for a vast sheep-raising industry such as they had developed at home. Soon thousands of sheep estancias covered extensive parts of the country. The Indians, finding wool warmer, gave up their cotton cloth and themselves became sheep raisers and wool weavers. The depopulated countryside suffered great damage as large herds of sheep, also goats, browsed the land, cutting it with their hooves. According to the authoritative account of L. B. Simpson, sheep and goat estates by about 1600 occupied an estimated area of 15,000 hectares. Horned cattle, introduced for beef and for draft power, multiplied rapidly in the new environment, overgrazed the land severely and menaced the milpas when they developed a taste for maize.

Spanish miners in their relentless search for precious metals speeded up deforestation to a disastrous degree. They needed much timber for mine shafts and huge amounts of charcoal in the smelting process. "Wherever a mining community (*real de minas*) was established, a diseased spot began to appear, and it spread until each mining town was in the middle of something like a desert" (Simpson, 1967). Add to this the city's demand for timber and charcoal, and it is no wonder that many mountains once clothed in forest now are almost bare rocky slopes where only goats can sustain themselves. Although in recent years the Mexican government has taken measures to improve the land and its productivity, the scars of centuries-long abuse are still visible everywhere. The example of Mexico must suffice to illustrate what happened in modern times to many lands opened up to European commercial exploitation.

## CONSEQUENCES OF THE INDUSTRIAL REVOLUTION

The Machine Age intensifies the processes by which mankind modifies its habitat. It greatly increases human control over energy, accelerates the use of mineral resources, and stimulates population growth and urbanization. In the nineteenth century, the impact was especially severe in the emerging manufacturing regions located on the coalfields. Patrick Geddes called the early phase of the industrial period, based on coal, iron, and steam engine, the "Paleotechnic Age," a time of crude exploitation of human and material re-

sources and of urban squalor. He hoped that it would be succeeded by the "Neotechnic Age," an age when the machine would be mankind's servant in achieving a high quality of life, with well-being and beauty in rural as well as urban surroundings.

It is the paleotechnic scene that William Blake had in mind when he spoke of "dark satanic mills," and that Charles Dickens described in his "Coke Town"—symbolic and symptomatic of a new type of urban life: "shrouded in a haze of its own . . . a blur of soot and smoke [where factory hands] worked, to the crashing, smashing, tearing piece of mechanism . . . all the year around, from the dawn of Monday, to the night of Saturday [amidst] the whirr of shafts and wheels . . . Down upon the river that was black and thick with dye . . . every dip of an oar stirred up vile smells."

The effects of the Industrial Revolution were not limited to the industrial districts as they spread from Britain to other countries. The new technology also brought changes in agriculture through the use of chemical fertilizers, farm machinery, and more rapid mass transportation to markets. European settlement on the grasslands of interior North America and Eurasia, and their remote counterparts in the southern hemisphere, would not have been possible without the railroad, steamship, power-driven harvester, barbed wire, and other inventions of the new era. As in the industrial regions, this technology caused undesirable side effects. Before considering these modern environmental problems, it is useful to examine a broader, more philosophical issue.

## ATTITUDES TOWARD THE ENVIRONMENT

Peoples of different times and places have viewed the relation between man and nature in a variety of ways. Essentially there are three concepts: (1) Man and nature live in harmony; (2) nature controls man; (3) man controls nature. Anthropological studies suggest that preliterate communities identify with their habitats; they feel they are part of a cosmic harmony which must not be disturbed. In more sophisticated form, this notion of man-in-nature appears in the writings of many Oriental philosophers, particularly of the Taoist

An automobile junkyard in rural Vermont. (Photograph—United Nations)

and Zen buddhist schools. Sometimes it crops up in Western thought as, for example, in the teachings of Saint Francis of Assisi.

The idea that human beings are subordinate to nature is less common. One can, of course, point to astrology or to the doctrine of environmental determinism (Chapter 2). The latter view is well expressed in Ellen Churchill Semple's famous prologue to her *Influences of Geographic Environment* (1911):

**Man is a product of the earth's surface. This means not merely that he is a child of the earth, dust of her dust; but that the earth has mothered him, fed him, set him tasks, directed his thoughts, confronted him with difficulties that have strengthened his body and sharpened his wits,** **given him his problems of navigation or irrigation, and at the same time whispered hints for their solution.**

However, on further reading one discovers, as with other environmental determinists, that such pronouncements are largely rhetorical. Implicitly or explicitly, these writers admit that man as a culture-shaped creature has considerable leeway in adjusting to the grip of his physical surroundings.

The third position—man as the master of nature—is the predominant attitude of Western civilization. The *Book of Genesis* contains the divine injunction that man subdue the earth. Probably more influential, certainly for modern times, were the secular philosophers of the Renaissance, such as Francis Bacon and René Descartes. Starting from the classical notion of a cosmic design, they searched for knowledge of the physical world that would make men "the lords and masters of nature." But was this control inherently benign and beneficial? Or could man as steward of the earth abuse his power? On the whole, the optimistic outlook prevailed: It equated man's scientific and technical advance with the idea of inevitable, boundless progress, which expresses itself in the landscape as an ever more perfect blend of natural and cultivated forms (Glacken, 1967).

Nevertheless, dissenting voices were not lacking. Around 1800, engineers studying Alpine rivers claimed that deforestation caused the sudden torrents which inflicted much damage on lowland settlements. Alexander von Humboldt was well aware of the dangers of using resources recklessly: "By felling the trees which cover the tops and sides of mountains, men in every climate prepare at once two calamities for future generations: want of fuel and scarcity of water." The scholar who most thoroughly grasped the implications of the cumulative force of human action was George Perkins Marsh (Chapter 2). He did not accept the reassuring thesis that man was part and partner of nature, progressing according to a divine plan. To the contrary, he believed "that man is, in both kind and degree, a power of a higher order than any other forms of animated life," a power which all too often, through imprudence or ignorance, disturbs nature's balance. In his *Man and Nature* (1864) he discussed in topical order man's influence upon animal and vegetable life, upon the woods, waters, and the sands, always emphasizing the unplanned, unforeseen, and uncontrolled changes which man had brought about. He hoped that by revealing the errors made in the past he could convince his readers, especially in America, of the necessity for wise stewardship in exploiting the earth's resources.

Although Marsh stressed the need for harmony he was, as Lowenthal observes, "more concerned with mankind than with the cosmos. It was not for nature's sake that he wanted to protect it, but for man's" (Lowenthal, 1958). In this respect he differed from romantics like Henry Thoreau who saw nature as the reflection of God and wanted to preserve it as the symbol of spirit-ual truth and moral law, the source of all creative thought.

In summary, although Western civilization shows a diversity of views regarding the relationship between man and nature, the dominant thought—certainly since the Renaissance—has been that man is the master. Modern science and technology could not have developed without this belief in man's mission. Now and then disagreement and warnings were voiced, growing in recent years to a crescendo of protest against the rape of the earth. Only time will tell whether the current "ecology" movement is a fad or the beginning of a momentous shift in attitude toward a more responsible management of our resources. The present concern can be better understood when viewed against the background of earlier apprehensions.

## CONSERVATION IN THE UNITED STATES

The story of how Europeans colonized the New World demonstrates the characteristic pattern of a species transferred into a new environment: quick dispersal into favorable niches, rapid growth, and reduction, even extermination, of vulnerable native life. In human terms it meant the exploitation of a new frontier with abundant resources, where clearing the forests, killing Indian and buffalo, plowing the plains, and mining the subterranean riches were taken to be the proper and self-evident means toward gaining the good life. Even so, from early colonial days onward there were scattered attempts at conservation. For instance, the Plymouth Colony passed ordinances in 1626 regulating the cutting and sale of timber. In 1681 William Penn as proprietor of Pennsylvania decreed that for every 5 acres of land cleared one must be left in forest. In 1832 George Catlin, artist and traveler, proposed the establishment of a reserve in the West to preserve the Indian and the buffalo.

Leading circles in America and Europe recognized the value of Marsh's work. He was called upon to shape irrigation laws in California, France, Italy, and Spain; he was quoted in proposals to plant trees on the Great Plains and to reverse the alarming deforestation of India. Although Marsh was not directly responsible for reserving public lands for the preservation of nature or for recreation, he doubtless strengthened the conservationists' arguments. Yosemite Park was created in 1864, the year his book was published. Yellowstone Park was set aside in 1372, with other national parks soon to follow. Compared, however, to the heedless exploitation of natural assets by fast-growing industries, the achievements of the conservationists during this period were modest indeed. The last hundred years have witnessed a growing concern about the abuse of the American environment but, curiously, the interest rose and fell in cycles as if each generation had to rediscover the anxiety in terms of its own experience.

## FOREST PROTECTION

By 1900 the realization that the open frontier had passed led many Americans to reflect on the prospect of diminishing natural wealth. In 1907 President Theodore Roosevelt launched the Conservation Movement, demanding an end to the activities of the "robber barons" and urging comprehensive administration of resources in the public interest. This new policy was especially designed to stop the raiding of forests. In this endeavor the President had the able assistance of Gifford Pinchot, the nation's first professionally trained forester but also a zealous publicist and astute politician. Through his labors over 50 million hectares were declared public domain, to be set apart and scientifically managed as national forests. Pinchot established the principle of constant annual yield by thinning and selective cutting. Like Marsh, he considered preservation of natural wilderness to be of secondary importance. "Forever wild meant to him forever mismanaged" (Pinkett, 1970).

Inevitably this view clashed with the philosophy of conservationists who, in the footsteps of Thoreau, insisted on the moral and esthetic values of undisturbed nature. Their spokesman was John Muir, founder of the Sierra Club. Taking issue with Pinchot's theory he stated: ". . . mountain parks and reservations are useful not only as fountains of timber and irrigating rivers, but as fountains of life. . . . Everybody needs beauty as well as bread, places to play in and pray in, where Nature may heal and cheer and give strength to body and soul alike." These conflicts between

conservation-for-use and preservation-for-beauty continue to this very day.

## SOIL CONSERVATION

Soil erosion moved into focus in the 1930s when a succession of dry years triggered dust storms on the subhumid Great Plains. The Dust Bowl disaster drew attention to soil erosion in other parts of the United States as well. In 1934 it was estimated that over the years man-induced erosion had substantially damaged over two-thirds of the country's land surface. Of this surface, 3 percent had been virtually denuded of its soil, 12 percent had lost over three-fourths, and 41 percent between one-fourth and three-fourths.

The ultimate cause of the devastation may be ascribed to the attitude of the American farmer who, in the pioneer spirit, creamed off the fertility of the land instead of carefully husbanding it. Contributing factors were of an institutional nature, among them forms of land tenancy. Quite commonly tenants or sharecroppers worked under a one-year contract, deriving no benefits from any improvements they might make. Therefore their only interest was to get as much out of the land as possible during the period of tenure. Also, in the large part of the country covered by the Federal Land Survey (Chapter 13), farms had been laid out according to section lines, which encouraged field division without regard to topography. All too often fields were plowed up and down the slopes. Because crops such as cotton, corn, tobacco, and various vegetables grow in rows on clean-tilled fields, their cultivation makes the land particularly vulnerable to erosion. The practice of dry farming in the subhumid western United States brought ever more land under the plow. During the fallow periods, especially in times of drought, the wind took hold of the loose bare soil. Overgrazing also destroyed the natural grass and scrub cover over vast areas of the plains and mountains, exposing the soil to removal by wind or water.

Public opinion became sufficiently aroused in the mid-1930s to insist on countermeasures. The need to cut down agricultural production during the depression years facilitated carrying out the program. Farmers were encouraged to practice contour plowing and to redesign the cropping pattern with fewer row crops and more

Disturbed Land, by States
(in Square Kilometers)

50

100

250

500

1,000

FIGURE **UNITED STATES: LAND SURFACE DISTURBED BY**
**19-3** **STRIP AND SURFACE MINING**

Before World War II most mining except for sand and gravel quarrying was done under the surface. Now more than four-fifths of the total United States production of ore and coal comes from surface mines, worked by gigantic earth-moving equipment. Since 1965, the dateline of this map, the amount of disturbed land has substantially increased, perhaps by as much as 50 percent in some states. Coal mining and sand and gravel quarrying cause most of the land disturbance, but indirectly they affect far more extensive areas through water pollution, landslides, isolation of large tracts of land, and mutilation of the landscape. The scale of the symbols indicating amounts of disturbed land is larger than the scale of the base map with state boundaries. The total amount of land disturbed by mining was 11,185 square kilometers (4,981 square miles), 1.38 percent of the total land surface of the United States (excluding Alaska and Hawaii). Data from Strip and Surface Mine Study Policy Committee, *Surface Mining and Our Environment,* U.S. Department of the Interior, Washington, D.C., 1967, as published in Detwyler, 1971, page 353.

close-growing ones, including pastures. Strip-cropping came into wide use—planting the land in alternate strips of close-growing and cultivated crops instead of in conventional fields. Grazing on the public lands of the West was restricted at certain seasons, and parts of the open range were fenced. These measures, and others designed to give farmers financial assistance, laid the foundation for a national soil conservation policy. Since then the work has been carried on, though less in the limelight. Although much has been accomplished, the land still suffers from annual losses through unnecessary erosion.

### THE ECOLOGICAL APPROACH

In the late 1960s a wave of anxiety about air and water pollution swept the nation and, to a greater or lesser extent, other urban-industrial societies. If disaster seemed close, it had been coming a long time and not without warnings. Beginning in the 1930s death from toxic smog struck communities in Belgium, England, and the United States. Radioactive fallout proved to be a real danger to man and beast. Lake Erie went "dead," and streams foamed with detergents. The Rhine became "Europe's sewer." Oil spills off the coast of England and California severely polluted adjacent shores. Surface mining destroyed even more land (Figure 19–3).

In addition to such events, voices sounded the alarm. In the academic sphere a "Marsh symposium" under the co-chairmanship of Carl O. Sauer, Marston Bates, and Lewis Mumford resulted in a tome of essays entitled *Man's Role in Changing the Face of the Earth* (1956), in which a number of prominent scholars and scientists reviewed man's use and, especially, his abuse of the habitat. But the book that more than any other shook the public's conscience was Rachel Carson's *Silent Spring* (1962). She castigated the thoughtless insecticide sprayers and pleaded for recognition of the ecologic ethic. Here lies the essential difference between preceding conservation waves and the current apprehension: Instead of focusing on a specific endangered resource— forest or soil—the present concern emphasizes the interrelatedness of forces and processes that threaten the total environment.

## CURRENT ISSUES

Now that "ecology" has become a household word and "quality of the environment" the popular slogan, one wonders why it took the general public so long to recognize the adverse effects of proliferating science and technology. Part of the answer lies in the psychological realm of perception. As long as smoke-spewing factories, rising slag heaps, and red brown rivers were considered signs of progress and prosperity, people accepted environmental pollution—if aware of it at all—as a normal part of life, a small inconvenience compared to the large benefits. Moreover, the dangers of pollutants grew slowly and unobtrusively through a complex series of reactions.

For instance, years passed before the harmful side effects of DDT, working through the food chain, were recognized, and still more before measures were initiated to ban the insecticide. It should be added, though, that even now there is no general agreement on the wisdom of this policy. Without an effective and cheap substitute for DDT, malaria may return and food supplies decrease. This is a minor risk for the advanced countries but a real hazard for many densely populated, underdeveloped ones.

### THE HURDLE OF IGNORANCE

Often a substance is suspected of disrupting ecological processes, but the exact way it works has not yet been discovered. Carbon dioxide acts in the atmosphere like glass in a greenhouse: transparent to sunlight, but almost opaque to heat radiation from the earth surface. Some scientists argue that this gas, accumulating in ever greater amounts from the burning of coal and oil, will warm up the earth. Consequently, the ice caps will melt, causing seas to rise and drown coastal areas. But others point out that the earth's average temperature has actually dropped slightly in the last thirty years in spite of the larger injection of carbon dioxide into the air. Perhaps the increasing dustiness of the atmosphere, by reflecting sunshine, cuts down incoming solar energy. But dust consists of a great variety of particles with different optical properties; some reflect sunlight, others absorb it. Until most of these particulates have been identified, any pronouncement on the nature of the dust hazard can only be tentative. The same uncertainty exists regarding the possible effects of water vapor that jet planes expel into the upper atmosphere.

In short, we know very little of how air pollution affects the global climate. Extensive research is necessary to pin down the basic facts concerning accumulation and distribution of carbon dioxide, water vapor, and the diverse dust particles before we can reach meaningful conclusions. We are equally ignorant regarding water pollution. In the last hundred years much has been learned about detection and control of bacterial pathogens and gross organic matter. Today's water supplies, however, particularly in urban-industrial areas, contain a host of chemical substances, still largely unidentified, which may pose serious health hazards (Figure 19–4).

Nor do we fully understand the effects of using nitrogen fertilizer instead of organic manure. It appears to disturb the natural nitrogen cycle, especially by wiping out varieties of nitrogen-fixing bacteria, but the exact nature of the process and its consequences are not yet grasped.

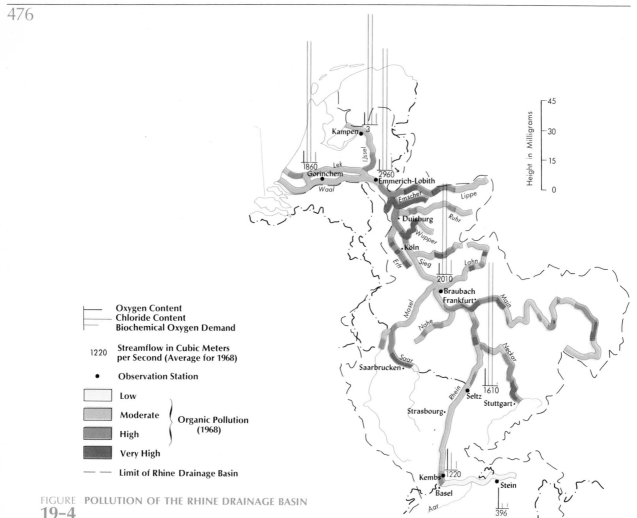

Height in Milligrams

Oxygen Content
Chloride Content
Biochemical Oxygen Demand

1220    Streamflow in Cubic Meters
        per Second (Average for 1968)

●       Observation Station

Low

Moderate        } Organic Pollution
                  (1968)
High

Very High

— — —   Limit of Rhine Drainage Basin

FIGURE  **POLLUTION OF THE RHINE DRAINAGE BASIN**
**19-4**

The Rhine and its tributaries have become open sewers for the heavily urbanized and industrialized areas within the drainage basin. This cartogram shows local conditions by various measures. The chloride content serves as an index of inorganic pollution which is not reduced by the self-purifying action of the water. The biochemical oxygen demand (BOD) indicates the amount of dissolved oxygen that bacteria need to decompose the wastes; the more contaminated the water, the higher the BOD. Since 1968, when these data were gathered, conditions in the basin have generally worsened. This figure is based on a cartogram in *Grote Bosatlas* (F. J. Ormeling, ed.), 47th edition, 1971, 32, with permission of Wolters-Noordhof, Groningen, the Netherlands. Source of the data: International Commission for Protection of the Rhine against Pollution.

Even if the harmful effects of a substance are known, suggested remedial action may open a new Pandora's box of troubles. A case in point is the proposal to replace chemical pesticides by biological controls, such as exposing insects to lethal infectious diseases. Although in principle this is a sound idea, such methods need careful evaluation lest the bacteria or viruses become runaway killers, agents of death to man, beast, or plant.

### THE ROLE OF ACADEMIA

Until quite recently the academic world, its tasks traditionally divided among departments, could not cope with the complexity of environmental problems. Each discipline dealing with biophysical phenomena handled its subject as though human action were to be ignored as a freakish interference in the natural processes. In turn, almost all social sciences focused on people as social beings and paid little attention to their relations with their habitat. Insofar as any discipline considered man's impact on nature, it did so within the confines of its own field.

Only two sciences were, in principle, better prepared for an integrated, comprehensive approach: ecology and geography (Chapters 1 and 2; also Detwyler, 1971, 3). Most ecologists, nevertheless, preferred to study pristine woodlands, pools, or coral reefs rather than ecosystems incisively modified by man. And most geographers, after rejecting the environmentalist view some fifty years ago, turned toward the human side of their field, neglecting its biophysical aspects. New training programs now under way should correct this deficiency. If so, geography may yet live up to the estimate of an eminent economist: "Of all the disciplines geography is the one that has caught the vision of the earth and the total system, and it has strong claims to being the queen of the human sciences" (Boulding, 1966, 108).

Actually the study of the manifold relationships between man and environment and their consequences is beyond the capabilities of any one discipline. *Man* always means man as part of a distinct society. This requires recognition of cultural differences in place and time. The term *environment* is now used in so many ways that it has become almost meaningless. First of all, it may refer to the biophysical ecosystem including air, water, landforms, climate, vegetation, soils, fauna and flora—"nature," for short, though nature modified by mankind. Second, the term may include not only "natural," but also constructed "artificial" features, anything from a peasant's hut to a dam or a megalopolis. In any case, these two kinds of environment are difficult to separate. What is a park? A cornfield? Often they are combined under such terms as landscape, milieu, physical or material environment. Third, the word environment is sometimes used to refer to the social group or groups in which an individual lives and works.

Inevitably, the wider the definition the vaguer the concept and the less operational value

it has. The same can be said of *ecology:* Once the name of a subfield of biology, it now suggests a method of approach, a way of seeing phenomena in their interdependence. In practice it means that the study of the mutual relations between human beings and their environment (however defined) must be broken down into specific sets of problems, but that each set, instead of being the domain of one science, requires interdisciplinary treatment. This course of action can strengthen conservation, which all too often has been a sentimental, missionary, or political movement without adequate scientific foundation to support its proposals for resource management.

## POLLUTION AND POPULATION

Inevitably a popular movement like the ecology crusade gathers under its banner a wide variety of views. One of them is that pollution results, or results mainly, from population increase and that consequently "zero population growth" (even better, a declining population) can cure most environmental ills. There are many good reasons to favor a reduction in growth, the sooner the better, and one of them is pollution abatement (Chapters 16 and 18). But this is another thing than saying that the population boom is the chief factor causing the degradation of the human habitat.

In recent decades most underdeveloped countries have gained population much faster than the developed ones, yet only occasional evidence shows that they have serious pollution problems. To the contrary, all available data indicate that the industrialized countries have experienced the greatest increase in pollution and at a rate much faster than their growth in population. The prospect for the near future underscores this trend. While the population in the United States is expected to grow about 12 percent between 1970 and 1980, the consumption of electricity will double and the use of water step up 50 percent. The reason is the increasing wealth, and thus consumption per capita. The chief of the Population Division, Bureau of the United States Census, concludes in a forecast of population and income (too lengthy to quote here) "that about two-thirds of the rise in expenditures for goods and services—and the concomitant increase in pollution, transportation and other problems accompanying it—would take place even if our population stopped growing tomorrow but continued to increase its income and to spend its money in the same old way" (Miller, 1971).

In relating population and pollution in industrial countries there is good reason to believe that distribution of people—or rather, maldistribution—contributes more to environmental stress than does population growth per se. Concentration in urban districts—with all the trappings of modern city life—places a massive burden on a specific locale. In 1970 over two-thirds of the United States' 210 million inhabitants lived in metropolitan areas. Considering present inner-city blight, commuter traffic jams, scarcity of nearby recreation space, and pollution of air and water, one wonders whether the quality of life will be affected by the continuing migration to the margins of metropolises.

It is worth noting that the well-known ecologist Barry Commoner takes the position that neither population growth nor increased affluence is responsible for environmental woes. Instead, he claims that the root of the trouble lies in changed consumption and production patterns, such as the substitution of synthetics for previously popular natural materials and the massive rise of power consumption in household appliances. Therefore, Commoner believes, we must change our economic system in order to survive. But he does not spell out how such an overhaul of society could be achieved.

## DEPLETION OF RESOURCES

The voracious appetite of the modern industrial world for raw materials raises the question of how long the earth can fill these demands. The question, not a new one (Chapter 18), is usually answered by polemical arguments. This is to be expected because all predictions depend on assumptions and because the scenarios of the future usually are intended to influence present behavior. Some writers start from the proposition that resources are finite; thus, the larger the consumption the sooner the exhaustion. Opposing this contention are those who see a resource as anything useful and therefore always defined in relation to people's knowledge and skill—their cultural achievement (Chapter 2). Many sub-

stances that are resources in the prevailing technology are indeed exhaustible—practically "finite"—but technical advance may create new resources. Accepting the latter point of view does not imply that we need not husband our present fuels and raw materials, but it allows a more imaginative outlook on the future. It reckons with the possibility that breakthroughs—comparable to those of domestication, steam engine, and nuclear energy—may occur again, even though we now lack the vision to describe their nature.

If one takes the pessimistic stance that depletion of the majority of our resources is only a matter of time, whether in the year 2000 or a few centuries later, one naturally feels uneasy about the rate at which advanced countries, from the United States to Europe and Japan, are using up the earth's raw materials. It is often said that one American consumes 25 to 50 times the amount one Indian or Chinese uses. This may well be true because it says in another way what we know about the contrast between developed and underdeveloped countries. What to do about this is less clear. Slowing down population growth in the industrial countries will have only a minor effect on the use of resources, far less than a drastic decline in consumption would have. But no country will voluntarily lower its level of living, especially not when it contains groups that have not even reached a reasonable and humane level of well-being.

If the developed countries, for the sake of conservation, were to reduce substantially their imports of raw materials, this would profoundly affect underdeveloped countries whose economic life depends on selling these commodities. The more one thinks about preventing depletion of resources the more complex and baffling the issue becomes. The need to conserve, reclaim, and recycle materials is obvious, but we still largely lack the techniques and the economic incentives.

## ECOLOGY AND ECONOMICS

Environmental clean-up will cost much money. Whether government or private industry bears the expense, each person as taxpayer or as consumer will in the end pay his share. But pollution is expensive too. It harms trees and crops, causes illness if not death in man and beast, damages materials, and depreciates property. These losses must be weighed against the bill for improving the human environment.

As long as air and water were considered free and inexhaustible, the industrialist could get rid of refuse without paying a penny. Society unwittingly bore these hidden costs. Now it insists that industry, including public utilities, must absorb the cost of waste disposal. As federal and state governments tighten and enforce standards, the financial outlay for antipollution gear will be substantial. Estimates for the near future indicate that the total annual expense for cleaning up the United States will add up to about 1 or 2 percent of the expected annual gross national product. In the long run, the benefits should far outweigh the cost.

Among the heaviest polluters are the petrochemical, pulp and paper, steel, and automotive industries, thermoelectric plants, and cities without adequate facilities to treat sewage and garbage. While most industries can assume the cost of reducing pollution, certain factories have found the additional expense too high to stay in business, and more will follow. Many of these plants are marginal, old, inefficient, or located poorly, about ready to cease operation anyway. Small towns that depend heavily on the payroll of one such plant are hurt badly by the shutdown. It appears unlikely, however, that the new antipollution laws will substantially alter the overall pattern of industrial location.

## THE WAY AHEAD

Mankind, in the very process of becoming human, withdrew from nature. Throughout the ages Homo sapiens increasingly learned to use the earth for material progress. In transforming the natural environment, much was destroyed but, in another sense, more gained. Now we must ask, have the losses outweighed the benefits? If so, is the trend reversible?

We should not underestimate human ability to learn from experience, or nature's capacity to recover from abuse. Depletion of natural resources and accumulation of wastes are the main facets of environmental deterioration. Ideally

there should be no waste. Pollutants can be useful substances in another context, as farmers have known ever since they learned to value ash for the swidden and manure for the field. We must learn to live, as it were, in a spaceship economy, marked by frugality, recycling, and above all, forethought.

The present mood of concern must develop into a deep understanding of the unity of the environment, an awareness that an assault on one part of our surroundings has repercussions elsewhere. Since it is impossible to take nature back to its virgin state, the only answer lies in striving for a new equilibrium. Applications of science and technology which have caused so much despoliation must now be bent toward cleaning up the habitat. Society must domesticate the machine and eradicate technological weeds. Mind and money should be devoted to raising the quality of the environment, with the same singleness of purpose as they were applied to space exploration in the 1960s.

Underdeveloped countries too will be confronted with modern forms of environmental abuse. It is far from certain that they will take warning from the distressing example of the industrial nations. The initial phase of industrialization puts a great financial strain on an underdeveloped country. The extra investment to control pollution and to conserve resources may seem a luxury it can ill afford. Japan's headlong rush to the top group of the world's industrial states and the consequent appalling environmental degradation shows what can befall a country when efforts toward economic growth are not balanced by measures to ensure the amenities of life. Will others like China and India, Nigeria and Brazil make the same mistake?

The rapidity with which urbanization is spreading over the world presents the greatest challenge to improving the environment. According to estimates of United Nations experts, in the year 2000 over 4 billion people (60 percent of the world population) will live in metropolitan areas, as compared with the 1.2 billion (40 percent) in 1960. Crowding together more and more people creates almost intolerable pressures on each city region.

It does not necessarily follow that the

countryside will be serene. The United States is the prime example of what happens when affluence and mobility combine to give easy access to the "great outdoors," the more remote and scenic the better. American recreational. space is being sold, subdivided, and "developed" at an alarming rate. From Lake Tahoe on the California-Nevada border to the Big Cypress Swamp in Florida, campers, second homes, resorts, and amusement parks degrade and mutilate natural treasures. The remaining open spaces are overrun by aircraft, speedboats, snowmobiles, and all-terrain vehicles that shatter the restorative quietude of mountain, lake, desert, and forest.

In the agitation to stop pollution, protection of the land itself has been almost forgotten. Yet, the United States urgently needs a comprehensive land-use policy to ensure an orderly and public-oriented management of the nation's domain. Several European countries already have put into effect plans to restrict areas to specific purposes such as agriculture, city building, industrial development, and recreation. One must hope that Congress will pass a land-use law before it is too late. The states should make similar plans—geared to the national guidelines—and coordinate existing or new regional programs within their borders.

Worldwide cooperation must supplement national efforts to make certain that good stewardship of the earth will not fail. A number of international organizations already occupy themselves with various specific problems, but from the modern ecological point of view—and from the plain old geographic one—the various activities lack integration. The agencies of the United Nations are only beginning steps that will rise above the piecemeal approach. Someday—and it already is too late to save much that is irreplaceable—an international agency may set uniform standards to control pollution of the seas, the stratosphere, and outer space. Equally important, it must establish rules to preserve treasures of wildlife and scenic beauty which, after all, are a heritage to be held in trust for all mankind.

## CITATIONS AND FURTHER READINGS

Anderson, E. "Man as a Maker of New Plants and New Plant Communities," in Thomas, W. L., Jr. (ed.), *Man's Role in Changing the Face of the Earth,* Chicago, 1956, 763–777.

Bach, W. *Atmospheric Pollution,* New York, 1972.

Borchert, J. R. "The Dust Bowl in the 1970s," *Annals of the Association of American Geographers,* 61 (1971): 1–22.

Boulding, K. E. *The Impact of the Social Sciences,* New Brunswick, N.J., 1966.

Bryson, R. A., and Kutzbach, J. E. *Air Pollution,* Association of American Geographers, Commission on College Geography, Resource Paper no. 2, Washington, D.C., 1968.

Burton, I. "The Quality of the Environment: A Review," *Geographical Review,* 58 (1968): 472–481.

California Tomorrow. *The California Tomorrow Plan,* San Francisco, 1971.

Carson, R. *The Silent Spring,* New York, 1962.

Commoner, B. *Science and Survival,* New York, 1966.

Curtis, J. T. "The Modification of Mid-Latitude Grasslands and Forests by Man," in Thomas, W. L., Jr. (ed.), *Man's Role in Changing the Face of the Earth,* Chicago, 1956, 721–736.

Dansereau, P. (ed.), *Challenge for Survival: Land, Air, and Water for Man in Megalopolis,* New York, 1970.

Darling, F. F., and Milton, J. P. (eds.). *Future Environments of North America,* New York, 1966.

Denevan, W. M. "Livestock Numbers in Nineteenth Century New Mexico, and the Problem of Gullying in the Southwest," *Annals of the Association of American Geographers,* 57 (1967): 691–703.

Detwyler, T. R. (ed.). *Man's Impact on the Environment,* New York, 1971.

Ehrenfeld, D. W. *Biological Conservation,* New York, 1970.

Fosberg, F. R. (ed.). *Man's Place in the Island Ecosystem,* Honolulu, 1963.

Glacken, C. J. *Traces on the Rhodian Shore: Nature and Culture in Western Thought from Ancient Times to the End of the Eighteenth Century,* Berkeley, Calif., 1967.

Golomb, B., and Eder, H. M. "Landforms Made by Man," *Landscape,* 14, no. 1 (Fall 1964): 4–7.

Hart, J. F. "Urban Encroachment on Rural Areas," *Geographical Review,* 66 (1976): 1–17.

Jacobsen, T., and Adams, R. M. "Salt and Silt in Ancient Mesopotamian Agriculture," *Science,* 128 (1958): 1250-1258. Reprinted in Detwyler, op. cit., 383-394.

Lowenthal, D. *George Perkins Marsh, Versatile Vermonter,* New York, 1958.

————"Not Every Prospect Pleases," *Landscape,* 12, no. 2 (Winter 1962-1963): 19-23.

*Man's Impact on the Global Environment: Assessment and Recommendations for Action,* Report of the Study of Critical Environmental Problems, Massachusetts Institute of Technology, Cambridge, Mass., 1970.

Martin, P. S. "Prehistoric Overkill," in Martin, P. S., and Wright, H. E., Jr. (eds.), *Pleistocene Extinctions: The Search for a Cause,* New Haven, Conn., 1967, 75-120. Reprinted in abridged form in Detwyler, op. cit., 612-624.

Meadows, R. W., Meadows, D. L., Randers, J., and Behrens, W. W., III. *The Limits to Growth,* New York, 1972.

Mikesell, M. W. "The Deforestation of Mount Lebanon," *Geographical Review,* 59 (1969): 1-28.

Miller, H. P. "Population, Pollution and Affluence," *Population Reference Bureau,* Selection no. 36, March 1971: 1-8.

Murphey, R. "Man and Nature in China," *Modern Asian Studies,* 1 (1967): 313-333.

Nash, R. *Wilderness and the American Mind,* New Haven, Conn., 1967.

Nelson, J. G., and Byrne, A. R. "Man as an Instrument of Landscape Change: Fires, Floods, and National Parks in the Bow Valley, Alberta," *Geographical Review,* 56 (1966): 226-238.

Nicholson, M. *The Environmental Revolution: A Guide for the New Masters of the World,* New York, 1970.

Pinkett, H. T. *Gifford Pinchot: Public and Private Forester,* Urbana, Ill., 1970.

*Resources and Man: A Study and Recommendations,* by the Committee on Resources and Man of the Division of Earth Sciences, National Academy of Sciences–National Research Council, San Francisco, 1969.

Salter, C. L. "The Litany of Tachai and the Foolish Old Man: Agricultural Landscape Modification in Mainland China," *Professional Geographer,* 24 (1972): 113-117.

Sauer, C. O. "The Agency of Man on the Earth," in Thomas, W. L. (ed.), *Man's Role in Changing the Face of the Earth,* Chicago, 1956, 49-69.

————"A Geographical Sketch of Early Man in America," *Geographical Review,* 34 (1944): 529-573. Reprinted in Leighly (ed.) [Sauer], *Land and Life,* Berkeley, Calif., 1963, 197-245.

————"Grassland Climax, Fire, and Man," *Journal of Range Management,* 3 (1950): 16-22.

Semple, E. C. *Influences of the Geographic Environment,* New York, 1911.

Shepard, P. *Man in the Landscape: A Historical View of the Esthetics of Nature,* New York, 1967.

Simpson, L. B. *Many Mexicos,* 4th ed., Berkeley, Calif., 1967.

Spring, D., and Spring, E. (eds.). *Ecology and Religion in History,* New York, 1974.

Stewart, O. C. "Fire as the First Great Force Employed by Man," in Thomas, W. L., Jr. (ed.), *Man's Role in Changing the Face of the Earth,* Chicago, 1956, 115-129.

Stone, C. D. *Should Trees Have Standing?: Toward Legal Rights for Natural Objects,* New York, 1975.

Thompson, K. "The Australian Fever Tree in California: Eucalypts and Malarial Prophylaxis," *Annals of the Association of American Geographers,* 60 (1970): 230-244.

Tuan, Y. F. "Man and Nature," *Landscape,* 15, no. 3 (Spring 1966): 30-36.

————"Discrepancies between Environmental Attitude and Behaviour: Examples from Europe and China," *Canadian Geographer,* 12 (1968): 176-191.

————*Man and Nature,* Association of American Geographers, Commission on College Geography, Resource Paper no. 10, Washington, D.C., 1971.

# EPILOGUE

## THE DIFFERENTIATION OF MANKIND

While Americans and Russians send spacecraft to the moon and Mars, primitive groups in New Guinea and Australia are just emerging from the Stone Age. What causes this wide range in development? Why do peoples behave in so many ways? Such questions can be answered from several viewpoints. First and oldest is the theological one: Divine Will has ordained the fate of earth and humanity according to its own rules. Second is the biological concept of evolution, introduced in the nineteenth century: Organisms, including man, diverge through natural selection in their environment. This book reflects a third view, which has come to the fore in the present century. It shifts the emphasis from environmental influences to cultural relationships. It does not discard physical environment and evolution. To the contrary, both receive deeper meaning by taking into account their relation to culture. The evolutionary process of Homo sapiens operates through cumulative transmission of collective experience rather than through anatomical change alone. "Mankind does not live in a state of nature, but in history."

The physical environment is not the dominant independent variable to which the human being—the selfsame creature everywhere—had to adjust. The view of this book, in contrast, is that each society projects its own common set of meanings and goals onto its habitat. To quote the geographer G. H. T. Kimble: "The most potent geographical factors in the world are not climate, soils, . . . or any other objective 'environmental' circumstance, but rather the shape these circumstances assume in the mind's eye, and the willingness of the mind to do something about them."

## CIVILIZATIONS

Sir Julian Huxley once characterized civilizations as "successful idea-systems," forming the steps in the stairway of cultural evolution. Each new civilization builds on the heritage of others, but derives its singular character from a mental breakthrough—a breakthrough somewhat like a mutation in an organism, creating a different variety. The new attitudes transform the societal structure, and realign the ties between the people and their land. Exactly what causes a civilization eludes us. Certainly no great one ever grew in quiet backwaters. Rather, they emerged at the turbulent confluence of many currents, some of native, many of foreign origin.

But civilizations fade away and others succeed them, usually rising in other locations. In western Eurasia, the crest of civilization moved from Middle

East to Mediterranean, and then to northwestern Europe. South and East Asia, as well as pre-Columbian America, experienced similar relocations. There is no reason to think that progress has found its final home in the North Atlantic community.

Although the dynamic culture hearths have shifted, they have so far been confined to relatively small segments of the earth surface. None have evolved in polar and subpolar regions, or in the mid-latitudes of the Southern Hemisphere, mainly, it would seem, because of environmental handicaps or peripheral location.

The present four major culture realms are the East Asian, Indic, Islamic, and Occidental. Their historical kinship is evident in the common economic roots: plow agriculture of grains, which has transformed the habitat into a man-made steppe landscape; domesticated herd animals; commerce and urban centers. Their superstructures are more diverse, although here too old links are apparent. Each has its spiritual basis in an ethical and religious ideology that demands supratribal if not worldwide adherence. Each has a written-down legacy of great thoughts and deeds that fosters awareness of its historic raison d'être. And each has its political basis in concepts of statehood and law.

## CULTURAL UNITY OR DIVERSITY?

Some five hundred years ago European civilization was simply one among several, and not a particularly distinguished one at that. Since then it has rapidly forged ahead, assuming since the Industrial Revolution the character of a hyperdynamic force. It is altering humanity as decisively as the introduction of agriculture did, some twelve thousand years ago. Its influence has expanded in three ways. Through emigration and settlement the European has overwhelmed the weak cultures in the temperate lands of North and South America, southern Siberia, Oceania, and the south tip of Africa. Through colonial rule Occidental culture has affected in various degrees most of the remainder of the world. And third, even those countries not politically controlled by Europeans or their descendants, have borrowed many Western traits, especially technical and economic ones.

The passing of the colonial era, while signifying political withdrawal, has not stopped the spread of Occidental culture. Quite to the contrary, the newly independent peoples need to develop their technology, economic organization, and social structure if they want to move forward, and in many cases this will involve more, not less, Westernization. However, each country must fit the alien ideas, institutions, and gadgets into its own culture pattern. In doing this, the independent country has more freedom in choosing what to accept and what to reject than was possible under a colonial administration. Moreover, it is not even desirable that Western culture, like a bulldozer, flatten out all that came before it. The philosopher Alfred N. Whitehead puts it this way: "Diversification among human communities is essential for the provision of the incentive, and material for the Odyssey of the human spirit. Other nations of different habits are not enemies: they are godsends. Men require of their neighbors something sufficiently akin to be understood, something sufficiently different to provoke attention, and something great enough to command admiration."

Different cultures, even the most humble ones, may harbor idea strains that could prove highly valuable in breeding new institutions to cope with as yet unforeseen situations. Burmese statesman U Thant's plea "to make the world safe for diversity" has meaning for the present as well as the future.

## FORCES OF OUR TIMES

The great forces that currently affect mankind are nationalism, progress, population growth, and urbanization.

*Nationalism* is the all-pervading political propellant of our era. It takes on many forms as it interacts with other ideologies—religion, capitalism, democracy, socialism, communism, racism, and so on—but, under whatever guise, it determines the present organization of earth space. Its positive value lies in transcending parochial interests and quarrels by uniting local communities into a greater whole and by inspiring them to common efforts for the general good.

But nationalism also has a negative side. At its worst it leads to wars on a much wider scale than tribal strife and impedes the international cooperation that the shrunken and interdependent world needs today. The trend seems to lead toward larger, multinational regional frameworks—and eventually, perhaps, to world federation. Whatever the future, the sovereign nation-state is as yet the accepted mold of political organization. Europe set the example; we now witness other culture realms in their slow and often painful process of nation building.

*Progress* through science, technology, and new forms of economic organization is the hallmark of modern Western civilization. Like the Occidental concept of the nation-state, the idea of material advance is now spreading throughout the world. But economic development requires more than importing machinery. Whatever its form, it demands changes in social organization and, above all, changes in attitude. Moreover, the ultimate goal must be to serve the social aims of each society.

These intertwined means and ends defy efforts to formulate a universally valid model for progress. Some countries will advance rapidly, others slowly, some through peaceful evolution, others by ruthless revolution. In the meantime, the Occident will race ahead with exploration of outer space, use of nuclear energy, industrial automation, and other applications of the computer's mechanical brain. One can but dimly perceive the opportunities—and dangers!—that mankind may encounter in these new ventures. Thus, while the West enters a phase which not long ago seemed mere science fiction, many societies just now are escaping the confines of a Babylonian technology.

Economic development, then, is a relative matter. Measured against the front-runners of the West, many underdeveloped countries climb uphill at an unbearably slow pace. But measured on their own ground, against their starting line only a generation or two ago, they have covered a remarkable distance.

It cannot be taken for granted, however, that progress is inevitable and automatic. History offers numerous cases of societies that disintegrated when confronted by an aggressive alien culture. Other peoples have tried, at least for a time, to ward off "the contagion of ideas" by building either visible or invisible walls. We cannot be sure that all countries will follow Western models, or that accepted ideas of progress will remain unchanged. Reluctance to give up cherished ways of life, or incompetence to guide the transformation, may effectively block economic development. The economist Kenneth E. Boulding once said of India that development there is difficult because its people have become so well adjusted to poverty.

Impatience with peoples who seem reluctant to abandon traditional values and habits should be tempered by the thought that the "brave new world" of the Occident shows a wide—and widening?—gap between the blind march of technology and the quality of life.

*Rapid population growth* in underdeveloped countries is now generally recognized as a major obstacle to their progress. While Western medical technology has curbed their death rates, traditional attitudes toward reproduction still prevail. Their governments must use a substantial part of the national savings to provide for the massive increase in population instead of investing in enterprises that will raise the levels of living. But again, one must guard against overgeneralization. Some countries, especially in Latin America and Africa, have large resource potentials which, if wisely used, should ease the pressure. Others, mostly in Asia, may double their already crowded and hungry populations in about thirty years. The last part of this century will be the critical period, either of successful transition to controlled well-being, or of decline to such depth of destitution that any upward move of the economy becomes virtually impossible.

Finally, there is the process of *urbanization*. For the last five thousand years cities have served as the mainsprings of creative thought and action. We can hardly think of a culture lacking urban centers that can qualify to be called a civilization. The difference, however, between traditional and modern societies is that while city life in the former can support only a fraction of the total population, in the latter it is the mode of life for the majority.

Evidently, the city will become the physical environment for most of humanity. People have always transformed their habitat, but never before have they been confronted with the stupendous task of creating a vast artificial milieu for multitudes. The nagging problem of population growth is magnified by the urban squeeze. Housing, transportation, recreation, education, water supply, sewage disposal, and other public facilities demand careful planning and tremendous investments. But this entire mechanical framework is only the means to serve cultural ends. An objective look at our own cities makes us realize the inadequacy of the material base and the confusion about the spiritual goals. If this is true for a wealthy nation with room to spare, it holds even more for poor and crowded countries without a long urban tradition. Jean Gottmann, contemplating the American Megalopolis, wrote that it "gives one the feeling of looking at the dawn of a new stage in human evolution." No wonder we have as yet only a blurred vision of the scope and quality of tomorrow's city.

These great forces of our era all have Occidental roots. Interrelated among themselves, they also interact in many ways with indigenous cultures existing in different environments, thereby creating variations on the general theme of change.

We geographers cannot lay aside our work and write "finis." Continuous change in societies and their habitats permits only tentative, interim conclusions. Old facts, too, show unexpected facets when reexamined with sharper analytical tools or viewed from a new angle. Beyond the horizon of present knowledge there is always the challenge of the unknown, spurring us on to further exploration.

But the pleasures and rewards of being curious about peoples and places are not reserved for the professional circle. Those who have learned how to observe the earth as the world of mankind, and how to perceive order in its diversity, have made a compact with geography that will prove stimulating and fruitful throughout their lives.

# INDEX

Page references in *italic* indicate maps or illustrations.

Aalen, F. H. A., 330
Abrimosov, P., 385
Acculturation, 29–30
Ackerman, E. A., 288, 304
Adams, J. S., 355
Adams, R. B., 15, 355
Adams, R. M., 256, 355, 467, 482
Afghanistan, 235, 296, *404*
Africa, 165–177
  cities of, 343–*344*, 438
  culture of, 195–198
  farmers of, 397
  housetypes of, *324*
  Islam in, 191
  labor migrations in, 437–438
  metropolises of, 362
  plantations in, 239–241
  population of, 395, 397
Age structure, 299, 406–407
Agglomeration, 262
Agricultural density, 450
Agriculture:
  in Bangladesh, 228–230
  beginnings of, 48–51
  in China, 227–228
  diffusion of, 54, 55
  in India, 228–230
  labor force in, *292*
  Mediterranean, 249
  modern, 66–67, 241–256
  origins of, 214
  plantation, 237–241
  and population, 227
  and settlements, 304–332
  in Southeast Asia, 230–232
  in Soviet Union, *252*
  and tenure, 242–244
  traditional, 225–237
  in tribal societies, 214–224
Aiken, C. S., 259
Ainu, *79*
Alaska, Eskimo of, 211–212
Alexander, J. W., 258
Allen, G. C., 285
Alonso, W., 268, 285
Alpines, 80–82
American Indians, 31, 66, 208–*209*, 211
Americas, the:
  civilization in, 54–56, *184*
  culture realms of, *184*
  early cities of, 341–342
  population of, 394–396
  (*See also* Canada; Latin America; United States)
Ames, O., 67
Ancient populations, 391–392
Anderson, E., 67, 466, 481

Andes, Central, 56–57
Angerdorf, *315*, 316
Anglo-America, 187–188, 316–325
  (*See also* Canada; United States)
Animals:
  domestication of, *48*–50
  extermination of, 214
  herding of, 235–237
Animism, 122
Anthropology, 8
Apartheid, 91–92
Aperchenko, V. S., 118
Arabic language, 108
Arable land, *459*
Arabs:
  cities of, 341
  culture of, 190–191
  Islam and the, 136–141
Aristotle, 30
Armen, G., 355
Armenians, 133
Ashton, T. S., 68
Asia, 109, 156–177, 191–195
  cities of, 362
  colonial cities of, 343–344
  industrial regions of, 279–280
  plantations in, 239–241
  population of, 395–397
  urban populations of, 438
  (*See also* Central Asia; East Asia; South Asia;
    Southeast Asia)
Asian highway, *296, 302*
Aswan Dam, 232, *233*
Athens, 333
Attitudes to environment, 470–472
Augelli, J. P., 198
Aurousseau, M., 355
Australia, 188, 254, 468
  cities of, 362
Australoids, 78, *79, 80*
Automobiles, 62, 63
Automotive industry, *263*
Awad, M., 256

Bach, W., 481
Bacon, E., 198
Baker, O. E., 14, 258
Bangladesh, 117, 166–168
  agriculture in, 228–230
  population of, 411–412
Bantu peoples, 90–92
Bantustan, 91
Baptists in U.S., *135*
Barbour, K. M., 422
Barlow, A. M., 368, 383, 385

Barrau, J., 224
Bartlett, H. H., 224
Bates, M., 43, 475
Beardsley, R. K., 256
Beaujeu-Garnier, J., 44
Bedford, R. D., 445
Behavioral environment, 34
Belen'kaya, V. D., 118
Belgium, 111–112, 276–278
Benneh, G., 224
Beri-beri, 454
Berman, M., 285
Berry, B. J. L., 353, 355
Bhardwaj, S. M., 143, 147
Bibliographies, geographical, 24
Bilingualism, 97, 110–113
Biogeography, 32
Biophysical environment, 27, *38–40*, 463–482
Birdsell, J. B., 92
Birth control, 402–408
Birth rates, 397–400, 402–408
Blacks in U.S., 86–90, 376–379
Blaut, J. M., 287, 304
Bloch, B., 119
Blood types, *75–76*
Bloomfield, L., 118
Blum, A., 59
Blum, H. F., 92
Blumenbach, J. F., 77, 92
Bobek, H., 44, 198, 204, 223
Bodin, Jean, 30
Boeke, J. H., 173, 177
Bogota, 370
Bohning, W. R., 445
Bombay, 389
Borah, W., 422
Borchert, J. R., 15, 348, 355, 385, 481
Borneo, *174*, 177
Boserup, E., 304
Boulding, K. E., 304, 477, 481, 485
Bourne, L. S., 355
Bowen, E. G., 118
Boxer, C. R., 68
Boyd, W. C., 82
Braidwood, R. J., 50, 54, 55, 67, 355
Brand, D. D., 414, 422
Brazil, 83
Breese, G., 386
Briggs, A., 355
Brigham, A. P., 42
Britain (see United Kingdom)
Brodsky, H., 355
Broek, J. O. M., 23, 177, 182, 194, 195, 198, 256,
  257, 331, 365
Bromley, R. J., 257
Brooke, C., 461

Brookfield, H. C., 304
Brown, R. H., 44, 317, 330
Bruk, S. I., 118, 422
Brunhes, J., 41
Brunn, S. D., 118
Brush, J. E., 355
Brutzkus, E., 304
Bryan, P. W., 42
Bryson, R. A., 481
Buchanan, K., 7, 327, 461
Buchanan, M., 471
Buchanan, R. O., 285
Buck, J. L., 257
Buckle, H., 31
Buddhism, 142–145
Buffon, G. de, 31
Built environment, 306–386, 464
Bureaucrats, 300–302
Burgdorfer, F., 44
Burgess, E. W., 349, 379, 387
Burghardt, A. F., 177, 356
Burton, I., 34, 481
Bushmen, 78, 79
Buttimer, A., 23, 41
Butzer, K. W., 68
Byrne, A. R., 482

Cactus, 468
Cahnman, W. J., 198
Calef, W., 258
California, 250–251, 365
Caloric intake, 453
Camel, 235–236
Cameron, R., 68
Cameroon, 222
Canada:
    bilingualism in, 111–113
    cities of, 364
    culture of, 188–189
    Eskimo of, 212–213
    Franco-Canadians, 163–165
    income in, 298
    languages of, 110
    manufacturing in, 271–275
    population distribution of, 35
    rural settlements of, 316–317
    steel industry of, 270
    (See also North America)
Canals, 61
Candolle, A. de, 67
Cape Coloreds, 90–92
Carr-Saunders, A. M., 393, 395, 422
Carson, R., 475, 481
Carter, G. F., 68
Carter, H., 118
Cartography, 9, 11
Cash crops, 218–222, 232
Caste, 141–142, 229, 311
Catholic Church, 132–133
Catlin, G., 472
Catudal, H. M., 177
Caucasoids, 78–83
Celtic Church, 133
Celtic languages, 108, 110
Central Asia, 341
Central Europe, 188–190
    industries in, 275–278
    migrations in, 430–433
Central places, 344, 349, 352–355
Centrality, 336–337, 353
Centuriation, 315, 323
Cereal importers, 459
Ceylon (see Sri Lanka)

Chad, 221
Chakravarti, A. K., 461
Chambers, J. D., 68
Chang, J.-H., 224
Chang, S., 355
Ch'angan, 342–343
Chapman, K., 285
Chappell, J. E., Jr., 42
Chardon, R. E., 258
Chicago, 353–354
Childe, V. G., 68
Chile, 5
China:
    agriculture in, 227–228
    cities of, 338–341
    civilization in, 53
    culture of, 192–193
    early migrations in, 80–81
    industrial regions of, 280
    migrations in, 439–441
    population of, 396, 414–416
    religion in, 146
    rural settlement in, 325–327
    and Southeast Asia, 194
    and the West, 58–59
Chinese in Malaysia, 174–177
Chinitz, B., 385, 386
Chisholm, M., 258
Cholera, 454
Chorley, R. J., 23
Christaller, W., 353, 355
Christianity, 124–125, 128–129
    in India, 168
Chung, R., 422
Cipolla, C., 422
Cities, 333–387
    in Africa, 307
    in Americas, 56–57
    blacks in U.S., 88–89
    emerging patterns of, 359–387
    government of, 384–386
    in Middle East, 51–52
    milksheds of, 248
    populations of, 360–361
    of third world, 438–439
City centers, 347–348
City planning, 369–373
Civilization, 179–198, 484–485
    of Andean region, 55–57
    beginnings of, 50–55
    in China, 53
    of Meso-America, 54–56
Clark, A. H., 147
Clark, C., 393–395, 422
Clarke, C. G., 177
Clarke, G., 68
Clarke, J. I., 257, 422
Classification:
    of cultures, 179–180
    of races, 76–83
Climates, 40
Clout, H. D., 330
Coalfields, 281–284
Coffee, 239
Cohen M, 100–101, 105
Collecting societies, 208–214
Collective farms, 243
Collins, D., 92
Colombia, 370
Colonial cities, 343–344
Colonialism, 165–177, 295–298
Colonization, 60, 83
COMECON, 163
Comitas, L., 446

Common Market, 161–162
Commoner, B., 478, 481
Communal tenure, 242–243
Communes, 228, 326, 327
Communication, 95, 96, 301
Communism, 147, 301–302
Commuting, 372–373, 427
Concentric urban theory, 349
Confucianism, 146
Confucius, 83
Conklin, H. C., 215, 224, 305
Connecticut, 274
Connell, J., 305
Conservation, 472–475
Constantinople, 341
Consumption, 478
    of energy, 293
Cook, S. F., 422
Coon, C. S., 92
Cooperatives, 249
Copper industry, 266, 282
Coppock, J. T., 258, 368
Coptics, 130–131
Corn Belt, 245
Cotton farming, 253
Coull, J. R., 462
Cox, K. R., 386
Crop farming, 245, 249–254
Crop and livestock farming, 311–316
Crosby, A. W., 68
Cultivation, 214–219
Cultural geography, 8, 32–33
Cultural landscape, 34–35
Cultural realms, 179–198
Culture:
    and geography, 32–33
    and nature, 27–46
    and race, 83, 104–108
    and religion, 121–122
    and resources, 33
    and society, 27–30
Cumberland, K. B., 214, 227
Cummings, F. H., 445
Curtis, F. S., 223
Curtis, J. T., 467
Cutler, H., 67
Cuzco, Peru, 57
Cyprus, 71, 83, 111

Dacey, M. F., 355
Dairy farming, 245–256
Dakar, 307
Dale, E. H., 177
Daniel, A. G., 68
Dansereau, P., 481
Darby, H. C., 44, 330
Darkoh, M. B. K., 285, 305
Darling, F. F., 481
Davies, H. R. J., 257
Davies, M., 283
Davies, W. K. D., 355
Davis, C. A., 93
DDT, 475
Dead language, 95
Dean, V. M., 305
Death rates, 397–402, 404–408
De Carvalho, C. M. D., 118
De Geer, S., 285
De Laubenfals, D. J., 93
Demangeon, A., 330
Demko, G. J., 422
Demographic transformation, 398
Denevan, W. M., 224, 481

Deniker, A., 78
Density of population, 450
Dependents, 299
Deshler, W., 462
De Souza, A. R., 288, 305, 439, 445
Detwyler, T. R., 43, 447, 481
Developed countries, 287–288
Development (see Economic development)
De Young, J. E., 330
Dialects, 95
   of eastern U.S., 106–108
Dickens, Charles, 470
Dickinson, R. E., 41, 330, 349–350, 356, 371, 386
Dickson, K. B., 305
Diet, 227
Diffusion, 28–29, 47–69
   of alphabet, 52
   between Americas and Old World, 58
   between China and the West, 58–59
   of cities, 336–343
   of hybrid corn, 29
   of industrialization, 261
   of papermaking, 58–59
   of plants and animals, 214
   of progress, 297
   of religions, 121–148
   of steam engines, 64–66
Dikshit, R. D., 177
Dimbleby, G. W., 68
Diringer, D., 52
Discovery, Age of, 60
Disease, 453–456
Distance, 20, 21, 268
Distribution, 17–19
   of human races, 78–83
   of languages, 96–101
   of rural settlement, 309–310
   of U.S. blacks, 88
Division of labor, 210
Dobyns, H. F., 422
Dobzhansky, T., 93
Dodgshon, R. A., 330
Doeppers, D., 147
Dog, 210–211
Domestication, 48–50, 466
Dominant genes, 73–77
Dominedo, F. M., 445
Donaldson, O. F., 93
Drake, M., 422
Drewe, P., 445
Dry farming, 5
Duncan, O. D., 462
Dunn, L. C., 85, 93
Durand, L., Jr., 258
Dussart, F., 330
Dwyer, D. J., 386

East, W. G., 177
East Asia:
   culture of, 192–193
   farming in, 227–228
   population of, 414–418
   rural settlement in, 325–328
Eastern Christianity, 129–133
Ecology, 16, 32, 474–475
Economic development, 37, 287–305, 486
   of Meso-Africa, 197–198
   plantations and, 240–241
   in plural societies, 173–177
Economic geography, 8
Economies, forms of, 203–208
   and development, 288
   tribal, 208–224

Ecuador, 66, 210
Ecumene, 40
Eder, H. M., 481
Edinburgh, 345
Education, 99
Egypt, 232–235
   early cities in, 338
Ehrenfeld, D. W., 481
Eisner, S., 355
Electric power, 266
Endemic disease, 455
Energy, 290, 293
England:
   open fields of, 313
   (See also United Kingdom)
Entrepreneurs, 300–302
Environment, 27, 38–40
   and economic development, 295, 304
   and economy, 203–208, 288
   and modern society, 463–464, 470–481
   perception of, 33–34
   and population distribution, 36–41
   and race, 78–82
Environmentalism, 30–31
Epidemic, 455
Epstein, H., 67
Esch, 312
Eskimos, 211–212
Estall, R. C., 285
Ethnic religions, 123–124
Europe, 60
   cities of, 340–341, 350, 365–368
   culture of, 184–191
   demographic transition in, 398
   farming in, 245–256
   forced migrations in, 430–433
   industrial regions of, 275–278, 281–284
   integration of, 161–162
   Jews in, 124–128
   labor migrations in, 435–436
   languages of, 102, 103
   metropolises of, 362–363
   migrations from, 428–431
   nations of, 151–165
   population of, 395–396
   religions in, 129–135
   superhighways in, 63
European Economic Community, 161–162
Europeans in Meso-Africa, 197–198
Evans, E. E., 330
Eversley, D. C., 422
Eyre, J., 257
Eyre, S. R., 43

Fabre, M., 93
Fairgrieve, J., 287
Farms, 309–332
Faruqui, I. R. al, 147
Febvre, L., 42
Fellows, D. K., 93
Fenneman, N. M., 14
Fertile Crescent, 50, 51
Fertility, 398–400, 402–408
Feudal system, 313–316
Field systems, 309–328
Fielding, G. J., 25
Fire, 47–48, 214
Fisher, C. A., 177, 198
Fisher, J. S., 258
Fishing, 458, 460
Fishing societies, 208–214
Fleming, D. K., 285
Flemish, 158–161

Fleure, H. S., 147
Flieger, W., 422
Food supply, 456–460
Forced migrations, 430–433
Forde, D. C., 43
Foreign aid, 298, 303
Forests, 473
Formal regions, 13
Forman, R. E., 386
Fosberg, F. R., 481
Foster, G. M., 43
Foust, J. B., 285
Francaviglia, R. V., 330
France, 113–115
   cities of, 351
Franco-Canadians, 110
Freehold, 243
Freeman, J. D., 224
Freeman, T. W., 41, 445
Frejka, T., 421, 422
French:
   in Canada, 163–165
   in Quebec, 316–317
French language, 113–115
   in Canada, 110
Fry, V. K., 223
Fryer, D. W., 242, 258
Fuchs, V. R., 285
Functional Region, 13, 15
Furnivall, J. S., 173, 177

Gad, G., 386
Gallion, A. B., 355
Garn, S. M., 92
Garner, B. J., 387
Gathering, 48–49
   in tribal societies, 208–214
   unspecialized, 208–211
Gaustad, E. S., 135
Gautama, 142
Gautier, E. F., 257
Geddes, P., 359, 386, 470
Geertz, C., 257
Genes, 73–83
Genetic drift, 74
Genetics, 73–83
Genotypes, 76
Genre de vie, 32
Geography, 7–25
   and culture realms, 181–182
   definition of, 7, 8, 16, 31
   and genetics, 73–83
   and history, 16, 21–23
   of manufacturing, 261–286
   of population, 391–404
   settlement, 306–386
   subdivisions of, 8–10
   urban, 333–387
   value of, 7
Georgia, 322
Germany, 218
   migrations and, 431–433, 436
   rural settlement in, 311–316
Ghana, 324
Ghettos, 375–379
   black, 88–89
Gibson, L. J., 285
Gilpin, W., 14
Ginsburg, N. S., 305
Glacken, C. J., 44, 472, 481
Glass, D. V., 422
Glassie, H., 324, 325, 331
Glazer, N., 381, 386

GNP, 290, 406–407
Goiter, 454
Goldschmidt, W., 43
Golomb, B., 481
Gottman, J., 150, 177, *248*, 355, 364, 386, 487
Goulet, D., 305
Gourou, P., 43, 224, 305
Grain farming, 251
Gravier, J.-F., 386
Great Plains, 13, *14*
Greece, early cities in, 338–339
Greek Orthodox Church, 71, 129–133
Green, C. M., 355
Green revolution, 229–230, *451*
Greenberg, D., 171
Greenland Eskimos, 212
Gregor, H. F., 258
Griffin, P. F., 422
Griffiths, I. L., 118
Griggs, D. B., 462
Gross national product (GNP), 290, 406–407
Grotewold, A., 23, 285
Groves, P. A., 386
Guatemala, 86
Guinea-Bissau, 74
Gutkind, E. A., 355

Hacienda, 237–238
Haeckel, E. H., 16
Hägerstrand, T., 426, 445
Haggett, P., 23, 445
Hahn, E., 67, 207
Haines, F., 223
Hair form, 77
Hale, G. A., 224
Haley, A., 93
Hall, A. R., 59, 69
Hall, E. T., 43
Hall, J. W., 256
Hall, P., 386
Hall, R. A., 118
Hall, R. B., 320, 328
Hamdan, G., 177
Hamm, M. F., 356
Hammond, M., 356
Hannerberg, D., 445
Hansa, 170–173
Hanseatic League, 340
Hardoy, F., 355
Haro, A. S., 386
Harries, K. D., 386
Harris, C., 44, 258, 262, 284, *349*, 352, 356, 388
Harris, D. R., 50, 67, 224
Harris, R. C., 331
Hart, J. F., 87, 93, 258, 331, 481
Hartshorn, T. A., 305, 386
Hartshorne, R., 24, 285
Harvey, D., 24, 386
Haugen, E., 118
Hawkes, J., 68
Head shape, 76
Heilbroner, R. L., 305
Herbert, D. T., 386
Herbertson, A. S., 43
Herding, *226*, 234–237
  in Africa, 219–220
Herodotus, 232
Heterogeneous peoples, 74, 78, *79*
Hettner, A., 184
Heyerdahl, T., 58
Hickey, G. C., 331
Higbee, E. C., 258

Hills, T. L., 317
Himayana, 141–*145*
Hinduism, 141–*143*
Hippocrates, 30
Historical geography, 9, 21–23
  of pollution, 391–404
History, 16
Ho, R., 257
Hodder, B. W., 305
Hoebel, E. A., 30, 43, 93
Hoffman, G. W., 177, 305
Hofmeister, B., 258
Hollingsworth, T. H., 422
Holzner, L., 355
Homogeneous peoples, 74, 78, *79*
Hookworm, 454
Hooson, D. J. M., 44
Hooton, E. A., 93
Horse, 211, 235, 236
Horst, O. H., 462
Horticulture, 250–251
Horvath, R. J., 223, 257, 386
House types, 309–332
  in U.S., 323–325
Howard, E., 386
Howe, G. M., 462
Hoyt, H., *349*
Hsieh, C., 257
Hsu, M.-L., 11, 44
Hsu, S.-Y., 147
Hudson, J. C., 331
Hughes, C. C., 212, 213
Hughes, J. W., 446
Human ecology, 32
Human geography, 8
Humboldt, A. von, 472
Humlum, E., 234
Humphreys, A., 285
Hunger, 452–455
Hunter, J. M., 331
Hunters, 48–49, 208–214
Huntington, E., 42
Hutchins, Thomas, 320
Huxley, J., 484
Hybrid corn, 29
Hydraulic landscape, 22
Hymes, D., 118

Ibadan, *344*
Ibos, 170–173
Ideolect, 95
Illiteracy, 300
Inca civilization, 56, 57
  cities of, 341–342
Income, *289*, *291*
  in Europe, *265*
  in U.S., *264*
Independent assortment, 73
India, *37*, 166–170
  agriculture in, 228–231
  bilingualism in, 111
  cities of, 341, *348*
  culture of, 191–192
  green revolution in, *451*
  industrial regions of, 280
  irrigation in, *231*
  languages of, *109*
  population of, 396, 411–412
  religion in, 141–*143*
  villages in, *229*, *311*
Indo-Europeans, 97–103
Indonesia, 77, 201, 328, 330
  populations in, 239–241

Industrial reconstruction, 264–265
  in South Wales, 283–284
Industrial regions, 271–284
Industrial revolution, 265–266, 282–283, 287–288, 344–346, 470
Industrialization, 64–66, 261–286
  and agriculture, 241–242
Infant mortality rate, 401, *449*
Infectious diseases, 455–456
Instituted regions, 13
Interaction, 19
Internal coherence, 16
Internal migration, 425–427, 438–444
Internally perceived region, 15
International languages, *112*
International migration, 426–438
Invention, 28
Iran, 302
Iraq, *339*
Iron industry, 269–271
Irrigation, 467–468
  in Egypt, 232–235
  in India, *231*
Isaac, E., 67, 147
Isachenko, A. G., 42
Isard, W., 355
Islam, 137–141, 190–191
Ismailites, *138–139*
Isolated state, 20–21
Isolation, 73–74
  and economic development, 296–297
Israel, 124–128
  migrations and, 433–434
Italy, 340, 380
  agriculture in, 249–250
Iwanicka-Lyra, E., 445

Jackson, C. I., *35*
Jackson, J. C., 355
Jackson, R. H., 331
Jackson, W. A. D., 198
Jacobsen, T., 467, 482
Jains, 168
James, P. E., 24
Japan, 193
  cities of, 308
  industrial regions of, 279–280
  population of, 416–418
  rural settlement, 327–328
Java, 201
Jefferson, M., 344, 350
Jefferson, Thomas, 323
Jenks, G. F., 258
Jews, 124–128
Johanneson, C. L., 67
Johnson, B. L. C., 462
Johnson, H. B., 24, 147, 331
Johnson, J. H., 331
Johnston, R. J., 356
Jones, E., 118, 355
Jones, H. R., 445
Jones, P. N., 386
Jordan, W. D., 93
Judaism, 124–128

Kano, Nigeria, 196
Kariel, H. C., 462
Kashmir, 169–170
Kaskaskia, *320*
Kaups, M., 118
Kaye, B., 224
Kenya, *18–19*

490

Keyfitz, N., 422
Khyber Pass, 296
Kibbutz, 243
Kiddle, L. B., 118
Kimble, G. H. T., 483
Kindleberger, C. P., 445
King, F. H., 257
King, R., 305, 462
Kirk, W., 34, 44, 68
Klassen, L. M., 445
Kluckhohn, C., 43
Kniffen, F. B., 323–325, 331
Knight, C. G., 220, 462
Knight, D. B., 177
Kolb, A., 198
Kollmorgen, W. M., 258
Koran, 137, 140
Korea, 193
Kormoss, I. B. F., 44
Kosinski, L. A., 44, 177, 422, 423, 427
Kostrowicki, J., 24
Kovalev, S. A., 331
Kramer, F. L., 67
Kristof, L. K. D., 177
Kroeber, A. L., 43, 180, 190, 198, 223
Kruschchev, A. T., 285
Kulischer, E. M., 446
Kurath, H., 107, 119
Kutzbach, J. E., 481
Kuznets, S., 305
Kuznetsk Basin, 279
Kwashiorkor, 455

Labor, 262–265, 272–273
    and agriculture, 242
    force, 290–291
    migrations, 435–437
Ladejinsky, W., 257
Lamaism, 144–145
Lambton, A. K. S., 257
Land Ordinance, 320, 323
Land reform, 243–244
Land survey, 309–310, 319, 323, 473
Land tenure, 227–228, 238, 242–244
Land use, 206–208
    in modern societies, 241–256
    in plantations, 237–241
    in Soviet Union, 252
    in traditional societies, 225–237
Landscape, 34–35
Langtvet, O., 331
Language, 47, 95–119
    and culture, 104–108
    in Europe, 102, 103
    in India, 167–168
    international, 112
    and landforms, 115–116
    in Nigeria, 170–173
    in Polynesia, 116
    and race, 104
    and society, 108–110
    in Southeast Asia, 194
Lapidus, J. M., 355
Lapps, 213
Latifundium, 238, 243
Latin America, 186, 438
    income in, 289
    plantations in, 237–239
    shifting agriculture in, 214–219
Latourette, K. M., 198
Layton, R. L., 331
Learmonth, A. T. A., 257, 462
Lebanon, 468

Lerner, M., 187, 198
Level of living, 289–291, 450–451
Levison, M., 68, 116
Lewis, D. T., 423
Lewis, E. T., 285
Lewis, G. M., 14
Lewis, O., 223
Lewis, P. F., 356
Lewis, R. A., 386
Lewthwaite, G. R., 42, 258
Liberia, 218
Li Choh-ming, 285
Lingua franca, 112–113
Linguistic family, 95, 97–103
Linguistic geography, 106–108
Literacy, 95, 99, 300
Livestock, 254
    in Africa, 219–220
    in India, 230
Livingstone, E. B., 93
Location, 10, 19–20, 23
    of cities, 333–336
    and economic development, 296
    of industry, 261–271
    isolated, 73–74
Loeb, E. M., 331
Logan, M. I., 285
Lomax, A., 198
London, 344, 368
    new towns near, 381–385
    pollution in, 463
    population in, 359, 374
Long-lot farms, 316–317
Lonsdale, R. E., 285
Loukotka, C., 119
Lowenthal, D., 44, 198, 446, 472, 482
Lowry, M., 85
Lucas, R. C., 34, 42
Lukermann, F., 44, 348, 354
Lutherans, 135
Lüthy, H., 68

Mabogunje, A. L., 305
McCarty, H. H., 285
McColl, R. W., 177
McConnell, J. E., 305
McGee, T. G., 438, 439, 446
McGlashan, N. D., 462
McIntire, E. G., 331
Mackenzie, R. D., 349, 379, 387
Mackinder, H. J., 33, 42
McNeill, W. H., 68, 198
Maconochie, A., 297
Mahayana, 144–145
Malawi, 86
Malaya, 174–177
    plantations, in, 239–240
Malaysia, 173–177, 232
Malnutrition, 452–455
Malthus, T. R., 447–448
Manchuria, 280, 439–441
Manners, J. R., 43
Manufacturing, 261–286
    in developing countries, 298
    labor force in, 292
Maps, 11
Marcus, M. G., 43
Market towns, 349
Markets, 262
Maronites, 130–131
Marriage circles, 85
Marsak, L. M., 68
Marschner, F. J., 319

Marsh, G. P., 34, 43, 472, 473
Marshall, J. U., 356
Martin, P. S., 466, 482
Marx, K. H., 448
Mass transit, 372–373
Massachusetts, 274
Mather, E. C., 258
Matley, I. M., 42, 257
Mauritius, 410
May, J., 454, 462
Maya, 343, 469, 470
Mayfield, R. C., 177
Meadows, D. H., 448, 462
Mechanization, 241, 255–256
Medieval cities, 340–341
Medieval population, 391–394
Mediterranean, 468
    agriculture, 249
    culture, 186
Mediterraneans, 80–82
Megalopolis, 346, 364–365, 369–370
Meillet, A., 100–101, 105
Meinig, D. W., 258
Meitzen, A., 331
Melezin, A., 259
Mellaart, J., 69
Merlin, P., 386
Merrens, H. R., 43
Meso-Africa, 195–198
    livestock herding in, 219–220
    plantations in, 239–241
    shifting agriculture in, 214–219
Meso-America, 54–56
Mesopotamia, 50–51, 337–338, 467–468
Mestizo, 186
Metallurgy, 50–52
Metes and bounds, 323
Methodists, 135
Métraux, A., 223
Metropolises, 359–360
    (See also Cities)
Mexico:
    early cities of, 323
    plantations in, 238
    population of, 412–414
    soil erosion in, 469–470
Meyer, J. W., 147
Michigan, 263
Middle East, 48–55, 190, 467, 468
    agriculture in, 51
    early cities in, 336–338
    Jews in, 124–128
Middle West, 275
Migrations, 425–446
    early human, 80
    from Europe, 428–431
    to Manchuria, 280
    metropolitan, 371
    in third world, 301
    to U.S., 428–431
    of U.S. blacks, 87–90
Mikesell, M. W., 43, 44, 257, 446, 468, 482
Milksheds, 248
Miller, H. P., 477–478
Milpa, 215–219
Milton, J. P., 481
Mingay, G. E., 68
Minneapolis, 12, 15
Minnesota, 12, 266
Mirow, N. T., 213
Mississippi R., 17
Mitchell, J. C., 344, 437, 446
Mobility, 425–446

Modern societies, 203–208
  cities of, 343–355
  industry in, 261–285
  land use in, 241–256
Modernization, 59–67
Mohammed, 137
Mongolia, 236–237
Mongoloids, 77–82
Mongols, 236
Monkhouse, F. J., 44
Monophysites, 130–131
Montagu, M. F. A., 93
Montesquieu, 31
Moodie, D. W., 224
More, Thomas, 297
Mormons, *135*, 318, *320*
Morrill, R. L., 386
Mortality, 397–402, 404–408
Mourant, A. E., 75
Mozambique, 166
Muir, J., 473
Muller, E. K., 386
Multilingualism, 97, 110–113
Multiple nuclei theory, *349*
Mumford, L., 34, 43, 338, 356, 368–369, 386, 475
Murdock, G. P., 224
Murphey, R., 257, 341, 357, 422, 482
Murray, M. A., 422
Muscovy, 189–190
Muslims, 137–141
  of India, 167
Mutation, 73
Myers, E. D., *181*
Myrdal, G., 303–305
Myrdal, J., 257

Naples, *380*
Nash, R., 482
Nationalism, 485
Natural selection, *73*
Nature:
  culture and, 27–46
  and mankind, 470–472
Nath, V., 257
Needham, J., 69
Nef, J. U., 69
Negritoids, 78, *79, 80*
Negroids, 78–82
Nelson, H. J., 357
Nelson, J. G., 482
Nelson, L., 331
Neolithic Age, 49–50
Neoplantation, 321–323
Nestorians, 130–132
Netherlands, 22, 244, 249
New England:
  house types, 324–325
  industry in, *274*
  rural settlement in, 317–319
New stone age, 49–50
Newspapers, *301*
New York, *378, 480*
  industry in, 271–272
  migrations to, *89*
  population of, 346–347
New Zealand, 188–190, 249, *250*
Ng, R. C. Y., 446
Nicholson, M., 482
Nigeria, 170–173, 196
  cities of, *344*
Nile river, 232–235
Nishi, M., 328, 331

Nodal regions, 13
Nomads, 54, 221, *226*, 234–237
Nordics, 80, 81–82
North America, 65
  (*See also* Anglo-America; Canada; United States)
Nostrand, R. L., 198
Nutrition, 452–455
Nystrom, J. W., 177

Oakley, K. P., 223
Occident (see Western civilization)
Oceania, population of, 395
Odering, B., 445
Ohio, 323
Old South, 321–323
  (*See also* South, the)
Old Stone Age, 47–49
Open fields, 311–316
Operational environment, 33, 425
Oren, P., 93
Orleans, L. A., 414, 416, 422
Orthodox Christianity, 71, 129–133
Ottoman Empire, 133
Overpopulation, 451–452

Pakistan, 123, 166–170
  population of, 411–412
Paleolithic Age, 47–49, 213–214, 464–466
Pampas Indians, 211
Pandemic, 455
Papermaking, 58–59
Papuans, 79
Paraguay, 111
Paris, 333, *351, 381*
Park, R. E., *349*, 379, 387
Parry, J. H., 69
Parsees, 168
Pasternak, B., 83
Pastoral nomadism, 235–237
  in Afghanistan, *234*
Patriarchates, 129–131
Pattison, W. D., 331
Patton, D. J., 259
Paullin, C. O., 147, 320
Peach, G. C. K., 386
Peasant society, 204, 205
Peet, J. R., 24
Peking, *326, 342–343*
Pennsylvania, 325
Peppelenbosch, P. G. N., 305
Perception, 33–34, 425
Periodicals, geographical, 24–25
Peru, 31, 57
Peucker, T. K., 44
Pfeifer, G., 33
Phenotypes, 76
Philippines, *440*
Physical features, 38–39
Physical traits, 76–77
Physiological density, 444
Pilgrimages in India, 143
Pillsbury, R., 357
Pinchot, G., 473
Pinkett, H. T., 473, 482
Piotrow, P. T., 422
Pirenne, H., 357
Pittsburgh, 334–336
Places, 13
Plague, *454*
Planhol, X. de, 147

Planning, city, 369–385
Plant domestication, *48–50*, 466
Plant location, 261–271
Plantations, 237–241, *246–247*
  in U.S., 321–*322*
Plural society, 173–177, 300–302
  U.S. as, 90
Pokshishevski, V. V., 387
Polders, 244
Political geography, 8
Polynesia, 116
Populations, 388–482
  age structures of, *299*
  and agriculture, 227
  of cities, 334, 346–348, 360–361, *374*
  density of, *12*
  distribution of, *18–19, 35–36*
  forecasts of, 408, 409
  of ghettos, 376–*378*
  historic, 391–404
  of London, 359
  and migrations, 425–446
  projections of, 398–400
  of U.S. states, 441–444
Porter, P. W., 44, 45, 218, 288–305, 439, 445
Potato, sweet, 58
Power, 64–66
  and industry, 265–266
Pre-Columbian cities, 341–343
Pre-Columbian culture, 183–185
Pred, A., 285, 353, 355, 357, 387
Prehistoric populations, 391–392, 394
Prehistoric societies, 465–467
Prescott, J. R. V., 178
Preston, R. E., 355
Price, A. G., 69
Prince, H. C., 44, 386
Printing industry, *263*
Privalovskaya, G. A., 286
Productivity, 225, 299, 450, 457–458
Progress, 485
  economic, 297–304
Protein intake, *453*
Protestantism, 132–137
Prothero, R. M., 44, 45, 422, 423, 462
Proudfoot, M. J., 446
Prunty, M. C., 259, 321, 331
Pryce, W. T. R., 199
Pryor, R. J., 426, 427, 446
Pueblo Indians, 208
Pugh, J. C., 171
Pulyarkin, V. A., 257
Punjab, 311
Pygmy, *79*

Quarters, city, 375–379
Québec, 163–165, 316–*317*

Rabbit, 468
Race, 73–83
  classification, 76–83
  and culture, 83
  definitions of, 86
  and economic development, 295
  and language, 104
  prejudice, 83–93
  segregation by, *378*
Railways, 61–62
Ranching, 254
Rapoport, A., 331
Ratzel, F., 32, 44, 115, 178, 425

492

Ravenstein, E. G., 426, 446
Raw materials, 266
Recessive genes, 73–77
Regional development, 264–265
Regions, 13–16
  culture, 179–180
  industrial, 271–284
Reindeer herding, 212, 213
Reitsma, H. S., 178
Relative location, 10
Religions, 121–148
  of Nigeria, 170–173
  of Southeast Asia, 195
  in U.S., 135–137
Renan, E., 150
Reproduction ratio, 398, 399
Reps, J. W., 319, 320, 355
Resources, 33–34, 478
  and development, 295, 304
Rhine, 476
Rhode Island, 274
Rice, 201, 225–227
Richardson, H. W., 305
Richardson, M., 305
Rickets, 454
Ritter, C., 32
Robertson, J. C., 35
Robson, B. T., 387
Rodgers, A., 286, 446
Roman Catholics, 132–133
  in U.S., 135–137
Roman Empire, cities of, 339–340
Rose, H. M., 93, 387, 422
Roseman, C. C., 446
Rostlund, E., 31
Roundy, R. W., 462
Rowland, D. T., 446
Rowland, R. H., 386
Rubber, 232, 239–241
Ruhr, 268, 281
Rumage, K. W., 25
Rundling, 314, 315
Russia, 188–190, 441
  (See also Soviet Union)


Saarinen, T. F., 34, 43
Sabah, 174–177
Sabbagh, M. E., 93, 178
Safran, N., 446
St. Paul, 12, 15
Salter, C. L., 482
Sánchez-Albornoz, N., 422
San Diego, 463–464
Santos, M., 305
São Paulo, 438
Sarawak, 174–177
Saskatchewan, 354
Sauer, C. O., 7, 34, 44, 48, 49, 55, 68, 69, 178, 223,
  465, 475, 482
Sautter, G., 24
Sauvy, A., 422, 451
Sawah cultivation, 201, 225–226
Saxony, 311–316
Scale, 10, 12, 13, 180
Schlippe, P. de, 224
Schnell, G. A., 422
Schumacher, E., 288, 305
Schwartzberg, J. E., 109, 147, 231
Scofield, E., 317, 331
Scotland, 345
Scurvy, 454

Sectionalism, 167–168
Sector theory, 349
Seibutis, A. A., 119
Semple, E. C., 42, 471, 482
Senegal, 307
Senior, D., 387
Serbs, 155–156
Services:
  and cities, 346
  labor force in, 292
Settlements, 306–386
Sexual selection, 73–74
Shatter belt, 151–157
Shepard, P., 482
Shia, 138–141
Shifting cultivation, 214–219
Shintoism, 146
Shortridge, J. R., 147
Sian, 327
Siberia, 190, 279, 441
Sidenbladh, G., 385, 387
Sikhs, 142, 167
Simmons, J. S., 462
Simmons, J. W., 446
Simoons, F. J., 68, 148, 257, 462
Simpson, E. S., 259
Simpson, G. E., 93
Simpson, L. B., 469–470, 482
Singapore, 174–177
Singh, K., 257
Site, 10
  of cities, 333–336
Situation, 10, 23
Sjoberg, G., 338, 357
Skelton, R. A., 69
Skin color, 76
Skoda, L., 35
Slave trade, 428
Sleeping sickness, 219–220
Smith, A. M., 119
Smith, Adam, 297
Smith, C. T., 423
Smith, D. M., 286, 305
Smith, E. G., 331
Smith, H., 199
SMSA, 346, 359
Social geography, 8
Social selection, 73
Socialism, 301–302
Societies, 27–30
  culture of, 179–198
  economies and, 203–208
  modern, 203–208
  traditional, 203–208
  tribal, 203–208
Society and languages, 108–110
Soil erosion, 473–474
Soja, E. W., 178
Solheim, W. G., 68
Sommers, L. M., 147
Sonnenfeld, J., 223
Sopher, D. E., 123, 148
Sorre, M., 41
South the, 321–323
  house types in, 325
  rural settlement in, 318–319
South Africa, 86, 90–92, 188
  labor migrations to, 437
South Asia, 191–192
  farming in, 228–231
  languages of, 109
  migrations in, 434–435
  population of, 411–412

Southeast Asia, 193–195
  agriculture in, 214–222, 230–232
  house types in, 328–330
  plantations in, 239–241
  population of, 396–397
  religions in, 141–145
Soviet Union, 188–190
  agriculture in, 252
  cities of, 368
  industrial regions of, 279
  metropolises of, 362–363
  migrations in, 441
  reindeer herders of, 212–213
Spain and colonies, 186, 237–239
Spate, O. K. H., 177, 257
Spatial distribution, 17–19, 427
Spatial interaction, 19
Spatial organization of cities, 352–355
Specialized gatherers, 209–214
Speech, 47, 95
Spencer, J. E., 223, 224, 327, 331
Spengler, J. J., 423
Spooner, B., 423
Spring, D., 482
Spring, E., 482
Springfield, M. A., 319
Sri Lanka, 86, 111, 401
Stamp, L. D., 423, 457–458, 461
Standard language, 95
Standard of living, 450–451
Stanislawski, D., 69, 178, 355
Steam engine, 64–66, 266
Steel industry, 269, 271, 282, 336
Stephenson, G. V., 178
Sternlieb, G., 446
Sternstein, L., 446
Steward, H. H., 69
Stewart, C. T., 355
Stewart, G. R., 108, 119
Stewart, O. C., 223, 465, 482
Stilt houses, 328, 330
Stoddart, D. R., 41, 43
Stone, C. D., 482
Stouffer, S. A., 446
Strassendorf, 314, 315
Stroyev, K. F., 259
Suburbs, 371, 373–374
Subways, 373
Sudan, 233
Sumerian cities, 337–338, 467–468
Sundquist, J. L., 446
Sunni, 139–141
Superhighways, 63, 64
Susman, P., 305
Swatridge, L. A., 387
Swaziland, 111
Sweden, population of, 418–420
Swiddens, 214–219
Sykes, P. A., 69
Symbol, city as, 336–337
Symons, L., 259
Szulc, H., 331


Taconite industry, 266
Taeuber, K., 93
Tamils, 175
Taoism, 146
Tatum, C. E., 148
Tax, S., 93
Taylor, C. C., 199
Taylor, G. T., 42

Technology, 47–69
  of steel industry, 269
Tempelman, G. J., 305
Tenancy, 243–244
Texas, 18–19
Theravada, 144–145
Third world, 287, 438–439
  cities of, 350–351
Thoman, R. S., 259
Thomas, W. L., 44
Thompson, E. T., 257
Thompson, J. E., 79
Thompson, J. H., 257, 285
Thompson, K., 43, 469, 482
Thompson, W. S., 423
Threshold, 353
Tielhard de Chardin, P., 287
Tocqueville, A. de, 163
Tokyo, Japan, 461
Tompkins, G. S., 317
Tools, 47–55
Toponyms, 108
Towns (see Cities)
Townsend, A. R., 199
Township and range, 319–321, 323
Toynbee, A. J., 180–181, 199
Tractors, 241
Trade:
  and development, 298
  in food, 459
Traditional societies, 203–208
  land use in, 225–237
Transhumance, 234, 235, 249
Transportation, 50–51, 59–64, 266–268
Tranter, N., 423
Trewartha, G. T., 317, 318, 327, 331, 332
Tribal societies, 202–203, 205–208
Truck farming, 250
Trudgill, P., 119
Tschudi, A. B., 257
Tuan, Y.-F., 25, 43, 482
Turkestan, 190, 236
Turner, R., 387
Twin Cities, 15, 384

Ullman, E. L., 349, 355
Underdeveloped countries, 287–288, 405–406
UNESCO, 257
Uniform regions, 13
U.S.S.R. (see Soviet Union)
United Kingdom:
  cities of, 345, 350, 367, 374
  and Common market, 161–162
  demographic transition in, 399
  industrial regions of, 275–277, 281–284
  industrial revolution in, 343–346
  new towns in, 381–385
  racial tensions in, 90
  rural settlement in, 316
United States, 188–189
  blacks in, 86–90
  cities of, 348, 364
  commuting in, 372
  conservation in, 472–474
  copper industry in, 266
  cotton farming in, 253
  dialects of, 106–108

United States:
  Eskimo of, 212–213
  ethnic groups in, 86
  farming in, 245–248, 250–251
  ghettos in, 375–379
  illegal immigrants, 431
  income in, 264, 289
  industry in, 263, 271–275
  internal migration, 441–444
  land surveys in, 319
  manufacturing, 271–275
  Midwest, 17
  migrations in, 87–90, 441, 444
  migrations to, 428–431
  milksheds, 248
  plantations, 237
  as plural society, 90, 151
  population of, 420–421
  ranching in, 254
  religions in, 135–137
  rural settlements of, 316–325
  steel industry, 269
  suburbs in, 373–374
  textiles in, 262–263
  urban renewal in, 381
  (See also North America)
Untouchables, 142
Ural-Altaic languages, 105
Ural Mountains, 279
Urban geography, 9, 333–387
Urban places (see Cities)
Urban populations, 334, 406–407
Urban renewal, 380–381
Urbanization, 334, 347, 486–487
Urbanized area, U.S., 347
Utah, 320
Uzozie, L. C., 224

Vance, J. E., 355
Van Paassen, C., 30, 41
Vavilov, N. I., 68
Venice, 333
Verdun, Treaty of, 158
Vermeer, D. E., 224
Vermont, 471
Vernacular, 95
Vidal de la Blache, P., 32, 41
Vietnam, migration in, 435
Villages, 309–332
Vitamin deficiency, 454, 455
Vogeler, I., 199
Von Humboldt, A., 32, 41
Von Thünen, J. H., 20–21

Wadham, S. M., 259
Wagner, P. L., 44, 106, 119, 223
Wagret, P., 259
Wahhabites, 139–141
Waibel, L., 20, 21, 24, 258
Waldhufendorf, 314–315
Waldseemuller, M., 9
Wales, South, 281–284
Walloons, 158–161
Wanklyn, H., 41
Ward, B., 305
Ward, D., 387

Ward, R. E., 256
Ward, R. G., 68, 116, 224
Washburn, S. L., 69
Watters, R. F., 224
Webb, J. W., 13, 24, 68, 116, 352, 357, 387, 427
Webb, W. P., 14, 259
Weber, A., 262, 267, 285, 286
Weber, A. F., 355
Weber, M., 121, 148
Welfare, cities and, 336–337
West, the (see Western society)
West Germany:
  industry in, 276–278, 281
  (See also Germany)
Western civilization, rise of, 59–64
Western Europe, 186–187
  cities of, 367
  industrial regions of, 275–278, 281–284
  nationalities of, 151–152, 157–163
  planning in, 370–371
  rural settlement, 310–316
Western society, 184–191, 484–485
  and China, 58–59
  Christianity in, 132–137
  and economic development, 287–305
  spread of, 30, 205–206
  technology and, 28
Wheat, 227
Wheat farming, 251, 255
Wheat trade, 253
Wheatley, P., 44, 355
Wheeler, J. D., 118
White, C. L., 365
White, L. A., 43
Whittlesey, D. S., 223
Wiesenfeld, S. L., 93
Wikkramatileke, R., 178, 257
Wild, M. T., 45
Wilkinson, H. R., 44
Wilkinson, J. C., 178
Willey, G. R., 54, 55, 69, 355
Wilson, R. K., 259
Winsemius, J., 387
Withington, W. A., 224, 258
Witthauer, K., 423
Wolf, E., 204, 223, 224
Wolff, P., 119
Wolpert, J., 426, 446
World Bank, 303
Wright, J. K., 24, 45, 320
Wrigley, E. A., 42, 423
Wright, H. E., 466, 482
Wycherley, R. E., 355

Yates, P. L., 259
Yaws, 454
Yeates, M. H., 387
Yellow fever, 454
Yinger, J. M., 93
Yoruba, 170–173, 344

Zaire, 99
Zelinsky, W., 44, 45, 135, 148, 331, 423, 446
Zero population growth, 420, 477–478
Zimmermann, E. W., 286
Zube, E. H., 44

# World:
## National Populations

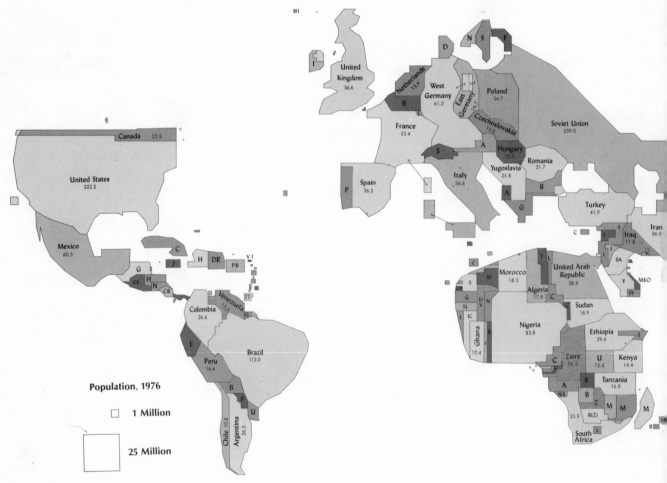

Canada 23.5

United States
222.2

Mexico
60.5

C

G

ES

H

N

CR

P

J

H

DR

PR

V I

TT

Venezuela
13.3

Colombia
26.6

G

E

Peru
16.6

Brazil
113.0

B

P

U

Chile 10.8

Argentina
26.3

**Population, 1976**

☐ 1 Million

☐ 25 Million

United
Kingdom
56.6

I

Netherlands
13.9

B

D

France
53.4

West
Germany
61.2

East
Germany
16.7

Poland
34.7

Czechoslovakia
15.0

N

S

F

Soviet Union
259.0

S

A

Hungary
10.7

Romania
21.7

Spain
36.5

P

Italy
56.6

Yugoslavia
21.8

A

B

G

Turkey
41.9

C

L

Iraq
11.8

S

J

SA

Iran
36.0

Y

M&O

SY

C

S

M

Morocco
18.3

Algeria
17.8

C

United Arab
Republic
38.9

Sudan
18.9

G

SL

L

UV

N

IC

B

Ghana
10.4

T

Nigeria
83.8

Ethiopia
29.4

S

Zaire
26.3

U

Kenya
14.4

C

A

R

Tanzania
16.0

N.B.

25.9

R(Z)

B

Z

M

M

M

South
Africa

L

R

M